# THE SKILLFUL TEACHER

## Building Your Teaching Skills

### Sixth Edition

Jon Saphier

Mary Ann Haley-Speca

Robert Gower

**Research for Better Teaching, Inc.** • One Acton Place, Acton, MA 01720 • (978) 263-9449 • www.RBTeach.com

**Library of Congress Cataloging-in-Publication Data**

Saphier, Jon.
The skillful teacher : building your teaching skills / by Jon Saphier, Mary Ann Haley-Speca, Robert Gower. — 6th ed.
 p. cm.
Includes index.
ISBN: 978-1-886822-10-8
 1. Teaching. 2. Learning. I. Haley-Speca, Mary Ann. II. Gower, Robert R. III. Title.
LB1025.3.S27 2007
371.102—dc22                                        2007007563

Printed in the United States of America
SIXTH EDITION

*PB Printing*        10 9 8 7 6 5 4 3 2

Published and distributed by:

Research for Better Teaching, Inc.
One Acton Place
Acton, MA 01720
978-263-9449 voice
978-263-9959 fax
info@rbteach.com
www.RBTeach.com

# Contents

## Part Three
## Introduction to Motivation 257

## Part Four
## Introduction to Curriculum 355

# Preface

We have written this book to assist teachers in their efforts to build greater competence in teaching skills. Our values are obvious. We believe that many things are important for good schools: curriculum is important; parental involvement is important; having a clean, safe building is important. But of all the things that are important to having good schools, nothing is as important as the teacher and what that person knows, believes, and can do. That is where the rubber meets the road in our business. In between the previous edition of *The Skillful Teacher* and this one, research has overwhelmingly supported this position (Gross, 1999; Mendro and Bebry, 2000; Muijis and Reynolds, 2000; Sanders and Rivers, 1996). Teacher effects dwarf all others on student learning.

A teacher's skill makes a difference in student performance, not only in achievement scores on tests (as important as that might be) but also in students' sense of fulfillment in school and their feelings of well-being. We do not mean to imply that being skillful substitutes for other human qualities, but we will argue that whatever else teachers do, they perform in the classroom and their actions set the stage for students' experiences. Therefore, only a skillful performance will do.

Our exploration of teaching in this book is guided by three key concepts: comprehensiveness, repertoire, and matching. Comprehensiveness refers to our efforts to understand teaching as a whole. We are working toward the day when one might say, "These are the areas that make up teaching. Know how to handle these things, and you have all the basic tools for the job."

Repertoire represents the fact that there is more than one way for teachers to handle any basic area of teaching. Repertoire is a concept that challenges teachers to develop a variety of strategies and behaviors for dealing with teaching situations. Matching is an idea that directs teachers to think about what behavior to pick from their expanding repertoires in light of the situation, the group, or the characteristics of individual students.

Throughout this book we revisit these three ideas again and again. As we define and describe each area of teaching, we take it through the range of options we have uncovered for handling it. Then we address the issue of matching for that area and what is known about it.

We propose that the skills of teaching include anything a person does that influences the probability of intended learning. That definition broadens the field for application of skill beyond classroom management and good delivery of instruction. Teaching skill includes motivating students and teaching them how to translate that motivation into effective effort.

Motivation is a huge variable in human performance of any kind. This is particularly true of student learning in a school setting where so many social and psychological factors may combine to support or obstruct students' attention and investment. Peer pressure, bullying, wanting to be "in" and accepted by classmates, feeling personally known and valued by adults, being pushed and supported to achieve at the same time, believing oneself to be smart or dumb in a subject—all these influence a student's confidence and effort in school. Being skillful at handling these things is just as important to successful teaching and learning as is expertise at one's content.

Teachers also need to be good designers of daily instruction just as architects are designers of houses. In the best of circumstances, a teacher starts from a well-designed unit in a curriculum that is congruent with the standards of the state and district. But curriculum units, even the best of them, do not provide the detailed scenarios of interaction and accommodation for the needs of individual students that good daily planning requires. Planning good lessons based on good curriculum guidelines takes a kind of teacher expertise altogether different from the types discussed above. Yet that planning and design expertise is also an indispensable teaching skill. Thus, new chapters on Planning and Curriculum Design appear in this edition. A new

chapter on Assessment emphasizes teacher skill at data analysis.

In *The Skillful Teacher,* we lay out the research-validated skills of teaching and organize these skills into four categories: (1) curriculum skills, (2) motivation skills, (3) instruction skills, and (4) management skills. Each of these four is divided into specific tasks of teaching. For example, one classroom management task is to keep the momentum of the class going without downtime for students, confusion over directions, or conflict over materials. A task of instruction is to ensure clarity and student understanding of important ideas by using tools from the repertoire of cognitive science. There are significant updates and expansions of the Clarity, Expectations, Personal Relationship Building, and Time chapters to reflect more recent research.

There are other areas where skillful performance is important: for example, skill at generating parents' involvement in their children's learning and skill at collaborating with one's colleagues. Those are topics for future volumes. In this book, we focus on the skills that foster successful in-class performance.

We have built the framework of *The Skillful Teacher* on a large number of specific teaching behaviors and situations so that it can be useful immediately as a tool for self-improvement, staff development, supervision, and teacher evaluation. The framework ties theory directly to practice. Extensive examples are provided to illustrate the teaching performances being discussed. It is our hope that in this way, readers will be able to understand their own teaching (or the teaching of others) more fully and accurately and, more important, will be able to control their own teaching so that it better serves their ends and the needs of their students.

In some sections, the sources we refer to are from the 1970s. This is not because the knowledge is obsolete or we did not apply diligence in updating our references. These are situations where important areas of knowledge have lost their magnetism and are rarely studied anymore, yet they remain important variables in teaching and learning. One example is the "say-do" principle of learning. Although it is out of fashion for researchers, knowing how to optimize perceptual input channels, particularly student talk about academic ideas, can make a significant difference in student learning.

We know that experienced teachers have tremendous personal practical knowledge about how to teach their subjects and about how to adjust to the needs of different children (Edwards, 1994). Much of our work in schools over the years has been facilitating teachers' working together in collaborative settings, forming study groups, and doing action research together. These are routes to increasing teacher capacity that translate directly into better learning experiences for children.

Teachers' personal practical knowledge is a hugely underused resource for school improvement. Putting it to work requires structures of time and space rarely seen: for example, bringing a task force of teachers together monthly to polish lessons on specific concepts (Stigler and Stevenson, 1991). In this approach, the task force develops progressive versions of the lesson, experiments and observes one another, and then presents the final result to their peers. Thus, all the teachers of a given concept have the benefit of their colleagues' finest thinking and active experimentation. The lessons emerging from this kind of collaboration are refined and effective, they have the commitment and ownership of the teachers, and they are available for each teacher's direct personal use with students. Working groups of teachers developing authentic assessments can also serve as dynamic professional learning experiences that draw on the personal practical knowledge of teachers. The term *professional learning community* (PLC) now applies to groups of teachers who operate this way. Good PLCs also examine student work together to identify patterns of student difficulty and design reteaching strategies for students who didn't get it the first time around. It is our hope that this text will serve as a resource not only to individual teachers but also to teachers who engage in this type of collegial study of their craft.

Because our profession has not acknowledged the existence or complexity of our public knowledge base on pedagogy itself, each generation of teachers has had to reinvent it, and most have gone their entire careers without discovering dozens of powerful tools and approaches that would have empowered their teaching. We hope this book is a step in remedying that situation.

We hold teaching to be a complex human endeavor requiring high-level thinking, decision making, and the capacity to form, consider, and weigh multiple alternatives. Reflection and decision making are central to our concept of the teacher's role. To make informed decisions, however, teachers need a full bank of available options to choose from, especially tried and tested options. They need systematic professional education that brings all the alternatives to their attention over time and enables them to acquire competence in using them. Then they will have the capacity to make decisions from both main sources of teacher knowledge: their own personal practical knowledge and that of their colleagues and the accumulated public pedagogical knowledge base of the field. *The Skillful Teacher* is our effort to organize and make available to all this second resource for teacher decision making: the repertoires of strategies and approaches that comprise our common public pedagogical knowledge base.

*Source Materials*

Edwards, J. "Thinking, Education and Human Potential." In J. Edwards (ed.), *Thinking International Interdisciplinary Perspectives*. Melbourne: Hawker Brownlow Education, 1994.

Gross, S. "Final Report, Mathematics Content/Connections Elementary Science in Montgomery County (Maryland): A Comprehensive Transformation of a System-wide Science Program." Montgomery (Maryland) County Public Schools, July 1999.

Mendro, R., and Bebry, K. "School Evaluation: A Change in Perspective." Paper presented at the Annual Meeting of the American Educational Research Association, New Orleans, Apr. 24–28, 2000.

Muijis, R., and Reynolds, D. "Effective Mathematics Teaching: Year 2 of a Research Project." Paper presented at the International Conference on School Effectiveness and School Improvement, Hong Kong, Aug. 2000.

Sanders, W. L., and Rivers, J. C. *Cumulative Residual Effects of Teachers on Future Academic Achievement*. Knoxville: University of Tennessee, Value-Added Research and Assessment Center, 1996.

Stigler, J., and Stevenson, H. "Polishing the Stone: How Asian Teachers Polish Each Lesson to Perfection." *American Educator*, Spring 1991, pp. 12–20, 43–47.

# Acknowledgments

A book that attempts to synthesize as much information as this one is obviously indebted to a host of authors and thinkers. The bibliography at the end of each chapter should indicate the range of individuals who have influenced our thinking.

We are grateful to the many educators in Brookline, Cambridge, Carlisle, Concord, and Newton, Massachusetts, whose participation in our early observational studies contributed to the original conceptual framework for this book. Specifically, Ginny Chalmers, Susan-Jo Russell, Suzanne Stuart, and Risa Whitehead opened their classrooms to us and held many important discussions with us about teaching. Peggy McNeill MacMullen was an invaluable part of the early brain trust that developed the framework.

Kim Marshall's detailed critique helped enormously in editing an earlier edition into more lucid, jargon-free prose, and Roland Barth performed a similar and much appreciated task.

We extend our gratitude to the team of Research for Better Teaching, Inc., colleagues and consultants—Marcia Booth, Ken Chapman, Greg Ciardi, Elizabeth Imende, Maxine Minkoff, Ned Paulsen, Alexander Platt, Laura Porter, Fran Prolman, Deb Reed, Ann Stern, Ruth Sernak, Kathy Spencer, Caroline Tripp, and Jim Warnock. They filtered a constant flow of refinements and suggestions from the teachers and administrators in the districts where they work. A special note of thanks to Caroline Tripp and Mary Sterling, who gave us invaluable guidance on style and voice as we prepared for this edition. All of this feedback added greatly to the book's substance and clarity.

The production process was skillfully guided by Susan Geraghty and Sandra Spooner. Leah Conn and Carole Fiorentino provided invaluable research and formatting support. Leah's editing and additions to the quizzes for each chapter will be prized by those who use these online resources at our Web site. Ivy Schutt managed in-house technology and permissions work with diligence and excellence. We also thank the new edition's copyeditor, Beverly Miller, for her high-quality work, Brenn Lea Pearson for the graphics and book design, Sylvia Coates for her thorough indexing, and Lisa Simons for the cover design.

Finally, we especially want to thank our spouses and families for their continuing support and understanding of the often demanding schedules of our work to advance the professionalization of teaching.

# About the Authors

**Jon Saphier** is the founder of Research for Better Teaching (RBT), a professional development organization dedicated to improving teaching and learning. In addition to *The Skillful Teacher*, Dr. Saphier is the author of several other books and articles on teaching, leadership, and school improvement, including *John Adams' Promise: How to Have Good Schools for All Our Children Not Just Some* (2005). Dr. Saphier devotes his time to long-term, in-depth, systemic change projects in selected districts. A masterful teacher, he conducts workshops, coaching sessions, and delivers keynotes that bring to life the principles and strategies described in *The Skillful Teacher*. In addition, Dr. Saphier is passionate about, and active in, public policy reform to promote the professionalization of teaching and leadership. Dr. Saphier has also served as a school administrator, staff developer, and teacher (K–12). In the last twenty-five years, he has coached over a thousand principals in instructional leadership and guided three large systemic school improvement projects.

**Mary Ann Haley-Speca** is a founding consultant and former director of training with Research for Better Teaching, Inc. During her twenty-three-year tenure with the organization, Ms. Haley-Speca has worked with teachers and administrators in urban, suburban, and rural public school districts and private institutions throughout the world, focusing on the study of instruction, school, and organizational culture; coaching, supervision, and evaluation practices; and professional development planning. She is the coauthor of two other popular RBT publications: *Activators* and *Summarizers*. She has served as a classroom teacher, staff developer, and program supervisor in the Hudson and Concord, Massachusetts, public schools. She is currently working as a full-time consultant with RBT on long-term projects in several urban and suburban school districts throughout the United States.

**Robert Gower** recently retired as a professor at the University of Massachusetts Lowell, where he helped develop the doctoral program in Leadership in Schooling. He is still active teaching online courses for the university. Bob's distinguished career includes being an elementary teacher, a principal, a researcher, a pioneer in the study of teaching, and a standout instructor and mentor for generations of graduate students. In 2007, he received the Faculty Excellence & Service Award and was recognized as a 2007 Honors Fellow by the University of Massachusetts.

# Introduction

*I'd ask to know what I was walling in or walling out.*

ROBERT FROST, "MENDING WALL"

Teaching is one of the most complex human endeavors imaginable. Both as teachers ourselves and as students and researchers of teaching, we have been awed by the immensity of the task of understanding teaching. We know that a good teacher is many things, among them a caring person. But a good teacher is also a skillful practitioner, meaning adept at certain specifiable, observable actions. Being skillful means you can do something that can be seen; it means different levels of skill may be displayed by different individuals; and it means, above all, that you can learn how to do it and can continue to improve at it.

Skillful teachers are made, not born. They have learned the skills they use, and others can look at what they are doing in the classroom and say what is skillful about it. Some skillful teachers do not have the vocabulary or the concepts for describing what they already do. They just "know" what to do and do it effortlessly and naturally—intuitively, some might say. This effortlessness is an unconscious, automatic kind of knowing—tacit knowledge, Michael Polanyi (1966) calls it. The limitation of this kind of knowing is that it is acquired only by a few, not given at birth, we want to repeat, but learned by them unpredictably, over time, in many different ways. And they can't pass it on to the rest of us because they can't say what they do.

There are some people, of course, who are not cut out to be teachers, just as some of us are not cut out to be race car drivers. No amount of skill training is going to make some of us into great race car drivers. But the great majority of us who are not born with a feel for the road in our fingertips can be taught the skills of race car driving and become competent at it.

Being skillful in teaching is an important theme of this book. As we develop that theme we want to be clear that we are not "walling out" from our conception of teaching certain important things, like being a human being. We value teachers who can feel a hurt, who know how to laugh and how to love. Being skillful is not in competition with being a thinking, feeling being. But we are highlighting the skillful part of being a good teacher in this book. There is more to good teaching than skill, but there is no good teaching without it. Skillful teachers are aware of the complexity of their job and work to be conscious and deliberate about what they do. They don't do what they do just because that is the way it has always been done, or because that's the cultural expectation of how it shall be done. They do what they do because they've thought about it and made choices from a repertoire of options that seem best. They want to control and regulate their teaching to have a positive effect on students, so they monitor what they do, get feedback, and try different things. Skillful teachers are determined that students will succeed. When that isn't happening they examine their programs.

Skillful teachers are clear about what is to be learned, clear about what achievement means, and clear about what they are going to do to help students attain it. And if one thing doesn't work, they make another plan that is also technically clear and well thought out.

Finally, skillful teachers are learners—always a student of teaching, as Joyce, Clark, and Peck (1981) say. Skillful teachers constantly reach out to colleagues with an assertive curiosity that says, "I don't know it all. No one does or ever will, but I am always growing, adding to my knowledge and skills and effectiveness." To skillful teachers, that openness and reaching out is an important element of professionalism.

# The Nature of Professional Knowledge in Teaching

## Areas of Performance, Repertoire, and Matching

Following is a list of important questions that all teachers need to consider regardless of the age, grade level, subject area, or courses they teach. Each of these questions is associated with a particular task—or what we will refer to as an area of performance—in teaching. We label the area of performance in italics following each question. Every one of these questions (and related areas of performance) is important unto itself and there is a chapter in this text dedicated to each. Collectively the questions and areas of performance address virtually all of the decisions, actions, and situations a teacher has to handle with students in classrooms.

There are a lot of other important kinds of knowledge and areas in which teachers need to function that are not addressed in these questions—like knowing their content deeply and working effectively with colleagues and with parents. We address these briefly later in this chapter. But these are not the focal point of this book. *The Skillful Teacher*—and these questions—focus on the instructional skills of interactive teaching.

*The Important Questions of Teaching*

1. How do I get students to pay attention and stay on task? (Attention)
2. How do I keep the flow of events moving smoothly and minimize downtime, delays, and distractions? (Momentum)
3. How do I eliminate disruptions while building responsibility and ownership? (Discipline)
4. How do I make concepts and skills clear and accessible to students? (Clarity)
5. How do I design more efficient and effective learning experiences? (Principles of Learning)
6. How do my personal passions show up in a "No Child Left Behind" world? (Overarching Objectives)
7. What do I need to know about my curriculum? (Curriculum Design)
8. How should I frame objectives so they precisely guide my planning and my students' learning? (Objectives)
9. How do I plan lessons that will reach all my students? (Planning)
10. How do I create learning experiences that develop the mind as well as the content? (Models of Teaching)
11. What choices do I have for differentiating learning experiences? (Learning Experiences)
12. How can I use assessment to inform instruction and improve student performance? (Assessment)
13. How do I get the most out of my space and furniture? (Space)
14. How do I time events and regulate schedules so that students get the most productive learning time? (Time)
15. What procedural routines are important and how do I get maximum mileage out of them? (Routines)
16. How do I communicate to students that what we're doing is important, that they can do it well, and that I won't give up on them? (Expectations)
17. How do I build good personal relationships with students and make them feel truly known and valued? (Personal Relationship Building)
18. How do I build a climate of inclusion, risk taking, and personal efficacy? (Classroom Climate)

We answer these questions by drawing on the rich knowledge base about teaching. This knowledge base is not a set of prescriptions or a list of behaviors known to produce effective learning (though there are a few of these). Rather, it offers options, or repertoires, for dealing with each area of the previous questions. It also asserts that effective teaching lies in choosing appropriately from among the options to match given students, situations, or curricula. In successful teaching, comprehensiveness, repertoire, and matching are what count: comprehensive awareness of all of the *areas of performance* involved in running a successful classroom; *repertoire* so that one has options to work with and draw on when addressing a given aspect of classroom life; and *matching:* making decisions about which tool will be most effective to use in a given situation. Ultimately, matching is the name of the game.

To illustrate this, consider a simple management concern: dealing with intrusions. A teacher is instructing a small group when a student outside of the group (Jimmy) is stuck on an item on a worksheet and approaches the teacher for help. The challenge for the teacher is maintaining the momentum of the instructional group while simultaneously addressing Jimmy's needs. There are several options for how the teacher can handle this:

(1) wave Jimmy off, (2) wave Jimmy in but signal him to be silent until there is an appropriate pause to give help, (3) redirect Jimmy to another student for help, or (4) proactively teach students what to do when the teacher is engaged in an instructional group. No one of these options is inherently better teaching. Each could be an effective and most appropriate response in a particular situation. For instance, if Jimmy doesn't have the confidence or social skills to approach another student for help, then waving him in may be better than redirecting. But if Jimmy is overly dependent on the teacher, waving him off may be the best choice, especially if the teacher believes Jimmy can do it himself if he tries again. The teacher's success in handling Jimmy will depend on whether she knows the options available for dealing with the situation and can choose the best response by matching the options to the specific situation.

There are many ways of dealing with each of the major areas of teaching identified in our list of questions, and skillful teaching involves continually broadening one's repertoire in each area and picking from it appropriately to match given students, groups, situations, or curricula. The knowledge base about teaching identifies choices available in each of these areas, available for anyone to learn, refine, and do skillfully. This book presents the options for each area, illustrates them with examples, and offers what is known about how to choose which is best at the moment.

Figure 1.1 illustrates the functional organization of the areas of performance in teaching. They rest on the foundation of essential beliefs, one of which is the belief that all students can learn rigorous academic materials at high standards. We make the case that the presence of this belief in individual teachers is the foundation of the drive to increase one's repertoire of teaching skills. Other beliefs in this foundation include the role of inter-dependence among educators in getting the job done for students, acknowledgment of the importance of collegial behavior to strong school cultures, the belief in professional knowledge as based on repertoires and matching rather than lists of effective teaching behaviors, and the belief in the need for constant learning. These beliefs are discussed in Chapter Two.

## Moves, Patterns, and Abstractions

Because these areas of performance together make up teaching it is important to recognize how they are related to each other. Some of the areas of performance have specific skills associated with them. We call these skills *moves* because they represent a brief action or a remark. Moves are quick, discrete, and observable behaviors. They can be counted if you so desire. Many teaching skills can be explained in terms of moves, and many of them turn out to be related to classroom management: attention and momentum, for example. The areas of performance that consist of moves occupy the bottom tier of Figure 1.2.

Other areas of performance involve teaching skills that are more patternlike: they can't be performed or seen quickly, for example, implementing a model of teaching. For instance, a teacher skilled using Taba's (1962) nine-step inductive model orchestrates a series of events and follows certain principles for reacting to students. The performance unfolds over time according to a certain regular and recognizable pattern. Being able to perform the pattern is the skill. It's a package: a cohesive, planned package that is greater than the sum of its discrete parts. Skillful teachers see moves as they stand alone and patterns of moves that make sense only when viewed as purposeful packages. The areas of performance that are *patterns* are in the middle tier of Figure 1.2.

**Figure 1.1. Map of Pedagogical Knowledge**

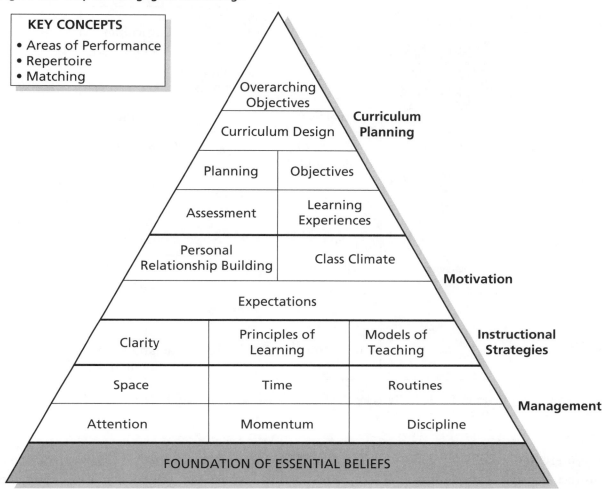

**KEY CONCEPTS**
- Areas of Performance
- Repertoire
- Matching

Overarching Objectives

Curriculum Design

**Curriculum Planning**

Planning | Objectives

Assessment | Learning Experiences

Personal Relationship Building | Class Climate

**Motivation**

Expectations

Clarity | Principles of Learning | Models of Teaching

**Instructional Strategies**

Space | Time | Routines

Attention | Momentum | Discipline

**Management**

FOUNDATION OF ESSENTIAL BELIEFS

**Research for Better Teaching, Inc.** • One Acton Place, Acton, MA 01720 • (978)263-9449 • www.RBTeach.com

And some of the important things teachers do skillfully are hard to see at all. These skills include choosing objectives, designing learning experiences, organizing curricula, and assessing student learning. The connections between actions and decisions become clear only over longer stretches of time or in conversation with a teacher because they are driven by big-picture blueprints (overarching objectives, curriculum maps, etc.). They are practiced before school, during planning, or after school while responding to students' work. These areas of knowledge and skill are *abstractions*.

Although not directly observable they nevertheless shape and account for what is going on in a classroom at almost all times. These areas of performance occupy the top tier of Figure 1.2.

These three kinds of knowledge—moves, patterns, and abstractions—comprise skillful teaching. The tasks of skillful teaching can also be grouped according to their function. The management areas of performance—Attention, Momentum, Space, Time, Routines, and Discipline—are the foundation of teaching. If those jobs aren't being handled, no learning can take place. They contain

**Figure 1.2. Three Kinds of Knowledge That Comprise Professional Teaching**

| Abstractions | Planning | |
|---|---|---|
| | Overarching Objectives | Curriculum Design |
| | Learning Experiences | |
| | Objectives | Assessment |
| **Patterns** | Models of Teaching | Class Climate |
| | Time | |
| | Space | Routines |
| **Moves** | Discipline     Clarity | Principles of Learning |
| | Attention | |
| | Momentum     Expectations | Personal Relationship Building |

Research for Better Teaching, Inc. • One Acton Place, Acton, MA 01720 •
(978) 263-9449 • www.RBTeach.com

the prerequisite skills for good teaching. The instructional areas of performance—Clarity, Models of Teaching, and Principles of Learning—deliver the goods; these skills come to life during interactive learning time in classrooms. The motivational areas of performance—Classroom Climate, Personal Relationship Building, and Expectations—help students generate the investment and put forth the effort that lead to successful learning. The curriculum areas of performance—Curriculum Design, Objectives, Planning, Learning Experiences, Assessment, and Overarching Objectives—contain skills that provide the blueprints for instruction. They stand behind and above instruction, motivation, and management. Management skills support and make possible instruction. Curriculum skills design

instruction. Motivational skills empower instruction. And instructional skills themselves deliver the goods. Altogether, these areas of performance delineate teaching: teaching is all of them.

## Six Types of Professional Knowledge

*The Skillful Teacher* is about the vast and complex field of generic pedagogical knowledge. Without solid skills in this area, many people entering teaching who are experts at their content and mature individuals transferring from successful careers in other walks of life quickly fail. We hope *The Skillful Teacher* can help prevent those unnecessary failures. But it is important to keep in mind how this knowledge base fits with others that are part of a fully

**Figure 1.3. The Knowledge Bases for Professional Teachers**

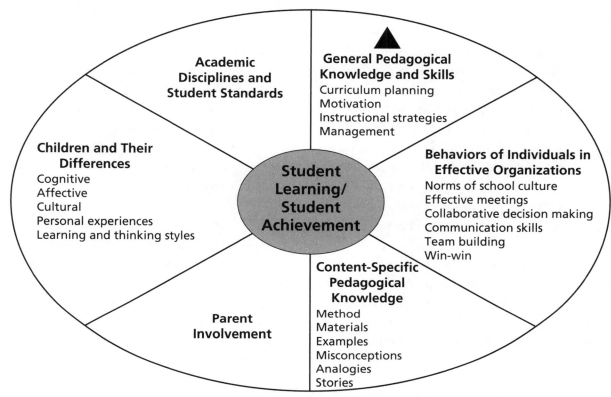

**Academic Disciplines and Student Standards**

**General Pedagogical Knowledge and Skills**
Curriculum planning
Motivation
Instructional strategies
Management

**Children and Their Differences**
Cognitive
Affective
Cultural
Personal experiences
Learning and thinking styles

**Student Learning/ Student Achievement**

**Behaviors of Individuals in Effective Organizations**
Norms of school culture
Effective meetings
Collaborative decision making
Communication skills
Team building
Win-win

**Parent Involvement**

**Content-Specific Pedagogical Knowledge**
Method
Materials
Examples
Misconceptions
Analogies
Stories

**Research for Better Teaching, Inc.** • One Acton Place, Acton, MA 01720 • (978)263-9449 • www.RBTeach.com

functioning professional teacher's repertoire. There are, of course, other kinds of professional knowledge that are central to successful teaching, which are shown in Figure 1.3.

There is a large set of tools for teaching specific to each content area. Lee Shulman (1986) described these as *pedagogical content knowledge.*

Content-specific pedagological knowledge includes knowing what analogies, examples, and visual representations best capture key ideas of the academic discipline; what experiments, equipment, models, and projects best develop student understanding; what prior misconceptions commonly interfere with learning; what real-world connections need to be made for students learning new academic content; what texts, stories, and other materials are available that are powerful resources for teaching and learning.

Another level of this kind of content-based expertise is knowing how to break the content into concepts and subconcepts, skills and subskills. It means that the teacher understands how the concepts and skills are connected to one another and how to bring these relationships to the attention of students. Every teacher must understand the network of concepts "that relate to the specific concept to be taught and how that network is connected to the content in the yearlong curriculum as well as to the curricula of the previous and following years" (West and Staub, 2003, p. 19). Liping Ma (1999) gives clear examples of how this kind of knowledge empowers good lesson and unit planning.

This knowledge is essential for successful teaching. Curriculum materials cannot be relied on to hold these connections, much less make them explicit for students. Curriculum materials are resources for teachers to draw on to create the best lessons for their students.

Skillful teachers are wary of curricula that prescribe a script that allows only one way of teaching. Such materials are marginally appropriate for paraprofessionals and provisional teachers who have no pedagogical knowledge of their own. But they ensure that a large proportion of students will not learn because their learning style is not matched to that one way of teaching.

In addition to generic pedagogy and content-specific pedagogy, four other important knowledge bases bear on the success of teaching and learning. Three of them are seldom found in teacher preparation programs or other systems that influence teacher capacity:

- Deep *knowledge of the academic discipline* itself and knowledge of the standards in the discipline that the state has adopted. Most states have raised standards for teachers' content knowledge and require a college major for secondary teachers in the field they will be teaching.
- *Knowledge of individual differences* in learners—cultural, developmental, and learning style—and how to include those differences in instructional decisions.
- *Knowledge of the behavior of individuals in effective organizations.* This kind of knowledge relates to effective teams, effective meetings, good communication, and problem-solving skills with other adults and the awareness of one's role as a teacher in building a strong school culture among the adults.

- *Knowledge of how to communicate effectively with parents and community.* This knowledge enables teachers to find multiple access channels to communicate to parents what they most want to know: that the teacher knows their child and wants the best for him or her. Beyond that is knowledge of how to connect parents and their children around homework and how to enlist hard-to-reach parents in communicating the value of education to their children.

When the public appreciates the complexity of successful teaching and the preeminent role it plays in student achievement (Sanders and Rivers, 1996), there will be a sea change in public policy: all these knowledge bases will be represented in a systematic way in teacher education and in the other levers of influence on teacher capacity (Saphier, 2005).

## Plan of This Book

Part One of this book addresses the management areas of performance, those most pressing and immediate needs for many teachers. Part Two addresses instructional areas, Part Three the motivational areas, and Part Four the curriculum areas (the design skills for decisions about what education is for, what shall be taught, and how to know if it has been learned). Thus, the chapters move from the specific and discrete to the complex, from those parts of teaching that are moves, to patterns of moves, to decisions about design.

Each chapter addresses a different area of performance. We frequently start by describing why the area of performance is important and how it relates to the bigger picture of teaching and learning. Then we define concepts and categories useful for understanding the areas of performance and look at each category to lay out the repertoire of ways teachers handle pertinent situations. We do this with examples as often as possible. Next, we usually examine what is known about matching teacher choices to students, situations, or curricula.

It is not absolutely necessary to read the chapters in order, but there are certain cumulative benefits that make that desirable. Good discipline, for example, builds on a foundation of teachers' skills with attention, momentum, expectations, and personal relationship building. A teacher who is struggling with a difficult class can turn to Chapter Eight on discipline, which has references back to specific management, instructional, and motivational areas of performance, and are the first places to check when working with difficult students.

## Uses of This Book

Our audience is teachers and others who work with them around instruction: supervisors, evaluators, instructional coaches, and staff developers. Even experienced teachers should check their skills against the repertoires available in each area of performance to see if there are ways to add to their range, effectiveness, and ability to match the diverse needs of students in their classrooms.

We hope through this book to build a common language and concept system for talking about teaching—not a dictionary of jargon, but a set of important and meaningful concepts about teaching that all educators can begin to use in common. Having language and shared vocabulary to describe what one does creates more conscious awareness of the most subtle aspects of practice, expands one's lenses for noticing causal relationships, and illuminates opportunities to constructively and creatively adjust and modify practice to achieve our goals. Furthermore if we can better understand each other, speaking and writing in clear and meaningful terms, then we can expect observation write-ups and evaluations of teaching to be more useful, supervision conferences to be more specific and productive, and staff development programs to be more focused.

We might also expect some of the barriers of isolation and loneliness between teachers to come down. We might expect conversation in teachers' rooms and other meeting places to be more open, more mutually helpful, and more about instruction. With a common professional knowledge base, discussing problems with each other might seem less an admission of personal inadequacy (a notion rooted in the intuitive teacher myth—that is, if good teaching is intuitive and you're having problems, then there must be something wrong with you) and more a matter of a professional challenge to tackle with knowledge and skills.

In undergraduate teacher education courses, student teaching, and graduate seminars, this same focus on skills and the development of common technical understandings should find a place. Technical understanding of teaching casts no aspersions on the importance of humanism or child development or detailed knowledge of age- and grade-specific content, methods, and materials. Student teachers in the primary grades, for example, would do well to know about unifix cubes and how to use them to teach place value. Similarly, student teachers in high school social studies would do well to know about the "History Alive" units and their uses. But teacher training (and in-service training) already deals with these things. In our development as a profession, it is time to deal with teaching itself.

*Source Materials*

"History Alive" Curriculum. Palo Alto, Calif.: Teachers Curriculum Institute.
　http://www.teachtci.com/prodev/compBackground.aspx

Joyce, B. R., Clark, C., and Peck, L. *Flexibility in Teaching.* White Plains, N.Y.: Longmans, 1981.

Ma, L. *Knowing and Teaching Elementary Mathematics: Teachers' Understanding of Fundamental Mathematics in China and the United States.* Mahwah, N.J.: Erlbaum, 1999.

Polanyi, M. *The Tacit Dimension.* New York: Doubleday, 1966.

Sanders, W. L., and Rivers, J. C. *Cumulative and Residual Effects of Teachers on Future Academic Achievement.* Knoxville: University of Tennessee, Value-Added Research and Assessment Center, 1996.

Saphier, J. *John Adams' Promise.* Acton, Mass.: Research for Better Teaching, 2005.

Shulman, L. "Paradigms and Research Programs in the Study of Teaching: A Contemporary Perspective." In M. C. Wittrock (ed.), *Handbook of Research on Teaching.* (3rd ed.). New York: Macmillan, 1986.

Taba, H. *Curriculum Development: Theory and Practice.* Orlando, Fla.: Harcourt, 1962.

West, L., and Staub, F. C. *Content Focused Coaching: Transforming Mathematics Lessons.* Portsmouth, N.H.: Heinemann, 2003.

# Teacher Beliefs

This is a book about how to make the knowledge base of teaching more accessible. It is also a book about teacher learning and a resource for it. There are certain beliefs about children, about teaching and learning, and about schools that bear heavily on a teacher's willingness to learn and what it is he or she feels impelled to seek to learn. We are convinced that some beliefs are essential to teacher learning. Without them, teachers will not be committed to stretching themselves fully or even commit themselves to that. Beliefs, which drive behavior, are often unexamined and are certainly resistant to change. But without understanding one's beliefs, it is impossible to understand one's attitude and motivation to learn new approaches to teaching.

One of these beliefs is about the nature of the knowledge about teaching itself.

Someone who believes there is no knowledge base on teaching will cruise on intuition and rely on the muse to inspire him or her toward improved performance. It is also easy to take the position that improving schools requires nothing more than recruiting superior people who know their content. The belief here is that any capable person who knows the subject matter can teach. In fact, this belief devalues the complexity of the work and hobbles teacher learning. And let there be no mistake, this position is abroad in the land and articulated frequently from pulpits of high visibility.

Another stance is to believe that the only real knowledge about teaching is internally generated through experience and that the only knowledge worth having comes from reflecting within and joining with peers to reflect together on teaching experience. Although this view is based on the valuable commitment to practice-based learning, it ignores the resource of public knowledge described in this book.

The belief that teaching knowledge consists of a prescribed set of effective behaviors is yet another unproductive mind-set. The nature of learning about teaching becomes reduced to the workmanlike task of following others' prescriptions for how to teach. Learn what the effective behaviors are, the story goes; then practice them and get good at them, and you will be a good teacher. (For commentary on the negative consequence of this belief, see Saphier, 2005).

For those who believe that teaching is intellectually complex, difficult, and demanding and that like that of any other true profession, its knowledge is based on repertoires and matching, then the doors of professional dialogue are opened wide. The need to learn with colleagues in examination of situation-specific questions comes to the fore, as does the need to reach out for new strategies and ways of thinking in the public knowledge base.

Think about why it is so difficult to get teachers to share their good ideas and successful practices openly at faculty meetings and other forums. Teachers who believe in the effectiveness paradigm assume there are right ways and wrong ways of doing things—effective and ineffective (or at least less effective). Suppose you share a successful practice that is different from what I do. The tacit inference, based on my effectiveness belief system, is that either you are right or I am—and you are either showing me up or trying to tell me how to do it right—which I'm not doing now. But if a school culture has internalized the belief in the complexity of teaching and the view of professional knowledge posed in this book, then I can hear your successful practice as an interesting alternative for my consideration, not a prescription for how to do it instead of the way I employ. So one belief essential to fruitful teacher learning and a strong professional community is about the nature of professional knowledge itself: that it is based on repertoires and matching, not effective behaviors.

The following sections examine a few other beliefs that we think are pivotal to teacher learning—beliefs that may be necessary to unleash curiosity and energy for teacher learning.

## Beliefs About Intelligence and Children's Capacity to Learn

Belief 1: *"You can get smart" (Howard, 1991, p. 12). Children's learning is primarily determined by their effective effort and use of appropriate strategies. "Intelligence" is not a fixed inborn limit on learning capacity. All children have the raw material to do rigorous academic material at high standards.*

Teachers who have internalized this belief believe it is their responsibility to:

- Communicate belief and confidence messages to all students
- Constantly reexamine their practices in light of student results
- Explicitly and implicitly teach their students how to mobilize effective effort
- Teach their students strategies for successful learning

Most Americans believe that intelligence is a fixed, innate entity that is endowed at birth, unevenly distributed, and determines how well a student can do. This belief in the bell curve of intelligence has huge implications for teaching and learning: that only a few students are smart enough to learn sophisticated academic material at high standards.

Teachers who believe that almost all of their students can achieve at a high level given the right conditions, that is, that students can increase their ability through application, focus, and good strategies, are almost driven to reconceptualize their role as a teacher. That reconceptualization would include being a teacher of strategies as well as a teacher of an academic discipline; it would include an implied obligation for the teacher to diversify his or her teaching to match different student learning styles. When a student isn't learning, it would drive the teacher to ask, "How might I approach this differently or alter the conditions?" And it would certainly imply developing the commitment to—and repertoire for—conveying high-expectation messages to students.

Others (Gould, 1996) have documented the history of this limiting view of intelligence, with its sad consequences for students. We present this history in Chapter Twelve, and make the case that intelligence can indeed be developed and that effective effort and good strategies are the principal determinants of academic success (see also Howard, 1991; Resnick, 1995). Our point is that a teacher's belief about the nature of intelligence and its limits (or limitlessness) forms a powerful frame around the motivation to expand his or her teaching repertoires. Anyone serious about professional development must address this belief system to unleash the full energy of adults to expand their capacity to reach all students.

## Beliefs About Learning

Belief 2: *Learning is constructed as learners assimilate new experience with prior knowledge.*

Teachers who accept this belief must construct learning experiences where the learners are active, applying knowledge and reflecting on its meaning out loud or in writing. It is their responsibility to create a balance between students' time receiving information and practicing skills and their time actively constructing, assimilating, and applying information in real contexts. This implies that teachers learn a variety of models of teaching and take it on themselves to learn how to develop the influence strand of Classroom Climate in this book (Chapter Fourteen). It particularly moves them to learn skills for making students' thinking visible (Chapter Nine) and ways to activate students' knowledge in relation to new concepts (also in Chapter Nine).

Belief 3: *Learning varies with the degree to which learners' needs for inclusion, influence, competence, and confidence are met.*

The psychological and cognitive milieu that teachers create has an enormous impact on what and how children learn. It is a teacher's professional responsibility to design an environment in which each child can succeed. Such an environment is characterized by community, mutual support, risk taking, and higher-level thinking for all. Teachers cannot narrow their self-definition to being representatives of academic discipline. They must think of themselves as teachers of students as well as teachers of a particular discipline. Influencing student motivation becomes part of their job description, along with teaching content. Thus, they become particularly interested in the skills for getting students to exert effective effort (see Chapter Twelve).

## Beliefs About Teachers and Teaching

Belief 4: *The nature of professional knowledge encompasses areas of performance, repertoire, and matching, not "effective behaviors."*

Skillful teaching requires informed and continuous decision making based on an understanding of multiple and interconnected areas of performance, repertoires, and matching versus learning a prescribed set of behaviors. Consequently, teachers are never finished learning. They must constantly enlarge their repertoire, stretch their comfort zones, and develop their ability to match students to reach more students with appropriate instruction.

Belief 5: *The knowledge bases of a professional teacher are many, diverse, and complex; and skillful teaching requires systematic and continual study of these knowledge bases.*

These knowledge bases include continuing development in knowledge about content, pedagogy, content-specific pedagogical knowledge, children and their differences, behaviors of individuals in effective organizations, and parent community involvement. For purposes of the category system here, *pedagogy* includes the study of curriculum design and planning. All of these are important areas of teacher knowledge in addition to interactive teaching skill.

Teachers must broaden their concept of professional development to include these domains and find ways to build repertoires in them.

## Beliefs About Schools and Schooling

Belief 6: *The total environment of a school has a powerful effect on students' learning.*

Teachers must participate actively with colleagues to shape the school as a learning environment. They must learn how to play a role in strengthening the institution and see themselves as players beyond the classroom, responsible for the system of the school. For this to happen, collegiality and interdependence need to be built into the fabric of their working relationships. Interdependence requires that they function as both leaders and team players and that they support a balance of autonomy and cohesion in curriculum and teaching practices.

Skillful teachers are leaders who take the initiative to influence colleagues toward ideas they value and move the school toward practices they believe will strengthen everyone. They are team players, collaborating with colleagues to improve the school and help individual students, and willing to give up some autonomy for actions implied by common visions and agreements.

The connection between teacher learning and this belief in interdependence and collegiality is that only teachers who have regular interaction with their colleagues through joint work can experience the benefit of their knowledge and the synergy of creating new knowledge with others.

Belief 7: *Racism exerts a downward force on the achievement of students of color that must be met with active antiracist teaching.*

Cultural and institutional manifestations of racism are carried over into school as the stereotypes, distortions, or omission of cultures other than Western European from curriculum.

The American view of intelligence as innate, fixed, and deterministic compounds the problem. It mingles with racism and creates the secret belief, articulated about once every several decades (Jensen, 1969; Herrnstein and Murray, 1994), that people of color, particularly African Americans, are less intelligent than whites. This induces differential teacher behavior toward students of color (Rist, 1970) and stereotype vulnerability (Steele, 1992) among the students themselves—that is, actual lower performance in situations where their race even subtly calls their ability into question.

All teachers need thorough education about these issues. They need information and experiences that will cause them to examine their tacit beliefs about people of color and the practices of society that reinforce them. And above all, they need to build culturally relevant teaching (see Chapter Fourteen) into their practice.

Readers could make the case for including other beliefs as well that can move teachers' behavior toward curiosity, sharing, reaching out to the knowledge base, and expanding repertoires. Our concern here is not to lay out a definitive set of beliefs; it is in posing the question, "How can we nurture beliefs that foster teacher learning and build supports for them into the cultures of our schools?" Without doing so, professional learning (and enduring school progress) is hamstrung.

We urge all our readers to join us in pondering this question and framing responses in action at their worksites, as we ourselves are trying to do at schools where we work. In addition, we offer one concluding thought: the most powerful lever for influencing teacher learning and beliefs may be teacher induction programs.

In the decade following the publication of this book, two-thirds of the American teaching force will turn over. In 2017 two-thirds of the teachers will be individuals who are not here now. Over their first three years on the job, their beliefs about teaching knowledge and its nature, collaborative work, how students learn, their conception of the role of a teacher, and their place in the ecosystem of the school will be formed and solidified through what they see modeled by significant figures around them, by what mentors tell and show them, by what colleagues help them discover, by what messages their administrators send to them about openness and seeking help, and by what support they experience for their own learning in college. Therefore, among all the possible avenues for teacher development, we put induction programs at the top of the priority list. Specifically we recommend these steps:

1. Train a large and dedicated corps of instructional specialists to be knowledgeable in adult development, observation and coaching skills, differential conferencing skills, and, above all, the knowledge bases of professional teaching. Expect them to spend three hours each week with their new teacher colleagues and to learn how to use teachable moments to help new teachers develop the beliefs outlined in this chapter.

2. Redefine building leadership (the principalship) to include leadership for strong culture with an emphasis on data analysis of student learning and design of reteaching, collegiality, experimentation, and reaching out to the knowledge base. Train, support, and evaluate leaders on their ability to deliver such leadership.

To check your knowledge about Teacher Beliefs, see the quiz on our Web site at **www.RBTeach.com/rbteach/quiz/FEBeliefs.html**.

## Source Materials

Gould, S. J. *The Mismeasure of Man.* New York: W. W. Norton, 1996.

Herrnstein, R. J., and Murray, C. *The Bell Curve: Intelligence and Class Structure in American Life.* New York: Simon & Schuster, 1994.

Howard, J. *Getting Smart: The Social Construction of Intelligence.* Lexington, Mass.: Efficacy, 1991.

Jensen, A. "How Much Can We Boost IQ and Scholastic Achievement?" *Harvard Education Review,* Winter 1969, pp. 1–123.

Resnick, L. "From Aptitude to Effort: A New Foundation for Our Schools." *Daedalus,* Fall 1995, *124*(4), 55–62.

Rist, R. "Student Social Class and Teacher Expectations: A Self-Fulfilling Prophecy in Ghetto Education." *Harvard Educational Review,* Aug. 1970, *40*(3), 411–451.

Saphier, J. *John Adams' Promise.* Acton, Mass.: Research for Better Teaching, 2005.

Steele, C. "Race and Schooling of Black Americans." *The Atlantic Monthly,* Apr. 1992, pp. 68–78.

# INTRODUCTION TO MANAGEMENT

**A**n effective management system paves the way for learning to occur with minimal interference and maximal nourishment. Part One therefore lays the groundwork for instruction.

Attention to each of six management areas—and the conscious choices made within those areas—can have a positive impact on the climate and tone of day-to-day classroom operations. This in turn will create an environment conducive to learning and achievement.

There are six important management areas:

- *Attention:* How do teachers get student attention, keep it focused on learning, and refocus it when it drifts? This chapter explores recent brain research and relevant guidelines that emerge for focusing attention. It also offers a vast repertoire of interactive tools that serve this purpose.
- *Momentum:* How do teachers anticipate, manage, or circumvent blocks to the smooth orderly flow of classroom life in order to preserve maximum time for learning? In this chapter, we identify eight categories of events teachers monitor to minimize disruptions to the learning environment.
- *Space:* How is the classroom's physical space arranged and used to support instructional objectives and signal what is important? This chapter examines repertoire and flexibility in furniture and seating arrangements with an eye to matching them to different forms of learning and ensuring easy access, visual and physical, to every student in the room. It also explores the ways in which space allocation and location of materials and resources indicate awareness of (and responsiveness to) students' psychological needs to feel a sense of ownership, privacy, and self-sufficiency.
- *Time:* What principles of time allocation do teachers need to use to guide the planning and implementation of successful learning experiences? The bottom line in this area of performance is maximizing student engaged and high-success time. This requires effective management systems, attention to pacing

and rhythm during instructional time, and structures for providing ongoing and meaningful feedback when students are engaged in independent work.

- *Routines:* What routines are important in order to maximize smooth operations and minimize wasted time and energy (teacher and students)? How do teachers ensure that students know what the routines are, why they are important, and how to carry them out? These questions are the primary focus of this chapter.

- *Discipline:* Vigilance in the above areas lays a solid foundation on which to build this sixth area of management. In this chapter we highlight the interconnectedness of areas of performance other than management: personal relationship building, clarity of instruction, design of learning experiences, the appropriateness of objectives, and the need to establish, communicate, reinforce, and uphold clear standards and expectations for behavior in order to help students learn what is appropriate and inappropriate, acceptable and unacceptable in a communal environment. Teachers also need to be prepared for the small percentage of students who, for any number of complex reasons, require something more. The chapter explains models of discipline that teachers can add to their toolkits over time for use with the most resistant students.

The most important issue overall for teachers regarding management is to keep their eye on the prize: developing, monitoring, and adjusting their management systems in ways that clear obstacles to student learning and help students to develop their identities as capable, respected, and self-reliant high achievers. Fred Jones (2000) defines classroom management as a "system that includes instructional strategies focused on making students independent and resourceful, motivational strategies that help students be more conscientious and accountable, and discipline strategies that reduce goofing off, set limits, and train students to be responsible and cooperate with one another." We think that sums it up pretty well.

*Source*

Jones, F. *Tools for Teaching: Discipline, Instruction, Motivation.* Santa Cruz, Calif.: Frederic Jones and Associates, 2000.

# Attention

## How do I get students to pay attention and stay on task?

Brain Research

A Continuum of Tools from Authority to Attraction

Analyzing Attention Behavior

Matching with Attention Moves

*Children are often criticized for "not paying attention." There is no such thing as not paying attention; the brain is always paying attention to something. What we really mean is that the child or student is not paying attention to what we think is relevant or important. Attention, as all of us know, is selective.*

PATRICIA WOLFE (2001, P. 80)

Focusing student attention on learning experiences is perhaps the most fundamental management challenge a teacher faces daily, hourly, and moment to moment in any classroom. In many ways, Attention is the bellwether area of performance among the group of management areas. Unless students are paying attention to the instruction, it does not matter how good the lesson may be. Engaging and involving students on task in large group, small group, or individual learning experiences is what Attention is all about—indeed, what management is all about. It is the precondition for instruction, the sine qua non for curriculum implementation.

## Brain Research

To determine what works and how to gain and maintain student attention most effectively and efficiently, it is prudent to consider how some of the brain research of the past two decades informs thinking. As Jensen (2000) put it, "The challenge for a teacher is knowing how to capitalize on the brain's attentional biases while also engaging students in meaningful learning." This challenge is twofold: capturing students' attention and sustaining their focus on what the teacher deems to be important.

## Building a Repertoire

Two generalizations derived from brain research have implications for classroom practice. The first, according to Jensen (2000), is that "the human brain is designed to selectively attend to stimuli . . . has a built-in bias for certain types of stimuli . . . and a natural prioritization process is occurring all the time, consciously and unconsciously" (p. 121). Second, key factors in the brain's initial filtering include novelty or contrast to what is familiar, intensity of stimuli, movement, and emotion. (Wolfe, 2001; Jensen, 2000).

These imply the need to design learning experiences that are vivid, varied, and delivered with passion and enthusiasm for the subject matter.

Learning experiences that begin with or incorporate an element of novelty or surprise grab attention: the physics teacher who introduces Newton's first law by ripping a tablecloth from under a place setting without disturbing the place setting, the math teacher who enters dressed as Cleopatra when she will be teaching about number systems and place value, or two teachers who stage an argument in front of class to introduce a lesson on conflict and conflict resolution.

Later in this chapter, we describe ways in which teachers keep students alert by doing things in the moment that are surprising or out of the ordinary (like breaking into song to give directions when student attention has drifted or randomizing calling-on patterns so a student never knows for sure when it will be her turn); ways in which teachers enlist interest in the content through the use of voice variety, gestures, challenges, and props; and ways in which a teacher wins student attention with positive emotional overtones such as praise, enthusiasm, humor, and dramatization.

That teachers need to build a repertoire of ways to capture the brain's attention is an important consideration here. Wolfe (2001) points out that although novelty is an innate attention getter, it is also short-lived. Repeated use of any particular strategy or format can result in habituation: the natural tendency of the brain to ignore a stimulus once it has become familiar.

Jensen (2000, p. 121) notes that the "brain is designed to attend selectively to stimuli, prioritizing on the basis of perceived importance and screening out that which seems to be less crucial to survival. The level of attention people apply to a learning situation is influenced or limited by their perception of its value." And Wolfe (2001, p. 83) holds that "two factors strongly influence whether the brain initially attends to arriving information and whether this attention will be sustained." These two factors are meaning and emotion. Thus, for students to want to attend, they need to know why something is important, personally relevant, and worthy of their attention. In Chapter Nine we discuss framing the learning for students—giving them the big picture of where a learning experience fits into a larger context—by sharing the objectives, explaining what it is they will be able to do as a result of a learning experience and why it is important to be able to do it, by activating their knowledge related to the topic, and by helping them make connections between what they already know and what they are about to study. In other words, teachers need to establish meaning for information being introduced.

## Attention Level

Attention level is determined by the interaction of various factors: sensory input (sources of information such as textbooks, videos, fieldtrips, etc.); data's intensity or perceived importance; and the brain's 'chemical flavor' of the moment . . ." [Jensen, 2000, p. 123].

Teachers need to consider the types of input or explanatory devices to employ when presenting information and ensure that they enable students with different modality strengths (auditory, visual, kinetic, and kinesthetic) equal opportunity to absorb and process information. (This is discussed in more detail in Chapters Nine and Nineteen.)

## Emotional State

Emotion drives attention, and attention drives learning [Sylwester, 1995].

All learning is state dependent: the physiological, emotional, postural, and psychological state learners are in will mediate content. And these states are related to the chemical "flavor of the moment" in the brain. Chemicals can be too high, resulting in hyper or stressed states; chemicals can be too low, yielding drowsiness. The learner's state can be influenced in the classroom with simple interventions [Jensen, 2000, p. 125].

Teachers need to recognize and do something when students' emotional states are either too low or too high to enable them to focus. They need to develop a repertoire of ways to induce emotional state changes or bring them into balance when the need arises. For example, to induce calm, Jensen suggests calling up predictable, ritual activities such as routine openings, closings, and greetings. When the need is to energize or motivate, teachers might introduce novelty or unexpected change. The former (inducing calm) points to ele-

ments of classroom climate (Chapter Fourteen), especially ways to create a sense of community and belonging. This also makes the case for strategic use of the principle of learning called Similarity of Environment (Chapter Ten). Another of the principles of learning, Vividness, highlights inducing surprise to energize. It underscores why doing something out of the ordinary to surprise or startle students can serve as an effective in-the-moment attention move.

## Laughter

Laughter has been shown to boost the body's production of neurotransmitters critical for alertness and memory. Some studies have shown that having fun and pleasant experiences improve the functioning of the body's immune system for three days [Fry, 1997, in Jensen, 2000, p. 125].

Teachers, like everyone else, need to enjoy the work they do, laugh with students, and see the humor in the everyday life of a classroom. One of us attended a presentation by a motivational speaker several years ago who put it this way: "If by 10 o'clock every morning we haven't had ourselves a good belly laugh, something is very wrong. It means we must be taking ourselves too seriously because working with a room full of children is very funny business!" Teachers need to give themselves permission to be silly or outrageous at times and draw the students into their mood. This can be done through the use of props, costumes, dramatization, or telling funny stories, among others. There needs to be a balance in designing learning experiences that are at once enjoyable and challenging (see the Feeling Tone principle of learning in Chapter Ten).

## Assessing the Challenge

Optimal learning occurs when there is a balance between level of challenge and level of existing knowledge or skills: if the challenge is greater than the skills, it can create anxiety; if the skills are greater than the challenge, boredom is likely.

This suggests that getting students into optimal learning states requires assessing the potential gap between the readiness level of the student and the challenge present in the learning experience. This sometimes calls for preassessment activities, analysis of the data, and differentiating the learning experience accordingly. (See Chapters Eighteen and Nineteen for more on each of these.)

## Physical Movement

> When the brain is fully engaged it is more efficient and effective. Vigorous physical activity is believed to increase blood flow to the brain. Cross lateral movement that works both sides of the body evenly and involves coordinated motion of both eyes, both ears, both hands, and both feet activates both hemispheres and all four lobes of the brain. As a result, "cognitive functioning is heightened and ease of learning increases" [Hannaford, 2005, p. 92].

This can have dramatic effects on learning. Intermittent physical movement throughout a learning experience is critical to maintaining the highest levels of attention. Jensen (2000) suggests starting a class period with two minutes of stretching to increase the overall alertness students bring to the learning experience. If learning experiences call for students to be sedentary for periods of time, the teacher needs to plan with movement in mind. The movement doesn't have to be a break from the focus of the lesson. But if students have a reason to move periodically (for example, get together with a learning partner seated in some other part of the room for two or three minutes of stand-up processing time; a team relay race where students go to the board one team member at a time to build a proof to a problem; groups working together to build a human sculpture representing the structure of an atom), chances are they will remain more alert and focused for longer periods of time. The movement breaks don't have to be long; they just have to be timely, occurring at least every twenty to forty minutes. Teachers who notice that attention is fading need to ask themselves how long it has been since students last moved.

## Learning Downtime

> Humans are natural meaning seeking organisms but excessive input can conflict with that process. . . . You can either have your learner's attention or they can be making meaning, but never both at the same time. The brain needs time to "go inside" and link the present with the past and future. Without this, learning drops dramatically. We absorb so much information non-consciously that downtime is absolutely necessary to process it all. The brain has an automatic mechanism for shifting (internal and external) and for shutting down input when it needs to [Jensen, 2000, p. 123].

When people are taking in information from any external source by listening, reading, seeing, or doing, for example, pauses must be built in systematically to give the learner time to absorb and organize . . . , reflect and process the information . . . , make connections, and construct personal meaning. If teachers don't consciously attend to this, the learner will do it anyway out of necessity and will appear to have stopped paying attention. In Chapter Nine, we discuss guidelines for how often and how long the pauses for processing should occur.

## Summary

Hence, a number of considerations and design principles serve as preconditions for students to be able to attend most fully:

- Frame each learning experience for students (Clarity).
- Use a range of auditory, visual, and kinesthetic explanatory devices when presenting information (Clarity).
- Pay attention to the feeling tone of the learning experience and mood of the students, and adjust where necessary.
- Consider preassessment to determine where students are currently in relation to where you want them to be by the end of the lesson, and design for differences in readiness levels of students.
- Pause regularly and periodically (every eight to ten minutes) to have students process what they are taking in before adding more information.
- Plan for at least two minutes of physical movement of some kind within every twenty to forty minutes of sitting time.
- Laugh with your students, and pay attention to the emotional climate in the room.

Without conscious attention to these considerations, teachers make the work much harder for themselves and their students, and the likelihood that students will be paying attention to what teachers want them to attend to is significantly diminished.

## A Continuum of Tools from Authority to Attraction

Skillful teachers lay the groundwork for focusing student attention by systematically incorporating the principles and guidelines cited above into the everyday fabric of classroom life. In addition to that, Figure 3.1 contains a wide range of in-the-moment moves that a teacher might use to capture, maintain, and recapture or refocus student attention. Teachers tend to need these most when a learning experience is whole-group oriented and teacher directed.

Within this general class of Attention moves, there are five categories: desisting, alerting, enlisting, acknowledging, and winning. The skillful teacher's repertoire for getting and keeping students on task should include at least a few moves from each of these categories. This is critical to being able to match the choice of move to what the situation warrants.

Keep in mind as we describe each of these that this list is meant to be an objective list of moves teachers make that get students' attention. In other words, we are describing every type of move we have seen or heard a teacher do that was for this purpose, but without judging the appropriateness, effectiveness, or relative merit of any individual move on the list. In order to determine the appropriateness of each of these moves, each teacher has to examine the context within which it is being used and its impact on students.

### Desisting

Desisting moves carry the message, "Stop what you are doing and shift your attention elsewhere," or "Get with it," and are most applicable when students are drifting off course. All the moves in this

**Figure 3.1.  A Repertoire of Attention Moves**

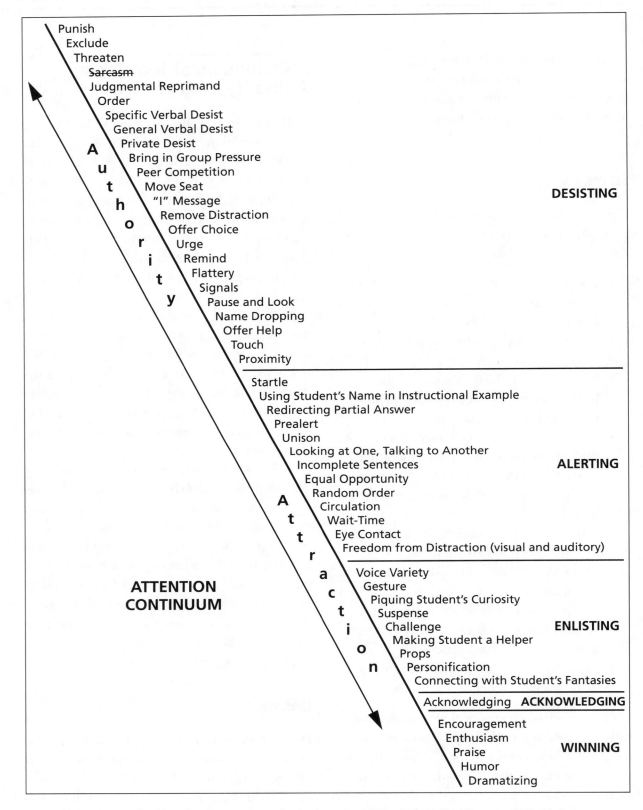

Punish
Exclude
Threaten
~~Sarcasm~~
Judgmental Reprimand
Order
Specific Verbal Desist
General Verbal Desist
Private Desist
Bring in Group Pressure
Peer Competition
Move Seat
"I" Message
Remove Distraction
Offer Choice
Urge
Remind
Flattery
Signals
Pause and Look
Name Dropping
Offer Help
Touch
Proximity

**DESISTING**

Startle
Using Student's Name in Instructional Example
Redirecting Partial Answer
Prealert
Unison
Looking at One, Talking to Another
Incomplete Sentences
Equal Opportunity
Random Order
Circulation
Wait-Time
Eye Contact
Freedom from Distraction (visual and auditory)

**ALERTING**

Voice Variety
Gesture
Piquing Student's Curiosity
Suspense
Challenge
Making Student a Helper
Props
Personification
Connecting with Student's Fantasies

**ENLISTING**

Acknowledging  **ACKNOWLEDGING**

Encouragement
Enthusiasm
Praise
Humor
Dramatizing

**WINNING**

Authority

Attraction

**ATTENTION
CONTINUUM**

**Research for Better Teaching, Inc.** • One Acton Place, Acton, MA 01720 • (978) 263-9449 • www.RBTeach.com

category are ways of telling students that they are doing something you want them to stop doing. Some are subtle, even silent. Others are more up front, out loud, and forceful. Some imply or state specifically what the students should be doing instead. Each can be a constructive way to signal you mean business and to get a student to shift focus or reengage.

The list that follows identifies a range of desisting moves, ordered from most forceful to least forceful, and gives an example of each. The general rule of thumb in the desist category is to apply the law of least resistance: use only the degree of directness and force warranted to reengage the student and maintain a calm disposition while delivering the message. Another consideration, especially with any of the more direct and forceful moves toward the top, is whether to deliver the message privately or publicly. The obvious benefit of a private message is to save face for the student.

1. Punish, or deliver a consequence for off-task or distracting behavior: "That will cost you half of recess." "You will be making up this time and the work this afternoon on your own time."

2. Exclude, or remove, the student from the situation that is distracting: "Leave the group, Michaela, and come back when you feel you are ready to focus."

3. Threaten with a consequence: "Stop it now or leave the group."

4. Sarcasm: *see page 25 for more information.*

5. Judgmental reprimand: "Stop that annoying tapping."

6. Order: "Get back to work now." "Sit on your hands until you're absolutely sure you're not going to touch anyone."

7. Specific verbal desist: Naming the behavior to stop and giving the student the appropriate

replacement behavior: "Stop dancing, Jim, and get back to your lab report."

8. General verbal desist: Vaguer language to stop a behavior: "Amanda, cut it out."

9. Private desist: General or specific but spoken to the student privately.

10. Bring in group pressure: "Rafael, none of us can leave for gym until you're with us." The classmates chime in, "Yeah, Rafael, come on!"

11. Peer competition: "John's ready. Are you, Beth?"

12. Move seat: "Jimmy, move over to table four, please." "You two are such good friends that you will be continuously distracted if I let you sit together."

13. I message: This has three parts: (1) a non-judgmental description of the behavior, (2) the way it makes you feel, and (3) the tangible effect: "When you are talking in your table groups while I am giving directions, it frustrates me. There are some real challenges to doing this task, and some of you are going to blow it simply because you won't be aware of what to look out for."

14. Remove distraction: Without speaking to her, Mr. Glade walks by Antonia and picks up the eraser she is playing with. He puts it in his pocket and walks down the aisle, continuing the discussion with the class.

15. Offer choice: Observing Antonia playing with the eraser, Mr. Glade says quietly, "Antonia, you can put it away or give it to me."

16. Urge: "C'mon, Jill, let's get in gear?" "Okay, let's settle down and be really good listeners."

17. Remind: "What are you supposed to be doing, Shelly?"

18. Flattery: "You're too conscientious to waste your time this way." "That kind of behavior is beneath your dignity. You are better than that."

19.  Signals: Bell ring, raised hand, piano chord, or something similar established with the students in advance and used routinely without verbal comment to call all activity and noise to a halt (momentarily or to make a transition). Or, without breaking the flow of talk with one student, the teacher holds up a hand in a "stop" gesture to a third student, signaling him to cease interrupting (or whatever else he's doing) and perhaps implying by facial expression and body language, "Wait a minute. I'll be right with you."

20.  Pause and look: Teacher pauses and looks at the child or group until the behavior ceases.

21.  Name dropping: Dropping a student's name into the flow of conversation (not to call on the student) but for purposes of attention: "Now the next problem—Jess—that we're going to tackle has some of the same elements—Jess—but the exponents are simpler."

22.  Offer help: "How can I help you get started with this, Hilda?"

23.  Touch: Teacher places a hand gently on the student's shoulder or some other neutral place—or points to a specific part of the text in front of the student. This may or may not be accompanied by the teacher's stopping the activity and making eye contact.

24.  Proximity: Being or moving physically near the student whose attention is wandering or likely to wander.

The reader will note in Figure 3.1 that we have crossed off sarcasm. By this we mean remarks that are intended to mock or deride a student: "Did you leave your head at home again, Grant?" "Imagine that! Grant is so busy watching what is going on outside that he doesn't know where we are in the book." "Mackenzie (who is combing her hair and looking in the mirror), your hair is ready for the cover of *GQ*, but I'd rather you were looking at the test tube and what is going on in it." We have represented it on the list because regrettably some teachers use it to redirect student attention and sarcasm usually does get students' attention: not only the student to whom it is aimed but to many others in class who may dive for (emotional) cover when it is delivered, hoping they won't be the next target. So an objective, descriptive list of attention moves would be incomplete without acknowledging sarcasm. But because it always involves some degree of personal derision—and because we are such powerful role models for students during these impressionable years—we have taken the philosophical position that it shouldn't even be considered as an option in any context. We believe the use of sarcasm is too costly to the overall psychological and emotional climate of the classroom and is at least a small killer of relationships.

## Alerting

Alerting moves are aimed at keeping students on their toes. Most of them function as moves intended to minimize distraction and attention dropout and maximize participation and engagement. As with desisting moves, the various alerting moves differ in the degree of force expressed in the move. From most to least forceful, these are:

1.  Startle: Doing something out of the ordinary or surprising to capture attention. Noticing that attention is wandering as a group listens to a recording, the teacher abruptly hits the Stop button and pops a question: "Why do you suppose Jefferson felt that way about Hamilton?"

2.  Using student's name in instructional example: "President Kiesha Royston sits impeached and convicted. Who then would

become president? And we thought life was tough under Kiesha! Now Vice President Christiane Baker becomes president. It's time to pack our bags and move to Canada!"

3. Redirecting partial answer: Wendy has begun to answer, and you say: "Take it from there, Andrew. How would you finish what Wendy is saying?"

4. Prealert: "That's right. Take the next one, Dwayne. Check him, Holly, and be ready to step in if he calls for assistance." (This is aimed at keeping Holly on her toes.)

5. Unison: "6 times 6 is—Jane? That's right. 8 times 8 is—everybody." The goal is to get all students to respond at once; other versions include students responding to questions or problems on individual whiteboards that they hold up all at once (see Chapter Seven ["dipsticking"] for more ways to do this).

6. Looking at one, talking to another: Looking at Royce, the teacher says, "Antonia, give us an example of—" (This lasts but a moment.)

7. Incomplete sentences: ". . . and so, as we all know, the thing that we put at the end of a sentence is a—" This might be accompanied by open hands and raised eyebrows at the group or hand gestures encouraging someone to respond.

8. Equal opportunity: The teacher establishes some sort of system (calling sticks or name cards, for example) so that students know they will each be called on sooner or later, and perhaps at any time. Students also know that they're not off the hook once they are called on and could be called on again at any time.

9. Random order: Students are called on out of sequence of their seating pattern so they can't predict when it will be their turn and therefore have to be alert.

10. Circulation: The teacher physically moves around the room while facilitating large group learning experiences.

11. Wait time: Intentionally inserting three to five seconds or more of silence after posing a question to the whole group, allowing thinking time for all to process before anyone responds. Or once a student has been called on, the teacher stays out of the way for at least five seconds so the student has the opportunity to construct a response. During the silence, the other students are induced to focus on that question silently in anticipation that it might be referred to them next.

12. Eye contact: The teacher makes frequent eye-to-eye contact with all students in a group.

13. Freedom from visual and auditory distraction: Arranging the room so that small group work takes place facing a corner or away from the main visual field in the room, or so that instructional or quiet work areas are separated from active and noisy areas. Alternatively, you direct the class, "Close your eyes and just listen."

## Enlisting

We call the third category *enlisting moves* because their purpose is to enlist, or sign up, an individual student's (or an entire group's) voluntary engagement in curriculum activities. These moves are intended to captivate students and sweep them away in the interest or excitement of the activity. They capture attention by emphasizing the appeal or attractiveness of the activity. Enlisting moves include these:

1. Voice variety: The teacher varies his speaking tone, pitch, volume, or inflection to emphasize points and add interest.
2. Gesture: Using hand or body movements to emphasize points or add interest.
3. Piquing student's curiosity: "What do you suppose could possibly have caused Alexander to behave in such a bizarre way?"
4. Suspense: With her back to the students, the teacher puts on a costume, a face, a wig, or something else; ten to fifteen seconds elapse while the students wait to see what the costume represents.
5. Challenge: "This next one will fool all of you!"
6. Making student a helper: "Jim, will you hold up those two test tubes for the group to see, please?" (Jim's attention has been wandering.)
7. Props: Using physical objects related to the content (for example, the take-apart human torso or hats to represent different vocations)
8. Personification, or attributing human characteristics to inanimate objects: "So, Sodium says to Chloride, 'How'd ya like to hook up?'" or "Now, if Mr. W were to walk through the door right now and look for things that started with his sound, what would he find to make him feel at home?"
9. Connecting with student's fantasies: "So the NFL drafts Ben and signs him for three years at $28 million a year. Which tax bracket is that likely to place him in?"

## Acknowledging

Sometimes students are inattentive for reasons that have nothing to do with what's going on in school or how skillful the teacher is. Some outside event is weighing on them (or exciting them)—for example,

their best friend refused to sit next to them on the bus this morning, their parents have just separated, they are playing in a championship game that afternoon. Or, hail the size of golf balls starts falling outside the classroom window.

At such times, merely acknowledging out loud to students your understanding of the distraction—or what's on their mind—can enable them to pay more attention in class. It is validating (and rare) to have one's feelings really heard, and simply acknowledging those feelings can facilitate attention. For example, saying, "I know you're excited about the hockey game tonight, especially with three stalwarts right here in our midst. But I'm asking you to put that on the shelf for a while, gang, because today's review is very important."

As another example, seven-year-old Sadé is distracted during reading group. Her glance shifts repeatedly to the place she left to come to group (a display of dolls from foreign lands that she was arranging). In a flash, the teacher sizes this up and, knowing that Sadé realizes that lunch will immediately follow reading, figures out that the child is feeling that she'll never be able to finish arranging the dolls. (After lunch can seem like forever to a seven-year-old.) So the teacher makes an acknowledging move: "Sadé, I know it's important to you to get all the dolls neatly arranged. You can devote yourself to that right before we go to lunch, I promise. Only now you need to work with us on this reading because we won't be doing this later. I'll make sure you get back there." Getting the dolls arranged may not seem important from an adult point of view, but such seemingly trivial matters can be consuming to children and block their involvement unless teachers perceive and respond.

Here is one more example. Perceiving that Marvin is concerned about something, the teacher makes this acknowledging move: "You're afraid you'll miss your turn at the listening station, Marvin?" Marvin nods. "Look, take your time, and do this paper well. I'll see to it that you get your turn as soon as you're done, even if we've passed you on the sign-up sheet."

Sometimes the teacher just asks, "Brenda, what's on your mind? You don't seem with us this morning." Further probing and active listening may or may not release this block. However, sometimes just talking about what's on the student's mind, without any solution from the teacher, will be unburdening enough to permit the student to reenter here-and-now tasks.

## Winning

Winning moves are similar to enlisting moves in that they are positive and tend to attract rather than force students' attention to the learning experience. However, we have distinguished winning from enlisting moves because winning moves focus students on the teacher, whereas enlisting moves focus students' attention more on the activity or the content. This is where teachers use their personality to mediate attention. The continuum of winning moves includes these:

1.  Encouragement: Prompting students' ongoing work, usually by means of voice quality and facial expression: "Keep going, you're getting it." A student says, "I don't know . . ." and the teacher responds, "Sure you do. What's one?"

2.  Enthusiasm: "That's a fascinating topic for a paper, Nikki! Wait 'til you see what's in this Web site!"

3.  Praise: "You really worked hard on that, Priya, and it shows everywhere!"

4.  Humor: Joking in a positive, supportive man-

ner, without sarcasm, that is mutually enjoyed by the students.

5.  Dramatizing: Acting out or performing material related to the lesson, or directing students to dramatize experiences. Here the teacher switches into role and speaks a line of dialogue through the persona of a character whose identity he has assumed, even if just for a single sentence: "Well, here I go into the den of smiling vipers." (The teacher has become newly elected President Abraham Lincoln entering his first cabinet meeting where all the officers think they'd be a better president than he and are in fact plotting to get rid of him.)

## Analyzing Attention Behavior

All of the types of moves from all five categories could be arranged along a single continuum whose rule is authority to attraction (see Figure 3.1). Moves and categories at the upper end of the continuum employ the most teacher authority most directly and firmly applied. As one travels down the continuum, the authority component becomes less and less dominant.

Thus, Attention is an area of performance of teaching that involves a more or less continuous scale of values along a functional attribute, the functional attribute being moves whose end is to engage, maintain, or reengage students' attention in the learning experience.

One way of thinking about the items in the figure is as a set of tools. Those in the desist category might be considered different types of hammers; those in the alerting category might be considered different types of wrenches; those in the enlisting category might be considered screwdrivers of various lengths, sizes, and tips; and so on. Just as a craftsperson would recognize the various categories of tools and the subtle differences among items within a category, so too can teachers study each of the categories and items on this list as discrete and distinct tools available for use. And any craftsperson would know that hammers are designed for certain types of jobs, wrenches for other jobs, and so on. They select the tool that is best suited (or matched) to a particular situation or job. So too it is with this tool kit for teachers: being familiar with and knowing how to use each of the tools is a goal to aim for over time. Acquiring a few of the tools in each of the categories—that is, building a repertoire from which you can pick and choose depending on the nature of the job—is essential to becoming a master of your trade.

One way to use this continuum is to profile one's own teaching performance. Which attention moves do I use? How many and which of the five categories do I use? What does my profile reveal about my attention repetoire? Some teachers have had colleagues or supervisors observe them to gather concrete examples of attention moves in their notes. Then later, using the notes as evidence, they check off on the continuum the moves the teacher made. A self-profile or the pattern of attention moves shown from such an analysis can be used to examine your existing repertoire and the appropriateness and effectiveness of your choices, which leads to the issue of matching.

## Matching with Attention Moves

The attention continuum is intended to be an objective list; that is, no judgments are implied about moves at the bottom being inherently better than moves at the top, or vice versa. We are arguing, in fact, that all the moves have a place, and each may be appropriate in a given context.

This array of attention moves offers a wealth of possibilities to classroom teachers. Teachers with well-developed repertoires in this area of teaching respond to different students in consistent but different ways. For example, the following descriptions illustrate how Mrs. T skillfully matches her attention moves to individual students.

Mrs. T knows that Daryl looks for power conflicts; he invites tests of will with her or any other authority figure. When she uses almost any of the desisting moves with him, he gets worse. For instance, he takes a specific verbal desist as a challenge to tap his pencil even louder and see what he can goad Mrs. T into doing, so she has learned to use alerting and enlisting moves with him. If he really gets out of hand, she will move firmly and remove him, but she often avoids the necessity for doing that and does get Daryl to pay attention by challenging him with a question, prealerting him, or by using the move of making a student a helper. She uses this last move when she sees him tapping the pencil and says, "—and so there really were four pyramids for the kings. Daryl, will you advance the PowerPoint to the next frame so I can point to things from the front?"

Monica is a different sort of child. Although she also engages in frequent off-task behavior, enlisting moves seem to overstimulate her. Mrs. T explains, "It's as if she interprets enlisting and winning moves as 'I-want to-be-your-friend' or 'I-want to-play' messages from me. She gets carried away with the interaction and focuses too much on me." While she looks for other ways and other opportunities to meet this need for closeness that Monica seems to have, during work times, Mrs. T uses midrange desisting and alerting moves (reminding, the look, prealerts) consistently, and successfully, with Monica when she's off task .

Different students—with different needs—require different moves, and skillful teachers deliberately match their moves to students. Some experienced teachers are intuitive about the way they differentiate these moves across their students, and they are known as effective classroom managers. They may not be able to explain why they choose what they do. They just seem to know that they have it right. Perhaps it is a subconscious acuteness they have at matching attention moves to various students.

Whether or not they have this intuitive flair, all teachers can benefit from reflecting on the patterns of inattention among their students and examining them in relation to the patterns of moves they seem to be making in response. They may discover that they are overlooking part of their available repertoire because they get so irritated with Adam, or that the repertoire could be enlarged, or that they could do better matching if they looked for the reason behind the inattention. Talking about a student (or a group) with a colleague using the attention continuum can be a highly engaging and productive activity.

To check your knowledge about Attention Moves see the quiz on our Web site at **www. RBTeach.com/rbteach/quiz/attention.html.**

*Source Materials on Attention*

Bennett, N. "Recent Research on Teaching: A Dream, a Belief, and a Model." *Journal of Education,* 1978, *160*(3), 5–37.

Brophy, J. E., and Evertson, C. M. *Learning from Teaching.* Needham Heights, Mass.: Allyn & Bacon, 1978.

Church, J., in collaboration with Hasenstab, J. *Teaching with T.E.A.C.H.* Emerson, N.J.: Performance Learning Systems, 1985.

Fry, W. "Role of Laughter." In E. Jensen (ed.), *Brain-Based Learning.* San Diego, Calif.: Brain Store Publishing, 2000.

Hannaford, C. *Smart Moves: Why Learning Is Not All in Your Head.* Arlington, Va.: Great River Books, 2005.

Jensen, E. *Brain-Based Learning.* San Diego, Calif.: Brain Store Publishing, 2000.

Martin, D. L. "Your Praise Can Smother Learning." *Learning,* Feb. 1977, pp. 43–51.

McKenzie, R., and Schadler, A. M. "Effects of Three Practice Modes on Attention, Test Anxiety, and Achievement in a Classroom Association Learning Task." Paper presented at the American Educational Regional Association, Boston, Mass., 1980.

Redl, F., and Wineman, D. *Controls from Within.* New York: Free Press, 1952.

Rosenshine, B. V. "Academic Engaged Time, Content Covered, and Direct Instruction." *Journal of Education,* 1978, *160*(3), 38–66.

Rowe, M. B. "Wait Time and Rewards as Instructional Variables: Their Influence on Language, Logic and Fate Control." Paper presented at the National Association for Research on Science Teaching, Chicago, Apr. 1972.

Sylwester, R. *A Celebration of Neurons: An Educator's Guide to the Human Brain.* Alexandria, Va.: Association for Supervision and Curriculum Development, 1995.

Tanner, L. *Classroom Discipline.* Austin, Tex.: Holt, 1978.

Wolfe, P. *Brain Matters: Translating Research into Classroom Practice.* Alexandria, Va.: Association for Supervision and Curriculum Development, 2001.

# Momentum

## How do I keep the flow of events moving smoothly and minimize downtime, delays, and distractions?

Provisioning

Overlapping

Fillers

Intrusions

Lesson Flexibility

Giving Notice Before Transitions

Subdividing

Anticipation

The concept of Momentum pertains to the smooth, ongoing flow of events in the classroom (Kounin, 1970). Teaching is full of pitfalls to momentum. When these pitfalls occur, students' concentration is broken, and they are distracted from or prevented from becoming involved in learning activities. They experience downtime—time spent waiting for things to get ready, get started, or get organized. When momentum is not maintained, students become bored or look for things to do, potentially filling their time by daydreaming or engaging in disruptive behavior. When momentum is effectively maintained, students experience smooth and rapid transitions from one event to another. Movement of students and equipment happens without bottlenecks, traffic jams, conflicts, arguments, or pushing and shoving. In this chapter, we examine the behaviors teachers perform to manage momentum and keep things moving along in the classroom.

In a general sense, many areas of performance relate to the concept of momentum. For instance, Attention does, insofar as students are kept interested or at least focused on learning experiences; Routines do, in that efficient design of routines for recurrent procedures expedites organizing and setting up, and speeds transitions; Expectations for work do, in that teacher persistence and clarity about how things are to be done enable students to work more automatically and make students individually efficient at moving from one thing to another.

Other areas of performance of teaching also bear on momentum: Personal Relationship Building does, in that students' regard for the teacher makes them less likely to resist or disrupt; Space does, in that effective arrangement of space facilitates students' finding things and getting involved and minimizes distractions; Time does, in that appropriate schedules provide for the ebb and flow of pupils' available energy and attention span, avoiding unreasonable demands.

Several of the curriculum areas of performance (Objectives, Assessment, and Learning Experiences) can also have an impact on Momentum. Mismatched material that is too hard, too easy, or inappropriately presented, can lead to bored or frustrated pupils who will certainly break the momentum of classroom flow.

In a broad sense, then, any mismatch of curriculum or instruction to students tends to break momentum. But to cast momentum so broadly is to subsume all of teaching under its umbrella. Indeed, any area of teaching performance, whatever the primary purpose of the behaviors it considers, does have a secondary effect on momentum. However, we believe that it is valuable to focus on aspects of teaching that relate primarily to maintaining momentum in the classroom. Therefore, we narrow our definition of Momentum to eight key subareas, or kinds of teacher behavior, whose primary purpose is to keep things moving along so that when ignored or improperly done, they break the orderly flow of events.

The eight categories of Momentum are an eclectic group, comprising items that pertain to maintaining or at least enabling student involvement in learning experiences, as all other management areas of performance do. But unlike the behaviors in other management areas of performance, which can be associated with other missions, these eight do not fit any other area of performance and are primarily aimed at momentum. They are called provisioning, overlapping, fillers, intrusions, lesson flexibility, notice, subdividing, and anticipation.

## Provisioning

Provisioning means having things ready to go—the space and the materials. With adequate provisioning, the teacher does not call a group of students together and then leave them for a minute to fetch something needed for the lesson from the closet. Students do not run out of needed materials during learning experiences so that they have to stop what they are doing and solicit new stocks from the teacher. (This does not preclude pupils' restocking themselves from known and easily accessible storehouses or supply points. It is when the supply point is out of paper, for example, that momentum suffers.) Materials are out and organized before the start of lessons, and the space is arranged as necessary before instruction begins. The room is equipped with things the students will need or are likely to need for the activities that may predictably occur over the day.

Provisioning, like much of the rest of good management, becomes conspicuous by its absence. Nevertheless, there are many observable signs of good provisioning. For example, for lessons, audio-visuals, technology, and demonstration equipment are set up in advance; the teacher writes information on the board behind a pulled-down map, so that the information is readily available when the map is raised; and handouts are stacked near the site of a planned lesson. For the room itself, activities, kits, games, listening stations, books, manipulatives, and problem cards are laid out in an orderly and visible fashion for pupils to find and engage; supply points are adequately stocked; and a CD-ROM is placed next to the computer. Next to it is a pad of paper with a note giving location codes for three different areas students are assigned to research that day. When provisioning is skillfully done, the small amount of teacher time spent provisioning the environment during the school day results in a maximum amount of time available for focus on students.

## Overlapping

We borrow the term *overlapping* from Kounin (1970) and expand on his definition: overlapping is the ability to manage two or more parallel events simultaneously with evidence of attention to both. "Manage" here includes two aspects of teaching performance. First is keeping in touch with what is going on in several groups, areas, or activities at once (the teacher may be involved in one, more than one, or circulating among several sites); it implies knowing the nature of the activity, the appropriate pupil behavior within the activity, and the current quality of the pupil's performance. Second is making moves to help pupils over blockages. Blockages may come from pupils' not understanding directions or not knowing what to do next, their inability to resolve interpersonal disagreements (for example, about sharing materials or about how to proceed next as a group), their encounter of material above their frustration level, attention wandering, or finishing an activity and needing help making or planning transitions to the next activity.

"With-itness" means that a teacher always knows what is going on in the room and shows it. It

is a prerequisite for overlapping (Kounin, 1970). This with-itness—a form of radar or "eyes in the back of the head"—is necessary for noticing and responding to misbehavior in its early stages. But in contrast to its disciplinary application, it is also the basis for overlapping several simultaneous instructional events, as it enables teachers to keep in touch with the flow of all of the events.

Building on with-itness, teachers make moves to keep momentum going when they notice a blockage or potential blockage. Here are a few examples of moves that maintain momentum by helping students avoid or work through blockages:

- The teacher, seeing a student nearing the end of an art project, says, "Where are you going to put it to dry, Jimmy?" Jimmy replies, "Under the woodworking table." The teacher responds, "Okay, fine. After that, you can finish the book you started this morning." The teacher has provided a focus for the closure of the activity and the transition to the next activity.
- As a pupil across the room appears stuck on his lab experiment, the teacher says, "Mark, ask Jane for some help if you're stuck."
- As the teacher sees a child using the last of the paint, he gestures for her to come over and reminds her to refill the paint jars when she's finished.
- When the teacher sees a group arguing over the position of a senator on a bill, she says to them, "Where could you find out for sure?" This is a way of directing the students back into constructive involvement.

The point of overlapping is that all of these moves to maintain the momentum of groups and individuals are made while the teacher may be instructing a punctuation skill group, listening to students in a group explain their thinking behind the math problem they are solving, holding a reading conference with an individual student, inspecting a pupil's lab report, or engaging in some other primary focus. The teacher makes the management move without leaving, interrupting, or seeming to remove attention from the primary focus but for an instant. It is an accomplishment to perform overlapping effectively at any time, and especially so when the teacher has a primary active role in a particular learning experience.

## Fillers

It happens regularly during the course of a day that teachers are caught with groups of students for short periods (from one to ten or fifteen minutes) where nothing is planned. Sometimes this happens in awkward places where standard classroom resources are not available, for example, outside waiting for a late bus, in the hallway waiting for a late class to come out of a specialist's room (gym, music), in an instructional group just ended where students have had it with work, yet when there isn't enough time to assign them anything else or even to let them choose and start some other activity around the room before it will be time to dismiss for lunch.

In such situations, what does the teacher do to prevent the disruption of momentum? Some may be inclined to comment, "Why does the teacher have to do anything? The students will just have to sit and wait, that's all. Students should know how to wait: it's an occasional and unavoidable occurrence in life. It's not up to the teacher to entertain them at these times." Yes, we would answer . . . a consummation devoutly to be wished. But it doesn't always work that way. For some groups not so in command of themselves and for

some situations, relying on students to patiently sit and wait can be an unreasonable expectation—and may result in disruptions. In such instances, teachers may pull out a filler to hold the class together for those few minutes, as these teachers did:

- Since the clock in her room is wrong, Mrs. M arrives with her first-grade class five minutes early for gym. There's no use trekking all the way back to the room; they'd just have to turn right around and return. So she asks the children to sit against the wall and move close together so they can all see and hear her. "While we wait for the other class to finish up, raise your hand if you can think of a word that rhymes with . . . *fish*." She calls on three students who give different rhyming words. "You're clicking this morning . . . Now . . . one that rhymes with . . . *lamp*." She calls on two more students.

- Surprisingly, lab teams 1 and 4 have finished their earth science experiments and write-ups early and put their equipment safely away. Ten minutes still remain in the period. Mr. L knows the remaining lab teams will be asking questions, and he'll need to be available for them. But to prevent downtime and fooling around for teams 1 and 4 (a distinct possibility with this class), he quickly writes eight science vocabulary words on the board and calls up those students. He gets them seated and started on a twenty-questions review game and is then back circulating among the experimenters in a scant forty-five seconds.

Sometimes fillers are not as directly curriculum relevant as in these examples. Primary teachers may just play Simon Says. A fifth-grade teacher may say, "Okay, without anyone looking at their watches, raise your hand when you think one-and-a-half minutes are up. Go!" (This game is a good way to quiet a noisy bus for a few minutes.) Secondary teachers may begin chatting with a class about current events or school teams. None of these is necessarily a waste of time, but it is worth distinguishing between fillers that pass the time and fillers that bring in something of the current curriculum.

## Intrusions

Sometimes a teacher's day can seem like a series of intrusions punctuated by moments of instruction. These intrusions take many forms: pupils wanting work corrected, wanting help, wanting directions clarified, or wanting disputes arbitrated; adult visitors; incoming messengers; public address announcements. Every intrusion has the potential to disrupt momentum, but teachers can handle intrusions in a way that minimizes their distracting influence on student's involvement with learning experiences.

Four basic levels of performance describe a teacher's ability to deal with intrusions:

1.  Allows intrusions to fracture momentum.
2.  Deals with intrusions in a uniform way. For instance, the teacher never allows students from outside an instructional group to ask questions (that is, doesn't tolerate intrusions of any kind); or always refers intruders to peers for help; or always has intruders wait nearby until an appropriate moment to help them arises.
3.  Deals with intrusions in a variety of ways using different ways at different times.
4.  Matches the response to the intrusion to the

characteristics of the students involved or to the particular situation. For example, this may mean that the teacher knows that Andrea (the child she's working with) has fragile concentration and that even a delayed response to an intruder will lose Andrea for good. At other times, it is the intruder's characteristics to which the teacher adjusts, sending off Charlie to get help from a peer because she knows that Charlie can handle that, but holding John in close while signaling him to be silent until she can briefly and quietly help him because she knows John doesn't have the confidence to approach a peer. In summary, while the situation is similar the responses are different and the matching may be to the student or to students in the group (those intruded on, or to the intruder).

Sometimes the teacher matches the response to the situation rather than to the student. For example, the case of a fast-paced verbal game involving a large group may prompt the teacher to brook no intrusions at all, even from a student the teacher would normally accommodate, in order to preserve the momentum of the game.

Like all of the areas of teaching in this book, intrusions remind us that the better we can match our responses to students or situations, the more effective we will be.

## Lesson Flexibility

What do teachers do when lessons or planned activities are bombing? How do they control momentum? We can distinguish four levels of teacher performance:

1. Press on with the lesson anyway.
2. Drop the lesson and switch to something else.
3. Keep the objective and try to teach it another way, or vary the format of the lesson.
4. Match a new format to the needs of the group, or adjust it for characteristics of individuals.

Here is an example of the last and most sophisticated level of lesson flexibility. A group of students is full of energy, charged up after physical education class. They are having trouble settling down for paper-and-pencil exercises on contractions. The teacher, sensing this, draws a grid on the board, puts contractions in it, and calls the students up to play a modified Concentration game in which they can actively participate. The teacher has simultaneously maintained focus on the instructional objective and the momentum of the lesson by matching the format to the on-the-spot needs of the students.

## Giving Notice Before Transitions

Momentum can be broken if students are not prepared for transitions (Arlin, 1979), for example, if they are abruptly directed to cease one activity and begin another without time to come to some satisfactory closure in what they are doing. This is especially true when pupils are heavily invested in their activity, as is often the case with creative-expressive endeavors. They resent having to stop what they are immersed in as much as a sound sleeper resents being rudely awakened.

Teachers anticipate and soften these transitions by giving students advance notice of when a transition is coming so they can get ready for it. For example, the teacher turns on a CD version of "Time Is Tight" and students know that by the time the song ends they need to have ended what they are doing and be ready for the next activity, or there is a digital timer projected on the smart board counting down the three minutes left for students to wrap up. Perhaps it is just a verbal warning, "two more minutes." To continue the earlier analogy, advance notice serves as the snooze button on the alarm clock.

## Subdividing

When groups of students travel through the room during transitions between activities or between phases of an activity (to line up, get their coats, go to the library, get microscopes, hand in papers), they sometimes get clogged in physical bottlenecks. These jam-ups result in crowding and general unpleasantness, and at the very least cause downtime while students wait for the crowd to thin. Subdividing (or fragmentation, as Kounin calls it) means anticipating these times and acting to prevent the jam-ups by dividing the groups into smaller units (individuals, pairs, tables, teams, children wearing sneakers) that move one at a time under the teacher's direction. Meanwhile, students not in the unit currently moving are occupied with finishing tasks, putting away materials, or other aspects of the transition (perhaps a filler).

Some teachers use their subdividing moves to reinforce items of recent curriculum. For instance, they dismiss students for the bus by asking multiplication facts or spelling words, calling on individuals, and allowing them to exit if they get the answer—"their ticket" some teachers call it.

The kinds of subdividing described above are most appropriate for primary age children. Older students who can manage themselves in situations involving potential jam-ups may simply be allowed to proceed. In this case, efficient teacher moves might include detailing several students to pass out materials to the rest; storing materials at access points that accommodate several students getting them at once; or sequencing or pacing activities so that small units of students naturally come up for materials (or pass the potential jam-up or down-time point) at different times.

## Anticipation

Anticipation is a quality of mind inherent in all seven situations described previously. But teachers possessing this quality exercise it in many subtle moments outside the boundaries of those seven. So we need a general grab-bag category to hold and describe such situations, and this is it.

Consider this incident. The teacher has given the class advance notice to get ready to go to the auditorium where a brass quintet will play for a middle school audience. "I hate concerts!" says Georgette. One minute passes; some students are putting things away. Two minutes; a few students are gathering by the door. Georgette is looking nobody in the eye and appears sullen. "Georgette, will you go down to the auditorium and see if the seats are set up for us?" says the teacher. Georgette goes. The class quickly lines up at the door, and the teacher sets off with them. They meet Georgette halfway there; she reports that the seats are set up and joins the class without protest as they proceed to the auditorium.

Skilled teachers perform this way every day. They anticipate trouble spots—incidents that will break momentum—and make moves to sidestep them. They move students out of the way of temptation, give resistant individuals face-saving ways to get out of self-made corners, anticipate situations or combinations of personalities that will break momentum and alter them—always before the trouble starts. Here are a few more examples of situations that benefit from a teacher's use of anticipation:

- When children are called to the rug or to a class meeting after cleanup, the teacher may anticipate that some will finish before others and that an ever-larger group will slowly be assembling in the meeting area and waiting without focus (the meeting won't start until they're all there). The same may happen with a middle school class that filters into the room in dribs and drabs before the bell and at the bell is dispersed all over the room. In both cases, by anticipating what is likely to happen, the teacher can arrange to be present at the meeting area doing something of interest to absorb the children as they arrive (riddles, general chatter, a game, a brainteaser, writing something of interest on the board, holding a novel object). Some groups left without a focus at a time like this will provide one of their own—wrestling, arguing, or other momentum breakers. A teacher who can recognize the potential of the group will anticipate these times and be there to greet them with some engaging activity as they arrive.

- Realizing that a small group will require much help and teacher time as they do follow-up work on a new geometry skill, the teacher will be sure the rest of the students are doing things they can handle comfortably, both in terms of procedures and directions and content. Otherwise the teacher may feel "nibbled to death by ducks," overloaded with demands for attention and help. As a result, the students will experience downtime, and momentum will falter. So on the spot, the teacher assigns a "challenge problem" that involves cumulative review and application of previously learned concepts from the previous section of the text (ones they can handle independently) to the bulk of the class and calls together four individual students for a ten-minute review of the new concepts taught.

Both of the previous examples involve anticipation and addressing the concern with a filler activity. Fillers and anticipation are related. Anticipation is the quality of mind that warns a teacher that without a filler at this moment, for this group, there may be trouble. But fillers are only one response showing anticipation. Anticipation is a bigger category than fillers. It is a kind of thinking, usually spontaneous, and often tacit, that says, "If I don't do X, momentum will break down here." X may be many things besides a filler. For example, Mrs. R, in ending a class meeting of first graders, picks children for the clay area first, then assigns other children to other areas. She does this because clay is the most popular activity and everyone wants to go there. She anticipates that if she doesn't deal with clay first and get it off everyone's mind, as well as reassure all children that they'll eventually get a chance there, it will be on everyone's mind while she tries to get the children to choose from among the other activity areas. Thus, the sequence in which she fills activity stations reflects her anticipation of what would happen if she didn't deal with clay first.

Anticipation is a difficult skill to observe, and for teachers to notice themselves applying, because those who excel at it typically perform anticipation moves spontaneously and intuitively rather than preplanning them. But teachers who experience difficulty in this area can often benefit from running advance mental movies of the day they have planned, especially if they do so out loud in the company of a colleague who's helping them problem-solve momentum issues. In this way, potential stumbling blocks to momentum may surface, and steps can be taken to avoid them.

## Conclusion

The Momentum area of performance is clearly concerned with teacher behaviors whose primary purpose is to minimize downtime, delays, and distractions and to keep things moving smoothly in the classroom in order to protect maximum time for learning within each of the subareas. Teachers perform a variety of moves specifically aimed at maintaining momentum. The more skillfully teachers select from their Momentum repertoire to match their moves to the needs and characteristics of the students or situations involved, the more smoothly and efficiently transitions are made and the more successfully momentum is maintained.

To check your knowledge about Momentum see the quiz on our Web site at **www.RBTeach.com/ rbteach/quiz/momentum.html.**

*Source Materials on Momentum*

Arlin, M. "Teacher Transitions Can Disrupt Time Flow in Classrooms." *American Educational Research Journal,* Winter 1979, pp. 42–56.

Doyle, W. "Making Managerial Decisions in Classrooms." In D. L. Duke (ed.), *Classroom Management: 78th Yearbook of the National Society for the Study of Education.* Chicago: University of Chicago Press, 1979.

Kounin, J. *Discipline and Classroom Management.* Austin, Tex.: Holt, 1970.

Pierson, C., and Mansuggi, J. *Creating and Using Learning Games.* Palo Alto, Calif.: Learning Handbooks, 1975.

# Space

Architects, interior decorators, and environmental engineers believe that the way things are arranged in space (including the space itself) makes a difference in how people function. These professionals make their living helping people to be happier and to function more efficiently through better use of the physical environment. Schools need to apply their insights to education for similar payoffs: increased satisfaction and productivity.

This chapter explores ways in which teachers can make the most advantageous use of classroom and school space. There are two equally important but different ways of looking at teachers' use of Space. One is to look at the way arrangements of furniture, materials, and space support the kind of instruction going on. What are the goals of the lesson? What kind of learning environment does it ask for? How does the use of space support the lesson? Since lesson goals and lesson forms change, space arrangements can be expected to change also. There are a variety of space arrangements teachers can use, and those arrangements can be rationally matched to the active form of instruction.

The second way of looking at Space focuses not on its varying uses but on how certain constant space-related issues of student life are handled: ownership and privacy. Different students have different needs in these areas, and there are ways that teachers can meet those individual needs. We look at Space in both of these ways.

## Matching Space to Instruction

Teachers experience a wide variety of office arrangements when they confer with school principals. Some principals speak to teachers across a desk; some have the teacher's chair next to the desk so that the conversation takes place across the corner of the desk. Other principals have their desk in a corner facing a wall and turn their chair around to confer. Still others leave their desk and confer with teachers around a coffee table where two or three chairs are set.

Each of those arrangements sends a different message about authority and uses physical setting to set the climate for the kind of interaction the principal desires. In the same way, teachers' arrangements of classroom space send messages about their image of the learner and the kind of learning they intend. Jacob Getzels (cited in Lewis, 1979) has associated four such images with four different patterns of classroom space.

First, he ties the "empty learner" image to the rectangular room arrangement: "In these classroom designs, which were the standard in the early 1900s and continue to be the most prevalent today, the teacher's function is to fill the learners with knowledge. Hence all desks face front in evenly spaced rows toward the front of the class and the source of knowledge, the teacher and his or her desk" (Getzels, in Lewis, 1979, pp. 155–156). Getzels next connects the image of the "active learner" to the square room arrangement: "In these rooms furniture is movable, arrangements are changed, the teacher's desk joins those of the children and the learner becomes the center" (Getzels, in Lewis, 1979, p. 156).

Getzels's third model is the "social learner" and the circular classroom: "Learning was perceived as occurring through interpersonal actions and reactions" (Getzels, in Lewis, 1979, p. 156). It is the shape that many affective education programs use today. One commercial affective education curriculum guide even calls its program "The Magic Circle." The final model is the "stimulus-seeking learner" and the open classroom: "Where learning centers, communally owned furniture, private study spaces, and public areas replace classrooms, halls, and traditional school furniture. The learner is seen as a 'problem finding and stimulus seeking organism'" (Getzels, in Lewis, 1979, p. 156).

Learners are, of course, all of these things. It is appropriate that students should sometimes be good receivers of information, sometimes active learners within teacher-planned tasks, sometimes heavily involved with each other in discussion, and sometimes shapers of their own activities. No one of these physical environments is the best; they are simply different and support different forms of learning appropriate to a particular lesson's goal.

Teachers can change space arrangements quite quickly for different purposes. One high school teacher we know sometimes has four different arrangements for four successive periods. The changes are made easily and quickly because the students know the basic formats and do all the moving of desks in one or two minutes, usually between classes. The teacher spends time at the beginning of the year explaining these formats to the students and doing a bit of practice arranging them, so the students can set up quickly from then on.

On one day we observed, the first class (seniors) started with desks in rows for a recitation and presentation lesson on Russian short stories. The second class (juniors) quickly rearranged the desks into clusters of six and began "committee work," that is, cooperative teamwork on planning and preparing analyses of various American playwrights' works. The teacher signaled the format as students were entering the room, asking the first few students to set up for committees as they came in. Others then joined in. The third class (sophomores), again on signal, quickly put the desks in a large circle around the perimeter of the room for a discussion of a class book-writing project involving elementary school children in a neighboring school. As a class, they were going to make some decisions and lay out a schedule for the project. The next period, a new class (also sophomores) had a drill-and-practice lesson analyzing themes for variety in sentence pattern. Their desks were arranged, as you may have guessed, facing the teacher.

Some basic arrangements lend themselves more easily to this kind of flexibility. For example, "Mr. Orr's grade five class sat at individual desks placed around the perimeter of the room [perhaps facing the wall]. The open area at the center of the room was used for more of the formal instruction and for small group activities" (Winne and Marx 1982, p. 496).

This type of arrangement gives students some privacy and insulation from visual distraction when they are doing individual work. For a class meeting or total group instruction, all they have to do is turn their chairs around and they're in a circle. They can go to tables in the middle for small group work, either with a teacher or in cooperative groups. Figure 5.1 presents some other arrangements of space to match different instructional situations. Figure 5.2 presents variations on these configurations.

## Twos

This configuration enables partner work for any number of teacher directions: "Compare your answers with a partner and reconcile any differences." "Turn to a partner and discuss how this character's action compares with other books we've read by Judy Blume."

The pairs of desks can be arranged in such a way as to give the teacher maximum visibility and also to create aisles of movement for the teacher to get proximity to each student quickly, either for one-on-one help or for regaining wandering attention.

## Circle

Either a circle or a "U" of chairs or desks enables eye contact among all the students and supports true discussion better than other arrangements. Many teachers report that the participation and interaction they want to induce among students in reform-oriented math classes simply don't happen as well with traditional seating arrangements. So for teachers who work to "make students' thinking visible" as we describe in Chapter Nine, this arrangement is highly desirable.

## Clusters

Students seated at clusters of desks or large tables support group work or committee work where students need to talk with teammates. The arrangement also supports tasks for which materials need to be spread out for sorting, arranging, comparing, or for making displays.

## Rows

This traditional arrangement supports solo student work, listening, viewing, and test taking. It minimizes social distraction but does not prevent teachers from pairing students up for periodic summarizing during instruction.

**Figure 5.1. Space Arrangements**

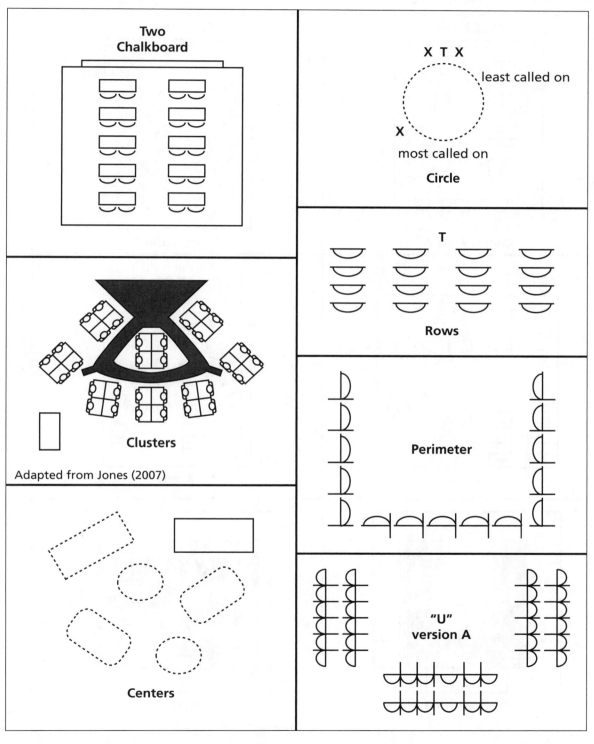

**Figure 5.2. More Space Arrangements**

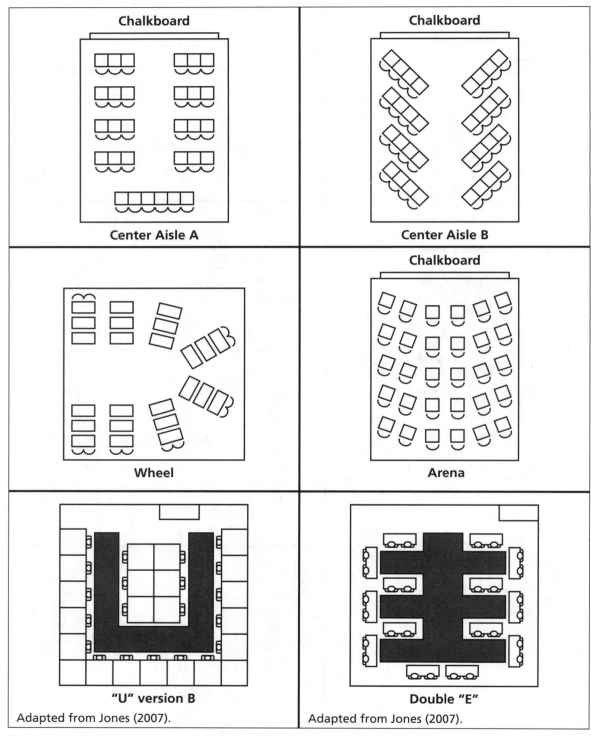

## Perimeter

In this arrangement, desks are placed around the perimeter of the room with the student chairs facing the wall. This arrangement reduces visual distraction, yet allows students sitting next to one another to consult each other and do partner work. The wall space in front of each student can be personalized with a corkboard and other displays pertaining to that student's classwork or personal artifacts.

If students simply turn their chairs around, a "U" is instantly formed for class discussion or for participating in a teacher-led lesson. This flexible arrangement also gives the teacher a clear field and open path for reaching any student quickly for help or management purposes.

The room has to be big enough so that all the students fit in the three-sided layout. The fourth side is usually the black- or whiteboard and presentation section of the room.

## "U"s

This arrangement packs in many students in large classes efficiently, yet it supports discussion, partner work, and proximity to the teachers. Teachers have a harder time getting close to students in the back row, but this is a good compromise for large class sizes.

## Centers

This arrangement is intended for academic periods when students are expected to move around to different stations or centers. Each center has a display or a task with materials the students are supposed to engage in. Traffic aisles between centers have to be clear and wide enough to facilitate easy student movement. This arrangement requires clear and accessible directions at each station and feedback mechanisms so students get information on how well they have done with the task.

A key consideration in examining use of space is to note whether it is a rational use. That is, are things arranged deliberately to best support the kind of instruction under way? If so, a second consideration is whether the arrangement varies when the instructional format or objectives change. Hence, use of classroom space can be classified according to one of the following statements:

- There is no teacher impact on space. The teacher takes it the way it comes (from the custodian, the previous period's teacher, tradition, or something else).
- Space is arranged according to a conventional design and used conventionally and consistently, without variation.
- The space is rearranged periodically but experimentally, without a clear rationale, mostly just for change itself.
- The space arrangement is constant but appropriate for instruction.
- The space is used flexibly for different instructional purposes at different times, matched to curricular goals.

Within a given arrangement of space, the placement of materials can further support instructional goals. Primary grade teachers are often particularly thoughtful about the placement of various items in relation to each other. For example, art materials may be placed near a creative writing area to encourage painting as a follow-up to creative writing. This kind of attention to location and activity flow, though, applies equally well to high school. A display of nineteenth-century American art may be placed over the supply table where students periodically go for assignment sheets and to turn in papers in an English class. The display might serve as a stimulus for a unit on American authors of the period. References and connections to the pictures can be made when the instruction starts.

## Ownership and Privacy

Lewis (1979) raises the issue of what spaces belong to the students in a classroom or a school. She provides the following list:

- Desk: This is probably the most valued and protected space. In traditional classrooms, it may be the child's only source of personal space. In more open classes, it may be shared with others or no longer be a part of the school furniture.
- Locker: Considered a convenience space, and also private if solely for the student's use.
- Special class seat: In music, art, and library, if seats are assigned, a certain degree of ownership will be attached to them.
- Chair: Often individuals and the group recognize individual ownership of chairs. Robert Sommer (1969) notes, "People who remain in public areas for long periods—whether at a habitual chair at a weekly conference or on a commuter train—can establish a form of tenure. Their rights to this space will be supported by their neighbors even when they are not physically present."
- Boys' or girls' room: This is definitely a child's space. The bathroom can be a private retreat for tears, anger, fights, secrets, mischief, and daydreams. In some schools, it becomes the communal news center for the

underground student communication network. In some secondary schools, it may become the property of a group of students, or it may be locked by the administration.
- Playground: This space is child owned and shared with other children. It is powerfully real and memorable, considering the relatively limited time spent in recess.
- Hall: Halls are no-man's-land in most schools, a public avenue. Nobody owns them, but they're very familiar territory. Perhaps the sense of ownership would be similar to that felt for one's lane or street at home. In secondary school, it is the hub of socializing.
- Classroom: In some rooms, children feel a sense of ownership for the whole room or sections of it. In other rooms, the desk may be the only owned space.
- School building: Feelings of ownership increase with the years spent in the building. Variations in intensity also depend on school philosophies, building dimensions, and the degree to which children participate in school activities [Getzels, in Lewis, 1979, p. 130. Reprinted with permission from the Copyright Clearance Center.].

Many students have a strongly felt need for a place of their own—not just a cubby or a mailbox—but a workplace to occupy that is regularly theirs. Adult readers may identify with this need. One of the authors consulted on a weekly basis with a school for several years without such a space, and it drove him crazy!

Left on their own, middle and high school students regularly take the same desk in a class. It becomes "their" seat. College students and adults do the same. As teachers plan classroom space, they should consider whether they have adequately met students' needs for ownership of space. That need varies considerably with individuals, as does their need for privacy.

Private spaces like carrels or, at the most private, individual practice rooms restrict visual distraction and noise. There are students who benefit greatly from having such places created for them or put at their disposal. Skillful teachers look for these individuals and match them with spatial arrangements that suit their needs. As they look at their classrooms and other school facilities (libraries, media centers), they ask themselves if enough private spaces have been provided to accommodate such students, because there are always some of them.

## Recommendations on Using Space

The literature on the use of school space is sparse, and the research is even thinner. A series of interviews we once conducted with teachers showed support for the following ten recommendations:

1. Materials students use should be visibly stored and accessible to facilitate efficient getting out and putting away.
2. Avoid dead space, that is, open, purposeless space whose use lends itself to random or illegitimate student activity.
3. In some settings, for reasons of safety or control, it may be appropriate for space to be arranged so the teacher can see all of it, with no blind spots. (In other settings this guideline may be inconsistent with goals relating to trust, privacy, and independence.)

4. Vertical space (walls, dividers, closets, and movable cabinet doors) should be employed productively—for example, for display, learning stations, or storage of materials, effectively increasing usable space in the classroom. Hanging artifacts or displays from the ceiling or multilevel use of space in addition to the floor (lofts, for example, or other erected structures) can increase effective usable space within a room.
5. Dividers placed on a diagonal with respect to the ninety-degree orientation of the walls can channel student movement and visual fields in interesting and deliberate directions.
6. Have a display area where students' work, art, and other kinds of products can easily be seen and examined.
7. Keep active areas distant from quiet areas in a room to minimize distraction and interference.
8. Keep adjacent activity areas far enough apart, or clearly bounded from their immediate neighbor, so as to prevent distraction and interference.
9. Have clear traffic paths connecting functional areas of the room that do not necessitate students' walking through one area (and disturbing things there) to get to another.
10. Empty furniture absorbs energy. Therefore, if you have fewer students than chairs in a secondary class, don't let the students spread out around the periphery of the room with empty chairs between them and you. Either eliminate the empty chairs, or move the students forward where they can be in contact with you and with each other.

Overall, the message we get from reviewing the literature on space and classrooms is to be deliberate about its use. Teachers can make instructional spaces more attractive, efficient, and flexible; in short, they can control and change these spaces to best support instruction in moving from lesson to lesson.

To check your knowledge about Space see the quiz on our Web site at **www.RBTeach.com/ rbteach/quiz/space.html.**

### Source Materials on Space

Abramson, P. *Schools for Early Childhood.* New York: Educational Facilities Laboratory, 1970.

Gross, R., and Murphy, J. *Educational Change and Architectural Consequences.* New York: Educational Facilities Laboratory, 1968.

Jones, F. *Tools for Teaching: Discipline, Instruction, Motivation.* Santa Cruz, Calif.: Frederic Jones and Associates, 2000.

Kohn, J. *The Early Learning Center.* New York: Educational Facilities Laboratory, 1970.

Kritchevsky, S., Prescott, E., and Walling, I. *Physical Space.* Washington, D.C.: NAEYC, 1969.

Lewis, B. V. "Time and Space in Schools." In K. Yamamato (ed.), *Children in Time and Space.* New York: Teachers College Press, 1979.

Marshall, K. *Opening Your Class with Learning Stations.* Palo Alto, Calif.: Learning Handbooks, 1975.

*School Review.* Whole Issue, 1974, *82*(4).

Sommer, R. *Personal Space: The Behavioral Basis of Design.* New York: Prentice-Hall, 1969.

Winne, P. H., and Marx, R. W. "Students' and Teachers' View of Thinking Process for Classroom Learning." *Elementary School Journal,* May 1982, pp. 493–518.

Zefferblatt, S. M. "Architecture and Human Behavior: Toward Increased Understanding of a Functional Relationship." *Educational Technology,* Aug. 1972, pp. 54–57.

# Time

## How do I time events and regulate schedules so that students get the most productive learning time?

Time as a Construct

Time Allocation and Efficiency

Pacing and Rhythm

*In their classrooms, expert teachers are very serious about time management. They view time spent with students as a precious commodity, like water, that if it is not handled properly, will slip through one's fingers without one's even noticing it.*

RICHARD JACOBS, ASSOCIATE PROFESSOR OF EDUCATIONAL ADMINISTRATION, VILLANOVA UNIVERSITY

Time is the currency of life, and teachers run the bank for their students about six hours a day, an enormously powerful position. They run the bank even for "free choice" times, where the options available are those offered or allowed by the teacher.

When students do what, in what order, and for how long is largely under the teacher's control, and we know from recent research that controlling it well has a big impact on student learning. This includes time spent in places other than the classroom, like the cafeteria. How long students spend in each of the environments the school offers and the quality of that time is something faculty members control.

This chapter is about being as deliberate as possible in managing student time use for maximum learning. It draws on the growing knowledge base of the field to help us be better time managers for our students. The issues of time management for students center on allocation, efficiency, and pacing. Investigating how we and our students are spending class time, and getting concrete and accurate data about that, is likely to yield some surprises and some interesting and useful insights.

## Time as a Construct

School effectiveness researchers over the past three decades have ranked time—and time-related instructional variables—either number one or number two on a list of eight to ten factors that are important to student achievement (Scheerens and Bosker, 1997; Berliner, 1990; Good and Brophy, 2000; Greenwood, 1991; Tindal and Parker, 1987; Marzano, 2000).

A superficial look at that research may prompt one to say, "So what else is new? Obviously if students spend more time on math and less time fooling around, they will learn more math." But researchers are consistently in agreement that it's not that simple: within reasonable limits, the issue is not about adding more time but rather about how time is used (Aaronson, Zimmerman, and Carlos, 1999; Evans and Bechtel, 1996).

Embedded in the research—and in the claims associated with it—is a delineation and hierarchical classification of various categories of time (see Figure 6.1). Starting with time in school, each of the categories in Figure 6.1 includes and subsumes those below and inside its circle. And the closer the category is to the core of the nested circles, the stronger the correlation is between time and student achievement. In this figure, *time in school* is the number of hours or days that a student should be, or is, in attendance.

*Allocated time* is the amount of time in school formally scheduled for instruction (versus noninstructional activities such as lunch, recess, and changing classes).

*Teacher instructional time* is the amount of allocated time the teacher is actually engaged with students delivering instruction or actively monitoring learning experiences (versus doing management tasks such as taking attendance and setting up equipment).

*Student engaged time*, often referred to as time on task, is the number of minutes that students are observably paying attention to and focusing on instructional material (versus waiting, daydreaming, fooling around, getting organized, and listening to announcements, for example).

*Academic learning time* is the portion of time students spend engaged in relevant academic tasks and performing those tasks with a high rate of success. Relevant academic tasks and a high success rate distinguish it from, and make it a subset of, student engaged time. For clarity, we will call it *high success time* here.

*Interactive instruction* is time spent directly with a teacher getting instruction (one to one, small group, or large group), as opposed to time spent alone doing seatwork or projects or working with a group that's not interacting directly with an instructor.

These categorical distinctions are very useful as a framework for studying this area of performance and for becoming ever more purposeful in maximizing its impact on achievement. Data show that teachers who study their time use make significant changes (Stallings, 1980) and get better student learning.

## Time Allocation and Efficiency

### Allocated Time

Allocated time, or time set aside for instruction, reveals something about the values of a district, a school, or a teacher. Time set aside for instruction and time set aside for instruction in specific subject areas are related but separate considerations in this category. An examination of each should yield data that reflect some consensus across a school about what is important and what the priorities are within those things that are important.

**Figure 6.1. Time Allocations in School**

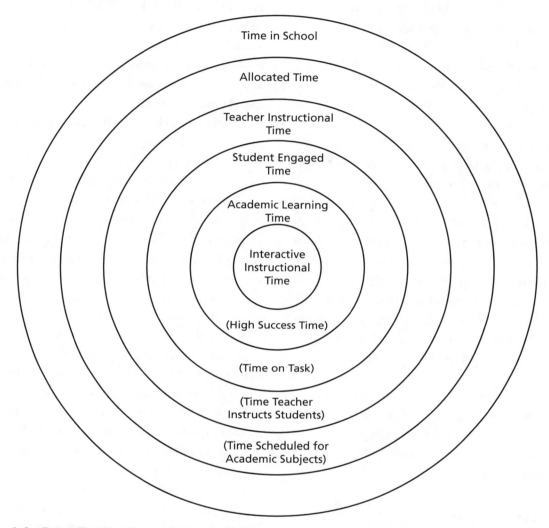

Time in School

Allocated Time

Teacher Instructional Time

Student Engaged Time

Academic Learning Time

Interactive Instructional Time

(High Success Time)

(Time on Task)

(Time Teacher Instructs Students)

(Time Scheduled for Academic Subjects)

**Research for Better Teaching, Inc.** • One Acton Place, Acton, MA 01720 • (978)263-9449 • www.RBTeach.com

It is likely that the current standards movement will press schools to pay more attention to, and reach more common agreements about, aligning time allocation with values and priorities and will result in providing some greater consistency or uniformity for students. Historically, however, while researchers have found little difference between time in school across schools, they have found some very big differences in allocated time for academic subjects, especially across elementary schools, and classes within a school where individual teachers tend to have more direct control over the daily and weekly class schedule. For example, Caldwell, Huitt, and Graeber (1982) found that:

> Time actually allocated for fifth-grade math ranged from 18 minutes to 80 minutes; allocated fifth-grade reading time ranged from 51 minutes to 195 minutes. Allocated time may also vary enormously within a class; for

example, in one study (Dishaw, 1977) one fifth-grade student spent 39 minutes each day on math while another student spent 75 minutes. These differences in actual allocated time suggest that some students may have two to four times as much opportunity to learn specific academic content as other students [p. 474].

Is it fair that because of a particular teacher's talents and inclinations, his or her class gets a great reading and writing program but practically nothing else?

At the schoolwide level, it is imperative that we examine how time is apportioned throughout the day, the week, and the school year and ask questions like these: What percentage of time in school is allocated and protected for instruction? How else is student time expended? Do the percentages match our priorities? How might we decrease the amount of allocated time not devoted to instruction?

Over the years, what amount of a student's time is spent learning what subjects? Is there some consistency and rationale to this expenditure of time? If not, then we are not really in control of the education we are delivering.

## Instructional Time: A Matter of Efficiency

Instructional time—the percentage of allocated time a teacher is engaged with students delivering instruction and actively monitoring learning experiences—might be referred to as time-on-task for the teacher.

Estimates of how much class time is devoted to instruction vary widely, from a low of 21 percent to a high of 69 percent (Conant, 1973; Marzano and Riley, 1984; National Education Commission on Time and Learning, 1994; Park, 1976). If we take the highest estimate of 69 percent as the upper boundary, we can conclude that of the 13,104 classroom hours theoretically available, only 9,042 hours are used for instruction. This comes to about 695.5 hours per year or about 3.9 hours per day (Marzano, 2003).

The research generally supports the positive impact of increasing the amount of instructional time. Walberg (1997) found a positive relationship between increased instructional time and learning in 97 percent of 130 studies (Marzano, 2003). One major study of eighty-seven secondary classrooms (Stallings, 1980) found the average engaged rate of teacher to students to be 73 percent. Some teachers used forty minutes of a forty-five-minute period to develop concepts; others used only twenty to twenty-five minutes (Good and Brophy, 2000). Teachers who had lower rates of interaction with students had classes with significantly smaller achievement gains (or no gain at all), especially for low-performing students. This is true even if students were on task most of the time. As Stallings (1980) explains, "The students are on-task, but the teacher is not teaching. In those classrooms where no gain was being made, the students were doing written assignments 28 percent of the time and reading silently 22 percent of the time, and teachers were doing classroom management tasks more than 27 percent of the time."

Maximizing instructional time requires organizing instructional activities and expediting noninstructional ones (preparing materials, taking attendance, managing transitions, dealing with discipline, and so forth) so there is a minimum of downtime and unsupervised learning time. Hence, how much of the allocated time we preserve for instruction is directly tied to classroom organization and management skills.

There is also a need to look at this category from a schoolwide point of view. Marzano (2003) proposes that "schools should make every effort to convey the message that class time is sacred time and should be interrupted for important events only, a message that is commonly conveyed in other countries." He cites Stigler and Hiebert (1999) who found that instructional interruptions (such as PA announcements) were far more typical in American classrooms than in Japan and suggests that we take measures to eliminate these by decreasing or eliminating announcements during instructional time, posting "Do Not Interrupt" signs on our doors, and referring to specific parts of class as academic learning time so students will understand the need to put forth greater effort to attend during those times.

## Student Engaged Time and Time on Task

Engaged time, a subset of allocated time, is the time that students appear to be paying attention to materials or presentations that have instructional goals. Although often used synonymously with the concept of time on task, Berliner (1990) distinguishes time on task as a subset—time a student is engaged in an appropriate learning task (for example, a student may be deeply engaged in mathematics work at a time that has been allocated for science).

Early studies (Fisher and others, 1978) reported that on average, students are engaged or attending for only a portion of allocated time—about 75 percent of it. But the range of student engaged time was very big—between 50 and 90 percent. Some studies (Stanley and Greenwood, in Greenwood, 1991, p. 11) have shown significant differences in academic engagement of high- versus

low-socioeconomic status (SES) student groups. They write, "On a daily basis high-SES students spent as much as 11 minutes (or 5 percent) more time per day engaged in writing, reading, and talking about academic matters than did their low SES counterparts. . . . At this daily rate, low SES students need to attend as much as one and a half months during summer vacation to obtain an equivalent amount of engaged time in one year. . . . Otherwise low SES students are at risk of academic delay and retardation because of their lower daily engagement rates."

While more recent reviews of the research can establish only a moderate correlation between engaged time on task and student achievement (Cotton, 1989), it is critical that we seize every opportunity to maximize engaged time for all students since it is the precursor to academic learning (high success) time.

Recent studies (Hunter and Csikszentmihalyi, 2003; Shernoff, Csikszentmihalyi, Schneider, and Shernoff, 2003) of student engagement, in which large numbers of secondary students used wristwatch devices to record their activity and feeling states eight times daily, found that students spend a majority of class time in noninteractive activities such as listening to lectures and doing individual seatwork assignments. Interactive activities such as participating in discussions (9 percent) and group or lab work (6 percent) accounted for only a small percentage of the total time. Engagement, measured as a composite of interest, concentration, and enjoyment, was higher in group and individual work compared to lectures, exams, or TV/video viewing. Students also reported being more engaged during "flow tasks"—those that students felt competent to complete and were high in challenge, compared to tasks that were low in challenge or that students felt were beyond their capabilities.

Differences in engagement rates were substantial. For example, 42 percent of students reported being attentive during low-challenge activities, whereas 73 percent reported paying attention during activities that were more challenging and required more skill (Emmer and Gerwels, 2006). Emmer and Gerwels cite other studies related to eliciting student interest. Mitchell (1993), studying secondary math classes, found that involvement in classroom materials was a strong predictor of student interest. Identifying two kinds of situational interest characteristics as "catch" and "hold" (elicitors and maintainers of interest), he found that group work, computers, and puzzles were three types of "catchers," and meaningfulness and involvement served to "hold." One of the best predictors of situational interest was involvement, measured by perceived enjoyment in the activity and "learning the material ourselves" and "doing something" versus listening to the teacher talk or "come in, take notes, go home, do homework and it's the same thing every day" (p. 436).

Other studies soliciting teachers' views (thirty-five of sixty-five teachers were secondary level) of how they engage students (Zahorik, 1996) found the most common method reported by all teachers was the use of hands-on activities. At least a third of the teachers also mentioned three other strategies: personalizing the content (linking it to prior student knowledge or experiences), building student trust (by using activities that permit students to share ideas and experiences, make decisions, and be involved in planning and making choices), and group work.

This research serves as an intriguing support for the kind of student discussions described in Chapter Nine, "Clarity," on making students' thinking visible and the twenty-two verbal behaviors.

Many of the areas of performance discussed in other chapters can serve as direct resources for positively influencing student engaged time and time on task. What follows is a list of other areas of performance related to increasing engaged time and specific subcategories that are most relevant to this concern.

*Management Areas*

- Attention moves, especially those in the alerting, enlisting, and winning categories (Chapter Three)
- Space arrangements that minimize distractions and facilitate learning objectives (Chapter Five)

*Instructional Areas*

- Clarity concepts: framing the big picture by communicating objectives, itinerary, reason for activities, and activating student knowledge to create context and establish relevance; choosing explanatory devices that engage auditory, visual, and kinesthetic learning modalities; and making cognitive connections and checking understanding broadly and frequently to ensure students understand (Chapter Nine)
- Principles of learning embedded in lesson design, including active participation, vividness, meaning, feeling tone, degree of guidance, say-do, knowledge of results and feedback, reinforcement, goal setting, and keeping students open and thinking (Chapter Ten)

*Motivational Areas*

- Classroom climate: addressing elements from all three strands (building community, creating an environment where it is safe to take intellectual risks, and cultivating personal efficacy) (Chapter Fourteen)

- Expectations: employing the critical attributes of communicating expectations regarding four kinds of standards and expectations and ensuring that all actions and interactions with students communicate three key messages: "This is important; you can do it; I won't give up on you" (Chapter Twelve)

*Curriculum Areas*

- Objectives: setting objectives that are challenging but made attainable for students (Chapter Sixteen)
- Learning experiences that are differentiated in input, process, and output to address differences in student readiness, interests, and learning styles (Chapter Eighteen)
- Assessment that is ongoing in a learning experience to get and keep students on track (Chapter Nineteen)

All of these areas of performance afford us resources and ideas for increasing our capacity to influence student engagement. As well, most of them serve as resources for maximizing academic learning time—the most significant time of all regarding student achievement.

## Academic Learning or High Success Time

In the research literature, the portion of engaged time that students are working on relevant academic tasks and performing those tasks with a high rate of success is referred to as academic learning time (ALT). We will simply call it "high success time doing important work." This is the category of time found to have the most significant correlation with student achievement.

Similar to findings regarding student-engaged time, the amount of high success time students experience across classrooms varies hugely. In basic skill work, for example, it was found to be anywhere from 16 minutes per day in a group of low-average classes to 111 minutes per day in a group of high-average classes. (High- and low-average does not refer to the ability level of the students; it refers to the teacher's ability to get more academic learning time for students [Caldwell, Huitt, and Graeber, 1982].)

Academic learning time says something about what kind of match exists between the current state of the learner, the material to be learned, and the design of the learning experience itself (Anderson, 1983).

High-average teachers provide "more than twice as much academic learning time as in the average case and more than six times as much as in the low-average case" (Caldwell, Huitt, and Graeber, 1982). These startling figures prompt a careful look at how our students are experiencing school time, since high-success time correlates strongly with achievement.

In order to increase high success time, we need to use time efficiently and structure learning experiences that enable students to be successful. Variance in high success time must be traced to the appropriateness of assignments, the diagnostic acuteness of the teacher, and the adequacy of instruction and direction giving before students are turned loose on individual tasks—in other words, our skill at clarity, structuring learning experiences, and matching objectives to individuals and groups. Many of the suggestions listed for engaged time can also serve as resources for attaining more ALT. And since scheduled time and allocated time set the upper limits for academic learning, or high success, time, it is worth considering things one can do in each of those categories to channel more available minutes toward this end. Finally, high success time can be positively affected by the degree to which students are engaged and interacting with the teacher, a category that researchers label interactive instructional time.

## Interactive Instructional Time

Instructional time is that portion of allocated time when the teacher is actively focusing in some way on instruction and facilitating learning versus attending to management issues. Engaged time is the portion of time the student is focused and attending to academic learning. Students may be on task but working independently of the teacher (for example, doing seatwork, written assignments, or silent reading) while the teacher is working with other learners. Hence, interactive instructional time is yet a smaller portion of both of those: the amount of engaged time in which an individual student actually experiences direct interaction with a teacher, whether it is in whole group, small group, or individual situations. And when it comes to this category, research findings have indicated the more, the better. The point is that when teachers are teaching, students are more likely to be learning, and that workbooks and other solo assignments that occupy students' class time don't teach—not a surprising finding when one considers the importance of teacher feedback, knowledge of results, degree of guidance, and other principles of learning.

In the past, this finding led some to advocate the direct instruction pattern of teaching for whole class groups as the most efficient form of instruction (Rosenshine, 1981). This recommendation really misses the point. In the direct instruction model, an individual student is not necessarily engaged and interacting with the teacher. For this model to maximize interactive instructional time, the teacher needs to draw extensively on strategies from outside the model: checking for understanding and building in processing and summarizing time for students in pairs and small groups so that the teacher can circulate and engage with individuals.

Furthermore, the direct instruction pattern (the "sage on the stage" model) is only one way to get teacher-student interactive time, and suitable to only one kind of teaching. There are learnings for which this pattern is clearly not the only or the best way—like teaching students to provide evidence for positions (see the Jurisprudential Model in Chapter Ten) or teaching the scientific method (see the Discovery Model in Chapter Ten). All the models of teaching in Chapter Ten can provide interactive teaching time, as can peer tutoring.

Thus it is important to put direct instruction in perspective. Direct instruction is effective for teaching skills, and it works to the degree that it provides high proportions of interactive instruction time. But there are other learnings besides skills and two dozen other models of teaching that can provide interactive instruction.

Another way to maximize interactive instructional time is by engineering lessons so that students are actively engaged in all phases of the learning experience (input, processing, and output). The teacher's role then is cast as the guide on the side: mediating, monitoring, and facilitating the learning process by providing guidance as needed, clarifying directions, responding to questions, posing questions to check for understanding and to stretch and extend students' thinking, and providing prompt and continuous feedback. This would be what we'd see, for example, in the most effectively designed and implemented cooperative learning experiences. What this actually sounds like is recorded in the Bodner scripts reproduced in Chapter Nine, "Clarity." Individualized programs are at high risk here. If they are poorly managed, students, though active and involved, may get only a few minutes a day with the teacher, and that is not enough. Teachers in this situation either need to do more group work or manage individualization so students get more feedback and guidance.

It is the attributes of interactive instruction that are important any way you can get them, and those attributes are, it seems to us: clear explanations, prompt feedback, knowledge of results, and appropriate degree of guidance. Good computer-based learning systems can provide these features.

## Time to Learn

Benjamin Bloom's work on mastery learning has added another important concept to the knowledge base about time: time to learn, or time a student needs under optimal learning conditions to reach some criterion of learning (Berliner, 1990). The idea is that most students can learn anything if they have the prerequisite pieces of knowledge and skills in place and are given adequate time to learn it. Giving them adequate time to learn doesn't mean giving them material and just waiting until they've gone over it long enough to absorb it; it means task analysis of new learnings, careful ongoing assessment, and reteaching loops for students who need it—and for only those who do. The view of time from mastery learning puts teachers on the spot along with students. Mastery learning brings with it a requisite set of assumptions: that all students are capable of achieving mastery of appropriate learning goals; that when learning isn't taking place something isn't yet right about how it is being presented to the student or the time given for the student to master it; that mastery is essential in order for the student to progress; and that modifications, adaptations, adjustments, and reteaching are all options available to support that happening. In other words,

one doesn't blame the students if learning isn't taking place. Instead there is a search for how to adjust, adapt, modify, and reteach until the student is on board and "getting it."

Mastery learning is a form of individualizing instruction. But individualizing means more than self-paced here, more than marching through programmed material. It means clear and comprehensive sequences of instruction laid out in advance, broken down into pieces, and with options for how to deliver instruction of those pieces to students. Above all, it means monitoring what students know and not giving up until they have met mastery criteria.

Finally it means planning reteaching loops and simultaneous extension activities for students who got it the first time around. Such a two-ringed circus presents management and planning challenges that are a stretch for teachers who are unused to managing multiple events in a classroom. In other words, mastery learning requires differentiating learning experiences (one size doesn't fit all) and is once again an example of how the areas of performance of teaching are interdependent and ever present. A sincere and focused effort to address and afford students time to learn requires an exploration of concepts addressed in the Momentum, Objectives, Learning Experiences, and Classroom Climate chapters.

## Time Audits

In the opening of this chapter, we suggested that getting concrete data about how time is spent in classrooms is likely to yield some interesting and useful insights, as well as surprises, all of which can serve as a productive foundation for creative problem solving around getting more currency for students to spend toward learning. Marzano (2003) refers to this as conducting time audits: gathering data that will reveal how much time in the day or a class period is devoted to actual instruction, how much time in class is generally taken up by noninstructional activities or management tasks, how much time individual students are focused and engaged, what they are doing or what is going on that distracts them, and so forth.

One of us once studied the time use of students in five classrooms of a K–5 school using a technique adapted from Engel (1977). He scanned the class every five minutes, making a notation for each student on a class roster. The notation captured what the student was doing and with what level of attention or involvement. From these data, a color bar graph was constructed for each student, color-coded to study activities showing student time use over a whole morning. Coded cross marks in black were overlaid on the color bar to indicate degrees of inattention or noninvolvement. Putting all the bars together on one graph for the class gave the teachers an enormous amount of information on individual students and patterns across the class. One teacher was losing a great deal of time in classroom management: passing out papers, setting up in the morning, and getting ready for transitions, for example. Another teacher had students with a low level of involvement due to social chatter at table groups—quiet and unobtrusive but nevertheless persistent and interfering with their work. Another teacher found her students were involved with individual tasks and projects, but sometimes received only five minutes of direct teacher instruction in the course of the day. All of these teachers made changes to increase their effectiveness after they saw the data. The changes involved more attention to momentum, rearranging space, rescheduling their own instructional time, and clarifying their expectations for student behavior. The point is that the obvious was not so obvious to them

until they directly faced objective data about their own students and their own classes. When they had the data, they were able to improve their effectiveness. Academic engaged time and student time spent in interactive instruction may sound obvious enough, but teachers who get the numbers on their own classes may find some new priorities emerging.

Although there are structured formal models to use to conduct this type of audit (Marzano, Kendall, and Gaddy, 1999), teachers could do much of this as action research in their own classrooms independently or with the support of a colleague present in the room. There are many kinds of data one might gather: noting starting and ending times of activities, transitions, and length of time spent on direction giving, for example. Comparing data gathered to what you might have predicted or anticipated the data would look like can lead to fine-tuning time estimates, problem identification, and pinpointing the means for using time more effectively. Or a colleague could collect data about how individuals or groups of students are spending their time: How much are they engaged and on task? When they aren't, what is going on? How much is interactive instructional time versus independent work? What kind of success are they having? The resulting data can be used to make adjustments and modifications that might increase student productivity and level of performance.

Leinhardt, Zigmond, and Corley (1981, p. 358) comment that "teachers must be vigilant in their search for children who are losing out. While the average off-task rate was 15 percent, some students were off-task more than 30 percent of the time. While the average amount of teacher instruction (in reading) was 16 minutes a day, the range was from 1.4 minutes per day to 35 minutes per day (within the same class). While the average time spent in silent reading was 14 minutes per day, some students spent no time at all reading silently. Fortunately, teachers can dramatically change the experience and performance of those students who seem to be losing out without changing things for those who are not." But first the teacher must become aware of who they are and how the time is being lost.

Good time management comes from handling a number of other areas of performance well. But when students are on task, productive, and experiencing success it is more than good time management; it is successful education. Seen this broadly, good use of student time is a criterion for good teaching, an outcome of all the things that go into good education. But there are some skills that are distinctly part of efficient time management itself. Let's look at an aspect of the time area of performance that allows it to stand on its own as an area of teacher skill.

## Pacing and Rhythm

Matching has been an important theme with each area of performance. We have advanced the notion that an area of performance contains a repertoire and that skillfulness comes in matching choices from it to individuals, groups, and curricula. So it is with pacing and scheduling. The same pace will not work equally well for all classes. Carolyn Evertson (1982) found that the way teachers paced activities varied greatly and corresponded to their success with high- and low-performing classes, but made quite a difference in low-performing groups. Students in low-performing classes have a clear tendency to drop in and out of participation, especially during seatwork. Some students refuse to participate at all. Evertson provides descriptions and commentary on two junior high teachers' classrooms to show how differences in pacing affect low-performing students.

We start with Teacher B:

[The teacher has just put the seatwork assignment on the board.] Marie says, "I don't have a book." The teacher says, "Look on those shelves," pointing. Marie says, "Those aren't ours." The teacher says, "Some of them are." Marie gets herself a book. Chico raises his hand and says, "I need help." About five students start the assignment right away. [There are twelve students present.] The others are talking, have their hands raised, or are going to the teacher's desk. The teacher says, "Come on up, Randy," when she calls on him. When he gets there, "Larry, leave him alone." Larry stands and visits by the teacher's desk. Chico puts his hand up again. The teacher says, "Chico, what do you need?" He says, "Help." The teacher says, "Okay, wait a second." Larry sits down by the teacher's desk and looks on as she tells him something. Chico calls out, "Miss _____, are you going to help me?" She says, "Yes, Chico, but come up here." He says, "Aw, Miss, it's too far." The teacher ignores him, and he goes to the teacher's desk [At this point, five students are at the teacher's desk.] [p. 182].

This classroom description shows rather dramatically the difficulty students in a lower-performing class can have in getting started and participating successfully in an activity. At one point, five students were at the teacher's desk, and most of them were waiting for help. (The teacher eventually helped nine students at her desk during this seatwork activity.) Having so many students in such close proximity to each other frequently created problems and led to misbehavior to which the teacher was forced to respond.

The dialogue also illustrates the poor task orientation that generally characterizes the lower-performing classroom. Chico's behavior here is typical of many other slow students. He did not take academic activities seriously, he was not willing to begin work on learning tasks, and he was not interested in participating. Poor task orientation on the part of one student can lead to disruptive behavior from others, as we find when we continue this activity:

> While the teacher is trying to work with Marie, Marie follows Chico's lead in teasing the teacher. She grabs the stapler. The teacher says loudly, "Uh uh, come on, Marie." Later, Marie grabs her paper away from the teacher, wads it up, saying, "You wrote on my paper. You're not supposed to write on my paper." Marie sits down. Billy, meanwhile, has continued to play around and talk to Larry. The teacher says sharply, "Billy, you come up here!" Larry says loudly, "That's exactly what Miss _____ says, and it works for her, too." As Billy scoots his desk up, Larry sings, "Row, row, row your desk."

When the teacher had to give individual attention to so many students, she could not monitor the class efficiently, and it was more difficult for the students to get the teacher's attention according to the prescribed procedure:

> Chico, who has his hand up, calls out, "Miss, I can't wait forever." The teacher says, "Just a minute." Mark yells loudly, "Miss!" The teacher ignores him and continues helping Marie. Then she goes to Pam, who has had her hand up for a long time. A girl calls out from the front of the room, "I need help." She has her hand up, but she calls out. The teacher looks at her and says, "Okay, I'll be there in a second."

It should be noted that two of these students here do not simply call out; they have their hands raised. However, they know that simply raising their hands is not as effective a signal as calling out. The teacher did not consistently enforce (in fact, hardly enforced at all) the rule against calling out under these circumstances:

> Chico calls out, "What time is it?" Billy tells him what time it is. The teacher ignores them both. Billy and Chico are trading epithets like, "Dumbhead." The teacher, helping the girls near the front, ignores them. Then, she looks up and says, "Chico, do you need something else to do?" Chico says, "No." The teacher says, "Then be quiet."

A basic conflict existed in lower-performing classes between two demands of the teacher: the need to help students and the need to control inappropriate, disruptive behavior. In this example, the teacher did not want to interrupt her interchange with the girls near the front, but she was finally forced to respond when the off-task behavior threatened to become disruptive.

The comparatively high achievement gain of Teacher F's lower-performing class recommends it for closer examination. Teacher F allocated considerably more time for checking and discussion of work (13.7 minutes) and the presentation of material—lecture or introduction to seatwork (14.4 minutes)—and considerably less time for the final seatwork activity (22.5 minutes) than was characteristic of the lower-performing classes in general. In addition, the lecture or introductory phase of seatwork was structured differently, frequently punctuated by two or more very brief, highly focused seatwork activities. In this class, the lecture or introduction to the final seatwork activity usually exhibited the following pattern:

> Teacher F goes to the board, where there are 25 numbers written, and begins rounding off the first one. He has the students do this on paper. He says, "I want you to do the first five." They are in columns of five. He continues, "Then put your pencils down." They are writing these numbers down and he moves around the room. He stops the class (after about 6 minutes) and asks David what his answers were. David frowns and says that he didn't get anything. "Who can help him out?" asks the teacher. Robert says, "I got it." The teacher moves on to the rest of the column and then goes on to the A column which should be rounded to the nearest hundredth. The students then do this column. Kermit calls out, "Are we going to have homework, too?" The teacher says, "I'll assign that in a minute." Kermit says, "Well, we don't have time to work on it if we're going to do all of these." Teacher F says, "Oh, we are not going to do all of these." The teacher goes to the board and asks for the students' attention and begins to go through the second column. He asks Jackie to help him round off the first, and she says she didn't get it. He says, "I just asked you to help." She looks at it and begins to try it. He walks her through the problem. (At this point, when there are approximately 10 minutes left, the teacher gives the seatwork assignment.)

Following is another instance of a lecture or discussion interrupted by brief seatwork periods.

> [The teacher] says that they will be talking about addition of decimals. He says that this is not really much different than adding whole numbers. The teacher has Johnny write the first problem out for him. He says to him, "Tell me what to put down." Johnny adds three and two and says that it's five. Then he adds six and nine and says that it's 15; put down the five and carry the one. The teacher then asks him, "Where do I put the one? Down here?" Johnny says, "No, you put the one over the eight." Then he adds the eight and gets nine. He tells him to put the decimal between the nine and the five. When he's through, the teacher says, "Very good." The teacher then starts asking them review questions on decimals. As he asks questions, he reminds students to "Raise your hands and tell me what place the decimal is in." The teacher calls on Gracie to do the second example on the board. She declines, and then the teacher goes on to call on Edward. Edward works through the problem and then says, "Tell me what's wrong." The teacher says to him, "Well, let's find out. How can we tell?" The students call out that they can subtract to check. At 9:28 the teacher puts up a third example. He tells the class that they'll be doing the assignment on their papers, and that they should go ahead and do number three to see if they can get it right. The teacher starts walking around checking to see if students are getting the problem right. There's some quiet talking in the room and the teacher is still walking around. At 9:41 the teacher says, "Let's look up here." (He works the problem on the board. After that, he assigns them another problem to do at their seats and walks around checking them.)

Teacher F copes with the problem of sustaining seatwork in his lower-performing classes by incorporating some of the seatwork into the lecture (or introduction to seatwork) in very brief segments, placing the responsibility for maintaining lesson continuity with the students for only a very brief period of time. The advantages of this format appear clear. First, a brief seatwork activity is more likely to have a high task orientation than an extended activity. Surrounding seatwork periods with lecture allows the more easily maintained lesson continuity of the lecture to help support seatwork. Second, these brief seatwork activities incorporated into the lecture enable the teacher to provide more immediate feedback than extended seatwork activities. The teacher can thus modify explanations during the lecture if necessary rather than interrupt a long seatwork activity, as frequently happens in lower-performing classes.

In summary, the lower-performing class of Teacher F presents an important contrast with Teacher B's lower-performing class. Teacher B had a significantly longer seatwork period and shorter checking and lecture activities, possibly adding to her difficulties inasmuch as seatwork is often a problematic activity in lower-performing classes. In contrast, Teacher F minimized this problem in his lower-performing class by reducing the length of independent seatwork activity, which contributed significantly to the higher task orientation of his class, as determined by observer ratings. The comparison suggests that long, extended seatwork activities are counterproductive, adding to management problems and minimizing good task orientation in low-performing classes.

Many middle and high school teachers have both high- and low-performing classes in their schedule. Are they able to make adjustments, as Teacher F above did, and pace classes differently for different groups? That is what we mean by pacing and rhythm. One can look to see if time is structured for certain individuals, as Teacher F did for a whole class. And the reasons for varying it certainly go beyond the global word *ability*. In the Evertson study, "ability" really meant achievement on California Achievement Tests. There was a distinction between high- and low-performing classes. There are many reasons for high and low performance besides native ability, with its implication about intelligence. Very capable but impulsive or disturbed students may learn best when their pacing is regulated for short bursts of highly focused activities. Skillful teachers look to create such arrangements for those who need it, while the rest of the class may be paced quite differently.

Most secondary teachers who make the shift from the traditional seven-period day to block scheduling find themselves needing to reexamine how they pace and chunk the period to maintain student engagement. It is not a question of whether students can stay focused for seventy-five to eighty minutes but rather how the activities in the overall period are structured and balanced: length of time; balance of information input, processing; and output; opportunities for physical movement at least every half-hour or so; and variety in interaction complexity (working alone, working interactively, participating in large group) that counts.

Another area of exploration regarding time and pacing has to do with students who are diagnosed with attention deficit disorder (ADD) or attention deficit hyperactivity disorder (ADHD). Educators and medical people alike with expertise in this area have expressed serious concern over the rapidly increasing percentage of students diagnosed and being treated with medication. From 1989 to 1995 the numbers multiplied fivefold to represent 5 percent of the school-age population (Barklay, 1995). "By recent estimates, there may now be as many as 4 million school-age (5–13 years old) children in the U.S. taking Ritalin or a similar prescription stimulant for the treatment of attention-deficit disorder (ADD) or attention-deficit hyperactivity disorder (ADHD). Ritalin production increased by at least 700% in the period from 1990 to 1998" (O'Sullivan, 2005, p. 302). According to figures from the U.S. Census Bureau four million children represent approximately 10 percent of children ages five to thirteen enrolled in school in the year 2000. Barklay went on to say, "We wish, hope, expect a drug to fix what's wrong without looking at other factors which affect the problem," for example, the structuring of the environment and the schedule.

In *Ritalin Nation: Rapid Fire Culture and the Transformation of Human Consciousness* (1999), psychologist Richard DeGrandpre argues that ADHD has more to do with changes in time expectations in our society than better diagnosis of a physiological problem. Children with ADHD "show a more limited sense of the past and, as a result, a more limited sense of the future" (Barklay in Wood, 1999). Chip Wood (1999) wrote about it this way:

> I see children who exhibit ADHD behaviors as suffering from temporal trauma. Sadly, they are serving as "canaries" in the cage of time, especially in our schools, where their failure to thrive should tell us something about their environment.
>
> School schedules speed up year after year, putting more and more pressure on children to manage a world filled with more transitions, extended curricula, less predictability, and less time to accomplish more. It's tough on all children, but for these "canaries" who have a heightened sensitivity to time pressures, it's impossible. Our society and schools are faced with two possibilities. One is medicating more and more children in an effort to decrease their sensitivity to our ever faster, less-regulated pace of life and education. Another is making changes in the structure and pace of school life to reduce temporal trauma for all of our children.

Clearly there is a lot to consider when it comes to this area of performance. At various points throughout this chapter, we have mentioned ways in which time issues are intertwined with other areas of performance in teaching. As we bring the chapter to a close, we offer a summary of many of those as they relate specifically to managing time efficiently and in service of supporting student learning and achievement.

*Minimizing Noninstructional Time and Developing Efficient Management Systems*

- Establish routines and procedures. Develop a plan for dealing with housekeeping issues (lunch count, attendance, permission slips, cleanup, announcements) so these don't compete with instructional time. (Routines)
- Delegate jobs. Teach students how to do some of the management tasks you would ordinarily do (wheeling the overhead projector into place, distributing and collecting materials, changing desk arrangements, or moving furniture to match the planned activity for the day) to reduce setup time and protect the maximum amount of time to be with them to guide their learning.
- Reward efficiency. Give students an incentive for being efficient with management tasks: a number of minutes that will be allocated for a preferred activity if they accomplish transitions within a prescribed period of time.
- Have instructional materials ready to go and supplies conveniently stored and readily

available to students so they can access and return them independently and efficiently. (Momentum: Provisioning, Space)

- Allow sufficient time for transitions to avoid a harried pace, but challenge students to be efficient, and teach them how to implement routines that save time. (Routines, Space, Momentum)

- Minimize time spent on discipline issues: Deal with disruptions and off-task behavior quickly, directly, privately when possible, and with the minimum it takes to get the students back on track. (Attention, Discipline)

- Recognize and reward students who are using time wisely and managing it well.

*Pacing and Rhythm During Instructional Time*

- Provide students with advance notice before transitions when they have been cognitively or physically engaged in a task or activity so they have time to shift gears. (Momentum)

- Start and end lessons on time with meaningful activities. The opening and closing minutes of lessons are the moments that are most naturally remembered. (Principle of Learning: Sequence)

- Plan for students to be actively engaged in important instructional (versus management) activities during opening minutes by activating knowledge for an upcoming lesson, recalling or practicing something previously taught, or recording objectives for the class in their notes and during closing minutes by summarizing and reflecting on what they have learned in class that day, answering a question related to the day's objective. Or use the closing minutes to give assign-

ments slowly and carefully, to pose challenging dilemmas for students to ponder (end without closure), or to get personal involvement or commitments from students on controversial issues or on contracts. The main point is to use them, not lose them by giving sharp focus and purpose to the beginning and ending minutes.

- Establish a routine where students anticipate coming in to class and starting immediately and independently on a three- to five-minute opening assignment. (Principle of Learning: Similarity of Environment)

- Calibrate time thoughtfully, and help students monitor it. When there is an activity students are expected to complete within a time frame, make sure it is a reasonable time frame, let them know what it is at the outset, and provide them with a way to monitor their pace accordingly (for example, a transparent timer on an overhead projector, intermittent pacing reminders, or student timekeepers within groups).

- Pause for students to process and make meaning. Pause every eight to ten minutes of direct instruction, and require students to process what they have been hearing, seeing, or doing so they have an opportunity to absorb it, register it in memory, and connect existing knowledge with incoming information. (Principle of Learning: 10:2 and Say-Do)

- Pulse the learning. Balance or chunk periods of direct instruction and information input with independent or small group opportunities for students to practice, apply, and get feedback and support with new learning tasks. Consider the length of chunks that are best suited to the performance level of the learners and the complexity of the material, and volley between input and guided practice accordingly.

- Allow time for thinking. After posing instructional questions to all students, pause and protect at least three to five seconds of silence so all have the opportunity to process what the question is asking and to construct a thoughtful response (Wait Time I). Pause again after a student answers to allow the response to be heard and absorbed by all and to give the student time to extend, modify, or elaborate on the thoughts she has expressed. (Wait Time II)

- Plan for physical movement. If a learning experience requires students to sit still for long stretches, plan ways for them to get intermittent physical movement (for example, stand and share, find a learning partner or other processing activities that require movement) at least every thirty to forty minutes to keep their brains functioning at their highest capacity. (Brain research on cognition)

*Maximize Engaged and Academic Learning Time*

- Balance the interaction complexity. Strike a balance between whole class, small group, paired, and individual learning time. Different learners have natural preferences, and too much of any one format can be a hindrance to learning. (Learning Experiences)

- Prepare students for independent work. Be clear in your explanation of what is expected, and have students summarize directions and expectations with partners to avoid confusion and helplessness when they are expected to begin the work. When appropriate, have students attempt an example while you circulate, and check

understanding before assigning a longer period of independent work to ensure that engaged time becomes academic learning time.

- Involve students in modeling and demonstrating work (being the teacher) prior to or after independent practice while you act as a guide on the side. This enables you to check understanding and keep students more actively participating.

- Monitor independent work. When students are working independently (alone or in small groups), consider it an opportunity to gather assessment data to inform instruction. Monitor the learning by walking around to find out how they are doing and to provide guidance and feedback, which will keep them on track and increase the amount of high success time for all of them.

- Accommodate different rates of task completion. Plan learning experiences so there can be some flexibility with the length of time individual students have to master skills or concepts and the degree of guidance they receive while doing so.

- Have relevant and meaningful supplemental work ready for students who finish tasks early. Often this requires planning for and managing more than one concurrent activity that students work on during an instructional period. (See Momentum: Fillers and Overlapping, Learning Experiences: Differentiation.)

- Collect data on how time is actually being used.

*At the School Level*

- Prioritize allocated time. Develop agreements about how much time should be allocated in the schedule for various subjects and curricular areas.

- Protect instructional time. Minimize or eliminate disruptions and intrusions into classrooms during instructional time; develop alternative ways to relay messages, make announcements, and touch base with teachers.

Probably there are no teachers anywhere who feel satisfied that they have had sufficient contact time with students to be able to accomplish all that they hope to, or all that they are expected to, in a given class period, day, or year. What we have tried to do in this chapter is show how multifaceted this area of performance is, suggest some ways in which one might thoughtfully and intentionally examine how students are spending this valuable resource, and encourage the collection of concrete data in order to discover ways in which we can take increasing control of time in order to get the highest rate of return on student achievement. To quote a respected colleague, "The quality of our teaching is what changes time in the classroom. As teachers we have the power to control the clock even if we often feel like the clock is controlling us" (Wood, 1999, p. 217).

To check your knowledge about Time see the quiz on our Web site at **www.RBTeach.com/ rbteach/quiz/time.html.**

## Source Materials on Time

Aaronson, J., Zimmerman, J., and Carlos, L. *Improving Student Achievement by Extending School: Is It Just a Matter of Time?* San Francisco: WestEd, 1999.

Anderson, L .W. "Policy Implications of Research on School Time." *School Administrator,* 1983, *40,* 25–28.

Anderson, L. W., and Walberg, H. J. *Timepiece: Extending and Enhancing Learning Time.* Reston, Va.: NASSP, 1993.

Baker, D. P., Fabrega, R., Galindo, C., and Mishook, J. "Instructional Time and National Achievement: Cross-National Evidence." *Prospects,* 2004, *34*(3), 311–334.

Barklay, R. A. *Taking Charge of ADHD.* New York: Guilford Press, 1995.

Berliner, D. C. "What's All the Fuss About Instructional Time?" In M. Ben-Peretz (ed.), *The Nature of Time in Schools: Theoretical Concepts, Practitioner Perceptions.* New York: Teachers College Press, 1990.

Bloom, B. S. "Time and Learning." *American Psychologist,* 1974, *29,* 682–688.

Brewster, C., and Fager, J. *Increasing Student Engagement: From Time on Task to Homework.* Portland, Oreg.: Northwest Regional Educational Laboratory, 2000.

Caldwell, J. H., Huitt, W. G., and Graeber, A. O. "Time Spent in Learning." *Elementary School Journal,* 1982, *82*(5), 471–480.

Conant, E. H. *Teacher and Paraprofessional Work Productivity.* Lexington, Mass.: D.C. Heath, 1973.

Cotton, K. *Educational Time Factors.* Portland, Oreg.: Northwest Regional Educational Laboratory, 1989.

DeGrandpre, R. *Ritalin Nation: Rapid Fire Culture and the Transformation of Human Consciousness.* New York: Norton, 1999.

Dishaw, M. *Descriptions of Allocated Time to Content Areas for the A-B Period.* San Francisco: Far West Laboratory for Educational Research and Development, 1977.

Emmer, E. T., and Gerwels, M. C. "Classroom Management in Middle and High School Classrooms." In C. Evertson and C. Weinstein (eds.), *Handbook of Classroom Management: Research, Practice and Contemporary Issues.* Mahwah, N.J.: Erlbaum, 2006.

Emmer, E. T., Evertson, C., Clements, B., and Worsham, W. *Classroom Management for Secondary Teachers.* Needham Heights, Mass.: Allyn and Bacon, 2002.

Engel, B. S. *Informal Evaluation.* Grand Forks: University of North Dakota Press, 1977.

Evans, W., and Bechtel, D. *Extended School Day/Year Programs: A Research Synthesis.* Philadelphia: Laboratory for Student Success at Temple University, 1996.

Evertson, C. "Differences in Instructional Activities in Higher- and Lower-Achieving Junior High English and Math Classes." *Elementary School Journal,* 1982, *82*(4), 329–350. Reprinted with permission.

Evertson, C., and Weinstein, C. S. *Handbook of Classroom Management: Research, Practice and Contemporary Issues.* Mahwah, N.J.: Erlbaum, 2006.

Ference, P. R., and Vockell, E. L. "Adult Learning Characteristics and Effective Software Instruction." *Educational Technology,* July-Aug. 1994, pp. 25–31.

Fisher, C. W., and Berliner, D. C. *Perspectives on Instructional Time.* New York: Longman, 1985.

Fisher, C. W., Filby, N. N., Marliave, R. S., Chaen, L. A., Dishaw, M. M., Moore, J., and Berliner, D. C. "Teaching Behaviors, Academic Learning Time and Student Achievement: Final Report of Phase III-B, Beginning Teachers Evaluation Study. Technical Report V-1." Sacramento: Commission for Teacher Preparation and Licensing, 1978.

Good, T. L., and Brophy, J. E. *Looking in Classrooms.* (8th ed.). Reading, Mass.: Addison-Wesley, 2000.

Greenwood, C. R. "Longitudinal Analysis of Time, Engagement and Achievement in At Risk versus Non-Risk Students." *Exceptional Children,* 1991, *57,* 521–535.

Hollowood, T. M., and others. "Use of Instructional Time in Classrooms Serving Students with and Without Severe Disabilities." *Exceptional Children,* 1995, *61*(3), 242–253.

Hunter, J., and Csikszentmihalyi, M. "The Positive Psychology of Interested Adolescents." *Journal of Youth and Adolescents,* 2003, *28*(1), 1–26.

Karweit, N., and Slavin, R. E. "Measurement and Modeling Choices in Studies of Time and Learning." *Educational Research Journal,* 1981, *18*(2), 157–172.

Leinhardt, G., Zigmond, N., and Corley, W. M. "Reading Instruction and Its Effects." *American Educational Research Journal,* 1981, *18*(3), 343–361.

Marzano, R. J. *A New Era of School Reform: Going Where the Research Takes Us.* Aurora, Colo.: Mid-Continent Research for Education and Learning, 2000.

Marzano, R. J. *What Works in Schools: Translating Research into Action.* Alexandria, Va.: ASCD, 2003.

Marzano, R. J., and Riley, A. Unpublished data. Aurora, Colo.: Mid-Continent Regional Educational Laboratory, 1984.

Marzano, R. J., Kendall, J. S., and Gaddy, B. B. *Essential Knowledge: The Debate Over What American Students Should Know.* Aurora, Colo.: Mid-Continent Regional Educational Laboratory, 1999.

Mitchell, M. "Situational Interest: Its Multifaceted Structure in the Secondary School Mathematics Classroom." *Journal of Educational Psychology,* 1993, *85,* 424–436.

National Education Commission on Time and Learning. *Prisoners of Time.* Washington, D.C.: U.S. Department of Education, 1994.

O'Sullivan, R. "Raising Children in an Age of Ritalin." *The Journal of Andrology,* 2005, *26*(3), 302–303.

Park, C. "The Bay City Experiment . . . as Seen by the Director." *Journal of Teacher Education,* 1976, *7,* 5–8.

Rosenshine, B. V. "How Time Is Spent in Elementary Classrooms." *Journal of Classroom Interaction,* 1981, *17*(1), 16–25.

Scheerens, J., and Bosker, R. *The Foundations of Educational Effectiveness.* New York: Elsevier, 1997.

Shernoff, D., Csikszentmihalyi, M., Schneider, B., and Shernoff, E. "Student Engagement in High School Classrooms from the Perspective of Flow Theory." *School Psychology Quarterly,* 2003, *18,* 158–176.

Stallings, J. "Allocated Academic Learning Time Revisited, or Beyond Time on Task." *Educational Researcher,* 1980, *9,* 11–16.

Stanley, S., and Greenwood, C. "How Much Opportunity to Respond Does the Minority Disadvantaged Student Receive in School?" *Exceptional Children,* Jan. 1983, *49*(4), 370–373.

Stigler, J. W., and Hiebert, J. *The Teaching Gap: Best Ideas from the World's Teachers for Improving Education in the Classroom.* New York: Free Press, 1999.

Tindal, G., and Parker, R. "Direct Observation in Special Education Classrooms." *Journal of Special Education,* 1987, *21*(2), 43–58.

Walberg, H. *Uncompetitive American Schools: Causes and Cures.* Washington, D.C.: Brookings Institute, 1997.

Walberg, H. *Improving Educational Productivity.* Aurora, Colo.: Mid-Atlantic Regional Educational Laboratory, 2003.

Wang, M., Haertel, G., and Walberg, H. "What Helps Students Learn?" *Educational Leadership,* Dec. 1993–Jan. 1994, pp. 74–79.

Wood, C. *Time to Teach, Time to Learn: Changing the Pace of School.* Greenfield, Mass.: Northeast Foundation for Children, 1999.

Zahorik, J. A. "Elementary and Secondary Teachers' Reports of How They Make Learning Interesting." *Elementary School Journal,* 1996, *96,* 551–565.

# Routines

**W**here would we be without routines in our daily lives: routines for getting up and ready for the day; routines for finding and sorting important items at home and at work; routines for doing certain recurring tasks? By "routine," we mean any recurring event or situation for which there could conceivably be a regular procedure.

Clearly, routines are essential to our daily lives. We all have hundreds of routines that we practice unconsciously; they become layered one on another, operate automatically, and free us for the more thoughtful and interesting projects we may wish to address. The same applies to the role of routines in the organization of classroom life. Good routines are important, even vital, to successful classrooms. When they are poorly thought out—or not thought out at all—the results are seen in disorganization, poor momentum, and often discipline problems.

Classroom routines need to be efficient and clear. The students need to know what the routines are and how to do them. We highlight those two

We appreciate the contributions of the following teachers who were kind enough to share some of their routines with us in this chapter: Nadine Bishop, Steve Bober, Peggy Bowlby, Jeff Levin, Ann Lindsay, Barbara Lipstadt, Betty Murray, David Negrin, Loren Robbins, Sally Springer, Gene Stamell, Bill Tate, Alan Ticotsky, and Joe Walsh.

ideas in this chapter, plus the idea that routines can teach. Routines themselves can be curriculum, by virtue of their particular purposes and the learnings embedded in them.

## Routines for What?

The Routines area of performance encompasses a variety of kinds of classroom routines. Some routines pertain to housekeeping (such as attendance, lunch and milk counts, getting and maintaining supplies, organizing boots and coats, cleanup, snack distribution). Other routines pertain to operational features of class business (making announcements; noise-level control; leaving the room; turn taking and population limits; what to do with the first ten minutes of the day or of the period; how to carry chairs, scissors, pencils). Still others pertain to work habits and work procedures (how to sit, how to study spelling words, use of lab equipment, procedures for using an easel, what form to use when preparing for literature circle discussion roles or solving nonroutine math problems and explaining your solution, a timetable and milestone chart of events to be checked by the teacher when students are preparing an oral presentation or a term paper). When skillfully performed, all of these routines are valuable ways of organizing and managing a class.

## Clear Communication and Standards

To get the most out of routines, teachers need to communicate them clearly. The first set of questions to ask about the use of routines concerns expectations: Do the students know clearly what's expected of them in the way of procedures and routines? Do they know what they're supposed to do?

Teacher behaviors that account for good communication of routines are similar to those for communicating expectations for work. Good communication of routines is:

- Direct: Routines are explicitly brought to students' attention.
- Specific: All important details are explained.
- Repeated to make sure students absorb them.
- Communicated with positive expectancy—a "you can do it" flavor.
- Modeled.
- Practiced until mastered.
- Tenaciously adhered to until integrated.

The same kind of thinking applied within the Expectations area of performance also goes into examining the appropriateness of the standards inherent in the routines and how the standards are adjusted (matched) for individuals and groups. Therefore, as with standards for expectations, standards for routines can be viewed along the scale below (see Chapter Twelve, "Expectations," for expanded definitions):

- None exist.
- Confusing: Standards are unclear.
- Low: The teacher demands less of students than she or he might.
- Too high: The teacher demands too much of students.
- Matched: Standards are appropriate for most students.
- High but reasonable: The standards are very demanding but attainable by students.

As with academic work, it is in our best interest and that of our students to match standards for routines to the needs of individual students or groups. (See Chapter Twelve for a discussion of various levels of matching standards.)

Now, with those issues under our belt, we're ready to move into new ground: What about the routines themselves? Why are they as they are, and how much mileage is being gotten out of them?

## Matching Routines to Purposes

The nature of classroom routines is determined by the teacher by abdication, negotiation, or directly. Seven levels of performance that describe teachers' use of routines can be distinguished:

1. No routines apparent for relevant events: ad hoc teacher reactions.
2. A few routines erratically followed.
3. Stable routines for most relevant events, with evidence of student training.
4. Stable and highly efficient routines for all relevant events.
5. Varied routines. The teacher modifies, experiments, uses alternative forms.
6. Routines are matched to the group.
7. Routines are matched to characteristics of individuals and mapped to goals for them.

This scale spans a range of answers to the question: Why are routines the way they are? They may serve efficiency, a valid and common orientation among teachers. They may serve a general goal: giving students security through the predictability of certain recurring events. They may map to more specific goals for groups or for the class as a whole, such as having students routinely record books they have read in a register so that they take some responsibility for a form of record

keeping and get to see and participate in building a cumulative index of their books read; or assigning teams to areas of the room for cleanup so that the children have to come to grips with group responsibility, handling the division of labor, and dealing with individuals who won't carry their weight.

Routines may be created or adjusted by teachers in the service of objectives for specific individuals. For example, in a primary grade class, Tim may start each day by taking down a few chairs and then moving into woodworking or clay—something with a motor emphasis, whereas Josh's starting routine may be worked out to reflect academics and time in a private space. In an older class in which students are routinely expected to check the board for morning assignments or for feedback from previous work, Clara may need a personal "greet" and escort over to the board or a folder of her own in which this information is placed. Tenth-grader Margaret may be asked to end each study hall with a log entry on what she has accomplished as a way of focusing her. Marvin may be asked to arrange the furniture for committee work at the beginning of each social studies period as a way of settling him down (and getting him to class on time).

Following are some examples of procedural routines that serve different purposes. Some serve efficiency and effectiveness—a worthy goal. These are related to momentum; that's the kind of efficiency meant here—an efficient flow of events without delays. For example, as students enter the room they pick up their name cards on a side table (this serves as attendance taking); work to be submitted goes in the red in-tray; extra handouts from the previous day's class are in colored and labeled folders on the windowsill; planners are open to today's date and on desk at the beginning of class for copying assignments due for next class. All of these are aimed at saving both student and teacher time and eliminating the "what do I do with . . ." or "where can I get . . ." time-killer questions at the beginning of class.

Other routines are aimed at increasing the effectiveness of cognitive learning. They are routines oriented toward academics—for example, word bank and word file are ongoing collections of words the children have found hard to spell. The student finds the correct spelling of a word, writes the word on a card, and then tapes the card to the word bank, a set of twenty-six pockets—one for each letter of the alphabet—mounted on the wall. Cards are later filed in a permanent word file for future use in spelling.

A third group of routines shows how much additional mileage can be gotten out of routines if they are used thoughtfully and deliberately. These routines reveal what many would call the hidden curriculum: the indirect personal and social learning students receive just from being present in a particular classroom. *Personal learning* refers to students' learning something about themselves or some ability that might be described in terms of character development rather than skill. *Social learn-*

*ing* refers to students' learning something about others, groups, or people together (cooperation, sharing). An example of such a routine is: "After I call on the first student to read, he in turn calls on the next reader." This keeps a larger percentage of the students involved. It also raises questions of fairness (boys shouldn't call only on other boys) and consideration of differential reading abilities.

We believe that teachers should be as aware and explicit as possible about their hidden curriculum, and it is through this area of performance that they can see much of it. If teachers want, they can make their routines serve multiple purposes.

To check your knowledge about Routines see the quiz on our Web site at **www.RBTeach.com/ rbteach/quiz/routines.html.**

*Source Materials on Routines*

Evertson, C., and Weinstein, C. S. (eds.). *Handbook of Classroom Management.* Mahwah, N.J.: Erlbaum, 2006.

Randolph, N., and Howe, W. *Self-Enhancing Education.* Palo Alto, Calif.: Stanford University Press, 1966.

Taylor, J. *Organizing the Open Classroom—A Teacher's Guide to the Integrated Day.* New York: Schocken Books, 1972.

# Discipline

"What do I have to do to get students to apply themselves to their work and stop fooling around and being disruptive?" That is the bottom-line question of Discipline. Many teachers spend a disproportionate amount of energy dealing with it; some leave teaching because they find they rarely deal with anything else. There is no question that good discipline is a prerequisite for good education. We must bring all of our best knowledge to bear on it to stop the needless dissipation of both teacher and student energy that it causes. We have the knowledge and the capability to retire this issue and to move on to the question most teachers are more interested in: "How do I build self-discipline and responsibility in students?" In this chapter, we address both questions.

The chapter is organized around the following assumptions:

- All behavior has an origin or cause.
- There are at least twelve different causes of inattentive or disruptive behavior.
- Effective responses to disruptive behavior are chosen from a repertoire to match the cause or causes.
- Effective discipline is built on a comprehensive approach that includes:
  - Laying a foundation of sound classroom management, solid instructional design

and delivery, and building relationships with students

o Establishing authority by communicating expectations, limit setting, and eliminating disruptions

o Building a strong classroom climate that nurtures cooperation, responsibility, and self-discipline

o Being familiar with more complex models of discipline that may be necessary to implement with a very small percentage of especially troubled or recalcitrant students

# A Comprehensive Approach to Discipline

Figure 8.1 summarizes the elements of a comprehensive approach to discipline and represents the necessary sequence of tasks to be accomplished for building a disciplined and orderly classroom. The diagram can serve as a resource for diagnosis and problem solving when discipline issues are interfering with classroom operations.

Following is a brief outline of the tasks that are necessary for good discipline. Each task has a tool kit associated with it; many of the tools are described in more detail in related chapters throughout the book.

## Task 1: Establishing Foundations of Classroom Management, Personal Relationships, and Sound Instruction

Begin by establishing a welcoming environment conducive to smooth management. This means making sure the environment in which the children live and work is set up properly, with routines, time schedule, procedures, and physical space, to facilitate smooth operation and minimize downtime and distractions; building relationships of regard and respect with students to signal that this is a place where they are valued as individuals; and designing and delivering instruction in a way that all students can experience both challenge and success. (See Chapters Three to Seven, Nine, Thirteen, Sixteen, and Nineteen.)

## Task 2: Eliminating Disruptions

Communicate through your actions that students can rely on you to maintain a safe and orderly environment. Even if you are totally committed to having a democratic classroom where students are responsible for their own behavior, this is necessary in order to garner the respect and significance you will need to create any classroom climate you care about.

Establishing authority and safety has three major subtasks. The first is establishing expectations for behavior with confidence and clarity and building a crystal-clear understanding of the rules and the social contract that will be the reference point for behavior. Involve the students to the degree possible in creating a social contract, and act out the boundaries of the rules so there is no ambiguity of what they mean. Later in this chapter we describe strategies for involving students in developing the rules.

The second subtask is to set limits by reacting with speed and decisiveness when behavior is inappropriate or disruptive. One does this by noticing when student behavior needs a response and responding quickly with the body language of meaning business (Jones, 2007) and any other steps that are necessary to preserve order and safety, both physical and psychological. Linda Lantieri (2001)

**Figure 8.1. Discipline Tasks and Toolboxes**

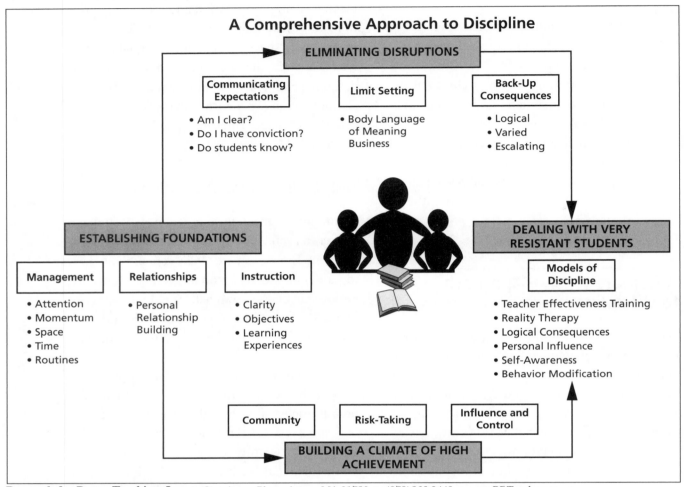

**Research for Better Teaching, Inc.** • One Acton Place, Acton, MA 01720 • (978) 263-9449 • www.RBTeach.com

shows the relationship of classroom order and psychological safety in the following quote:

> "Children do not always know what is safe for them or for others," said Dorothy. "Discipline and limits are a way we create a circle of safety for those not yet ready to do this for themselves. Picture these limits as a big hug—our strong arms encircling the child with comfort and safety."

Once we see discipline as an act of love and containment, we can be creative and responsive to the style and degree of discipline needed with a particular child or group. . . . When we distinguish respect from fear and provide limits to prevent children from harming each other, we are not defending our power as teachers; we are helping group members create the safety to be vulnerable and authentic with one another [p. 121].

The final subtask is responding to student behavior when necessary with consequences that are clear, swift, fair, and certain. This means having an escalating scale of consequences in mind and the backup systems in place.

## Task 3: Building a Climate of High Achievement

Build responsibility and self-discipline in classroom life. This means moving away from teacher control to building internal controls in the students and community responsibility for the classroom climate and environment. We address this topic later in the chapter and in much greater detail in Chapter Fourteen, "Classroom Climate."

## Task 4: Dealing with Very Resistant Students

Over the years, build a repertoire of advanced models of discipline to use for the most resistant students who have the most emotional baggage. This is not a target for beginners. Successfully mastering the first three tasks will take care of the vast majority of the discipline issues any teacher faces. But for the most intractable students, the sophisticated models of discipline will be useful from time to time. So after a few years of teaching experience, it is worth beginning to learn, one by one, the six classic models of discipline described in this chapter.

### How to Address the Tasks

These four tasks are sequential and must be handled in priority order. Experienced teachers may be working on the first three all at once from day one, but they are still sequential in the sense that each

task requires the one before it to be successfully in hand before accomplishing the next task. For example, if the environment is poorly structured (task 1), then the class operates chaotically and the teacher has a tough time catching all the disruptions and becoming a person of significance to the students (task 2). If the rules are unclear (see task 2), the teacher won't be able to deliver consequences for student behavior without being resisted and seen as unfair. If the consequences are not clear, certain, and fair from the students' point of view, not only will the worst disrupters start to get the upper hand, but the class as a whole won't invest in building a responsible, inclusive classroom community (task 3.)

There's no use doing the tasks backward either. No teacher can focus on climate building and teaching the students how to handle their own problems if the earlier jobs are not solidly handled. Hence, this sequence is a progression teachers can use to diagnose potential causes of discipline issues as well as to uncover myriad variables to adjust or fine-tune.

In this chapter, we address each of the task areas one at a time and lay out a repertoire of ways for accomplishing them. We begin by identifying a range of causes that lie behind disruptive or inappropriate behavior, the first four of which have to do with task 1: laying the foundations.

## Causes of Disruptive or Inattentive Behavior

All behavior has an origin or cause, and there are at least twelve causes of disruptive or inattentive behavior in classrooms (Table 8.1). We'll take a quick look at these causes and examine a few of them in depth.

Causes 1 to 4 all have to do with task 1: laying the foundations of management, relationship building, and solid instruction. All are related to aspects of teaching over which teachers have nearly complete control and when well executed can serve as preventive measures to discipline issues. The tools available for addressing these are described in greater detail in related chapters throughout this book.

Causes 5 and 6 are directly related to task 2: establishing authority and safety by ensuring that students know what is expected and how to do it. Causes 7, 8, 9, and 10 highlight characteristics that might be part of a student's makeup or natural or learned behaviors that collide with their otherwise instinctive tendency to cooperate and participate in school. Cause 11 suggests the need for task 4: becoming familiar with six sophisticated models of discipline for the small minority of recalcitrant, troubled students. Cause 12, student sense of powerlessness and alienation, is dealt with extensively in Chapter Fourteen, "Classroom Climate."

## Cause 1: Poor General Management

Competent handling of Attention, Momentum, Space, Time, and Routines forms a foundation for good behavior. Conversely, absence of their skillful handling creates distraction and fragmentation.

- Have you anticipated potential downtime, delays, and distractions and planned in advance for them? Are you periodically monitoring what and how students are doing when they are working independently? (Momentum)
- Before you begin instruction, do you ensure that students are focused and attending? Do you use strategies that will keep students alert and on their toes throughout a learning experience? When students resist or are unfocused, do you draw on a wide range of moves to bring them back, or does your repertoire collapse into repeated authorita-

**Table 8.1. Twelve Causes of Disruptive or Inattentive Behavior**

1. Poor general management: Attention, Momentum, Space, Time, Routines, Personal Relationship Building
2. Inappropriate work: too hard, too easy, or a glaring learning style mismatch: Objectives, Learning Experiences
3. Boring instruction: Learning Experiences
4. Confusing instruction: Clarity
5. Unclear standards, expectations, and consequences
6. Student ignorance on how to do the expected behaviors
7. A need for fun and stimulation
8. Value and culture clashes
9. Internal physical causes
10. External physical causes
11. Extraordinary emotional baggage
12. Student sense of powerlessness

tive moves that result in power struggles? (Attention)

- Are the space and furniture arrangements conducive to all students seeing the board and having adequate private or quiet time for working independently? Are all students within your visual range most of the time? (Space)

- Are time allocations reasonably matched (not too long or too short) to what students will need to complete tasks, participate productively in group activities, and sit still? (Time)

- Have you established routines for what to do when a student enters the classroom, needs help, is finished with work, and a myriad other aspects of daily classroom functioning so that you minimize downtime and unnecessary nagging and reminders? Do students know how to carry out the routines you have set? (Routines)

The bottom line here is that inattention to—or mismanagement of—Attention, Momentum, Space, Time, and Routines can leave students distracted, frustrated, or bored and tuned out, with downtime on their hands. When this is the case, it is likely that they will find an outlet somewhere for their energy and creativity, and that outlet may well be disruptive. One might argue that with prolonged boredom, disruptions are probably a sign of mental health and physical vitality in normal children. So when there are discipline problems, especially if the problems are endemic to the whole class, these management areas are the first places to look for causes and solutions.

The same holds true for personal relationship building with students. When teachers invest time in getting to know their students, show them

respect as individuals, and treat them fairly, most students tend to behave in kind. Gordon and Burch's *Teacher Effectiveness Training* (2003) devotes entire chapters to communication skills that contribute to positive and productive relationships with students. In the absence of a good relationship, it is far easier for students to act out, ignore expectations set for their behavior, and be resentful.

What this points to are the measures teachers can take to minimize discipline problems by applying the best of what they know in each of the areas of performance.

## Cause 2: Inappropriate Work

Even if the areas of performance already addressed are well managed, teachers need to make sure the work is appropriate for the students: challenging but attainable (Objectives and Learning Experiences). If it is too hard, too easy, or a consistent glaring mismatch to a student's learning style, the risk is frustration or boredom, either of which may induce disruptive behavior. Considering how to scaffold and differentiate learning experiences so that all students can productively work toward achieving an objective is an essential aspect of effective planning. But even if basic management is handled well and instruction is of reasonable difficulty, there may still be problems.

## Cause 3: Boring Instruction

Using the same format or activity structures day after day (too much lecturing, too many worksheets, low-level questioning, or something else) may also induce boredom and acting out behavior in some classes. Chapter Eighteen, "Learning Experiences," highlights variables to manipulate to provide balance and variety in lessons.

## Cause 4: Confusing Instruction

Confusing instruction induces frustration and boredom. Are concepts presented to students in ways they can absorb and understand? Do they have time to process and make sense of them? Does instruction align with what we know about different modality (auditory, visual, and kinesthetic) orientations, multiple intelligences, and variety in learning styles? Are we checking for understanding frequently across all students to ensure they are getting it as instruction proceeds? Do students know what they are expected to get out of a learning experience and why they are doing particular activities? All of these concerns are related to clarity of instruction; Chapter Nine, along with Chapter Ten, "Principles of Learning," can serve as a resource for minimizing confusion during learning experiences.

## Cause 5: Unclear Standards, Expectations, and Consequences

A more serious, and more common, cause of inattentive or disruptive behavior is unclear expectations and consequences: the intricate web of mutual understandings that goes with them may not be clearly established between teacher and students. We have yet to find a teacher with widespread discipline problems (rather than just one resistant child) who did not need help here. In Part Two, we specify the essential how-to's of building this web.

## Cause 6: Student Ignorance of How to Do the Expected Behaviors

Youngsters bring to school both the manners and the cognitive habits they have learned elsewhere. Failure to meet teacher expectations for lining up without running, listening to directions, lining up their work neatly on paper, or for putting materials away in an orderly way may simply come from the fact that they don't know how to do so. It is a fact that some kindergartners don't know how to walk rather than run in certain situations (which is to say they don't know how to predict consequences, control impulses, or plan physical movements). For some children, it is important to directly teach some of the hidden rules of school and formal behavior: classroom survival skills such as how to stay in their seat, how to participate appropriately, and where to put their things.

Some older students don't know how to categorize objects to expedite a cleanup, much less plan their time and movements during it. In these cases, teaching the behaviors step by step, not clever consequences or contracts, is the antidote to the disruptive behavior. There's no use trying to motivate youngsters to do something for which they lack the tools. Assumptions can cause teachers to overlook these possibilities. It may simply never occur to them that the deepening cycle of threats and punishments has its origin in simple ignorance. We urge teachers facing disruptive behavior to examine their students carefully. More often than is realized, teachers assume capacities that are not there in students' behavioral repertoires. In these cases, putting the behaviors into their repertoires is needed. A question not to overlook when trying to figure out a resistant class or individual is, "Do they know how to do what I am asking them to do?"

## Cause 7: A Need for Fun and Stimulation

Fooling around with friends is natural and healthy. Children would almost invariably rather fool around than do their work, so teachers should expect that and not resent it. Truth be told, we were probably like that too. (And it never completely goes away for some of us. Watch adults at faculty meetings.) This doesn't change in any way the teacher's responsibility to make instruction interesting and relevant or to make the rules clear and enforce student engagement. But it does perhaps temper irritation to remember the social urges and youthful energy that underlie some disruptive behavior.

## Cause 8: Value and Culture Clashes

Cultural clashes between teachers and students may underlie resistant behavior. This cause is rare but real and should be considered in classes where students' home life has strong ethnic roots in a culture different from the teacher's. In addition to ethnicity, another cultural dimension to be aware of is tacit rules—unspoken cues and habits—of different socioeconomic groups: "For example, being able to fight or have someone who is willing to fight for you is important to survival in poverty. Yet in the middle class, being able to use words as tools to negotiate conflict is crucial. Many times the fists are used in poverty because the words are neither available nor respected" (Payne, 2005, p. 60).

Other examples Payne cites include laughing when disciplined as a way to save face in matriarchal cultures; inappropriate or vulgar comments that may be the only language a child has learned for dealing with conflict; not following directions, which may be due to the absence of practice or procedural memory training; disrespectful behavior, which may be a result of not knowing any adults worthy of respect; and incessant talking, which may be a manifestation of the participatory nature of the culture of poverty.

The bottom line here is that children may be behaving in ways that are consistent with their own culture (racial, ethnic, or socioeconomic) but may be considered inappropriate in the culture of

school. It is imperative to examine inappropriate behavior with that in mind as a prerequisite to teaching replacement behaviors for students.

## Cause 9: Internal Physical Causes

Sometimes seemingly inattentive students in fact don't hear well. They fail to carry out directions not because they're daydreaming or willful; they simply mishear key words. We have known inattentive students to be diagnosed with hearing loss after several years in primary school and after much energy went into behavior modification and other focusing strategies for the children. Be sure to rule out physical causes when working with children who appear resistant or spacey. These include vision, organic hyperactivity, thyroid irregularities, fetal alcohol syndrome, drug dependency, attention deficit disorder, and a host of other possible physical problems.

## Cause 10: External Physical Causes

The environment of the class itself may be a mismatch for certain students, and a simple change of the environment can reduce or eliminate problems for them. The most obvious variable is the degree of structure in the class (Colarusso, 1972). High-structure environments leave students less choice in what activities to do when, with whom, and where in the room. Low-structure environments (which may nevertheless be highly planned and highly organized) have more student movement and more flexibility in who does what and when, since students are making more choices and are more in charge of their personal schedules.

For some children, the predictability and organization of a highly structured classroom environment represents a haven of comfort and security from an otherwise outside world (or home life) of uncertainty or chaos. A classroom in which daily schedules are published and adhered to, reasonable rules and routines are established and followed, supplies are orderly and accessible, and personal space (desk, locker, cubby, and so on) is assigned and controlled by them can render school a welcome environment for some students, fulfilling the basic human need to feel in control in ways they don't experience elsewhere.

In addition to structure, other environmental variables that might influence behavior include the amount and kind of auditory and visual stimulation in a classroom. Some people can completely tune out ambient noise, and others are highly sensitive to and distracted by it. This is also the case regarding the visual environment. The type or amount of lighting in the room can be a factor interfering with or supporting concentration for some students. Learning style experts (Dunn, 1994) highlight temperature and seating arrangements as additional variables that can affect learners. A room too hot or cold leads to physical discomfort that interferes with concentration. Thus, there are a number of environmental factors that might affect student behavior.

In *Teacher Effectiveness Training,* Gordon and Burch (2003) have some useful checklists for other ways to modify the environment. When considering how to improve students' behavior, teachers should look also at the appropriateness of the environments. They need to weigh how much these environments may be contributing to (rather than reducing) problems. The goal is to arrange them so that they do not play to students' weaknesses and trigger disruptive behaviors.

## Cause 11: Extraordinary Emotional Baggage

Some emotional baggage may be short term and its impact short lived: a feud with a friend, anxiety over a test, or a fight at home. Or it may be long term, cumulative, and more severe: great insecurity or fear over one's safety, being convinced one is a failure, and so on.

Some adolescents and even middle elementary students bring a sense of alienation and hopelessness to school that manifests alternately as withdrawal and disengagement or defiance and hostility. (Chapters Thirteen and Fourteen, "Personal Relationship Building" and "Classroom Climate" contain more guidance for these students than this one does.) The issue for these students is not discipline; it is motivation and meaning. Whereas the foundations for orderly classroom life that are presented in this chapter are necessary for alienated students, they are insufficient; those foundations will not be enough to get them engaged. Students who do not believe school has anything for them in life or who have given up on their own capacity to improve their lives through education require reaching beyond this chapter.

Hardest of all—despite all the best efforts in responding to these issues—there may still be a few students who resist learning and do not function in school. They may be passive and withdrawn or act out severely and consistently. The final section of this chapter addresses these students—the few, not the many; the troubled, not the norm. There are at least six major systematic approaches for dealing with resistant students, each cohesive and each different, and they are all effective if used with the right students.

## Cause 12: Student Sense of Powerlessness

Schools as institutions can resemble the army, prisons, and hospitals in the way they may systematically make students feel powerless. They can frustrate the basic human need for control by leaving little or no room for initiative, decision making, and leadership. This environment makes a significant percentage of children want to push back, and they do. If we use power skillfully, we can control these students—but we will probably also make them hate school and learn less. This is no pitch for free schools; learning is often hard work and requires doing assignments given by others, and that is okay. But without compromising high academic standards, teachers can structure classes so that students feel some ownership and control. Every increment of progress in this direction takes pressure off behavior management because students' energy starts to push with instead of against. Later and in Chapter Fourteen, "Classroom Climate," we will elaborate on how teachers can do this.

## Establishing the Foundation

In examining causes one through four of disruptive or inattentive behavior we proposed ways in which several of the management areas of performance (Attention, Momentum, Space, Time, and Routines) lay a solid discipline foundation. We also discussed the importance and benefits of investing in personal relationship building with students. Finally we highlighted instructional areas of performance (Objectives, Clarity, and Learning Experiences) that can serve as toolboxes for making the foundation structurally sound. Collectively these areas of performance afford us a huge framework for establishing preventive measures and for diagnosing and responding to issues that arise. This is the place to begin when dealing with discipline.

## Eliminating Disruptions

In Chapter Twelve, "Expectations," we describe four areas of classroom life where teachers set standards of performance: the quantity and quality of work, work habits and procedures, business and housekeeping routines, and interpersonal behavior. When it comes to discipline, we are primarily focusing on setting and communicating expectations in the last three categories. We use Figure 8.2 to describe the key issues in getting students to rise to the expectations their teachers set for them.

## Clarity and Conviction About Expected Behavior

The starting point here is the teacher. Do we (teachers) have clarity about what we want from our students? Do we have conviction about what we can reasonably expect from our students? The distinction here is an important one: clarity about what we want a student to do or measure up to is about setting standards of behavior; what we think a student will do—or is capable of doing—is about our beliefs and expectations. Each plays a critical role in the results we get from students. If we aren't clear about standards of performance, students won't know what we are asking of them. If we don't have conviction that students are capable of achieving a standard of performance, we aren't likely to inspire them to do so.

Is it reasonable to expect first graders to sit and listen at a classroom meeting for more than ten minutes? Are they capable of doing so? If you believe that your first graders will never be able to sit for more than ten minutes, they won't. Are your inner-city high school students too conditioned by street culture to give respectful silence to peers doing a mock debate? If we believe that, then disrespect is what we will observe.

Every year we work with at least one or two excellent teachers who are talented and caring people but whose effectiveness is reduced by their ambivalence about expectations. They are unsure how reasonable it is for them to expect and to push students toward more responsible and attentive behavior in class. They see the irresponsible behavior of

**Figure 8.2. Key Issues in Expectations**

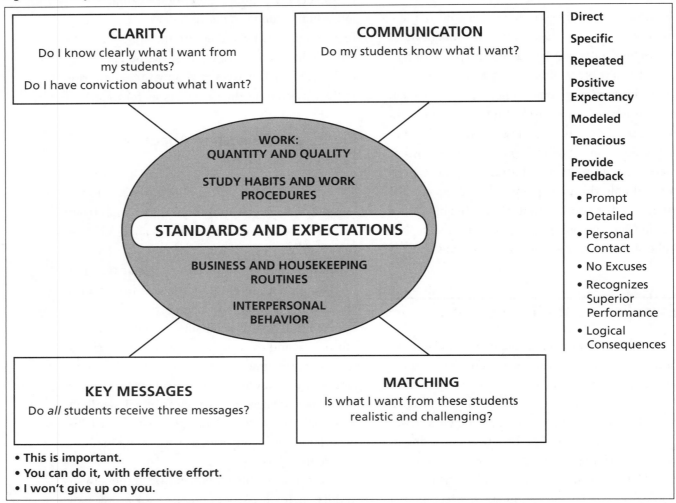

**Research for Better Teaching, Inc.** • One Acton Place, Acton, MA 01720 • (978) 263-9449 • www.RBTeach.com

students who appear out of control but have family and other problems and feel they must make allowances. They thus undersell the children and undershoot with their goals for student behavior. Who says first graders can't sit still in a circle and listen to each other for a fifteen-minute meeting? Who says ninth graders can't learn to function in self-organized task groups to plan and organize a project?

Again and again, we have seen it demonstrated that teachers can get what behavior they want if they work hard enough at it, are tenacious and determined enough, are committed to the idea that it is right and attainable behavior for their students, and are willing to teach the skills their students may need to function at that level. This is true even for some disturbed students, though they are more taxing, the setting may need adjustment, and this work will take considerably longer. Expecting anything less is ultimately a disservice to students. What you decide to "want," of course, can be unreasonable and age inappropriate, in which case what you get is what you deserve.

If you have a clear notion of what you want, and keep expecting, expecting, expecting, and say so out loud to students, with consequences when they don't measure up, with explanations of "why" over and over again, and with as much kindness and rationality as you can muster, you will get there. But first you must make some decisions about what is acceptable and unacceptable behavior and decide in order of priority what you want and that you will commit to getting it.

## The Taboo Exercise

The Taboo exercise is a useful first exercise for faculties to do together to get clarity, consensus, and conviction about behavioral expectations. Through the exercise, and the discussion it necessitates, people get clearer about distinctions between the most serious and unacceptable student behaviors that warrant uniform, immediate, and consistent responses and consequences from the whole staff, and about behaviors that are important to address or extinguish but far less serious and therefore not worthy of community time and investment. In the latter case, individuals decide how to address them.

The exercise begins with individuals privately and silently brainstorming behaviors they are bothered by and want to minimize or eliminate. They can record each behavior on a single sticky note. After brainstorming, they spend at least five minutes sorting each behavior, according to their own standards, into one of four categories on their own chart (Exhibit 8.1):

- Taboo—the most serious of behaviors. A student should do this only once because the reaction will be strong and total.
- Very serious—behaviors that are important to respond to, with swift and strong consequences. These are behaviors that would seriously threaten the social order and the climate if they were allowed, but they are not quite as serious as the taboos.
- No-no—behaviors that are against the rules and are responded to every time, but they are not a cataclysmic event. There are consequences, but the level of response is measured in comparison to the first two behaviors.
- Uh-uh—behaviors students shouldn't do and for which there are rules, like raising hands to speak in class, but enforcement may vary with conditions and mood.

Next, in small groups, teachers share what they have in each column and explain their reasons. Their task is to come up with a consensus chart. The resulting discussions are animated, informative, and productive. You can make something a taboo only if you have the power to do so with some social capital in the community to back you up. For example, many would like to make fistfighting a taboo anywhere on school grounds. In certain communities, however, because of the peer and adult culture, we do not have the power to make fighting a once-only occurrence. Therefore,

**Exhibit 8.1. Taboo Exercise Sheet**

| Taboo | Very Serious | No-No | Uh-Uh |
|---|---|---|---|
| Our reaction is so strong it happens only once. | We react strongly and take action. | We respond but don't get all worked up. | We enforce today but might ignore tomorrow. |

fighting is in the very serious category. People change their opinions, both up and down, about the significance of certain behaviors when they hear the rationale of others. A sixth grader climbing the chain-link fence in the recess courtyard moves up in Jim's mind to serious when he hears Clarisse's point about how dangerous a fall could be, especially with the occasional glass on the tarmac. Cursing moves down from a taboo in Marcia's estimation, although it is still extremely offensive to her, because she realizes how prevalent and almost colloquial it is in the student culture. She succeeds, however, in elevating cursing to a no-no behavior for Jim and Clarisse because she convinces them how important respectful language is to a focused academic environment.

These discussions lay a foundation for consistent faculty responses to student behavior and for determining what the consequences will be when a student violates them. They are particularly important in secondary schools, where students may experience wide inconsistency in adult standards across the five or more teachers they see daily.

## Do Students Know What Is Expected of Them?

The prerequisite for strength in this area is that students have a clear and unambiguous picture of the expectations for their behavior. Something must happen to get that information across. There are numerous ways this may be done: tell them directly, make up a chart, brainstorm, or negotiate the class rules at a class meeting. Expectations are sometimes not codified as formal rules or laid out all at once, but they become known to students through what a teacher reacts to consistently. However it happens, students must be clear about what we want from them, and we save a lot of time and

energy if we communicate expectations directly rather than leaving it to chance that students will figure them out. Furthermore, expectations must be specific so there is no misunderstanding or room for argument. It may not be enough to call for silent reading time. The class may need clarification on what silence means. Does it mean absolute silence, or whispering, or quiet talking? Can the students see the difference and modulate in a controlled way between those levels? If "silence" really means "quiet," then perhaps it really should not be called "silence" and vice versa. If students are supposed to arrive on time for class, does that mean being no more than two minutes late, being in the room when the bell rings, being in their seats, or being in their seats with notebooks open and ready to go? Where these boundaries are drawn is less important than that they are established clearly. There must be no doubt as to when a rule has been broken.

Mendler and Curwin (1999) describe a comprehensive strategy for involving students in rule making, called the social contract, to promote responsibility and respect and ensure there are clarity and buy-in regarding the rules of classroom interaction. After the teacher specifies nonnegotiable rules and establishes consequences, students work in small groups (or as a homework assignment) to propose rules for the teacher's and each other's behavior, including consequences—for example, "Rule: The teacher must call on students by their names. Consequences for violation: (a) Remind teacher of rule, (b) Teacher will apologize." "Rule: Teacher should check our papers in private and tell why something is good or bad, not just say 'good' or 'bad.' Consequences for violation: (a) Warning; (b) Teacher will give up a class period and set up 5-minute interviews with each student who wants more feedback on his papers."

Mendler and Curwin (1983) explain: "All of the rules and consequences are reviewed by the class to ensure proper understanding of what they mean. Role play is often a useful strategy to illustrate the exact meaning of a rule or consequence. For example some students want the teacher not to yell. It is important for the teacher to speak louder and louder until agreement is reached as to what constitutes yelling" (p. 73).

Then a careful process of decision making occurs in which the teacher and students decide which of the proposed rules and consequences will be incorporated into the contract. (For details see Mendler and Curwin, 1983.) Finally, students take an exam that tests their knowledge of the contract. All must be able to pass with a 100 percent score.

This novel social contract procedure accomplishes two things. First, students' developing rules for teachers gives them an added investment in making the process work. Second, the test for comprehension and the link to classroom privileges send the message that this contract is important and underlines the content of what the rules really are.

Developing the social contract for nonnegotiable and negotiable rules can take two or more periods. It begins with the teacher explaining the process for developing the social contract and explaining what makes a good rule and consequence:

- Good rules are clear, specific, and stated positively and precisely.
- Good consequences are clear, specific, logical, related to the rule; preserve dignity; and have a range of alternatives.

Students develop rules and consequences as a homework assignment or in small groups in class for the teacher and each other, while the teacher organizes all rules and identifies those that are nonnegotiable and those that are negotiable and their consequences. Then the teacher and students together discuss, clarify, and role-play all rules to ensure understanding. They use a decision-making process to determine which rules will become part of the contract and they establish unanimous consensus about the rules and consequences. ("Raise your hand if you do *not* want this to be a rule [or consequence]." Finally, they return to other rules and ask, "Can you reword this rule in such a way that you would be able to accept it?" And for those last two or three students who won't agree, "Would you be willing to live with it for a few weeks to see if it's as bad as you imagine?"

Mendler and Curwin (1983) recommend 70 percent agreement for negotiable rules to pass. Once the rules and consequences are established, the teacher administers the social contract test. Those who don't pass with 100 percent must retake the test. The contract is posted in the room, and copies are sent home to parents and to the administration. A week later, the class can renegotiate any rule and consequence that is not working or add new ones as needed. A monthly review meeting can assess how well the contract is working, and adjustments are made as needed.

The product of this work is the social contract. Most classes have class rules posted. But using the term *social contract* or *constitution* instead of *rules* suggests that the classroom is a community where teachers and students have mutual responsibilities and rights.

Some teachers call this beginning-of-the-year rules exercise "constructing a classroom constitution" or "bill of rights and responsibilities." A colleague of ours and a former classroom teacher, Dave Crump, used to start each school year by having his students develop a list of what they wanted to be able to count on as rights to be respected in their classroom that year. Once they had generated a good list, they would discuss what each idea meant and why it was important. Finally, they would vote on their top priorities and construct a manageable list of ten to fifteen rights that all promised to abide by. The final document was prepared, and each student signed it (Exhibit 8.2). When infractions occurred or conflicts arose around behavior, Crump would send students straight to the bill of rights to determine which of their rights had been violated—or which right they had violated—and to decide what a fair consequence might be. Frequently this deliberation and discussion diffused tension between peers, and by the time they were reporting back to Crump, they had pretty well resolved their issue.

Expectations need to be repeated often. That means, especially in the beginning of the year, restating and reminding students about expecta- tions and eliciting expectations from students just prior to events that may strain the behavior—for instance: "We're going to the auditorium now. What might it be like there as we walk in? What will we need to do? What should we keep in mind for our behavior as a good audience?"

Another useful strategy to clarify and rein- force expectations and build relationships with fam- ilies is early home contact with parents to establish a positive connection long before problems arise and to enlist their support and cooperation throughout the year in reinforcing the class con- tract. Fred Jones (2007) gives the following guide- lines for early contact with parents of elementary school children:

> Send home a welcoming letter to parents and students and attach a copy of general rules for the class. Call every parent sometime during the first few weeks of school. Make 5 calls a

**Exhibit 8.2. Sample Social Contract**

| *You Have the Right* |
| --- |
| To be called only by your given or chosen name. |
| To do your work without being disturbed by others. |
| To be treated with the same respect that all people should have. |
| To have your personal property right respected. |
| To ask questions when you don't know until you understand. |
| To get a good education and do your best work. |
| To have and express your own opinion, even when you disagree with others, including the teacher. |
| To know how you are doing in your schoolwork. |
| To be safe from someone hitting or harming you. |
| To have fun and play safely on the playground without being bothered by others. |
| Not to be criticized for things beyond your control or for things that you didn't know about. |
| To be by yourself sometimes. |
| To speak and listen to language that is appropriate for school. |
| Not to be teased for being different. |

*Source:* Reprinted courtesy of David Crump, principal, Harrington School, Lexington, Mass.

night—5 minutes long—so the job isn't burdensome:

- Introduce yourself.
- Briefly describe the highlights of your curriculum.
- Say something positive about the child—good news only. (If there is already bad news, save it for another day.)
- Discuss the classroom standards that you sent home. Answer any questions they might have about them. Ask for their support in conveying to their children the seriousness of the rules and structures of school.
- Ask about any special needs of the child: medical conditions you should know about? academic concerns they might have?
- Tell the parents that you need their help through the year. Acknowledge that they sometimes hear about a concern or issue before you will and request that they contact you if it is worrisome. State that in turn you would like to feel free to contact them if you hear about something worrisome. Underscore your desire to work together so that bumps in the road can be ironed out before they become "real problems."
- Conclude by inviting them to "Back to School Night."
- Consider a follow-up call randomly to one parent a week [pp. 155–156].

Here are Jones's guidelines for parents of children in secondary school:

- Make a welcoming phone call [as described for children in elementary school] to the parents of the 5 students in each of your classes whose misbehavior is likely to produce a parent conference before long.

- Intermittent calls. Pull the names of 2 students per class period per week. Call the parents over the weekend. Strengths and assets of the student will be the focus, but problems will also be discussed. It is amazing how an on-going, random, spot check system of feedback to parents can both put students on their toes regarding the following of classroom rules and generate good will from students and their parents. Literally *anything* personal says you care.
- Send a form letter home conveying the same information that might be conveyed over the phone [p. 134].

Teachers should have an attitude of positive expectancy embedded whenever they state and restate expectations. Positive expectancy has two aspects. The first has the sense, "Why of course you're going to do it!" This is not something the teacher says outright, but it is the assumption conveyed by body language and attitude. The other aspect of positive expectancy is encouragement and confidence—the "I know you can do it" attitude. It is often associated with positive statements of specific behaviors or questions ("Remember you want to raise your hand . . .") rather than direct desists ("Stop calling out!")

Explicit verbal "positive attribution" conveys expectations as well. Consider the following:

### Albert

The little boy, Albert, was standing near the teacher's desk and when he saw the drawings he promptly remarked, "They stink."

Brigit's smile vanished. The teacher took Albert aside, bent down to him and said, "You may not know it, but that hurt Brigit's feelings because she really worked hard on those pictures. Now, I'm sure if you knew that you were going to hurt her feelings, you wouldn't have said that about them. I don't think you'd ever want to be that kind of boy, would you?"

Albert swallowed, and with his face down, he muttered, "No." His teacher then took his hand and said, "Come, let's take a good look at her pictures together, and we'll tell her which one we like best."

The teacher did not simply scold and disapprove, although her approval was certainly at stake for Albert. What she did was remind him of a standard he already understood, but that had not yet become a guiding principle for his actions. Even though she didn't state the standard formally, her reminder that *It's bad to hurt people intentionally* came through very clearly.

Albert was induced to apply this standard to his actions because of two things his teacher did:

• She attributed underlying good intentions to him ("I'm sure if you knew that you were going to hurt her, you wouldn't have said that"). By doing this, she was granting him membership in the good persons "club"— a membership she assumed he desired. If he continued to ignore the standard, he'd lose his "membership"—not just because his teacher disapproved of him, but because the categories "person who intentionally hurts others" and "good" person are mutually exclusive. Research on children's understanding of logic shows that even five-year-olds can understand the idea of mutually exclusive categories.

• She asked him to define the kind of boy *he didn't want to be* (one who intentionally hurts others). By doing this, she was forcing him to choose whether or not he wanted to

keep his status as a good person. If he did, he'd have to use the standard as a guide for his behavior toward Brigit, as well as his future behavior toward others [Shulmand and Meckler, 1994, pp. 113–114].

Another way to convey positive expectancy is to be assertive in requesting appropriate behavior. Lee Canter calls for using one of four attention moves—eye contact, proximity, mentioning the student's name while teaching, and proximity praise—to redirect students back on task. Here's an example he gives for mentioning the student's name:

While at the board, the teacher notices that Tanya and Michael are off task and not paying attention. The teacher, in a matter-of-fact manner, continues the lesson saying, "I want all of you, including Tanya and Michael, to come up with the answer to this problem." As soon as their names are mentioned, Tanya and Michael immediately begin paying attention [Canter and Canter, 2001, p. 135].

If students counter with excuses or other diverting moves, Canter recommends the broken record technique:

TEACHER: Sue, I want you to raise your hand and wait to be called on before you speak. (Statement of want)

SUE: None of the other kids do.

TEACHER: That's not the point. I want you to raise your hand. (Broken record)

SUE: You never call on me.

TEACHER: That's not the point. I want you to raise your hand. (Broken record)

SUE: Okay, I will.

In this interchange, the teacher kept repeating (broken record) what she wanted from the child and would not become sidetracked by Sue's responses. The teacher maintained control of the interaction with the child.

In using this technique, you first need to determine what you want from the interaction with the student (for example, "I want Sue to raise her hand"). This becomes your statement of want and the gist of your interactions. You can preface your statement of want with, "That's not the point, but I want you to raise your hand" or "I understand, but I want you to raise your hand." No matter what manipulative response the student presents, if you respond with your statement of want—"that's not the point, I want you to . . ." the statement will be more effective (Canter and Canter, 2001, pp. 79–80].

This technique can be surprisingly effective, especially with students who are verbal. When you use it, you must know what consequences (or range of consequences) you are prepared to deliver if the behavior persists. Without that clear image, your assertiveness will be hollow. Furthermore, after reasserting the expectation three times, you must be ready to implement the consequence.

## Consequences

### Logical, Not Punitive

Rudolph Dreikurs (Dreikurs and Cassel, 1972) understood that punishment breeds resentment, whereas logical consequences begin to teach students the reality of the social order: every act has a consequence, and to avoid unpleasant results, they must behave in a way that will help to guarantee favorable results. Punishment is any aversive stimulus (like writing, "I will not throw paper on the floor," one hundred times) intended to discourage the recurrence of the behavior. The child will be less likely to do the behavior next time because this unpleasant thing may happen again. Logical consequences, however, are connected to the behavior in such a way as to feel like fair retribution for the violation. If a student has broken a rule against copying another's homework, a logical consequence is to have to do it all over again under supervision (rather than stay after school as punishment).

### A Range of Consequences

If each rule has an automatic consequence tied to it, you can get boxed into a corner. One consequence for each rule is a mistake. Mendler and Curwin (1999) cite the case of a teacher whose consequence for undone homework was staying after school to finish it. One day one of her best students said, "I'm sorry, Miss Martin, but my father was very sick last night. I had to babysit while he was taken to the hospital, and in the confusion, I didn't have time to get my homework done." The teacher is now in the dilemma of either being unfeeling and rigid ("I'm sorry, but you have to stay after school anyway") or letting the child off and teaching the rest of the class that good excuses can pardon undone work. This could have been avoided if the teacher could pick from an appropriate range of consequences for each rule. Mendler and Curwin (1999) devote two chapters to developing and implementing consequences and recommend four generic consequences that might be applied to most rules: reminder, warning, practice following the rule, and a written plan. Hence, for undone homework, the range of consequences might be: reminder; warning; hand in work before the close of school that day; stay after school to finish it; and conference with the teacher, student, and parent to develop a plan.

With this range of alternatives, Miss Martin could gently remind the child that homework is due on time and then ask how her father is doing. In this way she is implementing one of the prescribed consequences yet is not being overly rigid. With another student who had been late six times that month, she might make him stay after school and finish it. Fair need not always be equal.

### Delivering Consequences

Every time an expectation is not met, we must consistently react (meaning "react every time" though not necessarily the same way every time). The reaction may be anything from a reminder to a consequence, but something has to happen. Otherwise the students—especially resistant students—come to disregard the expectation or become confused over where it applies. The transgression usually cannot be ignored. (Sometimes we may choose to ignore certain behaviors when they are minor and calling attention to them would just reinforce them, or we may recognize them briefly.) The general mission here is to communicate to students that one's expectations are really one's expectations. We mean them. They get this message when they find we reliably call them on certain behaviors and usually there is a consequence (Rogers, 1987; Canter and Canter, 2001; Mendler and Curwin, 1999). Mere admonishing and reprimanding without action that goes beyond words usually sends the message that expectations are weak.

We must be tenacious about restating expectations and consistently reacting. Individuals and sometimes whole classes will test teachers to the limits on this. The thing is not to give up, even though misbehavior continues in the face of specific expectations consistently upheld. Some very difficult students will push to see if we really care (meaning care about them). If the reactions to the misbehavior are reasonable, appropriate, and fair, tenacity will carry the day.

Lee Canter (Canter and Canter, 2001) tells the story of an aggressive third grader who consistently abused other children verbally and physically. On several occasions, he extorted money from his classmates. At a meeting with the child's parents, the principal, and the teacher, a contract was signed that Carl would be excluded from school if he did any of the following things: threaten children, cuss them, extort money, or physically assault them. The parents agreed to follow through with the exclusion at home.

The next day, on the way into the classroom, Carl got into an argument with another student and roughly shoved him. Ms. S immediately went up to Carl and simply told him, "You pushed Sol. You've chosen to go home for the rest of the day!" Ms. S contacted the office, and the principal called Carl's mother, who came to get him. Carl went home and spent the rest of the school day in his room doing the work he would have done had he stayed in school.

The following day during a spelling assignment, another student refused to let Carl copy his work. Carl became angry and threatened to beat the student up. Ms. S, hearing this, told Carl what he had done and that he would be going home again. His mother picked him up, and he spent the rest of the day at home in his room. Carl behaved appropriately for the next two days. On the third day, during free choice, Ms. S observed him cursing and screaming at a girl who would not give him the puzzle that she was playing with. Ms. S repeated the same procedure of informing him of what he had done and that by behaving inappropriately, he had chosen to go home. For the first time, Carl became upset. He began to cry and say that he did not want to go home. Ms. S simply told him that "he made a choice" and would be going home.

As was typical, the third time was the charm. Ms. S's ability to deal assertively with Carl's behaviors let him know that his disruptions would not be tolerated. Carl thus chose to control his temper and behave in an appropriate manner with his fellow students.

It takes determination and tenacity to keep delivering consequences when the behavior persists. But without that tenacity, students will not believe teachers are serious about their expectations. Follow-through at the beginning of the year on plans such as the one Canter describes will be keenly observed by the rest of the class and lets them know you mean what you say. Inconsistency and lack of follow-through early in the school year are a common cause of school discipline problems.

One teacher we worked with developed the protocol in Exhibit 8.3 to keep herself neutral and clear because she knew Billy could thwart her resolve if she were not absolutely clear and consistent.

Canter elaborates on the virtue of persistence and consistency:

> Children may not care if you keep them after school once, suspend them every now and then, or send them to the corner infrequently. But there are few children who would not care if they knew that they would have to stay after school every day they chose to, even if it meant five days straight. There are few children who would not care if they knew they would be suspended every time they acted out, even if it meant three straight days of suspension. There are few children who would not care if they knew you would send them to a corner for their inappropriate behavior every time they chose to go, even if it meant five times a day.
>
> What we are trying to say is this: if you really care, the children will really care. If you are prepared to use any means necessary and appropriate to influence the children to eliminate their inappropriate behavior they will sense your determination and quickly care about the con-

sequences which they will have to face consistently if they choose to act inappropriately [Canter and Canter, 2001, pp. 109–110].

Almost any behavior we really want to get we can get if we have the determination because we do have the power. Does this mean that if one keeps delivering consequences persistently, the behavior is sure to change? First, it is possible to deliver a consequence over and over again consistently and have no effect. That can happen if the consequence is not strong enough, or if it somehow turns out to be a reward for the child. It can also happen if the behavior comes from a physical cause, ignorance, or a value clash. Second, the way in which the consequence was delivered in Canter's scenario had a lot to do with its success. The teacher did not blame, criticize, or humiliate the student; she simply but promptly went up to him, noted the behavior ("You pushed Sol"), and delivered the consequence ("You have chosen to go home for the rest of the day"). She pointed out that going home was the child's choice in this case since he knew that pushing Sol would lead to that. Thus, the teacher reacts with matter-of-fact emotion rather than anger. It is, in fact, easier to react that way when you know precisely what you are going to do. That knowledge (versus the helpless feeling when dealing with a child who seems outside your control) gives a teacher both confidence and calm, which allows for better judgments. So, being persistent with consequences can also fail if the consequence is not delivered in the right way.

The specific technique described in Canter's scenario is a strong one: systematic exclusion of a student to eliminate particularly disruptive and persistent behavior. But it can be very effective. Seymour Sarason (1971) describes another powerful exclusion technique (time-out in a colleague's classroom) that works without parents or contracts. It

**Exhibit 8.3. Sample Protocol for Dealing with a Challenging Child**

MEMORANDUM

TO:     Staff
FROM:   Ms. X
DATE:   May 15, 2008
RE:     Strategy to Help B

Here is the summary of our strategy for:

*Prevention:*       Before an activity begins, tell B.

                    If there is a change, alert him beforehand.

*Intervention:*     Rationale:

                    To help B be aware of his behavior and its effect on others.

                    To provide him strategies to cope.

*Strategy Steps:*

1. Nonjudgmental, nonhumiliating, private warning combined with statement of expectation and choice for B. For example: "B, you are _____. I expect you to sing the song. You have a choice: You can stop _____ and start singing, or if I need to speak to you again, you'll need to take some time out."

2. If B persists, call Mrs. L on intercom phone and ask her to connect you to Mrs. Q.

3. If Mrs. Q is not there, Mrs. L will contact another person and tell you where to take B. The code words are, "I need to send you a message."

4. Say to B: "You've made a choice by continuing to _____. You need to take some time out. Please go see Mrs. K."

5. If B balks, say, "B, you have a choice. You can either go on your own or if not, I will call Mr. S."

6. If B still doesn't go, say, "You've made a choice by not going on your own. I will call Mr. S."

7. Call Mrs. L to reach Mr. S. Mrs. L will cancel with Mrs. Q.

PRAY

I've provided words to use should you find that helpful. The key idea is choice and conveying to B that by acting in certain ways he is making the choice.

relies on the cooperation of another teacher into whose room the child is sent for exclusion. The host teacher has a special place the student goes to that is not fun and where the student does work. Details are presented in Part Two.

## Limit Setting with Escalating Consequences

A consequence should be logical and fit the infraction in terms of magnitude and perseverance.

Hence, it is important to develop a range of responses, from small to large. The general rule of thumb in limit setting is to apply the law of least resistance: start small and escalate only as necessary to extinguish the behavior. Knowing that we have a series of escalating consequences available enables us to remain calm yet firm and convincing when addressing inappropriate behavior. Remaining calm is essential to setting limits and establishing credibility and authority while preserving relationships of regard and respect.

Here is an example of a hierarchy of escalating consequences, which we explain in detail in the following sections.

1. Body language of meaning business/poker
2. Acknowledging a change in behavior and offering help
3. Quiet time
4. Verbal warning, privately delivered
5. Reeducation (cafeteria school)
6. Hold up a mirror (Simone story to follow)
7. Pulling the card
8. Letter home taped to desk
9. Account for behavior in writing
10. Time out in classroom
11. Time out in a colleague's room (see Sarason Gambit to follow)
12. Phone call home with student reporting in teacher's presence what happened
13. Parent conference with home reporting and consequences; contract signed by teacher, student, and parent
14. In-school suspension
15. Saturday school
16. Parent accompanies student to classes for a day as a condition for readmission (with parent supervision finishing work in isolation)
17. Deliver a student to parent at work
18. Suspension
19. Police
20. Expulsion

Let's go through these consequences one by one starting with the small ones.

## Small Consequences

### Consequence 1: The Body Language of Meaning Business

We owe a lot to Fred Jones (2007), who studied people with the "aura," the teachers with whom nobody seemed to fool around, and discovered that it was not magic that caused students to

respond to them. It was the subtle but specific, observable, and learnable body language they manifested. This body language communicated that they were serious about their expectations and would do whatever it took to get them met. They rarely had to do more than send body language signals, and they rarely had to implement backup consequences.

We recommend Jones's *Tools for Teaching* (2007) to all beginning teachers and any teacher struggling with discipline issues. The details of learning and implementing effective body language are spelled out at length there. To give readers an idea of the nature of this body language, here is a summary of steps from Jones's *Positive Classroom Discipline* (1987) for addressing off-task behavior. It begins with understanding never to go any further with the following limit-setting sequence than is required to produce the desired result:

- Notice
  - Notice the disruptive behavior . . .
- Excuse and square off
  - Terminate whatever you're doing, and say to the students you are working with, "Excuse me. I'll be right with you."
  - Turn completely.
  - Face the student squarely and look the student in the eye.
  - Make your face expressionless, arms hanging comfortably.
  - Take two relaxing breaths.
- Name
  - Say the child's first name only, in a bland tone.
  - Take two more relaxing breaths.
  - The student may fold, but if not . . .
- Move in (say nothing)
  - Walk slowly to the edge of the student's desk until your legs touch it.

- o Stand upright.
- o Take two relaxing breaths.
- The student probably folds, in which case you . . .
- Thank and move out
  - o Thank the student, genuinely and warmly.
  - o Wait fifteen seconds more.
  - o Go to the second student who was involved (if relevant).
  - o Thank him or her.
  - o Wait fifteen more seconds.
  - o Return slowly to the student you were previously working with.
  - o Wait for two relaxing breaths.
  - o Resume instruction.
- But if student didn't fold . . .
- Lean and prompt
  - o Lean over at the waist, resting your weight on one palm. (You're back at the student's desk.)
  - o Deliver a prompt on exactly what you want him or her to do next ("Carrie, you have two more problems to do. Let's finish them up").
  - o If the student starts working, wait for two relaxing breaths.
  - o Then do the "thank and move out" sequence.
  - o But in the unlikely event student still doesn't fold . . . .
  - o Palms (say nothing)
  - o Lean slowly across the child's desk, and place both palms flat on the far side of the desk from you (ooze, don't swoop).
  - o Look at the student for two relaxing breaths.
  - o When he or she resumes work, wait two more relaxing breaths.
- Then do Moving Out.

- Backtalk
  - o If the child displays helplessness, crying, denial, compliments, blaming, tangents, or accusing you of incompetence, say nothing and take two relaxing breaths.
  - o But if there's more backtalk . . .
- Elbow and prompt
  - o Bend your elbow, and place it on the child's desk.
  - o Repeat the prompt.
  - o If a second student chimes in . . .
- Camp out behind
  - o Stand slowly and walk around until you're between the two students.
  - o Lean your elbow on the table.
  - o Reestablish eye contact with the first student (blocking student 2).
  - o Take two relaxing breaths . . .
  - o Slowly move out.

Jones's premise is that limit setting in classrooms is like a poker game: students play a card (test limits by trying out behaviors) and wait to see what card we will play. If we "see them"—that is, respond in some believable way—the student generally "folds" (gives in). Sometimes we need to "raise them" again—escalate the consequence. The bottom line is not to play any higher a card than is necessary to get the child to fold. We must play the game with confidence and conviction, signaling that we are in control without needing to get emotionally rattled. This premise is embedded in the above sequence of steps.

Reading this list of steps does not enable one to learn and carry out body language poker successfully. One must practice it repeatedly and get feedback to do it well, as Jones arranges in his courses and we do in ours. We urge readers to take this information seriously (though the study and practice of this behavior is fun and does provoke lots of laughs) because it is so potent. If there was ever a good example of acting one's way into a belief, this is it. Practicing these behaviors is practicing an attitude as well—the attitude of teacher resolve and persistence—and developing confidence.

Here are accounts from three teachers who have been in our courses—one each from high school, middle school, and elementary—of their experience applying the body language of meaning business. All three were experienced teachers, well regarded and successful. They did not have significant discipline problems, but they still found learning these techniques well worth the effort.

### Charlotte Thompson—Newton North High School Science Department

I have been working on discipline this week. Luckily I have not gotten to the "palms and ooze" stage! In fact, I have noticed that by waiting for the students to turn squarely and completely around facing me, all problems were cut off at the pass. [She means a long pause after a desist move until the student has completely reengaged attention.] This week I stopped the class with, "Excuse me, class," and went over to two girls and quietly explained why it was necessary for them to stop talking. I assume because the entire class was watching me speak to them very quietly while leaning over their desk that they were a bit embarrassed. It did correct the problem.

I did have one student this week who was rather persistent in not settling down. I went over to his desk and just stared. Unfortunately, he seemed to enjoy that and did not cease his showing off. I got to step 6 with him, although I must admit I skipped step 5. I was not at all confident that he knew what to do, so I was

somewhat anxious to get to the prompt. He spends a good deal of time spacing out. But it did get him back to work and he stayed settled afterward for a pretty good length of time. [Reprinted courtesy of Charlotte Thompson].

### Jeanne O'Reilly—Middle School

Using the sequence sheet on body language, I decided to try it in class. The first day I used it, I was amazed at how easily and well it worked. In my first class, I never went beyond saying the name and taking the two breaths. For the purpose of this experiment, I want to focus on what happened with Phil. Phil is a good student, though easily swayed. He is very capable, and therefore though he disrupts the learning of others, his behavior rarely damages his own grade. He tends to infuriate his teachers.

On that fateful day, body language was really more in the back of my mind. I had been rereading the steps and finally decided to use it. I was at the front of the class leading a discussion when Phil started up with little comments to everyone within range. Normally I would walk over to a student like Phil not saying anything but just standing near him or behind him while continuing the discussion.

I almost surprised myself (as well as Phil) when I excused myself to the class, squared off, waited, and said his name as blandly as I could. He folded immediately. It occurred twice more, and that was it.

Well, I immediately began using it. My favorite thing about body language is how much it minimizes my own anger. I simply don't become as irritated, and the breaths really do keep me calm. My problem is remembering to use it. I find that when I'm tired or stressed, I lapse back. I do feel that this is one of the most valuable techniques I've learned any-where.

**Lisa Farmer—Elementary School**

There are times when children's behavior is inappropriate. In my kindergarten classroom, inappropriate behavior surfaces during our morning calendar meetings. The children usually talk and move about, switching places with their classmates. What I find most difficult is disciplining the behavior while keeping the momentum of the meeting. I decided to try the science of body language to see if more body language and less speaking would help at the meeting.

While I was beginning our morning meeting, Michael had his back to the circle and faced the blackboard talking to a friend. I called his name and made my face expressionless. He turned around and looked at me. When he saw my face, he looked at his classmates and quickly and dramatically sat down. He then gave me what I believe is a "smiley face." Because I kept looking straight at him, he looked down. I waited. He did look up again and found me still looking at him. What was most interesting was the reaction of the rest of the class. Michael's friend Adam turned around and followed Michael's lead in settling down. The others sat quietly watching. This first episode ended with my saying thank you and moving on to the calendar without interruption from Michael.

The first lesson I learned was that you can make a child aware of and stop inappropriate behavior with the bare minimum discussion. Without discussing it, the behavior stopped, and neither of us felt put down, angry, or uncomfortable. Though I have used a look or

eye contact previously, what made this effective was the waiting through two breaths. Since that first episode I have used this technique with other children and other situations effectively. During recent attempts, I have had to move close to the child, but I have never had to do more. One more important component is squaring off. The student seems to know you mean business because you are not moving.

"Body language poker," as Jones calls it, is a form of consequence for students who fool around. It is the lowest stakes and most common form of response successful teachers make to disruptive or inattentive behavior, and it eliminates most of it.

But teachers must have a clear series of escalating moves to reach for in order to have the confidence to implement good body language. "What if it doesn't work?" runs through every teacher's mind, especially beginning teachers. If the body language doesn't work (which, of course, it will almost all the time if done well), one can move up the hierarchy of responses and consequences slowly, always escalating only the minimal amount necessary to eliminate the disruptive behavior, confident in what you can do if you have to.

**Consequence 2: Acknowledging a Change in Behavior and Offering Help** This is a gentle and positive way of reprimanding and is similar to the desist move in the attention continuum called "offer help." The teacher talks privately to a student and says something like, "Jim, I notice you've had a hard time staying focused today. Is there some way I could help you get back on track?" or "What would help you refocus and get back on track?" Sometimes this will lead to help in the form of moving the student's seat.

**Consequence 3: Quiet Time** This consequence is really an opportunity offered for a student to regain composure and self-control when behavior such as excessive talking is getting out of control. "Juan, I think you need a little quiet time to regain your focus. What part of the room would be good for you to use?" Quiet time can be replaced with a walk around the classroom or a one-minute stroll in the hallway that the student takes to regain control and focus. It is different from time-out (consequence 10) because time-out is teacher enforced and the beginning and ending times are usually teacher determined. Teachers can work out a cuing system with individual students who do not read their own signals and indicate when it would be advisable for them to take such a quiet time. The agreement is that the reason for taking the quiet time is for the student to take the initiative to refocus.

**Consequence 4: Warning** Warnings inform individual students that they are getting near the threshold of receiving an aversive consequence. The warning can be delivered privately in the student's ear. "That's 1, Kiesha." Maybe when she gets to 3, the consequence becomes automatic. Students have to know what the consequence is, and everything we said in the previous section about consistent and certain implementation of the consequence must be carried out.

Warnings may also be delivered publicly by writing a student's name on the board and putting a stroke next to it for stage 2. These warnings are objective, low-affect moves that can be delivered without even mentioning the student's name or interrupting the flow of instruction in any way. Calm, neutrally delivered warnings avoid confrontation and blame, and convey the message that this is just the way of the social order, as Dreikurs would say.

It is not absolutely necessary that the students know exactly what will happen to them when they cross the threshold; in fact, it can even be more effective if they don't, as long as they know something will happen and they won't like it. And even if they don't know what will happen, you the teacher need to know the range of options you may actually carry out.

**Consequence 5: Reeducation** Cafeteria school is a favorite example of this consequence. Students who misbehave in the cafeteria are required to attend cafeteria school following afternoon dismissal or during recess. They receive a real "class" in cafeteria manners and appropriate behavior with modeling, practice, and testing. The unstated assumption is that if they knew how to behave properly, they would. This positive attribution of intent is slightly tongue in cheek, but not entirely. Many students in early grades, for example, do need practice in the impulse control and expected norms to contain their urge to run in hallways or wait quietly in audiences. The older the students are, the more aversive cafeteria school is. And the bonus is that students don't want to repeat being sent to it and don't form the usual resentment that detention or other punishments generate.

**Consequence 6: Hold up a Mirror: Simple Counting or Anecdotal Record Keeping** This consequence is about holding up a mirror to the student about his or her behavior. Here's an example of the first version: simple counting.

Latoya is always calling out and interrupting in class. It is impulsive on her part, and the teacher decides to use simple counting to highlight the behavior and call Latoya's attention to it. After a group one day, the conversation goes something like this.

"Latoya, do you know that you call out a lot without raising your hand? It's really distracting to me and unfair to the rest of the kids who want to speak."

"I'm sorry. I'll stop. I promise." (They have had these conversations before.)

"Are you really willing to work on it? Well, I'd like to help you. How many times do you think you call out in a lesson?"

"I don't know—maybe five?" (It's more like twenty-five.)

"Well, let's see tomorrow. I'll put a piece of masking tape on my wrist, and every time you call out, I'll put a mark on it without saying anything or stopping the lesson, but you'll be able to see me doing it and you'll know what it means. Okay?"

"Okay."

This technique can be highly effective in reducing habitual or impulsive behaviors when no more serious issues are involved than attention getting and impulsivity. Simply seeing the teacher make a stroke on the tape reminds the student of the goal: to reduce calling out.

"Oops," says Latoya, as she sees another stroke going down. Soon she learns to anticipate a stroke before a call-out and starts inhibiting the call-outs herself. Afterward, the teacher and Latoya can add up the total call-outs and set a goal to reduce the total tomorrow. A week of this may be sufficient to teach the self-inhibition Latoya needs to control calling out.

This technique and other forms of specific counting or record keeping about behaviors make students more aware of what they're doing and make the reduction of unwanted behavior a mutual teacher-student goal. The counting is the feedback to students about their progress and needs to be prompt, complete, and frequent (Van Houton, 1980). Students have to be willing to try for the technique to work. Sometimes a teacher count of a behavior before discussing it with students produces data with which to confront them. They may be so surprised by how often they behave inappropriately that the shock value will motivate them. Teachers can use the technique on a whole class as well as on individuals. Here the goal becomes lowering the class total of call-outs or whatever is the inappropriate behavior being brought to awareness.

Another version of this strategy is anecdotal record keeping: pausing to write verbatims of incidents when children have outbursts or interruptions, and then sharing the data with the student. The simple power of data without judgment is illustrated by the story of Simone.

### Simone Was Out of Control

I thought I'd tried everything—until the day I stumbled onto a solution that completely changed my teaching style.

Watching Simone, my tallest, lankiest, loudest third grader clunk around the classroom in my wedge-heeled shoes was enough to make anyone chuckle. (Teachers who've chosen comfort over style will understand my shoes weren't on my feet.) But Simone's frequent, disruptive outbursts were no laughing matter.

"Simone," I demanded stridently, "take off my shoes!"

"I was just trying them out," she replied, not at all abashed, continuing her jaunt around the room. Michael had the audacity to smile as she sallied past.

"What are you laughing at, stupid-face?" Simone snarled.

"Sit down, Simone," I intervened wearily, "and please try to remember that we don't call each other names here. You owe Michael an apology."

"I do not!" she exploded. "He laughed at me, and I don't like his ugly face."

Losing all remaining composure, I yelled, "Sit down and be quiet."

### I Was at a Loss

This was just one of many times Simone's inappropriate behavior upset me and unsettled the whole class. Sometimes her explosions were angry; sometimes they were rambunctious. But they were always frightening. Simone simply had no idea how overwhelming she was to me or to her classmates.

Despite all our troubles, I couldn't help liking Simone for her generosity and enthusiasm. And I know she liked me, too. She frequently brought me an apple in the morning, "For you, because you're the best teacher I've ever had," she'd announce as she put the apple on my desk. But our up-and-down relationship was underscored by the fact that I rarely got to eat my apples. Simone was usually angry at me long before noon, and when she got mad, she'd reclaim the apple or hurl it into the wastebasket. Many times, she'd jab her pencil into it with harsh, angry thrusts.

The pattern was set by mid-September. Several times a day, Simone would explode, and I would reason, cajole, placate, issue ultimatums—and too often yell—in vain attempts to control her outbursts. I'd already tried sending her to the principal's office, but she liked going there. I'd called her mother several times, but our conversations led nowhere.

Nothing was working, and I was exhausted at the end of every day. Correctly or not, I blamed Simone for how out of control I was feeling in the classroom. In truth, I was an emotional wreck—too caught up in the daily drama to think of a way out of my predicament.

### When Out of the Blue . . .

Though it was only September, I was beginning to look longingly to summer vacation as my only out. Then suddenly, and unexpectedly, I stumbled on an amazingly simple solution.

I was with a reading group—not Simone's—and the other groups were working independently. Suddenly, the relative calm was shattered by a spate of Simone's angry, hurtful words. I simply couldn't summon up the energy to play my usual role—rush over to her, reprimand her sternly, and try to make amends to whichever of the children was her victim. Instead, I thought to myself, *I'm going to write down what happened and by the end of the day I'll at least be able to remember what she did that was so horrible.* So I leaned over to my desk, picked up a yellow tablet and pen and began writing. When I had a verbatim record of her words, I looked over toward Simone to find her and most of her classmates staring at me. Sensing that the fireworks were over for the moment, I laid down my pen and returned to my reading group.

The next explosion occurred as we were about to begin a science lesson. Simone couldn't find her textbook, so she snatched Kara's book, screaming angrily: "Kara keeps stealing my stuff." Again, I reached for my tablet and began to write.

This time, Simone hurried over and demanded to know what I was writing. Showing her the tablet, I said, "I'm just writing down what you say and do." Seeing her words appear in front of her seemed to shock

Simone: she returned to her seat, and we had science without a single interruption.

By 3 o'clock, I noticed that whenever I saw Simone starting trouble or gearing up for an outburst, all I had to do was pick up my pen and she'd stop instantly. I kept up this new strategy. Within a week, Simone's tirades no longer controlled my classroom.

### It Was Magic

I was thrilled. Now that I could finally think straight, not only did I continue to wield my mighty pen but I had the time and energy to notice what Simone and her classmates were doing *right*. I began taking care to praise them for their *good* behavior. Consequently, there was more of it.

By now, I was completely enamored of my pen, and I began to experiment with extending its power. Whenever I felt overwhelmed or bewildered, I found I could clarify things by jotting down notes. It was a way of taking a step back and surveying what was going on.

*If this writing strategy works so well for me*, I thought, *why wouldn't it work for 8-year-olds, too?* I issued a new classroom rule. Henceforth, all complaints had to be in writing. I designed and duplicated complaint forms that provided space for the signature of the complainant, the name of the accused, and a description of the crime including date, time, conditions, corroborating witnesses, and details of any physical evidence. I stored the forms next to a "Complaint Box."

Initially, I checked the box each afternoon and rendered judgments and punishments. Soon, however, I hit upon the idea of rotating the judgeship. Committees were formed to review the complaints, eliminate frivolous claims, and decide valid ones. The students also

suggested punishments, although I retained veto power.

### Apogee and Apples

The new system made the children responsible for their own behavior. That made them feel powerful and more confident. They even began to come up with their own rules—such as the rule that no one involved in a dispute could sit on a committee that week.

Just when our classroom was beginning to look more and more like *The People's Court*, the number of disputes started declining. By spring, we were holding court only once a week, and the committee that reviewed the complaints rarely had more than one or two they considered valid.

Looking back over that year, I find myself saying a silent thank you to Simone. I've been reaping the benefits of what she taught me ever since that stormy September morning when I picked up a pen and started writing. Just as my pen and yellow tablet had come to signal serious intent to her and the class, the complaint form and a pencil reminded the children to stop and reason. As for me, besides enjoying the taste of success, I got to eat a lot of apples [Arnold, 1987, pp. 44–45].

**Consequence 7: Pulling the Card** This behavior from Fred Jones (2007) is a more developed form of the warning. To implement, you must have a card file on your desk with the name and home phone number of each student, including the work number of the parents. When misbehavior reaches a certain level, having already issued a warning to a student, you (1) catch the student's eye, (2) take a relaxing breath, (3) walk slowly to your desk without calling attention to yourself, (4) casually pick up the card file, (5) leaf through it, (6) pull the student's card while looking at him and lay it on the corner of your desk face up, (6) look again at the student without expression (Jones calls it "your best Queen Victoria face") as you place the card file back on your desk, and (7) resume instruction, giving the student one final look.

**Consequence 8: Letter Home Taped to Desk**  No discipline management technique comes with a guarantee, so what if the disruption continues even after you have pulled the card? How can you still stop the disruption without taking on the cost and risks of medium backup responses? The final response in your hierarchy of small backup responses is one more that comes from Fred Jones (2007): write a letter home to the student's parents and tape it to the student's desk with an appropriate warning. The procedure goes something like this:

1. Following at least two other warnings (small consequences), catch the student's eye, go to your desk, and sit down and begin to write a brief letter (five sentences or less) home: "Dear [parent's name]:

   Today in class I have had to deal with [briefly describe the behavior].

   I need your help.

   If we work together now, we can prevent this from becoming a real problem. I will call you tomorrow, at which time we can make a plan.

   Thank you for your help."
2. Sign the letter, and put it in an envelope.
3. Address the envelope, but don't stamp it yet.
4. Take the letter and tape it to the student's desk while privately letting him know it is a letter to his parents or guardians about his behavior in class:

"If I see no more of this behavior before the end of [the day or week] then, with my permission and in front of my eyes, you may tear up this letter and throw it away.

If, however, I see *any* more of this behavior, I will send the letter home or hand deliver it. Do I make myself clear?

For now, all I care about is getting some of this work done. Let's see if we can keep life simple" (pp. 316–317).

**Medium Consequences**

**Consequence 9: Student Has to Account for the Behavior in Writing**  Many schools require students who have been sent to the office to write an account of why they have been removed from class and sent there. The writing is not much of a nuisance for the student since he or she has nothing to do in the office anyway, and it gives the student a chance to make his or her side of the case. The writing is not such an aversive behavior. But when the writing has to take place in the student's own classroom and be given to the teacher who saw the behavior and called it, that is a different matter.

Some years ago, Viv Swoboda, now a principal but then an eighth-grade teacher, used the writing accountability technique to quell a rising tide of off-task behaviors. Here it is in her own words:

Because the class I have this year is particularly challenging and continually testing the established limits, I have done a lot of thinking about logical consequences for inappropriate activities in school. I am very conscious of how much school time gets wasted dealing with inappropriate behaviors, and how some students continually draw the class and me away from the day's lesson. I struggled with what would be appropriate logical consequences for the various class disruptions that I could consistently implement without giving myself a lot of extra work in the process.

I decided that I would develop a form that a student would have to fill out each time they did something inappropriate in school. I asked the students to respond to five questions:

1. What was your inappropriate activity in school?
2. Why was your activity inappropriate for school?
3. What are the negative effects that your inappropriate actions have on others?
4. What consequences would keep you from doing this inappropriate activity in the future?
5. Why is it necessary to have rules in order for a school to function smoothly?

I would give the student the form after asking them to stop the inappropriate activity. The form needs to be returned to me by 8:00 the following morning. Students knew I recorded the inappropriate activity in a notebook, but I usually didn't record it until after class because I try not to break the momentum any more than necessary.

In the beginning, there was a lot of complaining from the students every time I gave them a form to fill out. I had spent a lot of time talking about what I was doing and why and had asked for their suggestions for ways to eliminate the many inappropriate activities that happened during classes. I made a transparency of the form, went over the form with each one of my classes, and explained why I had included each of the questions. When it came time to use the form, I wasn't going to discuss it and continue taking time away from the les-

son. In the beginning, some of the students tried to engage me in a debate, but I simply gave them the form, reminded them I needed it back by 8:00 the following morning, and quickly tried to refocus the class on the lesson.

After two days, the students realized that they weren't going to draw me into a debate and that I was consistently going to ask any student who was doing something inappropriate to complete one of these forms. Ninety-nine percent of the students brought back the forms by the next morning. I had the 1 percent of students who didn't return the form complete it during their ten-minute break that occurs during the middle of the morning. It was torture for those students to have to sit at their desks and complete this form rather than be able to socialize with their friends. They decided they would rather complete the form for homework than give up precious time with their peers.

The number of inappropriate activities in my class has diminished tremendously. Before I started using these forms, there may have been twelve times a day that I might have spoken to students about doing something that was inappropriate in class. When I first started using the form, I would give out about six forms a day. Now I may pass out one form in three days.

I learned that my students really could control their inappropriate actions in school. This form really isn't a terrible punishment, but it is enough of an annoyance that it encourages most of my students to think before they do inappropriate things in class. This system has worked for me because it doesn't require a lot of my time. I keep the forms in a folder on my desk that I can reach easily, so I keep the break in the class's momentum to a minimum. Students asked what I was going to do with these forms. I told them it depended on whether the inappropriate actions stopped. Some students didn't want their parents or school administrators to become involved, and these forms were a clear record of who was disrupting the class.

After the students all saw the form, they felt there should be a question asking why they did what they did. They felt it was important for me to have that information. I will include that question on a revised form.

## Consequence 10: Time-Out in the Classroom

Time-out is an elementary technique not usually suitable in secondary school. It is often a feature in behavior modification programs and thus is unpopular with educators who prefer more child-centered approaches. Ruth Charney, however, one of the most humanistic and child-centered educators in the United States, devotes an entire chapter in *Teaching Children to Care* (2002) to implementing time-out. We recommend her version.

Marty is jostling Kintara for the second time in the back row of the rug area where classroom meeting has just started. "Marty, time-out."

Marty gets up from her seat and goes to the time-out chair, located in a visible (not central) area of the classroom. She sits for five minutes or until she receives a gesture from her teacher to return to her group. Signaled by her teacher's nod, Marty quietly returns to her place. There has been no explanation, no discussion. The unstated message is: "You know the rules. You know you are disturbing the meeting. You will be able to recover your controls and return as a member of the group" [p. 168].

Charney makes a point of introducing the procedure of time-out to the children carefully and completely. "It's a way that grown-ups help children get back in control. Children can also teach themselves to get back their controls and remember their rules. I stress that time-out is a job; it is work to recover your controls." Note the careful way Charney frames time-out:

Everyone forgets their controls sometimes and everyone forgets the rules sometimes. Children forget the rules, so do teachers and parents. Our rules make it safe and good for everyone in school. Not just me, not just Betsy—everyone. So it's very important that we respect the rules and use them. When we forget or choose not to use a rule we need to remember, we need a time-out. Time out is a special time to think about the rules we need to keep our classroom safe and good and to gather our own controls. Then we are ready to come back and join the group.

The key to using a time-out effectively is to pay attention to the small disruptions [see the echo of this principle in Fred Jones], the minor infractions and misbehaviors. If we use time-out correctly, children do not take the step from control to out-of-control. We take action before the lesson is in ruins, before self-controls deteriorate—the student's and our own. When we wait for things to get worse, we are rarely disappointed.

We don't allow the minor drumming on the desk to reach a crescendo. The nagging and nuisance-behavior does not go on until finally all our "buttons" are pushed. The background whispers and snide teasing are not ignored until fists fly and tears pour [p. 173].

A pattern of casual "shot-ups" is not allowed to grow into one of constant insults.

Noah may not call Mark "Fatty," even if he claims he's joking. Kevin may not use his superior size to push others aside, take a pencil or reserve first place in line. The group lesson might be stalled if I say, "Martin, the blackboard is this way!" for the fiftieth time between clenched teeth instead of saying, "Martin, time-out." The small side-shows will not devastate the lesson or the temper of the teacher. But, unless they are confronted, these "small disturbances" add up to constant noise and interruptions which drain and divert the best intentions. Often they are the very things we pretend not to notice.

Alex regularly careens around the room—his idea of walking is full speed ahead. He's a large boy, and he frequently bumps into the furniture, other children, and even largish teachers. He's quick to say "sorry" and express genuine regret, but if he slowed down he would hardly crash at all and no one would get hurt. Why make a fuss? He's only ten—he can't help it. But the fact is he *can* help it. He can move slowly and with planning—or not move at all.

It is important that children understand that they can help it. Minor disturbances are within their control [p. 175].

In the immediate enforcement of time-out, lengthy verbal explanations and negotiations are strictly avoided. Imagine if instead of the directive, "Time-out," the teacher had said, "Donny you need to go to time-out, because you are rolling a ball and not listening to Sherrill." Would Donny, now the center of attention, be more apt to agree or argue, "I *was so* listening . . ." An argument might lead next to a confrontation, and Sherill's sharing would quickly take second place to the duel between teacher and student.

If the teacher had just reached over and taken the ball from Donny, called his name or nudged him gently back into the activity, with no mention of time-out, wouldn't that be as effective and easier? My experience is that while reminders work occasionally, small disturbances usually keep erupting like popcorn—one after another that take the attention of the teacher and group. Time-out sends the message that you are *truly* expected to follow the rules [p. 178].

At the right moment—after a time-out—explanation and discussion help students construct meaning and take responsibility. At the wrong time—while a rule is being enforced—discussion stimulates evasion [p. 180].

We recommend readers read Charney's entire chapter (and book for that matter) to get the full flavor of this decisive yet humanistic version of time-out.

**Consequence 11: Time-Out in a Colleague's Room**
Time-out in a colleague's room was first written about, to our knowledge, by Seymour Sarason in 1971. It was intended for elementary grades. With modifications, we have used it successfully in high schools as well, including inner-city high schools. Here is Sarason describing the version for young children (see Exhibit 8.4 for a summary):

Relationship-building techniques for influencing the unmanageable child are indispensable to involving him constructively in the classroom, but they are usually insufficient to produce the dramatic suppression of hostile defiance that is necessary if he is to be allowed by the principal to remain in school. For the child's own welfare, therefore, it is necessary to work out with

**Exhibit 8.4.  How Time-Out in a Colleague's Classroom Works**

1. Introduction
   a. Introduce exclusion move to whole class with its causes and consequences. A way of helping students remember and follow rules that allow them to enjoy learning.
2. Implementation
   a. Give one private warning with specification of behavior.
   b. Give a public explanation of why the child is being removed.
   c. Remove the child, voluntarily or physically if necessary, or call the parent.
   d. Time-out is maintained for a half-hour.
   e. The child is excluded from participation or interaction with the second class.
   f. Review the situation with the class:

   Alternative ways the excluded child might have acted

   Reasons for the rule

   How to help the child follow the rules.
3. After-School Interview
   a. To help, not to embarrass, is the motive.
   b. The teacher hopes a warning will be sufficient in future.
   c. The teacher explains that it was the child who decided, by his or her behavior, when to be excluded.
   d. Show the child affection and respect.

*Source:* Reprinted by permission from Copyright Clearance Center, Sarason, 1996, pp. 165–167.

the teacher influence techniques that effectively suppress the child's defiant outbursts almost at once, unless teacher and psychologist feel that he would profit from a brief exclusion from school. The use of exclusion from school as an initial influence technique, however, is usually not nearly so effective with the defiant child as other measures. One of three techniques for suppressing defiant outbursts is implemented along with the relationship-building techniques in the case of each unmanageable child.

The most commonly recommended technique for suppressing defiant behavior is that of excluding the disobedient child from his classroom and placing him for half an hour in a classroom nearby. The success of exclusion depends on the preparation given by the psychologist to the teachers and school personnel involved, the support or toleration of the principal, and the *precise manner in which the teacher prepares her class and implements the technique* [italics added]. Any such dramatic recommendation, of course, requires the approval and comprehension of the principal, whose begrudging acceptance of the plan could undermine teachers' use of it. The principal must also participate in selecting the relatively experienced teacher with whom the unmanageable child's teacher pairs. Teachers have an antipathy to imposing on each other: the excluding teacher usually feels embarrassed about depending on another teacher, and the receiving teacher is concerned about her class being unsettled by the visitor. These understandable concerns must be recognized and assurance given that the plan may be stopped if it creates more problems than it solves. The participating pair of teachers must be fully briefed on the rationale and dangers in the plan so that they experience as few surprises as possible in implementing it. From our experience with the exclusion plan we now routinely brief participating teachers on several points. When a child is received in another room, he is to be given a seat at the back and excluded from any form of participation or interaction in the class. Before making this clear to teachers we occasionally found the excluded child excitedly participating in the receiving teacher's classroom activities. We also now prepare the excluding teacher for the problem of a child refusing to leave the room. He is to be carried out by the pair of teachers if he is in kindergarten through second grade. Older children refusing to leave their rooms are to be informed that unless they do so their parents will be phoned immediately. Never has a child refused to respond to either pressure. Never has an excluded child posed the slightest problem in the receiving classroom. Never has a child greeted the exclusion with anything but distasteful embarrassment.

So far the exclusion has the ingredients of an effective technique for suppressing defiant outbursts: it immediately terminates the disobedient behavior without introducing complications in either the receiving or excluding classrooms. Its unpleasant quality for the child renders it an effective influence technique in shaping more compliant subsequent behavior. The most significant source of power adhering to the plan, however, is probably not its unpleasantness per se but its decisive ability to

force on the consciousness of the child the limits beyond which he may no longer go; in short, to underline by dramatic action those rules that other children remember and obey through verbal injunctions alone. It also gives the teacher a measure of authority she had been lacking in verbal injunctions. If the plan is to maximize the child's chances of remembering and following classroom rules it must be introduced to the whole class not as an angry punitive retaliation by a distraught teacher but as a way of helping children to remember to follow rules that allow them to enjoy learning. It should be explained to the children repeatedly that a child will be excluded not because he is unwanted or disliked but because he needs the brief opportunity in another classroom to reflect on the rules he has been disobeying. By introducing the procedure to the entire class in a group discussion it does not appear as though the defiant child is being singled out; the shock of implementing the technique is reduced to more manageable proportion; and its rationale is communicated during a period of relative calm in the classroom. In their actual implementation of the plan teachers are cautioned against excluding children when they are furious with them, waiting instead until they have regained their composure. At that point the child is to be given one private, unembarrassing warning that clearly states that if a specific behavior does not cease he will be excluded. If several children are acting up defiantly they are to be warned publicly, but in no case is a child excluded unless he had one and only one private warning from the teacher to remind him clearly of the rule he is breaking and of impending exclusion if he does not stop disrupting the class. Contained in such private warnings must be the teacher's attempt to explain to the child how he is disrupting the class, together with whatever relationship-building techniques she feels appropriate and feasible. Should the child subsequently defy the warning intentionally, he is to be led out of the classroom by the teacher who explains to the entire class in the presence of the child why he is being excluded.

On returning to the classroom after delivering the child to the receiving teacher, the excluding teacher reviews the situation with her class, emphasizing the reasons behind the relevant rules and alternative ways in which the excluded child might have acted. Whenever possible her remarks are channeled into a group discussion that can be used to marshal the support of the class in helping the excluded child. Once children have expressed their expected bitterness toward the defiant child in such discussions, the teacher can elicit more sympathetic interest from them in helping him, especially when she points out that she needs help from the class in teaching the excluded child to follow class rules. Such discussion can be used to marshal the support of the class on a meaningful basis for the teacher to develop with her children a causal and change-oriented view of surface misbehavior. If the excluded child is to derive from his exclusion the maximum incentive and minimum discouragement to changing his ways, the teacher must schedule a short after-school interview with the child on the day of his exclusion. Like the class discussion, the follow-up interview is an essential ingredient in effecting a rapid suppression of his defiant outbursts. During the interview the teacher can explain how she excluded the child to help him remember class rules rather than to embarrass him, how she hopes that in the future a warning will be sufficient to induce the

child to control his behavior, how it is the child himself and not the teacher who decides whether he is to be excluded from the room. Finally, the teacher can use the interview to explore with the child whatever difficulties he is experiencing in the classroom, promising the child confidentiality if he wishes to reveal something personal. Throughout the interview the teacher makes clear her affection and respect for the child, indicating how his misbehavior is at least as discrepant with his own hopes for himself as it is with hers for him. The psychologist can be helpful in reducing the aversion some teachers express about "psychoanalyzing" their students. As long as they do not probe deeply and listen warmly and acceptingly to any problems the child discusses, their common sense and professional ethics, he tells them, are adequate guides. Most of the inner-city children who require psychotherapy will never receive it; thus the teacher's may be the only interest ever expressed in their emotional lives. Of course, the psychologist is always available to review with a teacher any material that baffles or disturbs her. We have never regretted encouraging teachers to conduct such therapy-like interviews, though we have played down the suggestion with some teachers more than others. One outcome of such interviews is that they establish an open line of communication between child and teacher by dramatizing the teacher's wish to help him by talking with him rather than by forcing him to change [pp. 136–139].

For older students, physical removal is obviously inappropriate, but most of the other features of Sarason's original design still apply. A receiving teacher, preferably in a grade widely separated from the student's, has to be identified, and a routine for accepting the student nonjudgmentally but in a nonreinforcing setting must be prearranged. The wide separation of grade level results in young children going to older children's rooms and vice versa. This adds to the aversive nature of the strategy because of the embarrassment or intimidation of being sent to such a room.

A monitoring adult, dean, or security officer may be needed to escort the student to be removed to the receiving classroom. And some work for the student to do should be sent with him or her as well.

### Consequence 12: Phone Call Home with Student Reporting What Happened in Teacher's Presence

The teacher calls the parent: "Mr. Palmer, this is Justin Rivera, your son's teacher. There's been an incident in class with your son, Michael, and I've asked him to explain to you himself what happened. Would you hold a second while I pass the phone to Michael?" If the student leaves out any important details, the teacher can remind him to insert them.

It is sometimes surprising how tough adolescents will turn to jelly after lots of hostile bluffing when you actually pick up the phone. If there is strong reason to expect physical abuse will follow at home, do not use this consequence.

### Consequence 13: Parent Conference with Home Reporting and Consequences; Contract Signed by Teacher, Parent, and Student

In this fairly heavy-duty consequence, the parents have been in for a conference with the teacher and perhaps the assistant principal as well. A behavioral contract has been written with certain behaviors and consequences at home as well as at school (Exhibits 8.5 and 8.6). Reports are sent home frequently about the student's behavior, and the consequences delivered at home are contingent on the reports from the student's teachers.

### Consequence 14: In-School Suspension

In-school suspension is a vehicle for students to evaluate their behavior and make choices. It is important that the suspension be framed that way for the student and carried out with that effect authentically. Those supervising the suspension room must see their role as helping a student evaluate choices and making a plan for successful reentry into mainstream classes. This counseling presence is important for a successful in-school suspension program.

### Consequence 15: Saturday School

Students who have been disruptive repeatedly during the week in school and failed to respond to consequences have probably missed significant amounts of class time. As a consequence, they may be required to come to Saturday School (usually Saturday morning from 9 to 12) where they must make up missed work. Staffing must be available to implement this approach, and it must be clear that Saturday School is not a place to "serve time" in a punitive sense, but rather a requirement to make up work the student missed during the week. Thus, it is required as a logical consequence of disrupting learning time, not an alternative way to sit detention.

### Consequence 16: Parent Accompanies Student to School

The embarrassment factor is at work in this consequence, which is both novel and effective from the middle grades on up. Here is an account of how one middle school implemented this consequence:

> Bob Browning spent a day at Wilson Junior
> High School in Hamilton, Ohio, some time ago.
> That in itself is unremarkable: Browning, after
> all, is president of the city's board of education.
> As he moved from class to class, taking his seat
> at student desks and quietly sitting through

**Exhibit 8.5.  Student Agreement**

### Smith Middle School
### STUDENT AGREEMENT

Smith Middle School is a place of learning and growing through a variety of experiences. Each student has the rights and privileges of our program as well as the responsibilities. Each student owns his behavior and the consequences of the behavior, good and bad. Upon entry to SMS, Daniel will be expected to abide by the code of behavior as described in general in our school handbook (pages 25 and 26). More specifically, he will be expected to demonstrate the following appropriate behavior:

Arrive to school on time daily.

Arrive to each class on time prepared with class materials, books, and writing utensils.

Complete all assignments (homework, classwork, and special projects) according to teacher direction and turn them in on time.

In class:          Pay attention.

Focus attention on the class lesson.

Any behavior that interferes with his learning or the learning of other students will not be tolerated. This includes:

Speaking out

Moving out of his seat

Looking around

Making sounds

If he does act inappropriately, the teacher will simply state, "David, this is inappropriate. If you do it again, you will report to the office."

If the inappropriate behavior continues:

Daniel will report to the housemaster, and the discipline referral form will be completed.

Mrs. Z will receive a copy of all discipline referral forms.

If two discipline referral forms are necessary in one day, Daniel's mother will be contacted, and he will have to go home for the day.

It is important to note that each referral involves the assignment of two demerits, and once the demerits add up to a suspension, it will be assigned.

Mature behavior is also expected in the corridors, cafeteria, gym, and locker room.

There will be no pushing, shoving, swearing, or insulting. The same results as described earlier will apply

Daniel will leave the school grounds at 2:05 unless he has been asked to stay for a teacher.

As is the case for all SMS students, Daniel is welcome to attend our roller skating, parties, dances, and special events. However, again as is the case for all SMS students, if Daniel's behavior warrants it, he will be asked to leave, and attendance in future events will be subject to review.

A meeting will be scheduled after Daniel has been at SMS for four weeks to review his behavior. It is important that he understand this STUDENT AGREEMENT and sign it.

_____ _____ (Principal)     _____ _____(Student)

_____ _____ (Housemaster)     _____ _____(Parent)

_____ _____ (Coordinator)     _____ _____(Chairperson)

**Research for Better Teaching, Inc.** • One Acton Place, Acton, MA 01720 • (978)263-9449 • www.RBTeach.com

**Exhibit 8.6. Educational Contract**

EDUCATIONAL CONTRACT

*Student's name:* Daniel
*Effective:* Nov. 15, 2007
*Review:* Dec. 15, 2007

**Classroom Behavior Expectations**

Daniel will arrive to class on time.

Daniel will come to class prepared. (Pencils, paper, book, etc.)

Daniel will speak out in class only after raising his hand and being recognized.

Daniel will conduct himself in a courteous and respectful manner.

Daniel will not interfere with other students' rights to learn, or the teacher's right to teach.

**Consequences**

*First Offense:* After a violation of the stated expectations, Daniel is required to leave the classroom and study in the Quiet Study for the remainder of the period.

*Subsequent Offenses:* On a subsequent offense within the day, Daniel is required to leave the classroom and will be sent home after the parents have been notified.

**Teacher**

After a violation of the expectations, the teacher will signal Daniel to leave the class and notify the office. The teacher will in no way influence Daniel to do or not do anything. (No urging, reminding, coaxing, encouraging, or scolding.) The teacher agrees to respect Daniel's right to fail or succeed on his own.

**Principal**

On notification of a violation of the expectations, the principal agrees to see to it that Daniel leaves the class if the signal given by the teacher is not acted on by the student.

**Student**

Daniel agrees that he is fully responsible for himself and that everything he does and does not do is done or not done by his own choice. He agrees to take responsibility for his failure as well as his success.

Cc: Mrs. X
  Mr. Y
  Ms. G
  Daniel's teachers

**Research for Better Teaching, Inc.** • One Acton Place, Acton, MA 01720 • (978)263-9449 • www.RBTeach.com

each period, some of the teachers got nervous. "They had no reason to," Browning says, "but it was understandable." Yet the most uncomfortable person in any of those classes was Browning's son, Sam, an eighth-grader, because Bob Browning wasn't in class in his official capacity. He was there in a more important role, as Sam's father and he was taking part in a program that subjects kids who break school rules to an ingenious—and devilishly effective—deterrent: bringing Mom or Dad to school.

"I got the idea accidentally," remembers John Lazares, Wilson's 37-year-old principal. "A kid came into my office whom I had seen a number of times for minor discipline problems— talking in class, being late, not bringing materials, driving the teachers crazy. I just got fed up and said, "The next time I see you, we're going to have your mother come in and see what we have to put up with all day." The reaction I got from him was, "Do anything you want, but don't have my mother come in." I'd never had this reaction from a kid before—and we've had kids arrested for drugs, suspended and expelled. He *begged* me not to have his mother come in. Something lit up in my head."

Situated in an industrial city midway between Cincinnati and Dayton, Wilson has a student body that reflects the city's racial, economic and ethnic diversity—and divisions. Until nine years ago, when a controversial new school superintendent began a citywide disciplinary crackdown, Hamilton's schools were scarred by violence, tension and drug use. By the time Lazares became principal last January, the school had a functioning code of conduct and an improving reputation. But up to 60 of Wilson's 860 students were expelled every semester, and dozens more were being suspended for everything from tardiness to fighting in school.

"One of the worst things that can happen to a child is to be suspended from school," says Lazares. "It's a waste. He spends three days at home for some little misdemeanor, and it makes him happy to be out of class. I decided to tell parents, 'Okay, if you'll come in and spend one day in class with that kid, I'll take the suspension away.'"

So, far, about 60 parents have put in their time at Wilson. "I thought it was great that I could come down and eliminate a little trouble for my son," Bob Browning says gamely. Sam was in trouble for missing detention. "I enjoyed it," says Ella Neal. "It helped me a lot to understand what the teachers had to go through and to understand my child much better." Her son, James, had been disrupting his seventh-grade class. Kids seem to improve dramatically when their parents come to Wilson. After-school detentions are down from 20 a day to zero on some days; expulsions have dropped to 11 since the program began. Only a handful of parents have refused to join what Lazares calls his Parent Involvement Program; many are eager to come. "For a lot of them, it's their first time in a school building since they graduated," he says.

On a recent morning, a few "veterans" discussed the program. "I was embarrassed," said Sam Browning. "One kid cried all day," said Shane Isaacs. Shane cleaned up his act when his parents simply met with the principal and *threatened* to go to class with him. "This is a tool for preventive discipline," says Lazares. "Kids who have seen other kids' parents in school stop causing problems, because they don't want their own parents to sit with them all day."

Punishment is only one aspect of the Wilson program. "In education, we're only as effective as the parents," says Lazares, "and now we have parents who call us once a week to check up on their kids' progress. If a child has been a discipline problem and goes for a while without causing trouble, I call them up and say, `You're doing something right.'" Each teacher now makes five phone calls—positive or negative—to students' homes every week. Lazares personally calls the parents of every child who makes the honor roll: 200 phone calls one week. "I want to notice those kids who do a good job," he says [Ryan, 1987, p. 10].

**Consequence 17: Deliver Student to Parent at Work** This consequence follows an escalating series of responses to a student's disruptive behavior. The parent, who should be no stranger at this point to the problems in school, is notified that a car is on the way over with the student.

**Consequence18: Suspension** We do not recommend suspension because it is usually a reward rather than a penalty, at least for older children. Students get unsupervised time away from school, lose academic time, and have more access to getting into trouble. It may become necessary, however, to separate a student from campus for a period of days where facilities are not available for in-house suspension. In this case, every effort should be made to arrange for the student to be in a supervised environment, perhaps some form of community service. Above all, when the suspension is over, a plan needs to be made with some accountability in it between the student, parents or guardian, and the school for the conditions of readmission to school.

### End-of-the-Line Consequences
**Consequences 19 and 20: Police Involvement; Expulsion** These extreme measures are obviously

the end of the line and require hearings and due process. We include them to complete the loop on the hierarchy of consequences.

## Recognizing and Rewarding Responsible Behavior Effectively

No discussion of consequences would be complete without examining positive consequences: how to respond to students—individual students or a whole class—who are meeting expectations. Canter and Canter (2001) recommend three guidelines for positive consequences: they should be things teachers are comfortable with, that students like, and that comply with school and district policies. Rewards might run the gamut from specific verbal praise ("Very nice job of managing your participation in the small group discussion and including everyone in the conversation . . ."), a chance to be the line leader or the messenger for the day, a "good news" note, a postcard or call home to parents, a positive note sent home addressed to the student, or a ticket that entitles the student to "purchase" items in the class store.

There is a case to be made that good behavior should not be rewarded; rather, it is expected and should be the norm, so there should be no reward system. Nevertheless, with certain classes where discipline problems are an issue, explicit reward systems can play a useful role.

Mendler and Curwin (1999) note that some rules can have only positive consequences when followed. They cite an example of a high school teacher who had a rule that paper airplanes could not be thrown in class during instructional time. The consequence for every week of no airplane throwing was that the class would have a paper airplane throwing contest. Mendler and Curwin report that "this creative contract stopped paper airplane throwing for the year" (p. 82). They believe there should be at least one positive consequence for each rule. In their earlier work, Mendler and Curwin (1983) suggested an approach to positive consequences that relies more on social praise delivered in private. They like to catch students being good and deliver both positive and negative consequences quietly so only the receiving student can hear. Thus, when the teacher is bending over a student to say something privately, the rest of the class doesn't know whether it's something like, "You have continued talking to neighbors despite two warnings. The consequence is you'll have to stay after class with me and work out a plan to avoid this behavior . . ." or "You've been focusing on your work and written two balanced sonnets this afternoon. That's what I call being productive!"

## Establishing Expectations at the Beginning of the Year

The opening weeks of a term or year are the prime time to ensure solid understanding of expectations, establish routines, and begin to build class cohesion. It is useful to think of this period as one of teaching or training for the students. Training requires practice; thus, if students are noisy and disruptive in the hallway, the teacher can say, "I can see we need more practice in hall walking from the way we just came back from gym," and take the class out for some practice right then. This is not punitive, but logical as a consequence.

Previously in the chapter we mentioned reeducation as a consequence and cited the example of cafeteria school. Mendler and Curwin (1999) cite a school that has an after-school class in cafeteria behavior, including practice and an exam for students who have been disruptive at lunch. Students must get 100 percent on the exam to "graduate." Nick Aversa, an eighth-grade teacher we've worked

with, spent the first part of every period in the first weeks of school rehearsing his students in how to enter class and get right to work. The routine included crossing the threshold to class and stopping all talking, finding a seat, getting out their notebook, and working on the opening activity for class. Initially he taught them why this was important and then walked them through a series of practices from hall to classroom. From then on, anytime someone forgot the procedure, the consequence was to go back out into the hall and reenter correctly. Nick would signal this by simply establishing eye contact with the offending student and then looking at the door. The student would know what he had to do.

**Standards for Student Behavior**  We have seen classes where the teacher's expectations for student behavior are lowered by the students; their behavior is so poor that the teacher concludes they *can't* behave any better. Watch out, though: the minute a person starts justifying behavior (or academic achievement for that matter) by saying, "What can you expect, given their environment," the students are in trouble. We are convinced that what you expect is what you get—not right away, of course, but eventually. The students may have to be taught how to meet higher behavioral standards, but they are not constitutionally, genetically, or environmentally unable to. There are examples all over the country that demonstrate that children from the most chaotic and deprived families and neighborhoods can behave perfectly well in school if the adults demand it, teach them how, and believe in them. (This does not include severely emotionally disturbed children who need special support to function in a school environment.) This last factor, "believe in them," is the subject of Part Three, "Motivation" (Chapters Twelve, Thirteen, and Fourteen). Students who don't believe school has any value for their future, especially in secondary grades, are much more likely to be discipline problems: they feel they have little to lose. So building their motivation to succeed in school has a strong bearing on their willingness to respond to the environment of responsibility and self-discipline that this next section is about.

Our point here is simply to alert readers to our responsibility, both in our individual classes and collectively for the school, to maintain the highest standard for civil and respectful behavior for our students.

# Building a Climate of High Achievement

## Giving Students a Real and Legitimate Sense of Control, Influence, Responsibility, and Power

At the start of this chapter, we proposed that teachers could structure classes so students felt some ownership and control of what goes on and that doing so could reduce discipline problems. However, this is no substitute for clear expectations and consequences. They should come first. We know a first-year teacher who never did get expectations and consequences sorted out that first year, but who nevertheless salvaged the year from total disaster by starting an individualized contract learning system. This system gave students some ownership and control by setting academic goals and providing them with good feedback. The students invested in it, and energy that might have gone into fighting the teacher went into meeting their learning goals instead.

But it was still a rocky year with less than optimal learning. If expectations had been established right from the beginning, her contract system

would not just have salvaged this particular class; it would have put it into orbit. So though we are strong advocates of the ideas to follow, our caution for any beginning teachers reading this section is to invest in getting expectations and consequences clear first.

There are three excellent approaches for giving students ownership in classroom life: (1) negotiating Mendler and Curwin's social contract, (2) using goal setting (see Chapter Ten), and (3) teaching through one of the five cooperative models of teaching (see Chapter Nineteen).

Sometimes teachers grant students ownership or a stake in classroom operations because they let the students in on something the teacher has noticed and invite them to work on addressing the problem. A high school English teacher in one of our courses shared the following example.

While studying the Clarity area of performance, he had an insight that he might often be playing guess-what's-on-the-teacher's-mind in his question asking. He shared this with his class the next day and asked if they concurred. They did. He then asked them what they could do about it, specifically what action class members might take if he victimized them with such a question or if they observed him doing it to someone else. After collecting ideas in a general class discussion, they settled on the following procedure: when students felt that they had been asked such a question, they could call the teacher on it and ask him to restate the question. Alternately, students who could not answer a question could redirect it to another student in the class by name. At other times the teacher would go around the class in order, asking review questions about the text read for homework. If the student could not answer a question or answered incorrectly, the next student would get the same question. If three students in a row failed to get the answer, the teacher would acknowledge that it was a poor question and rephrase it. The net result for these students, previously a low-performing class, was higher class participation and higher achievement. It is our belief, however, that there was a lot more going on here than simply eliminating guess-what's-on-the-teacher's-mind questions.

First, the teacher was showing fairness (Personal Relationship Building) in admitting that he could be the cause of a problem for students and looking in an open way for a solution. Second, these techniques gave the students some voice in determining the rules of the classroom game and controlling the flow of events.

Another way to give students influence and control is through incentive and reward systems. One teacher we know tried to increase students' motivation for doing homework assignments well. It had been his practice to give students daily quizzes based on homework readings. One day he told them that if they got four 100s in a row, they could earn a free 100 points that they might then "spend" on future quizzes at any time and in any way they pleased. They could skip some future quiz and take 100 on it, they could take 30 points of it and elevate a 70 to 100 sometime in the future, or just save the points. He found that students' efforts on homework assignments and quizzes dramatically improved, even those students who had already been doing well. Our hypothesis is that what was powerful about this technique was the way in which it gave students something to control: a bank account of earned points. Whether they earned them and how they would spend them was entirely within their control. (For the students already scoring well, perhaps it was insurance against future mishaps.)

Other teachers have replicated that technique but have eliminated the requirement that the four 100s be in a row: simply attaining four 100s earns the 100-point bonus.

These ingenious experiments suggest to us that there are many places in classroom life to look for ways to give students more legitimate control.

## Building Community in the Class

William Glasser's classroom meetings (Glasser, 1969), Gene Stanford's cycle of activities for developing effective classroom groups (Stanford, 1977), relationship-building activities (Wilt and Watson, 1978), cooperative learning (Dishon and O'Leary, 1998), the social competency program (Krasnow, 1993), and the responsive classroom program (Charney, 2002) are all approaches for building the kind of affiliation and harmony in a class that can prevent discipline problems. When relationships among class members are stressful or fractious (or both), these strategies can lower the pressure and productively rechannel energy that is going into fighting with one another.

Classroom meetings are a powerful practice for building a general sense of community in a class or handling problems such as scapegoating, bullying, and cliques. In *Schools Without Failure* (1969), Glasser describes in detail how to conduct classroom meetings and reports, "I haven't met a child incapable of thinking and participating to some degree in school if we let him know we value what he can contribute" (p. 97). That belief is essential for a teacher who wants to make classroom meetings work, because being nonjudgmental and accepting of student contributions is a key skill in leading meetings. The meetings are the vehicle through which students experience participation, the sense of being valued, and a sense of being part of something real. Class meetings are held regularly (at least weekly and preferably several times a week), with students and teacher seated in a tight circle. Teachers lead the whole class in nonjudgmental discussions about topics that are important and relevant to them. There are three types of meetings: open-ended meetings, social problem-solving meetings, and educational-diagnostic meetings.

In open-ended meetings, either teacher or students introduce a topic for discussion. One of the teacher's roles is to build a focusing question for the students around the topic, which can be anything of current interest to the students. In citing a meeting where the students wanted to talk about Disneyland, the teacher asked, "Who would like to go to Disneyland?" Almost every child responded affirmatively. "Suppose someone gave me two tickets to Disneyland and said I should give these tickets to two children in my class. To whom should I give the tickets?" In addition to translating open topics into focused discussions, teachers use skills of active listening and summarizing. Open-ended meetings begin building a sense of involvement with each other and lay the foundations for using the meetings for generating significant investment in academic work and the more difficult area of social problem solving.

Glasser's (1969) description of a social problem-solving meeting explains how classroom meetings can be used to improve some of the more intractable (and usually untreated) sources of disruptive behavior in classes:

> At another meeting, Mike was introduced as the topic. Physically overweight and not too clean-looking in appearance, with hair in his eyes and a very loud, offensive voice, and holes in all his tee shirts caused from biting and twisting and chewing on them, he was not pleasant to behold! Mike said he didn't like the class because they didn't like him. When asked why they didn't like him, he said it was because he was fat. The children eagerly disagreed. They said that had nothing to do with it. Mike wanted to know why, then. He was given the

> opportunity to call on those children he wanted to explain to him what they found offensive about him. Someone said it was because he wears funny hats to school, like the pilot's helmet he wore the day before. (Incidentally, he never wore it again.) Some said he dressed sloppily. Martin said it was because he said things that hurt people. For example, when Martin came home from Europe and showed the class several treasures that he brought to share, Mike said he didn't believe they were from Paris and that he bought the same things here. Martin said that hurt his feelings. David said that when he shared things with the class, Mike blurted out similar derogatory remarks. (Mike still has not cured himself of this, by the way.) John, who had become much more introspective and perceptive, said it was because Mike always made funny faces and looked up at the ceiling with a disgusted look on his face when people tried to talk to him. While he was saying this, Mike was doing just that. John said, "See, Mike, you're doing it right now, and you don't even know it." Mike was asked if anyone, in his opinion, went out of his way to be nice to him. He said, only Alice, whom he liked. Everyone giggled. Alice said she didn't care if everyone did laugh at her, she liked Mike and was not ashamed to be his friend. She liked being nice to him. We talked as a group about the importance of having one friend at least. The others found that no one really tried to go out of his way to be his friend, but each person would try to make some gesture to show they would try in the next week. They really rose to the occasion, but soon forgot about it and were their usual apathetic selves. However, no one seemed to go out of his way to be nasty, which was a change. Alice continued being nice to Mike, and the children stopped teasing her about it. Harriet, who was one of the girls

who was teasing Alice, apologized in a class meeting for doing so and she said she had once been teased for befriending someone without other friends, and that it took more courage to be his friend and yet she wanted to. She told Alice that even though it had hurt her feelings when the others teased her, she had forgotten and teased Alice and that she was sorry, and she could really understand how Alice felt. There has been a tremendous change in Mike this semester. He is not lackadaisical about his work or appearance, speaks more quietly, uses more self-control, plays a fairer game in the yard, gets along much better with others, and has more (or some) friends [pp. 152–153].

We have had teachers read this account and get scared off by it. It seems to some like opening wounds or beginning a process that could get out of control. Yet two teachers with difficult classes with whom we have worked have brought up comparable issues in their own classes and view their own series of meetings as among the most significant accomplishments of their careers. We are glad they took time to work up their courage, because they were also working up their skills at leading meetings on safer topics.

These kinds of issues can fester and hurt and drain students' energy, and bringing them out into the open with skillful leadership can make dramatic differences in class climate. Neither the teacher in Glasser's account nor those with whom we have worked were trained in counseling techniques. They were regular classroom teachers who had the courage and the commitment to want to help students build strong community within their classes and knew that there were large dividends for the effort in academic learning as well.

The teacher in the excerpt above decided that Mike could benefit from specific examples of how his behavior put others off and called for them. Furthermore, the teacher decided that it would involve Mike more (and make it safer for him) if Mike did the calling on other children. When the teacher asked Mike if anyone went out of his way to be nice to him, the teacher sensed an appropriate moment to turn the discussion around and focus on the positive. When the group talked about the importance of having one friend at least, the teacher asked a few key questions to guide the discussion that way.

Recognizing such key junctures and opportunities comes from the learning that occurs in undertaking social problem-solving classroom meetings. It is not the sort of thing one rushes into the first week of school, but these skills are within the grasp of most teachers. Overall, classroom meetings regularly practiced are one of the most significant climate builders for successful learning.

While he was teaching high school English, Gene Stanford (1977) came to the same conclusion and developed a carefully sequenced series of activities to build class cohesion over a year. He organized activities according to the stage of growth a class was in as it moved toward mature functioning. Students have to know something about one another before they can appreciate or become involved with one another, so Stage I is orientation. In Stage II activities explicitly develop norms of group responsibility (through teaching awareness of others), responsiveness to others (meaning good listening skills), cooperative skills, consensus decision-making skills, and social problem-solving skills. Stage III is coping with conflict; Stage IV is about productivity; and Stage V is about termination, that is, dealing with the end of the year, the end of the life of the group, and people's feelings about that. All this is integrated with an academic program and an emphasis on writing.

A number of models of cooperative learning structure academic tasks in such a way that students build affiliation, mutual understanding, and class cohesion. These models usually have students work in groups, with the activity structured so that either task completion or reward (or both) depends on everyone's participation. Yet groups are not penalized for having slow students or rewarded for having the best students in them. (For an excellent summary of how to implement these techniques, see Dishon and O'Leary, 1998. Cooperative models are also outlined in Chapter Nineteen of this book.)

This section of the Discipline area of performance has attempted to connect good discipline, meaning more narrowly an absence of disruptive and resistant behavior, with building a sense of community in the class. From our point of view, building community would be worthwhile in and of itself, but there is no denying it is also a powerful preventive force against discipline problems. Simultaneously, it is a wonderful source of strength for building environments that support the best kind of academic learning. The Classroom Climate chapter of this book has much additional material on these themes of ownership and community building.

## Dealing with Very Resistant Students

Now we turn to the most resistant students—those who continue to resist and disrupt despite clear expectations and consequences and despite the teacher's best efforts at creating ownership and building community in the class. These children bring heavy emotional baggage through the door with them every morning and act out their needs in disruptive behavior that is resistant to standard measures. Fortunately, there are not too many of them. Most of the students who initially appear to be in this category just need more clarity, conviction, and tenacity about expectations and consequences.

## Six Models of Discipline

This section explores six models for dealing with those most resistant students and how to choose from among them to match the apparent psychological needs driving the student behavior:

- Behavior modification
- Self-awareness training
- Personal influence
- Logical consequences
- Reality therapy
- Teacher effectiveness training

Implementing these models successfully is complex and requires guidance and practice beyond just reading about it. This section provides a solid grounding in their purposes and a framework for matching. It is our view that someone in each school should be an expert in all six models and, when a model is called for, be able to function as a coach to teachers for appropriate selection and effective implementation.

Each model has an intellectual parent, a central figure who has pulled it together and written extensively about it (except Behavior Modification, which has so many parents, aunts, uncles, and cousins it is hard to single one out). All six models are good when used appropriately, and no one of the six is inherently better than any other. We begin with a brief description of each:

- *Behavior modification* (discipline as behavior engineering) is a systematic approach to misbehavior based on the assumption that unproductive behaviors can be eliminated and productive ones substituted by analyzing and controlling one's environment and its rewards. Behavior modification systematically cuts off rewards for unproductive behavior, identifies substitute and more productive behaviors, targets these new behaviors explicitly with the student, and begins rewarding them on a schedule that starts out consistent and high in frequency and gradually becomes variable and lower in frequency. Behavior modification aims to work itself out of business as the new learned behaviors become inherently rewarding.

• *Self-awareness training* (discipline as self-control) teaches students to read their own signals so that they know when they're getting angry, afraid, frustrated, or whatever else leads to outbursts or other unproductive behaviors. They can learn a set of coping strategies to use when these things are starting to happen, coping mechanisms they eventually employ on their own. At the beginning, the teacher plays an active, verbal, and supportive role to the student, which gradually diminishes as the student moves toward greater autonomy with the system.

• *Personal influence* (discipline through personal regard) is based on strong mutual relations between the teacher and student. Teachers bring in enough of their outside-school life and accomplishments so as to earn some respect as a figure in the world, a person of some interest and significance beyond the immediate classroom environment. They then draw on this relationship, like money in the bank, and are quite firm with students when disruption occurs. They act quickly and decisively with consequences for disruptive behavior and let students know they are upset. They show their affect strongly but without losing control.

• *Logical consequences* (discipline as social contract) maintains a low level of teacher affect and draws on creative thinking to have students experience consequences that are logically connected to what they did. Power struggles with teachers as authority figures are avoided. Teachers analyze student motivations and use these analyses to help students understand themselves. Students learn about the reality of the social order through logical consequences consistently applied and do not get moral lectures. They are also not let off the hook. There is a strong orientation toward democratic

thought and the involvement of the group in establishing students' understanding of the social contract.

• *Reality therapy* (discipline as involvement) gets students to face and acknowledge what they are actually doing. A nonjudgmental but involved teacher gets students to evaluate what they have done in light of their basic needs. Students explore alternatives and are asked to make commitments to courses of action. This strategy is based on teacher involvement, follow-up, and tenacity. Students learn to face the reality of what they are doing and what that behavior is doing to their relations with others. This is a strategy for developing responsibility and self-worth through the involvement of someone who won't give up on them.

• *Teacher effectiveness training* (discipline as communication) gets teachers and students to clarify who really owns the problem, use appropriate skills, and, if it's a mutual problem, negotiate a no-lose solution using a set of sequenced moves. These solutions meet the needs of both the teacher and the student. It requires good active listening skills to find out a student's real need or real problem sometimes, and teachers need skill at sending "I messages" so students perceive the teacher's need. Good communication skills are required, and mutual respect grows from the problem-solving process.

To analyze the models, we use a framework, modified from Joyce, Weil, and Calhoun (2003), that uses the following categories: (1) definitions, (2) assumptions, (3) values, (4) goals, (5) rationale, (6) syntax (or steps), (7) principles of teacher response, (8) support system, (9) social system, and (10) effects. (For an update on four of the six models, see Wolfgang, 2004.)

To be able to implement these models is not terribly hard, but each does take real study and practice and each is distinctly different from the others in the teacher moves it calls for. The behaviors and skills one needs are probably not outside the existing repertoire of most readers—you probably have made every move somewhere in your life. It is their order and application that takes time to learn; and believe us they make a difference.

No one should think that by merely reading the balance of this chapter one is equipped to go out and do a model well. We issue this warning because we want the models to get a fair chance before someone who didn't really know how to do, say, Reality Therapy, comes back with no results after one try and says, "Oh, that didn't work for me." It can work for anybody if you know how to do it and apply it in the right cases. And that brings us to that matter of knowing when and who is the right case. Matching is the crux of this chapter— the crux of teaching itself. But before we go into what's known about matching with the six models, we feel it necessary to develop each one in more depth so you have more of a context in which to read about matching. So, there follow now six subsections elaborating each of the models; then will come the final and most important section on matching, Section V, with brief profiles of students for whom a given model is appropriate.

## Behavior Modification

An exemplar of this school of thought is CLAIM, a timeless book from CEMREL, written specifically for teachers on how to apply these principles in classrooms.

**Definitions**  The following definitions are derived from the application of the terms within CLAIM and are not necessarily consonant with definitions of the same terms elsewhere in the literature of behavior modification:

1. Reinforcement: anything that increases the frequency of a given behavior.

2. Punishment: anything that reduces the frequency of a given behavior.

3. Schedule: the relation of reinforcement to emitted behavior over time. Continuous reinforcement is reinforcement for every occurrence of the desired behavior. Intermittent reinforcement is reinforcement on an unpredictable basis for the occurrence of the desired behavior.

4. Extinction: elimination of a behavior, usually through elimination of the reinforcement, sometimes through pairing with punishment (negative reinforcement, aversive consequences).

5. Response cost: fines, usually in the form of removal of tokens or other forms of scrip redeemable for reinforcements.

6. Baseline: a record of the frequency of a given behavior over time before beginning selective reinforcement or extinction procedures.

7. Reversal: the restoration of a behavior to its baseline level, or near that level, when the selective reinforcement schedule is cut off.

8. Shaping: a gradual change in behavior accomplished through reinforcement of successively closer approximations of the desired behavior.

9. Prompting: giving necessary clues, hints, or prompts so that the subject can make the desired response in the presence of the appropriate stimulus.

10. Target behavior: the desired behavior to be achieved through application of behavior modification principles.

11. Contingency: the student response or behavior necessary to produce or earn the reinforcement; the job for which pay is given.

12. Fading: the gradual elimination of one reinforcer and its replacement by another reinforcer as the maintainer of the behavior.

13.  Modeling: imitating the behaviors of others that are producing reinforcements for those others.

## Assumptions

1.  All behavior is learned.
2.  Teachers cannot deal with the source of a student's problems outside the classroom.
3.  If unruly behavior exists and persists, the teacher has become responsible.

**Values**  The values are efficiency and effectiveness.

## Goals

1.  Illegal behavior will decrease in frequency and be replaced by legal behavior.
2.  Maximum academic progress possible for each student will be made.

**Rationale**  Systematic analysis of payoffs and systematic application of reinforcement theory to classroom behavior will yield an engineered environment most suited to maximum progress in learning. All behavior, even deviant behavior, is earning a payoff. If a teacher can identify the payoff and clip it, the behavior will be extinguished. If the payoff can be controlled and given for desirable (legal) behavior instead, the legal behavior will become established.

When misbehavior is reduced, the way is clear to efficient learning. Applying the same principles of reinforcement to learning tasks will effectively motivate individual students.

## Steps

1.  Pinpoint the target behavior—the behavior you want to occur.
2.  Observe deviancies from the target behavior.
3.  Chart a baseline rate for the deviancies systematically over a period of time (often weeks).

4.  Analyze what the reinforcement is for the deviancy, that is, what payoff the child is getting.
5.  Identify potential reinforcers for performance of the target behavior.
6.  Choose a reinforcer likely to appeal to the child.
7.  Design a progression and sequence of reinforcement for the child: the schedule of reinforcement, whether shaping will be used, and specific increments of behavior change that will be reinforced if shaping is used.
8.  Tell the student the target behavior.
9.  Design a method for observing and recording behavior frequencies.
10.  Apply reinforcement.
11.  Record behaviors.

## Principles of Teacher Response

1.  Reinforcement should be immediate.
2.  Beginning with schedules of continuous reinforcement, reinforcement should become intermittent to make target behaviors more firmly resistant to extinction.
3.  Use ignoring, fines, time-out from reinforcement, and simple aversive punishment to extinguish undesirable behaviors.
4.  If the program seems to be failing, reevaluate the reinforcers to see if they are really reinforcing, and look back at your analysis of what payoff the student is getting from the undesirable behavior. Maybe the error lies there.
5.  Associate social reinforcers with reinforcers in other categories (edible, activity, material).
6.  Attempt to fade to social reinforcers.

CLAIM takes the view that inherent satisfaction in performing academic activities like reading cannot accrue to a child until reading becomes part of his response repertoire. In other words, a student who can't read won't know reading can be fun. Therefore, behavior modification should be viewed as a transitional technique, to bring a child to a certain level where inherent reinforcers can take over.

In the realm of social behavior as well, a student may not know how to gain attention in socially acceptable ways. Behavior modification can bring him to a level of performance where he sees for the first time that other forms of interaction give him the attention he wants. If acceptable social behavior is not part of a student's learned repertoire of behaviors, he has no inkling that they can be reinforcing.

Thus, the strategic goal embedded in CLAIM's syntax is to fade out the material, edible, and activity reinforcers they teach teachers to use and wind up with the social and inherent reinforcers in effect.

### Support System

1. Appropriate reinforcers must be available in the categories chosen.
2. Time and personnel must be available to make the observations and record data for establishing baselines and compiling progress records once reinforcement is introduced.

### Social System

1. The teacher is the identifier, author, and dispenser and withholder of reinforcement. The student is the receiver, the one to whom "treatment" is given.
2. Authority rests clearly with the teacher.
3. Norms are established by the teacher and communicated to the students; conformance to norms is reinforced.

### Effects

1. The direct effect of CLAIM's interpretation of behavior modification should be attain-

ment of target behaviors by students as chosen by the teacher. Classroom deviancy becomes reduced, and on-task learning time becomes maximized. Learning carries on in an efficient and effective manner.
2. Implicit effects are to make for a passive student, accustomed to reacting in engineered ways to engineered reinforcements. An external orientation tends to develop a "payoff" mentality, though CLAIM tries to move against this tendency by fading to social and inherent reinforcers. Others have raised questions about the effect of life in the environment of systematic behavior management on creativity and on initiative.

### Self-Awareness Training

Therapists, teachers, and parents have used strategies from this model with children of all ages and also with adults. An understanding of the values of self-induced relaxation training and of self-control through inner speech may finally make us realize that people who talk to themselves aren't so crazy after all!

### Assumptions

1. Students may have no perception of the type, severity, or frequency of their behaviors.
2. Students may have no perception, or inaccurate perceptions, of their own feelings, their own interior states.

**Values** This model values the mental health of students. What is important is that students become aware of their feelings and actions so that they can come to terms with them. They learn to anticipate and control impulsivity, outbursts, withdrawal, and other erratic behaviors that are symptomatic of their lack of awareness of themselves.

**Goals** The goal of this model is to teach students to read their own signals and engage coping strategies when the signals cue them that they are about to "blow" or follow a dysfunctional pattern common to them.

**Rationale** Students who are disconnected from their own inner selves need help in perceiving what their actions really are. An impulsive youngster may have no awareness that he jumped to his feet, knocked a book off the table, bumped two children while running to the door, and stepped on a painting as he went by the easel. All that he's aware of consciously is that "it's time to go." An older student may not be aware that he is getting increasingly frustrated at not being called on in an instructional group, that he is drumming his fingers and clenching his fists precedent to an outburst where he will lash out impatiently. Both students need to recognize these situations and read inner cues about how they're thinking and feeling. They need to be aware that these are triggering situations and that something is happening inside them, before they can do anything about it.

This model directly addresses with students what the triggering situations are for them and then teaches them to become aware of their reactions as these situations develop. When they learn to read these reactions as cues to trouble, they need to know what to do. The self-awareness strategies offer a variety of techniques that students can learn, practice, and use under stress to cool off, control themselves, and continue functioning effectively in school.

**Steps** Three strategies are simple counting or graphing of behavior, relaxation, and self-coaching through inner speech (cognitive behavior modification).

*Simple Counting* An effective technique is simple counting or anecdotal record keeping, explained previously in this chapter.

*Relaxation* Which of us hasn't wished for some device to calm down a hyperactive class at one point or another? Progressive muscle relaxation (Bernstein, Borkovec, and Hazlett-Stevens, 2000; Johnston, 2001) is a process designed to reduce tension and reverse the effects of stress on the body. Based on a principle of muscle physiology (whenever you create tension in a muscle and then release the tension, the muscle has to relax), the process involves isolating one muscle group at a time, creating tension for eight to ten seconds, and then letting the muscle relax and the tension go. Consider this description:

> Relaxed muscles require less oxygen so the breathing pattern slows and deepens. The heart does not need to be beating so fast to carry oxygen out to tense muscles. Heart rate and blood pressure decline. The normal blood flow returns to the belly and digestion resumes. The belly is calmed. Hands and feet warm up. Such a series of bodily adaptations all start and fall naturally into place because the voluntary muscles are being directed into a state of relaxation. Soon changes in mood follow, and you become more calm and refreshed [Johnston, 2001, http://www.lessons4living.com].

Johnston provides a script of this process. In addition, Bruno-Golden (1974) and Koeppen (1974) have produced scripts for use with students to achieve progressive muscle relaxation.

For certain students, knowing how to relax can be a coping strategy against stress that might otherwise trigger disruptive behavior. In private or small group sessions, the teacher can instruct the student in the technique and gradually fade out the coaching until the student can self-instruct through a set of exercises with minimal teacher guidance. A point can be reached where only a cue to start from the teacher is necessary, and the student can carry out the exercise alone: "Robbie, you and I know you've been having a tough time controlling your temper these days, right? Well, I'd like to teach you something that will help. Are you game?"

Along with the training, teacher and student must discuss triggering situations, try to identify the settings and the conditions that set up the student for an outburst, and try to predict them. They need to talk about the student's inner feelings and the overt symptoms the student and teacher may observe as pressure builds up on the student. For students who are out of touch with their inner selves and have a great deal of difficulty talking about their feelings, the two of them may do better by focusing on objective, observable qualities of events: "It's usually when you're in small groups. You start to clench your fists, and your knuckles turn white." Ultimately students must be able to read their own signals and turn on their coping mechanisms before they lose control. Along the way, they may need help from the teacher to recognize these cues. A code word can be set up between them, or the teacher may have to intervene beyond cue giving in any one of the following ways that Wolfgang (1977) presents, getting more and more intrusive depending on how much control the student has:

- Proximity—looking on.
- "I see you starting to get out of control."
- "You're getting out of control. I will help."
- Physical interposing: verbalizing what the student is doing—or holding the student (for young children): "I won't let you hurt yourself or hurt others."

For less disturbed children, coping models simpler than relaxation can be employed. Students can take a walk in the hall to cool off or go to a private corner of the room. In both strategies, however, the teacher and students are confederates. They alone may be privy to the cuing system and the coping strategy. Students see the teacher as someone helping them to gain self-mastery. Teachers work to fade their active role to the minimum required to keep the student functional, delivering as much support as necessary but looking to reduce students' dependence on them.

Explosive youngsters badly out of touch with their feelings can be greatly helped by models such as this one but may need therapy in addition.

***Self-Instruction Through Inner Speech (Cognitive Behavior Modification)***   In self-instructional training, students are taught to use their inner speech to talk themselves through difficult situations in which they are struggling to contain impulses, remain in control, and employ alternate strategies. Teaching a student to alter his internal dialogue "will have directive effects on: (a) what the individual attends to in the environment; (b) how he appraises various stimulus events; (c) to what he attributes his behavior; and (d) his expectations about his own capacities to handle a stressful event" (Meichenbaum, 1977, p. 206).

One such approach is the think-aloud technique. Meichenbaum describes a program in which twelve aggressive second-grade boys were seen in small groups:

The program began with a "copycat" game, which introduced the child to asking himself the following four basic questions: What is my problem? What is my plan? Am I using my plan? How did I do? While the "copycat" was being faded, cue cards . . . were introduced to signal the child to self-verbalize. Over the course of training there was a shift from cognitively demanding tasks to interpersonal tasks. . . . Initial results . . . were quite promising. The results generalized to the classroom. The results of the Think Aloud training program take on particular significance when we consider [the] findings that aggressive boys had verbal facilities that were comparable to normal boys on various performance tasks, but that the aggressive boys failed to use their abilities to think through and plan solutions to problems. The self-instructional training program, Think Aloud, successfully taught such self-verbalization skills [Meichenbaum, 1977, p. 42].

In teaching these self-instructional strategies to students, teachers need to work with them alone or in small groups. Instruction starts with a situation that is often hard for the student to handle, for example, a transition where the job is getting from a class meeting or an instructional group to the door, lined up, and ready to go to lunch. We previously described a child who jumped to his feet, knocked a book off a table, bumped two children running to the door, and stepped on a painting as he ran by the easel. The internal dialogue we eventually want the student to carry on with himself might go like this:

*Defining the problem:* "Let's see, what's my job? To get to the line without bumping anyone."

*Focus attention on what to do:* "What do I have to do to get there? Start walking slowly; look where I'm going." "That's it; not too fast now."

*Self-evaluation, monitoring:* "Watch out for that easel rack." "How's it going? Pretty well."

*Self-reinforcement:* "Hooray! I made it!"

To teach a student to do that, the teacher has the student watch her act out the motions and verbalize out loud the dialogue above. Then the teacher asks the student to walk through the motions of getting to the door while the teacher again verbalizes the dialogue out loud. The sequence then proceeds through six phases (Meichenbaum, 1977):

| *Teacher* | *Student* |
| --- | --- |
| Gives out-loud self-instructions, performs motions | Watches |
| Gives out-loud self-instructions | Performs motions |
| Whispers instructions | Says self-instructions out loud, performs motions |
| Moves lips only | Whispers self-instructions, performs motions |
| Watches | Moves lips only, performs motions |
| Watches | Inner speech for self-instruction; performs motions |

Variations of this strategy are used with older students and with adults, but the principles remain the same. Students are taught to identify situations stressful to them so that they can prepare coping strategies. They are also taught to recognize their own signals of stress, so that when they are caught unprepared, they realize that they are on the edge of trouble and can spontaneously engage one of their coping strategies.

**Principles of Teacher Response** When the student loses control, the teacher steps in as strongly as necessary to restore it, but no more strongly than necessary; after all, the object is to build the student's own capacity for self-control. Alertness, cue giving, and minimal response consistent with safety are the watchwords here.

**Support System**  Teachers need time and access to students outside normal class time or the flexibility to get students alone in a private setting during class time. Teachers need to have identified in advance some triggering situations to work on with the student.

**Social System**  The teacher is a helping person in this model. Ultimate decision-making power on whether to use, and when to use, the coping strategies rests with the student, although the teacher is a trusted confederate and has the job of sending cues and prompts when the student is beginning to lose control.

**Effects**  Successful practice of this model reduces outbursts and disruptive conflicts for students who are impulsive and out of control. It also builds their self-confidence and sense of accomplishment: this is, after all, a kind of mastery they are achieving. As a result, doors open for them to more productive relationships with other students.

A related model, interpersonal cognitive problem solving, teaches youngsters alternative-consequences thinking. It is aimed primarily at young children and teaches them problem-solving strategies they can use to replace fighting, bickering, and resolution of conflicts by power alone. The following script from Shure and Spivack (1978) is illustrative. The teacher leads children to review their actions and the consequences of those actions and then to generate alternate actions that might get the child's need met:

TEACHER:  Dorothy, were you working with these puzzles?
CHILD:  Brian did too.

TEACHER:  Did you and Brian work together? (Teacher gathering facts of situation.)
CHILD:  Yes.
TEACHER:  Is it fair for Brian to pick them up by himself and for you not to pick them up?
CHILD:  No.
TEACHER:  Is it fair for you to pick them up and not Brian?
CHILD:  No.
TEACHER:  What is fair? (Teacher guides child to see problem from point of view of both children.)
CHILD:  Brian won't help me.
TEACHER:  Can you think of a way to get Brian to help you pick up the puzzles? (Child guided to think of solution to problem.)
CHILD:  I could ask him.
TEACHER:  That's one idea. What might happen if you did that? (Teacher guides consequential thinking.)
CHILD:  He won't help.
TEACHER:  That might happen. What else could you think of to do if he says no?
CHILD:  Hit him.
TEACHER:  You could hit him. What might happen then?
CHILD:  We'll fight.
TEACHER:  Maybe you'd fight. Can you think of a third, different idea?
CHILD:  You tell him.
TEACHER:  I could tell him. How will that help you when I'm not here? (Teacher continues to guide child to think of solutions to problem.)
CHILD:  I could say I won't play with him anymore.
TEACHER:  Is that a good idea?
CHILD:  Yeah.
TEACHER:  Why?
CHILD:  Cause then he'll help me.
TEACHER:  Maybe. See what you can do to get him to help [pp. 146–147].

The authors summarize the syntax embedded in this dialogue:

1. Elicit from the child his or her view of the problem in a non-accusatory way; for example: "What happened?" "What did the other child do or say?" "Why did he do that?" "What is it you want him to do?" "How do you know he won't do that?"

2. Ask the child, in a matter-of-fact fashion, why he acted as he did. "Why did you call him a dummy?" "Why did you feel like hitting him first?"

3. Guide the child to think about how he felt (feels) and how he thinks others felt (or might feel). You might ask, for instance, "How do you think he felt when you did that?" "How did you feel when he did that?"

4. Raise the question of how one can find out how another child thinks or feels. "How can you find out if he likes your idea?" "How can you tell if he is happy or sad?"

5. Ask the child to give his idea about how to solve the problem. "What can you do if you want him to let you do that (have that, let you play with him, stop hitting you)?"

6. Ask the child to think about what might happen next. "If you do that, what might your sister do or say?" "If you keep bothering him, what might happen next?"

7. Guide the child to evaluate whether he thinks his idea—regardless of its content—is or is not a good one, on the basis of his idea about what might happen next. "Is hitting back a good idea?" "Is trading a good idea?"

8. Encourage the child to think of different solutions to a problem, when relevant. "Can you think of a second different way to get him to give you a turn (let you play with them)?" "If they do not want to play now, can you think of something different to do that will make you happy? [pp. 229–230].

The responses of children indicate that they are more likely to take action when an idea is their own than when it is suggested or demanded by an adult. Although children at times need to take adult advice, experience indicates that when the child comes up with a solution he likes, he tends to move to action with a spontaneous motivation that stems from the natural connection between his thinking and his action. If his idea fails, he thinks again and may try another solution before reacting with impulsiveness, frustration, or withdrawal. He has learned a problem-solving style of thinking.

### Personal Influence

In this model, teachers build strong relations with students and use these relationships to motivate students toward more responsible behavior. Teachers make deliberate moves to enhance their personal significance to students and use their position of respect and regard and closeness to induce behavior change. They show high affect and high commitment; students find that their relationship with the significant teacher is a two-way street.

**Assumptions** Students are more motivated to behave and to do good work if they respect and like the teacher.

**Values** The things that are important in this model are student self-image and class order. The syntax reflects a conscious value that students build confidence in themselves as worthwhile people through a close relationship with a significant adult. It also has a clear commitment to class order and taking steps to stop disruption firmly when it occurs.

**Goals**   The first goal of the model is to build relationships between the teacher and resistant students in order to increase the personal influence of the teacher on students. The second goal is to establish clear expectations for behavior, with swift and consistent consequences for misbehavior.

**Rationale**   The relationship between teacher and student is like a bank account: it makes a student feel more comfortable, safe, and secure to have it. It enables a student to invest and grow, operating from a safe base to reach out tentatively to try new experiences. And it is something for both teacher and student to draw on in times of need. A good relationship with a liked and respected teacher will motivate students to try harder in their work and their efforts toward better behavior. It will also make a reproof from that teacher more telling.

In this model, teachers show students when they are upset with them: not losing control and ranting and raving, but showing anger, frustration, or disappointment. That means something to a student because the teacher is a significant person to the student. Students are less inclined to risk this relationship with a teacher through irresponsible behavior when the relationship is important to them. The teacher never uses the relationship as a threat or the denial of closeness as a punishment. In fact, after reprimands or episodes where students must be removed from the room, the teacher looks for the earliest possible opportunity to relate to the student positively in another context, to reassure and rebuild the relationship. Nevertheless, though the teacher does not use loss of love as a club, the very presence of the relationship acts as a healthy inhibitor of disruptive behavior from the student. It is healthy because wanting to please those who are important to us by acting responsibly is healthy. It is not the most advanced form of moral reasoning in the world, but for lonely and confused students it can be a definite step up.

Through this relationship, students can gain confidence, try harder, and succeed more in their work. From the stable base with the teacher, they can reach out and be brought into contact with other students in controlled settings, sometimes cooperative projects, so that they begin to extend their circle of successful relationships and begin to feel more worthwhile. As they can be accepted by more and more students, as they can see themselves as successful with others, so their capacity and desire to act in ways that will preserve these relationships grows.

**Steps**

1. Build a friendly relationship with an individual student aimed at closeness and open communication by looking for, and capitalizing on, moments for positive, friendly, one-to-one interaction:
   - A few minutes before class
   - A few minutes after class
   - Inviting student to have lunch together in the room once in a while
   - After-school projects
2. Practice active listening and other behaviors detailed under the personal relationship building area of performance.
3. Share with the class things about yourself that are interesting: travels, experiences, especially any accomplishment or proficiencies you have (like playing an instrument or some craft ability) that make you real and significant in their eyes without appearing boastful.

In general, this means showing these abilities rather than telling about them. Bringing them in to show and share is more likely to be interpreted as interesting than boastful if it is not overdone.

4. Connect the student with other students in safe and structured ways. For example, teach a young student a game, and then set him up for the first ten minutes of the day, typically a hard time for these children, to teach it to two other designated students. Have older students pass out materials or play designated roles in group projects.

5. In one-to-one interactions with the resistant students, let them know your expectations explicitly. If appropriate, make behavior contracts and record-keeping charts to help focus on what needs to improve and to keep track of progress.

6. When the student acts disruptively, react swiftly with consequences (which will frequently involve removal or isolation of some kind).

7. Always talk to the student afterward, calmly but expressing some emotion. Get the student to analyze what went wrong and what needs to be done.

8. Look for an early opportunity after a disciplinary episode with a resistant student to have a positive exchange about something (for example, "Gee, that's a nice piece of work, Youshen"), especially if you've been very tough about the discipline. The purpose is to reopen communication and establish that your relationship is still alive. The caution is not to overdo it so the student learns a reward (such as an after-school project) will follow most serious disruptions. Keep the relationship rebuilding low key, just enough to reopen and reassure.

9. Maintain frequent and direct contact with parents to involve them in the plan as much as possible.

### Principles of Teacher Response

1. Use active listening during relationship building.
2. Find or make opportunities to build relationships.
3. Show affect when disciplining.
4. Be calmer and more analytical in discussing the behavior with students.
5. Rebuild relationships in low-key fashion after tough episodes.

**Support System** To carry out this model, teachers need sufficient access and frequency of contact with students to build relationships. They also need to be consistent with consequences and follow-up. Where this is limited by modular scheduling, the school should consider a more self-contained class setting, or at least fewer teacher changes for this student. The teacher needs to have a set of consequences figured out in advance for the student (and perhaps rewards too, if this personal influence strategy is paired with behavioral contracting). These arrangements may require cooperation and agreement with other teachers or administrators. Know what you're going to do when the student's behavior crosses acceptable boundaries and gets too disruptive to continue instruction. Usually this will mean some form of removal to a mutual cooling-off room or other site. You have to know where.

**Social System** The teacher is the authority figure, and the norms for behavior come primarily from the teacher. The class may be intimately involved in setting rules in general, but even when democracy is part of the class's life and when it may be the way behavior norms are determined, personal influence does not intend to be a democratic model.

### Effects

1. Deviant behavior is reduced.
2. The teacher provides a role model of caring and of responsibility, to which the student begins to attach.
3. The student begins to build positive relationships with other students.

One more specific strategy that fits with this model: a well-thought-out and highly effective form of exclusion for disruptive students developed by Seymour Sarason and his associates. It appears in a book far removed from discipline: *The Culture of the School and the Problem of Change* (Sarason, 1971).

Sarason's strategy is a carefully sequenced set of steps to produce dramatic suppression of hostile defiance. The essence of it is pairing two teachers and removing the defiant student from one teacher's room to the other's. The success of the exclusion depends on the preparation of the personnel, their pairing, and the support of the principal.

Sarason attributes the effectiveness of the strategy to its ability to terminate defiant outbursts immediately and underline with dramatic action the limits beyond which the student may no longer go.

The procedure must be introduced to the whole class at once as a way of helping children remember to follow rules that allow them to enjoy learning. "It should be explained to the children repeatedly that a child will not be excluded because he is unwanted or disliked but because he needs the brief opportunity in another classroom to reflect on the rules he has been disobeying" (Sarason, 1971, p. 137). Sarason has used this strategy with students through fourth grade. We see no rea-

son why it cannot be applied successfully in higher grades as well.

## Logical Consequences

Dreikurs and Cassel (1972) sought to eliminate the authoritarian use of power by parents and teachers, which they saw as inappropriate in a democratic age and harmful to relationships between youngsters and adults. They blended Adlerian psychology with a technique for responding to misbehavior called logical consequences. Reacting with logical consequences is intended to take the acrimony—the child-adult power struggle—out of discipline and enable mutual respect to grow.

### Definitions

1. Natural consequence: an aversive result to a child's behavior that occurs by itself, naturally, without any human engineering or intervention (for example, a child who is tipping back in her chair finally falls over).
2. Logical consequence: an engineered aversive result to a child's behavior that is logically connected to the behavior.

### Assumptions

1. Equality is the only basis for solving discipline problems.
2. The fundamental human need is to belong, and it develops into a striving to function in and with a group in order to feel worthwhile.
3. All behavior is purposive. The goal of self-determined direction motivates children's behavior.

### Goals

1. Eliminate the "outright warfare" Dreikurs sees between delinquents and society, between rebellious youngsters and parents and teachers.

2. Apply Adler's first social law: the law of equality, the logic of social living that "demands recognition of every human being as an equal" (Dreikurs and Grey, 1968, p. 8).

3. Provide the means by which the student can function properly in an atmosphere of freedom ("properly" here meaning with responsibility rather than license).

4. Eliminate autocratic methods of discipline.

5. Eliminate the obnoxious behavior of the average American child who "fights with his brothers and sisters, refuses to put things away or to do homework or help around the house" (Dreikurs and Grey, 1968, p. 10).

6. Cultivate relations based on mutual respect between children and adults.

**Rationale**  The goals can be accomplished with an understanding of the causes of student behaviors and by not dealing with them by autocratic methods. Teachers' responses to behavior must manifest the reality of the social order by allowing students to take responsibility (and logical consequences) for their actions. When teachers and parents start generating responses to misbehavior from this framework of social reality, students will no longer resent, rebel, or feel oppressed because adult responses will no longer appear to be emanating from personal authority.

Furthermore, when the causes of misbehavior in individual students are understood, positive paths of action can be followed that relate to meeting the needs of the child. Thus, new responses to misbehavior based on democratic theory and positive programs of action to meet the needs of children who regularly misbehave will be the two prongs of the attack.

Students develop concepts, through learning, of what behavior will help them develop a place in the group. They may have the concept that cooperation will do so or that being the center of attention will do so. There are immediate goals behind every misbehavior. All misbehavior is the result of a discouraged student's mistaken assumption about the way to find a place and gain status.

Logical consequences has the student be impressed with the needs of reality, and not the power of an adult. The principle of dealing with each other as equals yields a relationship based on mutual respect. Students are teachers' equals now in their right and ability to decide for themselves instead of yielding to a superior force. Whereas punishment represents the power of personal authority, logical consequences, as the expression of the reality of the social order, operate at the impersonal level. Punishment says, "You are bad"; logical consequences say, "Your behavior yields this result." No judgment is made about "you" as a person.

**Steps**

1. Observe the student's behavior in detail.

2. Be sensitive to your own reaction to the student's behavior. If your reaction is "annoyance," the student's goal may be attention; when it is "threatened," the goal may be power; when it is "hurt," the goal may be revenge; and when it is "helplessness," the goal may be a display of inadequacy.

3. Give the student corrective feedback. Stop the student, reprimand him, and see how he reacts. If he stops, the behavior may be simply a bid for attention. If the misbehavior increases, its goal may have been to express power. If the student seems hurt, the goal may be revenge.

4. Confront the student with the four goals by asking one or more of these four questions in order—but after a cooling-off period from the moment of conflict.

- "Could it be you want me to notice you?" (Attention)
- "Could it be that you want to show me that you can do what you want to do and no one can stop you?" (Power)
- "Could it be you want to hurt me and the pupils in the class—to get even?" (Revenge)
- "Could it be that you want to be left alone?" (Inadequacy)

5. Note the recognition reflex, that is, which of the four questions the student seems to respond to verbally or with body language.

6. Apply appropriate corrective procedures depending on the student's goal as summarized in Figure 8.3.

When using a logical consequence, pick an appropriate type. There are a variety of types of logical consequence from which to choose, as the chart in Figure 8.3 reveals:

- *Choice.* The student can avoid the logical consequence right away by choosing to alter his behavior. If talking to a classmate is preventing a student from finishing his science exhibit, you let him handle and own the problem: he won't have anything to put on his desk for his parents to see at back-to-school night. You may point out his choice to the student, but let him have positive control over handling the outcome. The adult's action is nil.

- *Negative choice.* The teacher or parent points out what logical consequence will accrue to the student through the instrumentality of the teacher if he doesn't perform in a certain way. Not doing assigned work in school will result in his having to stay afterward to finish it. Having to finish it later is a logical consequence of not finishing it now. That's the way it is; staying after school is not viewed or presented as a punishment; it's just the way things are for people who don't finish their work.

The teacher has to stay after too to finish up her work and can't go until it's done. This is the social reality. This kind of logical consequence is considered negative choice here because the child is confronted with, "If you do X, then Y will happen." Y is an aversive consequence for the child.

- *Own medicine.* The child's behavior is given back. For example, interrupt the interrupter; make an unlivable supermess around the sloppy student. In effect, hold a mirror of his behavior up to the student. There ought to be a certain amount of humor and appreciation of rational limits when employing this technique, not vindictiveness.

- *No choice.* The teacher levies the consequence on the student right after the misbehavior occurs. What separates this from punishment is the logical connection the teacher must establish, at least in the student's mind, between the behavior and the consequence. No choice logical consequences can be immediate (removing two fighting children from a recess baseball game to sit out the recess) or a surprise, containing some element of novelty and originality (for example, the teacher has rock throwers on the playground start rounding up all the rocks they can find and then has them throw the rocks into a vacant lot to make the playground safer). Other examples given of original reactions sometimes smack of embarrassment. One morning the seventh grader who continually taps his pencil in an annoying way is given a crayon instead of a pencil; the teacher states, "If you cannot use a pencil correctly, you will have to write with this."

- *Satiation.* This means the same to Dreikurs as it does to behavior modification people: make the student do the illegal behavior over and over again until he is tired of it (have the spitball thrower chuck spitballs into a box all morning; have the wanderer walk around the room all afternoon).

Late in his career, Dreikurs concluded that logical consequences are most useful if the goal is

**Figure 8.3. Steps in Dreikurs's Model**

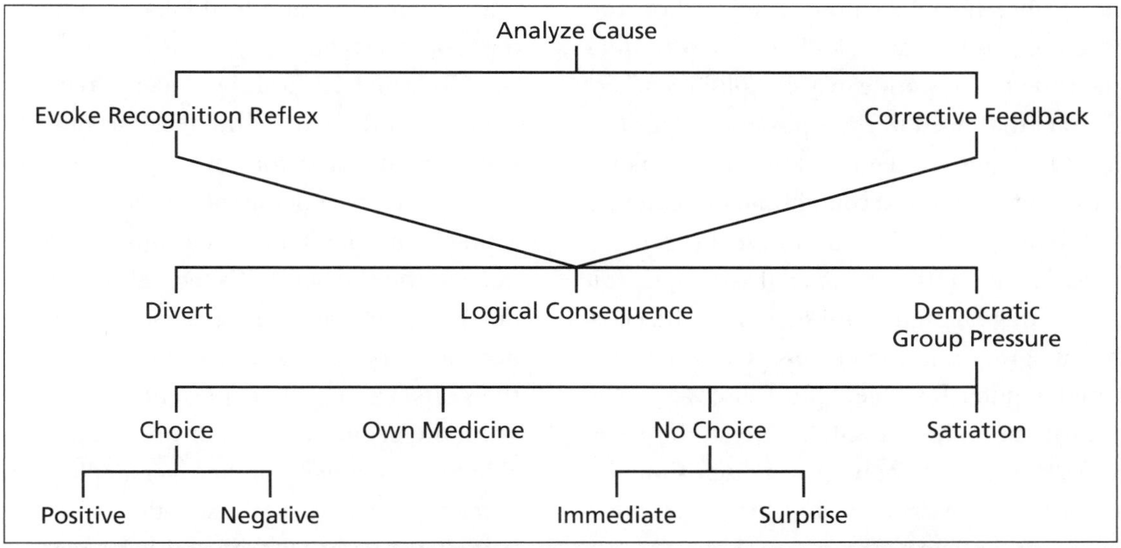

*Source:* Dreikurs, R., and Cassel, P. *Discipline Without Tears: What to Do with Children Who Misbehave.* New York: Hawthorn Books, 1972.

attention getting (Dreikurs and Cassel, 1972). With power or revenge, logical consequences may backfire and should not be used. Natural consequences are all right at any time, except against the feeling of inadequacy.

**Principles of Teacher Response**

1. Make sure the consequence is logically related to the misbehavior.
2. Present the consequence matter-of-factly, as an expression of the reality of the social order, not personal authority.
3. Make no moral judgments about the behavior or the student.
4. Be kind, and use a friendly voice; never act in anger.
5. Be firm. In a no-choice logical consequence, there really is no choice. This is what's going to happen to the student, and it must be carried through. Don't change your mind; don't give in; don't deviate from your announced procedure.
6. Act; don't talk. Too much talk (threats, warnings, explanations, exhortations) is the downfall of good discipline.
7. Be concerned with the present, not with the past. There must be no element of sin in the teacher's view of the misbehavior or any element of retribution for past offenses in the consequence used.
8. Never get involved in a power struggle with a student. You will always lose. Simply refuse to be engaged in this kind of conflict. Sidestep it.

Another way Dreikurs has of talking about the causes of misbehavior is to consider the four causes as goals of the student. The positive program seeks ways to meet these goals for the student without his having to misbehave.

While refusing combat, be aware of the cause of the conflict. If you diagnose "need to show and assert power" as the cause, look for opportunities for the child to show pride in accomplishment. Try to channel that need to show power into positive paths. If the cause is need for attention, look for opportunities to praise accomplishments, ignoring deviant behavior that is attention seeking. If the misbehavior stems from assumed disability, treat it with encouragement; ensure success in the classroom; and give responsibility that is carefully chosen and but publicly visible. If the cause is revenge, dig in for the long pull. Make the student feel liked. Dreikurs talks about group discussion and acceptance in this context, but leaves us with a direction rather than a syntax.

Use sociograms to gather data on popular and unpopular students, extroverts and introverts, he urges. Use this information in seating arrangements and class groupings to have isolates experience new skills of socialization and put compatible students together.

Have regular class discussions each week to consider class problems. Stimulate students to learn to listen, understand each other, and help each other.

The positive program has four thrusts, each responding to one of the four causes of misbehavior that Dreikurs cites. But unlike the syntax of direct response to misbehavior, the positive program consists of general principles of teacher response to be applied in a prescriptive manner rather than specific actions.

Encouragement is the utility infielder of this positive program, being applied to three of the four causes.

**Support System** The Dreikurs model is claimed to be most successful with children of elementary age. Beyond that age, more complicated and far-reaching motives add to the basic four with the onset of adolescence.

Effecting a logical consequence requires decisiveness on the part of the teacher and, in some instances, an ability for novel or original thinking (the surprise type of logical consequence). To levy a no-choice, immediate type of logical consequence, the teacher needs the self-confidence and quick response seen in experienced teachers who have developed a large repertoire of responses over the years. Failing the experience and the repertoire, the beginning teacher presumably must be able to think quickly on her feet, apply principles of teacher response to the situation, and develop a logical consequence for the misbehavior.

The teacher must keep his ego off the line and maintain a detachment that enables him to avoid power conflicts with children—another difficult challenge, especially for the beginning teacher who is inevitably involved to some degree with proving himself. It is this same kind of ego detachment on the part of the teacher that will permit the student to own his own problem in the choice, positive category. Furthermore, to try and convince a vicious-acting student that he is liked means liking an unlikable child, which demands a secure and giving, empathetic teacher.

Dreikurs's method demands firm, calm, non-judgmental ways of talking to students when handling misbehavior and the techniques of sounding out and structuring the expression of the group's feeling about the misbehavior. The space and time required for specific consequences may be considered. (Will there be someone around after school to supervise finishing work? Will shooting paper clips into a box in the corner of the room be too visibly distracting to the rest of the class in the setup of this room, or too noisy?)

**Social System** The teacher's role as autocrat is the target of the model. Get the teacher off the power pedestal, says Dreikurs; don't take the position of rule maker and enforcer as a personal role. Yet the teacher is the rule enforcer in the system; it's just that the rules are seen as not stemming from the teacher but rather from the nature of things, from the social reality. It is the teacher who devises the logical consequence for a misbehavior, and it is the teacher who makes sure that the logical consequence is applied. If the consequence would apply all by itself, it would be a natural consequence. Logical consequences require human intervention to be affected.

Rule making is more democratic. Students are included in the constitutional process. Nevertheless, the teacher holds and openly uses power in the logical consequences system, although this use of power is masked and blunted. Resentment that it might otherwise generate is reduced by having teachers avoid direct power struggles with children and by clothing the consequence in an attitude of detachment on the part of the teacher and logic in its relation to the misbehavior. It is not that power is used in a deceptive way, but rather that it is deceptive to think of the system as one that avoids the use of power. Logical consequences cultivate an attitude about power in teachers and children that seeks to associate it with social reality rather than personal confrontation; but it does not reduce or eliminate its use.

Dreikurs's last work (Dreikurs and Cassel, 1972), with Pearl Cassel, qualifies the use of logical consequences that meliorate the above conclusions. Logical consequences are sanctioned in this book against attention getting, and only there, whereas in previous books there was no such limitation. One does not use logical consequences when the student's goal is power or revenge or display of inadequacy. This, it seems to us, represents a shift of position from Dreikurs's earlier views. Taken at face value, this new position makes the Dreikurs model less reliant on power and more reliant on encouragement and such things as the use of sociometric data. This book has a chapter on the evils of competition in school situations, a new theme for Dreikurs, and a chapter on how to conduct democratic class discussions, not a new theme for him.

**Effects** The direct effect is that deviant behavior is reduced. In addition, teachers and students can relate to each other without the barrier of power struggles. Mutual respect is cultivated, and democratic practices are supposed to become more a part of classroom life. Students become more realistic in their view of the world and more appreciative of the social value of cooperation.

## Reality Therapy

Let us now examine a model of classroom discipline in which sanctions by teachers are eschewed. Several resources exist as background for this model. William Glasser in *Schools Without Failure* (1969) originally translated the principles of reality therapy into a series of steps (syntax) for teachers to use in responding to misbehavior. He expanded on this work later in the paperback edition of the book that was published in 1975 and again in *Choice Theory in the Classroom* (1998). In *Reality Therapy for the 21st Century* (2000) former coauthor R. E. Wubbolding continues the evolution of this model.

By using the steps Glasser laid out in this model, teachers can get students to take responsibility for their own behavior and for altering their behavior if it is not meeting their own needs for self-worth or respecting the rights of others to meet their needs. The result is a school climate of mutual respect, caring, and cooperative problem solving.

**Definitions** Glasser established his basic definitions in *Reality Therapy* (1965). Some have been translated into different vocabulary in the later iterations of the model but the meanings remain the same.

1. Respect: self-respect, a feeling of self-worth.
2. Self-worth: a feeling of value to oneself and to others; feeling that one is a worthwhile person.
3. Relatedness: being connected or involved with other people in a relation of caring.
4. Involvement: relationship with a person or persons you care for and whom you know care for you in return.
5. Love: involvement.
6. Responsibility: the ability to fulfill one's needs in a way that does not deprive others of the ability to fulfill their needs. A responsible person does what gives him a feeling of self-worth and a feeling he is worthwhile to others.
7. Realistic: an action's remote as well as immediate consequences are taken into consideration, weighed, and compared.
8. Identity: a state that results when one feels love and self-worth. In *Schools Without Failure* Glasser sees self-worth as necessitating confidence in one's knowledge and abilities in school. Love, in a school context, means social responsibility, caring for each other, and helping each other. Love is seen as the opposite of and the eliminator of feelings of loneliness and failure.
9. Success: an established identity; a state of having one's basic needs of relatedness and respect (or of involvement and self-worth) met.
10. Failure: a state where one's basic needs are not met.

To understand Glasser's model it is important to keep in mind the full and special meaning of his definitions of involvement, responsibility, realistic, success, and failure.

**Assumptions**

1. The basic human needs of all people are relatedness (involvement) and respect (self-worth).
2. All people are responsible for their actions.
3. All people are capable of acting responsibly, regardless of their background, past experience, or current environment.
4. A change in behavior will lead to a change in attitude.
5. The first five years of school are critical to the development of responsibility and the ability to succeed.

**Values**

1. Caring for one another, affection
2. Courage to attempt solutions to one's problems
3. Thinking versus rote learning in education
4. Relevance to the issues children face in their lives built into curriculum content

**Goals**

1. Achievement of personal success by individuals (defined as meeting the two basic needs of involvement and self-worth)
2. Achieving a social climate that manifests mutual respect, caring, and rational, honest, cooperative problem solving
3. Structuring the expression of affection in schools; creating a form for it; institutionalizing the expression of it; and making it a recognized part of the purpose and building it into the activities of school life

**Rationale** Success comes through being realistic, responsible, and right (which means acting in accordance with accepted moral standards). This can be restated: meeting one's basic needs of involvement and self-worth can be accomplished by considering the long-range consequences of one's acts, acting to meet the needs of others, and acting in accord with moral standards.

Achieving this kind of success requires involvement as a starting point. The child needs a significant other in her life about whom she cares and from whom affection is returned. When the child has that, she can then begin to relinquish action based on the pleasure principle, that is, immediate gratification. But involvement alone is not enough. After involvement exists, something must be done to raise the feeling of self-worth. The child can feel worthwhile only if she maintains a satisfactory standard of behavior. This means she must become capable of, and practice, self-evaluation; she must look at her behavior and judge whether it is responsible without depriving others of the ability to fulfill their needs.

Deviant behavior is unrealistic and irresponsible. Deviant behavior shows children have made bad choices about how to meet their needs. They can't make better choices unless they are involved with those who can. Discipline, which is what those who love give us, points out unrealistic and irresponsible behavior and helps the child become realistic and responsible.

**Steps**

1. "Make friends," says Glasser to teachers. "Become involved," he says to the therapist. "Establish a relationship," he says to both, "with mutual confidence in and expression of affection."

2. Ask, "What are you doing?" when a student misbehaves. This is identifying, verbalizing, and facing the reality of the behavior. This is a real step for some students, and not something they realize, much less ask, on their own.

3. Ask, "Is it helping you?" Judge the behavior. Behind the question is the thought that the behavior is not helping the child meet his basic needs. The teacher is not talking explicitly about the needs but simply asking for an evaluation of the behavior: "Is it helping you?"

Questions 2 and 3 may not be addressed by the students if the involvement is not previously established and if they do not know that there will be no punishment.

4. There is no punishment.

5. Make a plan. The teacher asks the student to make a plan to avoid the behavior or for how to cope with the situation in an acceptable way the next time it crops up. It is okay for the teacher to give suggestions and advice here, but the plan must be enough for the student so he can make a commitment to it.

6. Get a commitment from the student to carry out the plan. This can be verbal or written.

7. No excuses: "When will you do it?" And the teacher holds the student to the answer. No excuses are acceptable for not meeting the commitment. Although there is no punishment, the teacher holds the student to his commitment, and if the student does not meet it, the teacher asks the student to reevaluate the plan, make a new one, or renew his commitment. The process may need repeating over and over again. The teacher who is involved is willing to start all over again

repeatedly. But always there is the expectation and the trust that the student will finally meet it. The teacher never excuses or condones or makes allowances, or fails to hold students to commitments.

8. Class meetings. These form a regular part of the response system of the teacher to misbehavior (as well as a format for establishing the requisite involvement).

### Principles of Teacher Response

1. Point out the reality of the situation—of the behavior.
2. Never condone irresponsibility.
3. Focus on the present, not the past.
4. No punishment, no sarcasm, no ridicule. Sarcasm and ridicule are destroyers of affection, closeness, relationships, and involvement.
5. Don't avoid speaking in the first person. Say, "I want you to . . .," not, "we should" or "you should."
6. The environment should never be manipulated so the child does not suffer reasonable consequences of his behavior.
7. Handle class problems in class meetings.

There are three kinds of class meetings: social problem–solving meetings, open-ended meetings, and educational diagnostic meetings. Social problem–solving meetings are used to work out solutions to problems pertinent to the group or to any individual in the group. They are the kind of meetings that fit into the syntax of response to misbehavior. Open-ended meetings discuss questions of interest and relevance to the children's lives. In addition to making at least part of the day focus on issues of relevance to the students, these meetings perform a vital function in establishing involvement between the teacher and students and among the students themselves. Educational diagnostic meet-

ings are used to assess how well children are grasping aspects of curriculum and to plan future steps.

The leadership of social problem-solving meetings by teachers is also handled in accordance with certain principles:

- The solution to the problem is the focus of the discussion, never fault finding or punishment.
- The teacher remains nonjudgmental in his or her comments, though the students are not expected to do so. (Experiencing the feedback of his peers is one of the reasonable consequences a child suffers for an irresponsible behavior.)
- Conduct the meetings in a tight circle.
- Keep them short.
- Don't overdwell on a single problem student (three times in a row on a class bully would be overdwelling).
- Make the majority of class meetings in the other two categories (open ended and educationally diagnostic).
- Use class meetings as a vehicle for as much teaching of regular curriculum as possible.

### Support System

1. Heterogeneous, homeroom-based classes. The class must spend most of the day together as a social unit for the feelings of involvement with each other and with their teacher to develop.
2. No letter grading, so there is no labeling as failure.
3. The curriculum must have a "thinking" emphasis, so that it is relevant to issues in the students' lives.
4. There must be success in reading. Glasser sees this achievement as so much a part of social expectation about school and so necessary

for achieving feelings of success in school that special attention must be paid to its accomplishment in the design of school curriculum. To achieve it, he is even willing to dissolve the homeroom class unit for a portion of the day.

5. Probably most important, the teacher must be willing to make the personal commitment and self-investment to become involved with her students.

### Social System

1. The system is nonpunitive.
2. Students participate in rule making.
3. The constant willingness of the teacher to start again with a student who has not met a commitment expresses a confidence, a trust, in the student to eventually succeed. It also expresses a depth of involvement on the teacher's part.
4. The teacher's role is as a model of responsibility.
5. The teacher also has a role as a benevolent despot, not through punishment, but through rule enforcement and the holding of children to commitments they have made.
6. Rules are reasonable. Participation of students in the constitutional process tends toward making the rules more reasonable. But Glasser realizes and approves of the fact that adults serve as a major source for principles from which rules come. This is the practical reality. The statement that rules should be reasonable is something Glasser says to teachers and administrators knowing they will have and should have major decisions in what they will be.
7. The students are responsible for their own behavior and free to choose at all times what their behavior will be like. Their responsibil-

ity extends not only to themselves or even to the teacher, but also to all the other members of the class.

**Effects**  The direct effects are that social problems are worked on openly with an orientation toward solution, not blame, and that relevance is stressed in curriculum. There are nurturant effects as well: warmth and affection grow among students and between teacher and students, respect for each other's needs and rights is cultivated, and empathy develops as students' needs are met and their responsibility grows.

## Teacher Effectiveness Training

Thomas Gordon's teacher effectiveness training (TET) builds on the principles of the similar parent effectiveness training and has been translated into an in-service course offered nationwide to schools and school districts.

Gordon seeks to eliminate the conflicts and misunderstandings that cause poor relations between teachers and students by teaching them communication skills. The TET communication skills give students and teachers an alternative to power in resolving conflicts of needs. No longer does the teacher have to win at the expense of the student's needs (Method I), or the student win at the expense of the teacher (Method II). The no-lose Method III taught in TET enables both students and teachers to meet their needs.

### Definitions

1. Active listening: listening for the feeling and content (the encoded message) in a speaker's remark and feeding this back to the speaker.
2. I message: a nonjudgmental description of another's behavior, a statement of the behavior's tangible effects on you, and a

statement of the feelings generated in you by this behavior. These three elements in any order comprise an I message.

3. Gear shifting: switching into active listening after sending an I message.

### Assumptions

1. Acceptance enables change and growth. When a person feels he is okay as a person, accepted for what he is in the eyes of another, he will be receptive to changing his behavior. In addition to enabling change, acceptance is a near sine qua non for it. Someone who feels nonacceptance from a change agent resists the change. Gordon's base in Maslow and Rogers is evident here.

2. The Gordon system presumes relatively mentally healthy children; it is not designed for dealing with emotionally disturbed children.

3. A valued relationship exists between the teacher and the student. The system applies only when the teacher cares about the relationship and values it.

4. Students can take responsibility for and solve their own problems.

**Values**  Gordon values honesty and openness in communication. He values forthrightness in the recognition of and respect for one's own needs and those of others. He values nonjudgmental communication as an expression of that acceptance. He values the mutual respect of meaningful relationships where people, in caring about each other, try to meet each other's needs. He values behavior that facilitates the personal growth of others.

### Goals

1. Build a relationship between student and teacher whose result will be to make all teaching more effective.

2. Get students to take responsibility for their own behavior.

3. Increase the no-problem area and thus make more time available for teaching-learning.

**Rationale**  All classroom pupil behavior is either acceptable or unacceptable to the teacher. The rectangle in Figure 8.4 illustrates this universe of behavior. Everything above the line is acceptable; everything below the line is unacceptable. The placement of the line (and thus the size of the areas) varies with personality and within persons varies with time, mood, conditions, and environment. Whispering to a classmate may be acceptable one day and unacceptable another, depending on other factors in the teacher's life.

Another way of looking at the universe of classroom pupil behavior is problem ownership (Figure 8.5). A student's behavior is giving the teacher a problem, giving the student a problem (sometimes both), or giving no one a problem (like working on math problems, or going to sharpen a pencil in an undisruptive way). This no-problem area is called the teaching-learning area.

The causes of misbehavior are unmet needs of children and teachers. Instead of trying to identify and deal with these needs, teachers often use power, which results in poor relations with students;

**Figure 8.4.  Delineating Unacceptable and Acceptable Behavior**

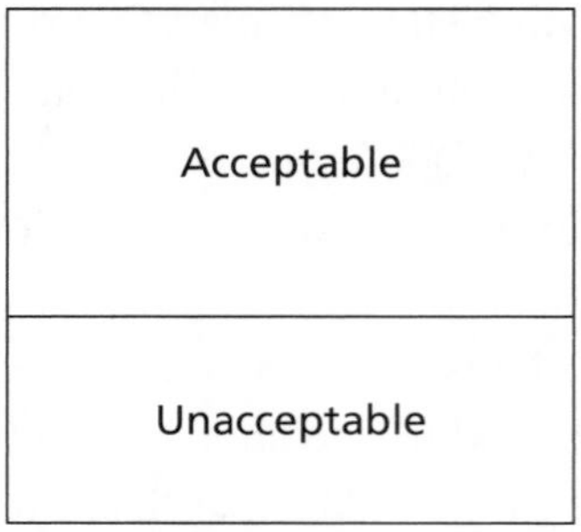

| |
|---|
| Acceptable |
| Unacceptable |

**Figure 8.5. Problem Ownership**

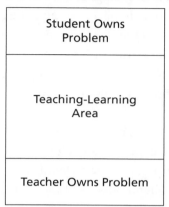

poor relations aggravate poor communication, and the circle goes around and around. Using communication skills to identify and meet teacher and student needs without the use of power is Gordon's strategy for reducing misbehavior.

**Steps**

1. Determine if a problem exists.
2. Own the problem. This one is harder than it sounds. The teacher owns the problem only if it is having a tangible effect on her. Adults often take responsibility for problems that are not really theirs. For example, Margie is dilly-dallying in the morning, is slow getting down to breakfast. Mother, who always has to harass her to get her to school on time, is a nervous wreck by the time the school bus finally leaves. Whose problem is this? Mother has made it hers. But who really owns the problem? Margie does. Right now Mother always solves it for her. If Mother lets Margie own her own problem, then Margie will have to deal with the consequences (walking to school, being late, waiting until Dad leaves for work and hitching a ride, also being late). If we choose to take responsibility for a problem

that is not really ours, it may begin to have some tangible effects on us (Mother is a tangible nervous wreck). But if we let the problem rest with its real owner, then only the owner feels the effects.

If the second-grade teacher is recapping open paint jars every night and mumbling about the irresponsibility of her class, whose problem is the paint jars? If the teacher lets the children own their problem of leaving paint jars uncapped and having only dried cake to paint with the next day, whose problem is it? If the students are working productively but noisily, and the class is next to the principal's office and the teacher is afraid the principal will get the wrong idea and give her a bad evaluation, whose problem is it?

3. Listen actively, that is, listen for the feeling content (encoded message) in the speaker's remarks and feed that feeling back to the speaker. ("What do you like in a girl, Dad?"—really meaning, "You're wondering what to do to get boys to like you.") Active listening tends to get at the real root of the problem, which may be buried under several layers of feeling. Good active listening extracts facts, meaning, and feeling content from heard remarks. While we are accustomed to listening for facts and meaning, we are not accustomed to listening for the important feeling content going on behind the remarks. If we are in the problem area, it may be this encoded feeling that is the cause of the problem, reflecting some unmet need. If we are dealing with a problem the student owns, "active listening" may help the student work his way through to a solution. But if the teacher owns the problem, I messages are brought to bear. Say that the room is too noisy for her tolerance and her conception of a level conducive to

learning, but the students aren't finding the noise offensive. The teacher sends an I message: "The noise level in this room is giving me a headache!" (description—effect). "I ache for some peace and quiet" (feeling).

4. Gear shifting. The I message may take care of the problem by itself. If the students have regard for the teacher and a satisfactory relationship with her, they may be motivated to change their behavior. But if they have a need of their own that is not being met, there is a conflict-of-needs situation. In this case, the teacher, after sending an I message, must gear-shift into active listening to identify the needs of the students. After a period of this, she may restate her I message. If both teacher and students own the problem, a no-lose solution may be called for.

5. Method III. This method is used only when it has been previously explained and "bought," at least for a trial, by the students. It consists of the following steps:
   • Define the problem in terms of needs.
   • Students and teacher mutually brainstorm solutions.
   • They mutually evaluate solutions.
   • They mutually pick one acceptable to both.
   • They determine how and when to implement.
   • They appoint a later date for reassessment of the solution and meet on the date.

6. Modifying the environment. Here the teacher takes the initiative to enrich, impoverish, restrict, enlarge, rearrange, simplify, systematize, or plan the environment, but not at the expense of the students.

**Principles of Teacher Response** In the no-problem area, the teacher can respond out of whatever framework she or he likes. But when there is a problem, the syntax provides clear steps to take, starting with defining and owning the problem. At the basis of all the steps are mutual respect and a desire to meet the other's needs. Principles of teacher response are empathy, separateness, facilitation, self-respect, and negotiation:

• Empathy is manifested in active listening.
• Separateness means allowing others to own their problems, not identifying with or assuming unto oneself the problems of others—letting people take responsibility for themselves.
• Facilitation means helping others find their own way to reach solutions to problems and facilitating their progress.
• Self-respect here means standing up for yourself too, not repressing your own needs, but recognizing, articulating, and seeking to meet them openly, all while helping others.
• Negotiation is the principle at the root of Method III solutions, the method called into play when there is a conflict of needs.

**Support System**
1. Active listening requires of the listener:
   • A trust in the ability of the student to solve his own problem.
   • Genuine acceptance of the other's feelings.
   • An understanding that feelings are transitory. ("I hate you!" Maybe he really does, at this moment, but not deeply, and probably not in five minutes.)
   • A real desire to want to help the student.
   • Separateness: an ability to psychologically separate yourself from another's problem, from identifying and assuming responsibility for the other, but not preventing you from helping.

- An understanding that students seldom start by sharing the real problem, which may be buried beneath several layers of feeling.

- Respect for the privacy of others, who may not want to reveal certain feelings to you or intend them only for your ears when they do.

- Time: enough time to go through the process.

2. I messages require of the sender:

- Honesty in expressing feelings.

- Risk: You are, after all, revealing a feeling to another person.

3. Gear shifting from I messages back to active listening requires significant ego control. With a strong need of your own, just expressed in the I message, suddenly you have to tune in to the other person's need and actively listen to it. (This is the most underrated and demanding aspect of Gordon's system.)

4. Method III requires that:

- Students understand what it's all about and buy it.

- Students believe you will do your part and not resort to power in the end.

- You have time to go through all the steps.

The elements of the support system pertain to attitudes and beliefs on the part of the teacher rather than physical supports. One must be a certain type of person, with certain understandings and beliefs, and have the time to carry out the system in a given situation, in order to make TET work.

**Social System**  Students and teachers are both conceived as individuals with needs to be respected and met. Whoever has the problem takes the initiative to send I messages to the person or persons whose behavior is having a tangible effect on them.

If the students are not skilled enough in sending I messages, the teacher is sensitive to their needs and uses active listening to bring them out. Conflict of needs is handled through the modified negotiation techniques of Method III or by having the teacher take the initiative to modify the environment so that the behavior goes into the no-problem area. Decisions are negotiated only when there is a conflict of needs. When acting in the no-problem area, there is nothing to prevent the teacher from taking the initiative and making instructional decisions based on other models of teaching.

**Effects**  The direct effects of the system, according to Gordon, are that "teachers like kids and kids like teachers"—that is, improved relationships. These improved relationships result from improved communication skills. Thus, the no-problem area expands in the rectangle, and more time is available for teaching and learning. More teaching and learning take place, and so teaching becomes more effective. The result of this humanistic approach is related to more effective teaching, but Gordon has a special understanding of "effectiveness."

There are nurturant effects as well. Remembering his base in Maslow and Rogers, and carefully reading his comments on the benefits of such things as active listening, reveals that "effectiveness" to Gordon means facilitating personal growth; that is what one becomes effective at doing. The new TET communication skills create better teacher-child relations, which manifest themselves in a changed learning environment of warmth, responsibility, mutual respect, and acceptance. The new learning environment facilitates personal growth and therefore simultaneously enhances academic learning.

Other nurturant effects are student modeling of active listening, I messages, and Method III techniques.

## Matching with Models

One of Dreikurs's statements has always struck us as significant: "All behavior is purposive." While his four "purposes" (attention, power, helplessness, revenge) don't seem nearly to cover the waterfront of motives behind misbehavior, the basic notion is a powerful one—people do what they do for a reason. They may not know the reason consciously, but it's always there. From this idea, we can recognize that behind all previous patterns of student misbehavior are needs, felt psychological needs that the student is trying to meet through the behavior. This doesn't mean we should excuse, accept, or accommodate the behavior; it simply tells us to figure out what the student is really trying to get through this behavior, which will help determine how to respond.

What the student may be trying to get, the unmet need that might be working actively inside him, might be:

| | |
|---|---|
| *Safety, security* | "I have enough trust. Things are at least minimally safe for me. I know what's going to happen next." |
| *Self-control* | "I can control myself. I'm not afraid I'll hurt myself or others." |
| *Affection* | "Somebody significant cares about me." |
| *Inclusion* | "I'm accepted in this group." |
| *Control as power* | "I have some control over my fate, over what happens to me." |
| *Self-esteem* | "I'm a worthwhile person." |
| *Recognition* | "Other people have esteem for what I've done, for who I am." |
| *Self-actualization* | "I'm realizing my potential." |

Most misbehavior need not be traced to unmet psychological needs. Students who test a teacher by calling out, passing notes, or doing a thousand other things may be doing nothing more complicated than simply testing the teacher. They're trying to see how much they can get away with. We're not talking about that here. We're talking about the one or two very resistant students who persistently misbehave despite solid classroom management, skillful instruction, ongoing attempts at relationship and climate building, and communication of expectations and limits.

The psychological needs listed above are arranged in sequence starting with the most fundamental. We will develop the hypothesis that there is a relation between the psychological needs driving a student's behavior and the most appropriate response strategy, along the lines shown in Table 8.2.

The six models are arranged, bottom to top, from those that demand the least maturity and competence of the student to those that demand the most. Students with unresolved needs in the early (lower) part of the sequence seem to be less mature emotionally and require models from the lower part of the continuum (behavior modification, self-awareness training). Students driven by later needs (such as control) seem better able to respond to more mature models (logical consequences, reality therapy).

Over a long period of time with a particular student, teachers should try to move up the chart. That is, they should start with models appropriate to the student's current needs, but help the student grow by moving into more mature models. In this way, they are moving students toward more self-discipline, even if they have to start off doing all the discipline for them (behavior modification). Students' growth toward improved mental health and emotional maturity is fostered by our ability to

**Table 8.2.  Matching Models to Psychological Needs**

| Psychological Need | Response Strategies |
| --- | --- |
| Self-actualization | Teacher effectiveness training |
| Recognition | |
| Self-esteem | Reality therapy |
| Control | Logical consequences |
| Inclusion | Personal influence |
| Affection | Self-awareness training |
| Safety/security/trust | Behavior modification |

modulate our models upward over time. If this seems like a big demand to be making on teachers—to master and practice appropriately six different models of discipline—we agree. Teachers aren't trained to do that in most university courses. But no one has to be an expert to start using this framework for understanding behaviors and trying to tailor responses. The fact is, we already have these students in our classes and we have to start somewhere. Getting to know and try the different models takes time and practice and proceeds much better if at least two teachers work on it together. But learning them is eminently doable, and an immense service to students who have no other stable anchors in their lives than their school and their teacher.

But let's backtrack. Where did we get the list of psychological needs to begin with? Historically many authors, such as Maslow (1962; see Figure 8.6), have brought to their work the notion of certain universal psychological needs shared by all humans. Some authors arrange them hierarchically.

"Hierarchically" to Maslow means that lower needs have the greatest strength until they are satisfied. For instance, if you're hungry, you don't worry much about social acceptance. If physiological and safety needs are met, social affiliation needs come to the fore. One tries to meet that need and it could account for much behavior we see. This same person, however, would not be driven strongly by needs for esteem and recognition; at least, that would not be the dominant force behind behavior until social affiliation needs were satisfied.

Maslow and others do not view these needs as developmental steps that once traversed do not need to be reworked. People move up and down the ladder according to current circumstances. If I lose my job, I am suddenly thrown two or three

**Figure 8.6.  Maslow's Hierarchy of Needs**

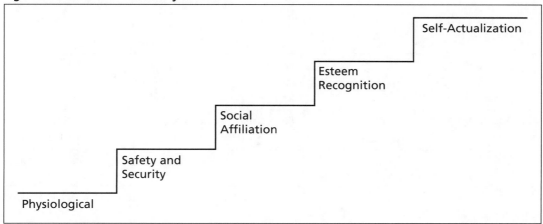

**Research for Better Teaching, Inc.** • One Acton Place, Acton, MA 01720 • (978) 263-9449 • www.RBTeach.com

steps down the stairs and begin operating out of my need for safety and security. If a student's parents get divorced, the same thing may happen.

In Table 8.3, we have spread out the basic psychological needs as described by a number of authors. Although each author uses different terms and highlights a different number of needs, there is considerable overlap among them, boiling down to eight basic needs that seem to be included by all the writers.

Note that we have included Erikson's eight psychological stages, or psychological crises, on our list, too. Erikson is a developmentalist; in other words, he sees these crises as stages that must be traversed before addressing later issues up the scale. And the crises usually do not reoccur once resolved, yet people (including children) can get stalled with unresolved crises at a lower level, which prevents their moving to healthy later stages of emotional development. What is relevant here is the connection between any one of Erikson's stages successfully navigated and the psychological need that gets met by that successful passage. There seem to be parallels between what Erikson sees happening—for example, during the crises of "initiative versus guilt"—and what Schutz (1967), Glasser (1986), and others see as meeting the basic need for control.

Taken together these writers seem to be sending some clear messages: (1) all humans have certain psychological needs in common, (2) the needs are related in regular ways (maybe hierarchical), and (3) needs drive behavior. When a basic need isn't met, it motivates observable behavior and enables us to account in some way for what we see.

How can we use those ideas to match resistant students with the six models? What is the relationship between a model a teacher may choose and the need that may appear to be driving the student's behavior?

In this section we offer some guidelines in answer to those questions, but the following caveat

**Table 8.3. Basic Psychological Needs**

| MASLOW | DREIKURS | SCHUTZ | GLASSER | ERIKSON | SUMMARY |
|---|---|---|---|---|---|
| Self-Actualization | | | | Integrity vs. despair  Generativity vs. sterility  Intimacy vs. isolation  Identity vs. identity confusion | Self-Actualization |
| Esteem  Recognition | Helplessness/ Competence | | Respect | Industry vs. inferiority | Self-Esteem |
| | Power | Control | | Initiative vs. guilt | Control |
| Social Affiliation | Attention | Inclusion  Affection | Relatedness | | Inclusion  Affection |
| | | | | Autonomy vs. shame | Self-Control |
| Safety/Security/Trust | | | | Trust vs. mistrust | Safety/Security/ Trust |

**Research for Better Teaching, Inc.** • One Acton Place, Acton, MA 01720 • (978)263-9449 • www.RBTeach.com

is necessary. We are not psychologists, and we are not trying to make teachers into psychologists. The last thing we want to do is to get teachers to label a student with a psychological need and begin "treatment." "Diagnosing" and labeling a student is always risky; it carries unintended consequences, even when done by health care professionals. Teachers should never diagnose, but they should try to use behavior to get clues to needs and make connections to models. That will be better than using one model with everyone as if it were *the* method of discipline, and it will be better than random, eclectic bouncing around with different models.

We are always trying to move students up the list toward the more mature models because a person who can respond to the reality therapy approach, for example, is more emotionally mature than a person who needs behavior modification all the time. In any given year, you may find yourself starting off with personal influence for Jimmy, but able to move to reality therapy by the end of the year. Many connections and transitions between the models are possible, but one always tries to move up the list with a student. Over a period of several years in a public school, we have seen skilled teachers move a student along from Behavior Modification in grades K and 1, to TET by grade 5. Other things outside the teacher's control must support a student's personal growth to enable dramatic progressions like that, but we are also quite certain it could not have happened without a team of teachers who shared this point of view and planned with each other to help the student grow.

### Six Typical Profiles

Figure 8.7 summarizes key elements of the six models we have discussed. Behavior modification is the most controlling of the models, and one thing we know about it is that it really works. If you do it well enough, you can get a student to do almost any-

thing, even high school students. Why would a teacher want to be so controlling? One reason might be desperation: the class (or the student) is so disruptive you can't think of anything else to do. Or students may simply not have in their repertoires the behaviors they need to function properly: not know how to pick up and put away, not know how to do assignments in order, not know how to meet deadlines, not know how to resolve a dispute without fists. Behavior modification can allow students to experience behaviors they would never try on their own and thus discover that there are other ways of doing things. Students in extreme inner states of insecurity or anxiety can be helped to function and get through the demands of the day by leaning on the strong structures of a behavior modification program. It supports them and helps them function during times when they are weak and confused. Rather than controlling in these circumstances, behavior modification is supportive, even protective. It stops the negative cycle of behavior that is destroying a student's relations with others and confirming a self-image that is probably already poor. It gives students a lifeline to hang onto until they can gain some control over themselves. And that is what we want to work for ultimately: self-control and self-discipline.

The self-awareness models are also suitable for students in tenuous emotional states. These students may intellectually know the difference between productive and unproductive behavior but be unable to control themselves. Their tempers often flare out of control; they don't trust themselves and have difficulty forming friendships. They may withdraw and spend a lot of time drawing, reading, or wrapped up in some objective activity. If they have a bent for science or art, they may produce outstanding projects, and in fact only through these projects do they build the superficial relationships they do have with others. They hate to talk

**Figure 8.7. Six Families of Response to Resistant Children's Behavior**

| REPLACING AND TEACHING NEW BEHAVIORS (Behavior Modification) | SELF-AWARENESS (Cognitive Behavior Modification) | PERSONAL INFLUENCE |
|---|---|---|
| Identify target behavior<br>Tell child/goal set<br>Clip reinforcers<br>Keep count<br>Reinforce approximations<br>Note progress to child<br>(Buckholt et al.)<br><br>Teach to think of alternatives, consequences of behavior, impulse control<br>(Shure and Spivack) | Looking on<br>"I see you're starting to get out of control."<br>"You're getting out of control. I will help" intervening/describing what you are doing<br>Hold<br>Teaching children to read their own signals, be aware of their actions and feelings<br><br>(Meichenbaum)<br>(Wolfgang) | Personal relationship building<br>Clear expectations of a significant other<br>Direct<br>Specific<br>Repeated<br>Positive expectancy<br>"You can do it"<br>Tenacity<br>Consistent reactions<br>Noticing<br>High teacher affect<br>(Hymes)<br>(Wallen and Wallen) |

| CONSEQUENCES | TAKING RESPONSIBILITY (Reality Therapy) | PROBLEM SOLVING (Teacher Effectiveness Training) |
|---|---|---|
| Teacher pairings<br>Limits<br>Warnings<br>Removal<br>Enlisting the class<br>(Sarason)<br><br>Creative and relevant logical consequences<br>No "battles"<br>Reality of the social order, not punishment<br>(Dreikurs) | What are you doing?<br>Is it helping?<br>What are you going to do about it?<br>Involvement<br>Humor, no excuses, tenacity<br>Seeing oneself as worthwhile and connected to others<br>(Glasser) | Teaching children to see their messages clearly, listen to others' messages accurately, and negotiate solutions<br>Active listening<br>"I" messages<br>Gear shifting<br>Method III<br>(Gordon) |

**Research for Better Teaching, Inc.** • One Acton Place, Acton, MA 01720 • (978) 263-9449 • www.RBTeach.com

about their feelings, in fact, are unable to, afraid to, and may refuse to if pressed. When they do speak about themselves, it is in connection with events and objects, not people or feelings. For young children in this plight, the strategies of Wolfgang (1977) and Lederman (1969) are on target. For older students, the self-instructional strategies of Meichenbaum (1977) are more appropriate, though forms of these are also useful with young children.

Students who are suited to the personal influence model often generate love-hate feelings in us. They have likable, charming, even lovable qualities. One moment you feel like hugging them, and the next you want to throw them through the wall. One-on-one they tend to be great; in a group, they can be poison, inciters, and show-offs. Curiously, they are often quiet in large groups where there is more anonymity, but incorrigible in small groups where the social tensions of establishing themselves with the others are too much for them. When they arrive in the morning, they may drift around the room, checking out what everyone is doing, moving from thing to thing, settling in nowhere. They have a need for affection and inclusion, which are often missing in their lives. In those morning meanderings, they are looking for their place, wondering where they can plug in, and they don't quite know how to connect. Their reputations and their relations with the other students don't make entry easy for them in unstructured situations. They long for friends, for closeness with other students and with the teacher, but they repeatedly behave in ways guaranteed to antagonize. The structure, the demands, the warmth, and the relationship building of the personal influence model help them bridge a difficult period in their lives.

With younger children, one may borrow from behavior modification to help these students gain more awareness and control over their most disrup-

tive behaviors. With older students, contingency contracting can help supplement the tough half of the personal influence model.

Some students say no, defy, and are openly challenging of authority at every turn. These students may be candidates for the logical consequences model. They refuse to do their work or do it only when they feel like it. They look for, and actually invite, power conflicts with authority figures. Such students can be tyrants in games with others and may do a considerable amount of bullying and outrageous pushing around of other students and of teachers too, up to the limit they can get away with. Their psychological need for control is driving the behavior—only the need has gone haywire, gone out of perspective, and is damaging these students and those with whom they come in contact. They have come to believe, as Dreikurs would say, that the only way they count in the world is by showing their power and controlling others. That is how they think they must act in order to be significant and worthwhile people. This mistaken belief must be changed if their behavior is to change in any way other than a temporary one.

Dreikurs's method avoids the power conflicts the student seeks and tries to teach the reality of the social order through logical consequences. These consequences do not represent the imposed power of the teacher, but rather the way things really work in the world. Thus, students can't get mad at the teacher and back into their old unproductive power game. They begin to see their behavior as having consequences for them because the behavior is incompatible with how the social order works, not because the adults "won't let me." They begin to learn something about the social contract. They are put in a position of seeing their behaviors in relation to what a society, a group, needs to function, and the group itself is used in classroom meetings to reinforce that message, which brings us to

Glasser's Reality Therapy and Classroom Meeting model, where the use of the group is more developed.

Candidates for reality therapy are students who are acting irresponsibly—students who are always forgetting books, showing up late, not doing work, missing appointments and obligations, blaming others, and not perceiving or at least acknowledging their own role in conflicts. These students may act quite disruptively, knocking over others' books, punching students they pass in the hallway, or slamming lockers. But they are not premeditated or deliberate about these acts in the same way as an attention seeker would be. They just seem to fall into these behaviors. They're like emotional drifters who are easily led into bad practices and bad company. When asked why they bumped into a student they'll likely say, "I don't know," and shrug. Given punishment and reprimands, they won't argue, won't comply, and won't change.

In reality therapy, students are brought up against the consequences of their behavior for their relations with other people. It is a more personal focus than the Dreikurs model, where the intended learning is that a particular behavior doesn't work in the world. Glasser's learning is more like, "It isn't working for me. Now what am I going to do about it?" This is toward the top of the scale of maturity among the six models because the responsibility for seeing, evaluating, and changing the behavior lies with the student, although an involved teacher is necessary to get the student into each step. Glasser, who doesn't focus much on the causes of misbehavior, likes to deal with the here and now. Many people, he believes, who act crazy can decide not to act crazy. They have the inner control to do that if they can go through the reality therapy steps and decide that it is worth their while to do so—if they have someone who's involved enough to walk the road with them and not give up on them. So Glasser might be inclined

to use reality therapy with students operating at quite a low level.

Classroom meetings broaden the sense of involvement from between teacher and student to include students with each other. Eventually through these meetings, students gain a place to talk to each other about what's on their minds. Resistant students get to hear how others are perceiving them, and the others are enabled to share those perceptions in a problem-solving environment.

A good candidate for teacher effectiveness training (TET) is a student who appears resentful, maybe sitting out his school time like a prison term, occasionally rebellious or wise, but usually functional. Work may be satisfactory or inferior. These students may feel the teacher never listens to them, and the teacher may feel they have no respect for or understanding of what school is all about. There is poor communication between teacher and student, and both feel their needs are unmet. Both are unsatisfied with their relationship in class even though overt conflict may not be frequent between them.

Such a student usually has a cumulative history of increasing hostility and seems ready to manifest it toward all teachers, unless they prove themselves otherwise. With other students, relationships are often fine. It is to adults that the student has begun to generalize the notion that "all they ever do is give orders, tell me what to do. They never listen." And the student has given up sending messages about his complaints.

TET can also be the right method for a student with a problem where, through active listening, a skillful teacher can help the student reach his own solution. TET isn't a model that lines up with a particular psychological need like some of the others do. It is the most mature of the models, because it calls on the student to have sufficient empathy or at least understanding to read a teacher's "I message" and be willing to respond through no-lose (or win-win) negotiation. Method III solutions themselves require listening and sending skills on the part of both parties that are difficult for very troubled students. Gordon himself says that TET is not designed for disturbed students. However, it is our experience that active listening and I messages are skills that are immensely valuable on their own, even when one is not using the whole TET model. Active listening is very helpful, almost necessary, in the self-awareness model, and "I messages" complement the personal influence model nicely. And, of course, active listening is the key skill for unlocking the longer-term resentment of the student profiled above.

To summarize, each of these six strategies is most appropriate for a particular kind of student. We have offered a typical profile for each of the six as general guidelines for matching and referred to psychological needs that may be behind the profile. To pick a strategy, a teacher must start with the student's behaviors. They should be written down—the what, when, with whom, how often, and where of these behaviors. Simply listing behaviors and circumstances, however, will not be enough. How a behavior is done (as reported by an observer) is important too, for from that "how," we will try to infer the motive behind it: Did Charlie knock over the books casually as he passed them, a kind of afterthought in his meanderings (reality therapy candidate)? Did he swagger down the aisle and knock them over with a cocky flick and insolent glare back (logical consequences candidate)? Did he let out some pent-up resentment simmering all morning and knock them over in exasperation (TET candidate)? Did he knock them over in an impulsive pell-mell rush to get to his seat (self-awareness candidate)? What are the other behaviors that make up Charlie's profile? In developing that profile, we may get closer to where Charlie is in life and see more clearly what strategy is most

likely to help him function successfully and grow emotionally.

It is interesting to reflect on how the teacher's role changes in different models (see Table 8.4). In TET the teacher is conceived as an equal to the student: both have their needs and their rights, and both participate in looking for no-lose solutions that will consider both of their points of view. In reality therapy, the teacher functions as therapist; though involved with and supportive of the student, they are no longer equals: the teacher is now a helping person who regularly and directly brings the student back to earth and makes him or her face facts. In logical consequences, there is more detachment yet, with the teacher now representing society. Teachers who use personal influence become admired authority figures to students. Self-awareness training turns teachers into coaches and systems designers and is not far removed from behavior modification, within which teachers are not only systems designers but operators of the machine.

As one goes down the list, the student's role diminishes and the teacher swells in authority, responsibility, control, and status. Conversely, as one goes up the list, the teacher diminishes in importance and the student grows as a fully functioning, socially aware person who can deal with life successfully. Through understanding teacher and student roles in the various models, we can broaden our perspective on the relations of the models to each other and underline the value of seeing them in a developmental progression. That perspective says to us simply: take students where they are and help them grow in maturity.

The arrows in Table 8.4 indicate some of the common progressions when students are able to respond to increasingly mature strategies. Behavior modification can help a student get in control enough to enter self-awareness training or respond directly to a teacher using personal influence. Both

**Table 8.4. Variations in a Teacher's Role Using Different Models**

| BEHAVIORAL CHARACTERISTICS | MODEL | TEACHER'S ROLE |
|---|---|---|
| resentment | T.E.T. | an equal person |
| irresponsibility | Reality Therapy | therapist |
| defiance & attention seeking | Logical Consequences | representation of society |
| impulsiveness | Personal Influences | significant other |
| ignorance or lack of control | Self-Awareness | coach & confederate |
|  | Behavior Modification | operating the system |

**Research for Better Teaching, Inc.** • One Acton Place, Acton, MA 01720 • (978)263-9449 • www.RBTeach.com

personal influence and logical consequences can be a springboard to reality therapy and classroom meetings. It is neither necessary nor appropriate to move through all six strategies with any one student. For a certain student, for example, the most natural step after personal influence may be reality therapy. At a certain point, the student may not need a teacher to act as his conscience but may be able to move directly to evaluating his own behavior.

When deciding to investigate the use of a model of discipline, consider these questions:

1. Have I gathered enough objective data on the student's behavior?
2. Have I presented the information to a team to get additional input and questions?
3. Have we come up with the best guesses as to the psychological need?
4. Have we picked a matched response model?
5. Have we worked out a coordinated plan for all teachers who contact this youngster?
6. Have we included the youngster's family in the plan?
7. Have we provided for periodic review and modification of the plan?

## Matching the Models: An Exercise in Analysis

Following are some profiles of students we have known. As you read them, consider which of the six models of discipline you think would be most appropriate and explain your rationale for your choice. This exercise is particularly beneficial when done with colleagues as a group.

### Shanda

Shanda seems on the edge of life. She's quite unpredictable. Sometimes she behaves like a lamb, looking at you with those beautiful brown doe eyes. She likes to cuddle and responds to warmth and physical affection. She will try her work for a while and some days (not often) gets quite involved in it. More often she does a little (or none) and is off around the room.

She'll grab things from other kids, push and shove, yell, and be combative. In class meetings or instructional groups, she may yell; when singing with a group, she'll be the first to degenerate into shouting or meaningless yells. Occasional periods of passive immobility, anger and striking out, and out-of-control behavior (throwing things, messing things) speak of deep inner sadness.

Shanda is six years old and from a single-parent home. Her mother is often not there when she returns in the afternoon, but she's not always sure which afternoons these will be. She has a key. She walks home with her brother who is five. Her mother is loving but unstable and troubled herself.

In large and small groups, whether for a class meeting or for instruction, she often bursts out of control: yelling, shouting, tugging, or pinching kids near her. She often smiles as she does this, as if it's a form of showing off, but she also responds quickly to teacher reprimands for a few seconds. The expression that flashes across her face when reprimanded shows acknowledgment that she's done something wrong, but then there she goes again. She is often removed from groups to a corner of the room or the hallway.

She doesn't get much work done and has a short attention span, but she is a bright child. She responds to warmth and cuddling and seeks out adult laps. She does considerable running in the room and lots of grabbing, fighting, and bumping. When removed from the group, she may sob deeply and genuinely for considerable periods of time. These periods of wrenching sadness and crying are not uncommon. Often she bursts into tears for no apparent reason.

You never know how she'll come in through the door. But what you see the first few minutes usually sets the tone for the day. A frequent scene is Shanda standing at the door, not coming all the way in, peering anxiously around looking at what is going on, being defensive about her space, probably getting bumped by a child behind her going in, and responding with a punch and angry face.

She will space out for short periods, looking sad and immobile; at other times, she may get quite involved with a story or a science activity. She can work cooperatively with other children, but these times often degenerate into fights over sharing or over real or imagined slights. She is easily set out of control, especially at transition times.

If you call for cleanup and lineup for lunch, she'll throw things in the general direction of where they're supposed to go (or just leave them where they lie) and run to the door. Frequent bumpings and fights result at these times. Running seems the only response she knows for a call to go from one place to another.

At times, she won't come at all, seeming not even to hear, being totally absorbed in blocks or clay. These periods of total absorption are less frequent than abuse of materials like sitting at the clay table making small balls and throwing them at nearby students or pretending a large shopping cart is a runaway car and crashing another child's shopping cart.

The only thing that seems to settle her down is physical restraint and cuddling. Sometimes you have to go through five or ten minutes of restraint.

## Ken

Ken is a ninth grader, though he looks a little young. He's always in hot water, though this happens rarely in class. Last week he got into a wrestling match—basically playful—with a buddy and destroyed a bed of spring flowers under the principal's office window by rolling all over them.

In private, teachers call him a "wild kid." He seems to live from moment to moment and to have no roots. Others can get him involved into almost any kind of mischief: stealing and vandalism (painting the dome of the new gym with silver spray-painted obscenities). He now occasionally thinks up a few things like that to do on his own.

He seems to act with no internal guidance system, an unguided missile; he has no goals, nothing to shoot for, nothing to get out of school. Beneath the rollicking prankster seems a fearful young man who, when caught and confronted with his deeds, shrinks visibly. When being addressed by the vice principal for discipline, he will not talk much, shrug his shoulders, look very depressed and alone. He accepts punishment, and it does absolutely no good. He makes promises and disregards them entirely.

### Freddie

Freddie seems out of contact with his body, ungainly and awkward, almost disconnected from his limbs. He looks as if he might bump into something at any moment without knowing it, and sometimes he does. He is eleven years old, tall for his age, and has a high-pitched voice.

He will come into the cafeteria, usually toward the end of the line. He walks with a lurching, shuffling gait, head bobbing. He will look around, head almost swiveling. By the time he's gotten through the line and to a table, he will be talking very loudly and a little wildly. Squeezing into a seat at a table, he may be abusive to adjacent children: "Hey, you slobbo, let me in!" Minutes later, there may be wild laughter, grabbing or throwing of food, and out-of-control behavior. The cafeteria overstimulates him, as do other large group settings.

Freddie is not hyperactive. In fact, in class he is most often completely absorbed in his work—his own work, that is, not the teacher's. He likes to draw fantastic machines and read about anything scientific, immersing himself in these activities at every opportunity and withdrawing from class participation.

In total class instruction and small group work, he calls out, does a lot of things seemingly to be center stage, and is often silly. If he can withdraw, he will just as soon pass these times covertly drawing or studying something that interests him.

He can get very angry at other students and has hurt a few with hard punches or by pushing them into desks this year. He loses his temper, has outbursts, and gets out of control.

He won't talk about his feelings and can't seem to respond to anything that asks him to talk from inside. He talks about things.

He knows a great deal about a number of scientific and technical topics and loves to repeat this knowledge to adults. As a younger child, he was a fanatical and knowledgeable dinosaur expert. In general, his mind absorbs facts and general information, but his lack of concentration seems to block him from making connections, from developing concepts you might expect from so verbally advanced a boy.

In skill work, like determining if a word would be on a given dictionary page or learning the algorithm for long division, he has very little patience; he tends to rip up papers if he doesn't get it right away. He won't ask questions, and when it's reexplained for him, he'll leap into applying what he's absorbed before the explanation is complete, almost with panic. Once he's gotten it, though, he can do it competently and generalize to new situations. He will race through work, however, and make many mistakes.

He doesn't have any real friends but does play with other children in such activities as fort building outside. He will not enter organized games readily, if at all. His play will be something that allows him to do his own thing, play his own part, focus his eyes and body on, say, the fort. His talk at these times will be about the fort or about some dramatic fantasy the children develop as they build the fort: "Hey, look at this cool slide here [that he's just made]. They'll be able to go ZOOM over the wall there." He will seldom look at another child as he speaks.

## Summary

We began this chapter with two questions that represent primary concerns related to discipline in classrooms:

- What do I have to do to get students to apply themselves to their work and stop fooling around and being disruptive?
- How do I build self-discipline and responsibility in students?

This chapter provides a wealth of options to consider that are within teachers' control and a range of possibilities for dealing with the neediest students. The twenty-one questions below serve as a summary of areas explored in this chapter and as diagnostic tools for prevention and management:

1. Do I use effective attention moves and make them promptly enough?
2. Do I maintain momentum in lessons?
3. Do I manage time and space well?
4. Have I established routines that will minimize downtime, delays, and distractions?
5. Do I build good personal relationships with students?
6. Is the work too hard or too easy for some students?
7. Do I vary instructional format and materials enough to avoid students being bored and to ensure that students of all modality strengths and learning styles can get it?
8. Is my instruction clear to all students? Do I check for understanding frequently and with all students to ensure they are with me?
9. Are the rules and consequences clear and specific enough to both me and to the students?
10. Do I communicate what I want from students in a way that is direct, specific, and repeated and shows positive expectancy (both "you can" and "you will")?
11. Do the students know how to do what I'm expecting of them?
12. Do I recognize and reward responsible behavior effectively?
13. Do I have a range of consequences rather than one rigid response for every transgression? Are the consequences logical rather than punitive?
14. Do I deliver consequences in a way that is consistent and tenacious, prompt, and matter-of-fact and indicates student choice?
15. Do I take sufficient time and care at the beginning of the year to establish all of the above?
16. Do I have high enough expectations for behavior no matter what the students' backgrounds?
17. Do I refuse to accept excuses?
18. Are there value or culture clashes between the students and me (or among students) that might account for distracting or disruptive behavior?
19. Are there physical reasons (hearing or vision loss, organic hyperactivity) that might account for a student's distracting or disruptive behavior?
20. Do I intentionally and explicitly build community in the class (knowledge about, appreciation of, cooperation with one another)?
21. Do I give students a real and legitimate sense of control, influence, responsibility, and power in class life?

To check your knowledge about Discipline see the quiz on our Web site at **www.RBTeach.com/ rbteach/quiz/Discipline.html.**

## Source Materials on Discipline

Adler, A. *The Problem Child.* New York: Putnam, 1963.

Arnold, J. "Simone Was Out of Control and So Was I." *Learning,* 1987, *16*(4), 44–45.

Aronson, E. *The Jigsaw Classroom.* Thousand Oaks, Calif.: Sage, 1978.

Bernstein, D., Borkovec, T., and Hazlett-Stevens, H. *New Directions in Progressive Relaxation Training: A Guidebook for Helping Professionals.* Westport, Conn.: Greenwood, 2000.

Bruno-Golden, B. "Progressive Relaxation Training for Children: A Guide for Parents and Children." *Special Children,* AASE/Box 168, Fryeburg, Maine (Fall 1974).

Buckholt, D. R., and others. *CLAIM—Classroom and Instructional Management Program.* New York: Walker, 1975.

Canter, L. *Classroom Management for Academic Success.* Bloomington, Ind.: Solution Tree, 2006.

Canter, L., and Canter, M. *Assertive Discipline: Positive Behavior Management for Today's Classroom.* Bloomington, Ind.: Solution Tree, 2001. Copyright © 1976 by Solution Tree (formerly National Educational Service), 304 Kirkwood Avenue, Bloomington, IN 47404, 800-733-6786. Used with permission of Solution Tree.

Charney, R. S. *Teaching Children to Care: Classroom Management for Ethical and Academic Growth, K–8.* Turners Falls, Mass.: Northeast Foundation for Children, 2002. To learn more about the Responsive Classroom© approach to teaching, you can visit www.responsiveclassroom.org. Reprinted with permission.

Colarusso, C. *Diagnostic Educational Grouping: Strategies for Teaching.* Doylestown, Pa.: Bucks County Public Schools, 1972.

Curwin, R. L. *Making Good Choices: Developing Responsibility, Respect, and Self-Discipline in Grades 4–9.* Thousand Oaks, Calif.: Corwin Press, 2003.

Dinkmeyer, D., and Dreikurs, R. *Encouraging Children to Learn.* Sussex, England: Taylor and Francis, 2000.

Dishon, D., and O'Leary, P. W. *A Guidebook for Cooperative Learning.* Holmes Beach, Fla.: Learning Publications, 1998.

Dreikurs, R. *Psychology in the Classroom.* New York: HarperCollins, 1957.

Dreikurs, R., and Cassel, P. *Discipline Without Tears: What to Do with Children Who Misbehave.* New York: Hawthorn Books, 1972.

Dreikurs, R., Cassel, P., and Kehoe, D. *Discipline Without Tears.* (2nd ed.) New York: Penguin Group, 1990.

Dreikurs, R., and Grey, L. A. *A New Approach to Classroom Discipline: Logical Consequences.* New York: HarperCollins, 1968.

Dunn, R. (1994). "The Dunn and Dunn Learning Styles Model: Theory, Research, and Application." In M. F. Shaughnessy (Ed.), *Education in the 21st Century* (pp. 131–141). Portales: Eastern New Mexico University Press.

Erikson, E. H. *Childhood and Society.* (2nd ed.) New York: Norton, 1963.

Ginott, H. *Between Parent and Child.* New York: Macmillan, 1965.

Glasser, W. *Reality Therapy.* New York: HarperCollins, 1965.

Glasser, W. *Schools Without Failure.* New York: HarperCollins, 1969. Reprinted with permission of HarperCollins Publishers.

Glasser, W. *Control Theory in the Classroom.* New York: HarperCollins, 1986.

Glasser, W., and Dotser, K. L. *Choice Theory in the Classroom.* New York: HarperCollins, 1998.

Gordon, T. *Parent Effectiveness Training.* New York: Peter Wyden, 1970.

Gordon, T., and Burch, N. *Teacher Effectiveness Training: The Program Proven to Help Teachers Bring Out the Best in Students of All Ages.* New York: Three Rivers Press, 2003.

Hersey, P., and Blanchard, H. *The Family Game.* Reading, Mass.: Addison-Wesley, 1978.

House, E. R., and Lapan, S. D. *Survival in the Classroom.* Needham Heights, Mass.: Allyn & Bacon, 1978.

Hymes, L., Jr. *Behavior and Misbehavior.* Upper Saddle River, N.J.: Prentice Hall, 1955.

Johnson, D. W., and Johnson, R. T. *Learning Together and Alone.* (2nd ed.). Upper Saddle River, N.J.: Prentice Hall, 1987.

Johnston, D. H. *Lessons for Living: Simple Solutions for Life's Problems.* Macon, Ga.: Dagali Press, 2001.

Jones, F. H. *Positive Classroom Discipline.* New York: McGraw-Hill, 1987.

Jones, F. H. *Tools for Teaching.* Santa Cruz, Calif.: Frederic H. Jones and Associates, 2007. Reprinted by permission.

Joyce, B., Weil, M., and Calhoun, E. *Models of Teaching.* Needham Heights, Mass.: Allyn & Bacon, 2003.

Koeppen, A. "Relaxation Training for Children." *Elementary School Guidance and Counseling,* Oct. 1974, pp. 14–20.

Krasnow, J. *The Social Competency Program of the Reach Out to Schools Project.* Wellesley, Mass.: Wellesley Centers for Women, 1993.

Lantieri, L. *Schools with Spirit: Nurturing the Inner Lives of Children and Teachers.* Boston: Beacon Press, 2001.

Lederman, J. *Anger in the Rocking Chair.* New York: McGraw-Hill, 1969.

Martin, G., and Pear, J. *Behavior Modification.* Upper Saddle River, N.J.: Prentice Hall, 1978.

Maslow, A. *Toward a Psychology of Being.* Princeton, N.J.: Van Nostrand, 1962.

Meichenbaum, D. *Cognitive Behavior Modification.* New York: Plenum Press, 1977. Reprinted with permission. www.melissainstitute.org.

Mendler, A. N., and Curwin, R. L. *Taking Charge in the Classroom.* Reston, Va.: Reston Publishing Co., 1983.

Mendler, A. N., and Curwin, R. L. *Discipline with Dignity.* Alexandria, Va.: Association for Supervision and Curriculum Development, 1999.

Payne, R. K. *A Framework for Understanding Poverty.* Baytown,

Tex.: RFT Publishing, 2005. Reprinted with permission.

Pierson, C. *Resolving Classroom Conflict.* Palo Alto, Calif.: Learning Handbooks, 1974.

Rogers, D. M. *Classroom Discipline: An Idea Handbook for Elementary School Teachers.* New York: Prentice Hall Professional Technical Reference, 1987.

Ryan, M. "Students Who Act Up." *Parade Magazine,* Jan. 18, 1987, p. 10. Reprinted with permission. Copyright © 1987 Michael Ryan. All rights reserved.

Sarason, S. *Revisiting the Culture of the School and the Problem of Change.* New York: Teachers College Press, 1996.

Schutz, W. J. *Expanding Human Awareness.* New York: Grove Press, 1967.

Sharam, S. "Cooperation Learning in Small Groups." *Review of Educational Research,* 1980, *50,* 241–272.

Shulmand, M., and Meckler, E. *Bringing Up a Moral Child: A New Approach for Teaching Your Child to Be Kind, Just and Responsible.* New York: Doubleday, 1994. Copyright © 1985, 1994 by Michael Schulman and Eva Mekler. Used by permission of Doubleday, a division of Random House, Inc.

Shure, M. *I Can Problem Solve. (ICPS): An Interpersonal Cognitive Problem-Solving Program.* Champaign, Ill.: Research Press, 1992.

Shure, M. *Raising a Thinking Child.* New York: Pocket Books, 1996a. Audiotape.

Shure, M. *Raising a Thinking Child Workbook.* New York: Holt, 1996b.

Shure, M. *Raising a Thinking Preteen: The I Can Problem Solve Program for 8- to 12-Year-Olds.* New York: Owl Books, 2000.

Shure, M. B., and Spivack, G. *Problem Solving Techniques in Childrearing.* San Francisco: Jossey-Bass, 1978. Reprinted by permission of Myrna Shure.

Slavin, R. E. "Cooperative Learning." *Review of Educational Research,* 1980, *50,* 315–342.

Stanford, G. *Developing Effective Classroom Groups.* New York: Hart, 1977.

Swap, S. "Disturbing Classroom Behaviors: A Developmental and Ecological View." *Exceptional Children,* Nov. 1974, pp. 163–172.

Van Houton, R. *Learning Through Feedback.* New York: Human Sciences Press, 1980.

Wallen, C. J., and Wallen, L. *Effective Classroom Management.* Needham Heights, Mass.: Allyn & Bacon, 1978.

Wilt, J., and Watson, B. *Relationship Building Activities.* Waco, Tex: WORD, 1978.

Wolfgang, C. *Helping Aggressive and Passive Pre-Schoolers Through Play.* Columbus, Ohio: Charles E. Merrill, 1977.

Wolfgang, C. *Solving Discipline and Classroom Management Problems: Methods and Models for Today's Teachers.* (6th ed.). Hoboken, N.J.: Wiley, 2004.

Wolfgang, C., and Glickman, C. *Solving Discipline Problems.* Needham Heights, Mass.: Allyn & Bacon, 1980.

Wood, S., Bishop, R., and Cohen, D. *Parenting: Four Patterns of Child Rearing.* New York: Hart, 1978.

Wubbolding, R. E. *Reality Therapy for the 21st Century.* New York: Taylor & Francis, 2000.

# INTRODUCTION TO INSTRUCTION

Part Two addresses the skills teachers use to deliver the goods: the cognitive knowledge and skills of the academic disciplines. Chapter Nine, "Clarity," summarizes many decades of research on cognitive science as it applies to successful teaching and learning. This is the material most people think of when they hear the word *teaching*. In this book we have defined *teaching* as a much bigger construct: anything a person does that increases the probability of intended learning. Nevertheless, Clarity skills are vital for creating successful learning experiences for students. They scaffold learning, make it accessible in varied and powerful ways, check to see if it has been assimilated, and get inside students' heads to identify misconceptions and confusions. The repertoires within Chapter Nine form a bedrock of good pedagogy.

Chapter Ten, "Principles of Learning," summarizes over a century of laboratory research by cognitive psychologists. This domain of teaching skill, neglected in recent decades and substantially missing from teacher preparation, is a powerhouse of technology for making learning efficient. Those interested in accelerating student learning and making it more durable will find a treasury of techniques here. Experienced and already successful teachers often exclaim on meeting this body of information, "Why haven't I heard about these principles before!!"

Chapter Eleven, "Models of Teaching," will appeal especially to readers five to fifteen years into their careers who are looking for intellectual stimulation for themselves and their students. This is the section of the knowledge base for designers who wish to craft lessons that develop thinking skills as well as academic knowledge.

The technology in Part Two is a rich resource for teachers when they are planning lessons. It is especially valuable for teachers working together in professional learning communities to come up with reteaching strategies.

# Clarity

Why is it that some people are better than others at getting us to understand things? What do they do to be more clear? Consider this episode: $2^2 \times 2^3 = ?$ is the problem and many in the class have gotten it wrong.

"What many of you did," says the teacher, "was to multiply the 2's so you got $2^2 \times 2^3 = 4^5$. That's wrong. It's $2^5$." He erases "$4^5$" and writes "$2^5$" in its place. "The 2 doesn't change." Then he moves on to the next problem.

The teacher has covered the problem, but he certainly hasn't explained it. The episode is notable for its omissions—for what didn't happen—more than for what did. The teacher didn't check to see if there was any understanding of the rule at work for doing this sort of problem ($N^a \times N^b = N^{a+b}$). He didn't ask students to explain to see if there was any conceptual understanding of why the rule works. He didn't do any explaining of the process for doing the problem. Importantly, he didn't elicit any student participation to see how many students and which ones might still be confused. For instance, he didn't check to see if any students could now do a similar problem. All he did was indicate wrong and right answers. There is little about this episode that is clear—to either the teacher or his students.

Clear teachers do far more than speak or lecture in an organized and easily comprehensible way, though that is not irrelevant to student understanding. These teachers guide student thinking in deliberate ways along a structured route engineered for thinking and learning. This is the scientific part of teaching. We can use what we know from a century of cognitive science to maximize the chances of students' assimilating, integrating, remembering, and being able to use concepts and skills. No content expert comes into teaching equipped to accomplish this skill-intensive job.

The area of performance we are calling Clarity means to cause mental acts within students' heads that will result in their understanding or being able to do something. It's what happens inside the students' heads that matters, not what the teacher is doing. Fortunately, what teachers do has a great deal to do with what goes on in students' heads if they use the knowledge base of cognitive science well. Unfortunately, as Graham Nuthall (2005) points out, it is possible to have a smoothly functioning, lively classroom where all the students appear happily occupied with worthwhile tasks and yet no mental acts conducive to learning are taking place.

This chapter is the heart of what people usually mean when they think of teaching: cognitive interaction. There are ten categories of teacher behavior in Clarity, each with its independent, deep, and validated research base, and we have divided them into five functions:

1. Framing the learning
2. Presenting information
3. Creating mental engagement
4. Getting inside students' heads (that is, cognitive empathy)
5. Consolidating and anchoring the learning (See Table 9.1)

We examine each of these categories of behavior and discuss the choices or repertoires available to us within each category.

# Framing the Learning

## Framing the Big Picture

This first group of behaviors clusters around the mission of framing the big picture. It is composed of behaviors that help students place new information in a larger framework of meaning in the beginning of a lesson.

- Communicating the objective: what the students will know or be able to do at the end of the upcoming instruction
- Giving students the itinerary, that is, the list of activities or sequence of events they'll be doing
- Reminding students of the big idea or essential question of which this lesson is part
- Explaining the reason for an activity—that is, how it helps meet the objective
- Explaining why the learning is worthwhile, why it might matter to learn this material
- Identifying criteria for success when a product or performance is involved

Research shows consistent correlation between these behaviors and improved student learning. We do not yet know with numerical accuracy the proportional role each plays in the ocean of factors that bear on student learning, but we do know that each matters and that there are a variety of ways to accomplish each of them. We know further that the repertoire of these ways has been developed by practitioners. That is where we have gone to discover the repertoires developed below and, indeed, in this whole book.

## Communicating the Objective

Communicating objectives lets students know what they will know or be able to do ideally as a result of

**Table 9.1. Clarity Concepts**

## I. FRAMING THE LEARNING

1. Framing the Big Picture by ensuring that students understand the following:

   - Objectives
   - Itinerary
   - Big idea/essential question
   - Reason it's worthwhile
   - Reason for activity
   - Criteria for success

2. Getting Ready for Instruction
   - Activating students' current knowledge
   - Preassessing
   - Anticipating confusions and misconceptions

## II. PRESENTING INFORMATION

3. Presenting Information through well-chosen Explanatory Devices:

   - Simple cues
   - Progressive minimal cues
   - Highlighting important info
   - Analogies
   - Diagrams
   - Translation into simpler language
   - Pictures or pictographs
   - Charts, whiteboards, Smartboards
   - Document camera or transparency
   - Audio and video recordings
   - Computer presentation software
   - Models
   - Mental imagery
   - Modeling thinking aloud
   - Graphic organizer

4. Speech
   - Avoiding "mazes" or "vagueness" terms
   - Matching to setting and student culture

## III. CREATING MENTAL ENGAGEMENT

5. Explicitness: Making explicit and not leaving to chance the following:

   - Intention of cues
   - Focus of questions
   - Necessary steps in directions
   - Meaning of references

6. Making Cognitive Connections: By teacher for student or by student at invitation of teacher:

   - Showing resemblance to student experience or something already learned
   - Asking students to compare and contrast
   - Extending to implications and future actions
   - Making transitions between ideas
   - Signaling shift in activity, pace, or level
   - Foreshadowing

## IV. GETTING INSIDE STUDENTS' HEADS (COGNITIVE EMPATHY)

7. Checking for Understanding

8. Unscrambling Confusions

9. Making Students' Thinking Visible

## V. CONSOLIDATING AND ANCHORING THE LEARNING

10. Summarizing

**Research for Better Teaching, Inc.** • One Acton Place, Acton, MA 01720 • (978) 263-9449 • www.RBTeach.com

the lesson. This teacher is making a clear statement of an objective by letting students know what they'll be able to do when the instruction is over: "Today we're going to learn how to write on paper what you've been telling me out loud in math groups—that you have one-half or one-fourth or three-fourths of a whole something. There is a special way of writing numbers that stand for those things and when we're done today you'll be able to use it." On the board she writes: "SWBAT [students will be able to] use math language with accuracy and understanding to represent simple fractional parts."

Most of us have been taught how to say and write behavioral objectives. That language serves a purpose, but it need not be used all the time. The example above happens to *be* a behavioral objective stated in language to match eight-year-old children, but the objective may not be a detailed behavioral one at all. Other language patterns can serve as well—for instance: "We're going to look at this film and see what we can learn about the personality characteristics of Hemingway the man." Once again, students are directed toward what they're supposed to focus on while viewing and know at the end of the lesson. Such statements frame the big picture, giving an overall orientation to what is to follow to help the students attend to what is important and to make sense of subsequent activities.

The main point in communicating objectives is to introduce lesson activities with something that casts them within a bigger frame, purpose, or objective, so that the students know what they're going to learn and what to focus on when they read, listen, or watch during instruction.

We have found that many schools now require teachers to write a daily objective on the board for students. That's a useful practice so that students have something to refer back to, but post-

ing it is nowhere near sufficient. It has to be accompanied by making sure students know what it is and what it means. The point is that learning is empowered when students understand what they are aiming to learn, and something has to happen beyond posting the objective on the board to assure that student understanding.

Certain forms of constructivist teaching do not need to start with an out-loud statement of the objective at the beginning of a lesson. Instead the lesson might be framed by a question to be answered through inquiry. In this way, students can channel their efforts and curiosity and focus their observations productively. For example, the objective for a math lesson in the elementary grades might be, "Students will be able to explain how a fractional part of an overall area can have different shapes within that area." Rather than state this at the outset of the lesson, the teacher might say, "How many different ways can you make quarters with rubber bands on this geoboard?"

The bottom line is that it is very important that we know in clear terms what the mathematical objective is and eventually cause the students to produce language that captures this understanding in their own words.

We don't really know if the students understand the objective unless we ask them. A physics teacher one of us knows regularly invites a visitor into his room, especially during lab periods. The students have a checklist where they get a bonus point if they explain the objective to the visitor, another if they explain how the activity they're doing serves the objective, and yet another if they can explain the relevance to life of what they're learning. Exhibit 9.1 presents the rubric used for this activity. Visitors are very popular with students in this classroom!

**Exhibit 9.1. Teacher Spot Check Rubric**

| Physics I | | | Pre-Archimedes | |
| *Teacher Spot Check Rubric* | | | *Name:* | |

For the teacher spot check, you will be graded by the following rubric.
You must have at least 2 rubrics completed that meet the standard.

| Standard | Exceeds Standard | Meets Standard | Comments |
| --- | --- | --- | --- |
| S7d: Student explains a scientific concept to others. | ❑ Explains how the activity will help them to learn the content.<br>❑ Makes a connection between activity and the real world. | ❑ Explains the activity to the visiting teacher.<br>❑ Knows the goal of the lesson.<br>❑ Explains what has been discovered so far in the activity.<br>❑ Explains what their role is in the activity. | |

*Teachers:*

If students don't offer up information unsolicited, please ask them probing questions regarding the items in the "Meets Standard" column.

If a student is unable to explain any one of the items in the "Meets Standard" column, do not give them credit.

Please initial on the appropriate line below.

Exceeds Standard _____

Meets Standard _____

Does Not Meet Standard _____

Teacher Signature: _____ Date:_____

*Source:* Reprinted with permission of Janece Docal and Jeff Schmitz.

## Giving Students an Itinerary

An itinerary is like an agenda or road map. It lists or delineates the sequence of steps that will occur over the course of an activity or period. It tells what activities will take place and in what order. For example, it is common to hear a teacher say, "This morning we'll be going over your homework answers and then looking at the material in the new chapter. Then we'll do some group work on your projects." This useful information gives students a mental sequence to follow and lets them know what to expect. Learners with sequential learning styles are particularly responsive to the practice of posting itineraries in a visible place.

Giving students an itinerary serves as a complement to the objective but doesn't replace communicating the objective itself. The objective specifies the learning outcome for students (the destination); the itinerary tells them how they will get there. An itinerary affords students the opportunity to keep track of what has happened, what is currently happening, and what's left to come. The true test of whether students have understood the objective of a lesson might be whether they can explain the connection between the events on the itinerary and what they are expected to know or be able to do when they have reached the end of the journey or the destination (the objective).

Giving clear directions and outlining what procedures students are going to follow (see Chapter Eighteen, "Learning Experiences") also complements, but does not replace, communicating an objective.

## Connecting to a Big Idea

This is the time in the lesson to reconnect the students with the big idea of the unit and perhaps the essential question that embodies it—for example, "The water cycle is one of the natural processes the earth uses to keep itself alive—and us alive too. We're exploring whether that cycle is in any danger and if we can do anything about it."

At the beginning of a unit, the teacher may spend considerable time developing these big ideas. And during the unit, teachers often remind students of the big idea at the beginning of a given lesson and connecting the objectives of the day with that idea: "After today's material on the drug influx from Mexico, we may have a new slant on the complicated question of United States immigration policy."

## Explaining Why the Objective Is Worthwhile

Communicating to students why the objective is worthwhile is the "Who cares?" question. Students may know exactly what it is about the Vietnam War that their teacher wants them to understand at the conclusion of the lesson; but they may not think it matters. For some students, understanding the usefulness or relevance of a learning objective makes a big difference in their investment in the lesson. Writing about "quadrant one learners" in her description of different learning styles, McCarthy (1987) makes the point that all learners need reasons for why they are studying what their teachers are asking them to learn. But knowing the reason is more than nice, it's *essential* for imaginative learners. She says that many teachers erroneously assume that students buy into learning because they see their teachers as experts who know what should be learned. "Students need reasons of their own. Giving them a reason, a need of their own for proceeding, is so simple and fundamental that one can only marvel that it is not done" (McCarthy, 1987, pp. 92, 94). We think, parenthetically, that this same generalization applies to all adult learning as well, whether it be in college courses, staff seminars, or professional development offerings. For all learners it will be useful to know why the topic is important to learn, and for a segment of each audience it will be essential.

It is particularly important for some learners (and useful to all) to know the reasons for understanding the principal causes of the Vietnam War and U.S. involvement: "The reason this is important to us is that the Vietnam War has causes in common with many other wars in history. If this country enters another war, it's likely that many of you will be urged to enter into the armed services and have friends who go to fight. Therefore, it will be important to you as citizens to be able to follow current events and the decisions of your leaders in government to see where we're headed. As citizens, you can make informed choices in voting for leaders who stand for policies you want. Our study here will help you decide in the future what you think we should fight for as a country—and at some point that choice is sure to be yours."

Although not as dramatic, we might be equally clear about why it is worthwhile learning geometric proofs; studying myth as a literary genre; or learning to identify by their attributes igneous, sedimentary, and metamorphic rocks. Giving reasons for learning doesn't necessarily happen with every lesson. Many lessons are taking students one increment further or developing their skill one degree higher on a particular objective. At the beginning of new units or topics, however, giving reasons for our objectives can be particularly appropriate. And it never hurts to remind students from time to time why something is important.

Preparing to deliver these reasons to students can be a useful exercise for us as teachers too. If we can't formulate a good reason for learning something, maybe we shouldn't be teaching it.

## Stating Reasons for Activities

Surprisingly, students often have no notion about the purpose of activities they are asked to do and make no link between activities and instruction they have just received (Tasker, 1981). "Reasons for activities" simply means telling students why they are asked to do a particular activity, that is, why the activity will help them learn something or contribute to a larger learning or task performance: "The reason we're doing this experiment is to show how hard it is to take data and record information simultaneously. You just can't do it. So like all scientists, we're going to have to extrapolate our readings. Remember that term from the graphs we worked on in the chapter?" Another example: "The reason we're doing these sentence combining worksheets is so you can use these same techniques to make your own writing more interesting in the adventure stories we're writing." These moves build a series of bridges back to objectives from individual activities and between activities themselves as is seen in Figure 9.1.

Sometimes the explanation shows students how the current activity fits into patterns of other

**Figure 9.1. Reasons for Activities**

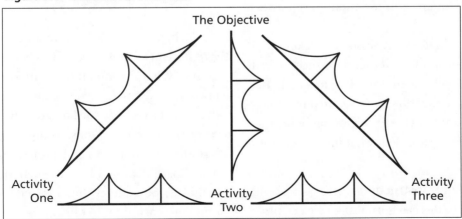

experiences they've been having or are about to have: "The reason I'm asking you to locate these references in the library database is to build up your speed and check your accuracy. You'll have to use this database a lot next month when you start your research papers, and I won't be around to help much of the time. So you've got to be able to use it independently to find books you want."

Without these explanations, many students do assignments mechanically, with minimal care and investment. They do them because they're "work" and you're supposed to do your work. But the work isn't leading in a meaningful way toward anything they understand. Teachers who have worked with learning styles and studied the intriguing work of McCarthy and McCarthy (2005) and Gregorc and Butler (1984) know that quadrant one learners—that is, big picture people—especially need to understand these connections.

### Communicating Criteria for Success

The criteria for success in a student task, often a bulleted list, reveal in detail what we really want the students to know or be able to do. Coming up with criteria is a planning skill; communicating them to students is a clarity behavior. Clear teachers don't keep criteria a secret; they make sure students understand them and can use them to self-assess their work.

Chapter Nineteen, "Assessment," takes up in detail the topics of rubrics, criteria for success, and exemplars of good student work that meet criteria. It's worth mentioning now, however, that providing these items to students at the beginning of instruction helps make clear exactly what the objective is.

### Getting Ready for Instruction

The behaviors in this category also take place prior to instruction with new material—sometimes in an earlier lesson—and increase the likelihood that instruction will be effective for more students. Two of the three (activating prior knowledge and pre-assessment) provide data for the teacher to take into consideration when finalizing the instructional plan, and may in fact provide data to inform the third: anticipating confusion.

### Activating Students' Current Knowledge

An activator is an activity designed to get students' minds active and in gear about a topic before they learn anything new about it. Research shows a cognitive payoff for student learning when teachers do this. Techniques that activate students' current knowledge about a topic not only get students' minds into a state of interest and heightened awareness, but can prevent the dreaded "Charlie Brown syndrome":

> Recall what Charlie Brown does when he gets a new book. Before he even looks at the book, he counts pages—625 pages—"I'll never learn all that!" He is defeated before he starts, before he has had a chance to realize that he does not have to learn all that. It is not all new. He already knows something about it. He has not given himself the chance to learn what he already knows about what he is supposed to know [McNeill, 1984, p. 34].

There are many different ways one might activate students' knowledge. A teacher might ask students, "What do you already know about X (the upcoming topic)?" . . . and as students brainstorm the teacher records (or has students individually record) their connections. As the concept or topic is studied, students can go back to these initial lists to compare what they have learned with their original ideas. Sometimes students find themselves fitting new learning into old charts, and sometimes they find parts of their old conceptions contradicted. In any event, having created an image of what they already know about a topic places a map before them against which they bounce (and into which they put) new information. It is in this way that activating serves the big picture.

Several variations of this idea (having students start with a blank piece of paper and fill it with what they already know or at least think they know to be true) are widely used in classrooms. "Know, Want to Know, and Learned" (sometimes referred to as "KWL" or the "three-column activator") is one such example used to preview and then summarize learning. As ideas are generated they are recorded in one of two columns: "What I Know" and "What I Want to Know." As students pursue the topic they review the initial chart and complete the third column "What I Learned." We use an alternate version in which the three columns are "Know," "Think I Know," and "Want to Know" (see Exhibit 9.2). We introduce a topic or show students a stimulus on a topic they haven't yet studied (headlines from a newspaper article, a picture on a book cover with the title) and ask them to share aloud their what they know, think they know, or would like to know about this. As they share ideas they assign them to one of the three columns. No discussion or question answering occurs during the building of the chart. This activity produces active participation, reveals student preconceptions, and generates student-owned agendas for reading or listening.

The charts are worth saving for a return visit after reading the piece or studying the topic. Some "knows" may turn out to be untrue; some "think I knows" are validated and others overturned; and all the "want to knows" should have been answered or might lead to follow-up research.

McNeill (1984) provides the following description of an activator called Semantic Mapping:

> Begin by asking pupils what they think of when they hear the word X (X is the topic they are about to read about). Free association is desir-

**Exhibit 9.2.  Sample KWL Chart**

| Global Warming | | |
|---|---|---|
| *Know* | *Think I Know* | *Want to Know* |
| | | |

able. As pupils offer their associations, list the responses on the chalkboard. Try to put the associations into categories.

For example, responses to "money" might be categorized into uses of money, kinds of money, denominations, consequences of having money, ways of earning and other associations. Help the pupils label the categories and then ask them to read the selection to learn more about X. It is fine to encourage pupils to pose their own questions about what they want to learn about X from the text. Next, after reading the selection, the class gives attention to the set of categories and pre-reading questions related to X. Pupils at this time add new ideas acquired from their reading, correcting and augmenting the original map [p. 10].

Although McNeill's description is of a semantic mapping exercise prior to reading a selection of text, note that it could be used equally well before doing an experiment, viewing a video, or interviewing a guest. The point is that the teachers are getting students ready for new information by calling up their own maps, or schema, of what they already know about the topic. The effect is to make students more cognitively ready to receive new information whether they are reading, watching, or listening.

Sometimes students need more than a blank sheet of paper (figuratively speaking) to surface prior knowledge and begin to make connections to a topic. There are other forms of activating that give students data to think about in relation to the topic. A wordsplash (Hammond, 1985) takes ten to twenty key words or terms from an article, story, or text chapter and "splashes" them at random angles and positions on a chart or whiteboard with the topic or focus of the article in the center (see Figure 9.2). In the sample following the words are about an animal, the paca, found in Central America. Prior to reading, students are asked to follow the rules of brainstorming in groups with a recorder as they respond to the following direction: "Generate sentences for each of these terms to show how you think they are related to pacas, which are rodents found in South and Central America." This technique produces wide student participation, higher-level thinking, focused reading, and better comprehension.

Many other techniques have been developed by practitioners and researchers in the reading and language fields and are well worth studying by teachers in all academic disciplines. They vary in terms of how much information is given to students and how much students are asked to generate themselves. Some take more time than others; some are verbal, some are visual; some require advance preparation of materials; others don't. What they all have in common is that students actively seek to make connections to an upcoming topic prior to beginning the study of it. Thus, all have the effect of getting students cognitively engaged and ready to receive.

The activators we described thus far have the purpose of getting students' minds engaged with a new topic. In addition to creating a desire to know and a sense of competence in students, some activators can also serve as assessments of students'

**Figure 9.2. Wordsplash**

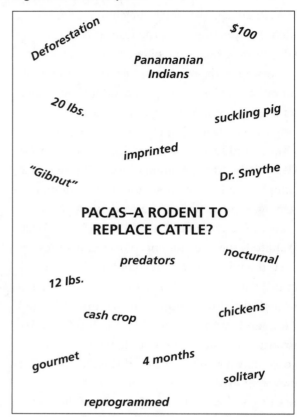

prior knowledge, getting us two for the price of one. A Sort Card activity in which students are given a set of cards each containing a fraction and are asked to sort them into categories based on their value can tell us quickly how well students understand and can identify equivalent fractions. Or giving students a set of cards containing vocabulary words, definitions, and sentences missing key (vocabulary) words and asking them to create triad matches of a word, a definition, and a sentence can give them and us a quick sense of what terminology is familiar and what needs to be explained or studied prior to introducing a new topic in science. There are many more ways to activate student knowledge and some also serve as preassessment tools. For additional examples, we refer readers to a separate publication, *Activators* (Saphier and Haley, 1993), which gives detailed directions for implementing twenty-four other techniques.

## Preassessing Students' Knowledge

Ausubel (1968) writes, "The most important single factor influencing learning is what the learner already knows. Ascertain this, and teach him accordingly." Gathering this information matters. If adequate prior knowledge is absent, even a great lesson on new material will go for naught. If students know more than we thought we can go faster. If they lack some necessary prior knowledge, then we need to alter the lesson plan and fill those gaps.

There are other direct ways besides activators to find out what students know. Preassessment devices provide this information. A brief quiz can serve this purpose, either a quiz the day before a lesson or a scan of the previous night's homework. The main point is to make sure students' prior knowledge gives them the readiness for the intended instruction. This is particularly important with vocabulary and concepts that are going to show up in a text and are assumed by the author to be available to readers.

## Anticipating Confusions and Misconceptions

A cartoon we have shows a little boy standing on his head on a bathroom scale. His friend reads the weight and says, "Your head weighs 43 pounds—same as your feet." As in the cartoon, students bring many misconceptions to instruction, misconceptions that can be resistant to change and interfere with instruction if they are not recognized and contradicted. One of the three forms of anticipating confusions and misconceptions (see Figure 9.3) means finding out what these misconceptions are and addressing them directly. Otherwise they will linger and distort students' assimilation of instruction (Eaton, Anderson, and Smith, 1984).

A series of investigations by science educators (Eaton, Anderson, and Smith, 1984; Eylon and Linn, 1988) revealed many misconceptions students have about how the world works: for example, "air is empty space," "my eyes see by direct perception" (rather than receiving reflected light), and "we have summer when the earth is closer to the sun." They bring these misconceptions to instruction, and unless teachers discover them, surface them and explicitly contradict them, students hold onto them and reconcile them with the instructional information. The resulting maps they create in their heads may seem logically consistent, but they're wrong and present serious obstacles to learning. This can happen even when the instruction is ostensibly clear as a bell—because of the failure to account for the misconceptions students bring with them to the instruction. And though the research is best developed for science concepts, there is no reason to believe the same thing does not happen with concepts from any discipline. We must be aware that students do not come to class as blank slates. Many of the activators cited earlier give us information about misconceptions students have on these slates.

In a second form of anticipating confusion, teachers use what they know about their students and their content to anticipate confusion and probable points of misunderstanding because the material is difficult to understand or easy to misinterpret. The teacher anticipates, for example, that when explaining free fall in physics, students might think *free fall* refers only to an object falling toward earth, straight down from a height. *Free fall,* however, means any situation in which an object is moving only because of the force of gravity. That includes the motion of an object in orbit around a central body, like the moon around the earth. It is accurate to say the moon is in free fall around the earth or that space shuttles are in free fall around

**Figure 9.3. Three Forms of Anticipating Confusion**

<table>
<tr><td>

**Predicting in advance common student misconceptions**

Based on your experience, and therefore being able to spend time contradicting the misconception and highlighting the correct idea. To do so, you may draw on a range of explanatory devices.

</td><td>

**Predicting in advance that the material will be hard to learn**

and drawing on a range of explanatory devices and frequent checking.

After a demonstration of the concept of density with two cups of cornflakes, one crushed and one not, the teacher sketches on the board and says, "Raise your left hand if diagram 1 is more dense, right hand if diagram 2 is more dense. Tina, tell me why you chose this one. Okay, everyone, in your notebooks, in three lines or less, define *density* and give one everyday example of something that is denser than something else."

</td></tr>
</table>

**Noticing or perceiving on the spot that students might not understand**

or might interpret differently something just seen or heard.

"Hold it, Todd. Look, everybody, see what happened? He did two steps at once in his head. First he . . ."

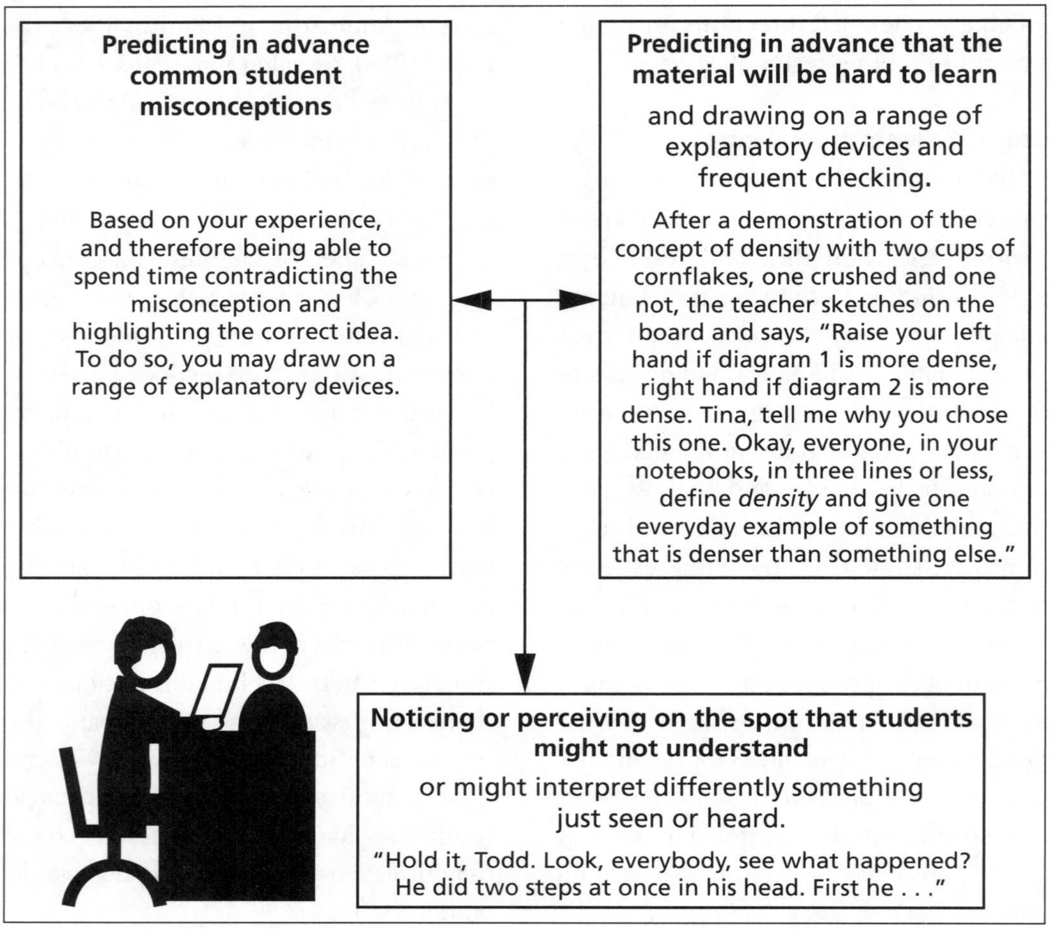

**Research for Better Teaching, Inc.** • One Acton Place, Acton, MA 01720 • (978)263-9449 • www.RBTeach.com

the moon when they are in stable orbit. *Free fall* in these situations means "falling around," that is, with circular motion of objects in orbit in space. By anticipating confusions, teachers become aware of when students are likely to have difficulty understanding and can spend time clarifying the material before students become confused.

Sometimes a teacher becomes aware of a possible confusion on the fly while teaching and makes a preventive move right then. A student is correctly solving an algebra equation but is manipulating terms in his head at a rate the other students might not be able to follow. So with an on-the-fly move to prevent confusing the other students, the teacher interrupts the student and says to the class, "Wait—see what he's doing here: he's doing two steps at once in his head; he's cross-multiplying and taking the square root. Okay, go ahead, Todd." This teacher has slowed the action for the benefit of the others and unpacked the two steps that Todd was doing simultaneously in his head, which the teacher anticipates the other students might not be able to understand.

Anticipating confusion is often one of the most subtle and difficult performances to observe because when one does this effectively, students do not in fact become confused: we "head them off at the pass," taking care of the potential lack of understanding before it develops. For this reason, it also represents a high level of sophistication in clarity.

It requires both the disposition and the ability to get inside students' heads and is the foundation of this entire set of Clarity skills. Teachers skillful at clarity want to know how it's going for their students and have a repertoire of ways for finding out. They have a degree of cognitive empathy for the workings of the learners' minds—an ability to put themselves in the learners' shoes—and that guides everything they do.

# Presenting Information

This section is about that part of teaching and learning after "activating" in which we are introducing new ideas and skills.

## Explanatory Devices

Explanatory devices are tools that can be used to present information and explain concepts within any approach to teaching. The repertoire of explanatory devices includes the following:

- Simple cues
- Progressive minimal cues
- Highlighting important information
- Translation into simpler language
- Analogies
- Diagrams

- Pictures
- Charts, whiteboard, Smartboard
- Document camera or overhead transparencies
- Audio and video recordings
- Computer presentation software
- Models
- Mental imagery
- Modeling thinking aloud
- Graphic organizers

Some of these are more linguistic representations (modeling thinking aloud and analogies), some are nonlinguistic (pictures, pictographs, graphic organizers, mental imagery), and others are more tangible and concrete representations (physical models). Given that learners take in information auditorily, visually, and kinesthetically, and that most learners are more dominant in one or two of the three modalities, we need to be strategic and balanced in our selection of explanatory devices to ensure equal opportunity for all learners. Are we explaining in ways that enable students to see, hear, and experience the content or concept? If not, we are cheating some learners. An advantage to planning with this in mind is that we are more likely to maximize the benefits of any individual explanatory device by enhancing how we use it. For example, we might want to use fraction rods (a physical model) to demonstrate the concept of equivalent fractions. Students will see the model and hear us talk through the explanation using fraction rods. But if we give each of them a set of fraction rods to construct the model along with us we incorporate the third (kinesthetic) modality. Nonlinguistic representations are especially critical when we are working with second language learners.

Because many of the explanatory devices are self-explanatory, we discuss here only six in more detail: progressive minimal cues, analogies, models, mental imagery, modeling thinking aloud, and graphic organizers, all of which can be powerful vehicles for supporting student understanding.

## Progressive Minimal Cues

In small group or one-to-one tutoring, a teacher often uses silent finger-pointing skillfully as a minimal cue to call a student's attention to an attribute of a word or a part of a problem he needs to look at again. The minimal part of the cue giving is important here: it's just enough to get students to look at what they need to but not so much as to deny them an opportunity for thinking out the error. For example, if a student reads "cot" as "cat," the teacher silently points to the "o" in "cot" as a minimal cue. If necessary, the teacher progresses up the scale of cues, making successive cues less and less minimal until the student gets it. . . . The next step would be to spell the word aloud, stressing the "O"—"c-*o*-t" but not telling the word.

## Analogies

Analogies help student understanding because they connect the new learning to something the students already know, and in some cases, they create visual images—for example: "The growth of a glacier is like *pancake batter being poured in a frying pan.* As more and more substance is added to the middle, the edges spread farther and farther out" (Ormrod, 2004, p. 245).

When appropriately chosen, they are effective devices for augmenting student learning (Bulgren, Deshler, Schumaker, and Lenz, 2000). Ormrod notes, however, that teachers must "point out ways in which the two things being compared are different, otherwise students may take an analogy too far and draw incorrect conclusions" (p. x).

## Models

A model can be a physical artifact that represents an idea or a concept to be learned. For example, the concept of multiplication can be represented by arrays of cut-out graph paper. In Exhibit 9.3, $1 \times 12$ is represented by one long column of twelve squares cut out from chart paper where the squares are one square inch; $2 \times 6$ is represented by two columns of six squares, also cut out from the same chart paper and taped on the board next to the $1 \times 12$ column; and another array of three columns with four squares in each column ($3 \times 4 = 12$) is taped right next to the other two. This presents a model of three different ways to multiply numbers and get the same product.

A model is something students can see and sometimes touch that represents the meaning of the concept, and it serves as a sense anchor in memory for the concept that teachers and students can use as common references for the idea: "Remember when we had the arrays of graph paper taped to the board? Well that's the kind of relationship that's going on in this word problem."

Exhibit 9.4 shows an additional set of models to represent multiplication in different real-world situations.

## Mental Imagery

One of the most powerful and least used explanatory devices is mental imagery. Mental imagery means making pictures in your head. When properly guided by teachers, students can use these mental pictures to understand physical states or processes; as analogies for concepts, for mood, scene, or context setting; or for improving memory of information or relationships.

Imagery has long been used in sports to improve physical performance (Whisler and Marzano, 1988). Athletes use mental rehearsal to

**Exhibit 9.3.  A Model of Three Ways to Multiply**

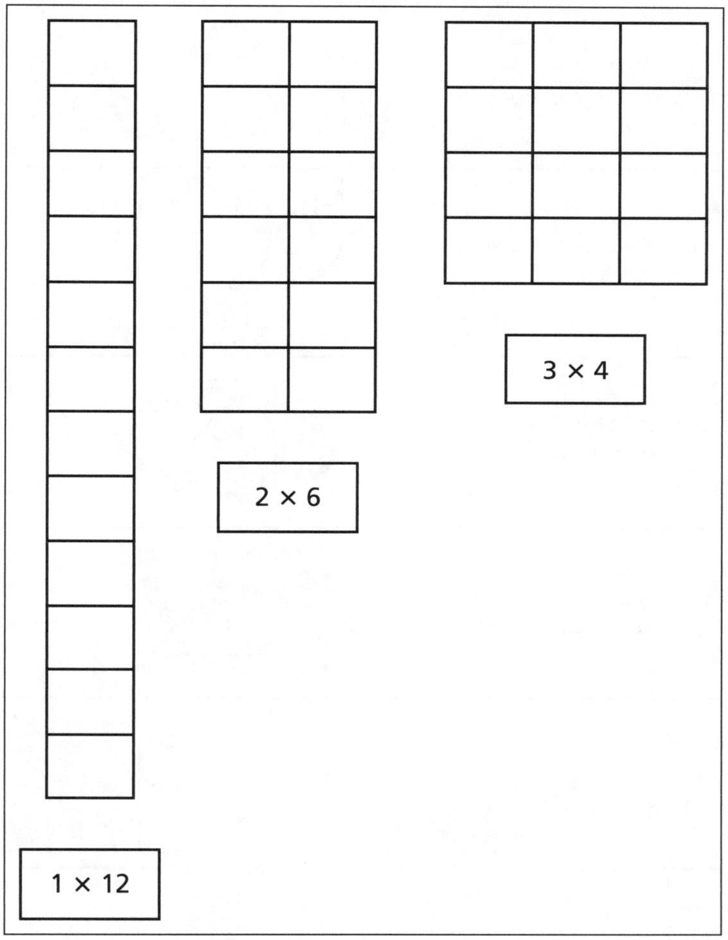

$1 \times 12$

$2 \times 6$

$3 \times 4$

focus their minds, concentrate, and practice and in the process improve their performance. In school, these same powers can be brought to bear to focus attention on academic material, elucidate meaning more clearly, and activate visual and right brain channels for stronger learning.

A guided imagery trip of a seed pod traveling from the mother plant to germination miles away can illustrate the steps and mechanisms of seed migration memorably. A trip inside an imaginary atom can illustrate properties of nuclei and electron orbits in ways that anchor new concepts last-

ingly, just as an imagery trip around a familiar playing field can anchor the concept of perimeter. Using guided imagery to reconstruct conditions inside the *Mayflower* prior to landing on the New England coast can make the study of the colony's founding vivid and real for students. Using imagery to have primary children see themselves reentering the room after recess, checking the assignment board for tasks, and walking slowly and quietly to their places can dramatically improve behavior at transitions. The uses of guided imagery are legion and cross all curriculum areas.

**Exhibit 9.4. Multiplication Models**

### • Equal Groups

Three bags of candy with 4 in each bag. How many candies?

$3 \times 4 = 12$

### • Allocation/Rate

Sue drove 3 miles each hour. She drove for 4 hours. How many miles did she drive altogether?

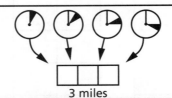

3 miles

$3 \times 4 = 12$

### • Array Models

Sue has a cupcake tray. It holds 4 cupcakes in each of the three rows. How many cupcakes does she have?

$3 \times 4 = 12$

### • Area Models

The room is 3 feet by 4 feet. How many square feet of carpet are needed?

$3 \times 4 = 12$

### • Scalar Models

Sue has $4. Tom has three times as much. How much money does Tom have?

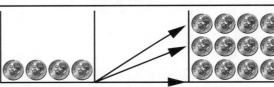

$3 \times 4 = 12$

3 times as many

### • Cartesian Models

She has 3 pairs of pants and 4 shirts. How many different outfits can she put together?

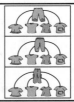

$3 \times 4 = 12$

### • Linear/Measurement Models

She measured 3 groups of 4 inches. How many inches?

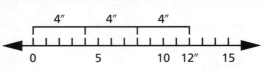

$3 \times 4 = 12$

*Source:* Unknown.

The following guidelines are useful for teachers planning imagery exercises with students:

- Clarify the purpose of the imagery—what you want to accomplish.
- Set the scene.
- Direct participants to get in a comfortable position, preferably without crossed limbs.
- Prepare and deliver a script with sufficient detail to evoke images.
- Pause at appropriate points to allow images to form.
- Use music if it seems to fit. "New age" or baroque pieces are often recommended.

Teachers need to be aware that in any class, there may be one or two students who are weak visual learners and cannot image easily. This is no reason to avoid using imagery; strengths can be built through practice. But it is a strong reason to acknowledge the possibility beforehand to prevent such a student blaming himself or herself (or blaming the teacher) for inadequacy. It is also a reason not to rely exclusively on imagery for teaching a particular piece of content.

Descriptions of successful imagery programs (Pressley, 1976; Escondido School District, 1979) often include having students speak about and share their pictures: "What do you see?" "Tell me about your picture." "What else can you see?" Researchers have demonstrated increased student comprehension, retention, and ability to make inferences from material treated in this way (see McNeill, 1984, for additional references).

## Modeling Thinking Aloud

When teachers model thinking aloud for students, they go through the thinking step by step as a student would, role-playing just what to do. This includes being puzzled, making mistakes, self-correcting, and checking themselves along the way.

Modeling thinking aloud is appropriate for any kind of multistep operation that uses problem solving. By doing the thinking aloud, teachers show students where the pitfalls are and how to get through common hang-up points, as well as model the appropriate steps. An example of modeling thinking aloud (partially) for organizing notes to write an essay on the Civil War might sound like this:

"Let's see. I've got all these note cards I wrote while I was reading the different books. Let me lay them out in front of me. [Lays cards out on table.] Hmmmm.

"Now how can I use them to figure out what to say? Maybe I can group them. Let's see . . . these three are notes about how different battles went, the mistakes and the good strategy moves. Okay, I'll put them together. . . . And these ones are about Lincoln hiring and firing the various generals. [Puts those together.] And these are about the stuff and money each army had behind it, and how they raised money in the North versus the South to pay for the army. [Puts those together.] . . . No, wait. This one with 'value of land' isn't really about financing the war. It's about farming and getting supplies. [Goes on grouping the note cards and saying out loud what she's thinking.]

". . . Okay, now I've got the groups. What's the point I want to make about each group? The topic sentence? . . . So this group, the generals. Well, Lincoln went through a lot of them before he found Grant. That could be the point. . . . Anything else? Well, actually he gave them each a long time and a lot of leeway before he fired them. They had to really mess up before he would relieve them of command. And they all did! Okay, that's my point then, two points really: that Lincoln gave them a lot of leeway to prove themselves, but he replaced them when they messed up. Now let's see, how will I frame that sentence?"

Subsequent modeling thinking aloud in this scenario might be for how to choose supporting details for the topic sentence from the note cards.

Modeling thinking aloud is done by a teacher in front of the class. It is a dialogue with oneself. Davey (1983) shows how the technique can be used to teach students a variety of comprehension strategies. For example, you role play coming upon a word you don't know in the text: "Hmmm, what does that mean? . . . better reread the sentence . . . still don't get it. Maybe I'll read ahead to see if it gets clearer. . . . Nope, still doesn't make sense. Let's see. Do I recognize any of its parts? . . ." In this way, the teacher can take a set of guidelines—reread; read ahead and back to see if the context gives a clue; look for parts you know, particularly stems, prefixes, and suffixes—and show what they look like in operation.

Modeling thinking aloud is one of the least seen and most powerful of the explanatory devices. It is especially useful in teaching any kind of problem-solving or step-wise procedure. Its essential attributes are:

- Internal dialogue made external
- Asking yourself questions
- Weighing alternatives and using criteria to choose
- False starts and self-correcting
- Persistence

### Graphic Organizers

Graphic organizers are "words on paper, arranged to represent an individual's understanding of the relationship between the words" (Clarke, 1990). They are diagrams, but a particular kind of diagram designed to represent relationships between ideas based on thinking patterns embedded in text structure, such as cause and effect, part-whole, comparison and contrast, description, or problem and solution.

Graphic organizers contain words instead of just pictures, and the form of the diagram represents a particular and generalizable kind of organizing structure or pattern of thinking. Graphic organizers are powerful devices not only for explaining and representing ideas and their relationships but also for having students summarize what they know. They help students:

- See the relationships of concepts and elements
- Organize information into a coherent structure
- Pay attention to important items
- Capitalize on visual learning and activate the right brain

When students are taught to use graphic organizers to record or summarize information, they also learn to be active readers and listeners.

There are a great many terms used for special-purpose graphic organizers: *mind maps, story maps, semantic maps, webs, concept maps, thinking maps,* and *clusters.* Some of them (mind maps, clusters, semantic maps) are used for recording a rapid flow of ideas and are taught to students for their own use in recording and organizing their thoughts prior to writing or research. Others (story maps) are used when students are reading literature to record plot line and character development in visual form. Still others (concept maps, a term commonly used in science and social studies) are used to record the relationships between concepts and facts in visual form and profile the essential attributes and nonattributes of concepts themselves (Bulgren, 1991).

Concept maps (Novak, 1991) and thinking maps (Hyerle, 1990) are graphic organizers where the form of thinking in the presentation of the material (for example, comparison and contrast) indicates use of a particular format for the diagram—say a matrix or Hyerle's "double bubble."

**Figure 9.4. Graphic Organizer for Comparing Life in 1776 to Today**

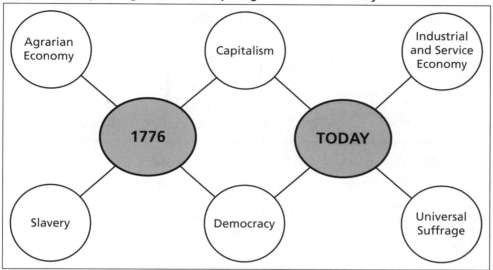

For example, if a text is comparing life in America of 1776 with life today, "1776" would go in one bubble and "Today" would go in the other (Figure 9.4). Circles between "1776" and "Today" with links to both would contain elements they shared in common, like capitalism and democratic form of government. Circles to the left and linked only to "1776" would contain elements unique to that time and not present today, for example, contrasts to current life like the agrarian base of the economy and acceptance of slavery. Circles connected at the right to "Today" and only to "Today" contain elements of society present now but not in 1776—elements that are contrasts to 1776 (like an industrial and service economy and universal suffrage). The form or thinking the author brought to the organization of the material would indicate which form of graphic organizer would be best for representing it (Figure 9.5).

Teachers can use graphic organizers to record class discussions and organize information they are presenting by drawing the organizer on the board as they go. This use will help students understand concepts and assimilate information. A higher goal, however, is to teach the graphic organizer forms to students themselves so they can eventually use them independently. At the end of this rainbow, then, one might hear a teacher make this assignment: "Take notes on your reading tonight and choose the form of graphic organizer you think most appropriate." This is asking students not only to be active readers, but also to be analysts of the form of thinking used to organize the information.

A research tradition in the reading field (McGee and Richgels, 1986; Heimlich and Pittelman, 1986; Armbruster, Anderson, and Ostertag, 1989) has demonstrated that graphic organizers improve comprehension when used as adjuncts to good instruction. Students learn that all text is written according to some structure of thinking, each of which has a corresponding graphic form that could be used to represent it.

Teachers can move students at appropriate rates toward independence with graphic organizers and toward being active thinkers and readers by phasing in these devices slowly, as in the

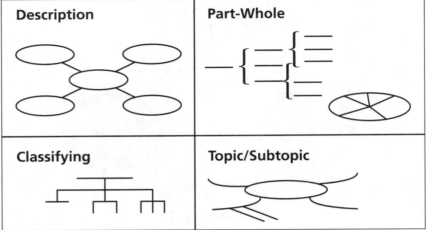

**Figure 9.5. Four Graphic Organizer Forms**

following sequence over a considerable period of time:

- Phase 1: The teacher makes the presentation or leads a discussion and records information using a graphic organizer as class discussion develops.
- Phase 2: The teacher chooses the form and fills in the main entries and subordinate entries as discussion proceeds. The teacher identifies the form of organizer being used and names the kind of thinking it represents.
- Phase 3: The teacher chooses the form, fills in the main elements of the form for the students, and has the students fill in the rest.
- Phase 4: The teacher chooses the form of the organizer, and students make all the entries.
- Phase 5: Students choose the form and make all the entries.

Graphic organizers are popular with teachers who are interested in teaching thinking skills, because identifying and naming the form of thinking behind the organization of the material under study automatically happens at mature stages with this device. Even students in the primary grades can understand ideas more clearly when they are represented through graphic organizers.

**Choosing an Explanatory Device**

To analyze your own use of explanatory devices, you can make a simple count of how many and which you have used in explaining and clarifying information. There is no evidence we know of that any one of these devices is better than another, but there is considerable support for variety in teacher presentation as correlated with effectiveness. Using a number of devices in lessons is one form of variety certainly. And common sense argues that by using a repertoire of these devices, a teacher can increase the likelihood of retaining students' attention and engaging their learning style. Given that these are explanatory tools, it is important to consider variety from the perspective of learning modalities. Do the explanatory devices you use afford students the opportunity to receive information through auditory, visual, and kinesthetic modalities? If not, is there a way to bring your teaching more into balance along those lines so that all learners, regardless of modality strengths, will have equal opportunity for absorbing it?

## Speech

### Mazes and Vagueness

Another teaching skill obviously involved in clear communication is the speech of the teacher. It must meet certain minimum criteria for diction, pronunciation, enunciation, grammar, syntax, and choice of words (appropriate vocabulary) in order for students to understand what is said. Smith and Land (1981) have analyzed speech patterns of effective and ineffective teachers. Their studies and those of others consistently show negative effects on students' achievement when teachers use "vagueness terms" and "mazes" in their speech. They give this example of vagueness terms (italicized in the following passage): "This mathematics lesson *might* enable you to understand a *little* more *about some things* we *usually* call number patterns. *Maybe* before we get to *probably* the main idea of the lesson, you should review *a few* prerequisite concepts. *Actually,* the first concept you need to review is positive integers. *As you know,* a positive integer is any number greater than zero" (p. 38).

This example illustrates mazes (with the mazes in italics): "This mathematics lesson *will enab* . . . will get you to understand *number, uh,* number patterns. Before we get to *the main idea* of the lesson, you need to review *four conc* . . . four prerequisite concepts. The first *idea, I mean, uh,* concept you need to review is positive integers. A positive *number* . . . integer is any whole integer, *uh,* number greater than zero" (p. 38).

As evident from the examples, mazes are false starts or halts in speech, redundant words, and tangles of words. Vagueness terms take many forms (see Table 9.2). Hiller, Fisher, and Kaess (1969) and Smith and Land (1981) presented evidence that vagueness occurs as a speaker commits himself or herself to deliver information that he or she can't remember or never really knew. It can also occur when a teacher does not wish to appear authoritative about information and allows a confused sense of personal relationship building to obscure clarity. Such confusion can occur when a teacher endeavors to be seen as open to student ideas and as a facilitator rather than an information giver. What results is a tentative teacher who uses many vagueness terms.

### Matching Speech

Beyond acceptable speech, there are some things that are not so obvious. Some teachers may speak in different ways to different students, perhaps varying their way of speaking by type of occasion too. The difference may be in the range of vocabulary used; the accent; the use of slang; the cadence, speed, or rhythm of the speech; or the formality or informality of the language (Joos, 1967). We can ask ourselves if we can speak to the students in their own language in language forms that are likely to be effective for explaining, clarifying, or elucidating . . . or better suited to the kind of interaction occurring.

### Respecting Speech

Ruby Payne (2005) makes the case that children of poverty have different language forms than middle class children, and that this difference, although not a deficit in complexity or sophistication, is an obstacle to success in school and in the workplace. She advocates explicitly teaching children of poverty how to translate their own informal language routines into standard English without labeling their nonstandard cultural forms as "wrong."

She modifies Martin Joos's framework and uses his term *formal register* to describe standard English story structure and his term *casual register* to describe the story structure found in certain American subcultures. Her resulting two ways of telling the Cinderella story is an amusing contrast of two cultural styles of storytelling—a contrast that was validated long ago by Shirley Brice Heath in her landmark *Ways with Words* (1983).

**Table 9.2. Vagueness Terms**

| CATEGORIES OF VAGUENESS OF TERMS | |
|---|---|
| **Category** | **Examples** |
| 1. Ambiguous designation | • Conditions, other, somehow, somewhere, someplace, thing |
| 2. Approximation | • About, almost, approximately, fairly, just about, kind of, most, mostly, almost, nearly, pretty (much), somewhat, sort of |
| 3. "Bluffing" and recovery | • Actually, and so forth, and so on, anyway, as anyone can see, as you know, basically, clearly, in a nutshell, in essence, in fact, in other words, obviously, of course, so to speak, to make a long story short, to tell the truth, you know, you see |
| 4. Error admission | • Excuse me, I'm sorry, I guess, I'm not sure |
| 5. Indeterminate quantification | • A bunch, a couple, a few, a little, a lot, several, some various |
| 6. Multiplicity | • Aspect(s), kind(s) of, sort(s) of, type(s) of |
| 7. Negated intensifiers | • Not at all, not many, not very |
| 8. Possibility | • Chances are, could be, maybe, might, perhaps, possibility, seem(s) |
| 9. Probability | • Frequently, generally, in general, normally, often, ordinarily, probably, sometimes, usually |

*Source:* Smith and Land (1981).

In Payne's formal register form, the story starts at the beginning and generally goes chronologically to the end. The most important element of the story is the plot. "A casual [informal] register story begins with the end of the story first, or the part with the greatest emotional intensity. The story is told in vignettes with audience participation in between. The story ends with a comment about the character and his/her value. The most important part of the story is the characterization" (Payne, 2005, p. 46).

Here is the formal register version:

Once upon a time, there was a girl named Cinderella. She was very happy, and she lived with her father. Her father remarried a woman who had three daughters. When Cinderella's father died, her stepmother treated Cinderella very badly and, in fact, made her the maid for herself and her three daughters. At the same time in this land, the King decided that it was time for the Prince to get married. So, he sent a summons to all the people in the kingdom to come to a ball. Cinderella was not allowed to go, but was forced to help her sisters and stepmother get ready for the ball. After they left for the ball, and as Cinderella was crying on the hearth, her fairy godmother came and, with her magic wand, gave Cinderella a beautiful dress, glass slippers, and stagecoach made from pumpkins and mice. She then sent Cinderella to the ball in style. There was one stipulation: She had to be back home by midnight.

At the ball, the Prince was completely taken with Cinderella and danced with her all evening. As the clock began striking midnight, Cinderella remembered what the fairy godmother had said and fled from the dance. All she left was one of her glass slippers.

The Prince held a big search, using the glass slipper as a way to identify the missing woman. He finally found Cinderella; she could wear the glass slipper. He married her, and they lived happily ever after.

Here is the casual register version; the bold type indicates the narrator; the plain type indicates audience participation:

**Well, you know Cinderella married the Prince, in spite of that old nasty stepmother.** Pointy eyes, that one. Old hag! **Good thing she had a fairy godmother or she never would've made it to the ball.** Lucky thing! God bless her ragged tail! Wish I had me a fairy godmother. **And to think she nearly messed up big time by staying 'til the clock was striking 12. After all the fairy godmother had done for her.** Um, um. She shoulda known better. Eyes too full of the Prince, they were. They didn't call him the Prince for no reason. **When she got to the ball, her stepsisters and stepmother didn't even recognize her she was so beautiful without those rags.** Served 'em right, no-good jealous hags. **The Prince just couldn't quit dancing with her, just couldn't take his eyes off her. He had finally found his woman.** Lucky her! Lucky him! Sure wish life was a fairy tale. Kinda like the way I met Charlie. Ha ha. **The way she arrived was something else—a coach and horseman—really fancy. Too bad that when she ran out of there as the clock struck 12 all that was left was a pumpkin rolling away and four mice!** What a surprise for the mice! **Well, he has to find her because his heart is broken. So he takes the glass slipper and hunts for her—and her old wicked stepmother, of course, is hiding her.** What a prize! Aren't they all? **But he finds her and marries her. Somebody as good as Cinderella deserved that.** Sure hope she never invited that stepmother to her castle. Should make her the maid [p. 32–35]!!

Payne has been criticized for generalizing about children of generational poverty so as to create a negative stereotype about behavior and language that is associated with income and class (Bomer, Dworin, Semingson, and Semingson, 2008; Gorski, 2006). In our view some of these criticisms are fair. Many families—white, black, or hispanic—who find themselves living below the poverty line have good standard, or as Payne would say, formal register English in their repertoires. The criticisms do not, however, invalidate her central message: the language of the "hood," the language of the barrio, the language of the neighborhood from which a poor child comes may not be standard English, but it has a rational structure and sophistication of its own. It should be respected and used as a base for explicitly teaching standard English.

The Cinderella story Payne calls *casual register* is actually in the language of black Appalachia similar to the story form Heath described in *Ways with Words* for the town of Tracton, which is subtle, sophisticated, but cultural and race specific rather than generically characteristic of poor families. Poor whites in the same region don't tell stories this way. In neighboring Roadville, the story syntax of the whites is also idiosyncratic, often containing proverbs or witty sayings, but different from the blacks. Heath (1983) concludes: "Both Tracton and Roadville are literate communities and each has its own traditions of structuring, using, and assessing reading and writing" (p. 230).

By calling formal register *middle class* English and associating casual register with poverty, Payne puts language patterns into economic categories, thus glossing over differences that are race and culture specific. The larger point we should take away, however, is that whatever the cultural roots of casual register for speaking and writing in children, they must learn standard English. Teachers need to recognize the validity of the cultural forms of speaking with which their children come, and use this understanding in instruction. Here are Payne's recommendations:

- Formal register needs to be taught.
- Casual register needs to be recognized as the primary discourse for many students.
- Have students write in casual register and then translate into formal register. To get examples of casual register down on paper, ask them to write the way they talk.
- Establish as part of a discipline plan a requirement that students learn how to express their displeasure in formal register.
- Use graphic organizers to show patterns of discourse.
- In the classroom, tell stories both ways. Tell the story using the formal story structure, and then tell the story with the casual register structure. Talk about stories: how they stay the same and how they're different.
- Encourage participation in the writing and telling of stories.
- Use stories in math, social studies, and science to develop concepts.
- Make up stories with the students that can be used to guide behavior.
- Tell students how much the formal register affects [life chances including] their ability to get a well-paying job.

# Creating Mental Engagement

This section is about cognitive tools available for making learning accessible to students. These tools work because they avoid obstacles to students' mental engagement and make connections.

# Explicitness

Explicitness is a category of behaviors—four different kinds in all—that stitch together instructional episodes. They unite the patches of the quilt in interactive teaching. When they're missing the patches fall apart, and so does the instruction. These behaviors are more visible, in fact, in their absence because of the confusions and cognitive gaps that occur when they are omitted. Explicitness means expressly communicating and not leaving to implication these four events:

- Intention of cues
- Focus of questions
- Necessary steps in directions
- Meaning of references

## Intentions of Cues

Effective explainers cue students explicitly to make the connections and use the kinds of thinking that will lead to learning the material. They leave no logical gaps. Teachers who are not explicit make assumptions (unfortunately, often faulty) about students' ability to read their cues or read their intentions. These teachers are often guilty of playing "guess what's on the teacher's mind" (or "guess why we're doing this"), a game that serves no purpose in learning and intimidates and confuses students. When giving explicit cues, teachers build little bridges for students between cues they give and how the students are supposed to use them. Here is an example of inexplicit cuing behavior. The teacher is attempting to build an image that will help students learn the word *concave:*

> Before defining "concave," Orr [the teacher] asked, "Where do bears sleep?" He thought students would create an image of a cave that would help them remember the definition. Both

students [we interviewed] noticed this odd question and understood that it was supposed to provide a device for learning the definition. However, neither perceived that this device was an image [Winne and Marx, 1982, p. 510].

Orr didn't have a bad idea here; he was just so inexplicit with his cue that the students couldn't use it. He intended the image of the cave to be a visual mnemonic: "When you stand in front of a cave, the space seems to belly away from you. Likewise, a concave surface curves away from you." If he had said that, the students might have understood his cue and been able to use it to remember what *concave* means.

### Focus of Questions

Sometimes the focus of questions isn't explicit and the result is another version of "guess what's on the teacher's mind." In the example above, there are several good answers to Orr's question: "Where do bears live?" But he wants only one from the possible universe of correct answers. Here is another example. A Latin teacher has a student read a question from an exercise in a text. "What type of question is that?" the teacher asks. The student does not respond. No other students volunteer or appear to know either. What the teacher really means is: Which of the six types of questions on yesterday's handout—questions with *quid, cur, quis, quem, ubi,* or *quo*—is this? He assumes the student realizes this, but the student doesn't. The teacher doesn't realize that "what type" is not a cue to the student to scan the six types on yesterday's worksheet and pick one. The universe of possible answers the student is scanning is not six choices; it is infinite, and so he is at a loss.

The teacher then directs the student to turn to yesterday's handout and read the first item. The student obliges. In a tired voice, the teacher says, "Okay, read the next item." The student obliges.

This second item is an example of the type of question from the exercise that confounded the student. The student finishes reading it. There is a pause. The teacher gives the student a wide-eyed look: "Well?" "Oh," says the student and goes on to identify the text line as a *quid* question.

This confusion would have been avoided if the teacher had been explicit about the mental operation he wanted the student to do: ". . . By 'what type,' Luis, I mean which of the six types we discussed yesterday. Check your handout compared to the text line you just read. Everybody else check, too, to see if you'll agree." Teachers who are explicit show students directly how what they're doing now . . . or next. . . will help them get to the learning goal.

Being explicit means looking for clear steps that enable learners to know why questions are asked and how directions or examples relate to learning tasks. "He always asks us questions we can't answer," is a common report that students make about unclear teachers. They can't answer questions because the teacher fails to define or at least reference the domain the question is tapping. Consider this episode: "What is good writing?" asks Ms. Arroyo, and she has a specified list of attributes in mind that she proposes to get up on the board. But the question is a "sucker" question: students are going to volunteer all sorts of plausible answers that don't fit in with her lesson plan. That would be okay if she were to collect them all, discuss them, and then perhaps compare them to the text list she has in mind. But instead she's going to say "no," and "that's not quite what I'm looking for," and invalidate much good student thinking as she develops (that's how her lesson plan puts it) her list. She doesn't really mean, "What do you think good writing is?" She means, "What do I think good writing is?" In other words, "Read my mind."

Another easy trap for teachers to fall into regarding explicitness is asking questions in series.

Good and Brophy (2000, p. 390) describe a teacher who in discussing the War of 1812 asks in one continuous statement, "Why did we go to war? As a merchant how would you feel? How was our trade hurt by the Napoleonic War?" The teacher is trying to clarify the first question and focus thinking on an economic cause of the war. In his attempt, he confuses.

Questions in series are a temptation when we ask a question and get silence from the whole class. We want to give a clue, so we ask another question that is intended to lead the students toward our focus. What we may accidentally do is jerk students' train of thought around and leave them confused as to what we are really after.

### Necessary Steps in Directions

We may direct students to begin tasks but inadvertently leave out necessary steps in the directions. This can happen when we make unwarranted assumptions that students understand the conventions for how certain tasks are done. A teacher who says, "Get together in groups of four or five and brainstorm as many endings as you can for this short story," has omitted to instruct groups to choose a recorder, so they all start brainstorming without one.

Another example is, "Fix these sentences and then move on to the next assignment." Some students have interpreted "fix" as "cross out and write over the words that are wrong" (which the teacher, in fact, intends). Others are recopying the entire sentences with the corrections, which is taking four times as long. As a result, they won't have time to finish the second assignment.

A still deeper way to get students to understand the focus of directions is to give a partial model of how to frame their thinking to carry out a task given to them. This can be a sentence starter. For example, we have asked students to contrast the reasons different politicians in the South gave for secession in 1860 and said, "So when you're answering,

you might say: 'Jones argued for the preservation of the rights of states to make their own decisions, *whereas* Smith thought preservation of the southern economy based on slavery was the main argument. He called this the Southern way of life.'"

Including specific language forms in sample answers ("Jones said X, *whereas Smith* said Y" or "Jones said X, *in contrast to Smith,* who said Y") and asking students to model their answers cues them to what their teacher meant by the direction. Language and thought are intertwined, so sharing sample language forms of exemplary answers when giving directions guides students with more precision into productive work.

Overall, the goal of this area of performance is to spell out completely what we mean in directions and not assume steps are obvious to students.

### Meaning of References

Sometimes we make references to famous people, ideas, events, or works that are intended to elucidate current instruction, but the students may not know the references and therefore they confuse rather than clarify. They may, in fact, detract from instructional effectiveness because as students try to puzzle about the reference by asking themselves what it means, they may miss the next one or two points that are made. For example, a teacher who says, "Reading James Michener's *Hawaii* can make one feel like Sisyphus, which becomes apparent by about Chapter 25." That sentence won't mean anything to students who don't know that Sisyphus was a cruel Greek king who was condemned to forever roll a huge stone up a hill in Hades, only to have it roll down again every time he neared the top. Therefore, to feel like Sisyphus means to feel hopeless about ever finishing.

Being explicit at times like these would not foreclose our using arcane references, but would cue us to explain them on the spot so students could benefit.

## Making Cognitive Connections

The behaviors identified in this section build bridges for students between items of academic material in ways that are engaging.

### Showing Resemblance to Something Students Already Know

It is useful to show how new learning resembles previous work or students' previous knowledge, "demonstrating to students how things we are talking about resemble what they already know" (Freidrich, Galvin, and Book, 1976). It is appropriate to make this move within many styles of teaching simply as a good clarifier. Here is an example of this move:

TEACHER: When we first worked on multiplying, you learned that it was related to addition . . . how?

STUDENT: Repeated addition.

TEACHER: Right! Meaning what?

STUDENT: Multiplying is like adding the same number over and over again . . . as many times as you're multiplying it by.

TEACHER: Okay, very good. Now this division operation we've been working on today is really a lot like multiplication, except what it's doing in short-cut fashion isn't adding a number over and over again, it's . . . what?

STUDENT: Subtracting it.

TEACHER: "Right! Everybody see that? Matt? Can you explain in your own words how division is like multiplication?"

STUDENT: It's the backwards of multiplying.

TEACHER: An interesting way to put it; I think you understand. Lily, what do you think Matt means by *backward*?

Here's another example from a beginning chemistry course:

TEACHER: So we've proven this welding torch burns hotter than the straight propane burner. Do you remember what we did at the beginning of the year, heating sodium chlorate in the test tube? What happened when we held a glowing ember over the tube?

STUDENT: It burst into flame.

TEACHER: How did we explain that?

STUDENT: Heating the sodium chlorate drove off oxygen and the oxygen made the ember burn faster and hotter.

TEACHER: Right! And a welding torch is like that. We've got these two tanks . . . [and goes on to show how a welding rig mixes two gases, acetylene and oxygen and that the presence of the extra oxygen vastly increases combustion temperatures].

The integrating of the old with the new that takes place here builds intellectual links between items of information in such a way as to keep the picture of the whole emerging chain visible too. As students learn the new item, they simultaneously see the whole chain that is now one link longer. The link and chain analogy may break down for bodies of information that relate in other ways—like a web, for example—but the Clarity move serves the same purpose: linking the new item with the larger picture of established knowns (Ausubel, 1968; Gagne, 1992).

Bulgren and others from the Institute for Research on Learning Disabilities at the University of Kansas use anchoring tables (Exhibit 9.5) to show in a visual and precise way exactly what the similarities and differences are between new and old concepts.

An anchoring table is a graphic organizer—in this case a special-purpose one—to compare and contrast new information to previously learned information. The steps for phasing in the use of an anchoring table with students are the same as those described for other graphic organizers.

**Exhibit 9.5. Anchoring Table**

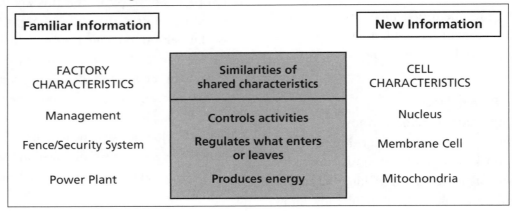

| Familiar Information | | New Information |
|---|---|---|
| FACTORY CHARACTERISTICS | **Similarities of shared characteristics** | CELL CHARACTERISTICS |
| Management | **Controls activities** | Nucleus |
| Fence/Security System | **Regulates what enters or leaves** | Membrane Cell |
| Power Plant | **Produces energy** | Mitochondria |

SUMMARY: A cell is a structure in which the nucleus controls activities, the membrane regulates, and the mitochondria produces energy.

The difference between this kind of integrating and "activating students' current knowledge" is that activating looks forward. It gets up on screen, as it were, students' existing conceptions. The associations or connections come from them as they see it at that moment. Thus, their minds are warmed up, and they have something to compare and contrast with the new learning when it comes along. What they already have may or may not be accurate, may be complete or incomplete. The purpose of eliciting the information from them is to get them thinking and give them a reference point against which to test the new learning. They may ask themselves: Is what we learn about chemistry, indeed, what we thought chemistry to be?

The purpose of showing resemblance to something students already know is to look backward. The teacher wants students to see that the new learning coming up really isn't so new or different (or so hard) and wants them to see that it fits in with something they already know—that there already exists a structure or a continuum in their heads to accommodate it.

## Asking Students to Compare and Contrast

"Compare and contrast the Hemingway short story we just read with the O. Henry story we read last week." This task makes students think. It calls for them to review each story, go into it, analyze it, and extract attributes of each author's writing to see how it is like or unlike attributes of the second author.

Compare-and-contrast tasks implicitly call for higher-order thinking in which one actively uses one's knowledge of the two items. You have to retrieve what you know and then manipulate it mentally. This is one of nine instructional practices that are included in Marzano's list of instructional strategies that have a high probability of enhancing students' achievement for all students in all subject areas at all grade levels. The effect sizes for this teaching practice are very high (1.61) for an average percentile gain of 45 (Marzano, Pickering, and Pollock, 2001.)

Comparing and contrasting lends itself beautifully to graphic organizers; skillful teachers draw on that powerful visual tool to empower the learning.

### Extending to Implications and Future Actions

Anything we do that causes students to think actively about academic material is an aid to learning. That is why questions that propel students to apply knowledge to a real situation (or to think about how they would apply it) augments learning:

"How might this court ruling affect criminal investigations?"

"What effect do you think this genetic finding will have on the way people live their lives?"

"How could you use this knowledge about area and perimeter if you were redoing your kitchen?"

Discussions that develop from such initial application questions can strengthen student understanding significantly if the teacher uses approaches consistent with those in the subsequent section on "making students' thinking visible."

### Making Transitions Between Ideas

These are brief, within-lesson transitions like segues made by an announcer and mostly applicable where direct instruction is taking place. (The teacher doesn't have the opportunity to guide transitions between items of information unless the teacher is leading the instructional activity.) In terms of clarity, these moves are verbal markers that help the student follow the road map as the teacher makes a left turn here, a right turn there, or circles back to the point of origin—for instance: "Okay, that word problem required us to multiply. Now let's move on to the next one and see if it is the same."

Notice the difference between that remark and a teacher who simply says, "Okay, let's move on

to the next problem." Telling the students to move on gets them from one place to the next but does not provide a transition. A transition move takes something about what has just been done and relates it to what's coming up immediately. It provides intellectual links like integrating moves do, but instead of linking to the learner's past experience or learning from other disciplines or other times, this link is between what has come immediately before and what's coming right now—in the lesson itself (Murray, 1991). Here's a good example: "So that's how the commercial banking system multiplies money deposited in checking accounts and creates new money. Now another way new money gets created is through consumer credit. Let's look at how all those plastic credit cards add to the banking system to create even more money."

### Signaling Shift in Activity, Pace, or Level

These moves are simple statements at transition points to prepare students for a change in the nature of cognitive work:

- Shift in activity: "Okay, that's all we're going to do with the lab reports today. Now let's take a look at the next chapter so we can preview the new material."
- Shift in pace: "We're going to pick up the pace now, so get ready for a little more action!"
- Shift in level of difficulty: "Now we're moving on to three-step problems instead of two-step, but still with the same operations."

### Foreshadowing

Consider these two teacher statements:

- "Well, you couldn't *have* two hydrochloric acid molecules on that side of the equation because it wouldn't balance. You don't have to worry about that now, but soon we will get to this notion that chemical equations must balance. When we talk about balancing equations, we'll be experimenting with the proportions of different chemicals that get used up in chemical reaction."

- "... And if you think Laura worked hard helping Ma around the house, wait 'til you see what she did with Pa Ingalls around hay making time. ['What's that mean?' a student asks.] Well, that's harvesting the hay and that was a very important part of farm life then ... now too. Anyway, hay making is coming up in a couple of chapters. I think you'll enjoy that section."

These examples of foreshadowing take a term or an idea that crops up and create a brief image of what it will be like or what it will be about. This is done so that when the students get to that point, it's not totally strange territory. "Oh, I remember we talked about that last week," a student may say to himself and start assimilating the ideas into his cognitive framework. Foreshadowing moves may crop up as moments of opportunity during instruction and are often unplanned. For instance, in the case of the second example above, the students had commented on how hard Laura works around the house, and their remarks made the teacher think of the days of hard labor she spent with her father making hay, so she brought it up for comparative purposes, knowing it was coming up in a few chapters.

When teachers end a lesson with an introduction or a forecast of what the students will be doing next, that is foreshadowing of a kind, but we tend to see that kind of a move as a cognitive transition: "Ladies and gentlemen, we're going to be using these vocabulary words today in our essays, so keep them handy and in a safe place." The difference is that a cognitive transition makes direct links

between what has just been completed and what's immediately to come in the flow of instruction—even if *immediately* is interrupted by overnight. Foreshadowing puts intellectual markers or hooks in place for items that are down the road and will not be dealt with the very next time the students work on this subject.

## Getting Inside Students' Heads: Cognitive Empathy

*Cognitive empathy* means the teacher is viewing the learning experience from the student's perspective and making decisions from that frame of reference. It is central to clarity and to good teaching in general because it enables teachers to know when students don't understand and then to zero in on what or what part of the material they don't understand.

Knowing when students don't understand and then determining what they don't understand are two different skills. Knowing when students don't understand suggests that teachers have means of checking for understanding during instruction. Determining what students don't understand implies that teachers have ways of unscrambling confusions that identify the specific points of misunderstanding and deal with them. Since both skill areas are important to clarity, we need to consider separately how teachers perform each.

## Checking for Understanding

We use the word *checking* to describe when teachers are trying to determine whether students are confused. When teachers are checking, they are reacting to the class, reaching out to students, and making a "yes ... no ... who?" judgment about whether understanding exists. There are four kinds of performance to consider here:

- Pressing on
- Reading body language
- Asking checking questions
- "Dipsticking," a term popularized by Madeline Hunter in the 1970s. It means taking a reading on the learning just as the oil dipstick in an auto engine gives you a reading on the oil level in the reservoir.

These are not mutually exclusive; we might be employing several of them at different points or simultaneously during the same lesson.

The first of these, *pressing on,* means we are not aware of or responsive to students' lack of understanding: *we just press on* with our explanations. Or, not being aware of the potential for confusion, we fail to give any directions for tasks that require explanation. Not checking and pressing on can occasionally be appropriate in fast-paced reviews of material previously taught if there has been thorough checking in the past and today our purpose is to highlight key terms or concepts. Even here, however, since checking takes so little time, it is wise to do it.

Second, we may check for understanding by *reading body language* that signifies confusion (postures and facial expressions, for example). Only when we notice such cues do we pause in our instruction. Relying on whether students appear to understand, however, can be risky. Students may provide no readable cues even though they are not following the instruction. For example, in a study of student thought processes during instruction, Peterson and Swing (1982) describe how students fooled observers who judged them to be attending to the lesson:

> Melissa's responses to the stimulated-recall interview suggested that she was not attending [although observers judged from her behavior that she was] and instead seemed to be spending much of the time worrying about her performance and the possibility of failure. For example, when asked what she was thinking after viewing the first videotape segment, Melissa replied: ". . . since I was just beginning, I was nervous and I thought maybe I wouldn't know how to do things." After viewing the second segment, Melissa said the following: "I was thinking that Chris would probably have the easiest time because she was in the top math group." After viewing the third segment Melissa responded: "Well, I was mostly thinking about what we talked about before—I was making a fool of myself." Finally, after the fourth segment, Melissa stated: "Well, this might be off the subject. I was thinking about my crocheting meeting 'cause I wanted to have it done" [p. 485].

Third, we may check more directly for general student understanding with periodic questions. We probe to see if students are still successfully comprehending the instruction. This checking may concern general understanding of content, procedures, or directions. It is worth pausing here for a minute to consider the use of recall and comprehension questions in checking for student understanding.

Recall questions call for factual answers that come directly from the material presented—for example, "What is the formula for finding the area of a triangle?" Comprehension questions can be answered only if students truly understand a lesson's concepts or operations. For example, the answer to, "What would you multiply to get the area of this triangle [one that has measurements marked, but no terms labeled]?" requires both the recall of the formula and an understanding of how to apply the formula to a specific triangle. Comprehension questions are those that can be answered only if students understand the concept being checked. Another example, "Why couldn't 'gobble' be on the page?"—where the guide words on the dictionary page are "hunt" and "mound"? Students can only answer that question if they understand how guide words bound the range of entries on a dictionary page.

Note that during "checking" we sometimes think we are getting a reading on comprehension, but in reality we are only checking recall of key words. "So the key elements of photosynthesis are . . . (chlorophyl) right and (sunlight) right; and one more . . .(carbon dioxide). Right. OK, you really do understand photosynthesis."

A fourth kind of checking for understanding involves *dipsticking*. Dipsticking occurs when the teacher is monitoring student understanding frequently and broadly across many students simultaneously. Hunter and her colleagues teach students to use signals—thumbs up, thumbs down, thumbs to one side—to send periodic messages to teachers about how well they understand something. There are any number of other forms of dipsticking teachers use to accomplish the same thing. For example, asking students, "Nod your head if you're with me so far," or calling for unison responses from the class can give a general reading according to how many students respond and how emphatic the response is.

These signals call for student self-assessment of whether they understand, but they may think they do when actually they don't. A more developed form of dipsticking gets an actual content answer from each student. In trigonometry, a teacher says: " When I call for the signal, hold up one, two, three, or four fingers to show in which quadrant the angle will terminate." In an English class, each student has cards that say S (for sentence), F (for fragment of a sentence), and RO (for run-on). The teacher says, "Hold up the appropriate card after I read each of the following."

These forms of dipsticking involve students' sending signals with their hands, cards, or another device. But dipsticking can be accomplished without signals. Some teachers pause in the middle of classes and give one-question quizzes . . . and then circulate and look over shoulders as students are writing to see how everyone is doing. Small numbers of college teachers around the country use electronic response devices at each student seat for a kind of dipsticking (Draper and Brown, 2004). This takes only a minute or two and gives an accurate reading of how well the students are understanding the material. The diagram in Figure 9.6 shows the relationship between signal and nonsignal forms of dipsticking.

Good performance on dipsticking is indicated when there is evidence that a teacher is taking constant readings across all (or at least most) of the students in the class to see if they're still understanding. Frequency and breadth characterize these readings of student understanding. Teachers may get these readings by simply asking a high volume of questions for a large number of students.

One can do dipsticking, that is, checking that is frequent and broad across the class, at either the recall or the comprehension level or both. But just because one is asking recall and comprehension questions doesn't necessarily mean dipsticking is taking place. They are overlapping but not necessarily inclusive sets. For example, one could be asking comprehension questions of individual students and moving on when the right answer was produced, thus not finding out if the rest of the students also understood (this is a frequent pattern in recitation lessons).

Dipsticking does not have to be a constant feature of every lesson. It could be out of place in

**Figure 9.6. Forms of Dipsticking**

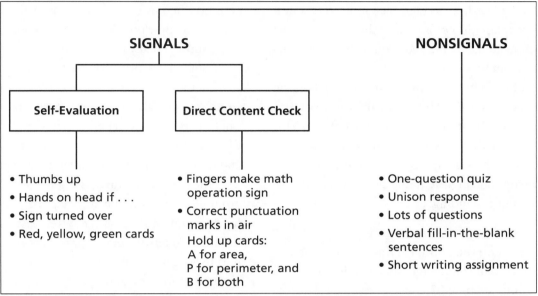

**Research for Better Teaching, Inc.** • One Acton Place, Acton, MA 01720 • (978)263-9449 • www.RBTeach.com

a true discussion where a line of argument is being developed or in a conceptual change lesson when students are encountering events in conflict with their native theories, constructing new theories to account for what they've observed, and testing the new theories. But even here there will be benchmarks when we will want to check students' understanding of something everyone should know. At those times, taking a true dipstick reading will provide much-needed information about who does and who doesn't understand.

## Unscrambling Confusions

When we detect that students are confused, the next clarity task is to find out what the students are confused about and tailor reexplanations accordingly. We call this *unscrambling confusions,* and it has a number of options to draw on:

- Do nothing at the moment.
- Reexplain.

- Isolate the point of confusion with pinpoint questions.
- Have a student explain his or her own current thinking.
- Persevere and return.

The first option, doing nothing in the moment, means making no response to the perceived confusion. There might be times when we acknowledge the confusion but do nothing to unscramble it right away: "I know this is a little difficult to see just yet, but hang in there, and I think it will make sense with a few more examples."

A second option is to launch into a reexplanation of the item. It may be slower or more detailed than the first explanation, or it may be a reexplanation using a different explanatory device. In either case we are presenting the same thing over again without any venture into the students' thinking.

A third option is to pose pinpoint questions to discover precisely where in the sequence of learning the student became confused. When that point is isolated, we swing in, economically omitting reexplanation of anything the students have already assimilated and move on with the reexplanation from there.

A fourth option is to ask students to describe or explain their thinking, to probe for how a student thinks about the concept or operation. This means to truly listen to the student and try to understand the student's frame of reference or way of conceptualizing the item. Questions can draw out the understanding:

- "How did you get that answer?"
- "How do you approach this kind of problem? Can you tell me what you did or thought about it?"
- "What did you try first? Why?"
- "What do you think this might mean?"
- "What does *city government* mean to you?"

In this way, sometimes we discover that apparently "wrong" answers aren't really wrong at all if we understand the student's assumptions and logic. As well, using the student's frame of reference with its meaning orientation enables us to reexplain the concept (or ask a series of questions that will bring the student closer to self-discovering the concept) from a vantage point that will have more meaning for the student. We might also discover that the concept turns out to be outside the boundaries of the student's thinking system, in which case it's an inappropriate objective altogether. And that is quite an important thing to find out.

The final option, persevering and returning, might be an integral part of the previous three but with an additional element: the return. We persevere when we find a student confused. We stick with the student who is confused, perhaps have several exchanges with him if time allows, and then, most important, come back to him later in the period to see if he really got it. This return visit may be accomplished by review questions or by asking the student to apply the idea in some other context to make sure he really understands it.

Sometimes there isn't time in the period for a teacher to unscramble all the confusions of all the students—a reality we all live with. In that case, what a perseverant teacher does is to note or record who specifically is still foggy on the new concept and make some provision for a return engagement with those students (arranging for a short small-group session right then and there perhaps, or asking Sam and Olivia to stop by after classes for a few minutes) to ensure that they will receive the support they need. (Notice how this option ties in with sending high expectations messages. In Chapter Twelve, we include students who don't get it yet as one of the ten arenas for sending the three key messages: "This is important; you can do it with effective effort; I won't give up on you.")

## Making Students' Thinking Visible

The context thus far for making students explain their thinking has been to unscramble confusions. The notion of making a student's thinking visible, however, has more reach. Consider the following:

> If you can both listen to children and accept their answers not as things to be judged right or wrong but as pieces of information which may reveal what the child is thinking, you will have taken a giant step toward becoming a master teacher . . . [Easley and Zwoyer, 1975].

> It was listening to their own students solve problems that made the greatest difference in [teachers'] instructional practice [Borko and Putnam, 1995].

> My definition of a good teacher has changed from "one who explains things so well that

students understand" to "one who gets students to explain things so well that they can be understood" [Reinhart, 2000].

These authors argue for the special importance of knowing what is going on inside students' heads. The behavior they are urging goes beyond the checking and unscrambling behaviors we have profiled so far in this chapter. They are part of a tradition of educational research that advises teachers:

1. Structure your interaction with students so you have frequent access to what and how they are thinking about the topics you are dealing with. This means asking them to frequently express, verbally or in writing, what that thinking is.
2. Get students engaged in explaining the rationale for their thinking and supporting it out loud.
3. Cause interaction and discussion among students about the thinking that surfaces.
4. Build a climate of safety and mutual inquiry among the students so they are not afraid of being wrong and will actively speak their minds (see Chapter Fourteen, "Classroom Climate").

These things happen by structuring the learning experiences so students are talking about their ideas and skills with one another or using them in some other active way to resolve a problem or answer a question (Applebee and Langer, 2003; Allington and Johnston, 2001; Cazden, 1992; Dillon, 1988; Mehan, 1974; Nystrand, 1997). Here are indicators David Perkins (2003, p. 5) looks for to see if, at appropriate points, student thinking is made visible to the teacher and to other students: "Are students explaining things to one another? Are students offering creative ideas? Are they, and I, using the language of thinking? Is there a pro/con list on the blackboard? Is there a brainstorm about alternative plans on the wall? Are students debating interpretations?"

Table 9.3 spells out the behaviors one sees when making students' thinking visible as a teacher commitment. We have titled this "Verbal Behaviors in a Class That Let Kids Get Smart" because there is a connection between these behaviors and the positive beliefs about students' ability that we introduce in Chapter Twelve, "Expectations."

These behaviors derive from a long tradition of theorizing and research on learning that is termed *constructivism*. This orientation supports classroom activity that is very different from lecture, presentation, demonstration, recitation, and frontal explicit teaching. The point of the research has not been to denigrate the explicit teaching of skills or the value, appropriately chosen, of times for presentational teaching. The point is that there is a wide range of situations where deep understanding and high operational proficiency are produced by posing problems or questions with properly supported climates where students' thinking is consistently invited, made

| Intention | Value |
|---|---|
| • To know what and how this individual student is thinking about the idea | • Curiosity |
| • To cause dialogue between and listening among students | • Student talk and interaction |
| • Provide encouragement, acknowledgment, and safety for students to risk speaking | • Classroom climate |
| • To make an idea clearer and more accessible through models, visuals, and sequence of questions | • Clarity |

**Table 9.3. Verbal Behaviors in a Class That Let Kids Get Smart**

### Teacher starts by asking a good open-ended question that gets students thinking. Then . . .

1. Asks students to explain the thinking behind their answers whether they're right or wrong.
2. Asks students if they agree or disagree with a student answer.
3. Asks students to comment or add on to a student's response or idea.
4. Creates and facilitates dialogue between students about their ideas.
5. Asks follow-up questions that are similar to ones just discussed to see if student really understands.
6. Asks students to make connections to something another student said or something else they know.
7. Credits meaning to student comments, even obscure ones, and probes for the student's thinking . . . and does the same with incorrect answers.
8. Uses wait time, allowing students to struggle, and dwells with the student's thinking, sticking with them.
9. Comes back to a student to check and clarify what his or her thinking is, given the comments of other students.
10. Asks questions to surface discrepancies between what the student says and the information in front of them: "How can that be? What's going on there?"

### Students:

11. Do the majority of the talking.
12. Are expected to explain their thinking.
13. Show they are listening to one another.
14. Are willing to admit confusion or not knowing.
15. Challenge each other's thinking nonjudgmentally.
16. Take initiative to explain another student's thinking, including how he or she might have made an error.
17. Who get it quickly take responsibility for helping those who don't.

### Other teacher observables:

18. Provides a clear visual display of the (mathematical) idea.
19. Gives encouragement.
20. Praises good thinking.
21. Validates students who acknowledge confusion.
22. Expresses confidence in the students explicitly.

**Research for Better Teaching, Inc.** • One Acton Place, Acton, MA 01720 • (978) 263-9449 • www.RBTeach.com

visible, and used as the interactive core of learning experiences. More and more research is confirming that, as Applebee and Langer (2003) stated, "Students whose classroom . . . experiences emphasize discussion-based approaches in the context of high academic demands internalize the knowledge and skills necessary to engage in challenging . . . tasks on their own." Behind the behaviors outlined in Table 9.3 lies a set of intentions and accompanying values.

In the 1950s and 1960s, researchers did studies in which they calculated the percentage of student talk to teacher talk in classrooms and compared the figures with student achievement. Their hypothesis was that teachers talk too much, and that when student talk fills more of the airspace in the classroom, more student learning would occur. The research findings were weak though positive. The question this research suggested was, "What kind of student talk matters?"

In the 1980s many provocative studies compared learning and thinking effects between student-led discussions and teacher-led discussions. In one condition, the English teachers got together to formulate the most provocative and interesting questions they could create and conducted discussions with students based on these questions. They wanted to provoke higher-level thinking. In the other condition, researchers simply seated the students in a circle and asked them to respond to the story and what thoughts it stimulated for them. The teachers facilitated a discussion completely fueled by the students' own reactions and questions. This second condition produced more higher-level thinking by the students and more insight and personal connections. (Eeds and Wells, 1989). Summarizing this literature, Lyons (1996) found that "students who participated in peer-led discussions have a better understanding of text, express themselves in more complex ways, approach text more

confidently, write better analytical essays, and are more focused on their reading related tasks."

The primary issue of interest was student ownership of the direction and the flow of the conversations in pursuit of their own reactions and interactions with their peers. The students' own thinking drove the event, and their thinking was visible to both teacher and other students.

Dillon (1981), pursuing another tack, had been researching what teachers called discussions and proposing that a true discussion should have a definition that separated it from a recitation, that is, an extended Q&A driven by the teacher's selection of questions. Such "discussions" were really oral tests conducted by the teacher, where the teacher moved on to the next question-producing point after the desired answer had been produced. To Dillon, a true discussion surfaced different points of view, and the teacher and students were in a more equal position intellectually in that the issues being discussed did not have definitive right answers. Thus, the idea of justifying one's position and providing evidence or rationale was essential to his definition of a true discussion.

Dillon took a different approach to getting students active in expressing what they were thinking from the people interested in peer-led discussions, but the content being taught was content where different points of view were possible, that is, where the content was not about scientific principles or mathematical certainties but about humanities topics where ambiguity often reigns.

Teachers at the time were interested in using such discussions to increase student participation and motivation and as ways to assess students' ability to apply in context skills taught in more direct instruction (for example, applying knowledge of the three branches of government to a discussion of whether the Supreme Court makes laws).

So we had on the table at this point the themes of (1) more student talk and talk that represents students' authentic thinking about the topic, and (2) the teacher as facilitator of that thinking. But surely, it was thought, this approach to surfacing student thinking would not be as applicable to content where precision, formulas, and algorithms were the order of the day. Then came three mathematics teacher-researchers: Magdelene Lampert and Deborah Loewnberg Ball, in Michigan, and Deborah Schifter in Massachusetts. Pioneers in what is now called reform-oriented math, they taught mathematics concepts and operations to elementary children with lessons that look much like the lessons of the Japanese mathematics teachers that drew such interest after Stigler and Hiebert's two TIMMS video studies. They put many fewer math problems in front of the children, and the children as a class and as groups were asked to solve them. When different answers were produced, children were asked to explain their thinking out loud, and other children were asked to comment. The climate was carefully constructed so that all thinking was encouraged, and students were asked to listen and respond to one another in the service of problem solving rather than being the first or fastest to get answers. Making student thinking visible in a context of problem solving and joint inquiry into mathematical principles was the ethos of the instruction and the value base of the way teachers chose to interact with students and have them interact with each other.

In the mid-1990s Lauren Resnick applied the term *accountable talk* to this kind of student discourse in which student thinking, supported by rationale or evidence, and a climate of mutual support and risk taking became a principle of learning that she advocated. Her students were urged to read Vygotsky (see Moll, 2001, for a summary of Vygotsky's influence on this movement) to establish the theoretical foundation for social learning and climate building.

Three other authors stand out for their work in raising our consciousness about the importance of making students' thinking visible. Throughout the 1970s, Bill Hull conducted a series of "Children's Thinking Seminars" where teachers met regularly to discuss cases of children's processing. Through logs, writing, and discussion, teachers were stimulated to reflect on the children's thinking to try to see how and why they were interpreting phenomena and doing problem solving as they were. Hugh Mehan (1974) analyzed classroom discourse between teachers and children and showed that children's "errors" in following directions were eminently logical interpretations of the adult talk when understood from the standpoint of students. Eleanor Duckworth (1981) conducted a series of investigations with teachers into youngsters' thinking in which the starting point was teachers studying their own thinking and learning processes. The outcome was that . . . "to 'give a child reason' became the motto, the aim, of much of the teachers' subsequent work. This was the challenge they put to themselves every time a child did or said something whose meaning was not immediately obvious. That is, the teachers sought to understand the way in which what a child says or does could be construed to make sense—they sought to 'give him reason'" (Duckworth, 1981, p. 6).

One of Duckworth's important messages was to point out that the main contribution of Piaget to teachers was not his stages of development but understanding his clinical interview technique "in which the adult role is to find out as much as possible about what the child himself believes about an issue" (Duckworth, 1981, p. 14). In addition:

> To the extent that one carries on a conversation with a child, as a way of trying to understand a child's understanding, the child's understanding increases "in the very process." The questions

which the interlocutor asks, in an attempt to clarify for him/herself what the child is thinking, oblige the child to think a little further, also . . . What do you mean? How did you do that? How does that fit with what she just said? I don't really get that; could you explain it another way? Could you give me an example? How do you figure that? In every case, those questions are primarily a way for the interlocutor to try to understand what the other is understanding. Yet, in every case, also, they engage the other's thoughts and take them a step further [p. 21].

Jill Bodner Lester, writing in Deborah Shifter's *What's Happening in Math Class* (1996), gives a wonderful image through dialogue of how talking mathematics and making students' thinking visible can unfold over the course of a year. She shows how a teacher adds layers of complexity and demand to what she expects students to do in becoming an interactive community of mathematics learners. It is also a developmental approach to creating a climate of safety and risk taking where children can come to a deep understanding of mathematical concepts.

Here are a few excerpts:

In order to engage children in thinking and discussion, I work to establish predictable classroom routines. Most days begin with a problem written on the board—which is read aloud twice, so that those who do not yet read well will have access to it. Then I ask the children to solve the problem mentally and to signal me when they have an answer. When everyone seems to be ready, I solicit answers and record each response on the board without comment. Our routine continues with a discussion of the answers that the children find troublesome or unreasonable. Then the children work in small groups to explore their ideas with concrete

materials and to find alternative solutions that support the correctness of their answers. Finally, the children and I gather in a circle on the floor to discuss the small group explorations and discoveries. This routine is introduced over time and plays an integral part in the establishment of a community of mathematics learners.

On the second day of school, we continued to explore the cube game in small groups. I joined Kelly, Nathan, and Isaac in a corner of the room. When I arrived, Kelly had one hand behind her back and was holding 7 cubes in front of her. Nathan was on his knees and leaning toward Kelly as he counted the cubes aloud one by one. Isaac was sitting apart from the group with his legs crossed. His attention appeared to be elsewhere.

I quickly assessed what I observed—Kelly and Nathan were actively engaged; Isaac was not—and decided to try to draw Isaac in.

*Teacher:* (I look directly at Isaac.) How many cubes do you think Kelly has behind her back?
*Nathan:* 13
*Teacher:* What do you think, Isaac?
*Isaac:* (Isaac looks uncomfortable. He squirms and moves a little farther away, his response barely audible.) 13
*Teacher:* What do you think, Kelly?
*Kelly:* (Kelly responds without the slightest hesitation.) 13.

I knew that the children solved the problem correctly, but I wanted them to begin to think beyond just answering—to focus on how they solved problems and why they chose their solution method. I looked from one child to the next, expecting my next question to be met with silence.

*Teacher:* How do you know that the answer is 13?

Nathan surprised me. He didn't seem to be the least bit put off by my question, and his explanation began to flow immediately.

*Nathan:* I knew it had to be 13. It had to be an odd number, 3 or 5. There's no 2, 4, 6, 8, 10. 7 + 3 = 10. 10 − 7 is 3. We have a whole 10 left. That's 13.

From what Nathan was saying, I could tell that he knew something about odd and even numbers, that he knew about grouping 10s and 1s, and he had used this knowledge to figure out his solution to the problem. However, I was still trying to understand the flow of his thinking, so I said, "I'm a little confused. I don't understand what you're telling us about odd numbers." Nathan's expression became a scowl. His left shoulder dropped, and he moved farther away from me. It was clear that he was annoyed with me and that my question made him feel uncomfortable. That was all right with me, as I wanted Nathan to think more deeply about his idea. I expected that he would eventually take on the challenge of my questions, if not today, then tomorrow, or next week, or next month.

[This is a key aspect of constructivist teaching: the push for students to think more deeply and take on the challenge of difficult material without fear of being wrong. . . . and the teacher's comfort with students struggling with ideas.]

Isaac now moved a little closer to the group. He had had time to think and appeared to be ready to risk sharing.

*Isaac:* There are 7 here. I counted up to 13 and 7 more. That's 20.
*Kelly:* (Kelly smiles and speaks quietly.) I started with 20 cubes and I counted out 7 behind my back. I counted backwards—20, 19, 18, 17,

16, 15, 14. The next number would have been 13. I knew there were 13 behind my back.

Each of the three children had solved the problem differently. Kelly had counted backwards from 20 in order to figure out how many cubes remained behind her back. Isaac had counted up to determine his answer, 13, and Nathan had both added and subtracted as he manipulated the odd and even numbers in his solution. Now I wanted the children to think about how it was possible that three seemingly unrelated solution processes could produce the same answer.

*Teacher:* It seems as if some of you solved the problem by adding and some of you solved the problem by subtracting, but you all got the same answer. How can that be?
*Nathan:* We're smart. We like to do it in different ways?
*Teacher:* Why does it work?
*Nathan:* (Nathan looks away and ignores me, directing his question only to the two children.) So, what's the answer?
*Isaac:* Let's count them.

In another example, the class was working on this problem: If there are nine boys and eleven girls in kindergarten, how many children are there in total?

When the children appeared to be ready, I asked, "Is there anyone who has an answer that he or she would like to share with us?" Children offered the answers 18, 20, and 19, all of which I recorded on the board without response. I accepted correct and incorrect answers—in the weeks to follow, as this procedure became routine, I would begin to ask the children whether any of the answers bothered them.

*Teacher:* How did you get those answers?

*Zoe:* (Zoe smiles.) I like to work with 10s. I took 1 away from the 11. I added it to the 9. That made 10 + 10. That's 20. (Zoe's smile gets even bigger.)

*Teacher:* That's interesting. Can anyone explain what Zoe did in his or her own words? (I want to be sure that the other children are following Zoe's thinking.)

As I waited for a response to my question, I looked around the room. The 25 children were looking right at me. This was different. Just two weeks ago they had been looking away and trying to avoid my questions. Slowly, a few hands rose. I called on Susan.

[This is evidence of a climate being developed where children will take the risk to think aloud in front of peers and teacher.]

*Susan:* (Susan always speaks softly. Her voice is very low, but the children are listening intently. The room is silent but for Susan's voice.) She started with an 11 and 9. She took 1 from the 11. Now it's a 10. She added the extra 1 to the 9. That's a 10, too. Then she added the two 10s and got 20.

*Teacher:* (I look directly at Zoe.) Is that what you were doing, Zoe?

*Zoe:* Yes!

*Teacher:* Does anyone have any questions? (I wait for a response. There is none.) Who else has a solution to share?

Several hands were raised, some waving furiously in my direction, others barely raised high enough to see. Isaac's was someplace in the middle, and I called on him.

*Isaac:* (Isaac sits upright in his chair. His voice is strong.) I added 11 and 9. I started with 11. Then I went 12, 13, 14, 15, 16, 17, 18, 19, 20.

*Teacher:* How did you know when to stop?

A puzzled look came over Isaac's face. He crinkled his eyebrows, squinted, and remained quiet.

*Laurel:* (Laurel leaps up out of her seat and shouts.) There are 9 numbers after 11!

There were nods and smiles everywhere. I was excited, too. Laurel had become so invested in figuring out what Isaac was thinking, she forgot that she is usually quiet and reserved. The other children—Sam included—who were nodding and smiling also must have been thinking about what Isaac was trying to do.

*Sam:* I did it that way, too!

Like Laurel, Sam had spoken out without having been recognized and looked around to see if there were any repercussions for speaking out of turn. There were none, so he smiled, wiggled in his seat a little, and returned his attention to the front of the room.

*Keith:* I have another way. I know that 9 is three 3s; 11 + 3 is 14; 14 + 3 is 17; 17 + 3 is 20.

*Kelly:* (Kelly is kneeling on one leg as she stands up beside her chair.) I pictured the cubes in my head. There were 11 of them, plus 9 more. First I counted them one way. Then I checked it by counting the other way.

Kelly walked forward and drew a picture of her solution on the board. There was a chorus of "Aah" and "Mmmm" after she finished. I thought about whether to look more closely at a particular solution, but I decided to let the children continue. They were discussing the math at hand in their own way, sharing their ideas and interacting with one another, and that was far better than focusing on me!

After a while the interactions among the children slowed, and I decided to intervene in order to add a different dimension to their analysis—assessment of answers for reasonableness.

*Teacher:* What if I were to say that there were 5 children in the kindergarten class? (My comments are greeted with laughter.)

*Jeremy:* Five doesn't make sense!
*Teacher:* Why not?

Jeremy shrugged, threw his hands up in the air, and grinned.

*Alec:* (Alec clears his throat in order to get everyone's attention.) I think that what he means is that 11 is more than 5 + 5.
*Jeremy:* (Jeremy is grinning from ear to ear. He nods.) Yeah!!!
*Teacher:* What if I were to say there are 40 children in kindergarten?
*Jeremy:* (Jeremy speaks out confidently.) 40 is way too much.
*Jamie:* Even two 11s aren't 40.

We have devoted substantial space to this history and the examples of what it sounds like in action because we want readers to know how important it is. This is a profound and important aspect of successful teaching. The research on making students' thinking visible is another way of saying, "Listen to the children." Over a five-year period, District 2 in New York City went from sixteenth to first place in math achievement by investing in the development of these skills broadly in all their teachers (Alvarado, Elmore, and Resnick, 2000). This kind of teaching takes a dynamic skill set that should be on every teacher's professional development agenda.

# Consolidating and Anchoring the Learning

## Summarizing

*Summarizing* is the final item in the list of instructional strategies for clarity. At the end of a lesson, it means explicitly pulling everything together for all to see or hear. Summarizing is also something that can be productive during a lesson.

Summarizing can be accomplished by the teacher or the students. That it happens is of primary importance; who does it is another decision. There are two principles of learning (see Chapter Ten) that underscore the benefits of summarizing at the conclusion of a learning experience: sequence and say-do. The sequence principle says that what happens in the beginning and end of events or experiences is what people tend to retain longest. Therefore, teachers who protect the last few minutes of class for summarizing increase the likelihood that the important ideas will stick.

The say-do principle means that whether learners take in information by reading it, hearing it, seeing it, or some combination of those, retention is limited on average to no more than 50 percent of what has been presented. It is when the learner has to shift from receptive into active mode with new information (putting it in his or her own words, talking about it, writing about it, explaining it to others, applying it), that retention rate grows on average to 70 to 90 percent.

In other words, when students must get cognitively active with the material, they have to personally reorganize the information and concepts they have received so that they can state them in their own words. Asking students to do the summarizing means asking them to say what they have learned in their own words. (It also means having to check their summarizing to see that it is accurate and complete.) It is the "in your own words" feature that is critical because it forces the learners to sift, reorder, and organize the information themselves. They can't just let the new learning lie on the library shelf of their minds as a memory trace. They have to pick up the pieces and put them together, and the very act of doing so strengthens the learning. Hence, teachers who ask students to do the summarizing themselves increase the likelihood that more of the learning will stick and that they will deepen their understanding of concepts. And when all of the students are involved in doing so simultaneously, another powerful factor is added: the principle of learning called active participation is engaged (see Chapter Ten).

There are many ways to accomplish this summarizing so that all students are involved. Keeping a learning log (Pradl and Mayher, 1985) is one way. Typically students make entries during the last five minutes of each period, responding to the following types of questions (Sanders, 1985):

- What did I learn today? What puzzled me?
- What did I enjoy, hate, accomplish in class today?
- How did I learn from the discussion or lesson?
- How was my performance in class?

Teachers can also ask students to do this orally, in pairs at the end of class, or at appropriate stopping points within class. Rowe (1983) has demonstrated that students' performance increases when two minutes are provided for them to summarize and clarify for each other in small groups after every ten minutes of teacher-led instruction. This "10–2 rule" provides students the same kind of opportunity to get active with the material in their own words. Tobin (1985) comments, "The results [of this technique] are consistent with our interpretation that students need time to process lesson content in information-dense subjects such as science."

Summarizing questions can be made specific and tailored to any content: "Based on our discussion so far, tell your partner the principal causes of the Civil War. Then have your partner tell them back to you." If the class has reached consensus on the causes, this is a summarizing of the information. (If the class has not resolved the question, having pairs work like this is more than summarizing, especially if they are asked to back up their respective arguments.) In addition, a teacher may ask students to summarize in writing (perhaps in notebooks) the main idea of each section in textbook chapters. Having to stop and summarize periodically as they read forces active cognitive processing; the children have to put what they have learned in their own words to write a summary. *Voila*, better learning. Studies have shown improved comprehension of text (not just stories) with convincing consistency (D'Angelo, 1983) when students do this kind of summarizing. And a number of writers have even offered useful models for teaching students how to do this summarizing-in-writing as they read (Hahn and Gardner, 1985).

In the introduction to this chapter we pointed out that Clarity as an area of teaching performance is about the things teachers do to support student understanding. In an earlier section of the chapter, we described teacher moves that help to clarify or frame the big picture for students: communicating objectives; giving itineraries; reminding students of the big ideas and essential questions for the unit and how a lesson relates to those; sharing the reasons an objective is important and the reasons for (individual) activities. We explored things to consider to get teacher and students ready for instruction: activate students' knowledge to create anticipation; anticipate confusions and do something to address them; gather preassessment data to plan where and how to begin where the learners are in relation to our objectives. Next, we discussed instructional moves to consider when presenting information: being intentional and using a variety of explanatory devices, monitoring your speech and language patterns to match to the group and prevent confusion; being explicit and not leaving to chance that students understand the intention of your cues, the focus of your questions, the necessary or critical steps in directions, the meaning behind your references; making cognitive connections for or with students by showing or exploring how new knowledge is like something students already know; providing cognitive transitions between ideas; signaling shifts; and foreshadowing. To monitor student understanding, we discussed the importance of checking to ensure all students are understanding, unscrambling confusion when it arises, and getting students to make their thinking visible. And the final concern is in protecting time for summarizing. Each of these is a functional aspect of the Clarity area of performance.

# Questioning

Questioning is done in classrooms for many purposes. We could say that it crosses nearly all the areas of performance in teaching. There are four main points about questioning that we want to highlight in this chapter. Each has large implications for practice:

- Questioning is not a unitary skill; it is an entire toolbox, and the tools selected should be matched to the instructional purpose. Figure 9.7 shows a variety of purposes for asking questions. Table 9.4 includes sample questions designed for each purpose.

- All children need to be engaged in conversation with higher-level thinking questions. This is especially important for children who are low in academic proficiency. Students who are three or four grade levels behind in literacy skills are still perfectly capable of higher-level thinking: inference, analysis, connection making. Furthermore, teachers need to engage them in this kind of thinking if they want to keep these children engaged in school.

- Questions should be planned when we are planning lessons, and planned with more specificity and detail than many of us are used to doing. Don't just plan the activities and topics for discussion and then wing it on what questions to ask as we go.

- Students should be taught to ask questions.

## Purposes of Questions

Questions are tools for accomplishing tasks. It is the tasks that matter, and being deliberate about what we are trying to accomplish with the question and having the repertoire of tools for accomplishing them. Question asking is not an independent and self-contained skill. A question is a tool, and not the only one, for stimulating many important student cognitions: framing, activating, connection making, analyzing, extending, applying, inferring, conjuring implications, checking for understanding, identifying points of confusion, implementing a model of teaching, summarizing, and other tasks. Rather than trying to develop questioning generically as some kind of skill, it is more productive to focus on what mental act we want to generate in students at a given moment and what move (perhaps a question) we will make to provoke it.

**Figure 9.7. Purposes of Questions**

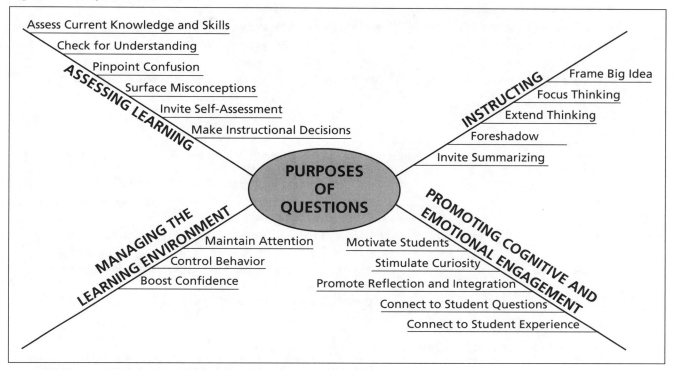

Assess Current Knowledge and Skills
Check for Understanding
Pinpoint Confusion
Surface Misconceptions
Invite Self-Assessment
Make Instructional Decisions

ASSESSING LEARNING

INSTRUCTING
Frame Big Idea
Focus Thinking
Extend Thinking
Foreshadow
Invite Summarizing

PURPOSES OF QUESTIONS

MANAGING THE LEARNING ENVIRONMENT
Maintain Attention
Control Behavior
Boost Confidence

PROMOTING COGNITIVE AND EMOTIONAL ENGAGEMENT
Motivate Students
Stimulate Curiosity
Promote Reflection and Integration
Connect to Student Questions
Connect to Student Experience

*Source:* Adapted from Bellon, Bellon, and Blank (1992).

## Higher-Level Thinking Questions

Here are some interesting statistics about teacher questions. Quite consistently studies show that about 60 percent of questions are recall or factual questions. The figure can rise to 80 percent recall in some classrooms (Cotton, 2000). Only 20 percent are higher level, and the remaining 20 percent are procedural. These are not good statistics for preparing students adequately for a twenty-first-century world.

Students who get instruction without higher-order questions score in the fiftieth percentile on tests compared to the seventy-fifth percentile if the same students engage in lessons where there are many higher-order questions (Gall and others, 1978). The reason for this is that higher-order think-

ing is inherently more interesting and it causes cognitive processing and organization of information that builds more elaborate mental structures. The point that matters is that all students should be brought to high levels of thinking with academic material through an appropriate balance of higher- and lower-level questions. To stretch students, teachers have to make sure all the students are invited equally into the thinking club, not just some.

Research on questioning does not say simply that the more high-level questions, the better. It does not say that low-level questions are useless:

The popular belief that lower level questions are less effective . . . has not been upheld. Achievement is related to the use of a variety of

**Table 9.4. Sample Questions**

| Purpose of Questions | Example |
|---|---|
| **Assessing Learning** | |
| Assess Current Knowledge and Skills | "Why do some objects float in water and others sink?" |
| Check for Understanding | "Can you tell me in your own words how photosynthesis works?" |
| Pinpoint Confusions | "What did you do after you entered the data?" |
| Surface Misconceptions | "Why do you think we have winter and summer?" |
| Invite Self-Assessment | "Which ones do you know well, and which ones do you need to practice tomorrow?" |
| Make Instructional Decisions | "Do we need more time on this?" |
| **Instructing** | |
| Frame Big Ideas | "What makes humans human?" |
| Extend Thinking | "Is this similar or different from the situation in Palestine?" |
| Deepen Thinking | "Go inside that now and tell me why that position might have made sense from his point of view." |
| Foreshadow | "Based on what we've explored today, why do you think the colonists decided to stay?" |
| Promote Transfer | "So how could you use this information about evaporation in your everyday practical life?" |
| Invite Summarizing | "What do you think were the most important points made in the discussion so far?" |
| **Managing the Learning Environment** | |
| Boost Confidence | "How would you do it, Tim?" [Tim is not confident of his math ability, but Mrs. Johnson has heard him propose a novel solution in his group. She wants him to present it to the class, knowing it will be appreciated by them and be a validating experience for Tim.] |
| Control Behavior | "How would you do it, Tim?" [Tim is starting to distract Millie, and Mrs. Johnson moves toward them while asking a question to get him engaged.] |
| Maintain Attention | "How would you do it, Tim?" [Tim's attention is wandering and Mrs. Johnson startles him back into focus.] |
| **Promoting Cognitive and Emotional Engagement** | |
| Motivate Students | "What product do you most want to design an ad program for?" |
| Stimulate Curiosity | "What do you know about voting and elections in this country?" |
| Promote Active Reflection and Integration | "What are three things you've learned, two questions you have, and one thing you don't understand yet?" |
| Connection to Students' Own Questions About Deeper Meaning | "What do you think the most important things are about having a family?" |
| Connect to Student Experience | "In 'Stone Soup,' does the villagers' reaction to the soldiers remind you of anything you've experienced in the neighborhood?" |
| | "What do you think the crime movie *The Negotiator* might have to do with international affairs?" |

**Research for Better Teaching, Inc.** • One Acton Place, Acton, MA 01720 • (978)263-9449 • www.RBTeach.com

**Figure 9.8  Map of Pedagogical Knowledge**

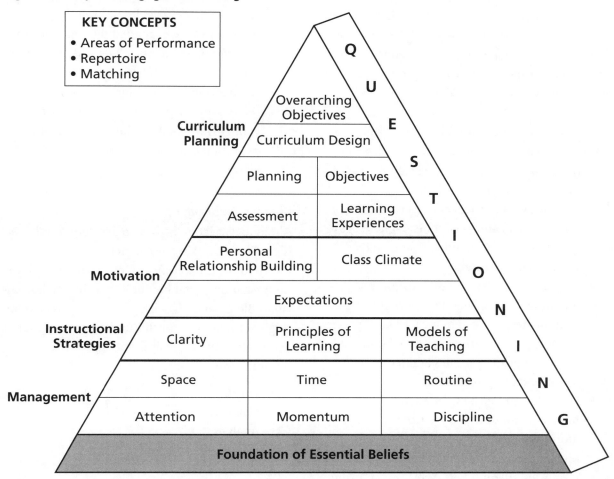

KEY CONCEPTS
• Areas of Performance
• Repertoire
• Matching

Overarching Objectives

**Curriculum Planning**   Curriculum Design

Planning | Objectives

Assessment | Learning Experiences

Personal Relationship Building | Class Climate

**Motivation**

Expectations

**Instructional Strategies**   Clarity | Principles of Learning | Models of Teaching

Space | Time | Routine

**Management**

Attention | Momentum | Discipline

**Foundation of Essential Beliefs**

QUESTIONING

**Research for Better Teaching, Inc.** • One Acton Place, Acton, MA 01720 • (978)263-9449 • www.RBTeach.com

questions designed to accomplish specific purposes. For example, a pattern of factual questions, student responses, and teacher feedback has been found to be the most functional mechanism for student achievement in basic skills. . . . [Furthermore] successful responding to lower level questions is a prerequisite for higher level learning. Students need a firm base of factual knowledge when they are engaged in higher level thinking activities. It is impossible to summarize or evaluate information that a person does not know or understand [Bellon, Bellon, and Blank, 1992, pp. 315–316].

At the conclusion of an exhaustive review of the research on questioning, Bellon, Bellon, and Blank (1992) concluded that teachers should plan questions and write them down in advance as part of the planning process to accomplish the learning objective of the lesson. If the objective of the lesson calls for analysis and application of information, they may need to ask quite a few recall questions first.

As always in skillful teaching, the balance of higher- to lower-level questions must be a match to the situation. But overall, there should be a high portion of higher-level questions for all students. Here is a summary of the research findings on higher- and lower-cognitive questions (Cotton, 1988, p. 5):

- In most classes above the primary grades, a combination of higher- and lower-cognitive questions is superior to the exclusive use of one or the other.
- Students whom teachers perceive as slow or poor learners are asked fewer higher-cognitive questions than students perceived as most capable learners.
- Increasing the use of higher-cognitive questions (to considerably above the 20 percent incidence noted in most classes) produces superior learning gains for students above the primary grades and particularly for secondary students.
- For older students, increases in the use of higher-cognitive questions (to 50 percent or more) are positively related to increases in on-task behavior, length of student responses, the number of relevant contributions volunteered by students, the number of student-to-student interactions, student use of complete sentences, speculative thinking on the part of students, and relevant questions posed by students.
- For older students, increases in the use of higher-cognitive questions (to 50 percent or more) are positively related to increased teacher expectations about children's abilities, particularly the abilities of students whom teachers habitually regarded as slow learners.
- The degree of improvement resulting from increases in both higher-cognitive questions

and wait time is greater than an increase in either of these variables by itself. Indeed, those who have examined the relationship between these factors tell us that, in a sense, they cause one another.
- Redirection and probing are positively related to achievement when they are explicitly focused on the clarity, accuracy, plausibility, and so on of student responses.

## Bloom's Taxonomy

All students need to be invited and supported to do higher-level thinking, no matter what their literacy level. To do this requires a clear framework for understanding what higher-level thinking is. Benjamin Bloom and his colleagues (1956) created the original framework for this understanding. Bloom and Krathwohl originally listed these levels for cognition:

- Recall
- Comprehension
- Analysis
- Application
- Evaluation
- Synthesis

Many grids, like the one in Table 9.5, illustrate the different levels of thinking with specific question stems and lists of verbs found at different cognitive levels.

Anderson and Krathwohl (2001) updated the original Bloom framework by adding the four kinds of knowledge to be learned to the picture: factual knowledge, conceptual knowledge, procedural knowledge, and meta-cognitive knowledge (Table 9.6). In addition, they redefined Bloom's "synthesis category" as "creating," by which they mean "putting elements together to form a coherent or functional whole: reorganizing elements into a new

**Table 9.5. Thinking Skills Model Categories**

| Category | Examples of Trigger Questions | Key Words |
|---|---|---|
| Knowledge | Define the word _____.<br>What is a _____?<br>Label the following _____.<br>Identify the _____ in this _____.<br>Who did _____? | Define, repeat, identify, what, label, when, list, who, name |
| Organizing | Compare the _____ before and after _____.<br>Contrast the _____ to the _____.<br>Differentiate between _____ and _____.<br>Classify _____ by _____.<br>Order _____ by _____. | Compare, differentiate, contrast, order, classify, distinguish, relate |
| Applying | How is _____ an example of _____?<br>How is _____ related to _____?<br>Why is _____ significant?<br>Predict what would happen if _____. Explain.<br>Choose the best statements that apply to _____.<br>Identify the results of _____.<br>Tell how much change there would be when _____. | Apply, demonstrate, calculate, complete, illustrate, show, solve, examine, modify, relate, change, classify, experiment, discover, dramatize, sketch |
| Analyzing | What are the basic elements (ingredients) in a _____?<br>What is/are the functions(s) of _____?<br>Inventory the parts of _____.<br>Categorize the _____ of _____.<br>Sort the _____.<br>What is the order of steps in _____? | Subdivide, categorize, break down, sort, separate |
| Generating | Hypothesize what will happen if _____.<br>Predict what would be true if _____.<br>Conclude what the result will be if _____.<br>What if _____ had happened instead of _____? | Deduce, anticipate, predict what if, infer, apply, speculate, conclude |
| Integrating | What would you predict/infer from _____?<br>What ideas can you add to _____?<br>How would you create/design a new _____?<br>What might happen if you combined _____?<br>What solutions would you suggest for _____? | Combine, integrate, modify, create, design, invent, compose, theorize, develop, devise, originate, revise, synthesize, conceive, project, hypothesize |
| Evaluating | What you would do if _____ happened? Why?<br>Judge what would be the best way to solve the problem of _____.<br>Why did you select that solution? | Evaluate, argue, judge, recommend, assess, debate, appraise, critique, defend<br>Evaluate whether you would _____ or _____. Why? |

*Source:* Reprinted with permission from Chris A. Carem and Patsy B. Davis, *Kappa Delta Pi Record*, Fall 2005, Kappa Delta Pi, International Honor Society in Education.

recording or having students record the powers on charts as we go. This is review, but I better be sure they are all clear on the differences. [recall question: enumerate the powers]

7. What are the similarities and differences between the judicial and the legislative branch powers? (Understanding [comprehension] question: compare and contrast)

This question will allow me to highlight how both the judicial and legislative branches deal with legislation, but one branch makes it, while the other reviews it if it is challenged . . . I should run similar comparisons for other pairs. (questions 8, 9)

10. What do you think the phrase *checks and balances* means? (Understanding [comprehension] question: interpret)

It might be good to have a visual here.

11. What are some examples of how one branch checks the power of another? (application question)

If they can't give good examples, we may have to stop here and use current events to go deeper. We'll see. I think I'll bring in newspapers from the past few days to have as a resource here.

12. Is checking different from balancing? (analysis question: differentiate)

13. Once we get understanding here, I think I can ask them, What do you think the founding fathers' rationale was for setting it up this way? (analyzing/inferring question: explain)

14. If we get this far I'd like to move them into application, like: How do you think the separation of powers will play out with the current bill before the state legislature to legalize gay marriages? (understanding question: prediction; also evaluate: conclude) I doubt we'll get that far tomorrow, however.

15. It would be good to go beyond the text and compare our system of checks and balances to other countries. Let's see, which countries might they know enough about? Oh . . . I can ask them to each pick one they're interested in and research it for the way checks and balances are present there, if at all, and then compare it to the United States. That will make a nice follow-up project and check for understanding. (application question; comprehension question calling for compare and contrast)

This teacher has planned a series of questions that establish the factual background students need to ask the higher-level questions later. Then she has deliberately alternated between comparison and contrast questions and analysis questions. Next she's asked an application question and finally has asked a large comparison question in the follow-up assignment that also invites evaluation.

Planning questions specifically and in detail can make a big difference in the quality of a class discussion and the development of student understanding and higher-level thinking. In fact, it's the only way to ensure those things happen.

## Other Dimensions of Questioning

In this section, we take a brief excursion into three domains of questioning not treated elsewhere in this book: invitational language, teaching inquisitiveness, and connecting with students' own inner needs for purpose and meaning.

### Invitational Language

Art Costa and Bena Kallick (2000) investigate the psychological effect of word choice and syntax in the way people frame questions. The point is that certain language forms in questions invite students to engage the question and other forms intimidate or close down thinking. Following are some examples:

*Making Questions Invitational*

- Use plurals: "What are some of your insights?" "What ideas do you have?"
- Express tentativeness: "What inferences might you draw?" "How might you address the problem?"
- Embed positive presuppositions: "As you think about the project, what will be some indicators you are progressing and succeeding?" "What are some of the benefits you will derive from engaging in this activity?"

*Questions That Miscue, Confuse, or Limit the Level of Students' Thinking*

- Verification questions: The teacher or students already know the answers. "What is the name of . . . ?"
- Closed questions: These can be answered "yes," "no," or "I can." "Can you recite the poem . . . ?" "Who can remember . . . ?"
- Rhetorical questions: The answers are given within the question or the teacher is not expecting an answer.
- Defensive questions: The questions lead to justification, resistance, and self-protection— "Why didn't you complete your homework?" "Why would you do a thing like that?"
- Agreement questions: The intent is to invite others to agree with an opinion or answer— "This is really the best solution, isn't it?" "Let's do it my way. Okay?"

## Teaching Inquisitiveness

Teacher questions are important, of course: they regulate the level of thinking in class discourse. But it may be more important to teach students to ask good questions themselves, not just be good at answering the ones their teachers pose. John Barell (2003) argues that making students inquisitive and giving them the opportunity and the intellectual tools to be so is one of the central purposes of education. Consequently, questions like the following frame curriculum units: "What goes on inside babies' heads?" "Why is music such a pleasure?" "What do collapses of past societies teach us about our own future?" "Why are most individuals and all human societies grossly underachieving their potentials?" Wiggins and McTighe (2005) have called such framing questions "essential" because they get to the center of what is interesting and important in a unit of study.

As an example of how inquisitiveness can be supported in students, Barell borrows from Matthew Lipman (1980) and asks students to identify what they find most interesting in their reading. Their thinking is elicited by these questions:

- What I find most interesting here is . . .
- The big ideas here are . . .
- I wonder why . . .
- What confuses me is . . .
- I can relate this episode/segment to . . .
- This makes me feel . . . [p. 107]

Barell goes on to point out that teachers would assess students on their ability to be inquisitive, that is, their ability to ask questions, if they truly valued that and presents a set of criteria for doing so.

Inquisitiveness *looks* like the following:
Students
- Look closely at things, explore
- Observe using a variety of senses (touch, smell)
- Show enthusiasm in facial expressions
- Seek out new ways of learning or things to learn about and create own problems to solve.

Inquisitiveness *sounds* like the following:
Students

- Ask a variety of questions: "Why?"; "How come?"; "What if?"
- Seek additional information: "Tell me more"; "Where else can I get information?"
- Make analogies: "This reminds me of . . ."; "It's like . . ."
- Reflect an "I enjoy" attitude: "This is fun!"; "I'd like more time to learn more."; "How exciting!"

Barell's book contains many scenarios at various grade levels and subject areas that show how teachers can set up conditions for students to develop these indicators of inquisitiveness. The emphasis is on the intellectual, the cognitive, and the curious. The examples are drawn from the fine collection of ideas and strategies in his book for developing curious minds and a particular environment in class to go with it. It's an environment that combines psychological safety so students will risk asking questions with the stimulation of fascinating phenomena students want to explore on their own terms. Barell writes, "Many teachers begin the year with a declaration of what's expected in the classroom. . . . This is an opportunity to tell students, 'I expect that you will become experts at asking good questions about what we are studying. Don't ever fear asking a question. Please don't sit there puzzling over some idea thinking everybody else understands it! They don't.'"

There are lots of other questions, however, that students bring to school with them, regardless of what questions teachers choose to pose: questions from their inner life—and important questions about meaning, purpose, and making one's way in the world. We think this should prompt us all to ponder: what place is there in school for those questions to surface and be respected, encouraged, supported?

### Including and Bringing Out Students' Basic Questions About Meaning and Purpose

It is our view that deliberately opening the space for such questions is a skill based on a personal commitment to the growth of students as people and that this skill is part of good teaching. When students can ask questions and discuss issues that matter deeply to them, the people and the place where those conversations happen is a place of power and influence in their lives. The classroom can be such a place, and this can be done within the curriculum. "Once a week [the students sit together] relating stories and feelings from their own lives that have been stirred by the required readings. Is there life after death? Is there a God? These same questions arise time and again when students anonymously set down their 'questions of wonder.' This domain of meaning and purpose is crucial to learning" (Kessler in Lantieri, 2001).

Space for questions like Why am I here? Does my life have a purpose? What does my future hold? needn't be present in any particular curriculum; it needs to be present in the heart of the teacher. And when it is, there are spontaneous discussions that arise from time to time in the regular curriculum material. The result of honoring these deepest thoughts, feelings, and questions of students is engagement in the regular curriculum and a commitment to learning beyond what one could otherwise expect. In other words, honoring what is deep and meaningful to students and inviting their engagement with it pays off in academic learning in ways teachers could never otherwise engineer with the best planning and the best cognitive science.

Parker Palmer's highly successful Courage to Teach program of retreats rests partially on its commitment to help adult teachers explore these questions for themselves and in a supportive community of professional companions: "This experience improves their classroom practice in significant ways through the development of genuine connections with their students and a growing capacity to 'teach from the heart,' and most feel that their students benefit tangibly from these changes" (cited in Lantieri, 2001, p. 146).

It is our view that honoring students' questions about meaning is especially important in schools for children of poverty. "If you don't have a place where the poor, marginalized, and young can find out who they are, then you have no hope of maintaining a free and civilized society" (Lamott, 2005).

To check your knowledge about Clarity Moves see the quiz on our Web site at **www.RBTeach.com/ rbteach//quiz/clarity.html.**

## Source Materials on Clarity

Allington, R. L., and Johnston, P. "What Do We Know About Effective Fourth-Grade Teachers and Their Classrooms?" In C. M. Roller (ed.), *Learning to Teach Reading*. Newark, Del.: International Reading Association, 2001.

Alvarado, A., Elmore, R., and Resnick, L. "High Performance Learning Communities Project: Final Report." Pittsburg, Penn.: Learning Research and Development Center, 2000.

Anderson, L. M., and Krathwohl, D. R. (eds.). *A Taxonomy for Learning, Teaching and Assessing: A Revision of Bloom's Taxonomy of Educational Objectives*. New York: Longman, 2001.

Anderson, V., and Hidi, S. "Teaching Students to Summarize." *Educational Leadership*. Dec. 1988–Jan. 1989, pp. 26–28.

Applebee, A. N., and Langer, J. A. "Discussion-Based Approaches to Developing Understanding: Classroom Instruction and Student Performance in Middle and High School English." *American Educational Research Journal*, 2003, *40*, 685–730.

Armbruster, B., Anderson, T. H., and Ostertag, J. "Teaching Text Structure to Improve Reading and Writing." *Reading Teacher*, Nov. 1989, pp. 130–137.

Arnaudin, M. W., and Mintzes, J. "The Cardiovascular System: Children's Conceptions and Misconceptions." *Science and Children*, 1986, *23*(5), 48–51.

Ault, C. R., Jr. "Intelligently Wrong: Some Comments on Children's Misconceptions." *Science and Children*, May 1984, pp. 22–24.

Ausubel, D. P. *Educational Psychology: A Cognitive View*. New York: Holt, 1968.

Bagley, M. T., and Hess, K. *200 Ways of Using Imagery in the Classroom*. Monroe, N.Y.: Trillium Press, 1987.

Barell, J. *Developing More Curious Minds*. Alexandria, Va.: ASCD, 2003.

Barell, J. "You Ask the Wrong Questions!" *Educational Leadership*, May 1985, pp. 18–23.

Baroody, A., and Ginsburg, H. "The Effects of Instruction on Children's Understanding of the 'Equals' Sign." *Elementary School Journal*, 1983, *84*(2), 199–212.

Belgard, M., Rosenshine, B., and Gage, N. L. "The Teacher's Effectiveness in Explaining: Evidence on Its Generality and Correlation with Pupil Ratings and Attention Score." In I. Westbury and A. Bellack (eds.), *Research into Classroom Processes*. New York: Teachers College Press, 1971.

Bellon, J. J., Bellon, E. C., and Blank, M. A. *Teaching from a Research Knowledge Base: A Development and Renewal Process*. New York: Macmillan, 1992.

Bennett, N., and Desforges, C. "Matching Classroom Tasks to Students' Attainments." *Elementary School Journal*, 1988, *88*, 221–234.

Black, H., and Black, S. *Organizing Thinking, Book II. Graphic Organizers*. Pacific Grove, Calif.: Midwest Publications, 1990.

Bloom, B. S., and Krathwohl, D. *Taxonomy of Educational Objectives: The Classification of Educational Goal*. New York: Longmans, 1956.

Bomer, R., Dworin, J., Semingson, L., and Semingson, P. "Miseducating Teachers About the Poor: A Critical Analysis of Ruby Payne's Claims About Poverty." *TC Record*, 2008, *110*(2).

Borko, H., and Putnam, P. T. "Expanding a Teacher's Knowledge Base." In T. Guskey and M. Huberman (eds.), *Professional Development in Education: New Paradigms and Practices*. New York: Teachers College Press, 1995.

Bragstad, B. J., and Stumpf, S. M. "How a Map Is Born." In *A Guidebook for Teaching Study Skills and Motivation*. Needham Heights, Mass.: Allyn & Bacon, 1982.

Brophy, J. "Teacher Effects Research and Teacher Quality." *Journal of Classroom Interaction*, 1986–1987, *22*, 14–23.

Brophy, J. "Teacher Praise: A Functional Analysis." *Review of Educational Research*, 1981, *51*, 5–32.

Brophy, J. E. "How Teachers Influence What Is Taught and Learned in Classrooms." *Elementary School Journal*, 1982, *83*, 1–13.

Bulgren, J. "Teaching Concepts: Concept Diagramming and the Concept of Teaching Routine." Lawrence: Institute for Research in Learning Disabilities, University of Kansas, Aug. 1991.

Bulgren J., Deshler, D., Schumaker, J., and Lenz, B. "The Use and Effectiveness of Analogical Instruction in Diverse

Secondary Content Classrooms." *Journal of Educational Psychology*, 2000, *92*(3), 426–441.

Burton, G. M. "Writing as a Way of Knowing in a Mathematics Education Class." *Arithmetic Teacher*, Dec. 1985, pp. 40–44.

Bush, A. J., Kennedy, J. J., and Cruickshank, D. R. "An Empirical Investigation of Teacher Clarity." *Journal of Teacher Education*, 1977, *28*, 53–58.

Carnine, D. "New Research on the Brain: Implications for Instruction." *Phi Delta Kappan*, Jan. 1990, pp. 372–377.

Carpenter, T. P., and others. "Using Knowledge of Children's Mathematics Thinking in Classroom Teaching: An Experimental Study." *American Educational Research Journal*, 1989, *26*, 499–531.

Cazden, D. B. "Revealing and Telling: The Socialization of Attention in Learning to Read and Write." *Educational Psychology*, 1992, *12*, 302–313.

Clarke, J. H. *Patterns of Thinking*. Needham Heights, Mass.: Allyn & Bacon, 1990.

Coffman, J., and Tanis, D. O. "Don't Say Particle, Say People." *Science Teacher*, Nov. 1990, pp. 27–29.

Cooper, C. "Different Ways of Being a Teacher: An Ethnographic Study of College Instructors' Academic and Social Roles in the Classroom." *Journal of Classroom Interaction*, 1980, *16*(2), 27–36.

Costa, A. *Teaching for Intelligent Behavior*. Orangevale, Calif.: Search Models Unlimited, 1985.

Costa, A., and Kallick, B. *Activating and Engaging Habits of Mind*. Alexandria, Va.: ASCD, 2000. Reprinted with permission.

Cotton, K. *Classroom Questioning*. Portland, Ore: NW Regional Education Laboratory, 1988. http://www.nwrel.org/scpd/3/cu5.html.

Cotton, K. "The Schooling Practices That Matter Most." Portland, Ore: NW Regional Education Laboratory, 2000. http://eric.ed.gov/ERICDocs/data/ericdocs2/content_storage_01/0000000b/80/27/d3/bc.pdf.

Crooks, T. "The Impact of Classroom Evaluation Practices on Students." *Review of Educational Research*, 1988, *58*, 469.

D'Angelo, K. "Precise Writing: Promoting Vocabulary Development and Comprehension." *Journal of Reading*, Mar. 1983, pp. 534–539.

Dank, M. *Albert Einstein*. New York: Franklin Watts, 1983.

Davey, B. "Think Aloud—Modeling the Cognitive Processes of Reading Comprehension." *Journal of Reading*, Oct. 1983, pp. 44–47.

Dillon, J. T. "Duration of Response to Teacher Questions and Statements." *Contemporary Educational Psychology*, 1981, *6*, 1–11.

Dillon, J. T. "The Remedial Status of Student Questioning." *Curriculum Studies*, 1988, *20*(3), 197–210.

Dishner, E. K., and others. "Attending to Text Structure: A Comprehension Strategy." *Reading in the Content Areas: Improving Classroom Instruction*. Dubuque, Ia.: Kendall/Hunt, 1992.

Doyle, W. "Stalking the Mythical Student." *Elementary School Journal*, 1982, *82*, 529–538.

Draper, S. W., and Brown, M. I. "Increasing Interactivity in Lectures Using an Electronic Voting System." *Journal of Computer Assisted Learning*, 2004, *20*(2), 81–94.

Driver, R., Guesne, E., and Tiberghien, A. *Children's Ideas in Science*. Philadelphia: Open University Press, 1985.

Duckworth, E. "Understanding Children's Understanding." Unpublished paper, Feb. 1981.

Duffy, G. G., and Roehler, L. R. "Improving Reading Instruction Through the Use of Responsive Elaboration." *Reading Teacher*, 1987, *40*(6), 14–19.

Duffy, G., Roehler, L. R., and Rackliffe, G. "How Teachers' Instructional Talk Influences Students' Understanding of Lesson Content." *Elementary School Journal*, 1986, *87*(1), 3–16.

Dunkin, M. J., and Biddle, B. J. *The Study of Teaching*. New York: Holt, 1974.

Easley, J. A., and Zwoyer, R. "Teaching by Listening: Toward a New Day in Math Classes." *Contemporary Education*, 1975, *57*(1), 19–25.

Eaton, J. "Research on Teaching." *Educational Leadership*, Oct. 1982, pp. 75–76.

Eaton, J. F., Anderson, C. W., and Smith, E. L. "Students' Misconceptions Interfere with Science Learning: Case Studies of Fifth-Grade Students." *Elementary School Journal*, 1984, *84*, 365–379.

Eeds, M., and Wells, D. "Grand Conversations: An Exploration of Meaning Construction on Literature Study Groups." *Research in the Teaching of English*, 1989, *23*(1), 4–29.

Edwards, J., and Marland, P. "Student Thinking in a Secondary Biology Classroom." *Research in Science Education*, 1982, *12*, 32–41.

Escondido School District. *Mind's Eye*. Escondido, Calif.: Board of Education, 1979.

Eylon, B., and Linn, M. C. "Learning and Instruction: An Examination of Four Research Perspectives in Science Education." *Review of Educational Research*, 1988, *58*, 251–301.

Fisher, D. *Instructional Design: The Taxonomy Table*. Corvallis: Oregon State University, 2005. http://oregonstate.edu/instruct/coursedev/models/id/taxonomy/.

Fogarty, R. *The Mindful School: How to Teach for Metacognitive Reflection*. Palatine, Ill.: IRI/Skylight, 1994.

Fogarty, R., and Bellanca, J. *Patterns for Thinking—Patterns for Transfer*. Palatine, Ill.: IRI Group, 1993.

Fortune, J. C., Gage, N. L., and Shute, R. E. "The Generality of the Ability to Explain." Paper presented at the AERA Convention, Chicago, 1966.

Friedrich, G. W., Galvin, K. M., and Book, C. L. *Growing Together: Classroom Communication*. Columbus, Ohio: Charles Merrill, 1976.

Gage, N. L. "Exploration of Teachers' Effectiveness in Explaining." Stanford, Calif.: Stanford University Center for Research and Development in Teaching, 1961. (ED O28 147)

Gagne, R. M. *The Essentials of Learning for Instruction.* (4th ed.). Hinsdale, Ill.: Dryden Press, 1992.

Gall, M. D., and others. "Effects of Questioning Techniques and Recitation in Student Learning." *American Educational Research Journal,* 1978, *15,* 175–199.

Galyean, B.-C. "Guided Imagery in the Curriculum." *Educational Leadership,* Mar. 1983, pp. 54–58.

Galyean, B.-C. *Mind Sight, Learning Through Imaging.* Berkeley, Calif.: Zephyr Press, 1988.

Garfield, C. "Peak Performers." New York: Random House, 2000.

Geller, L. G. "Conversations in Kindergarten." *Science and Children,* Apr. 1985, pp. 30–32.

Ghatala, E. S., Levin, J., Pressley, M., and Locico, M. "Training Cognitive Strategy-Monitoring in Children." *American Educational Research Journal,* 1985, *22,* 199–215.

Goleman, D. "Cues Are Easy to Misinterpret." *New York Times,* Sept. 17, 1991.

Good, T. L., and Brophy, J. E. *Looking in Classrooms.* (8th ed.). New York: HarperCollins, 2000.

Gorski, P. "The Classist Underpinnings of Ruby Payne's Framework." *TC Record,* Feb. 9, 2006.

Graham, S. "Teacher Feelings and Student Thoughts: An Attributional Approach to Affect in the Classroom." *Elementary School Journal, 85*(1), 1984, 91–104.

Gregg, C. I. "Teachers Also Must Learn." *Harvard Educational Review, 10,* 1940, 30–47.

Gregorc, A. "Learning/Teaching Styles: Potent Faces Behind Them." *Educational Leadership,* Jan. 1979, pp. 234–236.

Gregorc, A., and Butler, K. A. "Learning Is a Matter of Style." *Vocational Education Journal,* 1984, *59*(3), 27–29.

Hahn, A. L., and Gardner, R. "Synthesis of Research on Students' Ability to Summarize Text." *Educational Leadership,* Feb. 1985, pp. 52–55.

Hammond, D. *Wordsplash.* Rochester, Mich.: Oakland University, 1985.

Harris, P., and Swick, K. "Improving Teacher Communications." *Clearing House,* 1985, *59,* 13–15.

Heath, S. B. *Ways with Words.* Cambridge, England: Cambridge University Press, 1983.

Heimlich, J. E., and Pittelman, S. D. *Semantic Mapping: Classroom Applications.* Newark, Del.: International Reading Association, 1986.

Herron, J. D. "Piaget in the Classroom: Expanding What 'Good' Students Cannot Understand." *Journal of Chemical Education,* 1975, *52*(2), 146–150.

Hess, K. K. *Enhancing Writing Through Imagery.* New York: Trillium Press, 1987.

Hesse, J. "From Naive to Knowledgeable." *Science Teacher,* Sept. 1989, pp. 55–58.

Hiller, J. H., Fisher, G. A., and Kaess, W. A. "A Computer Investigation of Verbal Characteristics of Effective Classroom Lecturing." *American Educational Research Journal,* 1969, *6,* 661–675.

Hines, C. V., Cruickshank, D. R., and Kennedy, J. J. "Teacher Clarity and Its Relationship to Student Achievement and Satisfaction." *American Educational Research Journal,* 1985, *22,* 87–99.

Houghton, R. S. "Thinking Skills Model Categories, Trigger Questions, and Key Words Chart." In C. Caram and P. Davis(eds.), "Inviting Student Engagement with Questioning." *Kappa Delta Pi Record,* Fall 2005, pp. 19–23.

Hunter, M. *Mastery Teaching.* Thousand Oaks, Calif.: Corwin Press, 2004.

Hyerle, D. *Designs for Thinking Connectively.* Lyme, N.H.: Designs for Thinking, 1990.

Institute for Research on Teaching. "Kids Have Misconceptions." *Communication Quarterly,* Fall 1981, p. 4.

Institute for Research on Teaching. "Explicitness Is Key to Reading Instruction." *Communication Quarterly,* Winter–Spring 1984.

Johnson, D. R. *Every Minute Counts: Making Your Math Class Work.* Palo Alto, Calif.: Dale Seymour Publications, 1982.

Johnston, P. "Teaching Students to Apply Strategies That Improve Reading Comprehension." *Elementary School Journal,* 1985, *85,* 635–645.

Joos, M. *The Five Clocks.* New York: Harcourt Brace, 1967.

Kallison, J. M., Jr. "Effects of Lesson Organization on Achievement." *American Educational Research Journal,* 1986, *23,* 337–347.

Lamott, A. "In Steinbeck Country, We Said No to Closing the Libraries." *Boston Globe,* June 4, 2005. http://www.boston.com/news/globe/editorial_opinion/oped/articles/2005/06/04/in_steinbeck_country_we_said_no_to_closing_the_libraries?mode=PF.

Land, M. L., and Smith, L. R. "The Effect of Low Inference Teacher Clarity Inhibitors on Student Achievement." *Journal of Teacher Education,* 1979, *30*(3), 55–57.

Lantieri, L. (ed.). *Schools with Spirit.* Boston: Beacon Press, 2001.

Lester, J. B. "Establishing a Community of Mathematics Learners." In D. Schifter (ed.), *What's Happening in Math Class?* New York: Teachers College Press, 1996. Reprinted with permission of Copyright Clearance Center.

Liedtke, W. "Diagnosis in Mathematics: The Advantages of an Interview." *Arithmetic Teacher,* Nov. 1988, pp. 26–29.

Lipman, M. *Philosophy in the Classroom.* Philadelphia: Temple University Press, 1980.

Lopez, J. A., and Powell, A. B. "Writing as a Vehicle to Learn Mathematics: A Case Study." Paper presented at the Seventy-First Annual Meeting of the Mathematical Association of America, Jan. 1988.

Lyons, B. A. "Peer-Led Literature Discussion Groups: An Analysis of Recent Literature." 1996. http://eric.ed.gov/ERICDocs/data/ericdocs2/content_storage_01/0000000b/80/26/03/9f.pdf.

Margulies, N. *Mapping Inner Space: Learning and Teaching Mind Mapping.* Tucson, Ariz.: Zephyr Press, 1991.

Marino, J. L., Gould, S., and Haas, L. W. "The Effects of Writing as a Prereading Activity on Delayed Recall of Narrative Text." *Elementary School Journal,* 1985, *86,* 199–205.

Martin, J. *Explaining, Understanding and Teaching.* New York: McGraw-Hill, 1970.

Marzano, R. J., Pickering, D. J., and Pollock, J. E. *Classroom Instruction That Works: Research-Based Strategies for Increasing Student Achievement.* Alexandria, Va.: ASCD, 2001.

Marx, A., Fuhrer, U., and Hartig, T. "Effects of Classroom Seating Arrangements on Children's Question-Asking." *Learning Environments Research,* 1999, *2,* 249–263.

Marx, R. W., and Walsh, J. "Learning from Academic Tasks." *Elementary School Journal,* 1988, *88,* 207–219.

McCaleb, J. L., and White, J. A. "Critical Dimensions in Evaluating Teacher Clarity." *Journal of Classroom Interaction,* 1980, *15,* 27–30.

McCarthy, B. *The 4Mat Workbook: Guided Practice in 4Mat Lesson and Unit Planning.* Manchester, U.K.: Excel, 1987.

McCarthy, B., and McCarthy, D. *Teaching Around the 4MAT Cycle: Designing Instruction for Diverse Learners with Diverse Learning Styles.* Thousand Oaks: Corwin Press, 2005.

McGee, L. M., and Richgels, D. J. "Teaching Expository Text Structures to Elementary Students." *Reading Teacher,* 1986, *38,* 739–748.

McLean, T. J. "U. of Arizona 'Humanizes' Classes with Computers." *Dollars and Sense,* Sept. 1991.

McNeill, J. D. *Reading Comprehension: New Directions for Classroom Practice.* Glenview, Ill.: Scott, Foresman, 1984.

Mehan, H. "Accomplishing Classroom Lessons." In S. V. Cicouril (ed.), *Language Use and School Performance.* Orlando, Fla.: Academic Press, 1974.

Mett, C. L. "Writing as a Learning Device in Calculus." *Mathematics Teacher,* Oct. 1987, pp. 534–537.

Mills, S. R., Rice, C. T., Berliner, D. C., and Rosseau, E. W. "The Correspondence Between Teacher Questions and Student Answers in Classroom Discourse." *Journal of Experimental Education,* 1980, *48,* 194–204.

Moll, L. C. "Through the Mediation of Others: Vygotskian Research on Teaching." In V. Richardson (ed.), *Handbook of Research on Teaching.* (4th ed.). Washington, D.C.: American Educational Research Association, 2001.

Munk, T. "Thinking Skills Model Categories, Trigger Questions, and Key Words Chart." In C. Caram and P. Davis (eds.), "Inviting Student Engagement with Questioning." *Kappa Delta Pi Record,* Fall 2005, pp. 19–23.

Murdock, M. *Spinning Inward.* Boston: Shambhala, 1987.

Murray, H. G. "Effective Teaching Behaviors in the College Classroom." In J. Smart (ed.), *Higher Education: Handbook of Theory and Research.* New York: Agathon Press, 1991.

Novak, J. D. "Clarify with Concept Maps: A Tool for Students and Teachers Alike." *Science Teacher,* 1991, *58*(7), 45–49.

Novak, J. D., and Gowin, D. B. *Learning How to Learn.* Cambridge: Cambridge University Press, 1984.

Nuthall, G. "The Cultural Myths and Realities of Classroom Teaching and Learning: A Personal Journey." *Teachers College Record,* 2005, *107,* 895–934.

Nystrand, M. *Opening Dialogue: Understanding the Dynamics of Language and Learning in the English Classroom.* New York: Teachers College Press, 1997.

Ogle, D. M. "K-W-L: A Teaching Model That Develops Active Reading of Expository Text." *Reading Teacher,* Feb. 1986, pp. 564–570.

Ormrod, J. E. *Human Learning.* (4th ed.). Upper Saddle River, N.J.: Pearson Education, 2004.

Osborne, R., and Freyberg, P. *Learning in Science: The Implications of Children's Science.* Portsmouth, N.H.: Heineman, 1984.

Palincsar, A., and Brown, A. "When the Student Becomes the Teacher." *Harvard Education Letter,* 1986, *11*(2), 5–6.

Parsons, C. "Grading Teachers for Quality." *Christian Science Monitor,* Oct. 26, 1981, p. B1.

Payne, R. *A Framework for Understanding Poverty.* (Rev. ed.). Highlands, Tex.: aha! Process, Inc., 2005.

Perkins, D. *Making Thinking Visible.* Seattle, Wash.: New Horizons for Learning, 2003.

Peterson, P., and Swing, S. "Beyond Time on Task: Students' Reports of Their Thought Processes During Classroom Instruction." *Elementary School Journal,* 1982, *82,* 481–491. Reprinted with permission from University of Chicago Press.

Peterson, P., Swing, S., Stark, K., and Waas, G. "Students' Cognitions and Time on Task During Mathematics Instruction." *American Educational Research Journal,* 1984, *21,* 487–515.

Pradl, G. M., and Mayher, J. S. "Reinvigorating Learning Through Writing." *Educational Leadership,* Feb. 1985, pp. 2–8.

Pressley, G. M. "Imagery and Children's Learning: Putting the Picture in Developmental Perspective." *Review of Educational Research,* 1977, *47,* 585–622.

Pressley, G. M. "Mental Imagery Helps Eight-Year Olds Remember What They Read." *Journal of Educational Psychology,* 1976, *68,* 355–359.

Raths, J. "Enhancing Understanding Through Debriefing." *Educational Leadership,* Oct. 1987, pp. 22–27.

Reinhart, S. C. "Never Say Anything a Kid Can Say." *Mathematics Teaching in Middle School,* 2000, *5,* 478.

Ritchart, R. *Intellectual Character.* San Francisco: Jossey-Bass, 2002.

Ritchart, R., Palmer, P., Church, M., and Tishman, S. "Thinking Routines: Establishing Patterns for Thinking in the Classroom." Paper presented at AERA Conference, San Francisco, Apr. 2006.

Rohrkemper, M. M., and Bershon, B. "Elementary School Students' Report of the Causes and Effects of Problem Difficulty in Mathematics." *Elementary School Journal,* 1984, *85,* 127–147.

Rose, L. *Picture This: Teaching Reading Through Visualization.* Tucson, Ariz.: Zephyr Press, 1989.

Rosenshine, B., and Stevens, R. "Teaching Functions." In M. Wittrock (ed.), *Handbook of Research.* New York: Macmillan, 1986.

Rosenshine, B., and Furst, N. "The Use of Direct Observation to Study Teaching." In R. M. Travers (ed.), *Second Handbook of Research on Teaching.* Skokie, Ill.: Rand McNally, 1973.

Roth, K. J., Anderson, C. W., and Smith, E. L. "Curriculum Materials, Teacher Talk and Student Learning: Case Studies in Fifth Grade Science Teaching." Paper presented at the annual meeting of the National Reading Conference, Symposium on Teacher Explanatory Talk, Austin, Tex., Dec. 1983.

Roth, W.-M. "Map Your Way to a Better Lab." *Science Teacher,* Apr. 1990, pp. 31–34.

Rowe, M. B. "Getting Chemistry off the Killer Course List." *Journal of Chemical Education,* 1983, *60,* 954–956.

Sagan, C. *Cosmos.* New York: Random House, 1980, p. 199.

Sanders, A. "Learning Logs: A Communication Strategy for All Subject Areas." *Educational Leadership,* Feb. 1985, p. 7.

Saphier, J., and Haley, M. *Activators: Activity Structures to Engage Student Thinking Before Instruction.* Acton, Mass.: Research for Better Teaching, 1993.

Shifter, D. (ed.). *What's Happening in Math Class?* New York: Teachers College Press, 1996.

Sinatra, R. "Semantic Mapping: A Thinking Strategy for Improved Reading and Writing Development: Parts I and II." *Teaching Thinking and Problem Solving.* Mahwah, N.J.: Erlbaum, 1990.

Singer, H. "Teaching Active Comprehension." *Reading Teacher,* May 1978, pp. 904–907.

Smith, L., and Land, M. "Low-Inference Verbal Behaviors Related to Teacher Clarity." *Journal of Classroom Interactions,* 1981, *17*(1), 37–42.

Tasker, R. "Children's Views and Classroom Experience." *Australian Science Teachers' Journal,* 1981, *27*(3), 33–37.

Tobin, K. "Wait-Time in Science—Necessary but Insufficient." Paper presented at the annual meeting of the National Association for Research in Science Teaching, French Lick Springs, Ind., Apr. 1985.

Whisler, J. S., and Marzano, R. J. *Dare to Imagine: An Olympian's Technology.* Aurora, Colo.: Mid-Continent Regional Educational Laboratory, 1988.

White, R., and Gunstone, R. *Probing Understanding.* London: Falmer Press, 1992.

Wiggins, G., and McTighe, J. *Understanding by Design.* Alexandria, Va.: ASCD, 2005.

Winne, P. H. "Steps Toward Promoting Cognitive Achievements." *Elementary School Journal,* 1985, *85,* 673–693.

Winne, P. H., and Marx, R. W. "Students' and Teachers' Views of Thinking Processes for Classroom Learning." *Elementary School Journal,* 1982, *82,* 492–518.

# Principles of Learning

## How do I design more efficient and effective learning experiences?

Designing for Cognitive Impact

Designing for Motivational Impact

Technical Principles of Design

Principles Impacting Attention and Engagement

This chapter describes twenty-four packages of power, each one self-contained and ready for use by itself, each a possible addition to any teacher's repertoire, and each certain to increase the rate and durability of students' learning. A strong claim? Perhaps. But for once in education, a certain one.

What do these names mean to you: Ivan Pavlov, Edward Thorndike, Clark Hull, John B. Watson, Edwin R. Guthrie, Hobart Mowrer, Kenneth Spence, Edward C. Tolman, and B. F. Skinner? We don't hear much about them these days, yet these are men who approached learning as a phenomenon about which universal laws might be deduced and operating principles discovered, and they discovered quite a few of them. The tradition of their research goes back to 1885 (with Hermann Ebbinghaus) and is the strongest, longest, and soundest base we have in education for how-to recommendations. Taken together, their principles do not add up to a cohesive theory or approach to how to teach as we get from some of their modern counterparts (Jerome Bruner, David Ausubel, Jean Piaget). Instead, each of these principles was shown in its own way to make a contribution to learning effectiveness, and they lie scattered about the literature like so many precious stones waiting to be picked up. Many of them were collected in the 1970s and put into accessible form for teachers by Madeline Hunter and her associates. (*Teach More,*

*Faster* is an exemplary title of one of her books for teachers.) Nevertheless, these principles have not become part of the currency of in-service or teacher training or college teacher education.

As you read this chapter, you will recognize some of these principles from your own teaching. We find that most teachers routinely use six or seven of them intuitively, without knowing the labels you will learn for them here. Some teachers use more, some fewer. We have yet to find a teacher who uses them all, however, and so believe that there is something new in this chapter for everyone.

We have identified twenty-four of these principles in the literature (see Figure 10.1). What they all share in common is that each offers some sort of guideline for designing learning experiences. One might think of principles of learning like the spices used in food preparation: some seasonings are used regularly in most every dish a chef prepares (salt, pepper, sugar, parsley, to name a few) while others are used more selectively (cumin, tarragon, coriander). To a chef it is not a matter of the more spices the better but rather knowing the spices and applying them strategically where they will enhance the flavor. So too is the case with principles of learning: some apply broadly to most learning experiences (meaning, active participation, say-do) while others apply more selectively (isolating critical attributes, contiguity, mnemonics). Knowing the principles of learning enables us to apply them strategically to design gourmet learning experiences.

We have divided the principles of learning into four categories: those that offer guidance for enhancing cognitive impact, those that influence motivation, those that address technical aspects of design, and those that impact student attention and engagement. (For additional summaries and exten-sions of the principles, see Hilgard and Bower, 1966; Bugelski, 1971; and Hudgins, 1977.) When we get to Chapter Eleven, "Models of Teaching," we will be looking at teaching as a playwright looks at a script. We'll look at the design and sequence of the whole lesson and what discrete teacher moves have to do with the overall design of a particular kind of learning. We won't refer to any of these principles of learning then, but we won't be invalidating them either. They're always there and always relevant.

## Designing for Cognitive Impact

### Application in Setting (from Skill to Setting)

Students should practice new behaviors or skills in the settings and in the way those learnings will be used in life. Thus, spelling will more likely transfer to composition if spelling tests embed new words in sentences (perhaps from dictation). The ability to listen to others will transfer to real discussions and to conflict resolutions if practiced in class meetings and real or simulated disagreements. Notice that we used the word *transfer* in both of these examples. Application in setting is a principle that, when applied, makes it more likely that transfer will occur. As part of teaching for transfer, one is likely to see several instances of application in setting. Application in setting is something we see and give as a label to single-instance activities that are having students use a skill in some real-life context, such as identifying and labeling logical fallacies (the straw man fallacy) in arguments of current political candidates. But to claim teaching for transfer itself, there would have to be a series of such activities deliberately orchestrated so as progressively to distance the skill from abstract academic

**Figure 10.1. Principles of Learning**

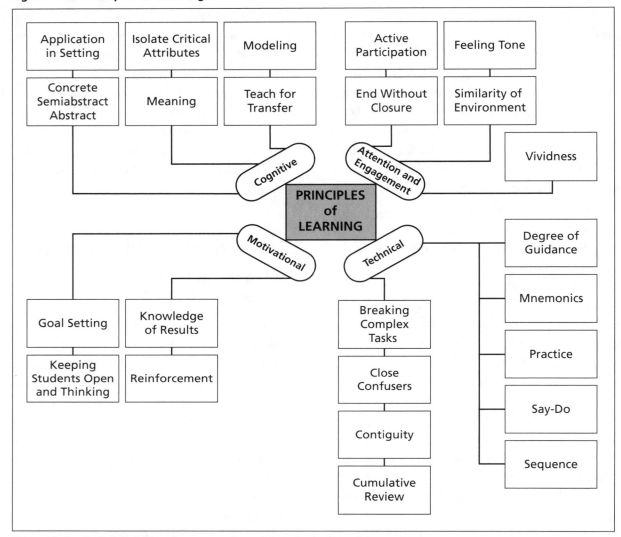

**Research for Better Teaching, Inc.** • One Acton Place, Acton, MA 01720 • (978) 263-9449 • www.RBTeach.com

contexts. Each of them singly may have been by itself an example of application in setting.

## Concrete-Semiabstract-Abstract Progression

Teachers using this principle begin with tangible or manipulative materials at one stage of instruction, move to pictorial representation of the same material, and at still later stages of instruction deal with the same materials with the students in purely abstract ways. This progression is effective not only with young children who are at Piaget's stage of concrete operation but also with adult learners. Dealing with concrete materials anchors images and experiences that later connect with and are summoned by the abstractions that refer to them. No one has to learn everything by experience (you don't have to be bitten by a rabid dog to learn they're dangerous), but experience anchors learning in a powerful way. Herron's 1975 study using models in chemistry instruction showed that using concrete materials was startlingly effective for developing concepts in college chemistry courses.

## Isolation of Critical Attributes

Teachers who practice this principle identify the critical unvarying attributes or elements of the item under study and label them. Particularly with regard to definitions of new concepts, they isolate the qualities or attributes essential to the concept, attributes "without which it is not" (without which the object is not the object but something else). For example, "What are the critical attributes that define an estuary?" The answer is "delta or fan shaped; at the bottom of a river; brackish water (part salt, part fresh); and sedimentary deposits at the bottom. Without any one of these four elements, we don't have an estuary."

Another example is for preparing students to write myths in their study of literary genres. It is very useful to develop the following list at the start:

- Heroic figures
- Magic
- Explains the origin of a natural phenomenon

These are the essential attributes—the defining attributes of myth. If any one of them is missing in a story, it's not a myth. Teachers can develop the list of attributes in a number of ways—for example, by having students read a variety of myths and extract what they have in common, consult reference books for definitions of myth, or tell students the attributes in direct instruction with examples. How-

ever it happens, that it happens can make a positive difference to learning.

A second way to use the principle has to do with concepts that are similar but different—perhaps concepts that are close relatives. For example, in comparing tattling and reporting, the teacher could develop two parallel lists of attributes and compare them. For tattling and reporting, the lists would be identical except for one item: intent. Intent (to get someone in trouble as opposed to giving needed information) is the critical attribute that discriminates tattling from reporting. Thought experiment: what is the critical attribute that discriminates prejudice from discrimination?

So far we have discussed two slightly different ways to use the principle: (1) listing the definitional attributes that make something what it is ("myth" for example) and (2) comparing two parallel lists of similar concepts to distinguish the critical attributes that separate the target concept (tattling) from its close relative (reporting). A third use helps us see which from among the many attributes that may characterize an entity are the critical ones—the ones it must have to separate it from the pack. For example, many mammals have hair and bear their young alive (rather than in eggs). But some mammals do not have those characteristics. All mammals, however, nurse their young. That is the critical attribute without which a mammal is not a mammal.

Through any of these three variations—isolation of definitional, essential, and critical attributes—this principle can strengthen learning.

When teachers highlight items as important, that is not isolation of critical attributes. Things can be important without being critical attributes—for example, "These four formulas may be the most important things to know in the chapter" or "These three events may be the most important things to know about the month preceding the

Civil War." Neither set of important things, however, is the critical attribute of anything. Highlighting important items is something teachers do deliberately and usefully to focus students' attention on more important items, but that is quite different from identifying the definitional attributes of a concept.

In exploring the difference between a developed and an underdeveloped country, the teacher may highlight certain critical attributes that define *developed:* for example, mechanized planting and harvesting, an efficient national market distribution system, and an infrastructure of highways and transportation networks. It is not enough, however, for this list of attributes simply to be presented in the text or on the board. The teacher must see to it that the critical attributes are generated, call the students' attention to them (or elicit them from the students), and then have students apply the attributes in deciding which cases (here, what countries) do or do not contain those critical attributes. When students can discriminate developed from underdeveloped countries through analysis of critical attributes in new settings or in studies of countries where they're not specifically asked to look at them as developed versus underdeveloped, then learning has transferred.

## Meaning

The more meaningful and relevant the task or application of information is to the students' world, the easier it is to learn. Teachers using this principle may make explicit references to students' personal experiences as a tie or a hook for connecting content with students' lives, or they may simulate the experiences in the learning activity or in some other way embed the new content in the students' meaning framework. One teacher using the principle gave us the following example: "The goal is to understand the difference between chronology and history. I do a two-part assignment. For one day, students are asked to keep a time line of their activities. The next day they are to write a narrative history of the one day for which they kept the time line, showing, where possible, a cause-and-effect relationship." This assignment makes a nice distinction between chronology and history around a context that has intimate personal meaning for the students: their own day's activities.

## Modeling

Learning can be enhanced by modeling new skills or operations and preserving these models for student reference during early stages of learning. After explaining and demonstrating the algorithm for two-digit multiplication (or the format for writing a book report, or anything else with procedures and steps), the teacher leaves a model showing the separate steps on the board as students go to work practicing examples.

Conceptual models that have visual representations of what concepts mean and how they work improve student recall of the concept and performance on problems that ask them to extrapolate from what they have learned (Mayer, 1989). For example, a lesson on radar included a five-step diagram that showed a sequence in which a radar pulse moves out from the source, strikes an object, and bounces back, with the distance determined as a function of the total travel time (Van Merrienboer, 1997). Perkins and Unger (1989) posit that powerful conceptual models have four characteristics:

- Analogues, which provide some kind of analogy for the real phenomenon of interest
- Constructed, which are fabricated for the purpose at hand
- Stripped, in which extraneous clutter is eliminated to highlight critical features

- Concrete, in which the phenomenon is reduced to concrete examples and visual images

## Teaching for Transfer (from Setting to Setting)

This principle is at work when teachers create a series of assignments or tasks in which the call for using a skill is progressively distanced from direct instructional settings.

Here is a good example of teaching for transfer. After differentiating fact (that which is immediately verifiable by the senses or that on which most experts in the field would agree) from opinion (a belief; evidence exists to support differing beliefs), the teacher has students label examples as fact or opinion: for example, "Mary is wearing a sweater" and "Mary is the prettiest girl in the class." Examples are made progressively more difficult ("Some people believe in reincarnation.") Eventually students are asked to generate the examples themselves. Then they are asked to bring in newspaper articles (a new setting) to analyze for fact and opinion. Finally, students are given cues to transfer their skill to settings where it isn't an assignment to distinguish fact from opinion, as in text readings.

Sometimes there is no need to do anything extra for transfer to occur because it happens by itself. If children have learned to borrow in subtraction, they will probably transfer the skill to the supermarket that very afternoon when buying supplies for a class party. But for many skills, transfer does not happen spontaneously, so we need to engineer a series of events that will induce it. The final event in the chain, the actual transfer of the skill to a new context, is one that students take by themselves. That is what makes understanding this

principle a bit tricky. We take students along a planned series of steps up to the edge of the water, but they have to jump in themselves for there to be evidence that transfer has actually occurred.

Ms. Crane, for example, is teaching her middle school students about characterization. They look at pieces of dialogue and physical actions of characters in stories to see what these pieces of behavior reveal about the characters. The objective is to learn to recognize how authors develop readers' images and understandings of characters through dialogue and physical actions. In the long term, Ms. Crane wants her students to be able to use characterization in everyday life, that is, to "read" people they encounter, making inferences about what they are feeling and thinking from bits of dialogue and physical actions the students observe. She wants them, in other words, to transfer their ability to recognize characterization as a literary device to their own ability to use it in understanding people they meet. After analyzing the text in novels for characterization, she assigns students to watch one of their favorite TV programs; they are to take down bits of dialogue or describe physical actions they see that are in some way indicative of the character's personality. Later in the week, her students are asked to bring in examples of characterization from their observations of people in their neighborhood or their family. She is thus progressively distancing their use of characterization from the academic context of novels they are reading and pressing them to use the skill in ever-closer approximations of real life.

If students have learned to read novels and plays for authors' biases, transfer has occurred if they then read nonfiction and magazine articles in the same way. Teachers encourage this kind of transfer by proper sequencing of assignments and pressing students to be aware of the multiple applications of their learning (Brown, 1989; Fogarty, Perkins, and Barell, 1991). This principle is easily confused with (but different from) application in goal setting, where a skill taught in an abstract setting is put to use right away in a realistic setting.

# Designing for Motivational Impact

## Goal Setting

The point here is goal setting by students. When students get involved in goal setting for their own learning, they learn more. In addition to being common sense, this conclusion is strongly supported by a line of research (Schunk and Gaa, 1981). When students take ownership for goals (either self-set, teacher set, or jointly negotiated), their motivation to accomplish them and their ability to self-evaluate (and self-regulate) increase.

Student goal setting will not happen by itself except for very motivated students. Teachers have to do something to facilitate the process—perhaps take a few minutes of class time for students to write their goal for the period (or the unit) on a piece of paper or hold periodic goal-setting conferences with individual students at timely intervals (like the beginning of new units or projects). These conferences can be quite short, but the goals chosen should be recorded and students should be asked later to evaluate how they did.

Student goal setting does not automatically lead to increased student performance. Certain properties of effective goals need to be present; they need to be specific, challenging but attainable, and able to be accomplished soon.

Specific goals contain items that can be measured, counted, or perceived directly as criteria for accomplishment. "Try my best" doesn't fit this mold; "Master the twenty spelling demons" does.

The more difficult the goal is, the more effort the student will expend, providing the goal is viewed as attainable. In guiding students to set goals, teachers have to help them walk the tightrope between what is "duck soup" and what is unrealistically difficult.

Finally, goals that can be accomplished in the short term work better than long-term goals. This does not mean long-term goals should not be set, only that long-term goals need to be broken down into short-term goals or subgoals with their own plans of action, if one is to be maximally effective in reaching them. Learning or work accomplishment goals for students seem to work best around specified skills and products and for time spans of one period to several days rather than over several weeks or months.

A common misinterpretation of this principle is that it means students are picking what they will study (that is, the content). This is not the case. Much more often (and usually more productively), they are setting goals about speed, quantity, or quality. Here is an example of a speed goal: The student makes a commitment to how fast he will do some amount of work:

TEACHER:  Glen, how many of these do you think you'll get done in the next half-hour?

GLEN:  I think this whole page.

TEACHER:  Really? Do you really think that's a reasonable amount?

GLEN:  Yes, I'll do it.

TEACHER:  Okay. Show them to me when you're done.

And here is a quantity goal:

TEACHER:  How many references will you use in researching that, Brenda?

BRENDA: About six.

TEACHER: Okay. If you think that's enough, put it down in your outline sheet.

There is no particular rate at which the researching must be done (except ultimately the deadline of the paper). It is a commitment Brenda makes to do a specified amount. The same kind of goal applies to how many books students will read for free reading, for example, or how many extra credit or supplementary exercises they'll do.

Quality goals are particularly interesting. In these goals, students make a commitment to how well they'll do something. This can take the form of targeting what aspect of their work they'll focus on improving. Teachers can give them the assignment to explain what they're working to improve (and maybe even ask for it in writing):

TEACHER: So, Jamie, what's your quality goal going to be on this paper?

JAMIE: I'm going to work on improving spelling and punctuation.

TEACHER: How about you, Tara?

TARA: My goal's going to be to use fewer tired words.

By getting students to set goals, teachers do not relinquish their ability to make assignments. They enlist the students in making personal commitments to speed, quantity, or quality. It is possible to have students choose content in some cases—"I want to learn everything I can about frogs," says Freddy. There are places where it will fit in with curriculum requirements and time available to help Freddy do so (especially if one of the teacher's goals is to stimulate and support an inquiring attitude). But it may be equally powerful to get students to set quality goals, thus involving them inevitably in self-evaluation to come up with a target for improvement.

In our experience, this principle of learning is one of the least practiced in education. If we devoted just a little time and energy to it, we might see big payoffs in student performance and in students' learning directly about self-regulation and self-evaluation.

## Keeping Students Open and Thinking Through Teacher Responses to Student Answers

Art Costa (1985) has pointed out that the way that teachers respond to student answers is probably more important than the questions themselves. Every time a student answers a question, a teacher does something. Similarly, if a student responds with silence because he or she can't answer the question or is slow to think it through, teachers still do something: give a cue, or refer it to another student, or offer to help. It is through these acts—repeated hundreds of times over a day—that teachers set a climate about whether it's safe to open one's mouth in this class. It is through teachers' patterns of actions at these moments that they exert a force either to keep students open and thinking or become a force to restrict thinking and risk taking.

This arena of classroom life—responses to student answers—is also an arena through which teachers send the three critical expectation messages: "This is important." "You can do it." "I won't give up on you."

## Knowledge of Results

Knowledge of results should be specific and timely. Practitioners of this principle give explicit feedback to students on their work as rapidly as possible after completion. The rationale is that this feedback has optimum corrective impact when most proximal to the student's engaging the materials and maximum communicative effect when it is both full and specific. (We note in Chapter Twelve that full and complete feedback is a form of respect by which teachers show students they value students' work enough to look at it closely.)

In twenty-first-century literature this teacher skill is called "feedback" more than "knowledge of results." In Chapter Nineteen, "Assessment," we go into considerable detail about how to give feedback to students in effective ways.

Here are two examples of knowledge of results:

- On completing a worksheet on social changes as a result of the Industrial Revolution, students see answers displayed on an overhead (or revealed from behind a rolled-up map). They correct their own papers and then ask clarifying questions of the teacher.
- Students correct their own workbook and worksheet pages from answer books, fixing all individual mistakes and explaining their errors.

Feedback from a teacher to students does not mean this principle is in operation, and finding out how they did on a test is not the principle. Students find out how they did at some point in every class, so there's nothing special about that. What is special (and what empowers learning) is feedback that is rapid, specific, and complete. Computer games give instantaneous knowledge of results, though not always with specific information about how to improve.

Teachers can claim they're using knowledge of results if they're giving students feedback about how they did *very soon* after they perform, along with an opportunity to self-correct or at least see what would have to be done to improve (Butler and Winne, 1995).

## Reinforcement

A reinforcer is anything that strengthens a behavior and can range all the way from edibles and tokens to teacher statements of recognition like, "You stuck with that hard one until you got it and you didn't give up!" Verbal reinforcement is the focus here because although it is so overworked in the literature and is so common a part of teachers' vocabulary, it is astonishing how little it is used skillfully. Many opportunities pass for applying this powerful stimulus to learning. The knowledge base tells us that verbal reinforcement should be precise, appropriate, and, when appropriate, scheduled from regular to intermittent.

*Precise* means that the statement should specify exactly what it is that the learner has done that is good: "You didn't rush today, and you got them almost all right" is better than "Good work." The student is much more likely to reproduce the high accuracy rate, which is due to not rushing, if not rushing is explicitly reinforced. When a teacher says, "You finished those problems and then you put your stuff away without my giving you any reminders, and you started on your writing. That's great," the student knows what is great.

Appropriate reinforcement is important. If a student doesn't want it, it's not reinforcing. Being praised in front of someone else may be embarrassing. Being told his handwriting is "nice" may turn off a sixth-grade athlete and get him kidded by his pals; more appropriate feedback for him might be, "John, you're one of our best ball players and I see your fine motor coordination is just as good as your coordination on the ball field" (Hunter, 1977). It is easy to see why studies of praise and reinforcement that count frequency of the behavior and look for correlations to student achievement can never get anywhere. Only appropriate use of reinforcement works.

Scheduling is the third important feature of reinforcement. B. F. Skinner discovered that behaviors established through operant conditioning become more stable and more durable if reinforcement is delivered with every occurrence of the behavior at first. But then reinforcement should skip occasional occurrences at random, and the span of unreinforced occurrences between reinforcers should gradually be lengthened. Use of intermittent scheduling to establish behaviors is more in line with a systematic plan for behavior modification a teacher might use to develop, say, hand raising versus calling out or promptness versus tardiness to class.

Although researchers agree universally on the positive effects of intrinsic reinforcement, a debate has raged for years over whether extrinsic reinforcers ought to be used. Chance (1992) has put the matter in perspective by pointing out the conditions under which extrinsic reinforcers are not only okay (meaning they do not damage students' motivation to do the activity when there are no reinforcers around) but are helpful to learning. Chance points out that extrinsic reinforcers include teachers' smiles, praise, congratulations, saying "thank you" or "right," shaking hands, a pat on the back, applauding, providing a certificate of achievement, or other behaviors that "in any way provide a positive consequence (a reward) for student behavior" (p. 203). Extrinsic rewards can decrease motivation to engage in a behavior (say, reading) if it is given as a task contingency, that is, for merely participating in an activity without regard to how well one does at it. But when rewards are success contingent, that is, delivered when students perform well or meet goals, there is no negative effect on engagement with the activity later when rewards are no longer given. Indeed, success contingent rewards tend to increase interest in the activity.

Intrinsic rewards are available to students only if they can perform sufficiently well in an area to get the reward, for example, if they can read well enough to get the pleasure of a good story. "While intrinsic rewards are important, they are insufficient for effective learning for all students" (Chance, 1992, p. 206) if one has to rely on them exclusively.

# Technical Principles of Design

## Breaking Complex Tasks into Simpler Parts

One often sees evidence of this principle when teachers are attempting to explain or clarify operations students have failed to grasp. The task is broken down into smaller parts, and one part, now isolated, is focused on for learning. For example, if students are having trouble with word problems, the teacher may have the students identify the central question and the operation called for without doing any computing. Or students may be asked to draw a picture of what happens in the problem as a way of conceptualizing it, again without any computing. This principle manifests as task analysis and ensures that sequential prerequisites for present learning tasks are established.

## Close Confusers

Ensure an adequate degree of original learning before "close confusers" are introduced. Teachers following this principle are careful not to confuse or weaken recently learned items—say, the letter "d"—by introducing too soon new items easily confused with it—the letter "b." In this example, the primary teacher will go on to "t," then maybe "f," then some other letters, all the while reviewing "d" in the expanding set of letters recognized and then finally introduce "b" as a new letter when "d" has been thoroughly learned and practiced.

To generalize the statement of this principle in other terms, teachers should not sequence new material so as to require fine discriminations between two contiguous terms when grosser discriminations can be used first. The making of fine discriminations can be demanded when at least one item of the content pair has had an adequate opportunity to be thoroughly learned. This is something to monitor in using textbooks where close confusers like rotation and revolution, weathering and erosion are introduced at the same time.

Similarly, exceptions to rules are not to be introduced until original rules are practiced and established sufficiently. Mindful of this principle, a secondary teacher writes:

> Constitutional law is a central part of any middle school social studies curricula. Instruction frequently involves explanations of the Bill of Rights, including illustrations of case law. For example, "freedom of speech" is usually tackled by considering yelling "fire" in a crowded theater. Before a teacher can realistically ask students to distinguish between acceptable and unacceptable forms of "free speech," he must be sure that they have a grounding in the basic concepts, including the important case law. Once they have this, they can examine a more complex situation.

## Contiguity

"First impressions stick" is one way of thinking about this principle. Events, objects, operations, and emotions close to each other in time and space tend to become associated in the mind of the learner. A first association, once learned, is hard to unlearn—whether it's calling Mary Ann, "Mary Lou" the first time you meet her and finding yourself doing so every time thereafter or adding the tens column first and then the ones and finding that a hard habit to break.

Learners should not be allowed to practice errors and build an incorrect association. Students who practice footnotes in the wrong format the first time find that the wrong model interferes with the right one when they finally learn it. This principle pertains mainly to paired-associate memory and procedural learning like vocabulary words and math algorithms, not higher-level thought questions. For memory learning, the implication for teachers is to anticipate errors where they are likely to occur and prevent these errors, even by giving the right answer where appropriate (for example, a new sight word) before a student has a chance to make a wrong guess (and thus learn a wrong association that must later be unlearned). Teachers should never allow a student to leave a paired-associate learning situation with a wrong answer; the last response that occurs should be correct.

Teachers should also be on the watch for potential negative emotional associations students may form. For example, students coming in to class after a recess full of fighting and negative emotions who are then introduced to a new topic may form negative associations with the topic that will interfere with their future learning. This is not the time to introduce poetry for the first time, for example. The teacher might preface the introduction to the topic with a brief activity that raises positive feelings in students.

## Cumulative Review

Any information or skill one doesn't actively use tends to be forgotten. Therefore, old learnings should be included in practice and drills of new material so that these old learnings are periodically exercised. As students move on in a skill sequence, the range and number of skills demanded in the practice exercises grow cumulatively to include all the old skills. To prevent practice tasks from becoming unwieldy when the range of skills is big, only a representative sample of them is included in exercises focusing on new material.

Certain skill sequences automatically cumulate old skills in new products without any design steps required by the teacher—for example, report writing. As students learn new punctuation and grammar skills, these are automatically practiced each time writing takes place and are expected to be done correctly. And as students use more elaborate language forms and learn to organize ideas better, these also are automatically expected to be continued in future writing. But other skill sequences require more deliberate design for cumulative review to take place effectively.

In drilling on flash cards to learn times tables, each new pack should contain a representative sample of all previously learned facts, and occasional packs should be reviewed entirely to solidify old learnings. In learning geographical features of a country in South America, the features should come up again and again in the context of the questions about the country's elections, political system, and economy. A violation of this principle would see students studying the geographical features of all the South American countries in sequence, then going back and studying all their political systems, then all their cultural highlights, and so on.

## Degree of Guidance

How much guidance will students need to get the most out of (or just to get through) the task? Guidance should be high with new tasks and withdrawn gradually with demonstrated student proficiency.

Evidence for this principle cannot be simply to observe teachers delivering different degrees of guidance to different students. Evidence must cite different degrees of guidance offered to the same student or group of students over time as they progressively show increased proficiency with the new material. This is sometimes difficult to see in short observations. Nevertheless, a teacher may introduce a new skill to a class and immediately provide adequate guidance in practicing it. This may mean working with just one group after introducing haiku to the whole class, while giving the rest of the class something else they still need to practice but without so much teacher guidance, and then rotating through the class with groups that focus on the new skill. Or it may mean the teacher puts on track shoes and gets around to everybody, giving guidance and help where needed. The latter is more time efficient if the teacher can pull it off (pulling it off is not so much a function of teacher skill as good judgment—what new material will or will not require more intensive individual guidance for students to be able to use it proficiently).

## Mnemonics

Teachers using this principle help students use mediational devices for remembering new learning—devices such as imagery, anagrams, or jingles ("30 days hath September"). Here is a familiar one:

Desert—*one "s," all alone in the desert.*
Dessert—*you get bigger in the middle if you eat too much of it.*

There are many mnemonic devices and a growing body of research comparing their effectiveness. For example, one particularly effective technique, the key word technique, is used for learning new vocabulary words and new terms. Students are asked to learn a key word (word clue) for the new term that sounds acoustically similar to it (for example, "purse" for "persuade"; "he's a date" for "hesitate"). Then students are asked to remember the content of a cartoon that contains the key word interacting in some way with the definition of the new term. Levin and others (1982) show a cartoon for the new vocabulary word *persuade.* One woman points to a purse in a store and says, "Oh, Martha, you should buy that PURSE!" Martha replies, "I think you can PERSUADE me to buy it." At the bottom of the cartoon is written, "Persuade (Purse): When you talk someone into doing something." In these cartoons, one character's utterance contains the key word, and the other contains the new term to be learned. Studies have been highly positive and uniform in demonstrating the effectiveness of this technique for learning new words (Levin, 1993).

Here are the steps in using mnemonic key words:

1. Think of a sound-alike or rhyming word you know that resembles the new word you're trying to learn. This word is the key word.
2. Make up a visual cartoon in which both the key word and the word to be learned are represented in the action or the objects.
3. Have dialogue between two characters in the cartoon, one using the key word and the other the word to be learned.
4. Make the dialogue meaningful, and arrange it so that the context of the dialogue and the cartoon illustrates the meaning of the word to be learned.

## Practice

Practice should be massed at the beginning of learning a new skill or operation (meaning frequent practice sessions, close together in time), then distributed over increasing intervals of time. The smallest unit of new information that retains meaning should be practiced at any one session and worked on for the shortest unit of time to allow the students to feel they have accomplished something. After they have achieved proficiency, they should practice learned items two or three more times to make the learning more permanent (overlearning). Unlike athletics and motor skills, where practice makes perfect and the more the better (up to a point), long practice sessions with academic skills quickly reach a point of diminishing returns.

For areas like the times tables, each fact is a unit of meaning on its own, separate from the others, and only one or two of them should be introduced at a time, embedded in groups of already known facts for drill. (Certain tables and groups of facts, however, such as the 10-times table, group all at once as a single unit of meaning.) In teaching students to analyze a story, a complex task, only one part would be assigned at first, say, identifying the setting; later would come describing the plot. In practicing a difficult piece of music, the student would practice not a page or a bar (which might be too small a unit to have meaning) but a measure.

Practice sessions should be short (two to five minutes) and frequent (twice a day rather than twice a week). This is quite at odds with the schedules we often see when students labor over workbooks in classrooms.

If a teacher wants students to practice writing news stories in a journalism course, the lead (that is, the opening sentence or paragraph that contains all the critical information of who, when, where, why, and what) is a meaningful unit. Students may be asked to practice writing just leads for frequent short practice periods before being asked to write entire stories.

## Say-Do

The more perceptual modes one engages for students—seeing, hearing, moving, touching—the better the learning will be. But in striving to increase the range of perceptual channels made active during learning, be particularly aware of the power of having learners say their learning out loud and get involved in using it to do something. The title of this principle, say-do, is meant to highlight the powerful effects achieved when these two channels for expressing learning are engaged.

What do we know about the relative power of various perceptual channels for acquiring information? How much do students retain over time if the only way they acquire information is to read it versus hearing it versus seeing it? What if they both see and hear the information? What if students were to read the information and then summarize their learning out loud to someone (read-say)? What would be the learning retention effects if students read information to acquire it, then had to summarize it out loud to someone, and then finally put the information to work by actually using it to do something? The graph in Figure 10.2 summarizes the relative effectiveness of different perceptual modes.

At first glance, the most surprising assertion in the chart is the magnitude of the boost in learning retention when "say" is added to the simple input channel of reading. The effect would probably be similar for see-say and hear-say, though there are no studies found to verify this claim. Studies of the effect of learning logs and dialogue journals confirm positive learning effects for hear-write and read-write (Pradl and Mayher, 1985; Fulwiler, 1987; Connolly and Vilardi, 1989).

To summarize in your own words, either verbally or in writing, what you have learned in a given experience is a complex cognitive act; it causes

**Figure 10.2. Relative Effectiveness of Different Perceptual Modes**

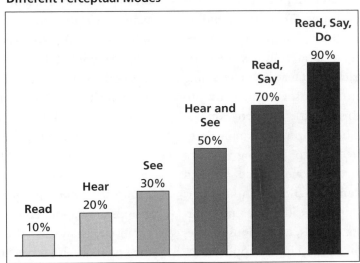

*Source:* This figure represents an amalgam of many studies.

search and retrieval of memory, organization of ideas, and summoning of language to recast the meaning in your own terms. It is logical that this complex set of cognitive acts would create neural networks and deepen memory traces.

The implications for teaching and learning are large. Foremost is the call to have students stop and summarize, either singly in journals or together out loud in pairs, what is important in a recent episode of learning. The need to create such pauses means that a teacher will build periodic summarizing into teaching as a regular practice.

The "do" part of this principle means getting students active as soon as possible using the materials in some realistic way.

Research has compared the relative effectiveness of perceptual channels, and there is a considerable literature on the effects of student verbalizations of their learning (Pauk, 1974; Webb, 1982; Morrow, 1985; King, 1990). One particularly well-designed study by MacKenzie and White (1982) comes close to including all the conditions in Figure 10.2. In their study of eighth and ninth graders' learning and retention of geographical facts, they involved learners in three different conditions to learn facts and skills in the geography of coasts, including information about landforms and plants. All three treatment groups studied a carefully designed programmed learning package of materials containing thirty-five pages and thirty-seven questions to encourage processing (Read). The program was supported by sixty photographs on 35mm slides (See). "Other characteristics of the program were statements of expected performance, worked examples and test items, practice at working new data, prompts to stimulate recall of relevant information and subordinate skills, indications of relevance of information to subsequent application, and transfer of verbal propositions to maps, diagrams and slides."

Treatment group 1 received the package described. Treatment group 2 went through the programmed package too and went on a field trip to a beach, two sets of cliffs, and two mangrove flats where the pictures in the program had been taken. The students were given an explanatory field guide designed to reinforce the information in the program they had done at school. A teacher guided them around the five sites, pointing out items in the guide. In the middle of the trip, students had to complete one set of questions. So in addition to the classroom-based instruction of treatment group 1, this group had a great deal more of seeing and hearing built in to their experience, as well as more calls to answer questions about the information.

Treatment group 3 also went on the field trip, but with some powerful additions: "At each site students received a worksheet, a map of the area, and a tide table. The teacher supervised while the students, individually and in groups, completed the tasks on the worksheets. Group discussions (Say) were held frequently. Students were continually required to do things (Do): observe, sketch, record, answer questions. Several unusual events were arranged, such as walking through the mud of the mangrove shore, tasting foliage for salinity, scrambling over cliff platforms, wading in the sea. It is emphasized that the students in [treatment group 2] saw the same things . . . and spent the same time at each site. They had information repeated to them more often, but did far less" (pp. 626–627).

The achievement results in this experiment were striking. In the initial achievement tests, both field trip groups outperformed the classroom-only group by a wide margin, but the two field trip groups were about equal to each other in student achievement means. After twelve weeks, however, the retention with respect to initial mean scores was 51 percent for the classroom-only group, 58 percent for the treatment 2 field trip group, and 90 percent for the treatment 3 field trip group. The addition of say and do together in this condition had a huge impact on long-term retention.

## Sequence and Backward Chaining

The first and last items in a series are the easiest to remember; the one just past the middle is the hardest. Learning can be accelerated by chaining a sequence backward from the last item, and sequences can be broken into small parts to avoid interference. This set of principles is applicable to rote learning and is easily observed when practiced in math fact and spelling drills or any other body of items in some sequence that students are expected to memorize (such as poems). Teachers can use this knowledge to improve the learning of items in the difficult positions. The sequence (or list) can be shortened or split in half so the difficult item becomes first on the shortened list. The order of items can be changed; the hard parts can be given extra practice; the hard items can be made more vivid (darker print, use of colors). A high school Latin teacher writes:

> Students are expected to learn ten new Latin vocabulary words each week. (1) They quiz each other from the list at the beginning of each class period for five minutes. (2) Then they drill alone on the ones they missed in the partner quiz. (3) They write the list in their notebooks along with the meanings, putting the ones they missed first and last in the reordered list (and second and ninth if need be). Words they know best are put in the just-past-the-middle position. They cover the answers with their hand and go down the list several times quizzing themselves. This procedure is repeated each day, with missed words in first and last positions. The whole thing takes about ten minutes, which I use to circulate and talk to individual students.

This principle of sequence and the importance of the first and last positions is also applicable to the use of time. What happens at the beginning and end of a class period (or day or term) is most easily remembered; thus, these spots should be milked to maximum advantage for learning. (See Chapter Six, "Time.")

# Principles Impacting Attention and Engagement

## Active Participation

In classes of teachers who use this principle, students are operating, responding, moving, and talking during the course of the learning experiences. Sitting passively and listening is not characteristic of learning experiences embodying this principle. Active participation of all students might not require small or large muscle movement or manipulation; it could conceivably involve written participation, with each student responding to each question, or it could be all verbal participation, with the setting structured in such a way that many students can talk at once (divided into pairs or small groups to reach consensus on something or debate some issue).

There are many techniques for structuring this kind of participation from students. For example, after finishing a presentation of the structure of an atomic nucleus and the meaning of atomic number versus atomic mass, the teacher says, "Okay, now explain to your neighbor the difference between atomic number and atomic mass." Teachers aware of this principle look for opportunities to make that kind of move.

## End Without Closure

Consider the impact of this teacher statement: "Think about three ways you might get out of this dilemma and be ready to share them with us tomorrow when you come in" (Russell, 1980). Leaving students without an answer and with something percolating overnight may be more effective in some cases than coming to a neat ending of each class with all issues resolved.

## Feeling Tone

Feeling tone propels learning in proportion to degree. This principle posits that students learn more and faster in proportion to the level of feeling provoked during the learning—positive or negative feeling. The rule is held to apply only up to a point. On one side, the more pleasurable the learning experience is, the more the learning will take place—up to the point where the pleasure takes over and begins crowding out the learning. There is, in other words, a point of diminishing returns for efforts to make learning pleasurable. When teachers raise the level of concern of students ("I'm going to check you all individually on this material this period"), learning is potentiated, but only up to a point. Too much concern turns into anxiety, quickly interferes with learning, and blocks it. Again, a point of diminishing returns is quickly reached.

Application of this principle sees teachers either making moves to make learning experiences enjoyable (without becoming hedonistic) or raising levels of concern ("We'll be having a quiz on this material sometime this week"), but neither to the extreme. Judging the extreme, or the point of diminishing returns, is not a judgment for which rules can be cited. To credit this principle as oper-ative, however, an observer would have to cite evidence of teacher moves to raise positive or negative feeling tone and be subjectively convinced (by watching student reactions) that extremes had not been violated.

## Similarity of Environment

Similarity of environment (actions, feelings, formats, routines) elicits the learner's mind-set to perform. This principle holds that certain features of the environment, when regularly associated with a particular type of learning or a period in which a type of attention or work is expected, trigger a mind-set in learners that "plugs them in" and turns on their operators for that particular kind of lesson or activity.

Therefore, teachers can regularly use repetitive formats for certain kinds of learning—when the environment assumes certain space, time, and routine features—to create expectational mind-sets in their students for that kind of work. For example, a science teacher we know has thirty lab coats hung on a row of pegs inside his classroom door. When students enter, they are expected to put on a lab coat and proceed to their seats. The lab coats signal a change of mind-set into being scientists.

In addition, teachers may warm up students for a lesson by doing an activity that starts them thinking the way they'll be asked to think in the lesson. For instance, suppose a teacher is going to do a lesson on outlining that requires students to categorize their ideas into topical groups. The teacher may warm up the class by playing Guess My Category. The teacher slowly develops the lists below on the board, writing the terms one at a time in the order indicated, under "yes" for positive examples of the category and "no" for negative examples. The students must guess the category to which the "yes" examples belong (in this example, "southern states"):

| *Yes* | *No* |
|---|---|
| Mississippi | New York |
| Virginia | Wyoming |
| Georgia | California |
| Kentucky | Iowa |
| Florida | Arizona |

When the game is over, the teacher says, "Now, the kind of thinking we were doing here is similar to what our minds have to do with facts in this outlining activity for today. Take out your note cards and . . ."

Russell (1980) points out that this activity is also an excellent sponge for students arriving in class (see the Momentum area of performance in Chapter Four). It gets them involved immediately with a meaningful activity yet does not penalize those who haven't arrived yet. Thus, it eliminates downtime and waiting.

## Vividness

The vividness, liveliness, energy, novelty, or striking imagery of a learning experience is thought to impress new learning on students more deeply through mediation of the attentional mechanisms. One can claim this principle to be in operation by virtue of observed student reaction to learning experiences, the "ooh-aah" reactions, the high level of arousal or emotion (surprise, fascination) attributed to observed student behaviors (wide eyes, open mouths, rapt gazes, unusual stillness). In trying to practice what he preaches, one of us once introduced a group of teachers to the principles of learning by pulling a series of small gift-wrapped packages out of a case labeled "idea bag" to high-light that each principle is discrete and valuable, self-contained and important.

## Summary

We have described twenty-four principles teachers can use to increase the rate and durability of students' learning. Following is a summary in alphabetical order:

1. Active participation: Encouraging through unison, checking with a partner, signals, and so on

2. Application in setting: Practicing new behaviors in settings where they'll be used

3. Concrete-Semiabstract-Abstract progression: Following as a progression with the introduction of new material

4. Breaking complex tasks into simpler parts: Down into simpler, smaller pieces; isolating trouble spots for focused work and practice; higher-frequency practice and repetition of new items

5. Close confusers: Ensuring an adequate degree of original learning before introducing close confusers

6. Contiguity: Don't allow practice of errors with paired-associate learning

7. Cumulative review: In practice, periodically including representative sample of previously learned material

8. Degree of guidance: High with new tasks; withdrawn gradually with familiarity

9. End without closure: But with follow-up at a later time, to invite percolation

10. Feeling tone: Fun, but not too much; worry, but not too much; raising level of concern

11. Goal setting: By students; ownership, specific, challenging; able to be accomplished soon, then over the longer term

12. Isolation of critical attributes: Highlighting and labeling the attributes

13. Keep students open and thinking: For example, supply questions for which answers are right, deliver promptly, and hold accountable

14. Knowledge of results: Promptly through monitoring

15. Meaning: Connecting to students' personal experience

16. Mnemonics: Devices to aid in memory (key words, images in sequence, jingles)

17. Modeling: Step-wise products, procedures, and processes preserved for student reference

18. Practice: Massed at beginning, then distributed; smallest meaningful units; short practices; overlearning

19. Reinforcement: Precise, regular, and intermittent

20. Say-do: Using all perceptual channels but emphasizing particularly saying and doing

21. Sequence and backward chaining: First and last are easiest; just past the middle is hardest

22. Similarity of environment: An activity that gets minds in gear for upcoming events

23. Teach for transfer: Engineering a planned sequence of activities that progressively distance the skill from abstract academic contexts

24. Vividness: And varying of practice formats.

To check your knowledge about Principles of Learning, see the quiz on our Web site at **www.RBTeach.com/rbteach/quiz/PLearning.html.**

*Source Materials on Principles of Learning*

Baretta-Lorton, M. *Math Their Way.* Reading, Mass.: Addison Wesley, 1976.

Barringer, C., and Gholson, B. "Effects of Type and Combination of Feedback upon Conceptual Learning by Children: Implications for Research in Academic Learning." *Review of Educational Research,* 1979, *49,* 459–478.

Beeson, G. W. "Influence of Knowledge Context on the Learning of Intellectual Skills." *American Educational Research Journal,* 1981, *18,* 363–379.

Bellezza, F. S. "Mnemonic Devices: Classification, Characteristics, and Criteria." *Review of Educational Research,* 1981, *51,* 247–275.

Blank, M. *Teaching Learning in the Preschool: A Dialogue Approach.* Columbus, Ohio: Merrill, 1973.

Brophy, J. "Praise: A Functional Analysis." *Review of Educational Research,* 1981, *51,* 5–32.

Brown, A. L. "Analogical Learning and Transfer: What Develops?" In S. Vosniadou and A. A. Ortony (eds.), *Similarity and Analogical Reasoning.* Cambridge: Cambridge University Press, 1989.

Bugelski, B. R. *The Psychology of Learning Applied to Teaching.* Indianapolis: Bobbs-Merrill, 1971.

Butler, D. L., and Winne, P. H. "Feedback and Self-Regulated Learning." *Review of Educational Research,* 1995, *65,* 245–281.

Chance, P. "The Rewards of Learning." *Kappan,* 1992, pp. 200–207.

Connolly, P., and Vilardi, T. *Writing to Learn Mathematics and Science.* New York: Teachers College Press, 1989.

Costa, A. *Teaching for Intelligent Behaviors.* Orangevale, Calif.: Search Models Unlimited, 1985.

Dunkin, M. J., and Biddle, B. J. *The Study of Teaching.* New York: Holt, Rinehart and Winston, 1974.

Ebbinghaus, H. *Memory.* 1885. Trans. H. A. Ruger and C. E. Bussenius. New York: Teachers College, Columbia University, 1913.

Fogarty, R., Perkins, D., and Barell, J. *How to Teach for Transfer.* Palatine, Ill.: Skylight Publishing, 1991.

Fulwiler, T. (ed.). *The Journal Book.* Portsmouth, N.H.: Heinemann, 1987.

Good, T. J., and Brophy, J. E. *Looking in Classrooms.* New York: HarperCollins, 1978.

Graham, S. "Teacher Feelings and Student Thoughts: An Attributional Approach to Affect in the Classroom." *Elementary School Journal,* 1985, *85,* 91–104

Haughton, E. "Aims—Growing and Sharing." In J. B. Jordan and L. S. Robbins (eds.), *Let's Try Doing Something Else Kind of Thing.* Arlington, Va.: Council for Exceptional Children, 1972.

Herron, J. D. "Piaget for Chemists." *Journal of Chemical Education,* 52(2), 1975, 146–150.

Hess, R. D., Dickson, W. P., Price, G. G., and Leong, D. "Some Contrasts Between Mothers and Preschool Teachers in Interaction with Four-Year-Old Children." *American Educational Research Journal,* 1979, *16,* 307–316.

Higbee, K. L. "Recent Research on Visual Mnemonics: Historical Roots and Educational Fruits." *Review of Educational Research,* 1979, *49,* 611–629.

Hilgard, E. R., and Bower, G. H. *Theories of Learning.* New York: Appleton-Century-Crofts, 1966.

Hudgins, B. B. *Learning and Thinking: A Primer for Teachers.* Itasca, Ill.: F. E. Peacock, 1977.

Hunter, M. *Motivation.* El Segundo, Calif.: Theory Into Practice Publications, 1967a.

Hunter, M. *Reinforcement.* El Segundo, Calif.: Theory Into Practice Publications, 1967b.

Hunter, M. *Retention.* El Segundo, Calif.: Theory Into Practice Publications, 1967c.

Hunter, M. *Teach More—Faster.* El Segundo, Calif.: Theory Into Practice Publications, 1967d.

Hunter, M. *Teach for Transfer.* El Segundo, Calif.: Theory Into Practice Publications, 1971.

Hunter, M. "Improving the Quality of Instruction." Paper presented at the ASCD Conference, Fifth General Session, Houston, Mar. 1977.

King, A. "Enhancing Peer Interaction and Learning in the Classroom Through Reciprocal Questioning." *American Educational Research Journal,* 1990, *27,* 664–687.

Levin, J. R. "Mnemonic Strategies and Classroom Learning: A Twenty Year Report Card." *Elementary School Journal,* 1993, *94,* 235–244.

Levin, J. R., McCormick, C., Miller, G., and Berry, J. "Mnemonic versus Nonmnemonic Vocabulary—Learning Strategies for Children." *American Educational Research Journal,* 1982, *19,* 121–136.

Mackenzie, A. A., and White, R. T. "Fieldwork in Geography and Long-term Memory Structures." *American Educational Research Journal,* 1982, *19,* 623–632.

Mayer, R. E. "Models for Understanding." *Review of Educational Research,* 1989, *59,* 43–64.

Morrow, L. M. "Retelling Stories: A Strategy for Improving Young Children's Concept of Story Structure and Oral Language Complexity." *Elementary School Journal,* 1985, *85,* 646–661.

Pauk, W. *How to Study in College.* Boston: Houghton Mifflin, 1974.

Perkins, D. N., and Unger, C. "The New Look in Representations for Mathematics and Science Learning." Paper presented at the Social Science Research Council Conference, "Computers and Learning," Tortola, British Virgin Islands, June 26–July 2, 1989.

Pradl, G., and Mayher, J. S. "Reinvigorating Learning Through Writing." *Educational Leadership,* Feb. 1985, pp. 4–8.

Pressley, M., Levin, J. R., and Delaney, H. D. "The Mnemonic Keyword Method." *Review of Educational Research,* 1982, *52,* 61–91.

Rosswork, S. "Goal Setting: The Effects on an Academic Task with Varying Magnitudes of Incentive." *Journal of Educational Psychology,* 1977, *69,* 710–715.

Russell, D. "Teaching Decisions and Behaviors for Instructional Improvement." Talk given at the Association for Supervision and Curriculum Development Convention, Atlanta, Ga., 1980.

Schunk, D. H., and Gaa, J. P. "Goal-Setting Influence on Learning and Self-Evaluation." *Journal of Classroom Interaction,* 1981, *16,* 38–44.

Sefkow, S. B., and Myers, J. L. "Review Effects of Inserted Questions on Learning from Prose." *American Educational Research Journal,* 1980, *17,* 435–448.

Trabasso, T. "Pay Attention." In J. P. DeCecco (ed.), *Readings in Educational Psychology Today.* Del Mar, Calif.: CRM Books, 1970.

Van Merrienboer, J.J.G. *Training Complex Cognitive Skills.* Englewood Cliffs, N.J.: Educational Technology Publications, 1997.

Webb, N. M. "Student Interaction and Learning in Small Groups." *Review of Educational Research,* 1982, *52,* 441–445.

White, B., and Horwitz, P. *Thinkertools: Enabling Children to Understand Physical Laws.* Cambridge, Mass.: BBN Laboratories, 1987.

# Models of Teaching

For students of teaching, few other efforts are as rewarding and as challenging as learning new models of teaching. Even the most mature and sophisticated of professionals can add to their repertoires and their power to reach a broader range of students. It is an ideal area of study for advanced professionals between their fifth and fifteenth year of teaching.

A model of teaching is a pattern of instruction that is recognizable and consistent. It has particular values, goals, a rationale, and an orientation to how learning shall take place (for example, by induction, by discovery, through heightened personal awareness, by wrestling with puzzling data, or by organizing information hierarchically). And that orientation is developed into a specific set of phases teachers and students go through, in order, with specific kinds of events in each phase. Each model of teaching is a particular entity with specific components, well worked out, and with markedly different appearances and effects.

Each of the dozens of models (Figure 11.1) is a design for planning lessons so as to achieve two outcomes: the teaching of content and the teaching of a particular kind of thinking. Almost any model can be used to teach a given piece of content; although the information learned may be the same, the intellectual experience for students will be different. For example, if Mr. Jones uses Taba's inductive model for a lesson on Hemingway, he wants students to learn not only about Hemingway but also to learn to think inductively. The model is carefully sequenced to get them into that kind of thinking. If he teaches through the jurisprudential model, he may want the same learnings about Hemingway, but he also wants his students to think like lawyers, taking positions and arguing them with evidence. If he uses the group investigation model, he may still want students to learn the same core information about Hemingway, but in addition he wants them to learn about group process, leadership, and coordinated plans of inquiry. If he uses the advance organizer model, he wants them to learn about hierarchical thinking and subordination of ideas. Models of teaching provide a way for teachers to be more articulate and precise about implicit learnings students take from instruction. They enable us to broaden the ways we instruct and thus broaden the range of students' intellectual experience in school.

Research over several decades has shown no one model superior to the others for achieving learning as measured by test scores. That only stands to reason, since that was not their intention. Models of teaching were not created to be more efficient hypodermics to inject knowledge into students' heads. They were intended to teach students how to learn and think in different ways. Educators can use a variety of models to match students' preferred learning styles and broaden students' capacity as thinkers and learners beyond their favored style.

Teachers who have multiple models in their repertoires may use several different ones in a day or even within a class period. Teachers who master additional models find themselves able to modulate across them like connoisseurs, thus giving professionalism a new dimension. Let us examine the models themselves, first with a more detailed description of what a model is and then with a look at a number of specific models.

**Figure 11.1. Families of Models of Teaching**

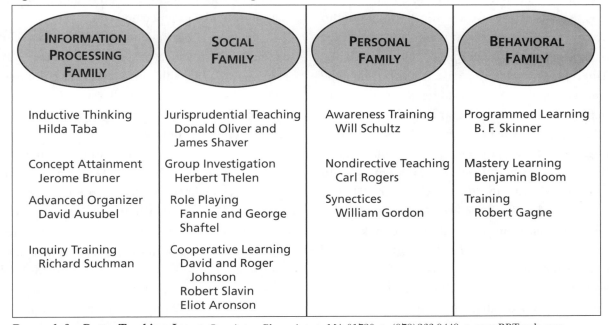

| INFORMATION PROCESSING FAMILY | SOCIAL FAMILY | PERSONAL FAMILY | BEHAVIORAL FAMILY |
|---|---|---|---|
| Inductive Thinking<br>Hilda Taba | Jurisprudential Teaching<br>Donald Oliver and James Shaver | Awareness Training<br>Will Schultz | Programmed Learning<br>B. F. Skinner |
| Concept Attainment<br>Jerome Bruner | Group Investigation<br>Herbert Thelen | Nondirective Teaching<br>Carl Rogers | Mastery Learning<br>Benjamin Bloom |
| Advanced Organizer<br>David Ausubel | Role Playing<br>Fannie and George Shaftel | Synectics<br>William Gordon | Training<br>Robert Gagne |
| Inquiry Training<br>Richard Suchman | Cooperative Learning<br>David and Roger Johnson<br>Robert Slavin<br>Eliot Aronson | | |

**Research for Better Teaching, Inc.** • One Acton Place, Acton, MA 01720 • (978)263-9449 • www.RBTeach.com

## An Example: The Inductive Thinking Model

The inductive thinking model has nine logical steps:

1. Enumerating or gathering data
2. Grouping
3. Labeling
4. Discriminating
5. Comparing
6. Inferring
7. Hypothesizing
8. Evidencing
9. Generalizing

This model, introduced by Hilda Taba, prizes developing students' ability to make inferences from data. Like all other models, it has a series of phases that unfold over time like acts in a play. Each phase looks and sounds different from the previous one, but like scenes in a play each is carefully articulated with the previous and the succeeding phases to achieve a cumulative effect.

A teacher who wished to use the model to present a lesson on Ernest Hemingway might start by showing a video biography of Hemingway's life. This is phase 1: gathering data. After the video, the teacher would ask students to relate items of information they remembered and would record the information on the board or on charts. The items might appear disconnected and random: "Had a fishing boat named the *Pilar*." "He went to Spain three times during the Spanish Civil War." "He had a house in Key West." "He liked to write early in the morning while sitting on a balcony overlooking the streets of Paris." Perhaps the class might collect two dozen such items that students would remember and contribute to the list. Phase 1 of the model always collects a database of some sort.

In phase 2, students would group the items from the database that belong together. They would look at the sentences on the board and put certain items together because they bear some relationship with one another.

In phase 3, students would give a title or a label to the groupings they were creating—for example, "Hemingway's work habits as a writer" or "Hemingway the outdoorsman" in which information about hunting on the Serengeti and fishing in Michigan would appear. Students around the class might group items in similar clusters, but there would also be some differences in the categories students created.

In phase 4, the students' groupings of the items about Hemingway would be displayed in some fashion for all to see (charts, overheads). In this phase, discriminating, students explain the thinking behind their categories. "What really made this grouping hang together?" The categories and the thinking behind them are compared and contrasted as the teacher guides the students through a discussion of the different ways the information could be grouped and why.

In phase 5, the students make inferences—for example, are any ideas occurring to them about Hemingway as a result of what they have done so far? Are there any inferences they would be willing to make about Ernest Hemingway as a man? In a recent demonstration lesson we did with adults, one person said at this point, "I think Hemingway was really a very lonely man." At no point in the video does Hemingway's biographer ever make that point explicitly, so no single item of information in it would ever lead a viewer to that conclusion. Yet as a result of having been through these phases and manipulating the data intellectually in the way those phases require, inferences such as this and others become available to students.

There are several other phases to this model, but we will not develop them in any detail. Our objective is only to show that the steps or phases in a model of teaching unfold in a planful way so as to lead students toward developing a particular way of thinking. We could summarize the first five phases of Taba's model by listing the key question of each phase:

*Phase 1:* What are the data?

*Phase 2:* How would you group the data?

*Phase 3:* What name would you give to your categories or groups?

*Phase 4:* What makes your groups hold together?

*Phase 5:* What inferences would you be willing to make about the topic?

# Eight Models of Teaching

The notion of models of teaching was introduced by Bruce R. Joyce in 1968 through *Teacher Innovator: A Program to Prepare Teachers,* funded by the U.S. Department of Health, Education and Welfare. In 1972, Joyce and Marsha Weil published *Models of Teaching,* which described a large number of models in detail. These descriptions have been updated in five subsequent editions (1980, 1986, 1992, 1996, 2000, 2003), which have added models and elaborated prior descriptions until we now have over two dozen models of teaching well described with anecdotes, examples, and outlines of steps. These books have been an important contribution to the literature on teaching because they made operational the theoretical approaches to learning developed by such luminaries as Jerome Bruner, David Ausubel, B. F. Skinner, William Glasser, Richard Suchman, Jean Piaget, and others.

To analyze each model of teaching, Joyce and Weil asked and answered the following questions for each theorist:

- What is the orientation to knowing and learning to know in this model? Does the teaching appear to be aimed at specific kinds of thinking and means for achieving it?
- What sequence of events occurs during the process of instruction? What do teachers and students do first, second, third?
- How does the teacher regard the student and respond to what he or she does?
- What teacher and student roles, relationships, and norms are encouraged?
- What additional provisions and materials (materials and support systems) are needed to make the model work?
- What is the purpose of the teaching? What are the likely instructional and nurturant effects of this approach to teaching?

The descriptions of these models display the range of teaching alternatives and allow comparison of their unique features. The language of models enables us to visualize clear patterns of action in teaching and learning. Thus, we can talk more precisely about what we might do if we taught a lesson through a different model; also we can talk more precisely about why we might do so and what the expected effects of using a particular model might be.

This chapter provides an introduction to eight models of teaching. Each is described in only the briefest details; in-depth study is required for gaining skill in them. We illustrate the range of models that have been developed and the wonderful menu for learning that lies before us. Most teachers already use one or two of these models, but few of us have been exposed to the full range, much less trained in the subtleties of implementing them and matching them to different students and curricula.

Our intention is to give a flavor for the different qualities of mind that models of teaching develop in students. Readers can focus further reading and learning on models that best meet their current priorities. And at the end of the chapter, we provide a bibliography of original sources on the models for readers interested in doing so to go beyond the chapter on a given model provided by Joyce and Weil. To make the models more vivid, we use a specific content in our survey: beginning geometry.

## Advanced Organizer Model

Advanced organizers are concepts derived from well-defined bodies of knowledge: mathematics, grammar, sociology, and so forth. The set of geometry concepts in Figure 11.2 illustrates a well-defined, integrated, and progressively differentiated set of organizing concepts.

**Figure 11.2. Progressive Differentiation in Geometry Concepts**

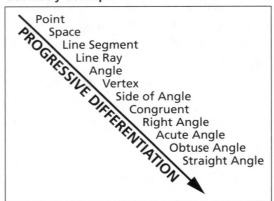

In the advanced organizer model, these concepts are introduced by the teacher progressively, one by one, through lectures, films, demonstrations, or readings. The student then applies the organizer and demonstrates mastery of the geometry concept. For example, the teacher might define an acute angle as any angle that is less than a right angle (less than 90 degrees) and then might clarify specifics through examples. In phase 2, the student might be asked to make a drawing that represents an acute angle and to label it ABC. From exercises such as this one, the teacher can determine student mastery, step by step, and integrate new ideas with previously learned content, which Bruner calls "integrative reconciliation" (Bruner, 1987). Then the teacher moves on to subsequent organizers.

A teacher using this model primarily seeks to advance the conceptual organizers of a body of knowledge and promote a meaningful assimilation of information. "Meaningful" means within the context of a hierarchical arrangement of knowledge. Students are expected to learn these organizers because they are basic and fundamental to academic knowledge. Some consider these conceptual organizers the bread and butter of school learning.

## Concept Attainment

Closely related to the advanced organizer model is concept attainment: learning by logic, analysis, comparison, and contrast. Instead of advancing the concept, the teacher presents the concept in the form of positive exemplars, and the students search for attributes to identify the concept (Figure 11.3). The teacher also uses nonexemplars that do not contain attributes of the concept to assist students in determining relevant attributes.

The student is expected to arrive at the concept inductively—to learn by identifying the salient features and formulating an abstract statement. The concept illustrated in Figure 11.3 is: "any angle that is greater than a right angle and less than a straight angle." The mathematical label is less important than the student's awareness of these defining attributes. Later the students can learn the name for this concept: obtuse angle. In the model of teaching, students learn the attributes of the concept first by deriving them.

The value of using the concept attainment model is that students learn not only the concepts themselves but the awareness of how concepts are formed from attributes. They acquire sensitivity to logical reasoning and a deepening regard for alternative points of view. These instructional and nurturant effects are learned through practice with concept attainment; the student in effect reconstructs knowledge through guided learning.

## Inductive Thinking Model

The inductive thinking model enables students to generate knowledge as if they themselves were scholars responsible for producing insights into factual reality.

Consider the array of data in Figure 11.4. Then ask a series of questions to lead students through a systematic sorting of the basic angles:

- What do you see?
- Which ones belong together? Why?
- What would you call them? Why?
- What do you notice about one of the groups?
- What similarities and differences do you see?
- What do these tell you about geometry?
- What do you think would happen if . . . ?
- What evidence would you use to support your guess?
- What can we say is generally true?

The likely concepts from such a logical process might more or less approximate formal knowledge of geometry, but there is no guarantee, nor does it matter to the teacher that a student doesn't know the concepts in advance. In this model, the teacher values student thinking: attention to logic, sensitivity to language, awareness of building knowledge, and concept formation. The

**Figure 11.3. Exemplars of Concept Attainment**

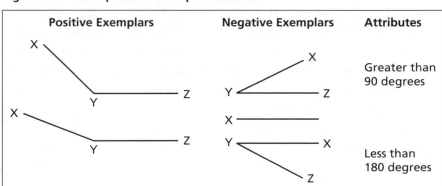

**Figure 11.4. Using the Inductive Thinking Model to Generate Knowledge**

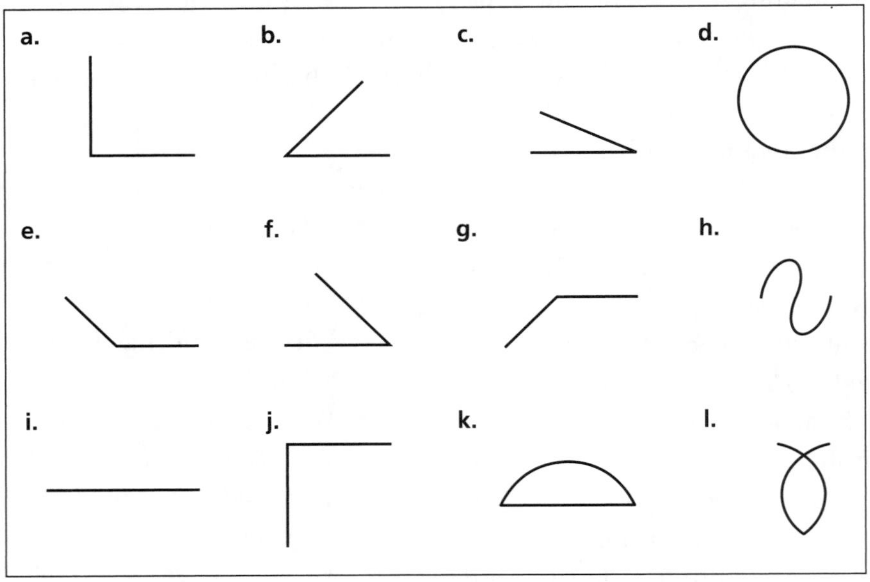

students work cooperatively toward building ideas about the shapes.

## Inquiry Training

In inquiry training, the student is expected to put his or her knowledge to work to solve a problem. In the process, there is more knowledge to be gained in both substance (mathematical knowledge) and process (inquiry training).

Let us say that the problem is to make two squares and four equal triangles out of a rectangle measuring 5 inches by 1 inch. To solve the problem, the student needs to construct a solution consisting of geometry concepts—a process of verifying relevant facts about objects, properties, conditions, and events—and simultaneously hypothesize possible configurations of space, shape, and size. For example, the student might think through the solution shown in Figure 11.5.

After being presented with the problem, students are encouraged to inquire together as a group while the teacher answers yes-no questions; seeks clarification; encourages student verifying, hypothesizing, and explaining behavior; and guides the group dynamics.

This model introduces a more tentative knowledge in which organized knowledge from the disciplines is synthesized and employed in the formulation of a solution. Mastery of knowledge is not the goal of instruction; rather, the student is expected to test out his or her own knowledge. In addition, students learn strategies for inquiry by witnessing their own inquiry behavior and learning to ask questions about objects, events, properties, and conditions. This happens when teachers and students go over their problem-solving behavior following the total class exercise. There is an interdependence in inquiry learning too. Students learn to listen well and use the insights of others for

**Figure 11.5.  Inquiry Training Solutions**

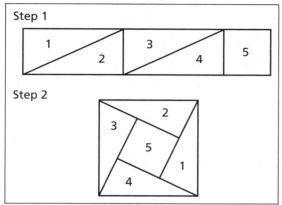

solving a problem. It also provides learners with experiences that prepare them for the uses of knowledge in actual situations.

## Awareness Training Model

The preceding models were developed from information-processing theory and represent traditional approaches to teaching. However, knowledge of geometric space and points in space can be a personal experience as well. Awareness training seeks to bridge the individual's own experiences with experiences of other people—in this case, those of a mathematician. Imagine students with a

rope who are able to experience geometric configurations equivalent to line segments and triangles (see Figure 11.6).

After experiencing geometry in this way, students would be encouraged to discuss their feelings and thoughts—that is, to give form to them in language within the social context of the classroom.

These experiences may appear elementary, but they are in fact extremely rich in personal relevance and serve to integrate knowledge and self. The teacher values the students' world and the students' ability to express themselves. In this model, personal awareness is held as a first type of knowing that can undergird subsequent learning. It takes advantage of the insight that we all like to be around people who can express their personal realities as well as those more commonly held by communities of scholars.

## Synectics Model

The synectics model has been derived from a set of assumptions about creativity and analogies. Creativity means seeing connections between the familiar and the strange and exploring new solutions to old problems. It means creating and attending to psychological states such as detachment, involvement,

**Figure 11.6.  Awareness Training Model**

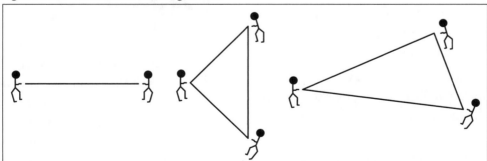

autonomy, speculation, and deferment. We attain these psychological states through analogies, which lead to the attainment and mastery of new and difficult material and novel vantage points for reconsidering problems. Both the means and ends of teaching are influenced by these assumptions.

In "Making the Strange Familiar," a title Gordon (1970) gives to certain phases of synectics, the teacher introduces the new material or content through lecture, video, or demonstration. Without comment, the teacher then solicits a possible analogy and asks students to describe it. To personify the analogy, the students act it out. Describing and acting out the analogy provide the particulars for the fourth and fifth steps—listing the similarities and differences between the analogy and the new material. Finally, the students return to the original material to examine and review it and to discuss details that might have been omitted from previous activity during the analogical thinking. Consider the following example:

Step 1: The teacher presents material on geometry.

Step 2: The students select an analogy—in this case, a tree.

Step 3: The students describe the tree in detail.

Step 4: The students act out being parts of a tree.

Step 5: The students point out similarities between the tree and geometry—for example, the "angle of the branches to the tree trunk" or "the points from where the branch begins to end."

Step 6: The students point out differences—for example, that the crooked branches are not straight lines.

Step 7: Teacher and students consider what aspects of geometry were not covered in the discussion of similarities and differences.

The synectics process induces creative thinking and mastery learning of content. It is both a personal experience that integrates geometry and personal knowledge and an analogical one that capitalizes on students' ability to make connections. In addition, it is a wonderful group experience. Those who diversify their efforts to learn through the synectics model achieve several goals: mastery of subject matter, analogical thinking, personal integration, fun, and group productivity.

## Nondirective Teaching

Learning is a personal experience. In this model, the individual experiences planning, responsibility, and a teacher who values the student's perspective. Acquiring responsibility for one's own learning and the skill to plan and develop those plans is no small matter. A teacher who wants students to become independent learners can use nondirective teaching to establish the interpersonal relationships that can facilitate personal productivity. The following conversation shows how this works:

MR. ROGERS: John, we're going to study geometry for the next three weeks, and I'm hoping each person will plan a personal project.

JOHN: What do you mean, Mr. Rogers?

MR. ROGERS: Well, what would you like to learn about geometry?

JOHN: I'll be honest: I never thought about geometry. To me it's just another school subject.

MR. ROGERS: I understand. We plan so much of your activity in school that it just doesn't seem right to have to think about it for yourself. However, it is important to me that you have this opportunity to set your own goals, to develop the project, and to share with me in assessing your progress.

JOHN:  I wouldn't know where to begin.

MR. ROGERS:  I'd like to help you. As a teacher I've learned a great many planning skills. I guess that's what makes this project so important to me.

JOHN:  What do you mean?

MR. ROGERS:  Well, I want you to learn to organize your own learning, to feel a sense of responsibility for where you're going and how you get there—more important, that you feel progress. I know you can do it, and I want to help you.

This type of experience for the student is not casual or mindless teaching. In its own way, it is a rigorous experience for both the teacher and the student. The teacher who normally plans and organizes instruction uses that knowledge and skill to facilitate the student's own efforts. It is necessary to share the student's anxiety and anger yet remain firm in efforts to support him or her. The student lacks the know-how to move along, but with courage, experience, and a sense of making progress, structuring learning becomes easier and more productive.

There are some persuasive reasons for using the nondirective teaching model. Students learn to take charge of their own school lives, not in the sense of excluding teachers and other students but in the sense that some part of what goes on is from the individual: it belongs to the student. Personal development is a goal. Students also become aware of their feelings and thoughts about themselves and others, and they are required to deal with them. Finally, students learn to plan and organize, carry out, and evaluate their own learning.

## Group Investigation

When a teacher thinks about teaching geometry, he or she is not often likely to consider social-oriented models of teaching because the traditions of mathematics education have been centered on the individual and mathematics content. Nevertheless, there are many opportunities for group activities that promote affiliation and interpersonal skills and also provide opportunities for collective inquiry and other problem-solving experiences. In this model, the individual gains mutual support during the time spent learning problem-solving behaviors. These are relevant to students not only during schooling but after graduation, when the application of mathematics is done in the workplace as members of teams.

Group investigation, a problem-solving model for groups of students, consists of the following events:

1.  Students experience a puzzling situation.
2.  Students discuss their reactions.
3.  Students identify the problem.
4.  Students make a plan and discuss roles.
5.  Students carry out the plan.
6.  Students reflect on their experiences.

In these events, the teacher guides the group dynamics and acts as a resource person. The social climate is cooperative.

An example of the application of group investigation to teaching geometry is how to measure heights. Such objects as flag poles, buildings, and trees are difficult to measure with devices, and getting students to plan and carry out original strategies for problem solving has both the effect of practical problem solving plus enhancing the more mathematical solution to the problem. The students need to explore aspects of the problem in practical ways, and their efforts to resolve these practical problems provide varied experiences, which help them appreciate a more generalizable solution.

In order to teach geometry through the group investigation model, a teacher has to appreciate both the instructional and nurturant effects of instruction. The experience involves respect for different people's points of view and knowledge construction, learner independence from the teacher, effective group process, a commitment to group inquiry and social dynamics, and disciplined inquiry. Group investigation synthesizes these value orientations. From an observer's vantage point, we need a polyfocal perspective to appreciate the richness of this model of teaching.

## Patterns of Instruction

Besides the models of teaching, there are three other common patterns of instruction in classrooms today: lecturing, recitation, and direct instruction, which probably between them account for the majority of what goes on in classrooms.

### Lecture

A good lecture is systematic and sequential and conveys information in an orderly and interesting way. Effective lecturers draw skills from the Attention, Clarity, and Learning Experiences areas of performance, as well as from the Objectives and Curriculum Design area of performance. The pattern of teacher behavior in lecturing, however, draws nothing from any internal theory of good lecturing or cohesive theory of learning. A lecture is a composite, with no secondary goal about learning how to learn. (When the lecture is a step in the advance organizer model, then the story is different.) Nevertheless, a good lecture is a worthwhile educational experience and certainly has a place in schooling.

A lecture is poor when the performance on one or more of the five areas of performance listed earlier is poor, not because of poor performance of a model called lecturing. A poor lecture may qualify as no teaching at all. Even an interesting speaker who holds students' attention or keeps them amused with clever anecdotes may be doing no teaching if the content is not organized around the course objectives and is not designed with the principles of organization in mind. Students can look forward to class and be well entertained but leave without having learned a thing.

### Recitation

A recitation is an oral test. The teacher asks questions, students respond, and the teacher makes value judgments on the responses. Its goal is to cover the material, go over it, ask questions, and see who knows what. By the time it's over, all the important material should be out (or have been said by someone and heard by all). Reviews for tests are often recitations. A recitation doesn't have a series of steps, but we could construct a list of events and qualities that might determine a good recitation:

- Covered all the material
- Highlighted important items
- Identified student confusions
- Got maximum student participation
- Took opportunities to stimulate higher-level thinking

For the rest, if we wanted to judge the quality of a recitation lesson, we'd have to go back to the management areas of performance of Attention, Momentum, and Clarity. Recitations have a place in school, but not as large a one as they seem to occupy. When a recitation is over, students and teachers are aware of who knows what, who has read the assignment, and who gets A's. As an educational experience used for more than an occasional review, it has no guiding principles or point of view behind it and little chance that the students will get better at learning in some particular way.

## Direct Instruction

Direct instruction is usually used for skill work and does have a series of phases, which Joyce calls a syntax:

1. The teacher states the aims of the lesson.
2. The teacher presents concepts or an operation.
3. The teacher gives examples or demonstrates.
4. The teacher asks questions to check student understanding.
5. Students practice with direct monitoring, feedback, help, and hints from the teacher, usually in the group.
6. Students practice alone (seatwork or homework).
7. The teacher corrects and decides whether to reteach, regroup, or move on.
8. The teacher gives frequent assessments.

Direct instruction lacks model status because it has no theoretical basis. It has no teacher-student response pattern or deliberate environmental conditions tailored to optimize a specified learning behavior among students. But we know that good direct instruction in groups with high time on task produces mastery of skills. Direct instruction reflects the current trends toward training, task analysis, and biofeedback. These preferences for instruction, which have evolved from the business community, reflect values of efficiency and effectiveness.

## Models Versus Patterns of Instruction

Lecturing, recitation, and direct instruction are prominent patterns of classroom instruction, and most teachers view them as models of teaching. But in theory and practice, they are not models at all. Models of teaching have elaborate theoretical statements and descriptions of patterns of behavior that teachers can be trained to perform. There are discrete teacher-student interactions that characterize one model and distinguish it from another. Models are similar to theatrical plays, though not so closely scripted; if teachers know the model, they can visualize the classroom activity before it occurs and use that image to monitor and regulate the flow of activity. The content and goals of models are equally distinctive. In one model, the content is derived from an academic discipline, such as mathematics; in another it may draw from recent student experiences for the content. A model will be chosen not only to convey content but to stretch the way students think and learn about learning.

Models of teaching allow teachers to ask of good teaching, "Good for what?" and to answer out of the things a particular model is designed to be good for (for example, logical thinking, inductive reasoning, personal self-organization, cooperation, and group skill).

## Update on the Models of Teaching

Some readers will notice the reference dates for these models of teaching range from the 1950s to the early 1970s. This indeed was a time of innovation in teaching, and many of the models of teaching were researched by scholars and elaborated by educators interested in classroom instruction. Some educators embedded specific models of teaching in curriculum materials made available during that period. It was a productive time in American education, a time during which instructional innovations flourished under the leadership of government-sponsored research and university scholarship.

What has happened between then and now? In many ways the models of teaching are fully developed approaches to helping students develop their thinking skills, and there are teaching guides with planning materials available to aid teachers and curriculum developers. Joyce, Calhoun, and Hopkins's *Models of Learning* (2002) recasts or refocuses these same strategies as models of learning. The authors describe their intent to teach thinking skills through curriculum implementation: "As we study the four families of Models of Teaching, we try to build a mental picture of what each model is designed to accomplish. As we consider when and how to use various combinations of models and, therefore, which learning strategies will get priority for particular units and lessons and groups of students, we take into account the types and pace of learning that are likely to be promoted" (p. 36). When teachers apply the models of learning to classroom lesson planning and planning units of study, the models often become fragmented. For example, the inductive thinking model has nine logical steps, but in a lesson a teacher might find only two or three of them. This is important. The original models of teaching or learning are complete packages, but in classrooms today, only part of the full model may be in use.

Consider a U.S. history teacher who asks her students to enumerate the possible causes of colonists' discontent prior to the Revolutionary War. Though she might be implementing the inductive model of teaching, which has nine steps, she might be able to implement only enumerating the causes and getting her students to explain them. In a specific lesson, it may not be not possible to implement all the steps in the model, but the fragment nevertheless can contribute to the larger process of inductive thinking and learning.

Bruce Joyce has always made the extra effort to test the validity of the models of teaching. We might think of him as an action researcher who uses the statistical effect size to measure the productivity of the models. Effect size is a comparison of mean scores. For example, a teacher could teach the same content using two different strategies or models of teaching and compare means scores to determine which approach was more effective. Over the years, Joyce has been able to show that different models of teaching are effective for teaching different student thinking skills.

Few educational researchers understand teaching and learning better than Joyce and his colleagues do. In the third edition of *Models of Teaching*, they write about the different models, the effects on learners of the different approaches to teaching, and the need to adapt teaching to different learners' styles. In describing the effects of models of teaching, they discuss selecting them on the basis of appropriateness and fit to the learner preferences for structure and varying degrees of task complexity. They write, "The models described in this book represent the capability to boost learning in nearly every domain and are characterized by a large range of degrees of structure and task complexity. Among them, they can reach nearly every learner. Careful selection should increase the probability of reaching nearly every learner in such a way as to boost the desired kinds of learning" (Joyce and Weil, 1986, pp. 418–419). The models of teaching offer students and teachers a range of effective approaches to both teaching and learning that provide a sophisticated palette for those interested in differentiated instruction.

What makes these models attractive to teachers is that teachers can help students build a repertoire of thinking skills: inductive reasoning, deductive reasoning, analogical thinking, inquiry training, concept building, and others. Joyce and colleagues write, "Debates about educational method have seemed to imply that schools and teachers should choose one approach over another. However, it is far more likely that for optimum opportunity to learn, students need a range of instructional approaches drawn from the information processing, social, personal and behavioral families" (2002, p. 70). Teachers can get excited about students having control over a repertoire of thinking skills as they work their way through elementary and secondary schools.

Joyce, Calhoun, and Hopkins (2002) help teachers refocus on learning. They ask teachers not just to think about their own teaching skills and strategies, but also to consider the kinds of learning taking place with these different approaches.

A second line of inquiry that Joyce and associates pursued became a significant influence on the school culture literature of the era. This was the evolution of peer coaching, the collegial school, and their work on professional development. From the very beginning, Joyce and associates used peer coaching to learn specific models of teaching. Learning the teaching models required an understanding of theory and practice, strategies and specific teaching skills, and savvy attention to adult learning. Teachers worked together to study the theory of the teaching models, identified the mini skills that make the models work in the classroom, practiced the models by simulating them in small groups (pairings and triads), and discussed the place of models in the classroom. Joyce and his associates worked with thousands of teachers over a twenty-five year period and evolved a peer coaching model that went from informal gatherings to a formal process called peer coaching.

Their model of peer coaching consisted of theory, demonstration, practice, practice with feedback, and application by teaching in the classroom with their students. Within a high school department, a staff of fifteen teachers might go through this sequence under the guidance of an expert consultant. The expert demonstrates the teaching model, organizes the peer coaching teams, and guides the practice and practice with feedback sessions. Ideally, the teachers circle through the peer teaching and peer coaching sessions enough times that they can return to their classrooms to practice with their students. Peer coaching is teachers learning with one another, adult with adult. Joyce found teachers learning together could be very powerful. (See "How to Learn a Teaching Repertoire," Joyce and Weil, 1986.)

Joyce and his associates began work on peer coaching in the early 1970s as an effort to help teachers learn different models of teaching and implement them in their classrooms. In the 1980s, their research on peer coaching focused more on small groups of teachers and on student learning and how teachers can create better learning environments. Joyce and Showers (1986) wrote, "There is no evidence that simply organizing peer coaching or peer study teams will affect students' learning environments. The study of teaching and curriculum must be the focus" (p. 12). Peer coach-ing involves teachers in sharing, planning, and talking about their experiences together. Coaching helps teachers implement new teaching strategies in their classrooms by helping them adapt strategies to their school curricula and find better ways to accommodate differences among students.

It wasn't long before the importance of a collegial school environment surfaced as a key condition for in-service professional development. Improving schooling requires promoting the evolution of the school organization and the relationships between the adults to find a model of schooling that fits the twenty-first century. Current trends include greater accountability, shared power and governance, and higher expectations for student achievement. All of this activity to rejuvenate the schools requires cooperation among teachers, school leaders, and public officials. Teachers must ask themselves: Am I prepared to work with formal knowledge of teaching and learning? Am I prepared to work with others to develop a collegial school and to create a professional environment for lifelong learning? Am I prepared to work toward more democratic schools for the twenty-first century?

Like a good case study, models of teaching have evolved from an innovation in teaching and learning to a full-blown theory of schooling and professional development. The current conventional wisdom about the importance of collaboration, professional learning communities, and deprivatizing teaching owes a debt that should not be forgotten to the forty-year history of those who developed models of teaching and peer coaching. In summarizing the task of professional development, Glickman, Gordon, and Ross-Gordon (2007) write, "For professional development to be meaningful to teachers and to lead to teacher renewal and instructional improvement, it must operate on two levels. First, teachers as individuals should have a variety of learning opportunities to support their pursuit of their own personal and professional careers. Second, teachers as part of a school and district organization should together define, learn, and implement skills, knowledge and programs that achieve common goals of the organization."

So as we go forward now, the models of teaching are there for our use in improving student thinking skills. Peer coaching is there to facilitate the process by which teachers learn new models and transfer that learning to their classroom teaching. We are still educating children by teaching them to read and write, but the school has a much larger purpose. Everyone in the school building has to grow stronger and better, and for that we need a different culture, a more collegial environment, and a school more accountable to itself and the public. The development of models of teaching play a significant role in the history of these growing perceptions.

We end with a summary of the major models of teaching and their theoretical underpinnings:

### Social Models

#### Group Investigation Model

Major theorists: Herbert Thelen, John Dewey
Mission: Development of skills for participation in democratic social processes through combined emphasis on interpersonal and social (group) skills and academic inquiry. Aspects of personal development are important outgrowths of this model.
Dewey, J. *Democracy and Education.* New York: Macmillan, 1916.
Thelen, H. *Dynamics of Groups at Work.* Chicago: University of Chicago Press, 1954.
Thelen, H. *Education and the Human Quest.* New York: HarperCollins, 1960.

#### Jurisprudential Model

Major theorists: Donald Oliver, James P. Shaver
Mission: Designed primarily to teach the jurisprudential frame of reference as a way of processing information, but also a way of thinking about and resolving social issues.
Oliver, D., and Shaver, J. P. *Teaching Public Issues in High School.* Boston: Houghton Mifflin, 1966.

#### Social Inquiry Model

Major theorists: Benjamin Cox, Byron Massialas
Mission: Social problem solving, primarily through academic inquiry and logical reasoning.

Massialas, B., and Cox, B. *Inquiry in Social Studies.* New York: McGraw-Hill, 1966.

## Laboratory Method Model (T-Group)

Major theorist: National Training Laboratory, Bethel, Maine; Leland P. Bradford
Mission: Development of interpersonal group skills and, through this, personal awareness and flexibility.

Bany, M., and Johnson, L. V. *Classroom Group Behavior: Group Dynamics in Education.* New York: Macmillan, 1964.
Bennis, W. G., Benne, K. D., and Chin, R. (eds.). *The Planning of Change: Readings in the Applied Behavioral Sciences.* New York: Holt, 1964.
Bradford, L. P. (ed.). *Human Forces in Teaching and Learning.* Washington, D.C.: National Training Laboratory, National Association, 1961.
Bradford, L. P., Gibb, J. R., and Benne, K. D. *T-Group Theory and Laboratory Method.* Hoboken, N.J.: Wiley, 1964.
*Human Relations Laboratory Training Student Notebook.* Washington, D.C.: U.S. Office of Education, 1961.

## Information Processing Models

### Concept Attainment Model

Major theorist: Jerome Bruner
Mission: Designed primarily to develop inductive reasoning.

Bruner, J., Goodnow, J. J., and Austin, G. A. *A Study of Thinking.* New York: Science Editions, 1957.

### Inductive Model

Major theorist: Hilda Taba
Mission: Designed primarily for the development of inductive mental processes and academic reasoning or theory building, but these capacities are useful for personal and social goals as well. The model was developed from a specific kind of thinking that underlies scientific inquiry.

Taba, H. *Teacher's Handbook for Elementary Social Studies.* Reading, Mass.: Addison-Wesley, 1967.
Taba, H. *Teaching Strategies and Cognitive Functioning in Elementary School Children.* San Francisco: San Francisco State College, 1971.

### Inquiry Training Model

Major theorist: Richard Suchman
Mission: Designed primarily for the development of inductive mental processes and academic reasoning or theory building. The generalized model of inquiry was developed from a general analysis of the methods employed by creative research personnel.

Suchman, J. R. *The Elementary School Training Program in Scientific Inquiry.* Urbana: University of Illinois, 1962.
Suchman, J. R. "A Model for the Analysis of Inquiry." In H. J. Klausmeier and C. W. Harris (eds.), *Analysis of Concept Learning.* Orlando, Fla.: Academic Press, 1966.
Suchman, J. R. *Inquiry Development Program: Developing Inquiry.* Chicago: Science Research Associates, 1966.
Suchman, J. R. *Inquiry Box: Teacher's Handbook.* Chicago: Science Research Associates, 1967.

### Biological Science Inquiry Model

Major theorists: Joseph J. Schwab, Jerome Bruner (curriculum reform movement)
Mission: Designed to teach the research system of the discipline but also expected to have effects in other domains; for example, sociological methods may be taught in order to increase social understanding and social problem solving.

Schwab, J. J. *Biological Sciences Curriculum Study, Supervisor. Biology Teachers' Handbook.* Hoboken, N.J.: Wiley, 1965.

### Advanced Organizer Model

Major theorist: David Ausubel
Mission: Designed to increase the efficiency of information-processing capacities to absorb and relate bodies of knowledge.

Ausubel, D. P. *The Psychology of Meaningful Verbal Learning.* New York: Grune and Stratton, 1963.
Ausubel, D. P. *Learning Theory and Classroom Practice.* Toronto: Ontario Institute for Studies in Education, 1967.
Bruner, J. *Actual Minds, Possible Worlds.* Cambridge, Mass.: Harvard University Press, 1987.

### Developmental Model

Major theorists: Jean Piaget, Irving Sigel, Edmund Sullivan
Mission: Designed to increase general intellectual development, especially logical reasoning, but can be applied to social and moral development as well.

Furth, H. G. *Piaget and Knowledge.* Upper Saddle River, N.J.: Prentice Hall, 1969.
Kohlberg, L. "Moral Education in the School." *School Review,* 1966, *74,* 1–30.
Piaget, J. *The Origins of Intelligence in Children.* New York: International University Press, 1952.
Sigel, I. E. "The Piagetian System and the World of Education." In D. Elkind and J. Flavell (eds.), *Studies in Cognitive Development.* New York: Oxford University Press, 1969.

### Personal Models

#### Nondirective Teaching Model

Major theorist: Carl Rogers

Mission: Emphasis on building capacity for self-instruction and through this, personal development in terms of self-understanding, self-discovery, and self-concept.

Rogers, C. R. *Client Centered Therapy.* Boston: Houghton Mifflin, 1951.

Rogers, C. R. *Freedom to Learn.* Columbus, Ohio: Charles E. Merrill, 1969.

#### Classroom Meeting Model

Major theorist: William Glasser

Mission: Development of self-understanding and self-responsibility. This has latent benefits to other kinds of functioning (for example, social).

Glasser, W. *Reality Therapy.* New York: HarperCollins, 1965.

Glasser, W. *Schools Without Failure.* New York: HarperCollins, 1969.

#### Synectics Model

Major theorist: William Gordon

Mission: Personal development of creativity and creative problem solving.

Gordon, W. J. *Synectics.* New York: HarperCollins, 1961.

Gordon, W. J. *The Metaphorical Way of Learning and Knowing.* Cambridge, Mass.: Synectics Educational Press, 1970.

#### Awareness Training Model

Major theorists: William Schutz, Fritz Perls

Mission: Increasing personal capacity for self-exploration and self-awareness. Much emphasis is placed on the development of interpersonal awareness and understanding.

Brown, G. *Human Teaching for Human Learning.* New York: Viking Press, 1971.

Schutz, W. J. *FIRO: A Three Dimensional Theory of Interpersonal Behavior.* New York: Holt, 1958.

Schutz, W. J. *Expanding Human Awareness.* New York: Grove Press, 1967.

### Behavior Modification Models

#### Operant Conditioning

Major theorist: B. F. Skinner

Mission: General applicability. A domain-free approach, though probably it is applicable to the information processing function.

Schramm, W. *Programmed Instruction: Today and Tomorrow.* New York: Fund for the Advancement of Education, 1962.

Skinner, B. F. *The Science of Human Behavior.* New York: Macmillan, 1956.

Skinner, B. F. *Verbal Behavior.* New York: Appleton-Century-Crofts, 1957.

Taber, J., Glaser, R., and Halmuth, H. S. *Learning and Programmed Instruction.* Reading, Mass.: Addison-Wesley, 1965.

To check your knowledge about Models of Teaching see the quiz on our Web site at **www.RBTeach.com/rbteach/quiz/MTeaching.html.**

### Sources for Models of Teaching

Glickman, C., Gordon, S. P., and Ross-Gordon, J. M. *Supervision and Educational Leadership: A Development Approach.* Needham Heights, Mass.: Allyn & Bacon, 2007.

Joyce, B., Calhoun, E., and Hopkins, D. *Models of Learning: Tools for Teaching.* Philadelphia: Open University Press, 2002.

Joyce, B., and Showers, B. *The Evolution of Peer Coaching: Educational Leadership,* 1986, *53*(6), 12–16.

Joyce, B., and Weil, M. *Models of Teaching.* (3rd ed.). Upper Saddle River, N.J.: Prentice Hall, 1986.

Joyce, B., Weil, M., and Calhoun, E. *Models of Teaching.* (7th ed.). Upper Saddle River, N.J.; Prentice Hall, 2003.

# INTRODUCTION TO MOTIVATION

**E**motions are everywhere. There is never an instant of waking life when they are not present and influencing the energy level we bring to tasks, the level of focus, the amount of investment. The chapters in Part Three address the things teachers do that influence the emotional state of students, either positively or negatively, and thus their capacity to invest in academic learning.

Students' attention and investment in academic tasks is affected by their relationship with their teachers (Personal Relationship Building); it is influenced by their interpersonal relationships with peers, the feelings of support and community on the one hand, or on the other hand feelings of fear and defensiveness against ridicule (Classroom Climate). And finally it is influenced by their own confidence that they can grow their ability to perform academic tasks versus self-doubt or belief in innate low ability (Expectations). For those who have wondered where the domain of feeling and the whole child enters into the picture of skillful teaching, this section is for you. Another way to cast these three chapters is that they circumscribe our influence on student motivation. Why are students motivated to work hard and learn? This question is important because motivation is the linchpin of student learning. Therefore, nurturing motivation where it doesn't seem to exist becomes part of our responsibility as teachers. For many children of poverty, part of our job is to plant motivation and grow it where it had not been before. We need to study that expertise and grow and develop our capacity to influence student motivation.

Do you accept that nurturing motivation is part of the classroom job? Consider this: the level of motivation any of us has is powerfully conditioned by people we consider significant in our lives, people who have power in their relationships with us and people we admire, respect, like, or love. The adults who are the most influential figures in children's lives outside their families are their teachers. They spend more time with children, in many cases, than *any* other adult in their lives, including their parents. Therefore, deliberately influencing student motivation is not a job we can dodge: we are significant figures in our students' lives and in the motivation they form to be learners. Because we are so powerfully positioned to influence it, we are throwing away legions of children if we choose not to engage this task.

What motivates students? Any one or a combination of the following factors could be at work:

- Students have an abiding interest because the material itself is relevant or because the teacher has developed activities that are varied, interesting, or a match for students' learning styles. (The Learning Experiences chapter of this book is where both these topics are addressed.)
- The students believe it will matter to them in some way if they do learn; they have a stake in doing well (Vision of a Better Life through Education). This is a very important part of motivation, especially for children of poverty, but it is beyond the scope of this chapter because it raises issues that expand beyond the four walls of the classroom. Whole school programs are created in pursuit of this goal. Schools that do handle the issue successfully, however, make deliberate connections with the community and show their students how school learning applies in the workplace and in life success (See Hightechhigh.org). Three additional factors that influence motivation are the topics of this section.
- Somebody significant in the student's life (a teacher) wants the student to do well. The teacher can be "significant" because the student looks up to her, that is, admires her. Or she can be significant because the student likes her and believes and feels she values and cares about her (see Personal Relationship Building chapter).
- A teacher can also be "significant" because he believes in the students and pushes them to realize the potential they don't see in themselves. The teacher believes the student *can* do well and builds the student's confidence that she is able to (Expectations chapter).
- The classroom culture supports and even encourages the students to do well. The place has a sense of community where students know each other and each member

is an important part. Risk taking is prized and protected. And students experience a sense of control and influence. All of this rubs off on the students' willingness to participate (Classroom Climate chapter).

Influencing students' motivation to learn happens in complicated ways, but in ways that we can see behaviorally and that are quite understandable. Therefore, the three chapters in Part Three take up the specific how-to's of this aspect of teaching by laying out the repertoires for building relationships, communicating belief and building confidence in students, and constructing classroom climates of community, psychological safety, and ownership.

Here's an example of how the three fit together:

Suppose one day I check for understanding and find you don't understand exponents. I then work with you after class to unscramble your confusions; I am using clarity skills, to be sure. But the fact that I take the *time* to do this and it's with *you*, that I pursue you to make the appointment and go out of my way to really help you get it—that's something I wouldn't do if I didn't value you. In fact, the whole episode conveys a Personal Relationship Building message: you are a valued person to me. I care about you.

Now in addition, while I am explaining common denominators to you, I may use phrases that are encouraging ("Yes, yes, keep it up") and I may express confidence in your ability to get it ("You're almost there. I know you're going to get this!"). So within this event is also the positive "I believe in you" expectation message.

When your friends hear you are staying late with me for twenty minutes and won't be going home on the bus with them, they are quite accepting of you putting out that extra effort; they don't make fun of you because you're staying with the teacher. The climate among the students in the class is supportive of one another putting out effort to learn and get help, either from each other or from the teacher.

The range of these behaviors in the exponents vignette above prompts us to ask: how do we conceptualize our role in nurturing motivation and inspiring it where it doesn't exist?

## The Anatomy of "Caring"

The expressions "caring" and "make students feel known and valued" have been prominent in recent literature. "Long after leaving school, [students] remember fondly and in graphic detail, those teachers who cared, and painfully those who did not. They may not recall the content these teachers taught, but their human impact is indelibly imprinted in their minds" (Gay, 2000, p. 49).

Whether one surveys the current literature on what's needed most to improve our schools or on what parents and students say when asked "What matters?" the resounding theme that emerges is *relationships* and the sense that people care. How does caring present itself in the classroom setting? "My teacher is really caring." "How do you know?" "I know he cares about me because . . .

- he won't let me get away with not doing my work. There's no escape!"
- he encourages me and makes me feel smart."
- he goes out of his way to help me when I'm stuck and makes sure I get it."
- he wants to know what I'm interested in and how things are going in my life."

In the Expectations chapter we will deal extensively with the first two student responses above. The Clarity chapter presents the tools for the third response. The final response—that he knows me and is interested in me—is directly connected to Personal Relationship Building.

This theme of students' needing a sense of caring will not go away, and dealing with it is a deep structure part of all our jobs.

*Reference*

Gay, G. *Culturally Responsive Teaching: Theory, Research and Practice.* New York: Teachers College Press, 2000.

# CHAPTER 12

# Expectations

How do I communicate to students that what we're doing is important, that they can do it well, and that I won't give up on them?

Standards and Expectations

Theories About Achievement and Development

Classroom Interventions

History of the Idea of "Intelligence" in the United States

*Nothing influences behavior so strongly as the clear expectations of a significant other.*

JIM STEFFEN, MANAGEMENT CONSULTANT

Classrooms are dynamic and complex societies that are rife with expectations: expectations that teachers have for students and that students have for teachers and for each other. These expectations explain a good deal of what we see in classrooms—the good and the bad, the productive and the wasteful. But the expectations themselves can't be seen; they hang in the air almost like an atmosphere; they exist only between people and they comprise a part of their relationship.

So what is it that teachers do to create an atmosphere in which high expectations are communicated clearly and convincingly to all students, not just some? In this chapter we explore Expectations as an area of performance in teaching by asking and answering a series of related and important questions:

- What are the meaning and significance of standards and expectations, and how does each impact the learning environment we create?
- How do students come to know what is expected of them (that is, what is important)?

We are indebted to Jeff Howard of the Efficacy Institute, Waltham, Massachusetts, for his pioneering work in emphasizing the primacy of effort in determining student achievement. His ideas are prominent in the "Attribution Retraining" section of this chapter.

- How do our beliefs about ability influence our behavior, the messages we send to students about their intellectual capacity, and our effectiveness in communicating high expectations to all students?
- How do students' beliefs influence their motivation to work hard and their confidence that they can achieve at high levels?
- What opportunities can we seize daily to influence student confidence and conviction that they have plenty of ability to learn?
- How can we teach students to exert their effort effectively?

Each of these questions addresses concerns that impact student learning and collectively they represent a huge positive or negative influence on the learning environment.

The opening quotation to this chapter contains two fundamental concepts pertaining to expectations. The first is the word *clear.* Students have to know with certainty what a teacher wants. The second is the phrase *significant other.* Teachers, like parents, are automatically significant others to students, if for no other reason than that they have power over them. If the relationship contains respect and regard (and perhaps affection), the teacher becomes even more significant. How such relationships get built is the subject of another important area of performance, Personal Relationship Building, discussed in Chapter Thirteen. In this chapter, we look at the expectations themselves and the process for communicating them. Finally, the assumption behind the opening quotation is that within limits, what you expect is what you get and that teachers can raise (or lower) students' performance by expecting more (or less) of them—quite a responsibility.

The bottom line of this area of performance is sending three key messages to all students:

1. This is important.
2. You can do it.
3. I won't give up on you.

Effective effort, not innate ability, is the key to achievement.

People of widely different personalities and teaching styles can and do succeed in sending these messages to students. Teacher success here is not a matter of style. From the lighthearted to the stern, from the free-flowing creative to the analytical, the best teachers find ways to convince students that they, the teachers, are believers—believers in the students and in the subject. Such teachers do not do so by magic or osmosis. Their words and actions, some quite subtle but nonetheless observable, send these messages and thereby make a huge difference in learning, especially to low-performing students. Figure 12.1 outlines the key issues for teachers to consider in addressing this area of performance.

## Standards and Expectations

The word *expectations* sometimes has dual connotations: (1) a standard of performance we are hoping for or (2) our anticipation (or prediction about) what one will be able to accomplish. Both are important constructs, and it is critical to separate and conceptualize each clearly, for each plays a significant role in creating an atmosphere conducive to student achievement at high levels. Throughout this chapter, we use the term *standard* to describe the level or type of performance a teacher wants from students and *expectation* to mean what a teacher thinks (believes or predicts) students will do. We now illustrate the nature and critical importance of each—and how they intersect with one another—to influence the messages students receive that impact performance and achievement.

## Standards: What We Want Students to Achieve

Standards signal to students what is important: what it is we want them to accomplish and how we want them to behave. In a classroom setting, there are four general categories for which teachers set standards of performance:

1. Quality and quantity of work
2. Work habits and work procedures
3. Business and housekeeping routines
4. Interpersonal behavior

Standards for the quality and quantity of students' work specify the characteristics of work

**Figure 12.1. Key Issues in Expectations**

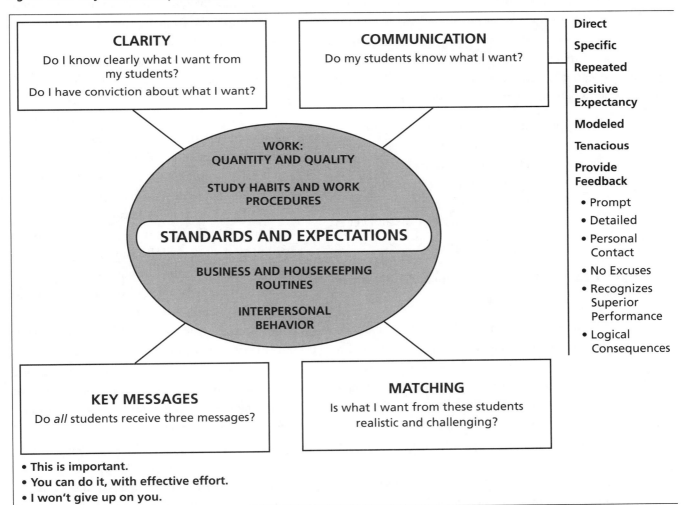

**Research for Better Teaching, Inc.** • One Acton Place, Acton, MA 01720 • (978) 263-9449 • www.RBTeach.com

that make it acceptable. These might include things like:

- Explaining how the student solved a problem in both pictures and words (quality)
- Supporting the hypothesis in a lab report with measured data (quality)
- Demonstrating proper form in four foul shots (quantity and quality)
- Responding to questions in complete sentences (quality)

Standards for work habits and work procedures pertain to how students go about their work, not the products of work themselves. We are talking here about ongoing habits and procedures that students are routinely expected to use in their work, not directions on how to do individual assignments. These might include things like:

- Responsibility and procedure for getting and submitting assignments when a student has been absent from class
- The process for previewing directions before beginning a task
- The procedure for entering class and getting started immediately on the "bell work" for the day
- What, when, and how often to update their independent reading log

At the beginning of the year, there may be repeated and direct attention to teaching these procedures to students, and the teacher will remind students of these ongoing procedures from time to time until they are established and working well. Eventually they won't be talked about at all. They just function, underlying the academic work students are doing.

Standards for business and housekeeping routines pertain to nonacademic work–related procedures such as:

- How attendance and lunch count are done
- Responsibility and procedures for cleanup in the lab or a work area

Finally, standards for interpersonal behavior pertain to how students should treat each other, interact with one another, and cooperate with the teacher:

- Treat every classmate with respect: listen attentively when they speak; ask questions when you don't agree with or understand them; be patient and quiet if they need time to think when you are finished speaking.
- When asked to work together with others, make every effort to work in a way that is helpful to everyone.

Each of these four categories of standards is considered separately because it is possible for a teacher to be very clear about what's important—and to have conviction that students will be able to achieve the standards set—in one category but not necessarily to be as clear in all four. As a result, teachers might find that they get great results, for example, on students following work procedures but inconsistencies or low performance when it comes to their treatment of one another or the quality of work they are producing. This signals an opportunity for teachers to step back and ask anew, "So what is it that I think is important? What is it that I want from students?" In other words, it suggests a need for teachers to clarify what they think is important and then to figure out how to communicate that convincingly to students.

In this chapter, we deal especially with setting and communicating standards for the quality and quantity of work and work habits and procedures. (For more about business and housekeeping routines see Chapter Seven, "Routines"; for interpersonal behavior, see Chapter Eight, "Discipline" and Chapter Fourteen, "Classroom Climate.")

So, deciding what is important is the first issue, followed by three others:

- Do my students know what the standards are, and do they understand what they mean? Just because I have gotten clear internally about what I want doesn't mean the students are similarly clear. Standards in all four areas need to be communicated to students explicitly, specifically, and repeatedly.
- Are my standards appropriately rigorous (challenging but attainable)?
- Have I scaffolded learning experiences to match the differential needs and readiness levels of individual students to ensure that all will progress toward meeting and achieving the standards I have set?

## Communicating Standards

How do teachers ensure that students know and understand what is important? There should be no secrets about what is expected and what it will look like when students are meeting those expectations. Let's begin by examining some behaviors that are common among teachers who create atmospheres of high expectations and get great results with students.

1.  *Direct communication:* The standard of performance is explicitly brought to students' attention, verbally, in writing, or through a visual model.

2.  *Specific communication:* The details of the standard for students' performance are clearly stated or otherwise spelled out. Criteria for success are delineated, and exemplars of student products or performances are shared and carefully examined with students. When the task or assignment is sufficiently complex or multifaceted, rubrics might be presented and explained—or developed with students (see Chapter Eighteen, "Assessment").

3.  *Repeated communication:* The standard is repeated often to make sure students absorb it.

4.  *Positive expectancy:* The standards are explained with an accompanying expression of teacher confidence (sometimes challenge) signaling "You can do this." Another version of positive expectancy has a more imperative quality: "Of course, you'll meet this expectation!" "It's what's done!" is the implication conveyed by tone and body language.

5.  *Modeling:* This has two meanings. The first is to show or demonstrate. A teacher may clarify for students what is wanted by performing the behavior or providing models. The purpose of this form of modeling is clear communication. The second meaning of modeling is to "practice what you preach." In regular practice and behavior, the teacher is a model of thoroughness, or self-evaluation, or courtesy, or whatever else is expected of students. Whether it's standards for procedures, interpersonal behaviors, work habits, or application of skills, students take powerful messages from observing how faithfully teachers follow their own dicta.

6.  *Personal contact:* There are frequent occasions of face-to-face interactions with students—before, during, and after class, even in the hallway. Perhaps they'll be jocular: "Hey, Noah! Before you get locked up in your shoulder pads this afternoon, you're going to see me with those corrections, right?"

7.  *No excuses:* Teachers hold students accountable, putting them on the spot when work is not turned in, is late, or is inadequately done

and not letting them off the hook by accepting inadequate explanations. Teachers give the work to students to correct or do over, set deadlines, offer help when necessary, or make provisions for students to get what they need to do the work (materials, peer tutoring, reteaching, or something else). "No excuses" means giving consequences that are intended to improve performance when performance is poor, without rancor or anger.

8. *Recognizes superior performance or significant gains over past performance:* When students do well, there is special recognition that highlights their accomplishment: posting especially good papers on a bulletin board, displaying a product in a public place, complimenting in front of the class, or a "Greatest Gains" award.

9. *Logical consequences for poor performance:* Equally important are consequences for poor or nonperformance. Something happens as a result of not doing homework or classwork or as a result of doing shoddy work, being late, sloppy cleanup, or the many other areas of student performance for which teachers have expectations so students become convinced the teacher means it.

Effective consequences are made clear in advance to students; are varied so there is a range of consequences rather than just one rigid one for each expectation; are logical rather than punitive; are delivered with appropriate affect; and teachers make it clear that the students have made a choice. (These attributes are developed in more detail in Chapter Eight, "Discipline"). Thus a student who chronically fails to do homework becomes a member of the "homework club" that meets two days after school and on Saturday mornings. The student can choose which day to attend but is required to attend for a minimum number of weeks until homework is caught up and starts coming in on a regular basis. A student who does poorly on a test is required to attend two after-school help sessions before taking the test again to earn a better grade, and will be granted the higher grade achieved in the retake.

10. *Tenacity:* This quality surfaces in response to resistance, and it subsumes repetition and consistency. When students resist reasonable teacher expectations and getting them met seems hopeless, teachers who struggle on nevertheless display tenacity. For example, a teacher goes to study hall to get a student when he doesn't show up for an extra-help session or reminds a student she's expected at 1:15 to go over some work and hands the student a sticky note saying, "1:15: Room 310!" as she leaves class. The messages are, "This is important; you can do it, and I won't give up on you." Effective effort is the key to achievement.

Tenacity is a quality or behavior that raises some interesting challenges and questions regarding the messages we send. On the one hand, the behaviors described have a quality of chasing a student in an effort to convince him that he can and must do it and that the teacher is there to ensure that he knows and sees that. Some amount of chasing is critical when dealing with students who don't necessarily believe in themselves and their capacity to do well—yet. On the other hand, the responsibility for ensuring that learning takes place cannot rest solely with the teacher. Students must do their part in order to develop ownership and, with it, the esteem that results from accomplishment. Decisions about how much to chase and when to back off—or get tough—and allow a student to experience the

**Figure 12.2. Tenacity Continuum**

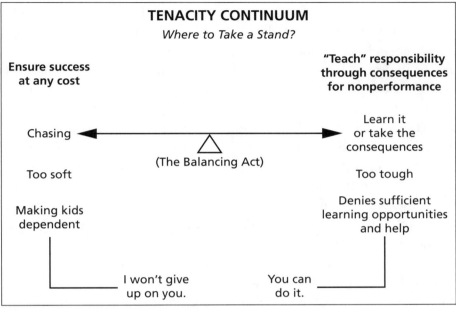

**TENACITY CONTINUUM**
*Where to Take a Stand?*

Ensure success
at any cost

"Teach" responsibility
through consequences
for nonperformance

Chasing ← → Learn it
or take the
consequences

(The Balancing Act)

Too soft

Too tough

Making kids
dependent

Denies sufficient
learning opportunities
and help

I won't give
up on you.

You can
do it.

**Research for Better Teaching, Inc.** • One Acton Place, Acton, MA 01720 • (978)263-9449
• www.RBTeach.com

negative consequences of his inaction can be an ongoing balancing act: How much chasing does a student need to internalize the message that a teacher really believes he can do it and cares enough to see him through it? How much support does a student need before he is ready to go it on his own? When is a student really prepared to assume more independent responsibility for his success? When is it time for the teacher to back off, hold the student accountable, and give him the reins to steer his own success? Chasing to the extreme can signal "the only way you can succeed is if I do it for you." Getting tough too soon denies a student the opportunity to succeed. For students with little confidence, the path we pursue along the tenacity continuum is rarely unidirectional. Instead it is more like an ongoing, calibrated dance to the left and right of center, ever attempting through our actions to keep two messages in balance: "You can do this" and "I won't give up on you," and all the while signaling "this is important"— this being whatever we are being tenacious about. The message of tenacity is that the teacher cares. The choice about how to display that with individual students is a matching decision (see Figure 12.2).

11. *Feedback on student work:* Academic feedback is more strongly and consistently related to achievement than any other teaching behavior (Fisher and others, 1978). This relationship is consistent regardless of grade, socioeconomic status, race, or school setting (Hawley and Rosenholtz, 1984). When feedback and corrective procedures are used, most students can attain the same level of achievement as the top 20 percent of students

(Levin and Long, cited in Bellon, Bellon, and Blank, 1992).

One powerful way in which standards are communicated to students is in the feedback they receive on their work. Findings like those cited previously have continued into the millennium (Marzano, Pickering, and Pollock 2001; Black, Harrison, Lee, Marshall, and William, 2003) Grant Wiggins (1993) defines feedback as "information about how a person did in light of what she or he attempted . . . actual versus ideal performance." It is the value-neutral part of what teachers say or write to students that identifies specifically how their performance compares to the standards established for that piece of work. What is apparent is the need to establish and communicate the standards of performance ahead of time to set the stage for feedback and to relate comments on student work to those standards specifically.

To be most effective as a means of communicating standards, feedback must be prompt (products are returned to students within a very few days of submission, and sometimes the same day) and detailed (feedback contains detailed remarks, notes in the margin, responses in a student journal, or verbal comments identifying what the student has and hasn't accomplished related to the standards established). See Chapter 19, "Assessment," for a more detailed discussion of feedback.

There are two remaining questions related to standards:

- Are standards appropriately rigorous (challenging but attainable?)
- How should learning experiences be scaffolded to match the differential needs and readiness levels of individual students to ensure that all will progress towards meeting and achieving the standards set?

These questions warrant equal consideration, but they are intimately tied to the other part of the overall picture: beliefs and conviction about students' capacity. Standards for performance won't be sufficiently rigorous if we underestimate the capacity of our students. Exploration of these questions follows the discussion of beliefs.

## Expectations: Beliefs About Capacity

Getting results for students is a matter of being clear on what we believe to be important (setting and communicating standards of performance) and having conviction that all students have the capacity to achieve those standards (expectations).

To have the conviction that all students can achieve in school, we have to perceive them all as having sufficient ability to do so and have confidence in our own capacity to meet students where they are now and move them incrementally toward meeting those standards. Both of these conditions can be seriously affected by the theories that we hold about people and their capacity to grow and develop.

## Theories About Achievement and Development

We explore two theories about innate ability and its relationship to performance and achievement. As you read, consider which of these theories dominated the environment in which you spent your formative years and how each of these theories plays out in your teaching.

**Figure 12.3. The Bell Curve**

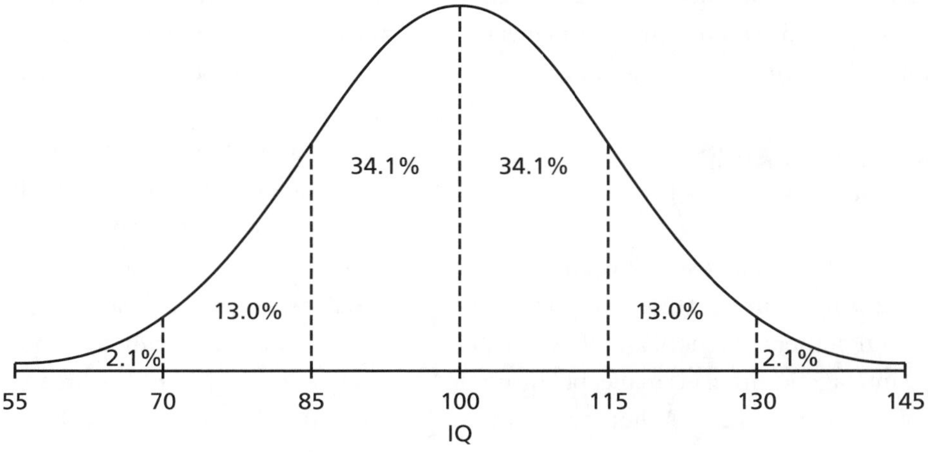

**Innate Ability Theory**

The innate ability theory about achievement and development is best represented by the bell curve (Figure 12.3), representing in this instance an uneven distribution of intellectual ability in human beings. Embedded in this theory are the following assumptions:

- Intellectual ability is a "thing," a unitary entity that is real.
- Intellectual ability is innate, that is, it comes with us as a package at birth.
- The amount of intellectual ability we are given at birth remains relatively fixed or stable throughout our lifetime. It doesn't vary much as we proceed through our lives, and we can't change or affect it much.
- Innate ability is unequally distributed: some of us are born with more of it than others.

- Intellectual ability determines how far a person can go and how well he or she can do, especially at academic material.
- Intellectual ability is measurable. We can test to tell how much of it a student has and arrange for each student to be in the right kind of educational environment for his or her abilities.

Most of us were raised in an environment that reinforced this theory and set of assumptions and we bought into those assumptions as if they were fact. This is not a statement of blame. It's a statement about the air we breathe in a society where this belief is played out more strongly than anywhere else in the world. These are undiscussed assumptions that dominated our country and our schools throughout the twentieth century and still have pervasive influence. Our contention is that these assumptions are flat out wrong. For a history of the concept of "intelligence" as it developed in the United States and evidence that it is malleable, see the Appendix at the end of chapter.

## The Effort-Based Ability or Incrementalist Theory

The effort-based theory posits that all children are born with sufficient innate ability to achieve anything asked of them in school and that this ability (in fact, intelligence itself) is malleable through effective effort (Figure 12.4). Whether a student does achieve and develop (get smarter) is not a matter of having the raw material or ability to work with, but rather believing he or she has what it takes (confidence) and investing effort effectively (working hard and acquiring knowledge and strategies for working smart). Another way of summarizing this theory is that "Smart is not something you are; smart is something you get (incrementally) by working hard and working smart" (Jeff Howard and Verna Ford, Efficacy Institute Maxim).

Indeed all teachers see differences in children every day in their classrooms, sometimes big differences: differences in readiness to learn, in speed of learning, in motivation, and clearly in current academic performance. Some students are way behind the others. But unlike an entity theorist, where the differences would be explained away as a matter of how much intelligence or innate ability one is endowed with, an incrementalist believes that all children have the intellectual capacity to eventually meet proficiency standards; it is not a deficient brain that is holding them back but any number of other variables, all of which can potentially be modified, accommodated, or influenced in some way.

Those who hold to this theory, when confronted with differences in children's development or performance, interpret the disparity as a function of disadvantages in their past that have created obstacles to their development and learning: limited experiences, absence of mediation or intervention, conflict of values related to school achievement, low self-esteem, mismatch in learning-teaching style, and myriad other possible causes, none of which is internally hard-wired in a person and all of which may be subject to change under the right circumstances. Students clearly have different aptitudes (a natural talent or ability for something), but they all have enough to attain proficiency in literacy and numeracy at rigorous standards.

**Figure 12.4 Incrementalist Effort-Based Belief**

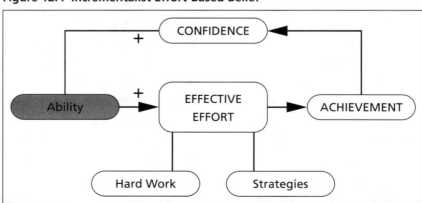

*Source:* Adapted from Efficacy Institute, Lexington, Massachusetts.

Two assumptions are embedded in this theory:

- There is no way of telling from children's attitudes, speech, cleanliness, clothing, record of past performance, and current performance what they are capable of learning and achieving if given time, motivation, and instruction that reaches out to meet their needs.
- Differences of color and culture have nothing to do with the capacities of children's brains.

Whereas the entity theory is deterministic, the incrementalist theory is optimistic. Those who espouse the incrementalist theory engage in an ongoing quest to discover what will enable students to turn on and take off.

Both explanations for achievement and development have been explored historically as part of a body of research referred to as attribution theory (Weiner, 1996; Nicholls, 1982; Dweck, 2002, 1999). Attribution theory is concerned with the explanations we give ourselves when we succeed for why we succeeded and when we fail for why we have failed. The research associated with it suggests that the explanations we give ourselves of the causes of our successes and failures (attributions) are based on our perceptions, and those perceptions and explanations ultimately influence our self-concept. They also influence our expectations for future situations, feelings of power and efficacy, and subsequent motivation to put forth effort. Weiner found four basic reasons to which individuals might attribute their success or lack thereof: ability, task difficulty, luck, and effort. Weiner arranges them in the grid shown in Table 12.1.

According to Weiner, successful, confident people attribute their success to internal factors (having the ability and exerting effort) and lack of success to the internal factor they control and can

**Table 12.1.  Attribution Theory**

|  | Internal | External |
|---|---|---|
| Constant (Stable) | Ability | Task Difficulty |
| Variable (Unstable) | Effort | Luck |

*Source:* Reprinted by permission from Weiner, 1972, 1974.

most readily influence (effort). Unsuccessful low-confidence people tend to attribute success to external factors (task difficulty: "Must have been an easy test," and luck: "I guess I just luckily studied the right chapters!") and lack of success to external factors (again, luck or task difficulty, those over which they have no control) with a secret inner fear that they really just don't have enough ability.

Young children believe success comes from effort; in fact, effort and ability are synonymous to them (Nicholls and Burton, 1982). But as they get older, some children start attributing academic success more and more to native ability rather than effort. This creates a bind, because the only possible conclusion for a child who is not doing well is that he or she must be dumb. Thus, many low-performing students opt out of school and quit trying by middle school because it's better to be considered lazy than dumb.

Dweck (1999) found that children (and adults) tend to be either entity theorists about intelligence and achievement or incrementalists. Entity theorists believe that intelligence is a thing—an entity that is fixed and responsible for any success; conversely, having low intelligence results in poor academic performance. Entity theorists take every assignment, every test, every task as an evaluation of their innate ability in a direct, causative way. These students form what Dweck calls a "performance goal orientation" toward academic work. Low performance (errors) indicates low ability. High performance indicates high ability. "I only like to do the things I already do well," says a girl who is an entity theorist.

Incrementalists believe that ability is built incrementally through effort and use of feedback from the environment. They form a "learning goal orientation," according to Dweck, where their goal is to learn something new rather than to prove themselves able, as is the goal of an entity theorist.

The consequences of these two internal theories of intelligence and the goal orientations that go with them are huge. Imagine the pressure a student feels who is constantly on trial, who experiences every academic challenge as a measure of self on a dimension so highly prized in our society: intelligence.

Not all students (or adults) are at the poles of the entity versus incrementalist continuum, but large numbers are. The closer students are to the entity pole, the harder it is to mobilize energy and strategies when experiencing difficulty. Instead they tend to interpret difficulty as a measure of limited ability and frequently give up. The closer a student is to the incrementalist pole, the more likely he or she is to treat difficulty and errors as data saying that working harder or working smarter (different strategies) is what is needed in order to overcome the difficulty.

This brings us around to why an examination of standards and expectations is so central to the work of teachers. The standards of performance

teachers set and the beliefs they hold about a child's capacity to meet those standards play a vital role in the messages sent to students and ultimately in what students are likely to achieve. So just how do these come together and play out in our classrooms?

## The Intersection of Standards and Expectations

Are the standards (or level of proficiency) targeted for students appropriately rigorous (challenging but attainable)? How strong is the conviction that all students have the capacity to achieve them? We could place each of these constructs (standards and expectations) along intersecting continua (see Figure 12.5) with the $x$-axis representing a continuum of low to high standards and the $y$-axis representing a continuum of low to high expectations. The standards a teacher sets and the expectations a teacher holds about students' capacity to meet or achieve those standards could be anywhere along those continua.

Figuring out where standards of performance should be set requires some knowledge of age-appropriate norms for students, clear proficiency targets in state frameworks, and some specialized knowledge of the population of the class in order to make valid judgments. Using these as guidelines, we need to strive to make the standards appropriately challenging but attainable for students.

The relative rigor of the standards and the degree of conviction we have about the capacity of students to achieve them will have an impact on how we behave and the messages sent to students. It is possible, then, to create several different kinds of scenarios that might be played out in a classroom:

• *High standards, low expectations:* The teacher sets high standards of performance but does not believe or expect that all children can or

**Figure 12.5. Standards and Expectations**

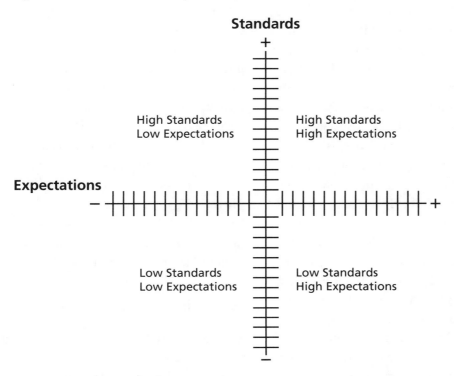

**Research for Better Teaching, Inc.** • One Acton Place, Acton, MA 01720 • (978)263-9449 • www.RBTeach.com

will achieve them. A teacher with this mind-set might say: "I set tough standards in this course. There's a certain amount of work to be done, and I expect everyone to do it. No excuses. Some will cut it; some won't. Some just don't have it—or have the drive—and will fall by the wayside. That's just the way it is."

• *Low standards, low expectations:* This plays out when a teacher has little conviction that students have the ability to achieve much and consequently sets low standards of performance. A teacher who holds this mind-set might say: "I don't ask much of these kids. School just isn't the place for them. They are borderline dropouts. They are going to end up in hourly wage jobs. They don't see the relevance of this course to anything they will do one day. I just want to get through the semester with them without a hassle. At least they are coming to class. I'll do some things to make it fun, and if they behave reasonably, they'll pass the course."

• *Low standards, high expectations:* This describes a teacher whose actions are based on little conviction that students are capable of meeting high standards but wants students to feel good about themselves. So he sets low standards of performance and celebrates students' meeting them. A teacher who has this mind-set might inflate student grades based on the amount of effort the student has invested rather than on what he or she has achieved. This can create a negative enabling situation: giving A's for mediocre performance with the delusion that the good grade will build student confidence.

• *High standards, high expectations:* This teacher sets high standards of performance, believes all students have the innate ability to achieve them, behaves in kind, and is determined to do everything in her power to help students get there. "I understand that kids in here have different degrees and kinds of developed abilities and speeds of learning. I know some of them have better backgrounds for getting this material, and maybe they're just quicker. But I also know what a quality performance is like from a student, and I know what it means to really know this subject. I press them all toward that standard of excellence. I make special provisions for the slower students to try to bring them along as far and as fast as they can go. I provide extra boosts and help those who need it, and I know they'll still move along at different rates and with different degrees of success. But the standard is there, and I differentiate instruction to match their needs, scaffold learning experiences to support incremental progress, and push them all toward ever-closer approximations of success. If they never get there, at least they learn about excellence and get rewarded mightily for their incremental steps toward it."

Many states have frameworks that provide overall proficiency targets that students should reach at end-of-grade level or end-of-course. In this sense the standards are externally set. The goal is to get all students to proficiency with these standards. But what about students who are way behind? We have to get push and pace in correct balance: accelerate the learning of students who are behind, and set standards of performance for them to reach each quarter or each year that put them on pace for proficiency at a targeted time in the future. The standard of performance we are talking about is one that represents an appropriate stretch: a stretch so that all the students who are behind can catch up to age-appropriate proficiency, and all the students already on pace can be stretched or deepened in appropriate ways.

The bottom line is that our beliefs influence our perceptions of individual students, and those perceptions influence how we behave—and ultimately what students achieve. We must consider how our perceptions about each student's capacity to achieve are influencing the standards of performance we set and the ways in which we behave daily. We communicate our impressions to students about their academic ability and capacity to achieve by subtle and indirect messages that students read and that influence their academic performance. Therefore, it is incumbent on all of us to take a step back and examine the mind-set we hold about innate ability and the limits or liberties we bring to students' learning as a result.

## Pygmalion in the Classroom

The notion that teachers communicate their impressions to students about their academic ability by subtle and indirect messages is not new. Many years ago in a landmark study, researchers Rosenthal and Jacobson wrote the famous *Pygmalion in the Classroom* (1968). They even made an appearance on the *Today Show*. They called attention to ways in which teacher perceptions of student ability result in differential treatment of students and have a positive or negative impact on their inclusion in classroom discourse and ultimately their performance in the classroom. Teachers were given falsified records of students' IQ scores: high-performing students might be represented as high, average, or low IQs and low performers as high, average, or low IQs. And that information, rather than the students' actual IQs, influenced how teachers dealt with their students and how the students achieved.

Cooper (1979) later organized these differential teacher communication behaviors into five categories:

1. *Climate:* "It was found that teachers who believed they were interacting with bright students smiled and nodded their heads more often than teachers interacting with slow students. Teachers also leaned towards bright students and looked brights in the eyes more frequently" (p. 393).

2. *Demands:* "Students labeled as slow have been found to have fewer opportunities to learn new material than students labeled as bright" (p. 393).

3. *Persistence:* "Teachers tend to stay with the highs longer after they have failed to answer a question. This persistence following failure takes the form of more clue giving, more repetition, and/or more rephrasing. Teachers have been found to pay closer attention to responses of students described as gifted. Teachers allowed bright students longer to respond before redirecting unanswered questions" (p. 394).

4. *Frequency of interaction:* "Teachers more often engage in academic contact with the high- than low-expectation students" (p. 394).

5. *Feedback:* "Teachers tend to praise high-expectation students more and proportionately more per correct response, while lows are criticized more and proportionately more per incorrect response" (p. 395).

There are twelve distinct behavioral items in these five categories, and they provide empirical evidence that teacher perceptions of a student's ability can lead to classifying students as "brights" and "slows" and to acting differently toward them, thus creating self-fulfilling prophecies. Here is a list of related questions you might investigate as you examine and reflect on your practice:

- Do I smile and nod more toward "highs"?
- Do I lean more toward "brights"?
- Do I look "brights" more in the eyes?
- Do I give "slows" fewer opportunities to learn new material?
- Do I stay with "highs" longer after they have failed to answer a question?
- Do I give "highs" more clues when they fail to get an answer—more repetition or more rephrasing?
- Do I pay closer attention to the responses of "the gifted"?
- Do I allow "brights" longer to respond?
- Do I have more frequent academic contact with "highs"?
- Do I give "highs" more praise per correct response?
- Do I give "lows" more criticism per incorrect response?
- Do I do any of the above more with girls than with boys, or vice versa?

Given that perceptions can have this kind of powerful influence on behavior, we ask our readers to consider the possibility that all children have the capacity to do rigorous work to high standards and to act as if that were so . . . to suspend disbelief and invest energy in searching for ways to create the conditions in which this would become a reality for all students. It is our contention that if we behave as if we can reach every child and we continue to strive to create the conditions that are optimal for their learning, we will see more miracles than we could have imagined and see more students reach proficiency than ever before.

What else might we see in classrooms where all students are perceived as capable of achieving high standards of performance? What would we be doing if we believed the effort-based incrementalist theory and acted out of that orientation? Those questions are the focus of the remainder of this chapter.

### High Standards—High Expectations

Commitment to the incrementalist belief can show up in teachers' behavior, classroom practices, school structures, and even conversations with one another. Teachers set standards of performance they believe to be rigorous, important, and appropriate; find out where students are in relation to those standards; and adapt instruction to accommodate students' differences in readiness levels (current knowledge or skills), learning and processing styles, and motivation. They don't pull back, give up, or dilute expectations and academic press for any of them.

They send positive expectation messages to all children regardless of their race or wealth, regardless of their learning or language differences. They seize every opportunity in regularly recurring classroom situations to reinforce the messages children get that their teacher believes they can do it and won't give up on them. Teaching policies and practices are conscientiously geared toward instilling in children life-liberating beliefs. Teachers teach students and parents about attribution theory and make effective effort an explicit agenda to combat the entity theory. They don't expect all students to learn at the same rate or meet standards at the same time, especially when there are wide differences in their prior preparation. But teachers take it as their responsibility to constantly examine and manage their biases for seeing current student performance through the lens of innate ability, teach children to believe in themselves, and explicitly teach them how to work not just harder but smarter with appropriate strategies. All teachers can create the conditions where unmotivated children

want to put forth the effort, and this should be an integral part of all our work. Some of what this commitment looks like at the school or district level is the focus of the excellent *Whatever It Takes* (DuFour and others, 2004).

In classroom practice, teachers invest in discovering ways to build confidence in students (belief in themselves and their capacity to achieve) and in teaching them how to invest their effort effectively.

## Classroom Interventions

Sending high expectation messages ("This is important, every single one of you can do it with effective effort: working hard and acquiring strategies, and, I won't give up on you.") and convincing students that they have the capacity to achieve at high levels (attribution training) is a moment by moment, everyday mission for a teacher. The actions are woven into the fabric of everything that transpires in class. This next section develops that premise by examining ten arenas of classroom life that afford teachers the opportunity to build student confidence.

### Building Confidence: Ten Arenas of Classroom Life

An arena is a place, structure, setting, or interaction in which regularly recurring events happen and can be observed. Many of the issues of differential treatment noted in Cooper's work are integral to arenas that recur daily in classrooms as teachers interact with students. The arenas listed below represent opportunities for a teacher to communicate behaviorally to students what is important and that he or she believes they have the capacity to achieve it:

1. Calling on students
2. Responding to student answers
3. When students don't answer
4. Giving help
5. Responding to student products:
   - unmet expectations
   - students doing well
   - significant change in performance
6. Dealing with errors
7. Grading
8. Students who don't "get it" yet
9. Grouping
10. Giving and negotiating tasks and assignments

Reflecting on these arenas and our practices within each of the arenas affords the opportunity to consciously align some of the most subtle behaviors and practices with sending powerful and positive high expectation messages to all students.

## Arena 1: Calling on Students

Calling on students is a way of inviting them to participate in classroom discourse, and to signal that their voice, thoughts, opinions, concerns, and questions are important. So in this arena we ask ourselves:

- Who gets called on?
- How do they get called on? By whom? Randomly? Systematically? Hand raising?
- How do I ensure that all are included?
- How frequently do individual students get called on?
- What do I do if students don't volunteer to participate?
- What are students called on to do?
- What level of thinking is called for in the question?
- Do I insert sufficient wait time (minimum of 3 to 5 seconds) after posing a question or a

prompt before calling on anyone so all students have an opportunity to process the question and construct an answer?
- What do I do to ensure that all can participate effectively?

The bottom line here is to examine the extent to which there is some sort of equal opportunity for all students. Whether it is answering questions, participating in a discussion, surfacing prior knowledge, or some other purpose for student participation, all students must get the message that their input is important, that they are capable of higher-level thinking, that their teacher believes they have important things to offer, and will ensure that their voice is represented and heard.

## Arena 2: Responding to Students' Answers

Another arena through which expectations are communicated is what teachers do right after a student has responded or spoken in class. This is a powerful arena, where the teacher's actions have embedded messages about what's important and about his or her belief in the student's capacity. Art Costa, professor emeritus at California State University, Sacramento, has pointed out that the way teachers respond to student answers is probably more important than the questions themselves. These are moments that happen hundreds of times a day, and what we say and do at these moments can influence the way students participate in lessons from that point on. Our responses to student comments or answers signal to individuals—and cumulatively to the whole class—whether it is safe to speak out, whether a student can risk trying something that's hard, and whether the climate is supportive of thinking and effort or punitive for not having the right answer.

Consider these ways that a teacher might respond to student answers to the question, "How do you find the area of a circle?"

- Criticize: "That's not even close. Come on, wake up!"
- Give the correct answer: "No, it's pi $r^2$."
- Redirect to another student after the first student's answer: "Judy, can you tell us?"
- Redirect to get more, build, and extend: "Okay. You're on the right track. Judy, would you add anything to that?"
- "Wrong" with the reason: "Not quite, because you left out the exponent." Then the teacher waits while the student tries again.
- Supply the question for which the answer is right, cue, or hold accountable: "That would be right if I asked for the formula for the circumference. Now do you remember anything about the use of exponents in that formula? [Now the student gets it right.] Right! And I bet you'll remember that after lunch if I check you too. I'll ask you then, and I bet you'll get it!"
- Wait time: Silence.
- Follow-up question to double-check or extend: "Can you tell me how you were thinking about that?"
- Acknowledge: "Um-hmmm."
- Restate in fuller language: "Okay. So you get the area by multiplying pi times the radius of the circle squared."
- Ask the student to elaborate: "Can you tell me more about what you meant by that?"
- Praise: "Way to go!"

Depending on how the teacher responds, a student may internalize one or more of the following messages:

- "I'm dumb."
- "Well, I muffed that one!"
- "My job is to guess the answer in the teacher's head and say it in precisely the way he's thinking it."
- "I muffed that one, and I should get back in gear. I know this stuff."
- "The teacher thinks I can think this one through and get it."
- "What I said was worthwhile, but there's more."
- "My teacher really listens to what I say."
- "My teacher really wants to know what I mean. There must be something worthwhile in what I said."
- "My idea wasn't as good as that one. Boy, I'm glad I didn't get called on."
- "Wow, I guess I did pretty well on that one."
- "It's not safe to risk an answer here unless you're really sure."
- "It is safe to risk an answer in here. If I don't get it, I won't be put down."
- "I can say what I think and be respected and accepted for that."
- "If I can't get it, I'll be helped to remember or figure it out."

It is likely all of us have received these messages at one time or another in our experience as students. Clearly the effects can be powerful. What the teacher does or says after a student responds in class can engage students and open their thinking or close them down; can make them feel more confident, curious, and encouraged to participate, or afraid, timid, protective, quiet, and defensive. Simultaneously, the effect is either to stimulate students to search, scan, wonder about, reflect, and in general think, or instead to try to get it right and shine, impress, and win (or protect themselves from getting wounded).

These responses form a repertoire. (See Exhibit 12.1.) No one of them is inherently best, most appropriate, or most effective. A teacher could create the context in which each of them, even criticizing (but not put-downs), could be appropriate. Matching is the name of the game. Several of them, however, are particularly effective for specific purposes and should be considered for inclusion into any teacher's repertoire. *Wait time* (or silence) is one such behavior.

In the late 1960s, Mary Budd Rowe discovered that if teachers purposefully paused and waited a minimum of three seconds or more after asking a question, many students who ordinarily did not answer did so, answers tended to be fuller rather than single words or phrases, and the answers were at a higher level of thinking. Rowe also discovered most teachers wait on average less than a half-second after asking a question before jumping in with cuing, redirecting, telling the answer, or restating the question. Her research continued for almost twenty years with similar findings. Waiting three to five seconds after posing a question is referred to as *wait time I.*

Waiting after a student has responded is called *wait time II.* This response behavior achieves similar desirable outcomes to wait time I: teachers tend to increase the cognitive level of their questions, and students increase the cognitive level of their answers, speak in more complete and more elaborate sentences, exhibit less tentativeness in their responses, and are more likely to start responding to each other and to comment on each other's answers (Figure 12.6).

While the idea of pausing for at least three to five seconds after posing a question or responding to a student answer appears to be simple and straightforward, most who have experimented with it will agree that it is initially uncomfortable and easy to forget to do. We are so used to filling silences with talk that unless we specifically commit ourselves to try wait time and get someone in to watch us trying it, we will likely fail to internalize this valuable behavior. Hence, it is a behavior where coaching or some form of peer feedback can be particularly helpful. The very presence of an observer reminds us of the commitment and increases the likelihood of successful practice.

Wait time—or "think time"—is a behavior we believe teachers should teach to students so they know what it means and why it is being used and so they can be comfortable using it themselves and honoring it when it happens in the classroom.

*Supplying the question for which the answer is right, cuing, and holding the student accountable* is another that we should include in our repertoires because it accomplishes several things. First, it salvages self-esteem. As Madeline Hunter says, "Our job is to help learners be right, not catch them being wrong. When someone is humiliated or feeling unworthy, their perception narrows." This strategy also strengthens a connection between the answer and the question it goes with by supplying that question. To use this strategy with every wrong answer would not be practical, but it is an excellent strategy to use frequently and especially when there's a question to link up with the wrong answer, often an item of recent learning.

The eight moves at the top of the continuum represent ways a teacher responds when a student has an (apparent or actual) incorrect answer. While there is nothing wrong with making it clear when an answer is incorrect, it does matter how a teacher says it and what he or she does next. Each of those moves is a different way of saying "no" or "not quite," but a common characteristic of all of them is that the teacher responds and then moves on to someone else.

The moves in the middle part of the continuum represent ways of sticking with students. Teachers

**Exhibit 12.1. Teacher Responses to Student Answers**

*Ways of moving on to another student*

Criticizes. "Come on. That answer shows no thought at all."

"No," and redirect to another student.

"No, then give the correct answer.

"No," with the reason, which may serve as a cue.

Cue, but move on to another student.

Move to another student if the first student doesn't answer.

Redirect to another student to add, build, or extend. "Would you add anything to that, Zach?"

Student authorized to call on another student to answer in his or her place.

*Ways of sticking with a student*

Supplying the question for which the answer is right, cuing, and holding the student accountable.

"No, but it's good you brought it up because others probably thought that too."

"Try again."

Validate what is right or good about an answer and then cue, sticking with the student.

Ignore the answer, and cue the student.

Wait time II.

Follow up with an expression of confidence or encouragement: "I think you know."

Follow up with an expression of confidence or extend.

Ask the student to elaborate.

Call for a self-evaluation of the answer.

Follow-up question to clarify: "Are you saying that . . . ?"

*Ways of acknowledging, affirming*

Acknowledge, "Um-hmmm."

Repeat the student's answer.

Restate the answer in fuller or more precise language.

"Right."

"Right," with the reason.

Praise or praise and extend.

**Teachers who convey positive expectations practice moves from the middle of this continuum.**

**Research for Better Teaching, Inc.** • One Acton Place, Acton, MA 01720 • (978) 263-9449 • www.RBTeach.com

**Figure 12.6. Wait Time**

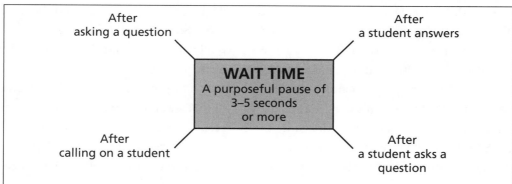

**Effects**

1. 300–700% increase in the length of student responses.
2. The number of unsolicited but appropriate student responses increases.
3. Failures to respond decrease.
4. Confidence increases—there are fewer inflected responses.
5. Speculative responses increase.
6. Teacher-centered show and tell decreases, and student-student interaction increases.
7. Teacher questions change in number and kind:
   • The number of divergent questions increases.
   • Teachers ask higher-level questions (Bloom's taxonomy).
   • There is more probing for clarification.
8. Students make inferences and support inferences with data.
9. Students ask more questions.
10. Contributions by "slow" students increase.
11. Disciplinary moves decrease, and more students are on task.
12. Achievement on logic tests improves.

*Source:* Rowe (1987).

who stick with students—especially if their initial response is seemingly incorrect—send messages that they have confidence in their students' ability to think through to an appropriate response. Giving a student a cue and lingering sends quite a different message from saying no and immediately calling on another student. Cuing the student but then calling immediately on another says the teacher doesn't really think the student has the capacity (or sufficient speed) to use the cue.

Whereas any response from this continuum might be effective in a given situation, the main point of this section is that teachers who convey positive expectations and build confidence and risk taking in students practice many moves from the middle of the continuum.

Sometimes teachers in our workshops wonder aloud how an instructor has enough time to do such sticking and cuing with students and still get through all the material they wish to. The fact is that it takes hardly any more time at all to do so—seconds more at most. Sticking with a student does not need to slow the rate of coverage (though for other reasons, such slowing down might be a very good idea). But consider the cost of not sticking with students who don't answer or answer incorrectly the first time; the individual student can easily feel inept at a moment like this—and consequently shut down cognitively. Also, by not sticking with the student, the teacher forfeits the chance to support a student's thinking and explicitly build confidence in his or her capacity to perform with academic material. Every long wait or period of silence when a student feels intimidated or unsure about a question is an opportunity to build confidence and capacity. Finally, it is not only the single response to an individual student that matters, but the pattern of responses over time that signals what the teacher thinks is important.

There are other responses as well to student answers. A *follow-up question* to double-check or extend (called a probe in research literature) is a way of checking to see if the student really understands the meaning of an answer or is just parroting. For example, a student might be able to recite "pi *r²*" without knowing that *r* stands for the radius of the circle. So a follow-up question might be, "And the *r* stands for . . . ?"

*Asking students to elaborate* on their responses helps the teacher know what they really meant: "Could you explain that further?" "I'm not sure what you meant by that, Jerry. Can you say a little more?" "You need to be more specific, Jane. How far exactly are you saying the fulcrum has to be from this end?"

*Acknowledging a student's answer nonjudgmentally* leaves the door open for further comment from other students or for adding to the original answer by the same student. ("So one possible explanation is . . . Thank you. What might be some others?")

*Restating in fuller language* is a move a teacher might do for the benefit of the other students—to make sure they understood what the answer meant. (Teacher asks: "Why do you suppose we celebrate

Lincoln's birthday but not all presidents' birthdays?" Student says: "He freed the slaves." Teacher says, "So you are thinking that he did something really important and that's how we decide whose birthdays to celebrate?")

*Praise* can be an effective response to a student answer, but only if used well (Dweck, 2002; Henderlong and Lepper, 2002). Brophy's (1981) definitive review of the research on praise summarized how to praise well. To be effective, teacher praise must be:

- *Specific.* It specifies exactly what is praiseworthy about the student's performance: "John, I'm impressed with the variety of verbs and sentence patterns you used in this composition. This is your best work so far."
- *Contingent.* The praise is dependent on successful student performance and not given randomly or for encouragement. Noncontingent praise (given randomly and sometimes for incorrect answers) is frequent and found "most often among teachers who have low expectations for student learning. Within any given class, it is most likely to be directed toward the lowest achievers. No doubt such praise is given in an attempt to encourage the student. However, it seems likely that to the extent that the students recognize what the teacher is doing, the result will be embarrassment, discouragement, and other undesirable outcomes" (Brophy, 1981, p. 13).
- *Genuine.* The teacher means it. The praise is not manipulative, or given to reinforce (that is, engineer) a specific behavior but reflects real appreciation on the teacher's part.
- *Congruent.* Gesture, tone of voice, stance, and posture send the same message as the

words. If the teacher leans back, looks away, and says in a bored tone of voice, "I can see you really worked hard on these problems, Freddy," Freddy is not likely to be convinced.

- *Appropriate.* The choice of words, setting, and style is matched to the particular student. Public praise to individual middle school students can embarrass them. Public praise for certain behaviors can make them want to crawl under the table: "Oh, John, your handwriting is so tidy and neat" (said to a macho eighth grader).

Brophy also points out that effective praise:

- Uses students' own prior accomplishments as the context for describing present accomplishments
- Is given in recognition of noteworthy effort or success at difficult (for this student) tasks
- Attributes success to effort and ability, implying similar successes can be expected in the future
- Fosters endogenous attributions (students believe that they expend effort on the task because they enjoy the task and/or want to develop task-relevant skills).

Each of the behaviors just described—wait time, supplying the question for which the answer is right, cuing, and holding the student accountable, follow-up questions, asking students to elaborate, acknowledgment, restating in fuller language, and praise—has research to support it as an effective teacher behavior (Costa, 1985; Dunkin and Biddle, 1974). There is similar support for redirecting in the literature and even a case for the appropriateness of criticism with certain students as long as the criticism is not a put-down (Graham, 1985).

These findings have been reinforced by subsequent research (Henderlong and Lepper, 2002; Dweck, 2002).

Since many of these response techniques are inherently worthwhile in and of themselves for stimulating thinking and attaining clarity, they are worth adding to all teachers' repertoires. And it is a good bet that among the list cited, there are several new ones for any teacher. (Least frequently seen, in our observations, are wait time, asking students to elaborate, and effective praise.) But beyond incorporating them into one's repertoire is the issue of matching. Are the response techniques being used appropriately in the right situation and with the right students? Wait time, for example, is less appropriate when asking low-level questions or doing drill. Giving students time to think and process is most effective when higher-level thinking is called for. Redirecting prematurely can deny a student the opportunity to think through an answer or refine one already given. Restating in fuller language can aid the understanding of the rest of the class, but if done unnecessarily or to excess can teach students not to listen to one another. The bottom line here, as elsewhere in the quest to understand teaching, is to work first to expand repertoires to respond more appropriately to more students in different situations, then improve the effectiveness of matching, and finally, skew responses to the middle part of the repertoire so as to take every opportunity to build confidence and capacity in students.

## Arena 3: When Students Don't Answer

Sometimes students are called on and don't answer or don't have a ready answer, and there is that loaded second or two in which we must make a decision: Do we get embarrassed for the student and want to get the spotlight off that child? Do we stick with the student, giving cues? Do we ask the question over again? Do we redirect the question to another student?

There is a progressive continuum of responses we might employ to keep students open and thinking when they don't answer:

- Use wait time I.
- Repeat the question.
- Cue.
- Ask a simpler question.
- Ask a fact-only question.
- Give choices for the answer.
- Ask for a yes or no response.
- Ask the student to repeat or imitate an answer.
- Ask for a nonverbal response (shaking the head or pointing).
- Instruct the student to say, "I need more time to think." Or "I don't know yet. Please come back to me."

The benefits of wait time have been described earlier. Simply enduring a little silence while Caitlin grimaces may give her the time she needs to come up with the answer. Modeling this behavior—taking time to think after a student has posed a question—can have a powerful influence too.

One of us once attended a session where David Perkins, codirector of Project Zero at Harvard University, was asked a question. (Project Zero's mission is to understand and enhance learning, thinking, and creativity in the arts, as well as humanistic and scientific disciplines, at the individual and institutional levels.) He turned his head, looked sideways, then up at the ceiling, and continued in silence for a full ten seconds. By this time I was getting nervous for David as a presenter and looking for something to say, some way to jump in and rescue him from what seemed like a paralytic attack. But just at that moment, David looked the

questioner calmly in the eye and delivered a brilliant reply, paragraphs long, with no wasted words. He didn't appear in the least ruffled. He had simply been comfortably thinking out his answer. It was I who had been uncomfortable with the pause, not Perkins.

Several other times in that session, similar pauses for reflection followed complicated questions from the audience. After the first time, I was not worried about David any more and spent the time thinking about the question too. In fact, Perkins's modeling of wait time for himself to think through an answer had an immediate effect on the class. The whole discussion became more reflective and thoughtful. And by having our instructor model his willingness to think before he spoke, we became more comfortable doing so. The result was to elevate the level of the entire discussion.

Turning to the other behaviors on the continuum, we see a progression where less and less is required of the student, until finally only imitation or headshaking is requested. This continuum was adapted from Good and Brophy (2000) for nonresponsive students. Their point is that students should not be allowed to practice nonresponsiveness but instead should be expected to participate.

"As long as they appear to be trying to answer the question, the teacher should wait them out. If they begin to look anxious, as if worrying about being in the spotlight instead of thinking about the question, the teacher should intervene by repeating the question or giving a clue. He or she should not call on another student or allow others to call out the answer" (Good and Brophy, 2000, pp. 192–193).

### Arena 4: Giving Help

Another arena of significance occurs when teachers give students help. This occurs in two ways: (1) students ask for help, or (2) students don't ask for help but the teacher gives it anyway (unsolicited help).

### Student Asks for Help

Giving help happens dozens of times a day. Read the following two scripts. In one, the teacher conveys positive expectations for the student. In the other, the teacher conveys negative expectations (Good and Brophy, 2000, pp. 229–230).

*SCRIPT 1*

STUDENT:  I can't do number 4.

TEACHER:  What part don't you understand?

STUDENT:  I just can't do it.

TEACHER:  Well, I know you can do part of it, because you've done the first three problems correctly. The fourth problem is similar but just a little harder. You start out the same, but then you have to do one extra step. Review the first three problems, and then start number 4 again and see if you can figure it out. I'll come by your desk in a few minutes to see how you're doing.

*SCRIPT 2*

STUDENT:  I can't do number 4.

TEACHER:  You can't? Why not?

STUDENT:  I just can't do it.

TEACHER:  Don't say you can't do it. We never say we can't do it. Did you try hard?

STUDENT:  Yes, but I can't do it.

TEACHER:  Well, you did the first three problems. Maybe if you went back and worked a little longer you could do the fourth problem too. Why don't you work at it a little more and see what happens?

An analysis of word choice and phrases in each of these dialogues illustrates how powerful a brief exchange between teacher and student can be on sending positive or negative expectations messages.

In the second script, the teacher asks, "Why not?" when the student say, "I can't do number 4." That's a "gotcha" question. If students know why they can't do it, they're able to move forward and ask for more specific help.

The teacher then responds to, "I just can't do it," with an injunction, "Don't say you can't do it," and a bit of moralizing: "We never say we can't do it." The teacher may mean that as an encouraging gesture, but whatever hope there is of being encouraging gets crushed by the no-win question: "Did you try hard?"

If the student has already been trying hard, only one conclusion is possible: "I must be dumb." And if the student hasn't been trying hard, then she or he must admit sloth.

The implication, though without much hope, is that maybe longer and harder will somehow put the student over the top. But the teacher gives no specific strategic help. "See what happens" is the parting shot, and the student is left feeling that not much more will happen.

In the first script, the teacher's first question—"What part don't you understand?"—credits the student with understanding most parts and asks him or her to zero in on the stumbling block. When the student stalls, the teacher explicitly expresses confidence in the student's capacity: "Well, I know you can do part of it, because you've done the first three problems correctly." Then the teacher goes on to give explicit coaching help and promises to return in a few minutes "to see how you're doing." The teacher will help but believes the student can do it. Nevertheless, the student won't be left hanging; the teacher will return as a safety net if there is still difficulty.

The point of studying these two scripts is to increase awareness of word choice and approach when students ask for help. With only subtle changes in what we actually say, we can convey confidence, point out how students can use what they already know, give strategies or cues as help, and check back at appropriate intervals—or we can moralize, simplify or dumb down the task, suggest inadequacies, hint blame, and convey—(sometimes masked behind polite words) that we really don't think the student is capable of doing the task.

One outcome we desire for readers of this section is that they will find themselves carrying a third eye and ear into their own classrooms. The third eye and ear are your own! And it is monitoring and giving you feedback as you speak when you are asked for help. What messages are you conveying as you interact with students to give help?

### Unsolicited Help

Graham and Barker (1990) and Zimmerman and Marinez-Pons (1990) found that when teachers give unsolicited help, students often conclude their teachers think the students are not able and need support. And some will then begin acting as if to confirm this belief. Another side effect of premature unsolicited help is that students learn not to struggle, that struggle is bad, that struggle means they are unable—which is exactly the way entity theorists plunge deeper into a subtractive belief system.

This is tricky, because teachers want to be available to the students who need the most support; we want, in fact, to arrange our time and other resources to deploy them efficiently in support of students who do need extra help. So how do we do so without inadvertently sending debilitating expectation messages? We think the answer lies in the subtleties of word choice and body language, as in these examples:

- Instead of going right over to Brian on the first problem and saying, "Need help, Brian?" Mr. Flood works with another child near him and watches how Brian is doing.

He is able to pick up early if Brian is struggling. "Trouble?" he says off-handedly while catching Brian's eye. "No," says the student. "Okay, a good scholar knows when to ask for help. So struggle is good. But be strategic, and ask me or someone else if you hit a wall."

- "Trouble?" Mr. Flood says off-handedly as he catches Brian's eye. "Yeah," says he. "Okay. So what part has you hung up?" "The whole thing." "Okay; now you can do this with a little coaching. What's the first step?"

Another recommendation is to make asking for help a rewarded behavior, used by "good students" or "scholars" in the culture of the classroom, when a student has used her own resources first. That way you won't have to give much unsolicited help. You can establish such a culture by teaching, practicing, and rewarding such behavior explicitly. It becomes part of the curriculum.

### Arena 5: Responding to Student Performance

There are many ways one might respond to student work, whether it is products they create or some type of skill-based performance. Among these are feedback, encouragement, suggestions or advice, praise and questions. "Good" feedback on student work is known to improve student learning. In fact, summaries of research on teaching skills show it to be one of the highest leverage skills for a teacher to master (Black, Harrison, Lee, Marshall, and Wiliam, 2003; Marzano, 2001). "The most powerful single modification that enhances achievement is feedback. The simplest prescription for improving education must be 'dollops of feedback'" (Hattie in Marzano, 2001, p. 96).

We describe the characteristics and the how-tos of good feedback in the Assessment chapter of this book so that we can show how teacher feedback fits as part of a constellation of skills related to assessment. These skills include involving students in generating criteria for good work, getting students to do self-assessments and goal setting, and making displays of data visible to the students.

Although we reserve the main discussion of feedback for the Assessment chapter, we do want to say a few words here about how feedback and other responses to student work serve as an arena in which the three key messages are sent (or negated). Threaded within a teacher's reactions or responses are tacit expressions of confidence (or no confidence) and embedded in the language we use are messages about how capable we think students are. First, if feedback is specific, detailed, frequent, and useful, the implied message is that we want the students to master the material and are giving them every support to do so. Otherwise we wouldn't take the trouble to create all the feedback.

Second, while "pure" feedback is nonjudgmental and simply identifies what students have or haven't accomplished in light of a set of established criteria or standards, the responses we make to student work often do and should include more than pure feedback: encouragement, appropriate leads and suggestions for how to improve it, and so on. This is especially true when responding to students' writing, both fiction and nonfiction. (See examples from Writer's Express in the Assessment chapter.) So it is important not only to give students a high volume of specific, useful feedback, but also to pay attention to the embedded belief messages that surround the feedback:

"Jim, you listed your findings in the lab report but never addressed the next two questions about the conclusions you draw from the findings and new questions this has raised. This isn't up to your best work." [Implied message: Jim, you are capable of good work.]

"So these are the parts you have to improve to have a first class essay." [Implied message: you can, indeed, make this first class. There are some parts of it to address and then you'll be there.]

"What help do you need in order to make this meet standard?" [Implied message: if you identify the help you need, the resources are here and you can meet the standard.]

"Now the only thing you have to do is get a really potent lead." [Implied message: you've done a good job and have met most of the criteria. If you get a potent lead you will have a complete and high-quality product.]

Readers may wish at this point to go to the Assessment chapter to learn about other aspects of feedback that serve student learning and student motivation. Our point here has been that the *moment of responding,* the actual event in which it is delivered, either verbal or written, is one of those moments when we need heightened awareness of our choice of words, our body language, and tone of voice so as to send a positive expectation message.

Connected to this arena are two other regularly recurring situations that call for reaction from us to students: when students don't meet the expectations we set and when there is a significant change in performance. Each of these situations represents an opportunity to reinforce effort as the cause of the results a student has produced (attribution training), and it is through these reactions that students get the message about how important something is and whether we believe they are capable of achieving the performance targets.

### Reacting to Unmet Expectations

When students do poor work, it is important they hear about it in a way that conveys our belief that they can do better, and that we are looking for investment of their effort because we believe it will pay off. Students may display reluctance or resistance when we react in a direct (and sometimes high-energy) way.

But students also can easily interpret low affect or a neutral or noncommittal response to low-quality work as an expression of our lack of interest or belief in them. It often is. And in the absence of a reaction, a large segment of students will not believe sufficiently in themselves to work hard or do well. This danger is particularly present for students who believe it's their innate ability that either enables or disables them to perform (Dweck, 2002). When students who hold this belief find something to be challenging or do poorly at something they attempt, they interpret it as confirmation of not having enough ability. These same students, according to attribution theory (Weiner, 1996), believe that when they do poorly, it is because of task difficulty—and underneath that belief, the damning suspicion that they are not bright enough. Thus, when students do poorly, going after them with high energy and affect becomes an implicit statement of belief in their ability and a call for more effort—an opportunity to retrain their attributions about what causes their success and failure.

### Reacting When Students Do Well

When students do well, it is important that the praise given to them attributes their success specifically to effort (and perhaps secondarily, by implication, to their having sufficient ability): "You came in for extra help, studied before the test, and took your time checking your answers before handing it in. And it really paid off!"

### Reacting to a Change in Performance

A significant change in performance, either dramatically better or worse, is another opportunity for sending expectation messages and attribution

retraining: "This is nowhere near the standard you're capable of. We need to figure out what is happening and what you can do to get back on track." A remark like that from a respected teacher can be a powerful spur to a flagging student. But what about the reverse?

Suppose a student with a D average gets an 83 on a test. The teacher stops the student on the way out the door and says, "You did really well on this test. Why do you think you did so well?" The student pauses, looks down, and mumbles, "Must have been an easy test." (Note the connection to external attribution—luck or task difficulty.) The teacher replies, "Easy test! I don't give easy tests; everybody knows that. And you got number 14 right. That was the hardest one. Now come on, what do you think you did to accomplish that?"

This teacher is trying to get the student to consider that not only does he have the ability to do well, but that there is something he has done to bring about this result (effort attribution). But if the student doesn't see himself as having that ability, he will more than likely be silent at this point in the dialogue. The suggestion behind the teacher's question can be threatening in several ways: "What if I *am* capable of good work? Will she expect it of me all the time? What if I tried and couldn't do this well again?" Another student may want to keep expectations low just to avoid working hard.

Still another possibility is that by challenging the student to think about why he succeeded, the teacher may be throwing him into social jeopardy. Segments of peer culture in schools are built around not doing academic work and dumping on school. To become a student and be seen as trying hard could be interpreted as a rejection of one's peer group. This syndrome recurs often for students of color where striving in school settings gets interpreted as "acting white" (Fordham and Ogbu, 1986). A teacher who seizes opportunities like the student doing unexpectedly well on a test needs to be ready to support the student through the thinking and the possible perceived risks: "Well, you think about it, and when you come in tomorrow, I'm going to ask you again why you think you did so well." Whether or not the student has a response tomorrow, the hope is that the student will start thinking about the possibility that he is capable of higher performance than he'd imagined and weighing the risks and rewards of trying hard. It is also a time for the teacher to devise strategies for how to work with him to provide support and scaffolds while he proves to himself that he has what it takes.

### Arena 6: Dealing with Errors

There are at least two ways in which any one of us can interpret errors or mistakes we make: as an indication of weakness or lack of ability or as an opportunity for learning and growth. If I believe errors are signs of weakness, I will avoid them at all costs. In fact, I will avoid topics and types of work where I think I may make errors so I don't have to face the "truth" about my low aptitude in that area. And I will get impatient with work that does not come easily or quickly because I will interpret the difficulty as a sign of my low ability. But if I interpret errors as feedback, that is, data to be used to indicate gaps I can fill or alternate approaches I must seek out, then I do not shy away from material I do not grasp quickly. This view requires an underlying belief in one's capacity to be able to understand the work ultimately by working at it (and a belief that it's worth the effort).

Teachers have the opportunity every time they help students deal with error to help them interpret it as data to deal with rather than as a low-ability message—for example:

- "You can do this if you have the right strategy, Carl, so you must need a different

strategy. Let's see, which ones have you tried, and which ones haven't you tried yet?"

- "You're able to understand stories when you have the right background knowledge, Julie. So there must be something the author is assuming about experiences you've had that isn't true. Let's see, what could it be? Show me one of the places you got confused."

- "Well, you do fine experiments when you understand what the task really is. So there must be something in the directions that didn't communicate. Take me through the lab setup, and show me where it's unclear."

Our intention here is to highlight the significance of students' attitude toward error and suggest how teachers might respond when errors occur so as to support the incrementalist view of intelligence and a learning goal orientation. (In Chapter Fourteen, "Classroom Climate," we examine how teachers build a climate for risk taking and confidence so that students learn to treat errors as opportunities for learning.)

### Arena 7: Grading

Grading practices send strong implicit messages about what is important and the teacher's beliefs in students' capacity. Consider the practice of allowing students to retake tests. Many teachers allow students to retake a test if they do poorly. What is significant here is how we determine the grade the student receives. Does the student get the higher of the two grades, signaling that demonstrated learning—and persevering toward that end—is what matters? Or do we average the second (usually better) score with the first to compute the final grade? Consider the implications of this practice and the messages it sends. Students who manifest genuine effort and reach equal proficiency with others (who got it the first time around) get lower grades. Thus, speed is rewarded over effort and all that may have gone with it (seeking appropriate help, consulting others, extra hours on the job, soliciting feedback and critique from others, goal setting). The implicit message this sends is that getting it the first time around—or faster—is more worthy or important than ultimately reaching high performance. We care more about speed than perseverance and demonstrating proficiency, for that is what we reward.

Some will argue that giving the higher score as the final score will encourage students to skip studying the first time, because they can always have another crack at it. We think, however, that very few students will be more inclined to put off study because they see retakes as a safety net. This has been borne out anecdotally with every teacher we know who has adopted the practice of allowing retakes. Students who adopt procrastination as a policy soon find themselves so far behind that the safety net doesn't help much. One teacher we worked with addressed this concern by requiring that students come for two after-school help sessions in order to be allowed to retake a test. This ensured that she and the student would have a chance to find out what kind of help and reteaching the student needed in order to be successful the second time. It also did away with the concern that students would abuse the retake system since a retake required extra investment of their time and effort.

Letter grading is another practice that sends strong implicit messages about what is important and our belief in student capacity. The A through F grading system is based on a belief that the purpose of schools is to sort students and identify those who get it and achieve proficiency and those who don't. But what if the purpose of schooling is to prepare all students to graduate with proficiencies that will equip them to be high-functioning, productive, competitive, and contributing members of society? What if we believed that society needs all students to meet the standards of the courses they take because the nature of the workplace and of the world requires all its citizens to be able to do problem solving, work with others, and use language effectively? What if we believed that what we spend time teaching and what students spend their time trying to learn is important enough that all students need to attain proficiency? What if we believed that all students have the ability to meet standards we set given adequate prior knowledge, sufficient motivation, and good instruction? Then the only grading system possible would be one based on mastery rather than sorting.

If that were the case, the only grades that would make sense are A, B, and "not yet," where "B" means "meets the standard" and "A" means "above and beyond the standard" or beyond the requirements of the course. Any student who has "not yet" met the standards of proficiency defined for the course or demonstrated mastery of the knowledge called for is not finished with the work of the course yet. The grade is an incomplete.

To adopt this grading policy, we have to take seriously our efforts to get all students to meet a standard (which requires being clear about what the standards should be and what they look and sound like). And opportunities must be available—after school, on weekends, in the evenings—wherever they can be found or created to offer students reteaching and additional help. We know of several high schools that have adopted and attempted to implement this policy. In one, faculty members and community volunteers are in the school on Tuesday and Thursday evenings and on Saturday mornings to help students finish their "not yets."

To be sure, this is a dramatic shift from the way schools have done things up to now; as a result, it calls on us to be inventive, creative, and relentless in seeking ways to overcome the obvious obstacles to implementing such a practice. But until there is this kind of shift, schools will continue through current grading practices to contradict any mission that seeks to convince students that the whole purpose of schooling is to show them that they have the ability to achieve and to ensure that they have adequate opportunities to do so.

The belief that all students can achieve high standards with rigorous academic material transforms nearly everything about the way we approach schooling, and grading is only the tip of the iceberg. The practice of giving "A, B, not yet" grades opens a positive Pandora's box of implied changes in instructional practices, staff development for expansion of teacher repertoires, and community support for quality schooling for all children. Chapter Nineteen, "Assessment," elaborates on what it takes to replace grading with more informative reporting systems.

### Arena 8: Dealing with Students Who Don't Get It Yet

It is a common event for a class to end with several students who don't understand the material yet. What, if anything, is going to happen so they have another chance? This is another of the regularly recurring situations where we can seize opportunities to build student confidence or miss opportunities and inadvertently signal to some students that there is no hope for them.

If we assume that some students won't or can't ever get it really, or get it only partially, we feel obligated to move on to new material and drop their gap in understanding by the wayside. "After all, they get what they can get. I can give them slightly different assignments [translation: less demanding] so they can feel success [what they really feel is shame]. I have to move on with the curriculum. After all, I have to get these kids ready for the Regents/APs/finals! I can't hold the others back!" The belief behind this statement is that the slower students couldn't really ever get the material anyway, and that getting all students to pass requires slowing down the whole class and dumbing down the standards.

But what if we really believe that all students can reach a high standard given hard work, effective effort, and adequate prior knowledge? What instructional practices would we be considering? We would provide time and structure to reteach for students who don't "get it" the first time around. In addition, we would employ all of the best practices in differentiating instruction and take the initiative to design courses, units of study, and lessons accordingly: preassessing readiness levels, analyzing the data we collect, and designing learning experiences that are geared to a common objective and standard of performance while incorporating options as to how students will arrive there. The options might include variety in how students take in information, how they process or practice what is to be learned, and how they are expected to demonstrate understanding and achievement of the objectives. The degree and kind of support is a variable that would be differentiated as well.

One possibility for differentiating support is setting up what some call a reteaching loop or a "scholar's loop" (Figure 12.7) as a regular classroom practice. For students who didn't get it fast or the first time around, a scholar's loop is a time and place where a concept or idea previously introduced is taught again or made available again to students with additional explanations, different examples, or different perceptual modes. It may or may not be teacher led. Other students or other adults may lead it. Self-directed learning experiences or computer simulations may be in the loop. But something happens for students who didn't get

**Figure 12.7. The Scholar's Loop**

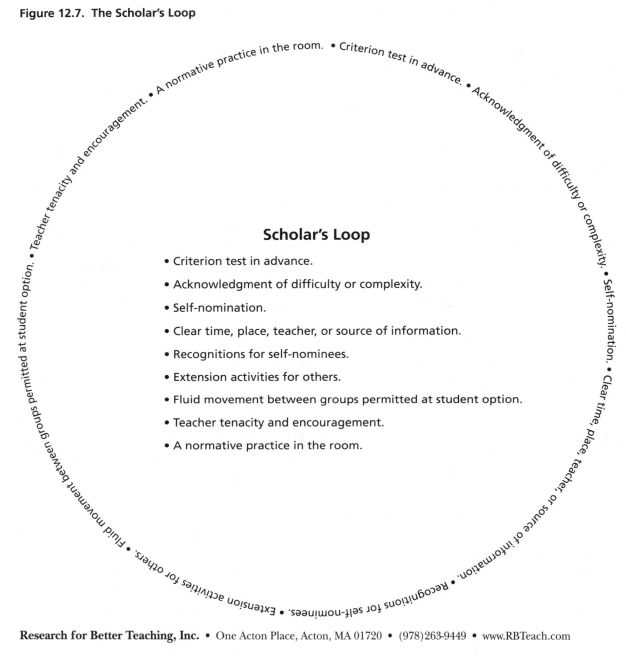

## Scholar's Loop

- Criterion test in advance.
- Acknowledgment of difficulty or complexity.
- Self-nomination.
- Clear time, place, teacher, or source of information.
- Recognitions for self-nominees.
- Extension activities for others.
- Fluid movement between groups permitted at student option.
- Teacher tenacity and encouragement.
- A normative practice in the room.

**Research for Better Teaching, Inc.** • One Acton Place, Acton, MA 01720 • (978) 263-9449 • www.RBTeach.com

it the first time around to ensure they do get it, and at the original level of rigor and at the original standard, not a watered-down one.

The loop has these components:

1. Students should be asked to self-select for the reteaching loop. To do so means they have to self-evaluate: "Do I really get this?"

2. Students need the clarity and aid of a criterion test or task given to them in advance so they can accurately self-assess. The learning target or the performance they are shooting for should be no secret.

3. The teacher creates and continually reinforces a psychological climate of safety and esteem for students who nominate themselves for the scholar's loop by:
   - Explaining to students when the process is introduced—and regularly reinforcing— that scholars are people who desire to understand something at a very deep level.
   - Explicitly acknowledging the difficulty of the material: "This is really quite difficult, because you have to get used to thinking about two things at once: identifying the relevant information and the relevant operation."
   - Praising the thoughtfulness of self-evaluation and the risk it takes to say one doesn't know something: "Good going, Kristina. You looked hard at your writing and decided to get a boost in this skill before moving on. You're going to know it very thoroughly when you're through, and probably incorporate this skill into your writing for life."

4. The teacher encourages the students who have entered reteaching while they're there. "Keep struggling—you've almost got it. I know you're going to get there. Try to put it in your own words now."

5. The teacher acknowledges difficulty and makes the reteaching loop a team effort: "I must not be saying it right. Manuel, can you take a crack at putting it in your own words and explaining it to Katrina?"

The most important part of the reteaching loop is the tenacity and expressed confidence of the teacher to each student that sticking with it will bring success. That means frequent assessments and follow-up with the students until they succeed.

Creating reteaching loops often requires breaking the class into groups and giving the other members of the class an enrichment or extension activity to apply their knowledge in new contexts. It takes extra time and effort to come up with those activities. There is no doubt that carrying out the belief that all children can learn to a high level calls for more work from teachers than if they allow those who don't get it first and fast to settle to the bottom of the tank. Sorting students has always been easier than teaching them.

One way to make the workload more reasonable in managing reteaching loops is to team-teach. Two teachers with a double-size class can divide up the preparation chores when they decide they need to have reteaching and extension activities. To summarize, reteaching loops are effective when they have the attributes shown in Figure 12.7.

Whether a student is successful in achieving a learning objective is highly dependent on the ways in which a skill or concept is presented, how the practice of that skill or concept is structured, and how students are expected to demonstrate their understanding and achievement of the objective. When a student hasn't gotten it yet, the concept of differentiation affords a wide range of lenses for considering what to modify in order to give the student further opportunities for success.

Planning differentiated learning experiences doesn't mean lowering the standards for some or all students and it doesn't mean individualized instruction. The objective and standard of performance for all students is the constant. What is differentiated are the routes, length of time, and degree of guidance available for students to make the journey. Thus, designing effective differentiated lessons requires being very clear about the mastery objectives and standards of performance for all students to achieve, knowing a lot about the students and gathering relevant data to inform planning, and drawing on content knowledge and instructional repertoires to incorporate variety: variety of sources and modes of information input, variety of structures and formats for students to practice or process and internalize new learning, and variety when it comes to assessment or ways in which students will be expected to demonstrate their understanding and achievement of an objective.

It is no small challenge to design differentiated learning experiences. To do so calls for a broad instructional repertoire, and implementation requires high levels of management skills. But we know it is what we have to do if we are to reach all of our students. Developing the capacity to offer this quality of learning experience for students must be the ongoing aim of any professional teacher if the goal is truly for all students to discover that they have what it takes to succeed in school and in life. (Chapters Eleven, Seventeen, and Eighteen present the keystones for differentiating instruction.)

### Arena 9: Grouping

The grouping of students for instruction is an arena that can send powerful messages about a teacher's belief in students' capacity—not because of the practice itself but because of several important variables associated with grouping students:

- The standards students are pressed to reach once they are in a group
- The flexibility of entry and exit from the group
- The quality of instruction
- The tenacity of the teacher and his or her expressed belief in the students' capacity to learn
- The understanding the students themselves have of why they are in a particular group

Many years ago, one of the instructors in our group at Research for Better Teaching was tracked with the lowest-performing eighth graders in his junior high school. This was true tracking: the students stayed together for all subjects and were put together on the criterion of prior academic performance—the classic low track. This placement might have condemned him to low performance and low expectations for the rest of his school career, but it didn't. The difference was that this teacher started the year saying to his whole group: "You've fooled people long enough. We know you have good brains and can do well in school. And we believe it's too important for your future to continue to allow you to do so poorly. So this year you're going to work as you never worked before, and learn more and do better than you ever have before."

The students' pace was accelerated, and the assignments and demands escalated significantly, as did the intensity of the instruction they received. By the end of the year, most of them had mastered two years' worth of academic content.

Well-documented examinations of tracking in the United States (Oakes, 1995, 1985) show conclusively that low-track students are systematically disadvantaged by low expectations, less opportunity to learn, less interesting material, and less interesting teaching. The studies show further that children of color, especially in urban areas, are particularly disadvantaged. Yet the inferred recommendation to eliminate tracking and do heterogeneous grouping in secondary schools appears to help matters little. The reason is that changing the structure won't help without changing teaching and changing beliefs and attitudes of adults and students. (The one exception to this generalization may be the practice of summarily eliminating the lowest track in multitrack schools and applying the standards and expectations of the next higher track to the lower-track students who are incorporated into the next track up.)

The research on heterogeneous grouping, synthesized from a number of original studies as well as two excellent research syntheses (Slavin, 1988; Gamoran, 1992), finds that the overall average achievement of students (referred to as "productivity" in the literature) in tracked and untracked schools is about the same. Tracked schools are not more "productive" than untracked schools—or vice versa. But tracked schools produce a bigger spread of student achievement than untracked schools. The highest-performing students do better in some tracked schools, probably because they are offered accelerated curricula (and boosted by the confidence of adults who expect them to do well). The low-track students do much worse in tracked schools than the lowest-performing students in untracked schools. On the surface, this seems to imply that untracking is good for low-performing students but cheats the most capable high-performing students of reaching their full potential.

Yet we know from individual studies that low-performing students in tracked schools can do well if grouped and given accelerated programs with high expectations for their success. And we also know that the most capable students in untracked

settings can be suitably challenged if their teachers are equipped to differentiate instruction.

The inferences seem clear:

- Eliminate the bottom tracks where multiple tracking is present.
- Help all teachers to internalize the beliefs and behaviors in this chapter for communicating high positive expectations to all students.
- Help teachers diversify their teaching repertoires and differentiate learning experiences so that top tracks can be collapsed and include a wider range of students without denying the highest-performing individuals their chance to be fully challenged.

Now let's look at the data from the elementary studies. Tracking in elementary schools doesn't seem to affect the achievement of either the high- or low-performing students much. Slavin (1993) argues that the reason for this low effect is that elementary tracking probably does not reduce real heterogeneity very much. Thus, the elementary tracks are still quite heterogeneous. Many authors, such as Jeanne Oakes (1985, 1995), speculate, though, that the damage to self-esteem and motivation that befalls elementary children labeled as low track is deep and permanent and shows up later in secondary school performance. Therefore, tracking children in elementary schools seems all loss and no gain. The one exception is that certain studies show that gifted students may be advantaged by homogeneous grouping in the elementary school. Many of their needs, however, can be met by differentiated instruction in the regular classroom by teachers who have extensive repertoires.

*Tracking* and *between-class grouping* mean that groups of students are sorted by perceived ability or prior performance. Tracking tends to mean students are sorted by general ability and grouped together for all their courses in secondary schools. In less rigid school structures, students can take high-track courses in some subjects and lower-track courses in other subjects. *Between-class grouping* is the term most often used in reference to elementary schools and means forming grade-level classrooms that contain students of similar ability.

*Within-class grouping*—often referred to as "flexible grouping"—means students are grouped temporarily for instruction in some skill, concept, or operation where they all need exactly that instruction; they are homogeneous in their readiness for and need of what the group is going to work on. The research on this kind of temporary grouping is strongly positive when the following four conditions are present:

1.  The students are heterogeneously grouped most of the day.
2.  The grouping reduces heterogeneity for a specific skill being taught.
3.  Grouping is flexible (it remains intact only as long as it takes for students to achieve the goal the group was formed to address).
4.  Teachers adapt the pace and level of instruction to the readiness and learning rates of the students.

Another elementary grouping model, the Joplin plan, though rarely implemented, has particularly strong positive findings in numerous studies on reading achievement. This is an elementary grouping model where students are assigned to heterogeneous classes for most of the day but regrouped throughout the whole school for reading instruction with others who need similar instruction, regardless of class or grade. Since strong positive research findings have never led to wide adoption of proven practices, this story should

not be a surprise. But it can be inferred that to implement a Joplin plan requires a high level of organization, leadership, and teacher communication, conditions absent in far too many schools.

What implications can we draw from the research on grouping? First, flexible within-class grouping should be used from time to time, even in high school classes, for focused instruction in specific areas where ad hoc groups need more input, guidance, or practice, as long as the four caveats cited above are followed. In order to do this within-class grouping, teachers need to have worthwhile activities prepared for the other students, be able to manage student engagement, and give feedback on progress to those not in the instructional group. Thus, the teacher must bring to bear well-developed repertoires of management skills in space, time, routines, and momentum and of planning skills to include selection of objectives, design of learning experiences, and assessment. (Ninety-minute periods or some other configuration of extended class periods prove especially useful because they give the flexibility to do small-group instruction within classes and still have time for whole-group activities and discussions.) The bottom line seems to be that good instruction for a wide range of students may require that teachers have the capacity to do small-group instruction, and good small-group instruction requires well-developed repertoires on a wide range of other areas of teaching performance.

Second, the greatest danger of tracking or grouping of any kind is that students get dull, skill-drill-oriented, remedial, dumb-downed instruction. The cost is not only their self-esteem but also their interest and motivation. Most likely they don't believe they are very capable, and they don't need poor instruction and meaningless curriculum to reinforce that belief. Low-skill, low-performing students, whether grouped together for instruction or not, must be involved in learning experiences about interesting and relevant topics. Above all, these students must be involved with higher-level thinking and discussions rather than passive work-sheet activities that call for little more than identification and recall.

For example, teaching approaches that make interesting discussions possible with low-skill secondary-level readers involve explicitly teaching these students reading comprehension strategies (like reciprocal teaching, Palinscar and Brown, 1984); text-text, text-self, and text-world connection making (Keene and Zimmerman, 1997); study skills like note taking, use of graphic organizers, and double-entry notebooks; and note studying within the regular curriculum. It also means teaching them discussion skills, discussion formats (literature circles, Socratic Seminars), and social skills.

We need to systematically build into students the capacity to use the good brains they have to interact successfully with higher-level thinking. It is a reminder that we are not only content specialists and teachers of subjects but also teachers of students. And that role includes teaching students how to use strategies and skills for more effective learning. This requires drawing on all the other material in this book on learning style, variety in learning experiences, clarity devices, principles of learning, and so forth to identify strategies and skills to teach to students explicitly and magnify their school competence as effective learners.

### Arena 10: Giving and Negotiating Tasks and Assignments

Chapter Nine, "Clarity," discusses many important aspects of giving assignments and tasks: ensuring that students know why they are doing the assignment (the purpose and objective), are clear about what to do (the directions), and know how their work will be evaluated (criteria for success). But when we give students assignments, we also convey messages about whether we think the task is hard or easy, whether we think students will struggle as individuals, whether we believe students will succeed, and whether we think success will depend on students' ability, effort, or luck. It is important to examine the messages we send students through the way we give assignments.

A teacher says to her sixth graders: "This weekend your assignment is to read the last three chapters of *Tituba* and be prepared to name the factors that you think contributed to a climate in Salem for the witch hysteria." So far that's pretty straightforward. The students may have some confusion about what "climate" or maybe even "factors" means in this context, but let's suppose the students know what's expected. No messages have been sent to individuals yet. How do they get communicated?

As the students go out the door, Ms. Hunt stops several of them for a private word:

- "Kaneisha, you should do really well on this. You've been reading carefully and taking good notes on each of the last two assignments. I think you're ready to put it all together."
- "John, how much time are you going to put in on this tonight?"
- "Marie, you're taking your book home, aren't you?" [Marie smiles and says, "Sure."] "Uh huh. Right!" [Ms. Hunt purses her lips.]
- "Do the best you can, George. At least read all three chapters."

Ms. Hunt has sent Kaneisha a high, positive-expectation message. She thinks Kaneisha is ready for a good performance that puts it all together.

It's hard to tell what message she has sent to John. If John is a slacker and she has communicated before that she thinks he is, then John may interpret her question to mean, "I don't think you're going to really do this, John." And John may be inclined to conform with that preconception. But maybe she has had a series of conferences with John and done goal setting with him around planning his time use for homework. Perhaps she is reminding him of the agreements he made and getting him to commit to a real number of minutes right now that she'll hold him accountable for the next day. Then the message is quite different from the slacker inference.

It sounds as if Ms. Hunt doubts Marie is going to take her book home. Her "Uh-huh. Right!" may give Marie license to skip the work—because her teacher expects her to.

George is getting a low-expectation message. The teacher will be content if he at least plows his way through the words in the book, but she doesn't expect him to be able to think through the question. At best, George will plow but not likely think. The expectation is no higher than getting through the three chapters. The expectation is actually less, since the teacher has said, "At least try," which implies that he won't be able to do it but that "trying" a little is expected.

These examples illustrate how the choice of words combined with body language communicates inner beliefs (the confidence we have) about what students can do and about what they will do on a given assignment. In addition to individual comments at the door and elsewhere, teachers sometimes communicate to a whole class at once about an assignment. If Ms. Hunt says, "Now this will be hard; it requires thinking back to all the other chapters we read too. But I know you can do it if you take your time and use your notes from our previous discussions," she is sending a high, positive-expectation message to the whole class at once. Acknowledging the difficulty of the task validates students' exerting effort. It's not supposed to be easy. (Calling a task easy is a no-win message. If it turns out to be easy, the student has no sense of accomplishment. Anyone could have done it. If children struggle and it was supposed to be easy, they may conclude they are stupid or not good enough at it; otherwise it would be easy.)

In addition to verbal messages to individuals and whole class groups, there are whole class messages that may be embedded in written direction sheets to students about assignments: "This problem set is important and is a good chance to raise your grade. Use this opportunity well."

We hope readers will listen to themselves during these daily and repeated moments when they communicate assignments and tasks to students—and especially attend to the side comments they make to individuals right after giving the task and the directions. In addition, we urge readers to seize these opportunities to send deliberately positive and encouraging messages to individuals who may be low performing, low motivation, and low confidence: "Charlene, this is a good one for you to show your stuff on. Now come on, dig in tonight. You've got a great brain, and I want to see you use it as a leader in tomorrow's discussion!"

## Summarizing Arenas and Their Significance

These ten arenas of classroom life represent innumerable opportunities for us to positively influence students' confidence in their capacity. They serve as specific tools for building life-liberating beliefs (see Table 12.2). The tools are subtle, simultaneous, and ever present. The bottom line is that we need to be aware of how we are using them, for the

**Table 12.2. Five Beliefs That Limit or Liberate Learning**

| Life-Limiting Beliefs | Life-Liberating Beliefs |
| --- | --- |
| • Mistakes are a sign of weakness. | • Mistakes help one learn. |
| • Speed is what counts. Faster is smarter. | • You are not supposed to understand everything the first time around. Care, perseverance, and craftsmanship are what count. |
| • Good students can do it by themselves. Competition is necessary to bring out the best in students. | • Good students work together with others and solicit help and lots of feedback on their work. |
| • Inborn intelligence is the main determinant of success. | • Consistent effort and effective strategies are the main determinants of success. |
| • Only the few bright can achieve at a high level. | • Everyone, not just the fastest and most competent, is capable of high achievement. |

*Source:* Saphier and D'Auria (1993).

consequences on student motivation and achievement are enormous. Our patterns of behavior should be consistent with the belief that all students can learn rigorous academic material at high standards. What we say regarding "all students can learn" must be congruent with what we do. If we seek to overcome the constricting grip of bright-slow class prejudice, which researchers are saying is an unfair restriction on the equality of educational opportunity offered to students, then we will consciously monitor any tendency toward the unholy thirteen behaviors Cooper identified. We will seize the opportunities present in each of these arenas to send high, positive-expectations messages to all students, press all students toward excellence, and give students lots of opportunities to exceed our expectations. Through these arenas, we can consistently send messages to students about what is important, that we believe they can do it through their effort and ours, and that we won't give up on them.

So what about getting students to believe that their effort really can and does make a difference? Earlier in the chapter, we summarized attribution theory as the study of the explanations people give themselves to explain their successes or failures. We also summarized Dweck's research suggesting that children have a tendency to believe that it is either their innate ability or their effort that primarily accounts for their success or lack thereof. In the arenas section of this chapter, we suggested that we seize opportunities in these everyday interactions with students to convince them that they have more than enough mental capacity to do high-quality work. We have attempted to make a strong case that teachers must do everything possible to convince students that each one of them has the capacity to do rigorous work to high standards and that it is investment of their effective effort (working hard and acquiring strategies) that will enable them to see that for themselves. This brings us to attribution retraining.

## Attribution Retraining and Teaching Effective Effort

Attribution retraining means getting students to change their attributions of success and failure away from factors over which they have little immediate control (luck, task difficulty, and innate ability) to the factor over which they have the greatest control: effort. Teaching effective effort means making students aware that effective effort (effort that results in achievement of a goal) is a combination of working hard and applying effective strategies. Emphasizing the strategy component with students is essential to giving them an explanation other than lack of ability when they are working hard and aren't yet seeing progress.

Teachers need to make attributions and effective effort explicit topics of conversation with students so that they are aware of the variety of ways that people explain their successes and lack thereof. We need to find out what the students believe about what makes someone successful and help them to see connections between their accomplishments and the effort they have invested to achieve them. A number of teachers in our courses have taught attribution theory directly to their students as a way to get the conversation started.

Students need to be taught what effective effort means and how to employ all six of its attributes (see Exhibit 12.2):

1. Time: Do I put in sufficient time to get the job done?

Although time alone is far from sufficient to accomplish difficult academic tasks, it is absolutely required. And it is true that some students truly don't realize that several hours of outlining, drafting, and editing may be required to make an essay meet a high standard.

2. Focus: Am I working efficiently and without distraction?

Work time should be efficient and low in distraction. There is plenty of latitude for individual style in defining focus. Some students don't find music, even loud music, distracting while they work. In fact for some it is a way of blocking out other environmental distractions. But talking to friends about the upcoming weekend or watching TV while doing academic work is not compatible with the concept of focus.

3. Resourcefulness: Do I reach out for help and know where to go for it?

Students need to know to reach beyond themselves for help, know how to do so, and where to go. Sources of help may be other people (study buddies, homework help centers, relatives) or other sources (reference books, online services, reference librarians).

**Exhibit 12.2. Effective Effort: What Does it Require?**

| It's not enough just to "try hard." By effort we mean these six things: | |
|---|---|
| 1. Time | An understanding of how much time it takes to do the job well. |
| 2. Focus | No TV or other distractions; concentrate only on the work! |
| 3. Strategies | If one approach isn't working, keep trying different ways until you find one that works. |
| 4. Resourcefulness | Knowing where to go and whom to ask for help when you're really stuck. |
| 5. Use of Feedback | Looking carefully at responses to your work so you know exactly what to fix. |
| 6. Commitment | Being determined to finish and do the very best work. |

*Source:* Based on a model developed by Jeff Howard.

4.  Strategies: What strategies am I using or could I use? Do I have alternatives when a strategy isn't working?

    Students need to know and use appropriate strategies to deal with academic tasks. A voluminous literature confirms that students do significantly better in academic work when their teachers explicitly teach them strategies for improving reading comprehension, organizing and revising writing, and reviewing, remembering, and summarizing (Paris, Wasik, and Turner, 1991; Pressley, Borkowski, and Schneider, 1987).

5.  Use of feedback: How or where can I get feedback on how I am doing? What does the feedback tell me about how to improve my performance?

    Good students listen to and look carefully at the feedback they get from teachers and use it to improve their performance.

6.  Commitment: When something is difficult, do I stick with it? Do I really try hard?

    Effective effort is grounded in will. You have to want to accomplish something to put out the effort and organize yourself to complete a tough learning task. You don't have to like it, but you do have to be committed to trying hard.

Some version of Exhibit 12.3 might be given to students periodically to reflect on a project they are submitting, or an exam they are preparing for, to keep in their minds what it means to invest effective effort.

Each of these attributes of effective effort has implications for things we can do to support students in investing their effort effectively:

- *Time:* It is worth discussing with students and coming to agreement about how much

**Exhibit 12.3.  Student Effort Checklist**

| Student Effort Checklist | ✓ |
|---|---|
| 1. Did I put in sufficient time to get the job done? | |
| 2. Did I focus efficiently and without distraction? | |
| 3. Did I reach out for help and know where to go for it? | |
| 4. Did I use different strategies and alternatives? | |
| 5. Did I get and use feedback during my work? | |
| 6. Did I stick with it even when it was hard? | |

time they should expect to spend on an academic assignment to meet high standards.

- *Focus:* Students have to have a clear idea of what the focus is, that is, the precise instructional objective. We need to create clear images for students of the performances they should be shooting for, and that means more than just telling the objective; it means showing them what meeting it would look like (communicating criteria for success and sharing exemplars where feasible). Focus also means eliminating distractions when studying.

- *Resourcefulness:* This means teaching students directly what resources are and how to use them. In a fourth-grade class one of us visited, groups of children were giving reports on Native American tribes. It could have been any fourth grade in America: models of hogans, teepees, longhouses, except for one thing. Every group started its report with a child's recounting where he or she had gotten the information, what the obstacles were, and how the child had overcome them. This was a teacher who had taught the students how to use outside help to get information, and who expected them to do so at every opportunity.

- *Strategies:* It is our responsibility to teach students how to use learning strategies. Regardless of the content area and grade levels we teach, we all need to be teachers of reading, writing, thinking, and reasoning strategies as they are requisite and transferable skills for learning in all disciplines. Students need to be taught how to use strategies such as these for doing academic work:

  o Graphic organizers, used for planning, note taking, and summarizing
  o Periodic summarizing, used to support retention and deepen understanding while reading, watching, or listening to information
  o Note taking to bring meaning to—and deepen understanding of—what the notes say
  o SQ3R (Survey, Question, Read, Recite, Respond), used to preview a reading to support comprehension
  o Mnemonic keyword technique, for memorizing

  We must also help students see how strategies can be transferred to other academic tasks. Otherwise, students may not think to use the strategies beyond the specific context in which we teach them. The how-tos of "teaching for transfer" are explained in Chapter Ten.

  Students should participate in constructing strategy lists ("Ways to Remember Something," "Effective Ways to Study for a Test," "Strategies for Getting Help") that hang on the classroom wall or go into their note-

books for future reference. Finally, students should have practice naming and evaluating the effectiveness of the strategies they have used, and identifying alternatives where necessary. David Perkins refers to this as developing reflective intelligence and proposes that it accounts for a significant dimension of a person's intelligent behavior (Perkins, 1995).

- *Use of feedback and praise:* Earlier in this chapter we discussed responding to student performance using feedback and praise among other types of responses. To use feedback and praise as a vehicle for attribution retraining we need to intentionally embed specific effort and ability attributions in our responses: "You've proven in your work all week that you have the brain power to do some very challenging problems. There must be some strategy you aren't using yet that would be the breakthrough on these. Let's look at how you are approaching them and do some brainstorming." "You really concentrated on organizing your ideas and taking time to plan before you wrote your final piece. Nice job!" "You stuck with the task—you never gave up—and now look at what you've accomplished." "When you saw that your first strategy wasn't working, you took another approach; and now look at the progress you've made on this."

- *Commitment:* To help students understand the importance of commitment and to mobilize them to make it, we need to teach them how to set goals that are specific, challenging, attainable, written, and revisited. (See Chapter Ten, "Principles of Learning.") Goal setting and having students review their goals frequently gives students the tools for making commitments that go beyond hopes and empty promises. It also causes students to self-evaluate and brings them in frequent contact with their teachers to share the evaluation and the data on which the goal was based.

Attribution retraining requires us to monitor our language and replace statements like "Good luck" with effort-oriented statements such as, "Give it everything you've got," and comments like, "Don't worry; it's easy," with statements like, "This is really challenging work. It's hard stuff, so give it your undivided attention, stick with it, recall all of the strategies you have for [whatever is involved], and you will get it." And when students have done very well, instead of saying, "You are so smart!" we need to say something like, "You have obviously really applied yourself, and your effort has paid off."

We need to talk with students about the life-limiting and life-liberating beliefs (see Table 12.2) and consider how classrooms and schools are designed to reinforce the life-liberating beliefs. (See Chapter Fourteen, "Classroom Climate.")

Finally, we might give students a tool for self-assessing their effort (separate from their achievement) and ask them to score themselves at the end of certain assignments or projects. Marzano, Pickering, and Pollock (2001) offer the rubrics in Exhibit 12.4, which pairs achievement with effort: the student scores both. Presumably, if one kept a running record of student achievement and effort using these rubrics, students themselves could draw conclusions about the connection between the two. This effort rubric focuses only on continuing to work or "pushing myself." An effort rubric could also include "using feedback" and "trying other strategies."

Here are some additional suggestions for teaching and reinforcing the value of effective effort, compiled by Ann Stern, a senior consultant at RBT:

- Tell personal stories of your effective effort.
- Ask students to recall times they succeeded because they didn't give up.
- Search for stories and examples of inspirational people students look up to who have achieved and excelled because of their persistence, determination, and hard work.
- Use literature. Share books about effort and where the central characters don't give up.
- Make effective effort a theme in your team or school.
- Recognize and celebrate effort: "You have really developed your skill in creating vivid images in your writing. All of your revision efforts paid off. This piece should be published!"
- Praise effort, not intelligence, in your choice of language.
- Prior to doing a task, have students identify what strategies they will use to be successful. Collect them on charts. Post and add to these charts as time and tasks go on.
- When students succeed, ask them to identify what accounted for their success, and hold them accountable for figuring out how their effort played a role.
- Saturate your environment with efficacy messages.
- Have students use the effort and achievement rubric in Exhibit 12.4 to score themselves and track the relationship between their effort and achievement.
- When a student says, "This is easy," reply: "It wasn't always easy. What did you do to get smart at it?"
- Have students visualize the actual physical moves (follow guidelines of mental imagery)

**Exhibit 12.4. Effective Effort Rubrics**

Scale: 4 = excellent; 3 = good; 2 = needs improvement; 1 = unacceptable

### A: Effort Rubric

4 I worked on the task until it was completed. I pushed myself to continue working on the task even when difficulties arose or a solution was not immediately evident. I viewed difficulties that arose as opportunities to strengthen my understanding.

3 I worked on the task until it was completed. I pushed myself to continue working on the task even when difficulties arose or a solution was not immediately evident.

2 I put some effort into the task, but stopped working when difficulties arose.

1 I put very little effort into the task.

### B: Achievement Rubric

4 I exceeded the objectives of the task or lesson.

3 I met the objectives of the task or lesson.

2 I met a few of the objectives of the task or lesson, but did not meet others.

1 I did not meet the objectives of the task or lesson.

| Student | Assignment | Effort Rubric | Achievement Rubric |
|---------|-----------|---------------|--------------------|
| Fri., Oct. 22 | Homework—5-paragraph essay re: *Animal Farm* | 4 | 4 |
| Wed., Oct. 27 | In-class essay re: allegory | 4 | 3 |
| Thurs., Oct. 28 | Pop quiz | 3 | 3 |

*Source:* Reprinted with permission from Marzano, Pickering, and Polluck (2001).

for arranging time and place for effective practice or study.

# Coda

The Expectations area of performance is an example of the way in which teaching is more a calling than a job. If successful teaching involves getting students to be believers in themselves, then that is a way in which this business resembles the clergy more than a craft. The thrust of this whole chapter is that we need to behave as if we believe that almost all students can learn rigorous material at high standards.

Different though we may be in our genetic endowment, if we could all do the incredibly complicated analytical task of learning to speak and communicate by age three, then we all have enough intelligence to do academic material well— that is, if we exert enough effective effort. The key word here is *effective.* Just exerting more effort—

harder or longer—is no guarantee of success for a struggling student.

Having completed four decades of desegregation, we are faced nonetheless with dramatic underachievement among blacks, Hispanics, and other people of color in our society. Communicating positive expectations and dissolving our stereotypes—perhaps even their stereotypes of themselves (Howard and Hammond, 1985)—is especially important. The roots of what people will do are planted firmly in their beliefs about what they *can* do. What are we as educators doing to help students, especially students of color, become believers in themselves as achievers? Avoiding the Pygmalion behaviors is a good start, but what's next? A steady stream of authors and researchers are telling us that new curricula and new tougher standards are not enough. "First, without a doubt, the indispensable characteristic of successful teachers in low-income-area schools is a positive attitude. It is not enough for a teacher to use the right words. The critical question is, what implicit and explicit messages are students getting from the teacher about their ability to learn?" (Frick, 1987). The more teachers can press for and attribute success to ability and effort as students go through school (rather than luck or easy work), the more success we will have with students of color—in fact, with all students. "If you have a C average or below, you should spend three hours studying for this test" means, "That's what it will take to get an A, and you can do it." This conviction about student capacity makes it incumbent on teachers to teach students *how* to exert effective effort; many come not knowing how to do so. That adds a new dimension to the job of teaching.

Maybe each school needs a person for shepherding that new job, a person in charge of "exceeding expectations," someone who shakes us up and goes around periodically reminding us to

reexamine what we are expecting and demanding of students in the way of performance. Perhaps that will be one effect of this chapter on readers. In the end, the hope and the promise of this area of performance is that it will elicit better performance from students and give them fairer and more equal treatment from us.

## Beyond the Skillful Teacher

In addition to individual teacher behaviors in the ten arenas, we need to look at the institutional structures of the school or the team or department. The three key messages show up here too, and schools that want to convince students they believe in them have available after-school help centers and homework clubs; online help services; extended schedules for middle and high school courses so students have extra time to finish the course requirements and the standards are not watered down; volunteer tutors; Title 1 funding reallocated from pull-out programs to after-school and weekend classes; alliances with community agencies to provide tutoring and support activities; and outreach to parents and families to ensure they understand why extra time is needed for study and mastery. In many poor communities, a major obstacle to motivation for students, especially high school students, is the absence of hope, the absence of faith that doing well in school would give them a chance at a better life. These students believe there is no payoff in store for investing in effective effort. The competencies they would gain from better school achievement are viewed as irrelevant to having a better life.

Such students have scant role models of successful people using their education to better themselves and their families, role models who used their skills to rise above damage and poverty. Schools that deal effectively with this situation have curricula and programs that bring students physically out of the school into the workplace where they can meet role models and mentors who look like them. A fully successful school in these circumstances has alliances with the community (churches, businesses, clubs, nongovernmental organizations, social service agencies) and uses all the resources it can muster to put social capital at the disposal of the neediest youngsters. Our society owes them that. Our democracy owes them that.

The peer culture also exerts a huge influence on students' willingness to commit themselves to academic learning. Jackson (2003) cites schools and programs that create "academic microcultures" and support children to develop a "student identity," that is, they see themselves as students and permit themselves to be seen by others as committed students. It is accepted, even cool, to be working on academic improvement of oneself. Sad to say, in most American city high schools, this student culture is rare. Whereas individual teachers can work on such cultures within the four walls of their classrooms, the job, especially in American inner cities and among the rural poor, is to build such cultures schoolwide. A book on the "how-tos" of this job building academic microcultures among students would examine the reward system of the school, extracurricular programs, and many other aspects of the social architecture of the institution.

To check your knowledge about Expectations see the quiz on our Web site at **www.RBTeach.com/ rbteach/quiz/expectations.html.**

## Source Materials on Expectations

Bellon, J., Bellon, E. C., and Blank, M. A. *Teaching from a Research Knowledge Base.* New York: Macmillan, 1992.

Bennett, N. "Research on Teaching: A Dream, a Belief and a Model." *Journal of Education,* 1978, *160,* 5–37.

Black, P., Harrison, C., Lee, C., Marshall, B., and Wiliam, D. *Assessment for Learning.* New York: Open University Press, 2003.

Blank, M. *Teaching Learning in the Preschool: A Dialogue Approach.* Columbus, Ohio: Merrill, 1973.

Brookover, W. B., and others. "Elementary School Social Climate and School Advancement." *AERA Journal,* 1978, *15,* 301–318.

Brophy, J. "Teacher Praise: A Functional Analysis." *Review of Education Research,* 1981, *5,* 5–32. Reprinted with permission of the publisher. © 1981 by the American Educational Research Association.

Cooper, H. M. "Pygmalion Grows Up: A Model for Teacher Expectations, Communication and Performance Influence." *Review of Educational Research,* 1979, *49,* 389–410. Reprinted by permission of the publisher. © 1979 by the American Education Research Association.

Costa, A. L. *Developing Minds.* Alexandria, Va.: Association for Supervision and Curriculum Development, 1985.

Covington, M. V. "The Self-Worth Theory of Achievement Motivation: Findings and Implications." *Elementary School Journal,* 1984, *85,* 5–20.

Cremin, L. A. *The Transformation of the School.* New York: Vintage Books, 1964.

Currie, J. "Early Childhood Intervention Programs: What Do We Know?" Brookings Roundtable on Children, Washington, D.C., 2000.

Dembo, M. H., and Gibson, S. "Teachers' Sense of Efficacy: An Important Factor in School Improvement." *Elementary School Journal,* 1985, *86,* 173–184.

Devaney, K. *The Lead Teacher: Ways to Begin.* New York: Carnegie Forum on Education and the Economy, 1987.

DuFour, R., Eaker, R., Karhanek, G., and DuFour, R. *Whatever It Takes.* Bloomington, Ind.: National Educational Services, 2004.

Dunkin, M. J., and Biddle, B. J. *The Study of Teaching.* New York: Holt, 1974.

Dweck, C. S. "Caution: Praise Can Be Dangerous." *American Educator,* 1999, *23,* 4–9.

Dweck, C. S. "Messages That Motivate: How Praise Molds Students' Beliefs, Motivation and Performance (in Surprising Ways)." In J. Aronson (ed.), *Improving Academic Achievement.* Orlando, Fla.: Academic Press, 2002.

Dweck, C. S. "Self-Theories and Goals: Their Role in Motivation, Personality, and Development." In R. Dienstlier (ed.), *Nebraska Symposium on Motivation.* Lincoln: University of Nebraska Press, 1991.

Dweck, C. S. *Self-Theories: Their Role in Motivation, Personality and Development.* Philadelphia: Taylor and Francis/Psychology Press, 1999.

Dweck, C. S. "The Role of Expectations and Attributions in the Alleviation of Learned Helplessness." *Journal of Personality and Social Psychology,* 1975, *31,* 674–685.

Fisher, C. and others. "Teaching Behaviors, Academic Learning Time, and Student Achievement: An Overview." *Journal of Classroom Interaction,* 1978, *17*(1), 2–15.

Fordham, S., and Ogbu, J. U. "Black Students' School Success: Coping with the Burden of 'Acting White.'" *Urban Review,* 1986, *18,* 176–206.

Frick, R. "Academic Red Shirting Two Years Later: The Lessons Learned." *Education Week,* Jan. 28, 1987, p. 20.

Gamoran, A. "Is Ability Grouping Equitable?" *Educational Leadership,* 1992, *50,* 11–17.

Good, T. "Classroom Expectations in Pupil-Teacher Interactions." In J. McMillan (ed.), *The Social Psychology of School Learning.* Orlando, Fla.: Academic Press, 1980.

Good, T. L., and Brophy, J. E. *Looking in Classrooms.* (8th ed.) Reading, Mass.: Addison-Wesley, 2000.

Graham, S. "Teacher Feelings and Student Thoughts: An Attributional Approach to Affect in the Classroom." *Elementary School Journal,* 1985, *85,* 91–104.

Graham, S., and Barker, G. "The Down Side of Help: An Attributional-Development Analysis of Helping Behavior as a Low-Ability Cue." *Journal of Educational Psychology,* 1990, *82*(1), 7–14.

Green, N. S., and Manke, M. P. "Good Women and Old Stereotypes: Retired Teachers Talk About Teaching." In P. B. Joseph and G. E. Burnaford (eds.), *Images of Schoolteachers in America.* Mahwah, N.J.: Erlbaum, 2001.

Hawley, W., and Rosenholtz, S., "Good Schools: What Research Says About Improving Student Achievement." *Peabody Journal of Education,* 1984, *61*(4), iii–vi, 1–178.

Henderlong, J., and Lepper, M. "The Effects of Praise on Children's Intrinsic Motivation: A Review and Synthesis." *Psychological Bulletin,* 2002, *128,* 774–795.

Hopfenberg, W. S., and Levin, H. *The Accelerated Schools Resource Guide.* San Francisco: Jossey-Bass, 1993.

Howard, J. *The Social Construction of Intelligence.* Lexington, Mass.: Efficacy Institute, 1990.

Howard, J. "You Can't Get There from Here: The Need for a New Logic in Education Reform." *Daedelus,* 1995, *124*(4), 85–92.

Howard, J., and Hammond, R. "Rumors of Inferiority." *New Republic,* Sept. 9, 1985, pp. 17–21.

Howe, M. J. "Prodigies and Creativity." In R. J. Sternberg (ed.), *Handbook of Creativity.* Cambridge: Cambridge University Press, 1999.

Hunter, M. "Improving the Quality of Instruction." Paper presented at Association for Supervision and Curriculum Development Conference, Detroit, March 1977.

Hunter, M. *Mastery Teaching.* El Segundo, Calif.: TIP Publications, 1982.

Jackson, B. D. "Education Reform as if Student Agency Mattered: Academic Microcultures and Student Identity." *Kappan,* Apr. 2003, pp. 578–585.

Johnson, S. M., and Birkeland, S. E. "Pursuing 'a Sense of Success': New Teachers Explain Their Career Decisions." Cambridge, Mass.: Project on the Next Generation of Teachers, Harvard Graduate School of Education, Oct. 2002.

Kamis, M., and Dweck, C. S. "Person vs. Process Praise and Criticism: Implications for Contingent Self-Worth and Coping." *Developmental Psychology, 35,* 835–847.

Keene, E. O., and Zimmerman, S. *Mosaic of Thought: Teaching Comprehension in a Reader's Workshop.* Portsmouth, N.H.: Heinemann, 1997.

Levin, T., and Long, R. In J. Bellon, E. C. Bellon, and M. A. Blank (eds.), *Teaching from a Research Knowledge Base.* New York: Macmillan, 1992, pp. 277–279.

Marzano, R. J., Pickering, D. J., and Polluck, J. E. *Classroom Instruction That Works: Research-Based Strategies for Increasing Student Achievement.* Alexandria, Va.: ASCD, 2001.

Means, V., Moore, J. W., Gagne, E., and Hauck, W. E. "The Interactive Effects of Consonant and Dissonant Teacher Expectancy and Feedback Communication on Student Performance in a Natural School Setting." *AERA Journal,* 1979, *16,* 367–374.

Nicholls, J. G. "The Development of the Concepts of Effort and Ability, Perception of Academic Attainment, and the Understanding That Difficult Tasks Require More Ability." *Child Development,* 1978, *49,* 800–814.

Nicholls, J. G., and Burton, J. T. "Motivation and Equality." *Elementary School Journal,* 1982, *82,* 367–378.

Oakes, J. *Keeping Track: How Schools Structure Inequality.* New Haven, Conn.: Yale University Press, 1985.

Oakes, J. "Two Cities Tracing and Within-School Segregation." *Teachers College Record,* 1995, *96,* 681–690.

Palincsar, A. S., and Brown, A. L. "Reciprocal Teaching of Comprehension-Fostering and Comprehension-Monitoring Activities." *Cognition and Instruction,* 1984, *1,* 117–175.

Paris, S., Wasik, B., and Turner, J. "The Development of Strategic Readers." In R. Barr, M. Kamil, P. Modenthal, and P. D. Pearson (eds.), *Handbook of Reading Research.* New York: Longman, 1991.

Perkins, D. *Outsmarting I.Q.* New York: Free Press, 1995.

Pressley, M., Borkowski, J., and Schneider, W. "Cognitive Strategies: Good Strategy Users Coordinate Metacognition and Knowledge." In R. Vasta and G. Whitehurst (eds.), *Annals of Child Development.* Greenwich, Conn.: JAI, 1987.

Resnick, L. "From Aptitude to Effort: A New Foundation for Our Schools." *Daedelus,* 1995, *124*(4), 55–62.

Rist, R. C. "Student Social Class and Teacher Expectations: A Self-Fulfilling Prophecy in Ghetto Education." *Harvard Educational Review,* 1970, *40,* 411–451.

Rosenholtz, S. J., and Simpson, C. "The Formation of Ability Conceptions: Developmental Trend of Social Construction." *Review of Educational Research,* 1984, *54,* 31–63.

Rosenthal, R., and Jacobson, L. *Pygmalion in the Classroom.* New York: Holt, 1968.

Rowe, M. B. "Wait Time: Slowing Down May Be a Way of Speeding Up." *American Educator,* 1987, *11*(1), 38-43, 47.

Saphier, J., and D'Auria, J. *How to Bring Vision to School Improvement.* Carlisle, Mass.: Research for Better Teaching, 1993.

Scott, D., Stone, B., and Dinham, S. "'I Love Teaching But . . . ' International Patterns of Teacher Discontent." *Education Policy Analysis Archives*, 2001, *9*(28). www.http:/epaa.asu.edui/ep-aa/v9n28.html.

Simonton, D. *Origins of Genius: Darwinian Perspective.* New York: Oxford University Press, 1999.

Slavin, R. "Ability Grouping: On the Wrong Track." *College Board Review*, 1993, no. 168, pp. 11–17.

Slavin, R. "Synthesis of Research on Grouping in Elementary and Secondary Schools." *Educational Leadership*, 1988, *46*, 67–77.

Smith, K. U., and Smith, M. F. *Cybernetic Principles of Learning and Educational Design.* New York: Holt, 1966.

Terman, L. *The Measurement of Intelligence.* Boston: Houghton Mifflin, 1916.

Vacca, R. T., and Vacca, J. L. *Content Area Reading.* (3rd ed.). Glenview, Ill.: Scott Foresman, 1989.

Van Houten, R. *Learning Through Feedback.* New York: Human Services Press, 1980.

Van Houtte, M. "Tracking Effects on School Achievement: A Quantitative Explanation in Terms of the Academic Culture of School Staff." *American Journal of Education,* Aug. 2004, pp. 354–388.

Weiner, B. *Theories of Motivation: From Mechanism to Cognition.* Chicago: Markham, 1972.

Weiner, B. *Achievement Motivation and Attribution Theory.* Morristown, N.J.: General Learning Press, 1974.

Weiner, B. "An Attributional Theory of Achievement Motivation and Emotion." *Psychological Review*, 1985, *92*, 548–573.

Weiner, B. *Human Motivation: Metaphors, Theories and Research.* Thousand Oaks, Calif.: Sage, 1996.

Wiggins, G. *Assessing Student Performance: Exploring the Purpose and Limits of Testing.* San Francisco: Jossey-Bass, 1993.

Writers' Express. *Teacher's Guide to Commenting on Polished Pieces.* Somerville, Mass.: Writers' Express, 2006.

Zimmerman, B. J., and Marinez-Pons, M. "Student Differences in Self-Regulated Learning: Relating Grade, Sex and Giftedness to Self-Efficacy and Strategy Use." *Journal of Educational Psychology*, 1990, *82*, 51–59.

# Appendix

## History of the Idea of "Intelligence" in the United States

Between 1890 and 1920, four historical trends intersected that gave the entity theory of intelligence deep purchase on the American imagination (Figure 12.8). During this period, massive waves of immigration brought new citizens by the millions to our shores. At the same time, the shift from an agrarian to an industrial economy created the needs that industry brings, the need for a stratified workforce: people to sweep the factory floor, people to work the assembly line, foremen to supervise the work, managers to staff and run the operation, capitalists to raise the money and govern the corporation. For the first time in U.S. history, there was a need to sort people for these new jobs, and waves of new people arriving to be sorted.

Coincidentally the science of measuring human behavior was getting a spectacular buy-in across the country as Frederick Winslow Taylor and scores of disciples were hired to study workers with a stopwatch and speed up their performance to make them more efficient. Speed and efficiency became valued commodities, and it became commonly accepted that human behavior of all kinds could be measured. This was an era of science and progress and measurement.

At the same time all of this was happening, from Herbert Spencer in Britain came the idea of social Darwinism (that "better people" will rise because they are "better," that is, more fit). And in turn-of-the-century America, the country of Benjamin Franklin, individualism, and self-reliance, it was almost inevitable that the notion of survival of the fittest be applied to competition among individual people as well as the evolution of species (Gould, 1981).

It became accepted that those who are at the top of society must therefore be better, and if we could simply figure out who were the more innately fit, we could sort people and invest resources accordingly. At about this same time, Alfred Binet in France had developed a test intended to diagnose specific aspects of mental functioning in children. This test was imported to the United States by J. M. Cattell and used (or misused according to Binet's description of its intended purpose) as an instrument to sort children based on the measurement of their innate ability, or IQ.

All of these forces together created an assumption, unchallenged for most of the twentieth century, that there was such a thing as intelligence, that it could be measured and quantified, and how much of it one has determines how far one can go. It surely explains how one does in school. Throughout much of the rest of the twentieth century, professionals spent considerable resources trying to design and refine instruments that would effectively measure and determine intellectual fitness (IQ, or

**Figure 12.8. History of the Concept of Intelligence**

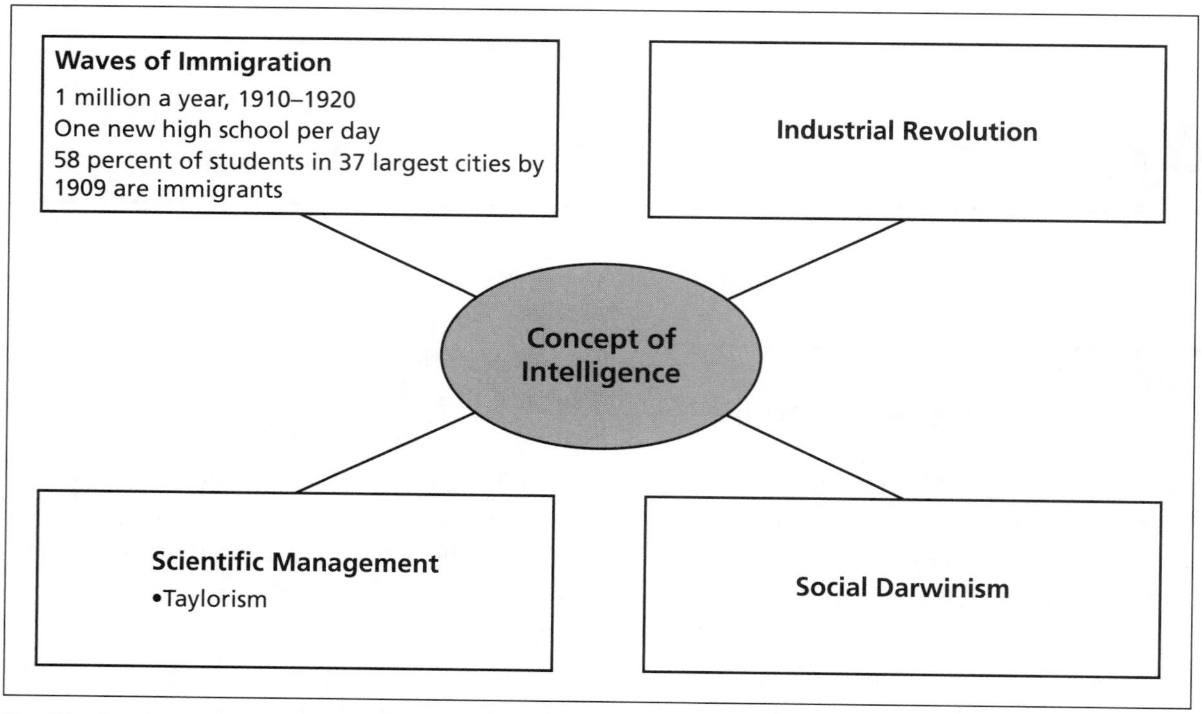

Note: Thanks to Greg Ciardi for first thinking this through and putting together this graphic.

innate ability.) Table 12.3 shows some of the important figures in the development of the entity view of intelligence.

## Challenging the Innate Ability Theory

The notion of innate ability as fixed and deterministic is not an easy or a comfortable one to challenge. Our everyday experience seems to confirm over and over again that all children are not formed with equal ability. Teachers see daily how quickly some learn and how slowly others do. So if one accepts the presumption of the bell curve (unequal distribution of intelligence), differences in observable learning rate or ability to perform skills are seen and explained as a function of natural brightness or gifts or aptitude for learning academic material. The accompanying belief goes something like this: "All children can learn, but they can't all learn as much. All children can learn, but many have limits of how rigorous the material can be. They can all learn more than they know now, but they can't all reach proficiency with high-level literacy and numeracy skills. That's just the way the world is. Why fight it?"

We should fight it because it isn't true; however, not only do most educators believe it at some level, so do students and their parents. Thus, the stereotypes children form of their own ability early in their lives serve as a self-limiting regulator on their expectations, their confidence, and their willingness to work harder or learn to work smarter. Each of us can surely remember a time when something happened or someone said something that convinced us we were inept, unable, or untalented in a certain area of performance. This conclusion, often formed at a young age, led to negative self-image in this area, to avoidance, and to self-perpetuating low performance. If one reaches such a conclusion about dancing or singing, it has some social effects. But if one reaches such a conclusion about academic ability, it can have profound and life altering consequences.

Consider the following information that challenges this model of innate and fixed ability. First, the correlation of measured intelligence with academic grades can be made to account for only 25 percent of variability in performance. ". . . IQ matters. It does not matter overwhelmingly—statistically, a correlation coefficient of .5 only accounts for 25 percent of the range of variation in [academic] performance, leaving 75 percent to be explained by other factors" (Perkins, 1995, p. 61). That figure includes borderline retarded children and children classified as gifted and talented. "If we were to reduce the spread to the normal range in a typical class we would probably be able to account for only 5 to 10 percent of the variability" (Jim Pelligrino, personal communication, June 2002). Hence, 75 to 90 percent of the variation in performance is probably attributable to factors other than measured IQ.

Similar findings apply to comparisons with measured intellectual ability of success in business. In predicting success among CEOs, Sigfried Streufert (1989) found that IQ didn't matter in the average range. From 96 on up, higher IQ is useless as a predictor or a correlate of performance. No matter how high a person's test scores were, it didn't get that person better performance as a manager.

Ironically, Binet himself explicitly took a position in opposition to the innate ability model:

## Table 12.3. Important Figures in Developing the Entity View of Intelligence

### England

1869: Sir Francis Galton (Charles Darwin's nephew) studies men of great reputation and distinction; in 1883 he starts a lab for the physiological measurement of intelligence; in 1886 he conceives of the idea of correlation coefficient; he founded the eugenics movement.

1895: Herbert Spencer argues intelligence is inherited and advocates mental testing.

1901: Karl Pearson, a student of Galton, succeeds in developing factor analysis as statistical technique: the Pearson product-moment correlation coefficient.

### United States

1890: J. McCattell, a student of Galton, coins the term *mental test* and in 1893 advocates these tests be given in schools. He begins publishing results.

1904: Charles Spearman calls the thing being measured "G," for "general intelligence."

1908: Alfred Binet develops a test for identifying learning disabilities.

1911: Edward L. Thorndike posits learning to be comparable to natural selection and thus comparable to neurological response times.

1911: Charles Davenport publishes *Heredity in Relation to Eugenics,* which becomes standard required reading in college courses.

1912: G. Stanley Hall advocates a differentiated curriculum for adolescents of differing ability.

1913: Henry Goddard translates and uses Binet's tests on immigrants at Ellis Island.

1916: Lewis Terman popularizes Binet's test and develops it; the Stanford-Binet is standardized with 100 as the mean; he advocates universal testing.

1917: Robert Yerkes administers intelligence tests to 1.75 million men entering the U.S. Army during World War I and creates the first norms based on a broad database.

1920: Walter Lippmann debates Terman in the *New Republic* magazine.

1925: Carl Campbell Brigham, author of the racist *A Study of American Intelligence,* is hired by College Board to develop the SAT.

1907–1928: Twenty-one states pass eugenics laws.

1. The scores [on the test] are a practical device; they do not buttress any theory of intellect. They do not define anything innate or permanent. We may not designate what they measure as "intelligence" or any other reified entity.

2. The scale is a rough, empirical guide for identifying mildly retarded and learning disabled children who need special help. It is not a device for ranking normal children.

3. Whatever the cause of difficulty in children identified for help, emphasis shall be placed upon improvement through special training. Low scores shall not be used to mark children as innately incapable [Gould, 1981, p. 155].

Intelligence is susceptible to development; with practice and training and especially with appropriate methods of teaching we can augment a child's attention, his memory, his judgment—helping him literally to become more intelligent than he was before. Intelligence was not a fixed amount, or a constant, or some Platonic, bounded essence. Intelligence was "educable." [Binet] advocated a "mental orthopedics" that "teaches children to observe better, to listen better, to retain and to judge better; they gain self-confidence, perseverance, the desire to succeed and all the excellent feelings that accompany action; they should especially be taught to will with more intensity; to will, this is indeed the key to all education" (Gould, 1981).

Second, what goes for "intelligence" can actually be increased. What goes for innate ability is actually the capacity to do certain discrete tasks that intelligence tests measure, and those capacities can be increased. Sustained increases in IQ points that endure long after the training is over result from the best of the twentieth-century programs aimed at increasing cognitive abilities, such as David Perkins's Project Intelligence (2–7 point increase) and the Carolina Abecedarian Project (cited in Neisser and others, 1996), an early childhood intervention program where the enrichment group scored higher than the control group at age two and were still five points higher at age twelve.

In Currie's (2000) review of the research on early childhood intervention programs, she cites the Milwaukee Project, which showed that participants in the program not only raised their IQ scores but maintained their advantage over the control group through the eighth grade. On measures of scholastic success, however, participants scored similarly to the control group. What does this tell us about IQ and achievement? As Currie puts it: "The Milwaukee Project suggests that an exclusive focus on IQ is unwarranted because other factors also contribute to children's success at school and in life" (p. 11).

Measured IQs in the United States have risen nine points per generation since 1932 (Flynn, 1994). The Wechsler and the Stanford-Binet are renormed every ten years, so this increase does not show up in publicly reported results. This suggests that if our grandparents (as children) were given the current IQ tests, they would almost surely perform in the retarded range based on today's scoring guides.

Does this steady advance in IQ scores mean we are actually getting smarter as a nation? What accounts for this rise? Could it be that ever more people go to school for more years and in school one develops skills (like vocabulary) that intelligence tests measure? Whatever accounts for it, one thing is sure: what the tests measure is susceptible to external influences that have led our population to be steadily more proficient at whatever it is the tests are measuring (Berliner and Biddle, 1995).

Third, there is a correlation between school achievement and measured intelligence, but it is the inverse of what the entity (bell curve) theory suggests. In short, considerable evidence suggests that schooling modifies intelligence.

In a study conducted in 1989, Israeli researcher-psychologists Sorel Cahen and Nora Cohen asked, "As you grow from year to year, does your measured intelligence determine your achievement at school, or does what you achieve in school determine your measured intelligence?" In other words, do children have to be intelligent to profit from schooling (as is widely believed in America), or do they have to have schooling to become intelligent? Although Cahen and Cohen used complex statistical methods, their findings were straightforward. They found that school achievement was a major factor in the prediction of intelligence test performance. In contrast, measured intelligence was only a weak predictor of school achievement. Thus, measured intelligence is strongly influenced by the opportunity to learn in school. Over the past fifty years, high-quality public education has been offered to larger and larger numbers of students in the industrialized world, and this fact explains why the average person today is measurably smarter than the average person was in the past. In 1910, only 10 percent of American children even entered high school. Today almost all enter (though nationwide about 80 percent graduate).

Other evidence supports this relationship between school experience and measured IQ. Torsten Husen and Albert Tuijnman (1991), distinguished educational researchers from Sweden and Holland, respectively, examined data from a study originally conducted in Malmo, Sweden, that looked at the IQs of 671 Swedish males over a ten-year period, from childhood to adulthood. Using complex statistical techniques unavailable at the time of the original study, the authors examined whether changes in measured IQ had occurred,

and if so what might explain these changes. Their conclusion was unequivocal: measured IQs had changed for many of the persons studied, and those who had experienced more schooling had also grown more in measured intelligence.

Thus, the characteristic that we call intelligence is not only dependent on inheritance and home background but is also influenced by schooling. Intelligence during the educative years is not a static and immutable characteristic. It appears to be quite dynamic and continues to be affected by environmental factors, particularly by access to high-quality schooling. Husen and Tuijnman concluded, "Schools not only confer knowledge and instrumental qualifications but also train and develop students' intellectual capacity. The results [of this study] suggest . . . that IQ as measured by group intelligence tests is not stable but changes significantly between 10 and 20 years of age. . . . [Apparently] schooling co-varies with and produces positive changes in adult IQ" (p. 22).

American psychologist Stephen Ceci (1991) reported similar findings. As a result of his research, Ceci concluded that the specific skills measured on intelligence tests and the processes underlying intelligence test performance are taught and learned in school. Ceci also estimated that these influences are substantial. A child could lose as many as six IQ points for each year in which he or she misses high-quality education from birth onward.

In brief, schooling matters. Genes and home environment are not the only contributors to intelligence. "A society that chooses to nurture and develop high levels of intelligence among its youth must also provide high-quality education for them. Poor schools, like poor home environments, have negative lasting consequences" (Berliner and Biddle, 1995, p. 49).

Fourth, regarding the popular belief in the heritability of intelligence: "heritability" is a statistical measure of the relation between a given trait and the presence of that same trait in a parent. Steven Ceci noted in a personal communication (2001):

> You can have high heritability [between parents and children, yet] large differences between children. An example from my 1996 book on intelligence, *A Bioecological Treatise on Intellectual Development,* is that the male sons of Japanese immigrants to the United States during the first part of the twentieth century grew, on average, five inches taller than their fathers despite heritability remaining approximately at .9! So heritability says nothing about *malleability* [see Figure 12.9].
>
> All this renders heritability a very tricky and not very useful or practical concept. . . . In my book I cite a famous adoption study that resulted in children's IQs going nearly 22 points higher than those of their biological mothers. Nevertheless the heritability estimate was quite high [between the children and their biological mothers].

Another interesting finding that challenges the belief that most of intelligence is inherited is a finding that the heritability of intelligence between young children and their parents is .45. But when the studies are done of the same children grown into adults and their parents, the heritability correlation is much higher: .70. Intelligence does change when measured over time, and as we get older, measured intelligence gets closer to what our parents scored. Here is one interpretation of how these numbers play out. "Smart" children (who had high IQ scores) born to low-IQ parents get dumber the older they get. Their IQ scores get closer to those of their parents. Therefore, the environment provided by lower-IQ parents drags their children's IQ down. But low-IQ children (who had low IQ scores as youngsters) born to smart parents get

smarter the longer they live. Their IQ scores get closer to those of their parents. Therefore, the environment that higher-IQ parents provide pulls the children's IQ up.

*Nature versus nurture . . . who is winning here?* Fifth, in people regarded as genius, a consistent characteristic is a huge investment of time and effort devoted to their area of interest and expertise. "Genius is 1% inspiration and 99% perspiration," said Thomas Edison. Studies of people of genius performed by Benjamin Bloom in the 1980s and recently by Howard Gardner and also by Michael Howe (2001) all find that geniuses are people who spent incredible amounts of time studying and practicing, literally immersing themselves in their area of expertise. In sports, music, scholarship, and research, this is the story one finds again and again: it's perspiration, not inspiration. These world-class performers were often undistinguished students in their school careers, and their performance in their chosen fields was often judged unpromising by their mentors. But they persevered.

Sixth, children who believe that ability can be increased do significantly better in school. Carol Dweck has shown this conclusively and repeatedly over a decade of research. She calls it the "incremental" view of intelligence, meaning a belief that intelligence can be increased in increments by working hard and working smart.

What all of this evidence suggests is that the variables that appear to have the most significant impact on a person's development and achievement extend well beyond—and are most likely far more significant than—any attempted measurement, perception, or comparison of a person's innate ability. These variables appear to include the quantity and quality of schooling one experiences, the amount and kind of effort one invests, and the belief one holds in the individual's capacity to grow ability itself!

**Figure 12.9.  Japanese Heritability**

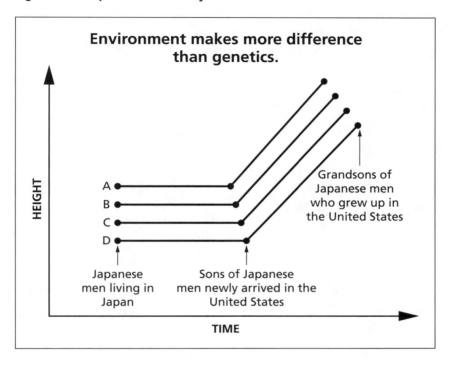

We propose an alternative way of explaining differences in human performance and achievement and will refer to this as the effort-based ability or incrementalist theory.

Jeff Howard has made the case repeatedly (Howard, 1995; Howard and Hammond, 1985) that the deeply ingrained American paradigm that intelligence equals achievement is both wrong and simultaneously the governing principle behind the design of our schools. Lauren Resnick agrees:

> What is the relationship between aptitude and effort? Early in the [twentieth] century we built an education system around the assumption that aptitude is paramount in learning and that it is largely hereditary. The system was oriented toward selection, distinguishing the naturally able from the less able and providing students with programs thought suitable to their talents. In other periods, most notably

during the Great Society reforms, we worked on the compensatory principle, arguing that special effort, by an individual or an institution, could make up for low aptitude. The third possibility—that effort actually creates ability, that people can become smart by working hard at the right kinds of learning tasks—has never been taken seriously in America or indeed in any European society, although it is the guiding assumption of education in societies with a Confucian tradition.

[In such an ability-bound view] students do not try to break through the barrier of low expectations because they, like their teachers and parents, accept the judgment that aptitude matters most and that they do not have the right kinds of aptitude. Not surprisingly, their performance remains low. Children who have not been taught a demanding, challenging, thinking curriculum do not do well on tests of reasoning or problem solving, confirming our original suspicions that they did not have the talent for that kind of thinking. The system is a self-sustaining one in which hidden assumptions are continually reinforced by the inevitable results of practices that are based on those assumptions.

It is not necessary to continue this way. Aptitude is not the only possible basis for organizing schools. Educational institutions could be built around the alternative assumption that effort actually creates ability. Our education system could be designed primarily to foster effort [Resnick, 1995, pp. 55-57].

By contrast, Lewis Terman (1916), dean of psychologists at the time our current educational system was taking shape, wrote: "The children of successful and cultured parents test higher than children from wretched and ignorant homes for the simple reason that their heredity is better" (p. 115).

The notion of effort-based intelligence turns this idea on its head, and in many ways effort-based intelligence is a much better fit with the democratic promise of a free society where education is meant to be the equalizer and schooling is supposed to give every child a chance to make something of himself or herself.

In the United States we don't have a guaranteed right to health care; we don't even have a guaranteed right to clean water. But Americans have a legally guaranteed right to education, no matter what their background. Schools can't offer that right equally to all children if they don't bring effort-based intelligence to personal interactions with children and parents, to teaching, and to an examination of our schoolwide practices.

*Source Materials on Malleable Intelligence*

Berliner, D. C., and Biddle, B. J. *The Manufactured Crisis: Myths, Fraud, and the Attack on America's Public Schools.* Reading, Mass.: Addison-Wesley, 1995.

Black, P., Harrison, C., Lee, C., Marshall, B., and Wiliam, D. *Assessment for Learning.* New York: Open University Press, 2003.

Bloom, B. *Developing Talent in Young People.* New York: Ballantine, 1985.

Cahen, S., and Cohen, N. "Age versus Schooling Effects on Intelligence Development." *Child Development,* 1989, *60,* 1239–1249.

Ceci, S. "How Much Does Schooling Influence General Intelligence and Its Cognitive Components?" *Developmental Psychology,* 1991, *27,* 703–722.

Ceci, S. *On Intelligence: A Bioecological Treatise on Intellectual Development.* Cambridge, Mass.: Harvard University Press, 1996.

Currie, J. "Early Childhood Intervention Programs: What Do We Know?" Brookings Roundtable on Children, Washington, D.C., 2000.

Flynn, J. R. "IQ Gains over Time." In R. J. Sternberg (ed.), *Encyclopedia of Human Intelligence.* New York: Macmillan, 1994.

Gamoran, A. "Alternative Uses of Ability Grouping: Can We Bring High-Quality Instruction to Low-Ability Classes?" Madison, Wis.: Center on Organization and Restructuring of Schools, 1992.

Gould, S. J. *The Mismeasure of Man.* New York: Norton, 1981.

Howard, J. "You Can't Get There from Here: The Need for a New Logic in Education Reform." *Daedelus,* 1995, *124*(4), 85–92.

Howard, J., and Hammond, R. "Rumors of Inferiority." *New Republic,* Sept. 9, 1985, pp. 17–21.

Howe, M. *Genius Explained.* New York: Cambridge University Press, 2001.

Husen, T., and Tuijnman. A. "The Contribution of Formal Schooling to the Increase in Intellectual Capital." *Educational Researcher,* 1991, *20*(7), 17–25,

Marzano, R. J., Pickering, D. J., and Pollock, J. E. *Classroom Instruction That Works.* Alexandria, Va.: ASDC, 2001.

Neisser, U. *The Rising Curve: Long Term Gains in IQ and Related Measures.* Washington, D.C.: American Psychological Association, 1997.

Neisser, U., and others. "Intelligence: Knowns and Unknowns." *American Psychologist,* Feb. 1996, pp. 77–101.

Perkins, D. *Outsmarting I.Q.* New York: Free Press, 1995.

Plomin, R. *Genetics and Experience: The Interplay Between Nature and Nurture.* Thousand Oaks, Calif.: Sage, 1996.

Resnick, L. B. "From Aptitude to Effort: A New Foundation for Our Schools." *Daedelus,* Fall 1995, *124*(4), 55–62. © 1995 by the American Academy of Arts and Sciences. Reprinted by permission from MIT Press Journals.

Sternberg, R. J., Grigorenko, E. L., and Bundy, D. "The Predictive Value of IQ." *Merrill Palmer Quarterly,* 2001, *47,* 1–41.

Streufert, S., and Nogami, G. Y. "Cognitive Style and Complexity: Implications for I/O Psychology." In C. L. Cooper and I. Robinson (eds.), *International Review of Industrial and Organizational Psychology.* London: Wiley, 1989.

Terman, L. *The Measurement of Intelligence.* Boston: Houghton Mifflin, 1916.

# Personal Relationship Building

How do I build good personal relationships with students and make them feel truly known and valued?

Why Good Personal Relations Connect to Student Achievement

Six Key Teacher Traits

*There are no insignificant acts of kindness, no forgotten words of encouragement, no meaningless hugs of congratulations. Long after students have forgotten day to day lessons, they remember who you are, what you stood for, and how you treated them.*

JIM MAHONEY (2003)

The long reach and powerful grasp of caring relationships in schools is well documented in close to seventy years of education research (Ancess, 2003), which suggests a strong association between student-adult relationships and student retention, achievement, and aspirations, especially in an urban context (Stanton-Salazar, 2001; Valenzuela, 1999). Emotional bonds with adults serve as a foundation for the development of intellectual and social competence in students (Newmann, 1993). The bottom line is that when teachers have regard and respect for students and vice versa, learning proceeds better.

Why do good personal relations have a connection to student achievement? What do people do to create these relations? What are the repertoires for developing and maintaining positive teacher-student relationships? These are the questions we explore in this chapter.

## Why Good Personal Relations Connect to Student Achievement

Geneva Gay (2000) writes, "I think interpersonal relations have a tremendous impact on the quality of teaching and learning. Students perform much better in environments where they feel comfortable and valued. Therefore I work hard at creating a classroom environment and ambiance of warmth, support, caring, dignity, and informality. Yet these psychoemotional factors do not distract from the fact that my classes are very demanding intellectually. Students are expected to work hard and at high levels of quality" (p. 197).

Positive teacher-student relationships are important to student achievement because they impact the climate and management of a classroom, they inform instructional design and delivery, and they influence student effort and academic engagement.

## Classroom Climate and Management

A teacher who invests time and energy in building relationships with students signals to them that they are respected and valued as worthwhile individuals, which most often results in students' liking and respecting their teacher. In turn, students will participate and contribute positively to the classroom climate and will be less likely to buck the program or become discipline problems.

In the face of positive relationships, students more readily accept rules, procedures, and disciplinary actions that follow violations of the rules (Marzano, 2003). Students who have neutral or negative relationships with their teachers are less inhibited from misbehavior and more likely to disengage during instruction. In one study of how ethnically diverse high school students who have experienced disciplinary problems explain the causes of conflicts with their teachers, Sheets and Gay (1996, pp. 86–87) note that "the causes of many classroom behaviors labeled and punished as rule infractions are, in fact, problems of students and teachers relating to each other interpersonally." So positive relationships contribute to a climate where there is greater energy available for—and devoted to—learning.

## Instructional Design and Delivery

The better we know our students as individuals, the more information we have with which to make instructional decisions: how to make the content relevant and personally meaningful, how to hook student interest, how to group students for academic tasks, how and when to intervene or offer support, and so on. When these decisions reflect awareness of student interests, background knowledge and experience base, characteristic behaviors, and learning style orientation and preferences, we are most successful in matching the learning experiences to the unique needs of our students. Thus, students have a greater chance of succeeding academically.

## Student Effort and Academic Engagement

Most significant of all is the connection that exists between teacher-student relationships, high expectations, and student achievement. This is where two areas of performance, Expectations and Personal Relationship Building, intersect with and complement one another.

"Adolescents are ready to work and achieve when they know that people care about them, that what they're learning matters, and that they possess the skills necessary to meet a given challenge. . . . Effective middle school teachers . . . recognize that if they do not meet their students' social and emotional needs, they will waste their content-area expertise. Students simply will not achieve academically when their affective needs go unaddressed" (Daniels, 2005, p. 52).

A strong positive relationship says to a student, "I value you and I care," which renders a teacher a significant adult in the student's life and therefore affords the teacher opportunities to demand (and support) more academic rigor of students. The relationship can serve as a vehicle for influencing academic identity, convincing students that they are capable of performing at high levels, and getting seemingly unmotivated students to come to school, stay in school, complete assignments, participate in class, and persist in the face of academic challenges. Teachers can use a relationship "... as leverage to help students transcend difficult and troubling times, develop personal discipline, and reconnect when they are at risk of dropping out" (Ancess, 2003, p. 63).

Hence, we see strong connections between Personal Relationship Building and several other areas of performance, most notably Classroom Climate (affording students a sense of safety, belonging, and willingness to risk), Discipline (and classroom management), Clarity and Learning Experiences, and Expectations (influencing students' willingness to work hard and to see themselves as academically able to achieve high standards). Some suggest that Relationship Building is the keystone to these other very significant areas of teaching performance.

## Six Key Teacher Traits

When students are interviewed about their relationships with teachers, there is a cluster of teacher characteristics or traits and certain classes of teacher behavior students repeatedly mention as important (Ancess, 2003; Johnson, 1976; Cushman, 2003; Figure 13.1). The traits are that teachers:

- Acknowledge them
- Value them
- Respect them

**Figure 13.1. Six Key Teacher Traits for Personal Relationship Building**

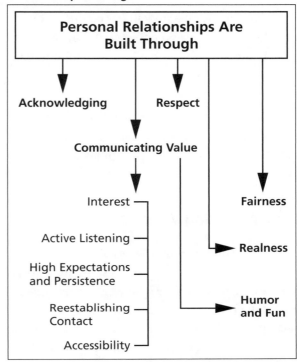

Research for Better Teaching, Inc. • One Acton Place, Acton, MA 01720 • (978)263-9449 • www.RBTeach.com

- Demonstrate fairness
- Exhibit realness
- Are open to humor and having fun

## Acknowledging

Students mention a variety of ways teachers make them feel noticed and acknowledged:

- Greeting students individually as they enter the room, pass in the halls, and so forth
- Welcoming them back when they have been out due to illness
- Making eye contact with them during whole group instruction

- Noticing when they aren't participating and encouraging them to do so
- Noticing when a student has confusion on his or her face and doing something about it
- Using procedures to ensure that all student voices are heard in class discussions

Acknowledging students is perhaps the first stage of another class of behaviors students cite as important in relationships with teachers: being valued.

## Communicating Value

One of our colleagues tells a story about a night she was helping her fifth-grade son with his homework. Right in the middle of reviewing for his social studies test, he put his pencil down and announced, "I had the best day of my whole school career today, Mom!" "Really?" she asked. "What happened that made it so good?" He replied, "Three times today when I was walking in the hall, teachers who have never had me in their classes passed me and said, 'Hi, Jon.' Mom, they knew my name and I never even had any of them as my teachers!"

We believe there are at least five subcategories of things students notice that give them a sense that the teacher values them: showing interest in them, being a good listener, communicating high expectations to them as individuals, reestablishing contact if there has been a reason to discipline a student, and being accessible to them.

### Showing Interest

Showing interest encompasses all the ways in which teachers make students feel important and show interest in them as individuals and as learners.

Showing interest in students as individuals includes:

- Knowing students' names and using them when addressing them in and out of class
- Knowing where they live and what their neighborhood looks like
- Listening carefully and actively learning about their concerns and fears
- Asking about their strengths and interests
- Finding out what their daily schedule looks like in and out of school
- Knowing what their responsibilities are outside school
- Getting to know these things early in the year
- Asking how their day is going
- Inquiring about them if they are out of school or ill

Teachers can make students feel important by:

- Connecting academic work to their interests
- Using their names in instructional examples
- Having brief one-on-one conversations
- Making time to see and be available to them outside class
- Asking what's bothering them when their facial expression says something is wrong
- Attending their extracurricular events to cheer them on

Showing interest in them as learners might include:

- Gathering data from them and teaching them about the types of learners they are
- Finding out what their positive and negative experiences have been thus far in school or in a particular subject area
- Finding out what they already know or have experienced in relation to a topic or skill to be taught

- Interrupting a lesson to check their understanding (frequently and broadly across the class)
- Getting their input at the close of class about what supported their learning and what hindered it and responding to what their responses reveal
- Finding out why a student might not be participating
- Finding out what they think is hard and what's not
- Finding a way to discern if they aren't comfortable participating in a large group
- Finding out how and with whom they are comfortable or uncomfortable working
- Showing interest in the subject matter taught and presenting material to students with passion and enthusiasm
- Making connections to their world so they see reasons why the material is worth learning

In an era when it is vitally important for adolescents to experience school as a stable, predictable, and hospitable place to be, Rodriguez (2005) underscores the importance of these efforts: "Solid teacher-student relationships give urban adolescents an anchor as they learn in an often unpredictable environment. To help students respond to our efforts, teachers must first acknowledge students as persons, legitimize their knowledge and experiences, and engage with them personally and intellectually. In doing so, educators recognize students as whole people and show them that they are valued, thereby relaying a message of hope" (p. 80).

### Being a Good Listener

"She really listens to me" is a common statement students make about teachers they like and respect. "I know my teacher cares because he takes me seriously when I share my personal and academic problems." Students yearn for teachers who are willing to listen and really hear what they have to say (Daniels, 2005). We believe there are at least two dimensions of listening that matter to students: focus and empathy.

Listening with focus means:

- Listening attentively and without interrupting
- Acknowledging (verbally or nonverbally) what is being said
- Inquiring for details rather than making assumptions when information is vague or unclear
- Checking understanding by paraphrasing or summarizing to ensure that we have heard accurately
- Posing reflective questions that invite further thinking or exploration of a topic of interest or concern to a student

Many teachers practice these behaviors naturally and at a less than conscious level in situations that don't involve intense emotion. However, in times of high excitement (enthusiasm, stress, tension, anxiety, frustration, annoyance, distress) on the part of the listener or the speaker, we need to be more conscious of monitoring these behaviors.

Listening with empathy means listening in a way that enables us to understand both the content of what the speaker is saying and the feelings that accompany the content. This is especially critical the more intense the emotional state of the speaker, the listener, or both, or in situations where one's perspective about something is quite different from the other's. Active listening, a core skill taught in communication and conflict management training, is a particular way of listening and responding to another person with the intent of coming to understand the other's point of view.

Active listening involves paraphrasing or summarizing what the speaker has said, and the paraphrase is an acknowledgment, as well as a check for understanding, regarding the content of their remarks and the inferred feeling state of the speaker. It is an attempt to signal to the speaker that he or she has been heard on multiple levels (content and affect). For example, when a student says, "I just can't do this work! These problems are too hard. There is no way I will ever get this done. I don't have enough time. I give up!" an active listener might say, "So you're stuck on these problems [content] and getting really frustrated [feeling]." A student who has come to class late, is without homework regularly, and has been falling asleep in class says in an after-school meeting with the teacher, "I have to drop this class. I have too much work to do; I don't have time to do homework. My boyfriend says I never have time for him. I have to baby-sit my little sister and brother every day 'til my mother gets home at night, and I have a job three nights a week to help pay our rent." The teacher says, "So you have several very significant responsibilities in addition to everything you are expected to do to keep up in school and you are overwhelmed with trying to balance it all." In both instances the teacher as listener is using the paraphrase of content and emotion to ensure that he has accurately understood what is going on for the student before offering suggestions, giving advice, or providing another perspective.

A teacher actively listening communicates concern for the student's personal feeling states and the desire to understand. Although it can be used manipulatively and insincerely, on-target and genuine active listening is the verbal behavioral embodiment of empathy. When combined with accuracy and respect (Egan, 1975), active listening makes children feel understood and cared about (Aspy and Roebuck, 1977; Rosenberg, 1999).

## High Expectations and Persistence

Students who have persistent teachers convey a message something like this: "You wouldn't take the time or exert the energy to push me and persist with me if you didn't think I was a worthwhile person. Especially if you do it with humor and some nurturing and encouragement, I know you value me. I warm to that and feel respected by it." They interpret communicating high expectations to students, holding them accountable, and supporting them in meeting the expectation as the teacher's regarding them as a worthwhile person. High expectations might be communicated in relation to:

- Academic performance
- Work habits
- Interpersonal behavior
- Being an active participant in class
- Showing up and being on time for class
- Taking responsibility
- Assuming leadership roles

That a teacher communicates high expectations constitutes the basis for relationship building. How a teacher does this is the central focus of Chapter Twelve in this book.

Persistence is what we do to "chase" when students aren't living up to expectations or performing up to par, when they are resistant, passive, or practice avoidance behaviors in the face of challenge. In short, when students don't yet see themselves as capable of achieving or measuring up, persistence signals our conviction that they can do it and we won't give up on them.

Persistence might show up as:

- Finding a student in the halls and reminding him he needs to see you

- Making extra time to work or be with a student
- Sticking with a student and explaining until he gets it
- Finding three more ways to explain something when the first three didn't work
- Wake-up calls to a student who is chronically late to school

Persistence and support are the left and right hands of effectively communicating expectations.

### Reestablishing Contact

When a teacher strongly reprimands a student (for example, sends the student out of the room) or carries out some high-voltage disciplinary move ("Stop that right now! You cannot destroy someone else's work. If you can't help him rebuild it, this area is closed to you for the day"), his or her relationship with that student may be under a cloud of tension (as it should be). After such incidents, the teacher who keeps good relationships looks to interact in a positive, personal way with the student around some other context. There is no apology in the teacher move or any implied backing down from the firmness of the previous move. It's simply a way of saying, "Okay, let's get in touch again. I still value you as a person." This is reestablishing contact: conveying the message that while the behavior was unacceptable, the teacher is not carrying a grudge and the relationship remains intact. It removes the tension between the teacher and student and gives the student an emotional entry back into the flow of activities.

### Being Accessible

Being accessible means making time available for students outside class time. It might be to provide extra academic help to students or support with personal or social issues students want to talk about.

Students notice when teachers are giving up their "own time" (lunch, before and after school, free periods) to be available to them, and they interpret this as a measure of the teacher's commitment to them (Ancess, 2003). And it's not enough just to say to students, "I'm available after class each day for help." Students have to believe we mean it and that coming to us will be a productive and confidence-building experience. Thus, we often have to say it again and again, and sometimes be even a bit more tenacious by requiring some students to show up until they see it is really not a punishment but a service to and for them.

## Respect

"Respect and fairness (equity) are identified as the prerequisites of effective teaching in the eyes of students . . . at all levels of schooling—from elementary to high school" (Stronge, 2002, p. 16). Respect from the student point of view has several faces and has some overlap with acknowledging and valuing them. Here are some examples of how students define respect (Ancess, 2003; Cushman, 2003; Gay, 2000):

- Treat us as valued and capable human beings.
- Give us chances to express our opinions and views without being put down.
- Involve us in decisions that will directly affect us.
- Speak to us with the same courtesy and respect you'd want from us.
- Treat each of us as capable of challenging work.
- Treat us as individuals and care about what's going on for us.
- Appreciate our differences and individual styles.

- Ask for our help or input when our peers are having problems.
- Treat our work and products we produce with care.
- Don't compare us to other students.
- Recognize why we might participate and why we might not. Afford us both options.
- Respond to our inappropriate behavior or unacceptable academic performance without denigrating us.
- Discipline us privately when the need arises.
- Respond to misbehavior at the individual level rather than holding the whole class responsible for the actions of one student or a small group.
- Be honest and matter of fact when rules are broken, and remind us why it matters.
- Remember that we are often insecure, and when we act in unacceptable ways, please be kind and respond with that in mind.
- Treat our mistakes as just that, and help us to learn from them.
- Correct our errors without using put-downs, making us feel dumb, or shaming us.
- Tell us what to do right.
- Try to work out behavior issues with us before calling home.
- Use our time well.
- Be prepared for class or give us something meaningful to do while we wait.
- Know your material, and present it enthusiastically.
- Teach interesting and important material.
- Use curriculum and activities that relate to our interests and strengths.
- Present ideas and activities in ways that we can relate to.
- Remember we need to stretch and talk periodically.

- Show interest in our success, and help us to get what we need from school.
- Display our hard work.
- Give us feedback on our work that shows you really examined it.
- Give us feedback that we can use to improve our performance.
- Follow through on agreements and commitments, and don't betray our confidences.
- Return our assignments in a timely manner.
- Behave in ways you expect us to behave.
- When we tell you things in private, keep them private.
- When we take risks, support us and protect our right to fail.
- Inspire us as a role model of what you expect from us.

It is also interesting to note how often in interview studies students comment on the appearance and dress of teachers they like. Perhaps students take good grooming and neat, clean clothes as a sign of respect and regard.

## Fairness

"Students know that by coming to school they are making a bargain with teachers, and they want it to be a fair one. . . . Whether they are 'hard' or 'easy' teachers, the adults who win students' trust and respect are the ones perceived as scrupulously fair in carrying out this usually unspoken bargain" (Cushman, 2003, p. 24). Fairness seems to be the absolute prerequisite for personal regard. Unless students perceive a teacher as being fair in making decisions that bear on them (making assignments, arbitrating disputes, giving help, choosing teams), they cannot begin to like him or her. On what basis, then, do students determine whether a teacher is fair? Here are examples of what students say (Cushman, 2003; Wubbels in Marzano, 2003; Kobrin, 2004):

- Let us know what to expect from you so we don't get taken by surprise.
- Let us know your plan: share the itinerary, objectives, expectations for work, and criteria by which you will assess our work.
- Tell us how you will grade our work before we do it, and give it to us in writing (in a handout or on the walls).
- Grade us fairly.
- Create reasonable rules, apply them consistently and fairly, and be flexible.
- Treat us consistently but also as individuals.
- Don't play favorites, alienating some of us while being friendly with others.
- Don't favor the students you think will do best.
- Don't make assumptions. Ask questions when there is something you don't understand.
- When there is conflict between two of us [students], be sure you hear both sides of the situation before delivering consequences.
- Let us know when you are displeased with our actions; don't just simmer until you blow up at someone.
- Warn offenders two or three times at most; then impose the consequence.

Students are asking us to keep no secrets about what will be expected of them academically and behaviorally, to inform them ahead of time exactly what we will use as a basis for assessing their performance, to give them feedback based on the established expectations, and to be treated as individuals capable of high performance. At the same time they ask that we monitor and avoid anything that could be construed as preferential or discriminatory treatment.

## Realness

"[Students] want teachers who . . . are willing to talk about their own personal lives and experiences" (Stronge, 2002, p. 15 ).

Because a teacher is in a position of authority, this dimension of relationship building is important to consider. Authority can act as a screen that distances relationships and obscures the humanness of thinking, feeling beings with life histories of experience. When young children address their teacher as "teacher" rather than by name, we get a glimpse of the teacher-as-authority mode. Children begin to see their teacher as real, as a person, only if the teacher lets them.

There are behaviors by which we can reveal aspects of ourselves that allow this image of authority figure to be tempered by images of teacher-as-real-person. Sharing anecdotes with students from our own lives and integrating appropriate personal experiences into explanations and presentations enables students to get to know us as people.

One of the strategies described in Chapter Three is an "I message," a statement a teacher might make to a student or students in response to an inappropriate or off task behavior. In an "I message" (Gordon, 1974), the teacher explicitly states his feelings and the behavior or circumstance that made him feel that way. When there exists a relationship of regard and respect, "I messages" can be another way to let students see their teacher as a person with feelings. Gordon reports numerous cases of children who, when confronted by "I messages," change their disruptive behavior: children who had no idea their behavior was affecting their teacher adversely.

## Humor and Fun

William Glasser (1998), says humor is a form of caring and that the need to have fun is one of the five basic human needs. Teachers need not be comedians, but those who respond openly to humorous moments or who can kid with students seem to strike particularly responsive chords. Students talk about liking teachers who are happy and smile a lot, have a great sense of humor, tell funny stories, can laugh at themselves, and can joke around and laugh when a student makes a joke that is funny, or when something genuinely humorous happens in class. In other words, they want to know that we know how to have fun and can enjoy doing that with them.

## Conclusion

The quality of relationships between teachers and students is a deep and constant backdrop to all that is transpiring in classrooms and one well worth examining. In analyzing our own teaching behavior (or observing another's teaching) for these traits, bear in mind that the appropriateness of moves from any trait may vary with the form of instruction or learning environment at any given moment. That these characteristic traits and behaviors are part of who we are with our students is critical; how we play them out is a matter of matching to variables like the age and grade level of our students, their cultural backgrounds and expectations, and ultimately their individual personalities and characteristics as learners.

To check your knowledge about Personal Relationship Building see the quiz on our Web site at **www.RBTeach.com/rbteach/quiz/PRBuilding.html.**

*Source Materials on Personal Relationship Building*

Allender, J. S., Seitchik, M., and Goldstein, D. "Student Involvement and Patterns of Teaching." *Journal of Classroom Interaction*, 1981, *16*, 11–20.

Ancess, J. *Beating the Odds: High Schools as Communities of Commitment.* New York: Teachers College Press, 2003.

Aspy, D., and Roebuck, F. N. *Kids Don't Learn from People They Don't Like.* Amherst, Mass.: Human Resource Development Press, 1977.

Brophy, J. "Teacher Praise: A Functional Analysis." *Review of Educational Research*, 1981, *51*, 5–32.

Brown, L., and Goodall, R. C. "Enhancing Group Climate Through Systematic Utilization of Feedback." *Journal of Classroom Interaction*, 1981, *16*, 21–25.

Cushman, K. *Fires in the Bathroom: Advice for Teachers from High School Students.* New York: New Press, 2003.

Daniels, E. "On the Minds of Middle Schoolers." *Educational Leadership*, 2005, *62*(7), 52–54.

Darling-Hammond, L. *The Right to Learn: A Blueprint for Creating Schools That Work.* San Francisco: Jossey-Bass, 1997.

Egan, G. *The Skilled Helper.* Monterey, Calif.: Brooks/Cole, 1975.

Ferreira, M. M., and Bosworth, K. "Defining Caring Teachers: Adolescents' Perspectives." *Journal of Classroom Interaction*, 2001, *36*(1), 24–30.

Fraser, B. J., and O'Brien, P. "Student and Teacher Perceptions of the Environment of Elementary School Classrooms." *Elementary School Journal*, 1985, *85*, 567–580.

Gay, G. *Culturally Responsive Teaching: Theory, Research and Practice.* New York: Teachers College Press, 2000.

Ginott, H. G. *Between Parent and Child.* New York: Macmillan, 1965.

Glasser, W, and Dotser, K. L. *Choice Theory in the Classroom.* New York: HarperCollins, 1998.

Gordon, T. *Teacher Effectiveness Training.* New York: Wyden Press, 1974.

Johnson, M. S. "I Think My Teacher Is . . ." *Learning*, Feb. 1976, pp. 36–38.

Joos, M. *The Five Clocks.* New York: Harcourt, 1967.

Kobrin, D. *In There with the Kids: Crafting Lessons That Connect with Students.* Alexandria, Va.: ASCD, 2004.

Lee, V. E., Bryk, A. S., and Smith, J. "The Organization of Effective Secondary Schools." *Review of Research in Education*, 1993, *19*, 171–268.

Mahoney, J. "What Matters: A Classroom Odyssey." *Phi Delta Kappan*, 2003, *85*(3), 235–238.

Marzano, R. J. *Classroom Management That Works: Research-Based Strategies for Every Teacher.* Alexandria, Va.: ASCD, 2003.

Mayeroff, M. *On Caring.* New York: HarperCollins, 1971.

McLaughlin, M. W. "Somebody Knows My Name." *Issues in Restructuring Schools,* 1994, *7,* 9–11.

Meier, D. *The Power of Their Ideas: Lessons for America from a Small School in Harlem.* Boston: Beacon Press, 1995.

Mergendoller, J. R., and Packer, M. J. "Seventh Graders' Conceptions of Teachers: An Interpretive Analysis." *Elementary School Journal,* 1985, *85,* 581–600.

National Research Council Institute of Medicine. *Engaging Schools: Fostering High School Students' Motivation to Learn.* Washington, D.C.: National Academies Press, 2004.

Newmann, F. M. "Director's Overview." *Issues in Restructuring Schools,* 1993, *5,* 2.

Noddings, N. "The Caring Teacher." In V. Richardson (ed.), *Handbook of Research on Teaching.* (4th ed.). Washington, D.C.: AERA, 2001.

Poplin, M., and Weers, J. Institute for Education in Transformation. *Voices from the Inside: A Report on Schooling from Inside the Classroom.* Claremont, Calif.: Claremont Graduate School, 1992.

Rodriguez, L. F. "Yo, Mister!" *Educational Leadership,* 2005, *62*(7), 78–80.

Rogers, V. R. "Laughing with Children." *Educational Leadership,* Apr. 1984, pp. 44–50.

Rosenberg, M. *Nonviolent Communications.* Encinitas, Calif.: Puddledancer Press, 1999.

Sheets, R. H., and Gay, G. "Student Perceptions of Disciplinary Conflict in Ethnically Diverse Classrooms." *NASSP Bulletin,* May 1996, pp. 84–93.

Sizer, T. R., and Faust, N. *The Students Are Watching: Schools and the Moral Contract.* Boston: Beacon Press, 1999.

Stanton-Salazar, R. *Manufacturing Hope and Despair: The School and Kin Support Networks of U.S. Mexican Youth.* New York: Teachers College Press, 2001.

Stronge, J. H. *Qualities of Effective Teachers.* Alexandria, Va.: ASCD, 2002.

Valenzuela, A. *Subtractive Schooling: Issues of Caring in Education of U.S. Mexican Youth.* Albany: State University of New York Press, 1999.

Wentzel, K. R. "Student Motivation in Middle School: The Role of Perceived Pedagogical Caring." *Journal of Educational Psychology,* 1997, *89*(3), 411–419.

# Classroom Climate

The research on classroom climate is thin but clear: thin because the volume of studies is much smaller than in the cognitive areas, clear because the findings are consistent across populations, ages of students, and subjects. Whenever students feel empowerment, acceptance, and safety to take risks and try things that are hard for them, they like school better and learn more (Moos and Moos, 1978; Haertel, Walberg, and Haertel, 1981; Fraser and Fisher, 1983; Fraser, 1986; Fraser, Malone, and Neale, 1989; Nunnery, Butler, and Bhaireddy, 1993).

That sounds like common sense, and it is, but the research in this area is approximately where research on clarity was thirty years ago. At that time, we knew that teachers who were rated as clear on a Likert scale got better results with students. We did not know, however, what they did in their practice to earn those ratings. We did not have a construct for the elements of clarity and how they were related to one another, an operational model for how they worked in interrelationship, or a sense of whether some of the elements were more important than others. We know a great deal more about clarity now. We can at least profile essential elements and have data to support their individual contribution to successful teaching and learning. The same is not true for classroom climate. We are still at the Likert scale stage.

Although the tradition of research on classroom climate has roots in the 1920s, Withall (1949) was the first to formulate a definition of the group phenomenon known as social-emotional climate. He noted

> a general emotional factor which appears to be present in interactions occurring between individuals in face to face groups. It seems to have some relationship to the degree of acceptance expressed by members of a group regarding each other's needs or goals. Operationally defined, it is considered to influence: (1) the inner private world of each individual; (2) the esprit de corps of the group; (3) the sense of meaningfulness of group and individual goals and activities; (4) the objectivity with which a problem is tackled; (5) the kind and extent of interpersonal interaction in the group.

Studies since then have examined high-inference variables and found better student achievement when the class is rated high on measures such as cohesiveness and satisfaction and low on measures such as friction, difficulty, and competitiveness (Fraser and O'Brien, 1985).

Overall, these studies show that "students' cognitive, affective, and behavioral outcomes are related to students' perceptions of psychosocial characteristics in classrooms" (Chavez, 1984; Battistich and others, 1995).

Four propositions speak to the importance of classroom climate:

1. The basic psychological needs of all humans make up an acknowledged and universal list: safety, self-control, affection, inclusion, self-esteem, recognition, self-actualization and freedom, and fun (see Maslow, 1962; Dreikurs and Grey, 1968; Schutz, 1967; Glasser, 1965, 1998).

2. The degree to which one's psychological needs are met determines how much of one's energy and attention is available for learning. If an individual is hurt and severely wanting on any of these needs, learning slows to a crawl or a halt. If these needs are adequately met, learning proceeds normally. And if they are met at a high level and nourished, learning flourishes.

3. Classroom climate directly influences how students do in school. It influences individually how their thermometers read on each of the basic psychological needs. It is a major variable shaping the degree to which each student's psychological needs are met during class time.

4. When the climate goes beyond meeting safety and security needs and develops strength on the important dimensions of climate—community, risk taking, and influence—learning accelerates (Figure 14.1).

**Figure 14.1. Psychological Needs and Student Learning**

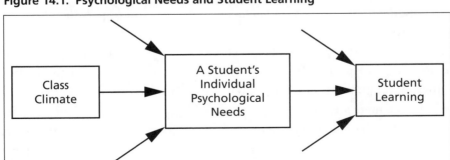

## Classroom Climate: What Is It?

Our operational definition of classroom climate is "the feelings and beliefs students have and the cumulative patterns of behavior that result from those feelings and beliefs regarding community and mutual support, risk taking and confidence, and influence and control." Community and mutual support are defined as an individual's feelings in relation to a group—feelings of acceptance, inclusion, membership, and maybe friendship and affection. Risk taking and confidence represent an internal, personal dimension that is influenced significantly by the reactions of others to one's behaviors. Put-downs and sarcasm, however subtle they may be, reduce one's confidence that it is safe to risk thinking and trying. A classroom climate that rewards effort and persistence deemphasizes speed and helps students learn that errors are merely opportunities for learning, not signs of personal deficiency. Influence and control represent the dimension of class climate that pertains to personal efficacy, defined as one's power to produce effects. It answers the following questions: To what degree do I as an individual get to make my presence felt legitimately in helping things function in here? How am I empowered to be a player, an influencer, someone who matters as opposed to a silent cipher whose existence makes no observable difference in the flow of life in the room, to say nothing of making choices about how I spend my own time? All three of these dimensions of class climate matter for student learning.

These three major strands of classroom climate are summarized in Figure 14.2, which treats each as a developmental aspect of climate—developmental in that there are stages of sophistication and maturity for each of the three strands, so a teacher planning to strengthen any of them would do well to plan activities and new practices with the stages in mind. The stages for the first strand, community and mutual support, are well treated in the developmental literature (Aspy and Roebuck, 1977; Wood, 1994a; Johnson and Johnson, 1995a). The stages in the other two strands are more hypothetical, though their elements are supported individually by research.

The sections that follow examine each strand separately and describe the meaning of each element in it. We also describe specific strategies and practices teachers can use to develop it.

## Community and Mutual Support

This dimension of climate describes the degree of inclusion, affiliation, and mutual support students feel with one another. When it is well developed, the student can say, "I feel accepted and included here. People are on my side. I can help others, and they will help me."

Within this dimension are five levels of development, each paired with a characteristic statement:

1. Knowing others: "I know these people and they know me."
2. Greeting, acknowledging, listening, responding, acknowledging, and affirming: "I feel accepted and included. People respect me, and I respect them."
3. Group identity, responsibility, and interdependence: "I'm a member of this group. We need each other and want each other to succeed."
4. Cooperative learning, social skills, group meetings, and group dynamics: "I can help others, and they will help me."

**Figure 14.2. Climate of High Achievement for All Students**

| CREATING A CLIMATE OF HIGH ACHIEVEMENT FOR ALL STUDENTS | | |
|---|---|---|
| **COMMUNITY AND MUTUAL SUPPORT** | **CONFIDENCE AND RISK TAKING** | **INFLUENCE AND CONTROL** |

Believing That . . .

| COMMUNITY AND MUTUAL SUPPORT | CONFIDENCE AND RISK TAKING | | | INFLUENCE AND CONTROL |
|---|---|---|---|---|
| Knowing others | Mistakes help | vs. | Mistakes = sign of weakness | Empowering students to influence the pace of the class |
| ↓ | ↓ | | ↓ | ↓ |
| Greeting, acknowledging, listening, responding, and affirming | Care, perseverance, and craftsmanship count | vs. | Speed counts Faster = smarter | Negotiating the rules of the "classroom game" |
| ↓ | ↓ | | ↓ | ↓ |
| Group identity, responsibility, and interdependence | Good students solicit help and lots of feedback | vs. | Good students do it by themselves | Teaching students to use the principles of learning and other learning strategies |
| ↓ | ↓ | | ↓ | ↓ |
| Cooperative learning, social skills, class meetings, group dynamics | Effort and effective strategies . . . main determinants of success | vs. | Inborn intelligence = main determinant of success | Students using knowledge of learning style and making choices |
| ↓ | ↓ | | ↓ | ↓ |
| Problem solving and conflict resolution | Everyone is capable of high achievement | vs. | Only the few bright can achieve at a high level | Students and their communities as sources of knowledge |

**Research for Better Teaching, Inc.** • One Acton Place, Acton, MA 01720 • (978)263-9449 • www.RBTeach.com

5.  Problem solving and conflict resolution: "We can solve problems that arise between us."

These relationships of warmth and inclusion don't get built by accident or by themselves. Teachers contribute to the strength and texture of the climate of inclusion and affiliation that students experience through their behaviors (Cabello and Terrell, 1993): their verbal interaction patterns with individual students, their means of handling conflicts between students, the cooperative structures they introduce for interaction among students, and their explicit teaching of social skills.

## Knowing Others

Gene Stanford, a high school English teacher, identified this strand of classroom climate as a developmental continuum in his 1977 book, *Developing Effective Classroom Groups*. He realized that the foundation of being a group member was knowing something about the others in the group. As a result, he regularly did brief get-acquainted activities (twenty-one listed in his book) in the early months of the school year with students in his classes.

Teachers who periodically take a few minutes several times each week to do these activities do not report time problems keeping up with the curriculum or studying what is required. These modest front-end investments in building community increase efficiency and time on task in the long run. (The same can be said for the other levels of community building in this strand.)

Dozens of books are available with excellent get-acquainted activities (Stanford, 1977; Shaw, 1992; Seigle and Macklem, 1993; Bennett and Smilanich, 1994) that are active and enjoyable. In People Bingo or the version called Find a Person Who, students mingle and try to get signatures in boxes of a grid where facts are listed about others in the group, for example, "Spent a year in France." Each student has to find the person matched to that fact and get his or her signature in that box. Some activities are lengthier, like structured interviews of partners. After the interview, the partners introduce each other to the class or to a small group based on the interview.

One of our favorites has always been Artifact Bags, which is just as popular among groups of adults as it is among fifth graders. Participants bring in unlabeled shopping bags containing five items that represent something about their lives or their interests. At each session, one participant chooses a bag at random and displays the items in it one at a time to the other participants, who are sitting in a circle. Participants try to guess who the owner is. After the fifth item is shown and described by the person who has been picking from the bag (some items may be too small for all to see thoroughly when just held up), the group makes a collective guess. Then the real owner reveals himself or herself and explains the significance of each item. There may be time to do two or three people at each session.

The popularity of this activity with adults signals how little opportunity there is in schools and school districts as workplaces to come to know one's colleagues. One doesn't have to take the whole faculty away on a retreat to pay attention to group building and relationship building.

Community-building strategies gain importance in the overall picture of classroom climate building for students as the forces of scheduling and course structures assume more importance starting in grade 6. These forces depersonalize and fractionate the sense of community for students.

## Greeting, Listening, Responding, Acknowledging, and Affirming

Have you ever noticed that in some settings (sometimes in whole towns) people look you in the eye, smile, and greet you when you walk by or enter their space? Beyond simply getting students information about each other, we should work on creating the conditions and teaching the skills of acknowledging and responding to one another. People who are greeted and acknowledged regularly feel affirmed and tend to be more available for learning. In the morning meeting structure at the Greenfield Center School in Greenfield, Massachusetts, the first activity uses one of the dozens of formats available for having the children greet one other around the circle. This is not a practice confined to the primary grades. Positive greeting is a form of acknowledgment worth fostering at any age. Wood (1994b) writes, "It is important for students [of grades 4, 5, and 6] to not only greet each other in the morning, but to learn to greet any member of the class in a friendly and interested way. Issues of gender, cliques, and best friends are developmental milestones for 9–13 year olds. Greetings help students to work on these issues in a safe structure every morning. It is the entry point for the teacher in her social curriculum each morning."

A sample greeting activity appropriate for the elementary grades is a ball toss greeting, which can be varied so that it will be challenging and build cooperation for older children. It begins with the children standing in a circle and greeting each other one at a time by tossing a ball. For example, Leslie starts the greeting by saying, "Good morning, John!" and then tosses the ball to John. He returns Leslie's greeting, then chooses another child in the circle to greet and toss the ball to. When the ball has been tossed to everyone except Leslie, it finishes by returning to her with a greeting. In a variation, the ball goes around one more time silently (with no greeting or talking) repeating the pattern it just made. Children will enjoy doing it several times this way and competing against the clock (Stephenson and Watrous, 1993).

Acknowledging and affirming one another can be structured into group meeting times. The social competency curriculum (Seigle and Macklem, 1993) uses Spotlight as an activity to affirm positive attributes and behaviors. One child is picked by the teacher (a different one each time) to be in the spotlight. The others then take turns giving the selected child compliments with specific examples: "Tim, it's nice the way you are considerate of other kids, like when you made room for me to get into the circle." Each child may speak only once and must address the child selected, not the teacher. The child in the spotlight listens.

Good listening can be taught explicitly. Students can be warmed up to the qualities of good listening by doing a mirroring exercise. Two partners stand and decide who will be the leader (person A) and who the follower (person B). Partner A puts his or her hands up and moves them around, palms facing partner B, who has to make his or her hands exactly mirror A's hands. After about forty-five seconds, the facilitator calls "time," and partners switch roles. A becomes the follower and B the leader. To do this activity well, both partners need to focus intently on each other. That sets the stage for direct teaching and practice of social skills, especially listening.

Direct teaching of children to listen involves role playing and practice. It can begin by asking students, "Think of someone who really listens to you. Why do you think that person does it?" Role-play listening attentively with the class, and have them tell you what they saw and heard. Record their answers. Next, have students describe someone they know who doesn't listen. Do a role-play with someone, and record what students say about the behaviors they heard and saw. Students are now ready to practice listening in trios: one listener, one speaker, and one observer.

Many teachers embed practice in listening in classroom routines—for example, by asking a student who wants to speak to summarize what the previous students said in a discussion. This request is thrown out randomly so students can't predict when they'll have to summarize.

## Group Identity, Responsibility, and Interdependence

Cooperative learning structures (see Kagan, 1992) and cooperative models (Johnson and Johnson, 1987; Slavin, 1986) encourage team building because they form natural groups where individuals are allied with one another. Creating a team name, a logo, or a banner becomes a natural way for getting the students involved with one another. On a higher level, students start depending on one another and see how they need one another. Jigsaw structures (Aronson, 1978) force interdependence because students must rely on their peers to learn certain material so they can present it to the others on the team. In a Jig-Saw, academic material is divided into parts and individual parts are assigned to team members. Team members study their parts and then meet in "expert groups" with other individuals from other teams who had the same part. In expert groups, the individuals compare notes and help each other prepare to go back to their home base teams and teach their parts to peers. Thus all members of a home base team are responsible for knowing all the information, but must rely on peers to get much of it.

Broken Squares is an activity often used to introduce students to interdependence. Five perfect squares, each 6 inches on a side, are cut into pieces, mixed up into five piles, and put in five envelopes (see Exhibit 14.1). Each team of five gets one envelope each. Their job, without talking or signaling, is to make five perfect squares. Individuals may not take pieces from anyone else; they can only give pieces away. When they give a piece to a team member, individuals may not put the piece in place in the person's puzzle; they can just give it to the person. Debriefing this activity with the questions listed in Exhibit 14.1 provides a fine entry point for discussing what happens if a person is ignored or withdraws or if a person tries to dominate the task.

Regular academic tasks can be adapted to the Broken Squares structure. An oak tag sheet with spelling words (or technical words or foreign language or English vocabulary words) can be cut up into a pile of individual letters. The letters are sorted randomly into five envelopes. Each of five team members gets one envelope. Their job as a group, without talking or taking pieces from another, is to build the words, spelled correctly. A poster of the words spelled correctly should be available for the group to consult while doing the task.

## Social Skills and Group Dynamics

The fourth level of community building focuses more explicitly on developing the skills to work effectively in groups. Social skills are taught in the manner of the Listening example already described. Class meetings become a common framework for teaching and exercising these social skills, which are often posted by name around the classroom. (Three excellent sources on how to run classroom meetings for social skill development are Glasser, 1969; Seigle and Macklem, 1993; and Wood, 1994b.)

Consensus-seeking exercises with an analysis of behavior and results afterward are useful. Tasks such as Lost in Space and Arctic Survival (Lafferty, 1992) give problems to teams from fifth grade on up that require prioritizing a list of items; for example, which ten of twenty potential items should be taken from a crashed plane if the group has to survive in subarctic conditions until rescued? Individuals do the task alone first, and then redo it with team members by sharing information and the rationales they used. The group choices almost always turn out to be closer to the expert's best answer than any individual's answer alone. Thus, the point is made about the benefits of pooling expertise and using consensus. After the activity, groups follow directions to examine the roles various members of the group played when they were working together. Valuable learning emerges about what behaviors individuals can do to make groups effective. Information emerges about blocking behaviors and what each individual could do to be a more potent group contributor next time.

Mysteries (Stanford, 1977) is another such structure. The clues necessary to solve a mystery are put on 3- by 5-inch index cards, and one clue is given to each student. The task is to identify the culprit with deductive logic by a process of elimination

**Exhibit 14.1. Broken Squares Activity**

### Directions for Marking a Set of Broken Squares

A set consists of five envelopes containing pieces of cardboard cut into different patterns which, when properly arranged, will form five squares of equal size. One set should be provided for each group of five persons.

To prepare a set, cut out five cardboard squares, each exactly 6" x 6". Place the squares in a row and mark them as below, penciling the letters lightly so they can be erased.

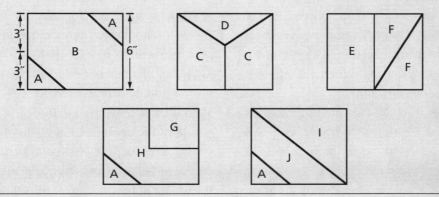

Lines should be drawn so that, when the pieces are cut out, those marked A will be exactly the same size, all pieces marked C, the same size, etc. Several combinations are possible that will form one or two squares, but only one combination will form all five squares, each 6" x 6". After drawing the lines on the squares and labeling the sections with letters, cut each square along the lines into smaller pieces to make the parts of the puzzle.

Label five envelopes 1,2,3,4, and 5. Distribute the cardboard pieces into the five envelopes as follows: envelope 1 has pieces I, H, E; 2 has A, A, A, C; 3 has A, J; 4 has D, F; and 5 has G, B, F, C.

Erase the penciled letters from each piece and write, instead, the number of the envelope it is in. This makes it easy to return the pieces to the proper envelope, for subsequent use, after each group has completed the task.

Each set may be made from a different color of cardboard.

### Directions

Each of you has an envelope which contains pieces of oak tag for forming squares. When the signal is given, the task of your group is to form five squares of equal size. Each square will be measure 6" x 6". The task will not be completed until five perfect squares have been formed.

### Rules

1. No member may speak.
2. No member may ask another member for a piece or in any way signal that another person is to give him or her a piece. (Members may voluntarily give pieces to other members.)

   (The letters on the pieces are irrelevant to the task; they are just for getting pieces back into the right envelope at the end of the exercise.)

### Processing "Broken Squares"

1. What happened first? What strategies were used in the beginning?
2. What were you (each individual) thinking about in the first few minutes?
3. What happened next? Did strategies shift? Were there different phases to how you functioned as a group?
4. Did someone make a move that shifted the group's approach or in some way broke the log jam?
5. Did anyone feel left out or appear to be left out?
6. What roles did each individual play in the group?
7. What did you become aware of about yourself regarding cooperation and competition?
8. What insight/awareness did you get about groups in cooperative tasks?

*Source:* Pfeiffer and Jones (1974).

if all the information from all the clues is available. The students who sit in a circle can read their card aloud but cannot give it to anyone else, and no student can read another student's card. This structure forces students to share information, organize it, and develop organization and leadership skills. As with all other such tasks, the analytical discussion afterward (called processing) is the most important part of the activity. It is here that students reflect on what helped and what obstructed the group's progress, and they make commitments about what they'll try to do better next time.

In Mysteries, the class is asked to make an accusation only when they all agree. If they are wrong, the teacher doesn't give the right answer but sends them back into the group to reexamine the evidence. In any event, after twenty minutes, the activity ends if the guilty party hasn't been identified, and the class returns to the task on another day.

The things students learn about successful group processes and individual social and task skills from these activities do not necessarily transfer into their everyday behavior unless teachers specifically plan for that transfer. Successful teaching of social skills requires (1) naming the skill, (2) creating an understanding of the utility of the skill in life, (3) modeling it, (4) having students practice it, and (5) giving students direct feedback on how they're doing. In addition to feedback from their teacher, having students process their own level of functioning in a group (that is, discuss it and self-assess) consistently correlates with better skill development and better academic learning (Yager, Johnson, Johnson, and Snider, 1986). The explicit teaching of social skills and the frequent debriefing or processing by students of how they did build an expectation through repetition ensures that the skills will be used generally in the classroom. (Transfer to set-

tings outside school is more likely to happen by following the guidelines of the principle of learning called teach for transfer found in Chapter Ten.)

## Problem Solving and Conflict Resolution

The final stage of development for a healthy classroom or school community is building the capacity of its members to solve their own conflicts. This work includes acknowledgment that conflicts are normal and that controversy, which is not the same as conflict, is actually good for learning.

Conflict is defined as a situation where the needs of two people are at odds, and the current course of behavior or action appears to make one the winner at the expense of the other. Conflict resolution means coming up with a solution that meets the needs of both parties or a compromise that both can live with.

Most conflict resolution models have similar steps and teach similar skills. For example, Thomas Gordon's (1974) model includes the skills of active listening and I messages, which are vital communication skills for enabling people to work through classic conflict resolution steps.

The following steps occur in most programs:

1. Recognize your anger, calm down, and collect yourself. Some programs teach relaxation or self-imposed time-out techniques for this stage.
2. Identify the real problem. Johnson and Johnson (1995a) break down the second step into valuable components:
   - Jointly define the problem as small and specific.
   - Determine what each person wants.
   - Determine how each person feels.

- Exchange reasons and rationale for positions.
- Reverse perspectives.

This stage can take some time. Many models advocate teaching students to identify their needs, not to speak in terms of actions or the solutions they want. Probing questions, clarifying questions, and considerable active listening are often required here. That is why a neutral mediator is often introduced into the process.

3. Decide on a positive goal. State a desired outcome in positive terms—for example, "We will both get enough time at the computer to rewrite our drafts."

4. Think of several solutions. Brainstorming techniques are often taught to students in this stage.

5. Evaluate the solutions, and pick one to try.

6. Make a plan. Often just picking a solution— "Share the computer time after lunch fifty-fifty"—isn't enough. A specific plan is needed designating who will do what, when, and where. The plan may need to be written and agreed to in writing.

7. Evaluate the plan to see if both parties are keeping their part of the bargain, if the plan is good, or if it needs to be revised. (For details and elaboration of these steps see Johnson and Johnson, 1995a.)

We are convinced that Johnson and Johnson (1995a) are right: every student, not just some, should be trained as a mediator. It is in being a mediator that students learn and internalize the skills of conflict resolution. Only then will they have the skills available for their own autonomous use when they get into conflicts themselves. The implication is that mediation training for all students is the most powerful model for teaching effective conflict resolution skills and getting students to transfer them into daily practice.

Social problem-solving meetings, as described by Glasser (1969), are an ideal forum for developing these steps and the skills to go with them.

In the only classroom climate study to investigate differential effects of climate variables by gender and race, Deng (1992) found that the achievement gap between blacks, Hispanics, and whites in mathematics and the achievement gap between boys and girls in mathematics widened when community was weak and tension was high. This finding underlines the importance of community as a variable in academic achievement for girls in math and perhaps for students of color in all subjects when classes are integrated.

## Risk Taking and Confidence

As we move from community building to the domain of risk taking, we examine what teachers can do to promote confidence and a safe atmosphere to "go for it." The five levels of this dimension of classroom climate are not as clearly developmental as they were in community because each level here is a belief rather than a set of steps. We believe that the foundation of intellectual risk taking in classrooms is built on internal beliefs about errors and what they mean, about speed of learning and what it signifies, and about the need to get it on your own as opposed to working with others and getting help. Productive beliefs about errors, speed, and getting help may be derived from one's basic belief about intelligence (that intelligence can be developed, and everyone can do well if they put in the time and use good strategies to learn). Whatever the relationships between these beliefs turn out to be, it is clear that we can identify a repertoire of teacher behaviors associated with strengthening each belief.

Table 14.1 shows the five beliefs introduced in Chapter Twelve, "Expectations," that underlie risk taking in their negative and positive forms. The positive beliefs are life liberating, the negative ones life limiting.

This risk-taking dimension of climate has to do with the amount of confidence a student has and the amount of social and academic risk taking the student will do. If it is well developed, a student might be able to say, "It's safe to take a risk here. If I try hard, learn from errors, and persist, I can succeed."

There remains a need to collect specific strategies and approaches for nourishing student risk taking. Some authors acknowledge the importance of risk taking but seldom explain how to cultivate it. For example, one writes, "A big piece of teaching for understanding is setting up social norms that promote respect for other people's ideas. You don't get that to happen by telling. You have to change the social norms—which takes time and consistency" (Lampert, 1990).

Here is another example. In a wonderful exposition on the practices of exemplary teachers who use cognitive strategies to move students from novice to expert in their problem solving in various disciplines, Bruer (1993) writes:

> The benchmark lesson on gravity begins 6 weeks into the course. By this time Minstrell [the teacher] has established a rapport with his class. He has created an environment conducive to developing understanding, a climate where questioning and respect for diverse opinions prevail, a climate where the process of scientific reasoning can be made explicit and self-conscious. Even veteran teachers marvel at how uninhibited Minstrell's students are in expressing ideas, suggesting hypotheses, and arguing positions [p. 42].

How does Mr. Minstrell get his students to be so uninhibited?

> A few days later, Minstrell and the class analyze their reasoning about the time it would take a 1-kilogram and a 5-kilogram object to fall the same distance. They run the crucial experiment—a miniature replay of Galileo's apocryphal experiment at Pisa. After both balls hit the floor simultaneously, Minstrell returns to the board where he had written the quiz answers. "Some of you were probably feeling pretty dumb with these kind of answers. Don't feel dumb," he counsels. "Let's see what's valuable about each of these answers, because each one's valuable. Why would you think heavier things fall faster?" [pp. 43–44].

Now we are beginning to get clues about creating this uninhibited atmosphere.

Here is a final example acknowledging the importance of risk taking:

> Inquiry teaching is difficult for teachers and requires skills that must be developed through intensive staff development. If a student whose answer is challenged does not trust the teacher, or the other students, the follow-up question, intended to cause the student to think more deeply about the subject, may have the opposite effect. The student may interpret the follow-up question as a clue that the initial response was wrong and that he or she is about to be made to feel foolish in front of the rest of the class. Threat seems to reduce our ability to think at higher levels, and what could be more threatening than public failure and ridicule?
>
> For this type of instruction to be effective, a teacher must create a classroom environment

**Table 14.1. Five Beliefs That Underlie Risk Taking**

| Positive Beliefs | Negative Beliefs |
| --- | --- |
| *On errors:* Mistakes can help one learn. | *On errors:* Mistakes are a sign of weakness. |
| *On speed:* You are not supposed to understand everything the first time around. Care, quality, and perseverance count. | *On speed:* Speed is what counts. Faster is smarter. |
| *On getting help:* Good students solicit help and lots of feedback on their work. | *On getting help:* Good students can do it by themselves. |
| *On effort and ability:* Consistent effort and effective strategies are the main determinants of success. | *On effort and ability:* Inborn intelligence is the main determinant of success. |
| *On effort and ability:* Everyone is capable of high achievement, not just the fastest. | *On effort and ability:* Only the few who are bright can achieve at a high level. |

where students feel safe to express their thinking, where they trust their teacher and fellow students, and where they understand the difference between criticizing ideas and criticizing people [Ellsworth and Sindt, 1994, p. 43].

This interpretation of the effect of removing threat—the threat of being laughed at, of feeling foolish, or of being wrong—is resoundingly confirmed by research on brain function (Sylvester, 1994). What then can we say about specific ways to strengthen a climate for risk taking?

## Errors

Americans tend to believe in the fixed, innate, and unalterable nature of intelligence. Most children learn early in school that mistakes are signs of weakness instead of data to use and an opportunity for learning. Cultivating the latter belief about mistakes is the very foundation for confidence and risk taking in the classroom. Thirty years ago, Jerome Bruner represented this idea when he said that a teacher's goal should be to help students "experience success and failure not as reward and punishment, but as information" (1997). People who

succeed in building this element of climate do so explicitly. Beverly Hollis, a teacher of reading in Sudbury, Massachusetts, writes:

At the beginning of the year, when students are reticent to answer and wait time has been exhausted, I ask my class, "Is this a life-or-death situation? No, well, so what if you're wrong then? This is one answer out of the trillion you will give in your life, so what if it's wrong? If it is wrong, I guarantee I won't let you leave until you've heard the right answer, and you'll probably remember the information much longer for having missed it. But most importantly, you will have taken a risk by giving an answer. So many insightful answers and comments are never made and, therefore, never discussed and further explored because you, as students, are afraid to be wrong. I don't want that to be the case in this room."

Having the ability to (1) risk being "wrong," 2) maintain a positive self-image if you are "wrong," and 3) move on rather than dwelling on a "wrong" answer are essential attributes for success, not only in school but throughout life. I talk with my students about risks in my personal life—my month-long wilderness canoeing trip—and risks I'm taking by teaching a concept or a unit in a particular way. I'll say, "I want to try something new I've learned in a class I'm taking, and I need your feedback." I always ask for my students' feedback after every unit. I tell them they can say they disliked a particular approach I used on the material covered as long as they offer positive criticism in pointing out what they didn't like and why, and if they offer alternatives or suggestions of what I can do to make it better. [Notice that in letting students critique her units, Ms. Hollis is giving them power.] I also give them choices about how they want to learn a particular unit and ask them to tell me why this would be the best approach to take. They love having "the power"! They have been incredibly perceptive, and as a consequence, they have been very accepting of my high expectations and my criticism when they fall short of the mark. I have students earn extra credit points to improve their grades on tests by listing what they were mixed up about or how they "messed up" on a test answer and what they learned. And, I openly and readily admit my own mistakes. Hopefully, this climate of honesty and risk taking allows me to correct students and myself without any of us feeling guilty or stupid for having made a mistake [used with permission from Beverly Hollis, a reading teacher in the Sudbury, Massachusetts, public schools].

Anna Shine of The New England School of English in Boston says:

One of the behaviors I encourage is making mistakes or guessing. I tell my students that I don't care if they are wrong, but I do care if they don't try, that there is no shame in trying and making a mistake or in falling short of their goals, but there is shame in not trying. And

worse than shame, a learning opportunity is not maximized. Again and again, I say to them, "Mistakes are not important; understanding is."

Obviously students will not take risks unless it is safe to do so. So, in my classroom, I try to create this environment, to make it safe to make mistakes because students can learn from mistakes. In fact, I reward students with big (two inches in diameter) gold stars in two situations. One is if they produce great work, and the other is if they produce great mistakes.

On the first day of class, when I show them my gold stars, they look at me as if I'm crazy. "A gold star for a mistake?" they think. "She doesn't know what she's doing." However, they soon learn that a gold star mistake is a mistake from which every student in the class can learn something. By making this great mistake, the student has provided everyone with a new learning opportunity, and the student himself has learned that it is safe to take a risk. By taking that risk, he grew (his knowledge and his confidence), the class learned, and he received one of the coveted gold stars [used with permission from Anna Shine, founder, The New England School of English].

In a similar vein, Terry McCarthy of the North Pole Elementary School in Fairbanks, Alaska, gives "bravery points" to students who have the courage to try hard questions or problems even if they're not sure they can get them. In these and other ways, thoughtful teachers deliberately create and nurture climates of risk taking and safety to make errors.

## Speed

A second belief about learning that children have is that faster is better instead of believing that care, quality, and perseverance are what matter. What do teachers do to disabuse students of the life-limiting belief in the virtue of speed versus care and perseverance?

In Chapter Twelve we described a policy on retakes of tests that would grant students as a final grade the higher score they got on a test or its retake no matter how many tries they took (assuming alternate forms of tests are available). This practice would replace averaging the test and its retake. Beyond that practice, giving only A, B, and "not yet" as grades signals that ultimate performance at high standards is what teachers are after, and nothing less will do. Getting there after suffering through a period of "not yet" does not make one's A any less valuable—just longer in coming.

Use of wait time, with an explanation of it to the class, is an everyday practice that reinforces thoughtfulness and perseverance rather than quickness. Mary Ann Pilat of the Wellesley, Massachusetts, Middle School uses a related practice, called the Level Playing Field:

> I explain to students that linear thinkers can come up with prompt answers to class discussion questions, but that gestalt, divergent thinkers, an equally legitimate learning style, often are stimulated onto side connections and thoughts by questions in class. So while following those interesting thoughts, the speedster linear thinkers have answered the question and appear to be getting all the answers. Divergent thinkers tend to participate less in class. So to make the playing field level for them in getting ready for a class discussion, I put the major questions we're going to discuss on the board and give everyone five minutes to think about them first before starting the discussion. I've been getting much greater participation from lots more kids, including some who never spoke in class before.

The final strategy for valuing care and perseverance above speed is the routine practice of reteaching loops described in Chapter Twelve. To make reteaching loops do what they can for classroom climate, nominating oneself for inclusion in a loop must be a behavior of high esteem and status in the class.

## Getting Feedback and Help

Another factor that obstructs learning and contaminates most classroom climates is the belief that "good students do it by themselves," instead of the belief that what makes good students is that they solicit help and lots of feedback on their work.

Teachers support the development of this belief by explicitly modeling and encouraging it and creating structures that manifest it. For example, the peer editing process in place in many writing programs can be applied to reports in other subjects; students would be expected to have peers critique their drafts according to commonly understood criteria and to do final drafts with their input in mind.

Other structures for mutual help can be made part of classroom routines:

- Students can take turns taking notes for the "absentee folder," which sits on a desk in the back of the room as a resource for absent students. When students come back after an absence, the notes help them catch up on what they missed, and the student who took the notes is available for personal help to the student who was absent.
- Teachers can organize students in groups or pairs of "study buddies" who are expected to help each other interpret assignments and prepare for tests.
- Various models of cooperative learning build in incentives for all team members so

that each member does well. Improvement of any individual's score on a quiz over that person's previous average earns points for the whole team. Team study time is provided so the members can help each other out (see Slavin, 1986).

Many other activity structures, such as Teammates Consult, Four Corners, Pairs Check, and Learning Buddies (Kagan, 1997), are available for helping students get committed to asking for appropriate help.

## Effort and Ability

To the degree that students believe intelligence is innate, fixed, measurable, and unevenly distributed, they will probably also believe that whatever quantity of intelligence they have is the main determinant of how they will do in school and elsewhere in life (Howard, 1993). It is difficult to be brought up in the United States believing anything else, for the concept of intelligence as an entity that regulates our possibilities is more developed and more influential here than in any other nation. In fact, the concept of intelligence as a fixed and measurable entity was created in the United States between approximately 1890 and 1920 (Gould, 1982; Oakes, 1985).

In this section, we move on to the consequence of this belief, to the fruits of its opposite, and how to transform students' belief into that opposite image. The opposite belief—the life-liberating one that fuels motivation and accelerates learning when it replaces the belief that innate intelligence is the main determinant of success—is that consistent effort and effective strategies are the main determinants of success (Howard, 1993). With these two things in place, everyone, not just the fastest and most confident, is capable of high achievement.

Attribution theory explains the dynamics at work in the two different belief systems (Weiner, 1972). The theory posits that the reasons we give to ourselves (the attributions we make) for our success when we succeed and for our failure when we fail have a dramatic impact on our future behavior. In fact, these internal explanations account for our future behavior. Teachers who want to help students change their beliefs about the value of effort and the importance of good strategies versus innate intelligence pursue positive behaviors in the ten arenas of classroom life described in Chapter Twelve. For example, they stick with students who don't answer quickly; they give cues and use wait time. The arenas through which the three messages—"This is important," "You can do it," "I won't give up on you"—are sent are also the vehicles for convincing students they have enough intelligence to do rigorous material well. What they need to do is work long enough, be resourceful, and learn strategies that will help them. Their teacher's responsibility is to teach them strategies explicitly.

## Influence

"Effective teachers know that to become engaged, students must have some feelings of ownership—of the class or the task—and personal power—a belief that what they do will make a difference" (Dodd, 1995, p. 65). This belief is echoed in two bodies of literature of the 1980s and 1990s. First, many frameworks for understanding thinking and personality style (Myers and McCaulley, 1985; Harrison and Bramson, 1982) find large percentages of people who have the need to be in charge or in control of at least certain aspects of their environment in order to function well. Second, the literature on constructivist learning and teaching posits that learning for true understanding requires students to construct their own meaning (Brooks and

Brooks, 1993). This involves owning their own questions and pursuing their own lines of inquiry with teacher guidance. These two literatures support the same proposition: successful teachers find ways for students to have some ownership and influence over the flow of events and the intellectual life of the classroom.

There are many ways to offer students choice and influence over their lives in school. One pertains to the social system of the classroom—the rules of the classroom game as opposed to the rules for interpersonal behavior one often sees posted on classroom walls. The rules of the classroom game pertain to social norms and procedures for conducting class discourse. They are often undiscussed and unwritten, though that is something we recommend changing. The teacher asks a question, the student responds, and the teacher evaluates is a typical cycle of discourse reflecting the "rule" that the teacher will control the talk in the room. Without losing control of the class or the curriculum, a teacher can permit students to participate in shaping and operating these procedural systems for discourse and business.

Another route to ownership and influence goes through learning style and choices. Many authors (Mamchur, 1990) urge giving students choices whenever possible about how to work on learning new concepts or carrying out assignments. Student choice making can be improved and empowered by knowledge about their own learning styles.

Finally, students can have some joint ownership of the intellectual life of the classroom through the way in which questions are posed and meaning is generated.

The five sections that follow might be thought of as levels of depth and sophistication in a strategic approach to giving students authentic influence in classroom life. Whereas you could work on them in any order or even simultaneously, it is useful to

understand which ones are more complex and why. Then you can choose them appropriately. You need not address the five issues sequentially and wait for a certain level of development before beginning practices aimed at another level. For example, there is no need to wait until students are stopping a class to ask for clarification before teaching students about their own learning style and how to use that knowledge to influence assignments. But it might be worth bearing in mind that the five approaches described do increase progressively in complexity. Therefore, if you are interested in developing student ownership and influence, you might start with the simpler and then move slowly to the more complex forms of student ownership.

## Stop My Teaching

"Stop my teaching" refers to empowering the students to use signals to tell a teacher when the instruction is leaving them behind. Katz (1992) talks about giving her son, a beginning teacher, some basic principles of practice for successful teaching:

> One of the things you always want to do as a teacher . . . teaching children old or young, doesn't matter who, you always want to teach the children to say to you things like: "Hold it; I'm lost." "Can you go over this one more time?" "Is this what you mean?" "Can you show me again?" "Have I got it right?" . . . ways in which you empower the learner to keep you posted on where they need help. If the children are very young you just say, "Pull my sleeve," whatever, as long as the child has the strategy to say to you "I don't get it." "I'm lost." "You're going too fast." "Hold it" and so on.

Teachers who take this injunction seriously develop signal systems where students can indicate on their own initiative that they are lost and want the teacher to stop and explain again. Hand signals like thumbs down held tight against one's chest could be such a signal. Or students could put red, yellow, or green cards on the corner of their desks like traffic light signals. Thus, teachers could get a quick visual read on how well students were understanding a discussion.

When the idea of stopping the teaching becomes part of classroom culture, other symbols or phrases come to represent the practice. One teacher told her class the story of a family vacation where she and her husband and six children stopped at McDonalds for lunch. Loading up hurriedly in the tightly packed van after their quick meal, they didn't do a head count and were four miles down the road before she said, "Where's Bobby?!?" Bobby was back at McDonalds.

The teacher now uses that phrase frequently in class as a coded signal: "Have I left you at McDonalds?" and the children also use the code to signal when they're getting lost. "Ms. Swift, I think I'm back at McDonalds!" The humorous shared code serves to authorize the practice of stopping the teacher's teaching, and the teacher's affirming reaction shows the practice to be a valued one that earns kudos for the child rather than a frown or a veiled accusation of inadequacy.

## Negotiating the Rules of the Classroom Game

Negotiating the rules of the classroom game means involving students in creating the routines and procedures of classroom discourse and class business. These rules are different from the rules of behavior that teachers and students commonly work out at the beginning of the year. The rules we are talking about here are usually tacit, underground, and unstated. They pertain to teacher-student and student-student interaction around such issues as questions and answers, class dialogue, and procedures and protocols for taking turns. Recitation lessons of teacher questions and student answers do indeed often turn out to be a game, where students try to win by getting the right answers and avoid losing by shrinking into invisibility when they don't know the answers.

Once in one of our courses, Dick Adams, a housemaster at Newton North High School in Newton, Massachusetts, asked his students if he had ever played Guess-What's-On-the-Teacher's-Mind with them. The concept had come up when we studied questioning techniques under clarity. Recall that teachers who play Guess-What's-On-the-Teacher's-Mind (GWOTM) ask inexplicit questions when they have a particular answer in mind but the way they ask the question allows for a universe of possible answers. "I don't ever do that, do I?" asked Dick. A number of slow, knowing affirmative nods came back at him from the students. "No . . . really? Give me some examples."

They did. And from that opening there proceeded a class discussion of how to conduct class discourse in such a way as to eliminate student pet peeves and increase productive participation. For example, they decided together that a student who couldn't answer a question could refer it to another student, whom he or she named. If three students in a row couldn't answer the question, Dick would conclude he had asked a bad question; then he had to ask it in a different way or ask students where the gap was.

His students became so excited over the way the class was going that they asked one of us to videotape it. We realized that the students were not just happy over the new dynamics and improved clarity of class discussions, but elated over having been a force that influenced the shape of the class itself. Students had changed the rules of the classroom game in collaboration with their teacher and emerged from the traditional nether region of passive ciphers to active and authorized players.

The point of this story is to raise the question: What opportunities do students have to influence the rules of the classroom game, to shape the form and dynamics of interaction and operation? How can teachers give them ownership in these rules?

## Teaching Students to Use Principles of Learning and Other Strategies

A third way to give students influence in classroom life is to share with them teaching and learning strategies we use ourselves. By including them in the secret knowledge of teaching and learning strategies, we give students choices, power, and license to control their learning.

Many of the principles of learning set out in Chapter Ten should be taught to students directly so they can use them to be more powerful learners. The same is true for a number of the explanatory devices in Chapter Nine. This is a good moment to review those principles to decide which ones you think would be most beneficial to turn over to your students as tools for learning. The more we are interested in empowering students and giving them choices, the more we will explicitly put learning at their disposal and urge them to use them autonomously.

Here are some of our nominees for principles and tools to teach to students:

- Sequence: Students can use this principle to sequence their own lists when studying vocabulary words (or anything else that is sequential in nature) so the items hardest for them are in the optimal first and last positions.
- Practice: Students can use knowledge of this

principle to optimize their personal practice schedules.
- Goal setting: Students can use this principle to set realistic academic and behavioral targets for improvement and make effective plans of action to meet them.
- Explanatory devices: Visual imagery and especially graphic organizers can become regular tools for students. Imagery can be used to pause during study and construct meaning in a visual way. Graphic organizers can become a habit as a note-taking technology through which students assimilate information as they read, hear, or see it. Teachers can integrate the use of these devices into assignments and work toward having students choose when and how to use them (see Chapter Nine).

While passing these strategies on to students, teachers who are aware of attribution theory and are committed to conveying the three expectations messages—"This is important," "You can do it," and "I won't give up on you"—will see they have a special opening. They will seize frequent opportunities to connect the use of these strategies with student success rather than let students attribute successful performance to intelligence. "Well, José, did you use any graphic organizers when you reviewed that chapter? No? Well, look—you're a strong visual learner. You and I both know that. Let's go over how to use that strategy with material like this. I know you can make it work for you!"

## Learning Style and Choices

"Students using knowledge of learning style" means teachers are not just using their knowledge of learning style to adapt lessons for the styles of their students; they are teaching the students about their own learning styles and the implications of those styles for what kinds of assignments will be difficult and what will be easier. Furthermore, they encourage students to use knowledge of their own styles to guide their study routines and even to ask for modifications in assignments that allow them to use their strengths. These steps set the stage for a more complex level of empowerment: giving students explicit choices over assignments, forms of tests, and forms of projects.

Many teachers have been to a workshop on learning style, and some may be trained in one or more of the learning style frameworks. These frameworks help them understand the similarities and differences in the ways humans take in, process, and express their learning. They also help in understanding the features of the learning environment and the different kinds of activities that work best for individuals. For example, some people learn best when they can talk and interact with others as they deal with new concepts. Others like to read, listen, view, and assimilate alone before interacting with others. This body of knowledge about learning style preferences can be a powerful vehicle for giving students ownership in classroom life.

Helping students understand their own learning style sets the stage for some important forms of empowerment. First, students can predict (and teachers can help them predict and prepare for) the difficulty of certain assignments or tasks that do not match their preferred learning style. If teachers have set the stage properly and taught about learning style, the value system associated with learning style frameworks enables students to see their difficulty in certain tasks as attributable to differences, not deficiencies. Second, the capacity to predict learning style match or mismatch to tasks enables students to mobilize extra effort and seek

help when appropriate. When teachers encourage students to use knowledge of their own learning style to do either of these two things, they are empowering them in significant ways.

The simplest place to start teaching students about learning style is with modality preference: visual, auditory, kinesthetic, or combinations of them. Simple modality preference tests (see Barbe and Milone, 1980) can be used to have students identify their preferences. Then teachers must look for (and share out loud with students that they are looking for) ways to vary their teaching to address different modalities.

Another framework for learning style differences that students can use in the same way is the left-brain–right brain or global-analytical framework. Dunn and Dunn (2001) provide another useful set for students to know about and for them to use to empower their learning effectiveness. Gregorc's (1985) framework provides a fourth and more complicated but highly useful cut at style difference. McCarthy's 4MAT System (2005) is a fifth and Gardner's multiple intelligences (2006) framework a sixth. Finally, the sophisticated Myers-Briggs provides a seventh.

All of these frameworks are worthy of study, and we believe they are an important part of teachers' professional knowledge. But for the sake of classroom climate and this particular dimension of influence, the point is to choose one of them and work on giving the framework to students, that is, teaching them to use it not to label themselves but to modulate their effort, seek help when appropriate, and sometimes take the initiative to alter assignments based on their self-knowledge from a learning style perspective.

Giving students license and encouragement to speak up in this way to ask for modifications of assignments brings us to the topic of choices. What kinds of choices do students get to make about their academic work, and how do they do it? Carolyn Mamchur (1990) writes: "Giving students choices may seem like a complex issue. But actually, it is dead simple. The rule is this: whenever you can give a student a choice of any kind, do it" (p. 636).

A "nonreport," an idea we found some years ago in *Mindsight* magazine, is a good example of students' influencing assignments and the shape of products. There is nothing particularly unique about nonreports. They are simply outside assignments—but with several major differences.

A nonreport is anything that does not fall into the category of straight written information. The task is to convince students accustomed to the way school is supposed to be that their teacher will accept and value their ideas. Their first question is usually, "What do you want?" since they know that pleasing the teacher is the quickest way to a good grade. Here is how a nonreport works:

1. Impress on students that a standard written report will receive no credit, since it does not meet the requirements of the assignment.
2. Make the assignment worth enough points so that not doing it will result in a substantial drop in grade. At first, there is a great risk in doing something not completely spelled out, so the risk of losing credit must be greater.
3. Create a grading scale that gives equal merit to content and to creativity (more loosely, to the effort the student has to make to personalize the knowledge he or she conveys).
4. Keep the topic very general, giving the students ample opportunity to select from among a wide variety of ideas. For example, if you are studying a unit on measurement, allow them to select anything at all dealing with measurement. Point out to them that there are few occupations (hobbies, sports, etc.) that do not contain measurement of some kind. Give them examples. Challenge them to name something that apparently has nothing to do with measurement—but be quick enough on your feet to find the measurement involved.
5. If they insist, and they may at first, give them a couple of examples of Nonreport-type formats (they are endless and limited only by imagination). For example, they could create a game, write a song, role-play a game show, do a slide or tape presentation, make a scrapbook, or build a model. But warn them that they will receive more credit for doing something you haven't thought of than copying something you have. And stick by that statement!
6. Perhaps most important, don't do this assignment unless you are willing to truly value the students' ideas. If you can't suspend your own idea of what is right or good and try to see the product from their point of view, they will never believe you again. But neither should you give credit for hastily conceived and executed junk. I once received a shoebox with a hole punched in one end that was labeled "Working model of a black hole." Hah!

I have found that giving 10 points for the idea, 10 points for the execution, and 10 points for the content, plus 5 for effort, works out well—a total of 35 points. The effort points come in when a person has had three weeks to do a project that might be reasonably well done but obviously took only 15 minutes compared to someone else who spent several hours. You can tell by looking.

The first time you do this, you will probably receive the usual assortment of collages, collections, and posters copied from books. But when these students see the more adventurous, creative, and "fun" projects getting all the praise, they will be more willing to let go a little the next time.

By the end of the first year that I had students do these projects, I turned them loose on a topic we had not covered in class: solar energy. They researched the topic, did their Nonreports—including a working parabolic solar cooker and a miniature solar greenhouse complete with Trombe walls made of plastic soft drink bottles—and presented them to the class, thus covering almost all the important aspects of solar energy—with no effort on the part of the teacher. One of the most rewarding aspects of these assignments is that, frequently, the students who usually get C's or D's in regular assignments really come into their own on Nonreports.

Nonreports allow students to plan, research, and execute. It evokes their creative potential and forces interaction with the content. Many students sought "experts" to help them and learned the intricacies of carpentry, photography, sound and art—because they wanted. And it is tremendously exciting to see projects come into the classroom that are far beyond anything the teacher would have assigned or expected.

*Source: Mindsight*, New Lenox, IL, 1989

We would add specific criteria for success that make it clear to students exactly what the attributes of quality work in the nonreport will be. For example, in the nonreport on solar energy, the criteria could be: (1) explains three different ways of converting solar energy, (2) discusses costs and efficiencies of various forms of solar energy, and (3) uses data to compare the efficiency of solar, fossil fuel, and nuclear energy. Students using these criteria could create dozens of different kinds of products to represent their learning, from radio shows to models to hypercard assemblies.

Randolf and Evertson (1995) give a simple example of student choice that suggests how plentiful the opportunities are for giving them:

> Ms. Cooper often delegated tasks that would typically be assigned [by her] to students. We have already described students as providing the text for writing class through Sharing Models/ Generating Characteristics. In this activity, students also took on the task of controlling the floor, which would traditionally be a teacher task. Areas of student control include deciding how to participate, getting the class's attention and leading the discussion by calling on peers. . . . Student readers usually stood in the front of the room, but Ms. Cooper gave students the option of reading from their desks. Students were given the same choice when they shared their rough drafts with the class. The fact that Ms. Cooper did not define this aspect of appropriate participation gave students choice in how to manage this aspect of controlling the floor [p. 22].

The ability of students to make choices and control the activity flow and the discourse within the group is partially responsible for the success of cooperative learning. In all cooperative learning models, students work in groups in which they control the dialogue, who speaks, when, and for how long.

## Using Students and Their Communities as Sources of Knowledge

This aspect of Classroom Climate building is about reaching out to and respecting what students bring to the classroom, their experience, and their questions.

### Constructivist Teaching

Constructivist pedagogy brings student influence to the intellectual life of the classroom and may be the most advanced level of student ownership. It is also the most complex and requires the largest paradigm shift for teachers; most of us, after all, were educated in schools where other people's constructions of knowledge were handed to us for consumption and digestion. Brooks and Brooks (1993) provide five overarching principles of constructivist pedagogy:

1.  Posing problems of emerging relevance to learners.
2.  Structuring learning around "big ideas" or primary concepts.
3.  Seeking and valuing students' points of view.
4.  Adapting curriculum to address students' suppositions.
5.  Assessing student learning in the context of teaching [p. 33].

There is still a place in good education for "active reception learning," as Ausubel (1963) puts it. But there is also a large place for carefully designed teaching that allows students to construct meaning for themselves.

Randolf and Evertson (1995) in their analysis of interactive discourse in a writing class describe this kind of pedagogy: "The construction of knowledge, which takes place through negotiation, depends on the redistribution of power from teachers to students. The fact that knowledge is presumed to come from students defines students as knowledge-holders, an identity usually retained by the teacher" (p. 24).

Constructivist teaching puts students in the legitimate role of knowledge generators and knowledge editors, whether in science, social studies, language arts, or any other academic discipline (Brooks and Brooks, 1993). The examples in the Randolf and Evertson study describe a series of lessons on literary genre. They show how teachers' conscious regulation of dialogue and interaction with students can make students genuinely empowered knowledge generators. For example, one teacher, Ms. Cooper, asked students to bring in examples of fables to share and discuss in class so they could extract the characteristics of fables from analyzing these examples. At one point, she asked the class to look for generalizations they could make about the morals of fables:

TEACHER: What can we say about the characteristics of morals? [Students offer some suggestions.] Maybe we need to explain what a lesson or moral is—how to be a better person. I'm going to put that up, unless you have objections.

LAURIE: They're trying to prevent you from making mistakes. [Teacher writes, "Stories are used to help you become a better person and not make mistakes."]

TIM: I disagree. Sometimes some of the things are wrong.

HILLARY: Can be [used to help you]. [Teacher changes "are" to "can be" in the sentence on the board: "Stories can be used to help you become a better person and not make mistakes."]

ONIKA:  But everybody makes mistakes.

TEACHER:  You're right [Adds to the sentence on the board: "or learn from characters' mistakes in the story."], but the purpose of the fable is to help you not to make so many mistakes.

In analyzing this episode, Randolf and Evertson (1995) comment:

> The discussion begins with Ms. Cooper's question. The answers she receives do not give her the information she wants, so Ms. Cooper supplies her own answer: a moral teaches how to be a better person. In stating her answer, Ms. Cooper clarifies her question: she is asking about the purpose of a moral. With this new information, Laurie is able to supply a response that Ms. Cooper validates by incorporating it into the characteristic she is writing on the chalkboard. So far Ms. Cooper is in the position of authority in the classroom: she initiates the topic, students respond with possible answers, and she evaluates them, rejecting all responses until she hears one that fits her expectations.
>
> The nature of the interaction changes, however, as Tim questions the characteristic that is the joint construction of Ms. Cooper and Laurie. In effect, Tim takes on the role of evaluator of the response, moving Ms. Cooper into the role of co-collaborator with Laurie. Ms. Cooper's response is thus demonstrated to be as open to evaluation as any other participant's response.
>
> Onika and Susan then join the deliberation, questioning the need for morals as they have defined them in class more than they are questioning the definition itself. Why, they argue,

should morals try to keep you from making mistakes, when you're going to make them anyway, and they help you learn? These contributions are initiations of a new topic, which Ms. Cooper responds to and evaluates by treating them as negotiations of meaning, signaling her acceptance by incorporating the new contribution into the statement on the board. Thus, the characteristic as it is finally stated is the joint construction of Ms. Cooper, Laurie, Tim, Hillary, Onika, and Susan [pp. 23–24].

Similar scenarios can be found in the literature for helping students construct knowledge in science and mathematics. This kind of teaching requires a role shift for some teachers of significant proportions away from being dispensers of knowledge to facilitating negotiation of meaning by students.

The role of the teacher in constructivist science teaching is often to involve students in predicting phenomena, then reacting to observed phenomena and constructing hypotheses, which they then test to account for their observations. For example, most students predict that heavy objects fall faster then lighter ones—which is incorrect. The hypothesis making and dialogue about subsequent experiments and explanations that constructivist teachers facilitate have similar qualities to the dialogue in the Randolf and Evertson example.

The changes that take place when teachers move to include more constructivist teaching in their repertoire are subtle but significant. The classroom does not look any different, and the assignments and topics may not seem much different. Where the changes show up is in dialogue with students and in the roles teachers and students are playing in the conversations they have in class. Though surface changes may appear small, the role shift is large, and the evidence is strong that the effect is large in student motivation, effort, and understanding (Newmann and Wehlage, 1995).

## Culturally Relevant Teaching

As we move toward the year 2020, when fully half of all children in the United States will be of color, it is especially important to be creating schools that acknowledge and value the culture of all students. Excluding these children's cultures from school artifacts, customs, arts, and curriculum not only demotivates but alienates significant numbers of students (Cummins, 1986). Ladson-Billings (1995) brings this argument into the more immediate domain of curriculum by pointing out that using the community as a source of curriculum experiences makes learning meaningful and active and also culturally relevant:

> Early in the school year, one teacher asked the students to identify one area in which they believed they had expertise. She then compiled a list of "classroom experts" for distribution to the class. Later, she developed a calendar and asked students to select a date that they would like to make a presentation in their area of expertise. When students made their presentations, their knowledge and expertise was a given. Their classmates were expected to be an attentive audience and to take seriously the knowledge that was being shared by taking notes and/or asking relevant questions. The variety of topics the students offered included rap-music, basketball, gospel singing, cooking, hair braiding, and baby sitting. Other students listed more school-like areas of expertise such as reading, writing, and mathematics. However, all students were required to share their expertise [p. 481].

Some may wonder how such open-ended assignments can be congruent with a school curriculum that contains specific skills the students are supposed to be mastering. By using practices described in Chapter Nineteen of this book, teachers can weave skill objectives for research, organization, and reading, writing, and speaking skills (or any other skills that are in the curriculum) into the criteria for good presentations by student experts. The point that Ladson-Billings makes is that the students own the knowledge they present, and the knowledge is acknowledged to have value. The "classroom experts" assignment is a practice that is congruent with augmenting student ownership and influence because the knowledge of students and the culture from which that knowledge comes—the students' own culture—is explicitly validated by a school learning activity.

Culturally relevant teaching is the topic of the article from which the Ladson-Billings excerpt comes. Culturally relevant teaching does not mean teaching about other cultures, though that can have value. It means validating the culture of students by including in-school learning experiences, topics, scenes, and knowledge that derive from the culture of the students themselves. It looks not only to individual students but also to the community from which the students come as a source of curriculum experiences:

> One teacher used the community as a basis of her curriculum. Her students searched the county historical archives, interviewed long-term residents, constructed and administered surveys and a questionnaire, and invited and listened to guest speakers to get a sense of the historical development of their community. Their ultimate goal was to develop a land

use proposal for an abandoned shopping center that was a magnet for illegal drug use and other dangerous activities. The project ended with the students making a presentation before the City Council and Urban Planning Commission. One of the students remarked to me, "This [community] is not such a bad place. There are a lot of good things that happened here, and some of that is still going on." The teacher told me that she was concerned that too many of the students believed that the only option for success involved moving out of the community, rather than participating in its reclamation [Ladson-Billings, 1995, p. 479].

## Classroom Climate Survey

This is a good point for readers to assess where they are in their thinking and practices with regard to classroom climate. We encourage readers to write answers to the survey questions in Exhibit 14.2 and compare answers in groups with colleagues.

To check your knowledge about Classroom Climate, see the quiz on our Web site at **www. RBTeach.com/rbteach/quiz/CClimate.html.**

**Exhibit 14.2  Classroom Climate Survey**

### Community and Mutual Support

1. How are students encouraged to get to know one another and to get to know other people?
2. When are students listened to, acknowledged, and affirmed as worthwhile, important, and cared-for people?
3. When do students learn group responsibility and interdependence?
4. What opportunities are there for learning social skills and cooperative learning?
5. How are conflict resolution strategies being learned and practiced in the classroom and around the school?

### Risk Taking and Confidence

1. What are the times when students are encouraged to take risks and find out it's okay to do so?
2. What do I do to disabuse students of the life-limiting belief in the virtue of speed versus care and perseverance?
3. When does the belief "good students solicit help and lots of feedback on their work" get communicated in the classroom?
4. In what ways do students learn that effort makes the difference?

### Influence

1. What are the times when students are in a controlling or influencing role?
2. What principles of learning are students knowledgeable about and encouraged to use?
3. What are the opportunities for giving control to students within the models of teaching being used?
4. What opportunities are there to have students be authentic knowledge producers and structure classroom discourse from the constructivist perspective?
5. What opportunities are there for students to be experts?
6. What are the ways in which the local community culture is viewed as a source of authorized curriculum and thus as a worthwhile source of knowledge?

**Research for Better Teaching, Inc.** • One Acton Place, Acton, MA 01720 • (978) 263-9449 • www.RBTeach.com

*Source Materials on Classroom Climate*

Aronson, E. *The Jigsaw Classroom.* Thousand Oaks, Calif.: Sage, 1978.

Aspy, D., and Roebuck, F. N. *Kids Don't Learn from People They Don't Like.* Amherst, Mass.: Human Resource Development Press, 1977.

Ausubel, D. P. *The Psychology of Meaningful Verbal Learning.* New York: Grune & Stratton, 1963.

Barbe, W. B., and Milone, M. N., Jr. "Modality." *Instructor,* Jan. 1980, pp. 44–47.

Battistich, V., Solomon, M. W., Solomon, J., and Schaps, E. "Effects of an Elementary School Program to Enhance Prosocial Behavior on Children's Cognitive-Social Problem-Solving Skills and Strategies." *Journal of Applied Developmental Psychology,* 1989, *10,* 147–169.

Battistich, V., and others. "Schools as Communities, Poverty Levels of Student Populations, and Students' Attitudes, Motives, and Performance: A Multilevel Analysis." *American Educational Research Journal,* 1995, *32,* 627–658.

Bennett, B., and Smilanich, P. *Classroom Management.* Ontario, Canada: VISUTRONIX, Bookation, 1994.

Berger, R. "Building a School Culture of High Standards." Unpublished paper. Shutesbury, Mass.: Shutesbury Schools, 1990.

Berman, S. "Educating for Social Responsibility." *Educational Leadership,* Nov. 1990, 75–80.

Brooks, J. G., and Brooks, M. G. *The Case for Constructivist Classrooms.* Alexandria, Va.: ASCD, 1993.

Bruer, J. T. "The Mind's Journey from Novice to Expert." *American Educator,* 1993, *38,* 6–15.

Bruner, J. *The Process of Education.* Cambridge, Mass.: Harvard University Press, 1977.

Cabello, B., and Terell, R. "Making Students Feel Like Family: How Teachers Create Warm and Caring Classroom Climates." *Journal of Classroom Interaction,* 1993, *29,* 17–23.

Charney, R. S. *Teaching to Care: Management in the Responsive Classroom.* Greenfield, Mass.: Northeast Foundation for Children, 1992.

Chavez, R. "The Use of High-Inference Measures to Study Classroom Climates: A Review." *Review of Educational Research,* 1984, *54,* 237–261.

Crocker, R. K., and Brooker, G. M. "Classroom Control and Student Outcomes in Grades 2 and 5." *American Educational Research Journal,* 1986, *23,* 1–11.

Cummins, J. "Empowering Minority Students: A Framework for Intervention." *Harvard Educational Review,* 1986, *56,* 18–36.

Curran, L. *Cooperative Lessons for Little Ones.* San Juan Capistrano, Calif.: Resources for Teachers, 1991.

Deng, B. "A Multilevel Analysis of Classroom Climate Effects on Mathematics Achievement of Fourth-Grade Students." Unpublished paper, Feb. 1992. (ED 348 222)

Dodd, A. W. "Engaging Students: What I Learned Along the Way." *Educational Leadership,* Sept. 1995, pp. 65–67.

Dreikurs, R. *Psychology in the Classroom.* New York: HarperCollins, 1957.

Dreikurs, R., and Grey, L. A. *A New Approach to Classroom Discipline: Logical Consequences.* New York: HarperCollins, 1968.

Dunn, R., and Dunn, K. *Teaching Students Through Their Individual Learning Styles: A Practical Approach.* Boston: Allyn & Bacon, 2001.

Ellsworth, P. C., and Sindt, V. G. "Helping 'Aha' to Happen: The Contributions of Irving Sigel." *Educational Leadership,* Feb. 1994, pp. 40–44.

Fraser, B. J. "Two Decades of Research on Perceptions of Classroom Environment." In B. J. Fraser (ed.), *The Study of Learning Environments.* Salem, Ore.: Assessment Research, 1986.

Fraser, B. J., and Fisher, D. L. "Student Achievement as a Function of Person-Environment Fit: A Regression Surface Analysis." *British Journal of Educational Psychology,* 1983, *53,* 89–99.

Fraser, B. J., and O'Brien, P. "Student and Teacher Perceptions of the Environment of Elementary School Classrooms." *Elementary School Journal,* 1985, *20,* 567–580.

Fraser, B. J., Malone, J. A., and Neale, J. M. "Assessing and Improving the Psychosocial Environment of Mathematics Classrooms." *Journal of Research in Mathematics Education,* 1989, *20,* 191–201.

Gardner, H. *Multiple Intelligences: New Horizons.* New York: Basic Books, 2006.

Gibbs, J. *Tribes: A Process for Social Development and Cooperative Learning.* (2nd ed.). Santa Rosa, Calif.: Center Source Publications, 1989.

Glasser, W. *Reality Therapy.* New York: HarperCollins, 1965.

Glasser, W. *Schools Without Failure.* New York: HarperCollins, 1969.

Glasser, W. *The Total Quality School.* New York: HarperCollins, 1998.

Gordon, T. *T.E.T.: Teacher Effectiveness Training.* New York: Peter H. Wyden, 1974.

Gould, S. J. *The Mismeasure of Man.* New York: Norton, 1982.

Gregorc, A. F. *Inside Styles: Beyond the Basics.* Maynard, Mass.: Gabriel Systems, 1985.

Haertel, G. D., Walberg, H. J., and Haertel, E. H. "Socio-Psychological Environments and Learning: A Quantitative Synthesis." *British Educational Research Journal,* 1981, *7,* 27–36.

Harrison, A. F., and Bramson, R. M. *The Art of Thinking.* New York: Berkeley Books, 1982.

Hodgkinson, H. Presentation to Phi Delta Kappan Annual Conference, 1993.

Howard, J. *The Social Construction of Intelligence.* Lexington, Mass.: Efficacy, 1993.

Johnson, D. W., and Johnson, R. T. *Learning Together and Alone: Cooperative, Competitive, and Individualistic Learning.* (2nd ed.). Upper Saddle River, N.J.: Prentice Hall, 1987.

Johnson, D. W., and Johnson, R. T. *Teaching Students to Be Peacemakers.* Edina, Minn.: Interaction Book Co., 1995a.

Johnson, D. W., and Johnson, R. T. "Why Violence Prevention Programs Don't Work—What Does." *Educational Leadership,* Feb. 1995b, pp. 63–68.

Johnson, D. W., and Johnson, R. T. *Learning Together and Alone.* (2nd ed.). Upper Saddle River, N.J.: Prentice Hall, 1987.

Kagan, S. *Cooperative Learning.* San Juan Capistrano, Calif.: Kagan Cooperative Learning, 1997.

Katz, L. "Five Keys to Successful Implementation of the Whole." Presentation to the Association for Supervision and Curriculum Development, New Orleans, 1992.

Kreidler, W. J. *Creative Conflict Resolution.* Glenview, Ill.: Scott Foresman, 1984.

Ladson-Billings, G. "Toward a Theory of Culturally Relevant Pedagogy." *American Educational Research Journal,* 1995, *32,* 465–491. Reproduced with permission from *American Educational Research.*

Lafferty, J. C. *The Subarctic Survival Situation.* Plymouth, Mich.: Human Synergistics, 1992.

Lampert, M. "When the Problem Is Not the Question and the Solution Not the Answer: Mathematical Knowing and Teaching." *American Educational Research Journal,* 1990, *27*(1), 29–63.

Lazear, D. *Multiple Intelligence Approaches to Assessment: Solving the Assessment Conundrum.* Chicago: Zephyr Press, 1998.

Lazear, D. *Eight Ways of Knowing: Teaching with Multiple Intelligences.* Chicago: Zephyr Press, 2003.

Mamchur, C. "But the Curriculum." *Phi Delta Kappan,* Apr. 1990, pp. 634–637.

Maslow, A. *Toward a Psychology of Being.* Princeton, N.J.: Van Nostrand, 1962.

McCabe, M. E., and Rhoades, J. *The Nurturing Classroom.* Willits, Calif.: ITA Publications, 1989.

McCarthy, B. *Teaching Around the 4MAT Cycle: Designing Instruction for Diverse Learners with Diverse Learning Styles.* Thousand Oaks, Calif.: Corwin Press, 2005.

Moos, R. H., and Moos, B. S. "Classroom Social Climate and Students' Absences and Grades." *Journal of Educational Psychology,* 1978, *70,* 263–269.

Myers, I. B., and McCaulley, M. H. *Manual: A Guide to the Development and Use of the Myers-Briggs Type Indicator.* Palo Alto, Calif.: Consulting Psychologists Press, 1985.

Nelson, J., Lott, L., and Glenn, H. S. *Positive Discipline in the Classroom.* Rocklin, Calif.: Prima Publishing, 1993.

Newmann, F. M., and Wehlage, G. G. *Successful School Restructuring.* Madison: University of Wisconsin, 1995.

Nunnery, J. A., Butler, E. D., and Bhaireddy, V. N. "Relationships Between Classroom Climate, Student Characteristics, and Language Achievement in the Elementary Classroom: An Exploratory Investigation." Paper presented at the Annual Meeting of the American Educational Research Association, Atlanta, Apr. 1993.

Oakes, J. *Keeping Track.* New Haven, Conn.: Yale University Press, 1985.

Pfeiffer, J. W., and Jones, J. E. *A Handbook of Structured Experiences for Human Relations Training.* La Jolla, Calif.: University Associates, 1974.

Poplin, M., and Weeres, J. *Voices from the Inside.* Claremont, Calif.: Institute for Education in Transformation, Claremont Graduate School, 1992.

Randolf, C. H., and Evertson, C. M. "Managing for Learning: Rules, Roles, and Meanings in a Writing Class." *Journal of Classroom Interaction,* 1995, *30,* 17–25.

Ring, K., and Cooper, S. *Mindsight.* New Lenox, Ill.: Institute of Transpersonal Psychology, 1989.

Scearce, C. *100 Ways to Build Teams.* Palatine, Ill.: IRI/Skylight Publishing, 1992.

Schutz, W. J. *Expanding Human Awareness.* New York: Grove Press, 1967.

Seigle, P., and Macklem, G. *Social Competency Program.* Wellesley, Mass.: Stone Center, 1993.

Sharan, Y., and Sharan, S. *Expanding Cooperative Learning Through Group Investigation.* New York: Teachers College Press, 1992.

Shaw, V. *Community Building in the Classroom.* San Juan Capistrano, Calif.: Kagan Cooperative Learning, 1992.

Slavin, R. *Using Student Team Learning.* Baltimore: Center for Research on Elementary and Middle Schools, Johns Hopkins University, 1986.

Solomon, D., and others. "Enhancing Children's Prosocial Behavior in the Classroom." *American Educational Research Journal,* 1988, *25,* 527–554.

Stanford, G. *Developing Effective Classroom Groups.* New York: Hart Publishing Co., 1977.

Stephenson, J., and Watrous, B. "The Morning Meeting Repertoire: A Collection of Ideas That Work." *Responsive Classroom* 1993, *5*(2), 8.

Sylvester, R. *A Celebration of Neurons: An Educator's Guide to the Human Brain.* Alexandria, Va.: Association for Supervision and Curriculum Development, 1994.

Vernon, D. S., Schumaker, J. B., and Deshler, D. D. *The SCORE Skills: Social Skills for Cooperative Groups.* Lawrence, Kans.: Edge Enterprises, 1993.

Wade, R. C. "Encouraging Student Initiative in a Fourth Grade Classroom." *Elementary School Journal,* 1995, *95,* 339–354.

Weiner, B. *Theories of Motivation: From Mechanism to Cognition.* Chicago: Markham, 1972.

Wentzel, K. R. "Social Competence at School: Relation Between Social Responsibility and Academic Achievement." *Review of Educational Research,* 1991, *61,* 1–24.

Withall, J. "Development of a Technique for the Measurement of Socio-Emotional Climate in Classroom." *Journal of Experimental Education,* 1949, *17,* 347–361.

Wood, C. *Yardsticks.* Greenfield, Mass.: Northeast Foundation for Children, 1994a.

Wood, C. *The Responsive Classroom.* Greenfield, Mass.: Northeast Foundation for Children, 1994b.

Yager, S., Johnson, R., Johnson, D., and Snider, B. "The Impact of Group Processing on Achievement in Cooperative Learning Groups." *Journal of Social Psychology,* 1986, *125,* 389–397.

# INTRODUCTION TO CURRICULUM

**P**art Four is about the thinking and design that go into planning successful instruction. The anchor and starting point of planning daily lessons is a good curriculum.

The standards movement has caused a rethinking of what good curriculum is and how to create it. Since schools are making the commitment to have all students reach proficiency, just presenting material and covering topics is no longer acceptable. Curricula must be designed so there is great clarity about what schools want students to learn and how to know when they do.

Chapter Fifteen, "Curriculum Design," describes what teachers should have in hand from the district so their planning is solidly rooted in the commitments made to what children are supposed to be learning. A good curriculum provides the intellectual superstructure from which teachers take guidelines for the direction and content of their lessons. In Figure Part 4.1 (which does, indeed, resemble a Melitta coffeemaker!), the curriculum is the top section; a teacher's thinking goes through this top to funnel down to today's objective. The neck of the coffeemaker is crystal clear thinking about the objective of today's lesson. But first the top funnel of good curriculum guidance is required so that the objective will be important, appropriate, and consistent with agreements about what should be taught.

Although getting clear on objectives is part of a bigger construct (lesson planning), it is such an important part that we devote all of Chapter Sixteen, "Objectives," to this topic. It is at the junction of the two sections of the coffeemaker because if anything goes wrong here, we get no coffee (no learning) at all. The planning never produces results because the objective is fuzzy or inappropriate. And fuzzy thinking about objectives is at the root of an enormous number of teaching and learning shortfalls in our schools.

When the objective is clear and appropriate, teachers can carry on with good planning for the experiences that are created for students in the actual lesson.

**Figure Part 4.1 Curriculum, Objective, and Learning Experiences**

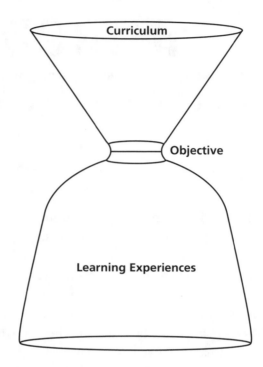

Chapter Seventeen on planning is a detailed exposition of the cognitive scenarios good teachers go through in their heads prior to instruction.

Together these three chapters form a piece. They need each other. Good planning requires good objectives to be anchored and purposive. A good objective needs a good curriculum behind it to be important and clear. Successful teaching requires that professionals be knowledgeable and skillful at all three.

Chapter Eighteen on learning experiences profiles the variables we control in designing, the texture of what students actually do. This is a chapter of particular interest to those who want to study differentiation of their instruction. The thirteen variables in this chapter are, in fact, a comprehensive layout of design features we can differentiate to address the learning styles of our students.

Chapter Nineteen gives us the framework to make assessment a tool for student learning, not just a measuring device. It also places emphasis on student ownership and the motivational opportunities inherent in good assessment practices.

Finally, Chapter Twenty, "Overarching Objectives," describes the way in which our core values can influence our instruction and have positive consequences for student learning.

# Curriculum Design

The curriculum for any subject or course at any grade level consists of a set of agreements between the district office (or academic department) and its teachers about the elements below. This chapter describes those agreements. Teachers need to understand the status of these agreements thoroughly if they are to be effective at choosing instructional materials for daily use, participating in curriculum development groups, and, most important, be skilled at planning good lessons. After defining and describing these agreements, we highlight the ones we believe are essential for every district to have and for teachers to use as a foundation for their lesson planning.

## Agreements of Curriculum

Records of the agreements that have been worked through can be found in curriculum guides in most schools and districts. The curriculum children actually receive depends on how faithfully these agreements are carried out.

These agreements are about (the asterisked items are the essential ones):

- Topics to be taught*
- Big ideas*
- Units of study organized around the big ideas*

- Learning expectations (or learning outcomes) for a grade or course*
- Uniform assessments (sometimes called benchmark assessments), especially final assessments, interim assessments, and unit assessments*
- Criteria for proficiency on assessment items*
- End-of-course samples of proficient student work (an exemplar everyone can look at to see exactly what the district really means by the learning expectation)*
- Pedagogical practices
- Pacing guides and curriculum maps
- Lesson plans
- Time allocations
- Instructional strategies
- Materials
- Resources

Many districts are not sufficiently explicit about what their curriculum is. An additional problem may be insufficient control over how it is implemented, even if certain elements are clear. Thus, the experience of children going from grade to grade may depend on individual choices teachers make about what to teach. It is important to know the stance your district has taken toward curriculum so you know what you're accountable for. Otherwise, there's a lot that can go wrong.

What can go wrong with curriculum? Consider the following possibilities:

- There isn't one.
- There used to be one. It might be around here somewhere.
- There is one, but nobody teaches it.
- There is one, but people teach what they want out of it, which means the students' experience is all over the place.

- There are no common assessments.
- The curriculum is the textbooks.
- The curriculum is neat activities, not a focus on student learning.
- There is a curriculum, but it does not match the standards teachers are responsible for.
- The curriculum office says what to teach, when, and for how long, with what materials, what methods, and exactly what to say as you teach it, making teachers feel as if they are in a straitjacket.

Districts that are clear avoid these problems and give teachers a solid ground on which to stand that balances cohesiveness, accountability, and professional decision making.

The agreements that comprise a curriculum (or absence of agreements) are about what is required, what is recommended but optional, and what is free choice for each of the elements (Figure 15.1). Exhibit 15.1 shows these elements in a grid that can be filled in with specifics to profile the status of agreements for any given curriculum.

It is certainly not necessary or even desirable to have districtwide requirements or uniformity on all the elements. We do advocate, however, having the three key elements in place that together define learning outcomes: end-of-course exemplars of proficient student work for a grade level or a course understood and used in common across the district for skills and academic content; uniform final assessments; and clear criteria for student success listed for interim benchmark assessment and the final assessment. The exemplars define for all to see what the standards are. When the interim or final assessment is a test (rather than a performance) the test items are quite important because, combined with criteria that define the desired level of performance, they end up defining the learning objectives. Without

**Figure 15.1. Mandala of Curriculum Agreements**

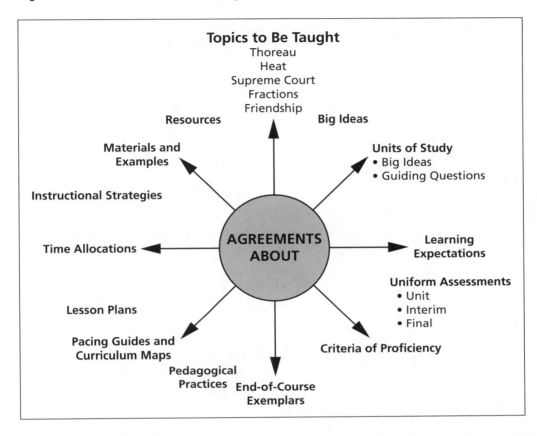

**Research for Better Teaching, Inc.** • One Acton Place, Acton, MA 01720 • (978)263-9449 • www.RBTeach.com

agreement on these things, it is impossible to know what the district's standards are.

For consistency purposes we also recommend uniform unit assessments across grade levels and courses and at benchmark periods, say, quarterly. That's the most basic level of having a curriculum that is coherent. On that basis, the district can say to parents, "We have consistency over the learning designed for your children."

Districts should, of course, also come to agreement about what topics students should study in academic units, with big ideas specifically identified. This keeps teachers' daily planning focused on the big ideas (enduring understandings). For pedagogical practices, we recommend an emphasis on formative classroom assessment and frequent feedback to students. (These items are required criteria in the "Standards for Accreditation" for K–12 schools issued by the New England Association of Schools and Colleges, 2000.) Finally, the foundation of any curriculum is a compact list of exactly what we want students to learn or be able to do (learning expectations or outcomes). The list should be one or two pages, suitable for handing to a newly hired teacher as a road map of the year. The items on this list should highlight the learning expectations that are essential versus those that are important or just nice to know.

**Exhibit 15.1. Matrix of Curriculum Agreements**

| Curriculum Element | Required | Recommended But Optional | Free Choice |
|---|---|---|---|
| Topics to Be Taught | | | |
| Big Ideas | | | |
| Units of Study<br>• Big ideas<br>• Guiding questions | | | |
| Learning Expectations | | | |
| Uniform Performance Assessments | | | |
| Criteria for Proficiency | | | |
| End-of-Course Exemplars | | | |
| Pedagogical Practices | | | |
| Pacing Guides | | | |
| Lesson Plans | | | |
| Time Allocations | | | |
| Instructional Strategies | | | |
| Activities, Materials, and Examples | | | |
| Resources for Teachers | | | |

**Research for Better Teaching, Inc.** • One Acton Place, Acton, MA 01720 • (978) 263-9449 • www.RBTeach.com

For the other items, we take no value position. What is required and what is optional should be a local teacher and school decision based on context and needs. It's simply that what the local decision is should be clear to all concerned (and it often isn't).

# Defining Elements of Curriculum

In this section, we define each element of curriculum.

## Topics

A topic is a bounded content focus: for example, the Civil War, fractions, Henry David Thoreau, heat, or French Impressionism. Topics are usually divided into a list of subtopics.

Wiggins and McTighe (2005) write about the overloaded curriculum and recommend choosing what is essential knowledge to teach as opposed to what is important and, finally, what is nice but not essential. Doug Reeves calls the essential items "power standards." He describes these as having durability and leverage because they are useful in a range of circumstances and academic disciplines. Graphing is an example. We apply our knowledge of graphs to reading newspapers, social studies and science textbooks, and directions for operating equipment we buy. The reason for making these discriminations is to enable teachers to prioritize the mass of material in their curricula. Agreement about which topics or skills are required is one way to take care of this need.

Themes are broad areas of inquiry thought to be of overarching significance, like social justice, understanding differences, how scientists think, and solving complex problems, that may run the duration of a course or a year. Not all curricula or school districts choose to embed themes in curricula. A theme by itself is an inadequate organizer for the topics in a curriculum or a unit, and excessive use of themes can lead to pure activity-based teaching ("Let's do friendship. I have some great books on friendship.") In contrast, an essential question for this topic might be, "What is friendship?" and the learning experiences might enable students to create a list of attributes for friendship. Properly chosen themes are really essential questions in disguise.

## Big Ideas

Big ideas (or enduring understandings) are important ideas that students should carry away from the study of a topic. A big idea is an understanding that is intended to last a lifetime. Examples are:

- "The planet's' resources are finite."
- "There is a conflict between acting in the long-term interest of the environment and the short-term interest of certain economic groups."
- "If you want to assess the effect of a change (mechanical, scientific, or even social), you have to hold the other variables constant while you experiment with changing one thing at a time."

An enduring understanding gets to the heart of the academic discipline. Table 15.1 provides some samples from elementary literacy and mathematics.

Big ideas are interesting and applicable. They give students a reason and a focus for studying smaller elements in the curriculum. They provide a cognitive hook for the item currently under study in a unit. It is important for a teacher to show how an item under study connects to a big idea. When that happens, it serves both a cognitive and a motivational purpose.

**Table 15.1. Enduring Understandings for Literacy and Math**

**Literacy**

Understanding is promoted by a reader's use of strategies and tools.

Different forms of print have different functions.

Knowledge about genre characteristics helps a reader construct meaning.

**Math**

Estimation prior to performing a computation helps ensure reasonable answers.

Any measurement other than counting produces an approximate rather than an exact value.

There is a one-to-one match between real numbers and points on a line.

*Source:* Weston, Massachusetts, public schools.

Curriculum is also empowered by well-chosen guiding questions (or essential questions) to frame and motivate the lessons. A guiding question is a fundamental query that directs the search for understanding. It is open-ended and succinct, and it contains emotive force and intellectual bite. It raises other important questions and frames outcomes as culminating insights derived from inquiry. Everything in the unit is studied for the purpose of answering it. "What is worth fighting for?" "Where do waves come from?" "Who was a great person?" (Traver, 1998).

## Units of Study

A unit is an organization of student experiences that are sequenced deliberately to create a cumulative effect. The unit package provides materials for students to study, materials for teachers to use

for advancing ideas and skills, student tasks, directions for student activities, and a host of supplementary ideas and guidelines for teachers to use. Not all units contain big ideas, but they should.

Certain segments of elementary reading, writing, and mathematics instruction may not be organized into units, but rather be considered continuous strands of instruction. Primary reading curriculum is an example where a balanced literacy approach uses guided reading of sequenced texts to develop a wide range of skills arrayed on a continuum. Even without units of study, however, teachers can still teach for big ideas.

Table 15.2 summarizes key terms from the Wiggins and McTighe model and shows their relation to one another as well as to goals for units and the mastery objectives for lessons.

Good units are planned backward from a clear image of what we want the students to be able to do at the end. The end-of-unit assessments are designed right after the identification of the big ideas. This is in marked contrast to the dominant twentieth-century method, where the topics were picked first, then the activities were designed, and then the students were tested by assessments designed at the end. The two approaches are summarized in Figure 15.2.

## Learning Expectations

The following statements are taken from state standards documents and are examples of what might be given to a teacher to identify the knowledge or skills fourth graders are expected to master by the end of the year:

- Students will be able to identify the meaning of common idioms and figurative phrases (English Language Arts)

**Table 15.2. Examples of Curriculum Technology**

| Examples for Examining Curriculum Terminology | Example 1 | Where You Might See It |
|---|---|---|
| Overarching theme of year | What is a just society? | On a banner over the board |
| Enduring understanding (big idea) | There is a tension in foreign affairs between acting in one's national self-interest and respecting the national sovereignty of others. | This generalization may be brought out in class discussion, sought in student learning logs, or converted into a question for essays or debate, for example |
| Essential question (guiding question) | Is the U.S. military justified in actively intervening in internal affairs of another country? If so, when? | In a corner of the board or in materials framing the unit |
| Broad content goal for a two-week study—a unit objective | The Panama Case: Using Defense Department and State Department documents from the period, as well as news reports from the *New York Times* archives, students will be prepared to compare and contrast the cases of the Falklands, Grenada, and Panama. | Assignment sheets |
| Specific mastery objective (performance indicator) for the next two days—a lesson objective | Students will be able to explain the mechanisms and sequence of steps in the drug trade through Panama in the 1980s. | On the board as class begins and shared explicitly with students |

| | Example 2 | On a banner over the board |
|---|---|---|
| Overarching theme of year | What is a just society? | |
| Enduring understanding (big idea) | The planet's resources are finite. There is a conflict between acting in the long-term interest of the environment and the short-term interest of certain economic groups. | This generalization may be brought out in class discussion, sought in student learning logs, or converted into a question for essays or debate, for example |
| Essential question (guiding question) | When is it appropriate to promulgate regulations for environmental safety that will cost jobs? | In a corner of the board or in materials framing the unit |
| Broad content goal for a two- or three-week study—a unit objective | Using online national databases and reports from the EPA and the electric power industry, students will be able to take a position and defend their cases for raising or not raising pollution standards at electric power plants. | Assignment sheets |
| Specific mastery objective (performance indicator) for the next two days | Students will be able to use statistics about rising air pollution 1960–2005 and rising use of fossil fuel from multiple sources to graph the power industry's contribution to air pollution. | On the board as class begins and shared explicitly with students |

**Research for Better Teaching, Inc.** • One Acton Place, Acton, MA 01720 • (978) 263-9449 • www.RBTeach.com

**Figure 15.2. Design Sequence: Old Model, New Model**

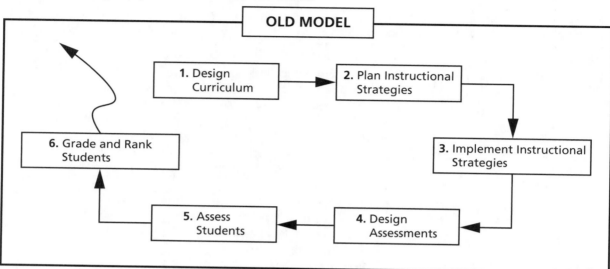

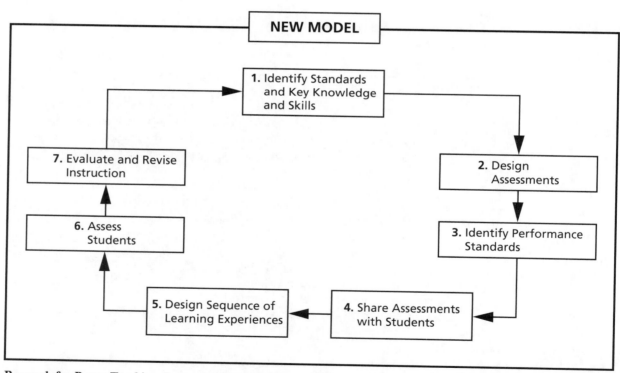

**Research for Better Teaching, Inc.** • One Acton Place, Acton, MA 01720 • (978) 263-9449 • www.RBTeach.com

- Students will be able to express an opinion of a literary work or film in an organized way, with supporting detail (English Language Arts)
- Students will be able to use concrete objects and visual models to add and subtract common fractions and represent answers in lowest terms. (Math)

These statements are typical of those found in standards documents across the fifty states. A more comprehensive list of such statements can serve as a simple map of what to teach.

However, these statements do not specify the level of difficulty or complexity of the reading or the comparison that the students are expected to produce. These statements of learning expectations do tell us for what student performances we will need exemplars, but they don't spell out precisely the level of performance expected or the criteria for determining proficiency. So it is one useful resource in need of others.

## Uniform Performance Assessments

Good curriculum contains specifications for evidence of student learning, specifically tasks, assignments, tests, and quizzes that would produce this evidence. This evidence may come from observations of student performance, interviews consisting of question-and-answer exchanges with students, and sample student products. Such assessments may also include performance tasks, products, and projects that are uniformly given to all students across a grade level in a given subject to evaluate student mastery of the material at the end of a unit. As curriculum gets more developed, uniform assessments come every quarter, not just at end of the course or year.

## Criteria for Proficiency

The uniform performance task is not quite enough. We need explicit, public grading criteria as well. For example, consider this learning expectation: "Express an opinion of a literary work or film in an organized way, with supporting detail." The criteria for success are:

- Include an introduction that summarizes the work's genre, plot, or main point
- A statement of your opinion
- Three details to support your opinion
- One text-to-text connection
- Summary

These criteria direct us to scrutinize a student product for specific features that, if present, allow it to be evidence of proficiency.

Criteria are sometimes represented in analytic rubrics, devices designed to show relative and specific degrees of completeness of student product in relation to specific criteria. It is the criteria behind the rubrics that are most important, however. Rubrics are not always needed, but criteria are.

## End-of-Course or End-of-Year Samples of Proficient Student Work

An end-of-course or end-of-year sample of proficient student work (often referred to as an "exemplar") is a template against which to compare evidence that an important proficiency has been met by a student. It embodies in a finished product and makes concrete exactly what we expect students to be able to do in a particular academic area at the end of a semester or school year. These are, for example, sample student responses to data-based questions that meet criteria for proficiency, writing products that show the level of skill students are expected to display, projects, problems solved, lab reports written, and videos of verbal presentations, among others.

A benchmark is a specific performance to shoot for that marks progress toward, not final attainment of, a higher goal. Runners set themselves targets or benchmarks that gauge their progress toward a winning time. They feel good when they pass the benchmark, but their training isn't over yet. The benchmark signals that a significant increment of improvement has been passed. Thus, there should be more benchmarks in a course or grade level than just one at the end of the course or semester. There can be as many or as few as are appropriate for the content or skills being learned. In guided reading in the primary grades, each alphabetical level of book is a benchmark of a sort. A child moving up from "M" to "N" books has passed a benchmark with specific observable performance associated with it. In many schools, quarterly assessments are developed to spell out intermediate levels of performance on the road to final proficiency.

## Pedagogical Practices

A pedagogical practice is a commitment to a form of instruction that has a research base or perhaps a philosophical base. For example, a district or a curriculum department may have a commitment to writing across the curriculum, in which case all teachers may be asked to have students keep written learning logs of some kind in which they reflect on their learning each day. Or the school may have a commitment to cooperative learning, or project-based learning, or integration of technology, or a certain balance of formative and summative assessment that they expect as well as student self-assessment and goal setting. Such com-

mitments might show up in how curriculum is constructed and implemented. Above all, such practices if expected should be explicit to all and part of induction for new teachers.

## Pacing Guides

A pacing guide is an approximate timetable that lays out how much time it usually takes to complete each set of lessons of each unit of study. This is particularly useful to teachers who haven't taught a curriculum before.

A scope and sequence chart often lays out a sequence of topics or skills for a content area but does not give a sense of how long components take to learn under normal circumstances.

A curriculum map (Jacobs, 1997) is a diagram that shows the development from year to year of content and skill knowledge. This allows a school and district to avoid repetition ("But we learned about latitude and longitude in fifth grade and seventh grade . . .") and make sequencing of content rational, reinforcing, and without gaps.

## Lesson Plans

Lesson plans are detailed implementation scenarios that specify the learning objectives and experiences students will go through and tasks they will be asked to do. Many other components may be part of the scenario too, like motivators, activators, descriptions of equipment to use, pages in books, and assessment devices. We devote Chapter Seventeen, "Planning," to this important topic.

Lesson plan samples are often part of good curriculum guides, but detailed plans for individual lessons should be made up by teachers who use the unit plan as the framework and district lesson plans and materials banks as resources to draw from. This is because good planning requires teachers to think deeply about the content, analyze what prerequisite skills and knowledge will be fundamental to understanding the new material, and consider that in light of what they know about their students, they need to plan preassessment, determine how to best present a concept to match needs and background knowledge of their students, anticipate confusions students may have during a given lesson, and so on. Thus a detailed implementation scenario should stem from the teacher having dug into the content herself and determined how to support all students in achieving the lesson objective.

## Time Allocations

Certain districts mandate how many minutes per day must be spent on certain subjects in elementary school. In some places, this can go so far as how many minutes within the language arts block are spent on guided reading, interactive writing, free reading, and other topics. These time allocations may be recommended, mandatory, or nonexistent. It all depends on what is decided would be best in the local context and what has been clearly agreed.

## Instructional Strategies

It is also possible that there are some schoolwide or grade-level commitments to particular instructional strategies, like the use of certain graphic organizers, of selective manipulatives in math, and of particular discussion formats or reading comprehension strategies. Sometimes they are integrated into curriculum designs. In contrast to pedagogical practices, which are big conceptually, such as constructivism and active learning, an instructional strategy is small, such as modeling thinking aloud, "Carousel Brainstorming," and so on.

## Activities, Materials, and Examples

At a very detailed level, it may be expected or perhaps only recommended that teachers use particular instructional materials, like fraction bars for math or the History Alive Curriculum or a particular apparatus to illustrate acceleration as a principle of Newtonian physics. Required use of certain textbooks adopted districtwide falls in this category.

## Resources for Teachers

Depending on the size and budget of the district, any of the following resources may be available for teachers to draw on:

*Print Materials*
- Curriculum guides
- Lists of recommended books and materials
- Unit guides
- Recommended Web sites
- Sample lessons
- Curriculum libraries of great units

*Physical Materials*
- Math manipulatives
- Science apparatus

*Human Resources*
- Building-based curriculum specialists
- Staff development on planning skills
- District curriculum specialists
- Staff development on analysis of data
- Staff development of teachers
- Culture of sharing units and materials
- Professional norms of joint planning

*Other*
- Collections of instructional materials available for loan

- Association memberships
- Funds for attending content-area conferences and professional development workshops

A distinction must be made between materials and resources. *Materials* are tangible items used to implement lessons, to teach the curriculum. *Resources* are what teachers use to prepare themselves to teach it well.

## A Lesson Looked at from a Curriculum Point of View

Lesson plans are guided by the curriculum but not necessarily spelled out in the curriculum. Let us define a lesson as *a time span when a teacher takes a bounded chunk of material from a unit or a topic and creates an experience or a series of experiences for students.* The idea is that when the lesson is over, most of the students have learned whatever was the target, whether a skill (for example locating places by latitude and longitude) or a concept (for example, the separate powers of the three branches of the U.S. government and their checks and balances on each other).

This definition of a lesson is thus tied to material to be learned rather than to time. A lesson can take more than one class period. If a lesson is good, it will have most of the following parts, although not all may be used in a single class period because some steps are coming later or have already happened:

- Precision: A clear statement of objective in mastery language (what students will know or be able to do) exists, plus other elements profiled in Chapter Seventeen.

- Connections: There are links with similar lessons being taught elsewhere in the district with regard to rigor, consistency, and alignment.
- Rigor: The standards for proficiency are high enough.
- Consistency: "Proficient student performance" has the same meaning throughout the school or the district.
- Alignment: What's supposed to be taught is actually taught and actually tested.

## Lesson Planning and Instruction

The implementation of a lesson is marked by unplanned behaviors that come from a teacher's instructional repertoire and decisions made on the fly that are not always premeditated:

- Checking for understanding that is frequent and broad to identify when to slow down, stop, or reteach, and for whom
- Unscrambling confusions that gets students to make visible their thinking, assumptions, or processes
- Explicitness
- Cognitive connections

Teachers design lessons that are based on what is in the curriculum. The lessons teachers design may or may not draw heavily on district support materials, unit guides, and other resources. But the lessons themselves, that is, the sequence of activities and tasks students do daily, are formulated by the teacher as designer. They are not specified and required in the curriculum. This does not mean that the teacher has to make them up from scratch each day. It's just that in a district that values professionalism, the teacher makes choices about what the appropriate activities and tasks are for students. The teacher is a designer of student work. To prescribe what teachers should do in lessons can be insulting to professionals and deny students the benefit of informed professional decisions about the how, when, and how fast of instruction.

We do wish to acknowledge that for novice teachers and paraprofessionals, it may be appropriate to provide scripts of what good presentations or questioning would sound like and to prescribe in considerable detail how to set up materials and get students to engage them. But such scripts should be used only as needed for inexperienced personnel and only until their diagnostic and planning skills reach professional levels. Table 15.3 shows the relationship of lessons, units, and courses.

## Indicators of a Well-Developed and Coherent Curriculum

Besides the existence of good curriculum documents (blueprints, frameworks, and guides), one might find:

- Book closets and audiovisual repositories where materials consistent with the curriculum are stored and accessible to teachers.
- A compilation of assessments that are uniform and used by all teachers of a given subject or topic
- Talk at grade level or department meetings about curriculum implementation and improvement
- State standards and framework documents readily available

**Table 15.3. Relationship of Lessons, Units, and Courses**

| | Duration | Central Elements | Measurement by | Records |
|---|---|---|---|---|
| **Course** | Semester or year | Overarching theme<br>Proficiency targets<br>　Exemplars<br>　Criteria<br>　Rubric | Benchmark performances or products<br>Final examinations<br>Comprehensive orals | Certification of proficiency (3 on a 4-point scale)<br>Credits<br>Final grade |
| **Unit** | Weeks or months | Big ideas/enduring understandings<br>Guiding/essential questions<br>Evidence of learning | Projects<br>Unit tests<br>Performances | Grades tied to rubrics |
| **Lesson** | One to three class periods | Mastery objectives | Observation<br>Inspection of student work<br>Quizzes<br>Products<br>Q&A interviews | Checklists<br>Gradebooks<br>Anecdotal notes<br>Running records |

**Research for Better Teaching, Inc.** • One Acton Place, Acton, MA 01720 • (978) 263-9449 • www.RBTeach.com

- Individual classrooms outfitted with a copy of relevant standards and curriculum guides
- Banks of exemplars of student work at proficiency for various units and skills available for teachers
- Lesson plan banks of exemplary lessons available
- Time built into the professional development schedule for improving the teaching of specific units or topics in the curriculum

## Conclusion

The common understandings and agreements here about good curriculum not only enable us to achieve consistency in our teaching, but also to agree on common maps about what is important to teach. The elements can also be used as a template for design in a district that is in the process of creating curricula.

In addition, common understanding of exactly what student performance schools are shooting for and what good performance would look like is a prerequisite for effective team meetings when grade-level teachers or middle school and high school teachers who teach the same content meet together. Teachers can't collaborate to look at student work and problem-solve about how to teach certain items better if they're not teaching to the same standards and in agreement about the criteria for good performance.

Our hope is that teachers know what questions to ask about the agreements their schools and districts have made regarding what to teach and what good student performance should look like. In addition, this chapter should serve as a guide for what work needs to be done when teachers serve on curriculum development committees. And finally, we hope that it is apparent how important a clear and consistent set of curriculum agreements is for planning cohesive instruction that can move all students to proficiency.

The next two chapters profile the teacher skills required to move from curriculum to the planning and implementation of good lessons based on that curriculum.

To check your knowledge about Curriculum Design see the quiz on our Web site at **www.RBTeach.com/rbteach/quiz/CDesign.html.**

*Source Materials on Curriculum Design*

Gagne, R. M., & Briggs, L. J. *Principles of Instructional Design.* New York: Holt, 1974.

Jacobs, H. H. *Mapping the Big Picture.* Alexandria, Va.: Association for Supervision and Curriculum Development, 1997.

Reeves, D. B. *Making Standards Work, 3rd Edition: How to Implement Standards-Based Assessments in the Classroom, School, and District.* Denver: Advanced Learning Press, 2002.

"Standards for Accreditation." New England Association of Schools and Colleges, 2000.

Taba, H., Durlin, M. C., Prenhul, M. C., & McNaughton, A. A. *A Teacher's Handbook for Elementary Social Studies.* (2nd ed.). Reading, Mass.: Addison-Wesley, 1971.

Teachers Curriculum Institute. History Alive Curriculum. Palo Alto, Calif.

Traver, R. "What is a Good Guiding Question?" *Educational Leadership,* Mar. 1998, pp. 70–73.

Tyler, R. *Basic Principles of Curriculum and Instruction.* Chicago: University of Chicago Press, 1949.

Wiggins, G., & McTighe, J. *Understanding by Design.* (2nd ed.) Alexandria, Va.: Association for Supervision and Curriculum Development, 2005.

# Objectives

In Chapter Fifteen, we made the case that a clear and challenging curriculum is an anchor of instructional cohesiveness. It provides the common focus that ultimately grounds professional talk at such places as team meetings. Now it is time to move down one level of abstraction from curriculum to daily lessons, particularly the role of a clear objective in that lesson.

A clear objective articulated by a teacher in terms of student mastery is the indispensable anchor of good daily lesson planning. The quality of one's thinking about objectives during planning directly accounts for the effectiveness of student learning experiences. A clear objective serves as a control tower, always in touch with and carefully guiding the planning for the glide path, the approach, and the landing. In this chapter, we show how that is so and provide guidelines for crafting good objectives.

The teacher skill in this chapter is a thinking skill. It is employed before a lesson takes place, yet it is responsible for how the lesson looks and sounds. It is also a hinge for how much student learning takes place. The quality of teacher thinking about objectives accounts for much of what we see (or don't see) in classrooms.

## Thinking in Terms of Student Mastery

It is easy to lose track of where you're going if you don't think or write objectives in terms of student mastery. A teacher can get tied to materials and activities and have students involved and liking their classes, but be achieving uncertain, erratic, and unpredictable results. Student involvement and enjoyment of school are important goals, but they do not by themselves make for effective teaching and learning.

Madeline Hunter, former director of the UCLA Lab elementary school, used to tell a story that illuminates how fuzzy thinking about objectives can dilute learning. She finds a kindergarten teacher holding her head amid a room that's a mess of paper and glue. There are mimeographed turkeys all around on which children have been pasting squares of colored tissue paper to make Thanksgiving collages. Madeline asks what's been going on. "Well, it was an art experience for the kids," is the reply. The exchange then continued:

MADELINE: Why did you go to the trouble of mimeographing the turkeys? Why not just give them a piece of paper and the tissue and let them be creative, express themselves?

TEACHER: It really wasn't that. It was really a lesson in eye-hand coordination.

MADELINE: Well, then why didn't you have them outline the turkey? You can't tell whether they stayed within the line or not when they've got them pasted all over the turkey.

TEACHER: Well, it really wasn't that. It was a lesson in conservation.

MADELINE: Conservation!

TEACHER: Yes. The kids have really been very wasteful of paste. So I was trying to teach them to put just a tiny piece of paste on.

MADELINE: Then why didn't you give them a piece of paste, or a paper of paste, and see how much of their turkey they could finish before they ran out of paste? You can't tell if there's a cup of paste under some of these turkeys.

TEACHER: Oh, for cryin' out loud, can't kids just have fun?

MADELINE: Sure they can have fun. What do your kids like to do?

TEACHER: The thing they like to do best is just chase out on the school grounds.

MADELINE: Why didn't you take the last half-hour and go around, supervise them while they chased, and you wouldn't have this mess to clean up [Hunter, 1977].

## Five Kinds of Teacher Thinking

There are five kinds of thinking relevant to lesson planning. Each of the five has an important place in planning, but if any one becomes an exclusive mind-set, the instruction that results can have significant gaps for students. In the sections that follow, we profile these five kinds of thinking.

### Coverage Thinking

One kind of thinking during lesson planning is what content or skill is to be addressed or "covered" in the lesson (an event in history, Impressionism, converting fractions to decimals, the preterite tense, dribbling a basketball, the biography of a particular writer, two-part harmonies, and so on) When a teacher is thinking about coverage, she is thinking in terms of her part in the lesson. She is going to present, describe, explain, demonstrate, or cover identified information, events, procedures, or processes. As central as this concern is to any lesson, there is a danger when our planning stops here or when we think of what we are covering as the objective of the lesson ("My objective tomorrow is to cover the material on gas attacks in World War I."). This outlook will negatively influence the quality of the teaching and consequently the learning that takes place. A teacher who confuses coverage with objectives focuses on getting through everything without thinking about student learning. What becomes important is covering the agenda and presenting the information within the time frame of the lesson. When the agenda is covered the lesson is done. The teacher has taken the information out of her head and put it "out there." She is not necessarily doing it in a way that is guided by what is in the students' heads before she starts. And she doesn't know if it passed through the nether regions of "out there" into students' heads when the lesson is over. When planning is driven by coverage thinking alone, we tend to do minimal—or superficial—checking for understanding, less intellectual exploration, and less integration with other learning. Instruction tends toward recitation.

## Activity Thinking

Another consideration in designing lessons is thinking about what activities we want students to do: researching information on a Web site, answering questions, watching a film, building a model, solving problems, conducting an experiment, discussing a reading, and so forth. The focus shifts now from what the teacher will do to how students will participate in the lesson. Once again, this is a very important aspect of lesson design: what will students do to take in information, process it, and internalize it? This becomes a liability only if the focus rests on activities alone—students being busy—without examining the activities in light of

an important learning outcome or weighing decisions about what activities students will do in terms of how well each activity supports achievement of an intended lesson objective. Without such a focus, it is possible that an activity is not teaching what should be taught or that the activity can be completed without students' learning anything.

"Write a story," for example, may be the activity for after lunch in a primary grade room. To get the children involved (make the activity more fun, more attractive, more motivating), the teacher has textured wallpaper pieces they can use to make covers for their "books" and is going to help them bind their books. The quality of stories ranges from complete plots with beginnings, middles, and ends to random pictures with no text at all. While binding each book, the teacher asks the children about their stories: some make comments; some don't. The teacher is focusing on the binding and keeping the flow of students moving. An observer in the class sees no evidence that there is any particular feature the teacher is looking for in the stories. She is making an effort to be positive about some aspect of each child's work, but appears to be looking for nothing in particular. The real goal is just that the students produce stories of any quality and make books to put them in. This is activity thinking in isolation from other important planning concerns. The teacher might not have intended that, but no other conclusion is supportable.

When teachers' prime planning concern is about activities, they miss opportunities to underline the critical learnings, make connections between learnings for students, and check and evaluate student learning. A teacher thinking in terms of activities is concerned more with what students are doing rather than with what they are learning. Sometimes this confusion shows up in assessment. Criteria for success might focus more on the visual appeal or mechanics of the product versus the content substance that indicates achievement of important learning outcomes.

## Involvement Thinking

Another important concern in lesson planning is to get all students engaged in the learning experience. This can be accomplished in many ways: by using examples that are relevant to students (a lesson on the court system for eighth graders that features a case of police shutting down a party: kids are arrested for transporting beer even though they did not actually drink it); by causing movement, interaction, and exchange of opinion among students; by presenting discrepant events that arouse curiosity. When a teacher plans how information will be presented or activities are shaped and varied to accommodate a variety of learning styles, differing levels of background knowledge, or degrees of readiness, we see the most complex level of this aspect of planning and the effects show up in the classroom. There is strategic consideration about how to present and have students process information in a variety of modalities, whether students should do activities individually, in pairs, in small groups, or as a whole class; there is often choice and variety available to students. We see evidence of this kind of thinking when teachers design differentiated learning experiences for students. The idea is to make the learning inviting and accessible to all students, provided, that is, that all of the concerns and decisions about student engagement are in relation to a particular learning outcome for the lesson.

Here again, if student involvement or engagement becomes the dominant concern without being considered in light of a clear learning objective, things will look very different. When a teacher says, "My objective tomorrow is to get all students

to react personally—say what they'd do if they invented a horrible weapon. Would they turn it over to the government?" he is confusing involvement thinking with objectives. There is no learning outcome implied; success will be measured by whether or not students participated, rather than by what new learning has occurred or is in evidence.

Or consider the following scenario of a teacher talking about a lesson: "My students love to do word searches, so I make up one with their spelling words in it, and they do it for seatwork. They really have fun with them. They really got into that word search today!" But when we ask how it helped students learn to spell the words the answer is, "I'm not sure. I assigned it because I thought they'd like to do it, and they do." As it turns out, there is no evidence that word searches improve students' ability to spell the words they find. It may improve their ability to scan complex data fields for visual information; some may develop systematic searching strategies for finding the words more efficiently. But this was not the objective, and students who learn systematic search are learning it at random and incidentally, not through any deliberate approach.

Studies of teacher planning (conducted by having teachers think aloud) have shown that activity thinking and involvement thinking have tended to dominate planning. Planning lessons that are engaging for students is important; it is a good thing to do. But student engagement is not enough for learning. They have to be engaged with activities that are carefully designed to lead to desired learnings.

Secondary teachers sometimes report that when they plan for students to be actively involved in learning experiences they encounter initial resistance: some students would rather sit back and be passive than be held accountable to actively participate. Perhaps some of the resistance is a reaction to experiences they've had in the past where learning experiences were poorly designed or managed. Perhaps it also says something about what they have become accustomed to expecting: that the teacher is the one who does most of the work! If that is their misconception, it is time to teach them otherwise and to show them through well-designed learning experiences that their active participation is the only way they will be the ones learning. And similar to the case we made earlier, this means thoughtfulness about how to structure and monitor activities and ensuring that we function as facilitators keeping students on track with the learning outcomes.

If we think of a learning experience as a journey students will take, then coverage, activity, and involvement thinking are like planning the details of the trip: the routes to take, stops along the way, possible alternate routes, what transportation to use, how to make it interesting, and so on. But the next two kinds of thinking—determining and articulating the objectives or student learning outcomes—are of the highest order of importance in lesson design. To continue the previous metaphor, the objectives identify the destination of the trip. Hence, they need to be determined before decisions are made about what to cover, what activities students will do, and how things will be designed to maximize student involvement.

## Mastery Objectives Thinking

If the objective is mastery of the spelling words, then the teacher will do something that should increase the likelihood that the students will spell the words correctly: perhaps quiz each other in pairs and then make a list of the words they missed and go through a practice routine of seeing, saying, writing in the air, and retesting, over a ten-minute period. Then clearly there is a mastery objective at work for the students.

Perhaps a teacher says, "My objective for tomorrow is for students to be able to distinguish between rational, amoral, and moral reasons for political decisions from the list of positions we will generate in class." If he focuses on student learning, there will be lots of checking to see what students know, perceive, or can do. When the goal is mastery, timetables are flexible, and what's important is that students learn well, even if less material is covered.

When teachers plan with a focus on mastery objectives they ask themselves certain questions: (1) "What exactly do I want students to know and be able to do when this lesson is over?" (2) "How will I know they have learned it, that is, what will I take as evidence the objective has been met?" Thus, thinking clearly about objectives also means thinking about assessment and how to gather the data that will enable us to determine where student learning is in relation to the targeted objective.

Two major issues to consider in identifying the mastery objectives for a lesson are as follows:

- Is the objective precisely worded so that the learning targets are clear to both teacher and students?
- Are the objectives appropriate, that is, aligned with the district or grade-level curriculum standards?

We address the alignment issue later in the chapter.

When it comes to the language of an objective we have identified several attributes that ensure a focus on student learning. All mastery objectives start with the learner as the subject: "Students will be able to . . ." or other language to that effect (for example, "Participants will demonstrate that they can . . ."). Then comes the all-important verb. It has to be an action verb that can be observed—for example, "*explain* in their own words," "*make* a model that displays . . . ," "*list* the evidence that supports," "*describe* the attributes of . . . ," "*compare and contrast* the elements of . . ."

Verbs that are about unobservable processes cannot stand by themselves in a statement of a mastery objective. Such verbs are *understand, appreciate, witness,* and *see,* for example. You can, of course, use these verbs if you then go on to say how the students will show that they know or understand.

You know it's a good objective if you can answer this:

- What is each student going to walk away with inside his or her head that wasn't there before, that is, something the student can understand and explain or something he or she can do as a skill?
- How will I know the students can do this?

Our colleague Mary Sterling suggests the following sentence structure for framing objectives: "Students will demonstrate an understanding of . . . [know] by . . . [able to do]" Teachers in her courses practice framing their objectives in this form. Then they ask one another: Is the "able to do" deep enough and strong enough to convince you that they know? In pairs, Sterling asks teachers to exchange their statements and single-underline the "know" and double-underline the "able to do" parts.

The next phase of making a clear objective is identifying the criteria for success for evaluating whether the student work meets the objective.

The more precise and mastery oriented teachers are, the more time they spend thinking about how they will assess student mastery. The more time they think about that, the clearer they get on the criteria for a student product that would meet the standard of mastery they want. That is, clear thinking about objectives must precede developing a student task whose product will signal mastery. The development of that task or product, in turn, invites listing the criteria and level of performance on each criterion a student has to meet to reach the objective. (See Exhibit 16.2 for criteria for success.)

For example, say you want your students to be able to explain how the checks and balances built into the U.S. Constitution work. That's a mastery objective but without criteria. The criteria for meeting that objective are that they could describe a situation in which each branch has checks on others. That's six examples they have to come up with: how the executive exerts checks on the legislative; executive on judicial; legislative on executive; legislative on judicial; judicial on executive; judicial on legislative.

Or perhaps your mastery objective is that students can explain the variables that influence the rate of evaporation for a liquid. What criteria would you use to assess they met that objective? There are three variables involved in how fast liquid evaporates: surface area, air velocity, and temperature (air pressure might be included also as a variable for more advanced students). So one criterion is that they include all three in their explanation. A second criterion is that they know the correct relation of each variable to evaporation: the bigger the surface area, the quicker the evaporation; the warmer the temperature, the quicker the evaporation; and the faster the air velocity, the quicker the evaporation. They have to address each of the three variables and describe the relation of each to evaporation. How well do they have to do so for it to count as mastery? It is to answer

**Exhibit 16.1.  Lesson Objectives**

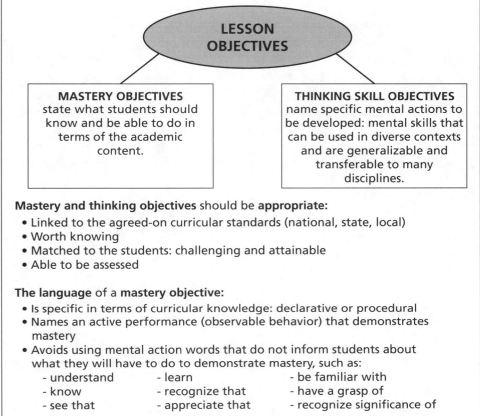

**Research for Better Teaching, Inc.** • One Acton Place, Acton, MA 01720 • (978)263-9449 • www.RBTeach.com

this question that rubrics are developed (Chapter Nineteen, "Assessment").

This way of thinking goes directly from the objective to the creation of the assessment, and all before designing the actual experiences or selecting the materials to use in the lesson. This is the new model of curriculum design described in the previous chapter.

**Exhibit 16.2. Criteria for Success**

**Definition**

Criteria for success are the qualities the must be present for performance and products to meet the standards and be deemed successful. "What are the criteria?" means:

- "What should we look for in examining students' products or performances to know if they were successful?"
- "What attributes should we use to judge the effectiveness of the product or performance?"
- "What counts?"

A list of criteria (and exemplars) enable students to assess their current performances in light of the target performance. Criteria for success do not state what the teacher will do. They do not state what the student will do. Criteria for success name or describe the characteristics of the product performance, so the subject of the criteria should be the product or performance.

*Examples of some criteria for products*

1. The lab report
   - lists all the steps for the process of _____
   - explains your observations
   - explains your conclusions about the relationship between _____
   - uses technical terms correctly
2. Your learning log
   - summarizes the major events in the chapter
   - identifies the central conflict and progress toward its resolution
   - includes your own reflections on the decision that the protagonist is making in her attempt to deal with and solve her problem

**Examples of some criteria for a performance**

1. Your oral presentation
   - clearly states your position on the topic
   - presents the arguments supporting your position
   - supports all arguments with reason and evidence
   - responds to arguments opposing your position
   - is accompanied by visuals (e.g., charts, overheads, chalkboard, handouts)
   - is loud enough for everyone in the room to hear easily
   - may be spoken with notes but not read
   - is fluent in delivery and confident in tone (which means you practiced!)
2. Your sharing of your independent reading tells
   - the title and author of your book
   - the most interesting part so far
   - at least one vocabulary word that is new or interesting to you
   - a prediction of what will happen next

**Research for Better Teaching, Inc.** • One Acton Place, Acton, MA 01720 • (978)263-9449 • www.RBTeach.com

## The Match Between Stated, Lived, and Worthy Objectives

So far we have said there are the four kinds of thinking in lesson planning: mastery, involvement, activity, and coverage. They are not mutually exclusive and tend to be cumulative. A teacher planning in terms of student learning has to consider activities, involvement, and what will be covered. But the acid test for clear objectives thinking is that these three are aligned in service of the mastery objective.

This is an interesting lens to use in reviewing classroom events. Inquiring into the nature of thinking about objectives will often help solve puzzles about why certain pieces of teaching are going awry or not fully living up to their promise.

Sometimes the objective as stated (and written on the board) does not match the objective in action, that is, the objective that the activities appear to be aiming for. And it could be that neither one exploits the full potential of what could or should be the objective, that is, a worthy objective.

One of us recently visited a freshman world history class with a high school principal. Before class the teacher explained that her objective was for students to see how Napoleon's invasions and conquests spawned nationalism as a strong force in European countries that had previously been socially and politically fragmented. This was because the people united against a common enemy (Napoleon) and saw themselves as having common cause.

During the first part of the class, the teacher gave a lively lecture about Napoleon's big military mistakes and students appeared highly engaged. At the teacher's direction students were copying into their notebooks the main points she was putting on the board. At the conclusion of the lecture, students were assigned to triads to locate information in the text about Napoleon's big mistakes.

Reflecting later on what actually took place in that class it was difficult to determine how the activities of the day matched either the objective she had stated in our earlier conversation or what she had written on the board ("Students will understand the impact of Napoleon's reign on Europe."). Because Napoleon's reign had many different effects on Europe, it was even unclear from the board what specific effect she wanted students to "understand."

Her presentation, the notes students took, and the small-group activity focused entirely on Napoleon's big military mistakes. There was no mention of nationalism in the lecture or the activities. Although the text addresses the whole issue of Napoleon's impact on nationalism in several of the countries he invaded, students were directed to research his mistakes, thus missing the bigger picture or more important objective.

Later during the class while students were working in triads, we questioned individual students about the meaning of nationalism. Three-quarters of them couldn't explain it.

We think this vignette highlights two important points:

1. When objectives are unclear or not fully formulated in the teacher's mind, both teacher and students may work hard but miss the point. The intended learning may be lost.
2. A lesson like this and the available material in the text could serve many worthy objectives if the teacher dug deeply into the material as part of the planning process.

Given what was in the text and what other learning needs these students revealed, including not knowing what nationalism was to begin with, a number of other objectives could have been worthwhile choices (see Table 16.1). Because there was not any checking for understanding going on, the only verifiable accomplishment, if we are really

**Table 16.1. Stated Objectives, Lived Objectives, and Worthy Objectives**

| Stated Objective | Lived Objective | Actual Experience | Worthy Objectives |
|---|---|---|---|
| *(What's posted on the board or written in lesson plan. It might even be what the teacher tells the students the objective is.)* | *(Objectives that are being addressed through the activities the students are participating in)* | *(What the students are actually doing)* | *(Learning targets that would benefit the students most)* |
| • Students will understand the impact of Napoleon's reign on Europe. | • Students will be able to name Napoleon's three big mistakes. | • Students will listen to a presentation on Napoleon's big mistakes and copy the teacher's board notes into their notebooks. | • Students will be able to explain what nationalism is and how it shows up in the modern world.<br>• Students will be able to explain how Napoleon's foreign invasions stimulated nationalism in every country he touched.<br>• Students will be able to explain how Napoleon's arrogance led to suffering and death for millions and also led to his downfall.<br>• Students will be able to organize main ideas and subordinate ideas they extract from the text into Cornell-style notes.<br>• Students will be able to use three conventions in textbooks (section titles, color cues, and sidebars) to guide their reading. |

honest about it, was to get the students to copy her notes off the board.

## Generic Thinking Objectives

A fifth kind of thinking about objectives is practiced by teachers who, in addition to aiming to teach concepts, information, and skills, wish to develop particular thinking skills in students at the same time.

Let's go back to the word search. Suppose you want students to learn something about systematic search as a strategy. That's the kind of skill we use to look through a collection of nuts and bolts for a particular size, or scan a map for Maple Street and know only that it's somewhere on the page.

A teacher who wants students to learn strategies for systematic search would certainly talk about how different children were going about looking for the words: comparing approaches and strategies, giving names to the different strategies, listing them on the board, asking students where

else they could use these strategies or what other kinds of tasks would be good places to try them out (transfer), and so forth. This teacher has a generic thinking objective: an objective to develop a thinking skill apart from any particular content knowledge.

Consider a seventh-grade social studies class working on a chapter about Bedouins of the Arabian desert. There's a lot of information in the chapter—facts and concepts galore. But their teacher wants them to learn more than facts. She wants them to learn about hierarchical relationships—not just relationships in Bedouin life, but the nature of hierarchical relationships in general, how to find them and represent them. So she adds something to the assignment, asking them to identify key terms from the chapter and make a diagram that shows their relationships to one another. Now something more is required. Figure 16.1 shows two diagrams that students might draw.

**Figure 16.1.  Diagrams for Learning About Hierarchical Relationships**

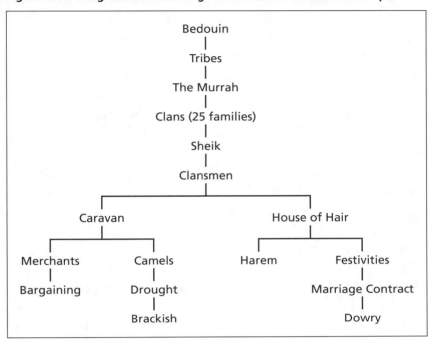

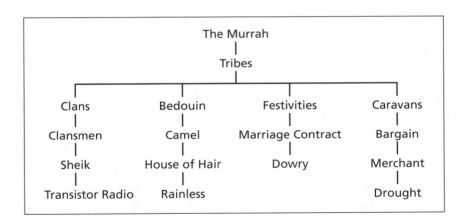

Note the different kinds of thinking behind these two diagrams. The first has terms arranged subordinately according to size. The Murrah is one of many tribes. Each tribe (Murrah included) is composed of clans of about twenty-five families, and each clan is headed by a sheik. Each family is organized around a patriarch and inhabits a "house of hair" (a Bedouin dwelling) with a harem. Then the relationships shift to category groupings.

The second diagram shows relationships that are random and nonlinear. The diagram seems to have been created by free association rather than consistent application of some particular kind of logic.

Now students compare their diagrams in small groups and explain the kind of relationships their connecting lines represent. They talk to each other about their thinking and later in a total class discussion will develop in particular what hierarchical or subordinated relationships mean using their examples. The teacher will use those words (*hierarchical*, *subordinated*) because the objective for this and for the upcoming series of lessons is that they become able to do that kind of thinking, whether it's around Bedouins, sports, or computer programming. The objective here goes beyond mastery of content, though it includes that. It aims to develop a particular thinking skill.

There are literally dozens of thinking skills that may be targeted and taught simultaneously with and through academic content. But it takes consciousness and intentionality to ensure that improving students' thinking capacity or skills is the focus of a learning experience. When we bring this lens to lesson design we ask ourselves, "What thinking skill or processes could I teach or reinforce in this lesson and how might I engineer activities and assignments so that that kind of thinking will be an instructional focal point?" (Table 16.2 describes a wide range of such thinking skills taken from a taxonomy created by Deb Burns.)

## Distinguishing Thinking Skill Objectives and Mastery Objectives

There is an important distinction between thinking skill objectives and mastery objectives. They are both, to be sure, a form of mastery. In the latter, the goal is for students to master knowledge (for example, be able to explain the causes of the Civil War) and operational skills (for example, write with good grammar; solve three-step word problems; locate points on the globe with latitude and longitude). In the case of thinking skill objectives, the goal is for students to master a generic form of thinking skill, like comparison and contrast, or understanding one's assumptions, or defining the real problem before listing solutions. Put another way, the

goal is for students to learn or get better at a particular mental process and be able to transfer it to material other than today's content.

Let's say that your geography lesson today includes being able to list the attributes of an estuary: (1) fan-shaped land formation, (2) at the mouth of a river, (3) containing sedimentary deposits, and (4) filled with brackish water. But more generally, aside from today's geography lesson, you want your students to know that many concepts have a set of attributes that define them, and all the attributes need to be present for the concept to be the concept. You want them to be able to analyze the attributes of an item. That's a generic thinking skill. An example would be to use the attributes of representative democracy to analyze which of two countries, both of which appear to have elections, are really democracies (for example, compare Iraq in 2007 with Israel).

Merely giving assignments whose fulfillment calls for certain thinking skills is not teaching the thinking skill, just as round-robin reading, which calls for students to perform reading, is not necessarily teaching them anything about how to get better at reading (Duffy, Roehler, and Rockliffe, 1986). For example, asking students to compare and contrast the motives of the North and the South at the beginning of the Civil War does not teach students anything about the act of comparing and contrasting two things if they do not already know how to do that.

Almost everything teachers ask students to do requires them to think in some way. But only when they are deliberately and explicitly teaching a particular kind of thinking skill that can be named can we say that there is a thinking skill objective. If you want your students to learn thinking skill X, you may repeatedly give them tasks that call for it, that is, do a task that requires the thinking skill to complete it correctly. But you may not have clarity

**Table 16.2. Taxonomy of Thinking Skills**

### ANALYTICAL REASONING SKILLS

**Identifying Characteristics**

The ability to identify the numerous, distinct, specific, and relevant details that distinguish a specific idea, object, or event; the ability to generate a "rich" description

**Recognizing Attributes**

The ability to assign a name or label to the general or common features and factors within a set of data

**Making an Observation**

The ability to use purpose setting to select relevant attributes, tools, or procedures to guide a data gathering experience

**Discriminating Between Same and Different**

The ability to discern and make fine distinctions between the characteristics of various objects, ideas, or events

**Comparing and Contrasting**

The ability to use purpose setting and common attributes to identify commonalities and discrepancies across numerous sets of information

**Categorizing**

The ability to group similar objects or items according to previously established, essential attributes or characteristics

**Classifying**

The ability to use purpose setting and relevant attributes to sort, organize, and group information

**Criteria Setting**

The ability to identify and quantify the most useful standards that can be used to evaluate item or items for their worth

**Ranking, Prioritizing, and Sequencing**

The ability to place items or events in a hierarchical order according to a quantifiable value

**Seeing Relationships**

The ability to compare ideas or events to identify the regularity between two or more attributes in a relationship that yield a reliable or a repeated scheme

**Predicting**

The ability to use pattern recognition, comparing, contrasting, and identifying, and anticipate likely events in the future

**Determining Cause and Effect**

The ability to identify the varied and most powerful reasons for, or results of, a given event or previous action

**Making Analogies**

The ability to identify a relationship between two familiar items or events and similiar items or events in a novel situation for the purpose of problem solving or creative productivity

### ORGANIZATIONAL THINKING SKILLS

**Memory**

The ability to readily bring from long-term memory relevant, stored facts and information

**Summarizing**

The ability to give a brief review of essential information that has been read, heard, or observed

**Metacognition**

The ability to consciously monitor, describe, and reflect on one's own thinking process

**Goal Setting**

The ability to identify the most desirable end state of a problem situation

**Formulating Questions**

The ability to develop relevant inquiries that will provide needed information to solve a given problem

**Developing Hypotheses**

The ability to use prior observations to develop a possible explanation for the apparent relationship between two or more variables

**Generalizing**

The ability to use repeated, controlled, and accurate observations to develop a rule, principle, or formula that explains a number of related situations

**Problem Solving**

The ability to define and describe a problem, to identify the ideal outcome, and to select and test possible strategies and solutions, revising and evaluating as necessary

**Decision Making**

The ability to use appropriate criteria to select the best alternative in a given situation after careful consideration of the facts, possibilities, consequences, and one's personal values

**Planning**

The ability to develop a detailed and sequenced program of action to achieve an end

### CRITICAL THINKING SKILLS

**Inductive Thinking**

The ability to draw an inferential conclusion on the basis of repeated observations that yielded promising, consistent, but incomplete data

**Deductive Thinking**

The abililty to draw a logical conclusion in which the premises were related and supported the argument under discussion

**Determining Reality and Fantasy**

The ability to distinguish between information that is fanciful and imaginative and information that is true to life and derived from the real world

*(Continued)*

*Source:* Reprinted with permission from Burns, D. E. (1993). *A Six Phase Model for the Teaching of Thinking Skills.* National Research Center on the Gifted and Talented. University of Connecticut.

**Table 16.2. Taxonomy of Thinking Skills** *(continued)*

**Determining Benefits and Drawbacks**

The ability to weigh the advantages and disadvantages of a given idea or action

**Identifying Value Statements**

The ability to recognize statements within an argument that reflect appraisals of worth that cannot be documented through objective means

**Identifying Point of View**

The ability to recognize the various individuals or groups that may have differing sets of observations or priorities that influence their perspective on a given argument

**Determining Bias**

The ability to distinguish between statements in an argument that can be proven and those statements that reflect personal beliefs or judgments

**Determining the Accuracy of Presented Information**

The ability to verify the authenticity and precision of the evidence presented in an argument

**Judging Essential and Incidental Evidence**

The ability to categorize information within an argument into useful and less useful categories

**Determining Relevance**

The ability to distinguish between points in an argument that are related to the topic under consideration and those points that are distractions and not related

**Identifying Missing Information**

The ability to identify the information that is needed to evaluate the strength of an argument; information that may have been purposefully omitted from related data sources

**Judging the Credibility of a Source**

The ability to judge a source of information within an argument as believable, reliable, valid, and worthy to be considered

**Determining Warranted and Unwarranted Claims**

The ability to distinguish between claims that can be proved and those that cannot be proved

**Recognizing Assumptions**

The ability to discriminate between information that is commonly accepted as true and information that is assumed to be true without any proof of evidence

**Recognizing Fallacies**

The ability to recognize errors in conclusions drawn from deductive or inductive reasoning that is used to support an argument

**Detecting Inconsistencies in an Argument**

The ability to identify contradictions or incompatibilities within an argument

**Identifying Ambiguity**

The ability to identify words or phrases within an argument that have two or more possible meanings so as to be unclear, indefinite, vague, and subject to personal interpretation

**Identifying Exaggeration**

The ability to identify words or phrases within an argument that overstate, magnify, or overemphasize beyond what is accepted as fact

Determining the strength of an argument The ability to identify the theme, reasons, and evidence used to support an argument or proposal

**CREATIVITY SKILLS**

**Fluency**

The ability to generate numerous ideas or alternatives to solve a problem that requires a novel solution

**Flexibility**

The ability to generate a wide variety of ideas or alternatives to solve a problem that requires a novel solution

**Originality**

The ability to generate novel, unique, and rare ideas or alternatives to solve a problem that requires an innovative solution

**Elaboration**

The ability to generate a large number of minute details or descriptions that explain a specfic and novel solution to a problem

**Imagery**

The ability to visualize a situation or an object and to mentally manipulate various alternatives for solving a problem related to the object or situation without benefit of models, props, or physical objects

**SCAMPER Modification Techniques**

The ability to use a checklist (substitute, combine, adapt, modify or minify, put to new use, eliminate, reverse, rearrange) of techniques to guide a comprehensive search for appropriate strategies to modify and improve a product by altering one or more components of the original product

**Attribute Listing**

The ability to identify appropriate improvements to a press or project by systematically considering modifications of the various attributes of the original product

**Random Input**

The ability to see a relationship between an apparently irrelevant word or phrase, selected at random, and a potential and creative solution for a given problem

**Brainstorming**

The ability to work with a group of other people to withhold judgment while identifying various innovative and numerous alternatives for solving a given problem

**Creative Problem Solving**

The ability to use a multiple-step process to identify, research, and plan to solve a subproblem that requires a novel but relevant solution in order to remedy or alter a problem situation

**Synectics**

The ability to identify an analogous situation to a given problem set and to use that relationship to identify a solution to the problem at hand about what it takes to get them there, and you may not have the true commitment to go the extra step of teaching the thinking skill explicitly.

When teaching a particular thinking skill is a real objective, we advise naming the thinking skill, teaching it, coaching it, and arranging for the children to get feedback on how they're doing with it—all this in addition to having them practice it. If a teacher has a thinking skill objective for children (rather than just an assignment or a task that *calls for* thinking), the teacher should:

1. Name the skill.
2. Deal explicitly with how to do it (for example, model aloud with the steps or have students share strategies for doing it).
3. Highlight steps.
4. Give tips and coaching pointers.
5. Have students practice with feedback.
6. Evaluate how the students are doing with the thinking skill.

Unfortunately, we usually see only step 6. That's not teaching a thinking skill; that's testing for it and hoping the students will learn the skill from the test or the task.

Table 16.3 summarizes the five kinds of thinking about objectives described so far and Figure 16.2 shows them in a graphic relationship.

The explicit teaching of thinking skills has a marvelous literature of its own. Tishman, Perkins, and Jay (1995) describe school structures and practices that support the explicit teaching of thinking skills. In fact, they are interested in fostering schools where thinking dispositions such as open-mindedness, strategic spirit, and inquisitiveness are core values of the institution. Similar positions are taken by Barell (2003) and Costa and Kallick in their excellent "Habits of Mind" series (2000). Teachers and leaders who want these things for their children have an overarching objective for what a school should be. An objective to teach an individual thinking skill like comparison and

**Table 16.3. Five Kinds of Thinking About Objectives**

| Name | Language Used | The Purpose |
|------|---------------|-------------|
| Generic thinking skills: Student centered—centered on ways that children function intellectually | "Analyze relationships between concepts and diagram them hierarchically." | For students to express or develop a certain kind of thinking skill |
| Mastery of academic knowledge or skills: Student centered—centered on what children will learn in the way of new information or skills | "Be able to describe to each other the principal causes of World War I." "Measure distance using scale on the map." | For students to know or be able to do something specific |
| Involvement: Student centered—on how children will react | "After giving a dramatic reading of the story, I'll solicit their opinions and get them involved in a discussion." | For students to be visibly involved—at least to participate actively and at best to be excited and have fun |
| Activity: Student centered—on what children will do | "They'll look at the filmstrip, then make a map of the South, then answer the questions at the end of the chapter." | For students to finish certain tasks |
| Coverage: Teacher centered—on what the teacher will do, what agenda to get through | "First I'll discuss the heat of reaction; then I'll go over endothermic reactions, entropy, enthalpy, and then review valences." | To mention or get students to mention ideas |

**Figure 16.2. Nested Thinking Behind Objectives**

## Thinking Behind Objectives

**THINKING SKILLS OBJECTIVES**
What thinking skills do I want students
to be able to use?
How will I know if they can do it?

**MASTERY OBJECTIVES**
What do I want students to know or
be able to do when the lesson is over?
How will I know if they know it or can do it?

**INVOLVEMENT**
How can I get students
really engaged?

**ACTIVITIES**
What activities could students
do to gain understanding or
to develop these skills?

**COVERAGE**
What knowledge, skill, or
concept am I teaching?

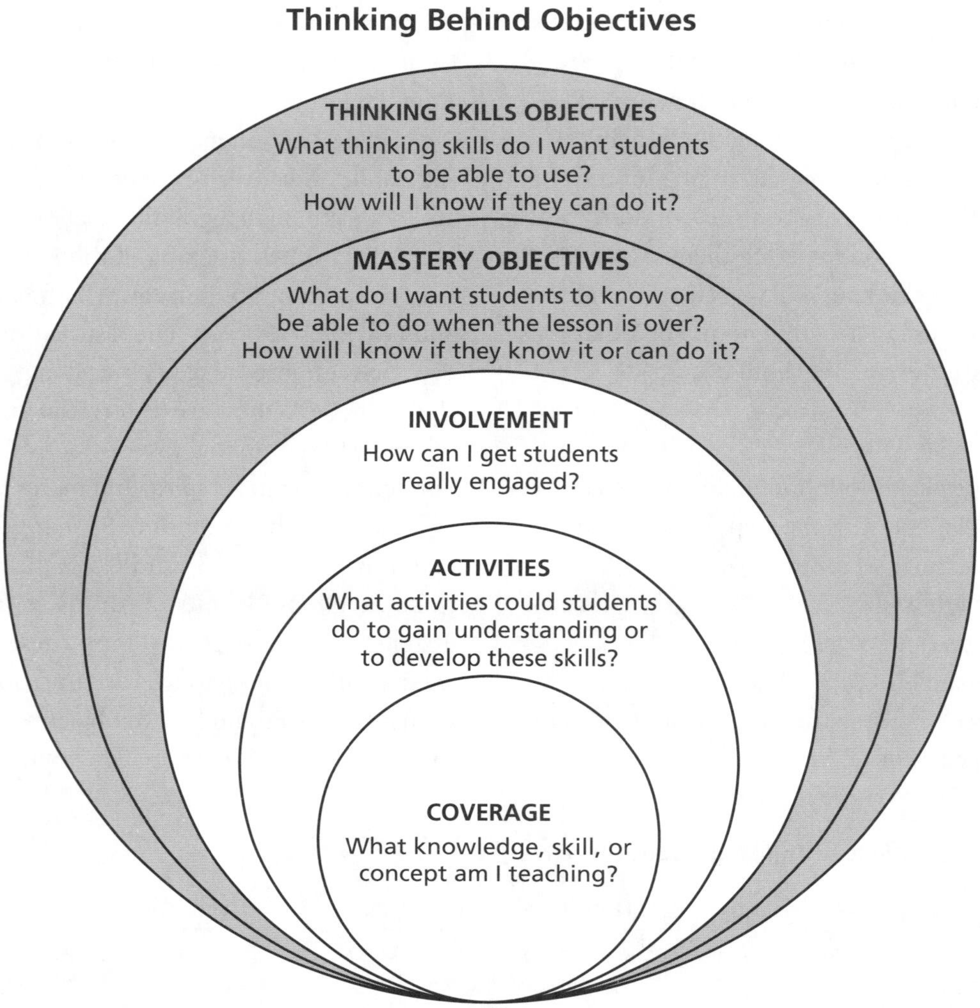

**Research for Better Teaching, Inc.** • One Acton Place, Acton, MA 01720 • (978) 263-9449 • www.RBTeach.com

contrast is well nourished when an entire school decides to make developing minds a core value.

## Nested Thinking Behind Objectives

No one can teach a thinking skill objective without having some content for the students to apply it to, so a teacher who is teaching to a thinking objective almost always has a mastery-of-knowledge or skills objective too. That is why the thinking circle in the diagram in Figure 16.2 includes the "mastery of knowledge and skills" circle. But the reverse is not necessarily true: A teacher can be teaching for mastery of knowledge without necessarily aiming to teach a particular thinking skill.

Similarly, the way in which the other circles in Figure 16.2 are nested shows the overlapping relationship of different kinds of teacher cognition during planning. For example, one can think "coverage" without having any activities for the students to do, but there cannot be activities without having some content the students are dealing with. To give another example, a teacher can have activities without any clear notion of what she wants students to learn. But she cannot have a true mastery objective without having both something for the students to do (activity) and some content on which to do it. Thus, the mastery of knowledge and skills circle contains the other two.

## Teacher Thinking and Lesson Planning

We have made the case that there are pitfalls when coverage, activity, or involvement thinking dominates planning. Since the real goal of coverage thinking is to get through material, such teaching is predictably characterized by more teacher talk, more lecture, and less checking for understanding.

Activity thinking tends to produce classes where students are often busy, sometimes working in groups. There may be good record-keeping systems on student completion of tasks and assignments, but activity thinking, when it dominates, tends to produce classes where students are clear on neither what is to be learned nor the criteria for quality work.

Involvement thinking adds higher energy and more fun, but classes may look essentially the same as those that are activity based.

In previous chapters, we have presented repertoires and argued that all behaviors in a repertoire can be good if they are an appropriate match to the student, situation, or curriculum. The repertoire argument needs to be modified, however, to be valid for the five kinds of thinking about objectives. Activity thinking or coverage thinking is not good enough if one never gets as far as mastery thinking in preparing for lessons.

On the other hand, fully developed planners—teachers who have clear images of what they want students to know and be able to do—still have to identify content for coverage. They still have to invent or find activities that could logically lead stu-

dents to master the intended learnings. Good planners, in fact, ask the key questions involved in all five kinds of thinking in Figure 16.2, but they start by answering the mastery question thoroughly: "What do I want students to know or be able to do? How will I know if they know it or can do it?"

Teachers who are logical, linear, and analytical like to start with a statement of the mastery objective and proceed deliberately to develop assessment criteria and criterion tasks. Then they identify activities and materials that fit in with this objective.

Many of us have "neat" activities or materials we love to use or think will be highly engaging for students. But this is a dicey place to start the planning process, because there is a tendency to warp the objective to fit the activity we love. There may be a need to give up certain engaging activities we are attached to if they do not directly help students learn something they are supposed to be learning.

Each of us in teaching, in looking back at a class we taught or observed, ought to be able to infer a clear statement of what students were supposed to be able to do at the end. And that something needs to be part of the curriculum to which our school or district is committed.

A clear objective creates an image of what a student will know or be able to do when the instruction is over: a picture in your mind, a sentence of inner speech you say to yourself, or a written statement. What's important is that the image is framed from the students' point of view. The objective is a clear picture that the teacher has of desired student performance, which then becomes a clear picture for the students too.

We would argue that all objectives can be framed as a clear image of student performance—even objectives pertaining to attitude or appreciation. Second, we argue that objectives that are not thought through in this way typically wind up with coverage thinking, activity thinking, or involvement thinking, and all three of these are weaker than mastery thinking. Third, we argue that mastery thinking improves teaching by leading teachers to do more goal stating with students, more checking, more feedback according to criteria, better record keeping, and more diagnosis of individual student needs.

Let's return to the first point: all objectives can be framed as mastery learning objectives (creating a specific image of what a student will know or be able to do). How about attitude objectives?

## Objectives About Social Skills and Attitudes

Objectives need not be solely about cognitive topics. Pairs of students are coaching individuals on a certain bookkeeping procedure, and we infer that there is an objective about cooperation and helping others in the room. Deirdre is excluded from the class meeting (first grade) and sitting near (though facing away from) a pile of blocks. We hear a few remarks and see some body language from the teacher that leads us to conclude she has an objective in mind for Deirdre: take responsibility and clean up; you can't get out of your responsibilities to others by pouting and stalling.

Mr. Caswell wants students to develop a positive attitude toward classical music. How would he know if he'd accomplished that? What does he mean when he says, "I want my students to appreciate Beethoven"? He might mean that he expects knowledge of the intricacy and subtlety of the design of a Beethoven symphony to generate respect. Further, he may believe that for some people, having to listen in a focused way to the symphony as they analyze its parts will lead to aesthetic enjoyment. All of that may be his concept of "appreciation": respect through knowledge and liking through repeated experience. If that is his concept, it will lead him to do certain activities in class

aimed at generating specific student performances: performances like being able to analyze parts of the symphony and label a score, describing in words the principles by which Beethoven developed and restated themes, or identifying the different symphonies. All of these student performances he can picture because he has thought about what "appreciation" means. But if he doesn't translate "appreciation" into some sort of student performance in his head, then what Mr. Caswell does with students in class may be random in its effect; he will not be looking inside their heads to create anything in a planful way. He will be operating outside their heads with activities and presentations that may or may not contact anything inside students. Who can tell? Without that image of the student performance he's aiming for, Mr. Caswell may do activities that lead to no performance or to an opposite student performance.

Objectives that say "students will be exposed to" make us uneasy. If you're going to "introduce" students to an idea or "expose" them to an experience, do you expect anything to stick? If you do, you can say what it is and go for it specifically. If you don't, why are you exposing them to the idea to begin with? ("All you get from exposure is a cold," quipped Jim Kilroy of Tulane University.)

Here is another way of looking at this: A teacher without an image of the student performance sought is likely to pick activities that inadvertently get another performance—or no performance. If you don't specifically know where you're going, why would you expect to get there? If you do get there, it will be by accident or luck, and certainly will take a lot longer. If you look at the students who are along for the ride in such a class of twenty-five students, some may peel off and get to the destination on their own, despite the instruction. Others never arrive.

So again, the big question is, Was there a clear objective? When you reflect on the class period, can you infer a clear statement of what students were supposed to know or be able to do at the end? If you can't, the students probably can't either. And if they can't, that's trouble. It doesn't matter if the objective is on the board, but it does matter that the students can tell you what it is, and with understanding. We do encourage teachers to write lesson objectives on the board; but unless they do something to ensure that students understand it we might as well save the board space.

Maybe the teacher stated the objective, and the job of identifying it is easy; or maybe the objective is written down somewhere in the book, on the worksheet, or in the packet. That is nice when it happens (and valuable for student learning), but often that is not the case. To determine whether a mastery objective is really driving the lesson, an observer to the lesson should be able to look back on what she saw and heard and infer it accurately. We must be able to go back over the lesson from an outsider's point of view and say, "Well, clearly from what I saw and heard, the objective must have been for students to identify the five parts of a story (protagonist, antagonist, conflict, plot, climax) and be able to find examples of them in the story read for homework." Maybe the teacher never said that in so many words, but clearly that is what students were supposed to learn how to do. The students too should know what the objective is. They should be able to make some such statement of objectives if asked at the end of the period. A teacher who does know what the student performance should look like is able to share an exemplar of such performance with the students and also share the criteria that make it an exemplar. At the very least, this teacher has the criteria thought out, listed, and available for the students.

In our work, we have found that the question "Was there a clear objective?" can be answered by "yes," "no," or "yes but fuzzy." The type of class most likely to look like a "no" or a "fuzzy" on objectives is a rambling discussion that touches assigned material in an erratic way or not at all or that covers course material without making relevant connections between items or making links to other course material. Another "no objectives" class has some students doing busywork, often on worksheets, about material they already know or have mastered. Calling this "reinforcement" won't wash. Practice has its place, of course, but the practice must be strengthening a learning that needs it.

## Level of Difficulty

"'Not too hot, not too cold, but j-u-u-u-st right,' said Goldilocks. And she ate it all up." Even before J. McVicker Hunt (1961) named it the "challenge of the match," educators were striving to make the work given to students not too hard and not too easy, but just hard enough to stretch them toward optimum rate of learning. The problem of the match makes teachers look at where students are now and ask, "How big a bite can I give them for the next increment of learning?" For example, judging the size of the bite for six second graders may lead their teacher to teach fractional notation and adding of fractions with common denominators in the same lesson. They can grasp that. The students in an eleventh-grade German history class may not only assimilate the background and content of Bismarck's "blood and iron" speech but also in the same class explain it in terms of Bismarck's character.

If you think this sounds like individualizing, you're right. It is individualizing the number of learnings tackled at once and their pace—the size of the bites of learning—to individuals and groups.

There are many other variables that the term *individualizing* may include. Most of those variables are about how the learning shall proceed. Here we are talking about what, and how much, shall be aimed at for learning, regardless of the how.

What evidence might there be that the size of the bite was a good match for a group of students? Perhaps there was some initial struggling but then grasping of new ideas; perhaps moments of silence followed by student questions and clarification of difficult concepts; perhaps episodes of puzzlement culminating in "aha!" reactions; perhaps there was diligent note taking. Negative evidence is easier to spot: confusion, dismay, frustration, or mute silence for work that's too hard (or inadequately presented); boredom as pencil tapping, looking around, chatting, or sloppiness for work that is too easy. (Easy work is far from the only cause of this litany, but it should be checked out when the behaviors occur.)

It is possible as well that none of those overt behaviors may be present, yet the objectives might still be mismatched to the students. In that case, only a knowledge of the students' prior work in relation to the demands the teacher is making could help us have a conversation about the appropriateness of the objectives. Discussing these choices with one another at team meetings with prior student work to look at is a very productive use of time.

## Detailed Behavioral Mastery Objectives

In the 1960s Popham and Baker (1970) and Mager (1962) popularized the writing of detailed behavioral objectives in which criterion levels for performance were specified as well as the conditions under which students would perform them—for example, "Given ten multistep word problems involving multiplication and division, students will complete them in a half-hour at 90 percent accuracy." This movement, which eventually became the butt of jokes and a target of scorn, had aimed to sharpen thinking about student outcomes and improve accountability for student results.

Particular kinds of content do lend themselves well to very detailed behavioral objectives, typically operational skills that can be observed at criterion levels of mastery (mathematical manipulations, decoding in reading, and technical writing skills, for example), but this same kind of objective may not serve instruction so well when one attempts to apply it to an area like cooperation. How can a teacher meaningfully specify a criterion level for mastery with respect to cooperation? He could have a student discriminate cooperative from noncooperative behavior at a criterion level in stories read or video clips viewed, but how useful would that be?

Different levels of specificity in language serve best with different types of content. Thus, teachers need to use different kinds of objectives and use the language most suited to the content at hand. The use of detailed behavioral objectives for an art curriculum or an oil painting course might well trivialize that content.

But what about the teacher who uses general language in objectives for material that would lend itself nicely to detailed behavioral objectives? Here's an example: "Children will add three-digit numbers with medial zeros competently." What is "competently"? Here Popham and Baker (1970) would argue that a criterion level for mastery is essential for sharpening the delivery of skills and the evaluation of who knows what.

## Objectives and State Standards

The standards movement represents a commitment of educators all over the country to raising the academic rigor of school curriculum. The impetus for this movement was alarming national reports in the

**Figure 16.3. Education Required for Jobs, 2000–2010**

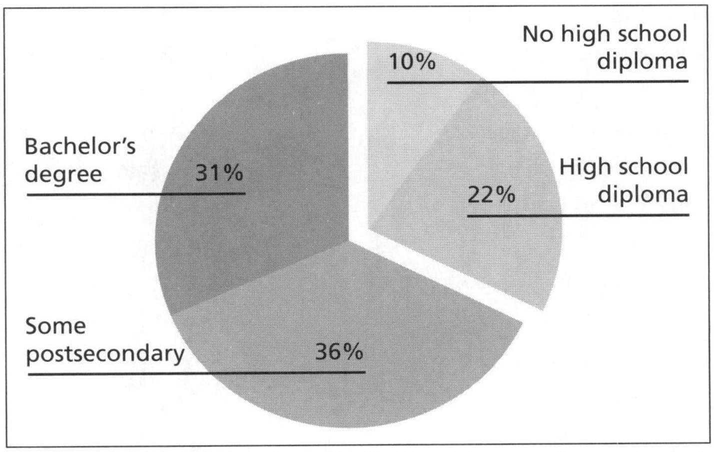

*Source:* Carnevale and Desrochers (2003). Materials selected from *Standards for What? The Economic Roots of K–12 Reform,* Educational Testing Service, 2003. Reprinted by permission of Educational Testing Service.

1980s and international comparisons in the 1990s that were not flattering to student achievement in the United States.

Equally important, the standards movement also became an equity movement based on the realization that students need a twenty-first-century education if they are to succeed, and that can't mean something radically different in Des Moines than in Detroit. We need to standardize the skills and concepts we offer in schools to achieve consistency, and more particularly, equity by teaching the same skills and concepts to children of poverty as to children in schools serving affluent children. If schools underexpect and underoffer higher-level skills to children of poverty, they will continue to offer them unequal educations and unequal chances in the race of life.

This equity in educational rigor is especially needed now since, as Project Achieve cites, "more than two-thirds of [new] jobs will require some postsecondary education. The jobs requiring the most education and offering the best pay are the fastest growing" (Figure 16.3).

So how does this movement translate into educational practice? The first level of response has been to create state standards documents that attempt to promulgate high and uniform learning expectations for all students in the state. The actual standards in documents published by the states are general statements about the kinds of competency students should have in the academic subjects. They are not very specific: they define the broad areas of knowledge and skill. In New York, for example, Standard 3: Mathematics—Elementary, is: "2. Students use number sense and numeration to develop an understanding of the multiple uses of numbers in the real world, the use of numbers to communicate mathematically, and the use of numbers in the development of mathematical ideas." The meaning of this general statement becomes slightly more focused when such documents give indicators of what meeting that objective might look like:

Students:

- Use whole numbers and fractions to identify locations, quantify groups of objects, and measure distances.
- Use concrete materials to model numbers and number relationships for whole numbers and common fractions, including decimal fractions.
- Relate counting to grouping and to place-value.
- Recognize the order of whole numbers and commonly used fractions and decimals.
- Demonstrate the concept of percent through problems related to actual situations.

Standards documents then sometimes give sample pieces of evidence to show a student was meeting the standard:

- Count out 15 small cubes and exchange 10 of the cubes for a rod 10 cubes long.
- Use the number line to show the position of 1/4.
- Figure the tax on $4.00 knowing that taxes are 7 cents per $1.00.

Some states move down to yet another level of specificity by listing within content topics exactly what the learning expectations (sometimes called "content expectations") are for a grade level. Within the second-grade content expectations document for the State of Michigan we find these expectations for working with unit fractions:

N.ME.02.18 Recognize, name, and represent commonly used unit fractions with denominators 12 or less; model 1/2, 1/3, and 1/4 by folding strips.

N.ME.02.19 Recognize, name, and write commonly used fractions: 1/2, 1/3, 2/3, 1/4, 2/4, 3/4.

N.ME.02.20 Place 0 and halves, e.g., 1/2, 1 1/2, 2 1/2, on the number line; relate to a ruler.

N.ME.02.21 For unit fractions from 1/12 to 1/2, understand the inverse relationship between the size of a unit fraction and the size of the denominator; compare unit fractions from 1/12 to 1/2.

N.ME.02.22 Recognize that fractions such as 2/2, 3/3 and 4/4 are equal to the whole (one). Work with unit fractions

So we have "standards," "indicators," "sample evidence," and "learning expectations," each derived from the previous one, and each more specific in telling a reader what students are supposed to know and be able to do (Figure 16.4).

But as readers, we do not know the level of difficulty, the nuances, and the level of quality expected from a student in these areas until we see the actual student task that will assess it and a sample of student work that meets the standard. At this writing, state standards documents are still quite varied in the level of specificity they provide educators and parents in their states. They also differ in their content. Generating more agreement across states is one of the reasons for the formation of Project Achieve in 1996.

The objectives that a teacher comes up with for a given lesson serve the purpose of breaking down the general statements of state standards into an appropriate outcome that is measurable for each student at the end of a particular lesson. In other words, they break down the large objective in the state standards into the smaller pieces of learning that their particular students need to master en route to the bigger objective. The Michigan second-grade content expectation, for example, is, "For unit fractions from 1/12 to 1/2, understand the inverse relationship between the size of a unit fraction and the size of the

**Figure 16.4. Standards and Indicators**

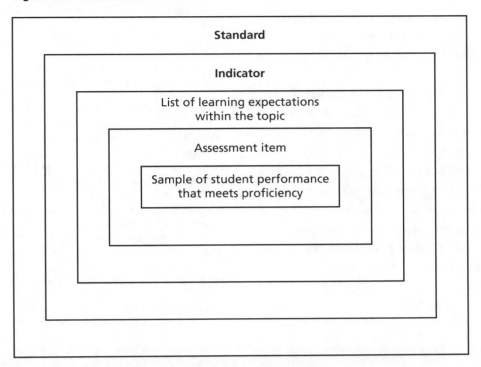

denominator; compare unit fractions from 1/12 to 1/2."

No one can create a single lesson that enables students to do that. Today's lesson may have as its objective an understanding that students need first in order to comprehend the inverse relationship described in the Michigan content expectation. Perhaps the prior understanding they need is this: "Students will be able to explain that the denominator in fractional notation tells us how many equal pieces the whole is divided into."

Perhaps, more significant, our own class observations have shown us that many students don't yet realize that they can't compare two fractions unless they are both describing the same whole. That's a common misunderstanding. So today's objective needs to focus on that, and that understanding isn't in the state standards at all.

Daily lesson objectives derive from a teacher's ongoing assessment of what students understand and need to learn next on the route to meeting standards prescribed for their course. Most lesson objectives should be related to accomplishing a state standard, but the objective for a given lesson will probably not be found in the state standards documents.

Teachers should always know what standard a given lesson is related to. That is why some districts require teachers to write the related standard on the board as well as the daily objective. That practice is supposed to exert a discipline on teachers to be sure the two are related. All too often, however, the standard written on the board, accurately copied from a state standards document, is too abstract to be of much use to anybody in understanding the fit of today's lesson either for students, teacher, or a supervisor who visits.

Teachers need to know the relation of today's objective to the standard they are working on all right, but the most important alignment is that the objective of the day be on target for the needs of the students.

This chapter has been about the significance of clear thinking about objectives and how such thinking creates an objective that can serve as the control tower to lesson planning. In the next chapter, we spell out the dimensions of how such planning should proceed, including the importance of students' knowing what the objective is.

To check your knowledge about Objectives see the quiz on our Web site at **www.RBTeach.com/ rbteach/quiz/objectives.html.**

## Source Materials on Objectives

Alexander, L., Frankiewicz, R., and Williams, R. "Facilitation of Learning and Retention or Oral Instruction Using Advance and Post Organizers." *Journal of Educational Psychology*, 1979, *71*(5), 701–707.

Barell, J. *Developing More Curious Minds*. Alexandria, Va.: ASCD, 2003.

Bussis, A. M., Chittenden, E. A., and Amarel, M. *Beyond Surface Curriculum: An Interview Study of Teachers' Understandings*. Boulder, Colo.: Westview Press, 1966.

Carnevale, A. P., and Desrochers, D. M. *Standards for What? The Economic Roots of K–12 Reform*. Princeton, N.J.: Educational Testing Service, 2003.

Clark, C. M., and Yinger, R. J. "Teachers Thinking." In P. L. Peterson and H. J. Wahlberg (eds.), *Research on Teaching*. Berkeley, Calif.: McCutcheon, 1979.

Costa, A., and Kallick, B. *Habits of Minds* series. Alexandria, Va.: ASCD, 2000.

Duffy, G., Roehler, L., and Rockliffe, G. "How Teachers' Instructional Talk Influences Students' Understandings of Lesson Content." *Elementary School Journal*, 1986, *87*(1), 3–16.

Hunt, J. M. *Intelligence and Experience*. New York: Ronald Press, 1961.

Hunter, M. "Improving the Quality of Instruction through Professional Development." Presentation at ASCD, Houston, 1977.

Joyce, B. R., Clark, C., and Peck, L. *Flexibility in Teaching*. New York: Longman, 1981.

Mager, R. R. *Preparing Instructional Objectives*. Palo Alto, Calif.: Fearson, 1962.

National Commission on Excellence in Education. "A Nation at Risk." Washington, D.C.: Department of Education, 1983.

Peterson, P. L., Marx, C. W., and Clark, C. "Teacher Planning, Teacher Behavior, and Student Achievement." *American Educational Research Journal*, 1978, *15*, 417–432.

Popham, W. J., and Baker, E. L. *Systematic Instruction*. Upper Saddle River, N.J.: Prentice Hall, 1970.

Saphier, J. D. "The Parameters of Teaching: An Empirical Study Using Observations and Interviews to Validate a Theory of Teaching by Linking Levels of Analysis, Levels of Knowing and Levels of Performance." Unpublished doctoral dissertation, Boston University, 1980.

TIMSS (Trends in International Mathematics and Science Study). Department of Education, National Center for Education Statistics, 2003 and 1999.

Tishman, S., Perkins, D., and Jay, E. *The Thinking Classroom*. Needham Heights, Mass.: Allyn & Bacon, 1995.

Tyler, R. W. *Basic Principles of Curriculum and Instruction*. Chicago: University of Chicago Press, 1949.

Waxman, H. J. "Productive Teaching." In H. C. Waxman and H. J. Walberg (eds.), *New Directions for Teaching Practice and Research.*. Berkeley, Calif.: McCutchen Publishing, 1999, pp. 74–104.

Wise, A. E., and Okey, J. R. "A Meta-Analysis of the Effects of Various Science Teaching Strategies on Achievement." *Journal of Research in Science Teaching*, 1983, *20*(5), 415–425.

Zahorik, J. A. "Learning Activities: Nature, Function, and Practice." *Elementary School Journal*, 1982, *82*, 309–317.

# Planning

This chapter is about planning lessons, the small daily packages of crafted instruction within units. (For the important teacher knowledge base about unit design, see Chapter Fifteen and the excellent work of Wiggins and McTighe, 2005, on backward planning.) Well-designed units are still only general blueprints to what a teacher will do tomorrow with the twenty-eight students in front of her. Good planning skills for daily lessons stand behind good teaching.

Instructional coaches, department chairs, and administrators often find they get more payback from planning conferences with teachers than from observations with feedback. This will be true when the teacher's growing edge is issues relating to clarity and the other areas in Part Four.

## Curriculum Units, Lesson, and Spontaneous Teaching Skills

The centerpiece of planning is the lesson: the planned time period when students engage content through experiences that teachers have designed. A lesson plan is the detailed implementation scenario that specifies what the teacher does and what the students are expected to do during a bounded chunk of time devoted to a particular mastery objective (see Chapter Sixteen, "Objectives"). It may take more than one class period to complete a lesson so defined. Therefore, certain elements of the lesson, like activating student current knowledge, may take place on Monday, and most of the feedback on student work may be observable on Tuesday. These two class periods as a package comprise a complete lesson on, say, the separation of powers in the U.S. government. That lesson, in turn, is part of a unit on the U.S. Constitution. The design and overall construction of the unit may be in the district curriculum guide. But the actual plan for individual lessons probably is not, and should not be, in the curriculum guide. Designing lessons and crafting student work is the teacher's job, and curriculum guides and other district materials are supposed to be helpful resources for how to do so.

Good curriculum specifies the "what" of teaching, which should include the big ideas and enduring understandings students are expected to take away from units of instruction. Curriculum documents may also specify other agreements about instructional approaches, like an agreement that students will be writing about their interpretation of mathematical ideas. But it is teachers who plan the "how" of lessons that need to be designed in advance for each day. And then during lessons, teachers make spontaneous moves that weren't planned at all, and couldn't have been, but that are drawn mindfully from their repertoires of skills like "probing a student's thinking" to understand why they're confused.

This chapter is about what skillful teachers do the night before. In their planning, they:

- Check in with the big ideas of the unit
- Articulate the mastery objectives for themselves after digging deeply into the content
- Decide how to communicate objectives to the students
- Decide what evidence would demonstrate mastery of this lesson objective

- Analyze evidence about previous student learning (perhaps yesterday's quiz or homework) so they know where to focus
- Plan pacing and subgrouping
- Pick materials, models, examples, stories, and cases to use
- Anticipate confusions, especially language and vocabulary meanings, and identify requisite prior knowledge students might not have
- Design and choose learning experiences
- Check that learning experiences are logically linked to the intended learning
- Decide how to collect evidence of learning during or concluding this lesson
- Plan how students will make their thinking visible and public
- Plan how to get students to summarize

In addition, they may:

- Plan how to get students' minds in gear at the beginning
- Predict how much time will be needed for each task or activity and plan other environmental variables (space, management routines) that may need to be arranged
- Plan the effective effort strategies that may be employed or taught
- Plan how to diversify for different learning styles
- Plan certain key interactive moves like an opening question
- Decide who may need assistance or extensions during the lesson and provide for it
- Plan what extensions and challenges will be provided for students who are ready for them
- Plan how and when to explain the homework and its connection to today's lesson

This chapter now expands on these points and looks at planning decisions a teacher could conceivably make. These steps are important for planning any class regardless of whether it's a literature discussion in AP English, second graders circulating at math learning stations, a seventh-grade earth science lab, or whole class direct instruction in the U.S. Constitution.

Some of the decisions are not applicable in certain classes. Don't get the idea that if one doesn't go through all twenty-one decisions, the planning is poor. In certain situations, some decisions above are not applicable. In primary grade literacy, for example, in a guided reading group with three first graders on book "D," there is no decision about materials. The leveled books are the materials. Checking for understanding is continuous as children read, and objectives may be slightly different for each of the three children. A teacher conducting lessons based in curricula that use inquiry models of teaching might not start by clarifying objectives for students (though they would be developed at some point later). For the first lesson or two on representative government, for example, there is no "evidence from yesterday" about how much progress students have made toward mastery (though there might be a preassessment to find out what they already know or think they know about representative government.)

# The Twenty-One Planning Decisions

The decisions that follow are divided into two sets. The first thirteen are basic and indispensable decisions for any lesson planning. The second set of eight decisions is important too, but these topics are at a finer level of specificity. Good planning allows quite a bit of flexibility about the order in which a teacher addresses these issues, and as we have noted, not all of them need to be addressed for certain lessons. In general, the decisions don't have to be addressed in a linear fashion in the order presented. This should reassure nonlinear thinkers who hate lists and recipes. The first five decisions, however, are so important for getting focus in one's teaching and getting student results that we are going to ask even the creative-random among you to think these through thoroughly before going on with your planning.

## Thirteen Basic, Indispensable Decisions

Plan before instruction begins with these basic decisions:

1. Check in with the curriculum, the standards you're working on, and particularly the big idea (enduring understanding) that's on the table to be sure the lesson you're planning connects explicitly to it.

2. Articulate the mastery objective of this lesson (or series of lessons) to yourself fully. Say exactly what the students will know or be able to do, or do better, at the end of the lesson. Dig into the content to examine its nuances and central ideas before arriving at this statement.

3. Plan how to communicate the objective to the students with unmistakable clarity in language they will understand. How are you going to get them clear about what they're trying to learn? Will you generate essential questions and criteria, give exemplars, or share assessments you will be using?

4. Decide what evidence you will use as confirmation of student mastery. (They may not meet it tomorrow, but having this end in mind is the fulcrum of good planning.)

5. Give careful attention to the evidence from yesterday (or . . . whenever else is relevant) about who "has it" and who doesn't. Also look carefully at those who have it so well they're ready for an extension or deepening activity.

6. In light of the evidence from yesterday's work (or from your preassessment if this is the first lesson in the series), plan the pace and grouping or subgrouping if appropriate for differentiation of instruction. This includes the size of the bite (how big an increment of learning) you will aim for in this lesson. It also includes whether you need to do some preteaching for some students and some reteaching for some students who didn't get it yesterday. It means coming up with extensions and challenges for those who got it quickly.

7. Pick materials, including exactly what manipulatives, pictures, diagrams, pieces of text, equipment, and media will best make the learning accessible to the students.

8. Anticipate confusions especially about vocabulary and concepts to be used, and preteach if necessary. Anticipate misconceptions, and plan how to surface them and contradict them.

9. Choose student learning experiences:
   • Instructional strategies you will use. . . (e.g., demonstration, modeling, thinking aloud, minilecture with graphic organizer). Pay particular attention to how you can embed reading strategies in your routines for engaging text.
   • Tasks, exercises, and activities the students will do.
   • Hooks that will engage student interest.
   • The sequence of student tasks and teacher-guided strategies within the lesson most likely to develop the concept, skill, or understanding.
   • How to preteach essential vocabulary or concepts that some student may lack.

10. Check that doing the task will logically lead to learning the intended skill or concept.

11. Decide when and how you will gather the evidence of student learning during or after the lesson.

12. "Plan how students will make their thinking and understanding public" (West and Staub, 2003, p. 13; see "Making Students' Thinking Visible" in Chapter Nine).

13. Select a strategy for getting students cognitively active in summarizing and assimilating their new learning.

## Eight Implementation Detail Decisions

Next come eight implementation decisions:

14. Decide how you will get students' minds in gear for this lesson at the beginning, activate their prior knowledge, and find out what they already know.

15. Arrange the environmental variables (space, routines that may need to be preplanned or taught) and how much time you predict will be needed for each task or activity.

16. Choose the effective effort strategies you may explicitly teach or that you may ask students to use (e.g., student self-evaluation, use of "effective effort rubric").

17. Decide specific interactive moves you should make (key steps in directions, key questions to ask, cues to give, connections to past learning . . .) "to make sure important ideas are being grappled with and will be highlighted and clarified" (West and Staub, 2003, p. 12).

18. Decide how to diversify for different student learning styles.

19. Decide how much support, cuing, and help students may need while doing the work, including deployment of other people who may be in the room.

20. Decide "what extensions or challenges you will provide for students who are ready for them" (West and Staub, 2003).

21. Choose homework and how and when to explain it and what it's for.

In the next sections we comment on each of these decisions and some of the fine points in their meaning.

## The Finer Points About the Basic and Indispensable Decisions

Although most of these decisions may seem relatively straightforward, some further discussion and concrete examples may help to clarify the importance of giving each our thoughtful attention during planning.

### Decision 1: Check In with the Curriculum, the Standards, and the Big Idea

You could do a good lesson on consonant digraphs in second grade and get away without connecting it to a big idea. The same is true with density in eighth-grade science or separation of powers in eleventh-grade U.S. history. Most of us who are veterans have taught our way through the decades without making connections to big ideas. But our students would have been better off if we had kept big ideas in mind and made explicit connections for them when appropriate.

The big idea in the second-grade lesson may be a theme we're pursuing all year long: "You can get tools for figuring out any word you don't know, and this year we're filling in our tool box so you'll be able to sound out any word!" Perhaps in your curriculum, the word is *strategies,* and the big idea is that "we're learning to be strategic readers." "As readers we're in charge, and we have lots of different strategies to reach for if we don't know a word." So in today's lesson, digraphs are explicitly connected to phonic clues, a strategy different from the one the class worked on yesterday (which was reading the whole sentence and skipping the unknown word to see if that enabled the children to guess).

Another example is about how the Constitution designs separation of powers of the three branches of government into the working of our republic. Teaching how that operates and why (checks and balances) is a standard U.S. history objective. This learning (and, in fact, most other teaching points, regardless of academic discipline) becomes more compelling and more interesting to students if they see it as connected to something that's bigger and inherently important. That's what a big idea or enduring understanding is—something important to connect the learning to that is motivating. One possibility of a big idea for the separation of powers might be: "It takes vigilance to preserve the balance of powers our founding fathers built into the Constitution. Every few decades you can find an episode in history where an interest group tries to assert its power by strengthening one of the branches above the others. So far, we've managed to counter those campaigns, but it hasn't been easy."

A big idea like that stimulates a strong reason for students to understand the operation of separation of powers because they're going to be asked to use it to analyze historical episodes that could have derailed the U.S. democracy and perhaps analyze current efforts to swing power to one branch.

### Decision 2:
### Articulate the Mastery Objective for Yourself

See Chapter Sixteen, "Objectives."

### Decision 3:
### Plan How to Communicate the Objective to the Students with Unmistakable Clarity

The next step for planning a lesson is thinking deeply into the content to be learned today. What the students are supposed to be learning is usually listed at a high level of abstraction in the standards document of the school district (or state) and the list of learning expectations for the course. But to plan a lesson that works for the children today, we need to be much more specific than that.

Before we think about assessment, student activities, meta-cognition, differentiated instruction, designing questions, or student motivation, we must look at the materials in the curriculum at a finely grained level to find out what the content is that the students are supposed to learn. Maybe it's a skill; maybe it's a concept; maybe it's a body of information (facts); maybe it is a combination of these. But first we must determine exactly what it is supposed to be and express this in concrete and precise language.

So get the book, get the lab manual, get the novel, get the problem set . . . whatever . . . that the students are going to engage today, and examine it in detail. Here are examples from different grade levels and subject areas.

#### Elementary Mathematics

First-grade students are asked to fill in blanks in number patterns. The first one is:
"2, 4, ____, 8, ____, ____. What is the rule? _____."

The second one is: "The rule is go back four each time. 34, ____, 26, ____, 18, ____, ____."
There is a number line on the page to help them.

A student who can count by 2s may see that the first example is a pattern of counting by 2s, and then might just swing in to using that memorized pattern to fill in the blanks. Is that what you, the teacher, want this exercise to be about: applying memorized counting-by-two patterns? If so, that would be fine. But perhaps the learning is supposed to be about number lines and how to use them as a visual tool for understanding addition. The rule is "add two" with each increment, and that means jumping two spaces on the number line. Are you sure your students know how to apply repetitive rules to adding on a number line? Do they need any instruction or practice before you turn them loose for independent work? What exactly is the most developmentally appropriate idea mathematically and the most important learning for the students to get out of this?

What about the second task on the sheet: a subtraction model. That means going to the left on the number line, "backward" on the number line, decreasing in value. But the numbers in the task, though going down in value, go from left to right on the page, the "up" direction on the number line, which is the opposite of how one would go on the number line to carry out subtraction. Will that be confusing? Do you expect the students to use the number line to get their answers, counting back four units with each move? Are you using the terms *addition* and *subtraction* yet? What vocabulary is appropriate for where the students are in their learning? What does a student have to know in order to do this second example? Should you do the second example at all today?

These are the kinds of questions we need to ask ourselves about the content before planning other aspects of the lesson. And the starting point is looking at the actual materials to see what the learning objective should be for the students, given what they know and what the next step for them should be.

**Seventh-Grade Science**

The textbook chapter is full of information about the interaction of ocean waves and landforms, including the names of many landforms that get created (for example, *spit, headland*). There are also terms that pertain to the processes that ocean movement cause (*erosion, deposition*) and there are terms related to these processes (*sediment, glacial moraine*). So amid all this information, what is the most important learning that students walk out the door with?

We have to do a close reading of the chapter ourselves to answer that question. Such a close examination of the text reveals that the main point is that *waves alter land*. Everything else in the chapter is about different aspects of the phenomenon: ways that happens, what the landforms look like, and the names of these different forms. But the main thing is for the students to understand that the ocean with its waves and currents is constantly altering the shape of the coastline and that these changes have consequences for human and animal life. If the activities of the lesson are not designed so every student walking out the door could say that in his or her own words, then the lesson hasn't been properly planned.

The next step after formulating a clear statement of the mastery objective is to communicate it to students. This is not a simple package handled by writing an objectives sentence on the board (though there's nothing wrong with that). It's fine to tell the students what the mastery objective is, but just telling them doesn't mean they understand it (or care about it). The essential questions and enduring understandings that are embedded in good curriculum help with "Why should I care?" For example, we may be studying the separation of powers to answer the larger question, "Is the Supreme Court taking over the legislative function, and is that OK?" When Grant Wiggins said, "Assessment is the Trojan horse of school reform," he

meant that through assessment, students (and parents and everyone else too) finally "get" what you really wanted them to learn. Therefore, giving the students the assessment (yes, the test) in advance gets people really clear about what the learning is supposed to look like.

Communicating what you really want students to know or be able to do includes explicitly showing them the performance task you expect them to do at the end of the instruction, ideally with a list of criteria, exemplars of products that are done well, and rubrics for scoring the exemplars. It may also include having students develop their own criteria or having them analyze "not yet" examples since we all get clearer about what something is by also knowing what it is not. (See Chapter Sixteen.)

So far we have advocated planning explicitly how to (1) make a clear statement of objectives, (2) show the assessment task, (3) give criteria, (4) share exemplars, and (5) explain rubrics. Having all these ready up front would be the fullest way to communicate objectives to students in a no-secrets classroom. You don't need all these, of course, when the learning targets are small. If students are learning the skill of using latitude and longitude to locate a place on the globe, they don't need a rubric. But many student products assigned (essays, lab reports, stories, oral reports) could have all five of these elements available for students. Math and science problems that exemplify the skills students are responsible for can be given to students in advance along with solutions worked out just as you want them to be able to do on the assessment.

If you expect the students to explain what powers each branch of government has and how they check and balance one another, you wouldn't give them the whole exemplary essay that answers the question in text, but you would tell them the aspects of checks and balances you want them to be able to comment on and not leave them to guess. ("Be able to explain how the legislature uses the confirmation process and the budget process to influence the court; show an example of how the court tests the constitutionality of legislation and can overturn it; be sure to explain how influence is exerted in at least one significant way between each of the following: legislative on executive, legislative on judicial, executive on legislative, executive on judicial, judicial on executive, judicial on legislative.")

Choosing and communicating objectives in primary grade literacy and numeracy looks a little different. If you're doing guided reading with three first graders on a book at the "E" level, you are working on a developmental continuum with each of the three children. Your records identify different skill elements to focus on with each child. Maisha is ready to work on fluency and reading with more natural speech rhythm; John is ready to master sound blending with "e" and "i" words; Darcy is ready to master the voice changes signaled by periods and commas. (Notice we haven't said "Maisha needs . . ." "John needs . . ." It's not that they're needy; it's that they are mastering the skills of reading that are next for them developmentally.) They're all reading the same book, seated with you at the same time. As each child reads, you give cues and small pieces of instruction in line with what skills they're developing: "Now, Darcy, pay attention to the comma in the sentence coming up; I bet you'll be able to make it sound just like talking!" Note the expression of confidence in her.

## Decision 4:
## What Will You Take as
## Evidence of Student Mastery?

What's the test item or performance that, if a student could do it successfully, you would take as

evidence of mastery? It may be as simple as looking over a student's shoulder and seeing her set up a three-step word problem correctly after reading it. It could be hearing a student explain to you how the executive branch exerts influence over the judiciary through the appointment process. The point is this: it is extremely important for us as teachers to get this performance in mind clearly before we begin a lesson. This performance becomes the anchor for everything else we do in the planning process. Thus, when we get to designing learning experiences, we will ask: Would question X or activity Y likely lead students to be able to do this performance?

Having envisioned specifically what performance we want from each student, we are much more likely to assess the children frequently and use those data as feedback for them and for ourselves about the effectiveness of the instruction. Both kinds of feedback are essential to successful teaching, and both have their origin in the planning of lessons.

## Decisions 5 and 6:
## Analysis of Evidence and
## Planning Pace and Grouping

When planning a lesson, we should consult data from the students' performance yesterday (or . . . whenever else we last got data). This information will help us decide about our pace for the class tomorrow. Obviously if our students showed on the quiz (or in the learning logs) that they don't understand what the purpose of the executive branch of government is, we will not move forward with the judiciary. More likely though, we discover from the evidence that a few students don't get it and the rest do. That's the way it is with most things taught at any given time. So now in our planning we have to design something so that the four students who are still foggy about the executive branch and its powers can get clear.

Before generating options for how to handle this situation, consider the attitude this step represents. We are saying that if four students didn't show evidence of understanding what they were doing in today's class, it is our responsibility to come up with a plan tonight so they will understand by the end of tomorrow (or soon). We can't say, "I taught it; they just didn't learn it," and move on with the rest of the class, leaving four students with this gap, . . . or move on with the hope that it will become clear to them through ensuing activities. We have to plan something to happen for them that will make it clear, and if possible, plan it for tomorrow.

That's what teachers are for, that is what professional decision making and diagnostic expertise and knowing how to reach diverse learners is all about. If all the job entailed was being a content expert and going through the material, then anyone who knows the material could teach. But if making sure the students *learn* the material is what the job is about, then the job requires professional expertise about planning and teaching. That is the position that stands behind these pages on Planning Skill. One option is to set up the class in groups for the first fifteen minutes debating whether the executive, particularly the president, has the authority to launch a punitive military strike against a country that has been proven to sponsor a terrorist group against the United States. While the groups are debating the question and coming to a position, you could take aside the four students who still have confusion about the purpose of the executive and reteach yesterday's lesson in a different way, with diagrams and frequent checking for understanding of each of them.

Another option is to make an appointment with the four students at the beginning of class to see you for supplementary instruction during X block, which the school has reserved for tutoring and extra help: "Gang, evidence from yesterday's quiz shows me you four need another go-round from me on the executive branch. We didn't get it done yesterday. I'm sure you can master this information, but I must have thirty minutes with you all together during an X block. Does it work better for you today or tomorrow?" (Notice the positive attribution statement in this language and the joint assignment of responsibility for the teaching and learning between teacher and students.)

Here is a third option. All year you have been working on a climate of mutual help and community building in the class. Thus, students who have received feedback that they're struggling with a concept can ask for help from their peers. Asking for and giving help has become a valued and praiseworthy behavior in the class and become scheduled into the rhythms of class routine. So at the beginning of tomorrow's class, you say, "Okay, before we start, does anybody want help with any of yesterday's material?" Three of the four hands go up: "Who's willing to give them a briefing [the term the class has adopted for peer tutoring] at lunch or some other time today?" Hands go up; the students who ask for help pick someone, as is the class routine. You thank and praise all who have entered this process, quickly by name, including the volunteer helpers who weren't picked.

While this is going on, you walk past Jerome, who didn't raise his hand for help but should have, and gently say, "What about you, Jerome?" "I'm goin' to ask my Dad tonight," he replies.

How you respond to Jerome depends on the context variables: whether it's good Jerome will ask his dad, whether Jerome is an isolate and you're trying to build connections between Jerome and others in the class, and all sorts of other possibilities. The point here is not how to handle Jerome, but that you have a deliberate plan you decided to implement the night before to deal with what the evidence told you: that four students don't get it yet.

There are many options besides these three, and no argument is made that these three are superior to others. We are making the argument, however, that a teacher has to come up with something to deal with the situation and that doing so is part of planning the night before.

### Decision 7: Pick Materials

This is the favorite part for many of us. In fact, some us like to start planning here because we have materials we love to use, materials the students have enjoyed in the past, and materials we think are engaging and clear. Beware! This is a habit that can lead to engaging activities that are unconnected to what the students are supposed to be learning.

Maybe you have a great case study you like to use when you study pollution in earth science. You've never seen a better one. And you love to show the movie *A Civil Action* to drive the point home about corporate responsibility as a wrap-up. But does the case study help you make the main point of the unit: that proactive environmental cleanup has social costs as well as social benefits?

You could use the case to make that point if you had some additional data to go with it. That is, you may find a place for your favorite materials in this series of lessons you're preparing, but start with the mastery objective and the evidence you would take that students had mastered it. Then go back and see if your favorite materials still fit or if they can be modified to fit the objective more precisely.

### Decision 8: Anticipating Confusions

When planning lessons, it is enormously helpful if the teacher's experience base allows him or her to predict what will be difficult or confusing for students about upcoming concepts or skills. Teachers use those predictions to develop something particularly clear or vivid for explaining that concept, warn the students in advance that this is particularly hard and they should thus ratchet up their focus and attention, do something to surface the confusion explicitly and explicitly contradict it, or tailor materials and the tasks students are asked to do to address that confusion.

Student confusions are often rooted in their different understandings of the words and terms used. For example, in the primary grades when students are given a set of seven tiles and a set of four tiles and asked how many more there are in the larger set, there is a confusion that prevents them coming up with 3 as the answer. It's a language confusion. They tend to focus on the word *more*, identify the bigger set, which has more, and count how many are in it. Thus they give the answer 7. We have seen teachers design excellent activities for students that nevertheless don't do the job, because they didn't anticipate this kind of confusion.

One meaning of "how many more" in a mathematical question is "how many *extra* in the bigger set if you match up the two sets one-to-one." Failure to use that language or in some way address the language confusion of the children delays the learning and causes confusion that is evident despite an otherwise excellent design for materials and tasks. Anticipating this confusion might have led to a different sequence of activities (like saving the introduction of the subtraction algorithm for later) and different language in the directions to the students with the task.

## Decisions 9 and 10:
## Designing Learning Experiences and Checking That Learning Experiences Are Logically Linked to the Intended Learning

The next aspect of lesson planning is the design of student learning experiences. Schlechty (2000) says that the center of teaching skill is the work we create for students to do. That is congruent with what Ralph Tyler (1949) said long ago when he pointed out that learning proceeds from what the students do, not what we do. But what the students do derives from the tasks we set them and the preparation (instruction) we give them for those tasks. A learning experience is more complex than just designing tasks for students, although it includes the tasks. It is smaller than a lesson because a lesson can shift gears and contain several learning experiences. Every time the activity changes, the learning experience changes. A lesson typically changes activity structure every now and then so as not to bore students.

A learning experience may be the teacher presenting, a Q&A session, a demonstration, student group work, and all manner of cognitive activities and formats. In this stage of planning, a teacher may choose a strategy to help students understand, like developing a graphic organizer of the three branches of government or doing a think-aloud with an approach to problem solving in math. And interspersed with these activities is a sequence of tasks for students: solve this problem; respond to this inference question; compare notes with your neighbor; determine the most important variable, and defend your choice; make a table of data; come up with a topic sentence. The design of the students' cognitive experience in a lesson is under our control. And clearly doing that well has a tremendous influence on children's

opportunity to learn. Thus, planning the minute-to-minute unfolding of those learning experiences in some detail is a vital component of teaching skill.

Let's start with student tasks. We select or make them up for students to do, some during the lesson and some afterward for homework. The key question is, "Is the doing of the task likely to lead students to learn the learning?" This is not a trivial question.

Let's say that students are asked to trace a map of Africa, fill in the names of the countries, and color it in. This is part of a unit on Africa. Some outcomes a teacher might reasonably want in the unit are for students to be able to name African countries if they are shown an outline of the shape without the name; identify which countries have coasts and which are inland; estimate the relative size of African countries in relation to each other; and explain the relationship between the country's location and water supply to its climate and growing season. Any of these might be worthwhile goals, but none of them will be realized by drawing an attractive map. There is nothing wrong with each student going home with an attractive, accurate map of Africa, but additional events and assignments must be planned if they are to learn something.

If we want students to be able to name the countries, then we make up a game where that is required. If we want students to know which countries are inland, then we have them highlight these countries on the map in a certain way and memorize a list; if we want them to know the relative sizes of the countries, then we have them estimate how many cut-outs of given countries can fit inside a to-scale cut-out of, say, the United States and construct a table of comparisons from smallest to largest. If we want them to understand the placement of the country on the continent in relation to climate and growing season, then we have them color in the map by topological features and write sentences about the patterns of crops and closeness to the equator. It should be logically conceivable that the doing of the task assigned to students could (though not necessarily by itself will) lead them to the intended learning.

Our point is this: look carefully at the activities you select for students to do in relation to the mastery objective and ask yourself if doing that task is connected to the precise learning you're aiming for. Fun activities do not ensure worthwhile learning.

### Decision 11: Decide How and When to Gather Evidence of Student Learning

Each lesson should produce data we can use for deciding how many students "have it," who doesn't, and who is ready for moving ahead. If we don't have data of some kind to look at as we're getting ready to plan, then there was a hole in our planning or implementation yesterday.

### Decision 12: Decide How Students Will Make Their Thinking and Understanding Public

The sequence of activities should include a way for students to be talking, writing, and doing in interaction with each other around the content of the class in such a way that they can respond to one another and that the teacher has access to their thinking.

### Decision 13: Plan How to Get Students Cognitively Active in Summarizing

The "Summarizing" section in Chapter Nine, "Clarity," described the significance of this behavior. The planning implication is simply that time needs to be provided for it to occur, and the actual mechanism for summarizing may require some preparation.

## The Finer Points About Implementation Decisions

These questions are slightly less critical than the ones above, but they can often determine the success of a lesson.

### Decision 14: Getting the Students' Minds in Gear

This item means choosing and using an activator (see Chapter Nine). No lesson hinges on doing or not doing this strategy. It is particularly useful, however, when starting a new topic like "taxes" or "weather" because it can surface many misconceptions we can deal with later.

### Decision 15: How Much Time Will Be Needed for Each Task or Activity

Do a fast-forward time-lapse mental movie in which you imagine the activities playing out. Will they fit in the time allotted? Plan other environmental variables: space and routines, if necessary.

### Decision 16: Plan the Effective Effort Strategies That May Come into Play

This is an uncommon element in lesson planning. We have included it because teaching the students how to exert effective effort is a commitment of ours personally, and we think it should be in the background all the time, waiting for opportunities to be included in any lesson. (We have profiled these strategies in Chapter Twelve, "Expectations.") Suffice it to say here that we should scan those ideas often during lesson planning to see which ones can be included today, especially strategies like student self-identification of errors and self-correction.

### Decision 17: Plan Interactive Moves

This includes planning your questions so as to guide thinking appropriately (see Chapter Nine).

A related question is what mediating do we have to do as teachers so the students can take advantage of the available learning by doing the task. For example, if we want students to be aware of the proximity of the African country to the equator and the effect of that on climate, we could have them draw the equator on the map at the beginning. Then say, "Now as you're drawing in countries, figure out how you'll record in a separate data table how far they are from the equator. Later I'm going to ask you to show some connection between their location and their crops and growing season. Who wants to predict what we may find?"

These moves cue the students about a line of inquiry that they will be pursuing about geography, climate, and crops. It also gets a few predictions out for the students to be thinking about as they're working on the map: "Mr. Rodriguez, I think the countries close to the equator will have a lot of desert and grow crops only close to rivers." Without some deliberate structuring for students' cognition while working on the map, they may produce a great map without any cognition at all related to what you want them to know. Students can trace and label a perfectly beautiful map while at the same time socializing. Good planners decide in advance on structuring moves that increase the percentage of student attention and cognition that is spent on the desired learning.

A number of the Clarity moves (like activating students' current knowledge or explicitly telling students the reason for the activity they're doing)

fit here. Of particular importance is planning the questions to ask so as to guide thinking along productive paths and stretch the thinking of all students to higher levels. (For more detail on this, see the section on designing questions in Chapter Nine, "Clarity.")

### Decision 18: Plan How to Diversify for Different Student Learning Styles

The simplest and most practical level of diversification is the set of variables we've laid out in Chapter Eighteen, "Learning Experiences." If you have all the issues above under control, then it is time to see how you can vary perceptual mode, grouping structure, and so on to match and stretch student learning preferences. To go deeper into this topic, explore McCarthy (1987), Gregorc (1977), Dunn (1978), and Tomlinson (2004).

Another potential decision (we call it 18a) is to plan how and when to check for understanding. Acknowledging that this is often done on the fly, it may be helpful to flag a check-in point during planning to make sure we stop and get some data from all the students about how clear we are. Such a point would be where we're shifting gears or subtopics, and failure to understand the previous topic would ruin a student's understanding of what you are about to explain in the next five minutes. For example, in automotive class, you've just finishing explaining the four-stroke cycle of a piston in the internal combustion engine. You're about to explain the significance of spark plug timing, that is, how close to top dead center of the compression stroke the plug fires. But if the students have any confusion about what is happening in the compression stroke and that the valves are all closed, thus holding in the gas air mixture, they won't understand the significance of spark timing at all. You'd better stop here and check for understanding.

### Decision 19: Decide How Much Help an Individual Student May Need and from Whom

This item is related to planning pacing and grouping. If you have aides, paraprofessionals, or volunteers in the room, this is where we plan who is deployed with whom.

### Decision 20: Plan Extensions or Challenges for Students Who Are Ready for Them

Some students will get the instruction quickly and be left sitting on their hands unless we plan an extension activity that will stretch them. This activity needs to be one that they can do with help from peers or on their own since we will be working with those who don't get it yet at this time.

### Decision 21: Plan Homework

The homework should be good homework. Good homework has the following characteristics:

- Students understand how it is connected to their learning
- It advances the students' understanding of a concept
- It generates fluency with a skill or ability to apply a skill in a more difficult or different context
- It gives students the background information they need for upcoming in-class work

But beyond its quality, plan how you're going to explain the connection between today's class and tonight's homework to students.

## Conclusion

This, then, is planning: a carefully executed cognitive scenario, really a set of cognitive tasks in an extended scenario. It is not intuitive or easy, and not to be done hastily, but it is clearly learnable and coachable, though often not developed sufficiently in teacher preparation. Good planning draws on—and is related to—many of the concepts developed in Chapters Nine (Clarity) and Twelve (Expectations) and is described in Exhibit 17.1.

Much checking for understanding (Clarity) is not generally planned in advance (though it is often wise to identify certain benchmark moments for checking). Successful teacher checking is broad and deep and springs spontaneously from the teacher's repertoire during interactive teaching. This chapter is about the elements that show up during a lesson that do *not* spring spontaneously from an acquired repertoire in the way attention and momentum moves do or checking and unscrambling do.

A virtuoso may make sensitive and skillful moves on the fly during instruction, but if these moves are not done within a well-designed plan for students, learning is limited.

Consider an analogy to sports. A virtuoso player may dazzle us with his or her performance in one part of the field, but unless there is a game plan that is solid and appropriate, the team won't win despite its talented players. The teacher in a classroom is like a player-coach. She is on the field interacting with individual students, making plays, and making a difference. But the teacher is also responsible for the conditions of the game: the quality of the learning experiences designed for the students, the careful attention to data about current student performance that will underlie teacher choices, the careful planning of questions, groupings and the series of tasks for students, the quality and frequency of feedback that has been engineered for the students that day, the structures and systems that build student confidence and promote effective effort. All of these aspects of students' experience unfold every day, and the more design

**Exhibit 17.1. Relationships Between PLANNING, CLARITY, and EXPECTATIONS**

| Planning Decisions | Clarity Move | Expectations Arena |
|---|---|---|
| 1. Recall big idea | Framing the big picture | |
| 2. Articulate mastery objective for today | | |
| 3. Plan how to communicate objective | Communicating objective | |
| 4. Envision evidence you'll take as sign of achievement of mastery of objective | Criteria for success | |
| 5. Analyze evidence from recent student work | | |
| 6. Plan pace and subgrouping | | Grouping and "reteaching loop" |
| 7. Pick materials | | |
| 8. Anticipate confusions | Anticipating confusion | |
| 9. Identify presentation strategy and student tasks | Explanatory devices | |
| 10. Check match of student task with objective | | |
| 11. Plan how and when to gather evidence of student learning | Checking understanding | Calling on and responding to students |
| 12. Plan how students will make their thinking public | Making thinking visible | |
| 13. Plan how to get students to summarize | Summarizing | |
| 14. Decide how to get students' minds in gear | Activating knowledge | |
| 15. Plan space, time, routines | | |
| 16. Plan effective effort strategies | | |
| 17. Plan interactive moves (cues, questions) | Explicitness-questioning | |
| 18. Plan how to diversify | | |
| 19. Plan student assistance | | |
| 20. Plan extensions and challenges | | |
| 21. Plan homework: what, why, and connections to today | Making connections | Feedback and grading structures |

and thought that are behind them, the better the learning will be. A big part of the skill of successful teachers is knowing how to plan these and other elements of sound instruction. Planning happens off the field, the night before.

To check your knowledge about Planning see the quiz on our Web site at **www.RBTeach.com/ rbteach/quiz/planning.html.**

*Source Materials for Planning*

Dunn, R., and Dunn, K. *Teaching Students Through Their Individualized Learning Styles.* Reston, Va.: Reston Publishing Company, 1978.

Gregorc, A. F., and Ward, H. B. "A New Definition for Individual." *MASSP Bulletin,* 1977, 20–26.

McCarthy, B. *The 4Mat System.* Barrington, Ill.: Excel, 1987.

Schlechty, P. *Shaking Up the Schoolhouse.* San Francisco: Jossey-Bass, 2000.

Tomlinson, C. A. *How to Differentiate Mixed Ability in Mixed Ability Classrooms.* Alexandria, Va.: ASCD, 2004.

Tyler, R. *Basic Principles of Curriculum and Instruction.* Chicago: University of Chicago Press, 1949.

West, L., and Staub, F. *Content-Focused Coaching.* Portsmouth, N.H.: Heinemann, 2003.

Wiggins, G., and McTighe, J. *Understanding by Design.* (2nd ed.). Alexandria, Va.: ASCF, 2005.

# Learning Experiences

## What choices do I have for differentiating learning experiences?

Sources of Information

Resources

Personal Relevance

Type of Interdependence

Degree of Supervision

Self-Expression

Degree of Abstraction

Cognitive Level

Structuring

Grouping and Interpersonal Complexity

Information Complexity

Sensory Channels

Scale

The main point of this area of performance is to enable you to survey the activities you offer to students so that you can describe them in a new way. This new way may give you a fuller picture than you have had before of what students are experiencing in your class—or it may give you a picture of what they are not experiencing, that is, the characteristics your learning experiences do not have. This information could lead you to make one of the following statements:

- "That's fine. It's okay not to have these features. What I'm doing is really on target for this curriculum, and those wouldn't be."
- "Well, there are some things I'm not doing that would be good to do. I'd like to do them, but there's just so much time. I think I'll put them on the back burner for now and look into adding them when things slow up a bit."
- "Well, there are a few things I hadn't thought about much before. They'd be really good, and I'd like to try them now."

The point is that you should be able to look at your teaching, or that of someone else, and see more than you have before and then make some decisions based on new understanding. You may come away from this chapter newly aware, or perhaps reminded, of some important things that you can design into students' experiences.

This area of performance is constructed from the students' point of view. We ask first, "What are students experiencing in their environment? What are the attributes of the activity? What is it like from the students' angle to be doing this?" Then we ask, "So what? What difference does it make? Of what importance is what students are experiencing on this particular attribute? What does it mean about their overall school learning?" This enables us to make choices, because the shape of the learning experience is, after all, something we control as teachers.

We analyze a student's learning experience almost as if it were a real, tangible thing, like a rock. It isn't tangible, but it is real and has describable attributes like a rock does. Supervision, for example, is an attribute with three possible values (or options): independent, facilitated, or directly supervised. Which are students experiencing right now? They may be closely and directly supervised right now and independent later in the day. Their learning experience may change based on this attribute, and when it does, it's a different learning experience.

A learning experience takes place over a time span with a beginning, middle, and end. It can be quite short—a matter of minutes—or extend to hours. When it changes on significant attributes, it's a different learning experience.

This kind of analysis yields a full and accurate picture of what the student is experiencing in a planned activity. We can look at activities over a period of time and see what patterns and ranges are built into these experiences. Then we can decide if the range is appropriate. Are we ever giving students a chance to work cooperatively, for example, or is it always competitive or individualistic? Which sensory input channels are stimulated? Do we ever use the kinesthetic channel? What is the balance between concrete and abstract in our teaching? This area of performance provides a set of questions with which to survey our teaching periodically and see if we are offering what we want to offer. Finally, this area of performance gives some sharp-focus lenses for looking at matching and adjusting learning experiences for individual students or groups.

In the following sections, we describe the attributes of learning experiences one by one and lay out the possible forms each may take. You may choose to profile yourself as you go, noticing which of the options characterize learning experiences you offer and then deciding if those choices are broad enough and appropriately matched to your students.

## Sources of Information

### Definition

You can examine learning experiences to determine whether the information the students are working with is *conventional*—from conventional sources such as a text, a reference book, you, or some other source that gives the information to them—or *constructed*—meaning that the students constructed the knowledge through some process of their own, such as observation, experiment, interview, deduction, induction, application of logic, discussion, debate, or questioning.

Looking something up is always a conventional source of information. The student's own initiative, objective, and choice of learning experience may be behind the act of looking up, for instance, design features of an airplane, but the source of the information is still conventional.

## Significance

It is significant to know whether students are ever challenged or put in positions where they are able to use their own resources as active agents for the generation of knowledge new to them, as opposed to receiving information that has been assembled, organized, or predigested for them. Neither source of information is better than the other, but they are clearly different in their effects on the learner. If teaching uses either source to the exclusion of the other, we are led to ask whether learners have sufficient balance in their educational program.

# Resources

## Definition

Students may use any one or more of the following resources in the course of their work:

- A text
- The teacher
- Peers
- Parents
- Interviews with outside people (other than parents, teachers, or peers)
- Observation
- Audiovisual material
- Online services or electronic sources
- Reference books
- Their own imaginations or experiences

This attribute is an index to the breadth of resources brought to bear on the student's learning experience and can tally a simple count of how many are used.

## Significance

Over the course of a student's education, we would expect all of the resources listed to be used. In any one course, grade, or class, you would ask which resources and how broad a range were appropriate and desirable, and compare that with the reality. In examining an individual student's educational experience, you could usefully ask how many of these resources were brought to bear across different courses and evaluate the fit of the operating range of resources to the intentions of the program.

# Personal Relevance

## Definition

On this attribute, learning experiences are found to be *contrived, simulated,* or *real.* The degree to which the learning experience relates to aspects of life that have personal meaning to the students is indexed here. Does it connect to their real world outside school?

Doing a workbook page containing problems of adding money in the form $124.35 + 3.50 = ?$ would be judged as contrived, since calculating the answer on a workbook page is not connected to the students' world of experience outside school. But if the class has set up a model store selling grocery items (or anything they might find in a real store), and the students are buying items using play money (or even real money), then this activity simulates real experiences from the students' lives. If the class takes a trip to a supermarket and spends money it has made through some project to buy supplies for a party, and they collect, purchase, pay for the items, and get change, then the activity is judged real: it is integrated, connected, and related directly to the real world.

*Contrived* in this sense does not have a negative connotation. Much of learning and knowledge construction is contrived in that it does not simulate or reproduce the reality outside school, nor could it. It is impractical for almost all of us to learn about the history of India by visiting historic Indian sites (though that would be nice). And aspects of historical study necessarily require reading books and other contrived (versus real) experiences to proceed effectively with the learning. There is no general value implied in this attribute that real learning experiences are superior to contrived ones. Students do not have to leave school on a field trip to enter the realm of real learning experiences either. The act of painting is real no matter where one does it. Painting is painting and not a simulation of painting, whether or not one does it in school or in an art studio. The same applies to creative writing or other aesthetic work of any kind. Having a debate is a real experience between the debaters and not simulated just because it is not taking place in a court of law or a legislative chamber. Many experiences in school are inherently real for students. Settling a dispute with another student over how to share materials is a real experience in which students play a deliberate role and act as mediators according to certain designs.

## Significance

Many educators believe it is important that as many learning experiences as possible connect to students' real world of meaning—their world of experience outside school. One school of learning theory holds that such learning experiences are more effective, more powerful, and more lasting in effect (Dale, n.d.). The student, it is said, has a con-

text in which to embed the new information and because of its relevance to his personal life is more impelled to attend to and participate in what's going on. This then guarantees a level of involvement on the part of the student with the learning experience that will maximize learning. To people of this persuasion, it is important to know how much realness is characteristic of learning experiences being offered. Early childhood educators and open classroom educators are especially interested in this attribute of learning experiences (Bussis, Chittenden, and Amarel, 1976).

Regardless of one's beliefs about the learning theory of personal relevance, it is a distinction we can make among learning experiences. It produces data to bring to an analysis of teaching-in-action in comparison with teaching's intentions. We can look at curriculum designs to see where and how often opportunities for realness exist and how appropriate such experiences might be to the content and the learners. We can evaluate the efficiency of a curriculum in terms of the balance among contrived, simulated, and real experiences that is best for accomplishing the objectives of the instruction in the time allowed.

# Type of Interdependence
## Definition

Johnson and Johnson (1987) first set out a three-point typology for learning experiences: *cooperative, competitive,* and *individualized.* (They don't use the term *learning experiences;* they say *goal structures.*) A learning experience specifies the type of interdependence existing among students—the way in which students will relate to each other and the teacher. One might say they have taken a specific aspect of the social climate—that aspect related to competition and its presence, absence, or opposite—and defined it in detail:

> When students are working together to find what factors make a difference in how long a candle burns in a quart jar, they are in a cooperative goal structure. A cooperative goal structure exists when students perceive that they can obtain their goal if and only if the other students with whom they are linked can obtain their goal. Since the goal of all the students is to make a list of factors that influence the time the candle burns, the goal of all the students has been reached when they generate a list. A cooperative goal structure requires the coordination of behavior necessary to achieve their mutual goal. If one student achieves the goal, all students with whom the student is linked achieve the goal. When students are working to see who can build the best list of factors influencing the time a candle will burn in a quart jar, they are in a competitive goal structure. A competitive goal structure exists when students perceive that they can obtain their goal if and only if the other students with whom they are linked fail to obtain their goal. If one student turns in a better list than anyone else, all other students have failed to achieve their goal. Competitive interaction is the striving to achieve one's goal in a way that blocks all others from achieving the goal. Finally, if all students are working independently to master an operation in mathematics, they are in an individualistic goal structure. An individualistic goal structure exists when the achievement of the goal by one student is unrelated to the achievement of the goal by other students; whether or not a student achieves her goal has no bearing upon whether or not other students achieve their goals. If one student masters the mathematics principle, it has no bearing upon whether other students successfully master the mathematics principle. Usually there is no student interaction in an individualistic situation since each student seeks the outcome that is best for himself regardless of whether or not other students achieve their goals [Johnson and Johnson, 1987, p. 7].

Johnson and Johnson have an observation checklist with a series of yes-no questions for classroom organization, student-student interaction, and teacher-student interaction. The outcome scores of the checklist are three percentage figures for the three possible goal structures. There is a recognition that a learning experience will rarely be exclusively cooperative. From the percentage figures of Johnson and Johnson's observation checklist, one could make a statement about the dominant quality of the learning experience along the attribute of competition.

An important body of research literature has emerged on the effectiveness of cooperative learning for cognitive as well as affective ends. This is accompanied by an emerging technical literature on how to do cooperative learning. At least five forms of cooperative learning are developed and available for teachers to try (Exhibit 18.1). They are arranged in the table in the order of the demands they place on students for interaction and communication skills (from least demanding on the left to most demanding on the right).

If you want to rate yourself on this attribute, you will want to be able to look at a single learning experience and characterize its dominant quality: cooperative, competitive, or individualistic. For example, in certain science lab courses we have

**Exhibit 18.1. Five Formats for Cooperative Learning**

| Team Games Tournament | Student Teams, Achievement Divisions | Jigsaw | Johnson and Johnson | Group Investigation |
|---|---|---|---|---|
| | Whole class instruction ↓ | Divide material into 5–6 parts for 5–6 students on a team ↓ | Task given to groups ↓ | Puzzling, interesting situation ↓ |
| | 4–5 students on a heterogeneous team quiz each other, and do worksheets | Members learn their parts solo ↓ | Social skills training and debriefing ↓ | Explore student reactions ↓ |
| Tournament, tables with 3 students of equal ability representing different teams. They play games using academic material: Winner, 6pts.; Second, 4 pts.; Third, 2 pts. ↓ | 15-minute written quizzes students take alone ↓ | Teams disband. Individuals from different teams who have the same item form an "expert group" to coach each other and prepare presentations for their teams. ↓ | Groups decide how to divide it up to produce a single cohesive product ↓ | Formulate study task with large group ↓ Form subgroups taking a subtask of larger project ↓ Organize, assume roles, plan ↓ |
| Newsletter recognizes winning team (and first-place scorers) | Students earn points for their team by improving on their own prior performances ↓ Winning teams posted | Teams reassemble for peer teaching ↓ Individual tests | Groups work together; do job ↓ Receive group grade | Independent work, study ↓ Groups analyze progress and process ↓ Plan presentation and display ↓ Evaluation by class of group's contribution |

**Research for Better Teaching, Inc.** • One Acton Place, Acton, MA 01720 • (978)263-9449 • www.RBTeach.com

observed, groups of students worked together sharing apparatus, ideas, and information as they performed a common experiment. This we considered significant cooperation. At the same time, these students were recording experimental results in individual notebooks the teacher graded separately.

Different groups of students were at different places in the sequential programmed curriculum. Some were working alone, either because no one else was at the same place as they or because they wanted to work alone (which the teacher allowed). Students took tests individually when they felt ready. Individual pretest feedback was given by the teacher to students, and tests were graded individually. This was significant evidence for calling the learning experience individualistic. In this lab course, there were no observed instances of students' comparing test scores in a competitive way, though in interviews teachers cited cases where that happened. Indeed, even if we had observed students' comparing scores, it wouldn't necessarily merit a judgment of competition as a value of the learning experience on this attribute since what one student earns on the test has no bearing on the score of any other student. It could be argued that comparing test scores reflects competitive qualities inherent in humans, the culture, in the process of testing itself ("Whadjaget?").

The kind of competition we looked for was one designed into the learning experience by the teacher or the curriculum—something like a team game, a contest for speed or accuracy involving a group of students, or a recitation period where a student gives right answers in competition with peers. Many competitive forces emanating from students themselves, peers, parents, or the culture and community may affect student behavior. These forces are not examined here. This attribute looks at aspects of the design of the learning experience that set up, by virtue of that design, interactions that are competitive, cooperative, or individualistic in nature. Only students' behavior of these three types that is encouraged or arranged by the design of the learning experience will enable us to make a judgment on this attribute. Competitive, cooperative, or individualistic behavior of children that cannot be attributed to the design of the learning experience that comes from some other source is deemed irrelevant to the judging of this attribute.

In the case of the science lab course, competition would not be scored as a significant quality of the learning experience because whatever of it there was couldn't be traced to the teacher or the design of the learning experience.

## Significance

It is not hard to get a discussion started among educators, parents, or even passers-by on the street about the merits or evils of competition. It is a condition of life we have all experienced and about which we all have formed some values. This attribute of teaching calls attention to teachers' ability to control in aware and deliberate ways how competitive, cooperative, or individualistic the experiences of students are in schools. Educational decision makers bring different values and different histories to their settings, as has always been the case. But whatever their decisions about the shape of learning experiences, these decisions can be informed and deliberate if made by professionals who know the full implications of their acts. This attribute provides tools for surveying your own teaching to see how much cooperation or competition you are putting into students' experiences. It also offers resources for getting the balance you want.

In this attribute, as in all the other attributes of learning experiences we have touched, there is an analyzable nature, an emergent reality to the experience students have on each attribute. That experience is in the form it is because an educational decision maker has made it that way—either deliberately or in ignorance. Each attribute is controllable, alterable, and subject to change by educators who seek to be knowledgeable and deliberate about the environments they create for learners.

## Matching

There is matching if the teacher differentiates deliberately among groups or individuals as to the competitive, cooperative, or individualistic quality of learning experiences.

## Degree of Supervision

### Definition

Students may be directly supervised by a teacher who checks on what and how everybody is doing, may be independent and responsible for their own work, or the teacher may facilitate their work by being available as a resource person and occasionally intervening with suggestions, recommendations, or stimulating questions (Dunn and Dunn, 1978). As we reflect on the learning experiences we design, the number of these three possible conditions present in our teaching—*supervised, facilitated,* or *independent*—can be counted.

### Significance

A limited range on this attribute—for example, a teacher who always supervises all learning activities—excludes certain kinds of learning in a classroom. The breadth or narrowness of range on this attribute is something we can look at for its nurturant effects on students, that is, the effects on them of living in an environment of that kind. We can then ask if that is what we intend. And we can, of course, compare this range of supervisory modes and the nurturant effects attached with the goals of the curriculum.

### Matching

Teachers who discriminate among students on how much supervision they require or can tolerate so as to maximize their performance match the amount and kind of supervision they provide to the characteristics of students. Jane flourishes if left to work independently much of the time, checking in occasionally for conferences with the teacher. Working under direct supervision for the bulk of the day unnecessarily limits her learning experiences. But Moira can't seem to get herself organized; she'll have several false starts and then may socialize away her morning if she is not directly supervised in her work. Her teacher provides much direct supervision for her and much independence for Jane. The same kind of distinction can be made for subgroups of the class and would enable us to conclude yes for the matching on supervision.

## Self-Expression

### Definition

Students may or may not be given the opportunity to express something of themselves in a learning experience. If they are given such an opportunity, the self-expression may be delivered through drawing, creative writing, performing, speaking, or building or construction of some sort. Merely to respond or recite is not to express one's self as meant here. Expressing one's self means expressing something that is unique to the individual or expressing some standard information in a way that encourages students to bring something of themselves to the expression. An assignment to diagram mitosis for biology (though different students will embellish the product to different degrees) is a prescribed product that has the student express mitosis, not himself or herself. An assignment to represent the "1812 Overture" in paint is also prescribed but frees the student to express things unique to him or her that are stimulated by the music. A recitation question asking a student to summarize Turner's frontier thesis does not allow self-expression as would a question asking a student to say how he would have responded to the offer of free western land had he been alive a hundred years ago.

## Significance

The significance of this attribute relates to the value placed on self-expression by those responsible for the educational program. Data on the attribute tell us what we have and enable us to raise the attribute as an important and perhaps overlooked aspect of learning experiences over which program designers and teachers have control. And as before, we can compare realities with intentions, where intentions about self-expression have been considered by program designers and made explicit.

## Matching

We may look to see if the ways in which we encourage expression of the self also allow differences in ways students can best do that expressing. If matching were present, one would see not only a range on this attribute but also negotiation or direct planning of students' activities where they were asked to or permitted to express themselves in ways different from other students.

# Degree of Abstraction

## Definition

Learning experiences can be scored as *concrete, representational* (iconic), or *abstract* (Bruner, 1966). Concrete means manipulative: students are touching or seeing real objects that are integral to the learning experience. Iconic means representational: a picture, image, or other facsimile of real objects is embedded in the materials with which the learner is interacting. Abstract means symbolic: words or thoughts are the stuff of which the learning experience is made without support from facsimiles or concrete objects.

## Significance

We can compare the range of levels of abstraction offered to the nature of the content and make judgments concerning appropriateness. Similar comparisons can be made in consideration of the age and learning style of the students. We might expect to see teachers of young children designing more concrete experiences than at other grade levels. But it has been acknowledged for several decades in learning style models that reliance on concrete models and examples is characteristic of some learners no matter what the age.

## Matching

Because students of the same age are often at different levels with regard to their ability to process abstract information, we might expect a teacher to discriminate among students and adjust the level of abstraction of the learning experiences offered to characteristics of individual students. Conrad Toepfer (1981) and others have applied these insights to the typical middle school curriculum and found that much of it demands formal operational thinking of students, a kind of thinking that, according to their statistics, only 12 percent of American youngsters are capable of at age twelve. Toepfer makes a strong case that teachers who match the level of thinking to the students' capacity for abstract thinking, especially in the plateau period of twelve to fourteen years of age, make a huge difference in school failure rates. He and his colleagues recommend testing students for their level of thinking (onset of concrete operations, concrete operations, initial formal operations, established formal operations) and accommodating instruction to the stage. Intelligence, he points out, is different and uncorrelated to stage thinking. Super-bright youngsters go through the same Piagetian stages of growth and in about the same proportions per given age as students of normal and below-normal IQ.

This attribute of learning experiences bears a hard look if we are to meet the needs of all students at all ages, stages of development, and learning style orientations.

# Cognitive Level

## Definition

In Chapter Nine (Clarity) we discussed questioning and Bloom's Taxonomy (and Anderson and Krathwohl's update of that Taxonomy) as a framework for designing questions requiring different levels of thinking. We can examine learning experiences to see what cognitive level of performance they ask of students. We can also look across learning experiences we offer to identify the range of thinking embedded in them and count the number of levels for which evidence can be produced.

## Significance

Researchers have long investigated the number of higher-level questions teachers ask students in verbal interaction. The research implies that the more higher-level questions there are, the better, and studies have attempted to correlate the proportion of higher-level questions with student achievement (Winne, 1979a). However, large doses of high cognitive levels may be quite inappropriate for students who have not worked through lower levels with the same material. When we considered the Models of Teaching area of performance in Chapter Eleven, we saw that for certain models (like Taba's), it is the order in which cognitive operations are demanded

of students that is important, not the raw amount at any level.

Focusing on the cognitive level embedded in learning experiences offered by a teacher enables us to collect data on the range offered. Any predominance of one or two particular levels will prompt us to ask, "Why?" If a teacher or a curriculum has some specific thinking objectives in mind, we can compare intentions with reality.

## Matching

Tailoring or adjusting learning experiences on the same or similar material so that the cognitive level demanded is different for different students is evidence that we are differentiating cognitive level across students. The danger in such differentiation is if we deny to low-skill students the opportunity for higher-level thinking. This pattern appears when one holds low expectations for students derived from impressions of their lower innate ability. Thus, instruction becomes more drill oriented and less interesting for these students, deepening their cycle of failure and their subsequent rejection of school itself.

The point here is to be aware if we are limiting the involvement of certain students with experiences from the higher levels of Bloom's taxonomy. We can differentiate learning experiences appropriately for different students in many ways, including pace. But we should look for ways to offer the full range of cognitive levels to both high- and low-skill students.

# Structuring

We have all heard people refer to students who need a high degree of structure. We have often wondered exactly what is meant by that *structure* and discovered, not too surprisingly, that people mean different things: that the student has to be closely supervised or that the task has to be broken down into small pieces and the student told exactly what to do, when, and how. We find out how structuring is being handled when we give directions. We would have called this section "giving directions" except that giving directions is only one way that activities get set up. Sometimes students are asked to set procedures, and sometimes teachers and students negotiate what to do and how. One way to analyze differences in instruction is to examine how much and where these different kinds of structuring are occurring: by the teacher (high structure), negotiation (moderate structure), or students (low structure). Another question to ask is if we differentiate among students along this attribute of who structures activities. That is matching.

When teachers give directions, they often structure (that is, make decisions and give instructions about) the content to be worked on, the procedures to follow, the behavior to do (for example, "write," "discuss," "compare," "listen"), the form of student products, and the point of closure (signaling when it's over). Content, behavior, procedures, products, and closure are the five components of structuring. Exhibit 18.2 identifies each of these

aspects of a learning experience and the choice points one has for either increasing or decreasing the degree and kind of structure embedded. Thus, the degree of structure in a learning experience is largely a matter of whether or not decisions are being made and who is making them.

## Content

Content means information or objects dealt with at the item level. Who decided, introduced, or is responsible for the presence of the particular items students are working with? Making reliable assignments of responsibility here requires being clear on the unit of analysis. Just how big or small is an item? Some examples will help (see the top of page 422).

At the most general level, the teacher is almost always responsible for content. In the example where students debate the pros and cons of busing, the teacher probably (though not necessarily) introduced the subject. The teacher is responsible for the topic—the area being treated—but clearly that is above the item level. If teachers are responsible for the responses the students are producing in that they ask factual or leading questions, then they are responsible for the content. But if the

**Exhibit 18.2. Who Decides**

| | No one decides | Student decides | Negotiation | Teacher decides |
|---|---|---|---|---|
| | | *Low structure* ————————————➤ *High structure* | | |
| 1. Content | | | | |
| 2. Behavior | | | | |
| 3. Procedures | | | | |
| 4. Products | | | | |
| 5. Closure | | | | |

*Source:* Reprinted by permission from Ann Berlak.

| Activity | Item | Responsible Party |
|---|---|---|
| Recitation or review of Civil War battles with teacher leading questioning in chronological order, seeking identification and sequence | Pieces of information elicited from students | Teacher |
| Teacher says, "Read this book and answer the questions at the back." | The book, the questions | Teacher |
| Teacher says, "Pick a book you'd like to read, and summarize it verbally for me." | The book | Student |
| Although the use of time is structured by the teacher in the item above and the behavior and writing are also structured, the content—what is operated on, written about—comes from the student. | | |
| Teacher suggests, "Use the blocks to make a model of the store we visited." | Model of store | Teacher |
| Although the student controls the shape of the product, what the store will look like, the item on which he is operating—blocks—and the model of a store were directed by the teacher. If the student were free to represent the store in any medium he chose (paint, clay, or something else), then the behavior would have been attributed to the student as the shape of the product, but the content would still be the teacher's decision about what to represent. | | |
| Class discussion about the pros and cons of busing to integrate public schools; teacher serving as facilitator and clarifier, not taking a stand, trying to get students to show their positions. | Arguments, positions, and evidence for positions | Students |
| Following a discussion of movies, students form interest groups to study selected aspects of movie production: special effects, casting, script writing, shooting schedules. Students nominate themselves into groups, and teacher mediates which groups may form and the membership. | Special effects, casting, shooting schedules, script writing | Negotiated |

students are bringing in information not directly tied to the teacher's questions, items, or objects that could not be the only reply to the question or the lead-in of the teacher, then the students are responsible for the content at the item level (though perhaps not the general topic).

What can be said about a discussion where the teacher starts off being responsible for the content, say, a recitation, and then switches to more open-ended exploration of the same material, and all within the same discussion: "And now what would you have done in General Lee's position? Do you think he did the right thing? Can you justify your position?" Here the responsibility for content has shifted from teacher to students, and an important attribute to the learning experience has changed. We will be interested in knowing what other attributes of the learning experience have changed.

For individual learning experiences, we can note who is responsible for the content at the item level. Across learning experiences, we can note which of these parties are responsible if we survey a number of lessons: teacher, student, or negotiation.

## Behavior

To determine who has structured the student behavior within the learning experience, the question is to ask what verb describes what the student is doing. Who is responsible for that operation (verb) being the operation: the teacher, the student, or negotiation? The student is reading, writing, summarizing, responding verbally, building, or painting. Who chose that? These are questions to ask of individual learning experiences. Then when we look across learning experiences and note our range on structuring of behavior, we ask how many of the three possibilities we've exercised. (Or perhaps none was exercised.) It may be that we have a behavior in mind for the learning experience but fail to state it. This is of no consequence if the behavior is obvious or understood by the students. ("Doing" a page in a workbook is understood to mean, "Follow the directions on the page," which almost always calls for a written response in a blank or on a line.) But if the behavior is not clear to the students or we didn't fully think it out ("What do we do, Mr. Jones?"), then we could conclude "none" here. For example, "Do the next chapter in your book," may mean, "Read and answer the questions at the end," "Read only," or "Read for the general idea." Unless some routine has been established for what "reading a chapter" means, we could conclude this is "none" on structuring behavior.

## Procedures

Procedural moves set the details of who and how—for example, dividing a class into teams for a spelling bee, giving directions for a worksheet exercise, and describing the procedure in a concept attainment game. Included in this category are the negotiations, which may go on at some length, when students are given the opportunity to decide how they want to go about studying a given content area. Procedures may come from the teacher or from the students, or they may be negotiated. Which are the following?

- "We are going to divide the class into three groups. John, Gary, and George will be in group 1."
- "First we're going to do worksheets. Then I want you to write down the items that were difficult, and when you've done that, we'll discuss those items."
- "We're going to go around the circle here, and each of you will tell us something you read about Hemingway and I'll write it on the board."
- "How shall we do this? Shall everybody participate?"
- "John has suggested that we invite the editor of the newspaper to speak. Do you agree that this is a good way to begin our study of journalism?" (Joyce, 1969).

It may be that we have some procedures in mind for the learning experience but fail to state them. In that case, there is no structuring of procedures. If we say, "Work on your folders, boys and girls," and within each folder there is a structuring of procedures for each child in the form of a note ("Charlie, do the first two worksheets and then bring them to me for checking"), then the procedures are structured by the teacher. But if it is unclear what the procedures are to be because we have failed to state them or failed to think them out and don't explicitly ask students to make decisions about procedures, then one might conclude "none."

## Products

Who determines the form of the tangible products: teacher, student, or both together?

- Teacher: "I'll tally votes here on how many thought the Civil War represented progress versus setbacks." The tally is the product.
- Student: Any creative or expressive activity (painting, creative writing) makes a student responsible for the form of the product.
- Negotiated: "How shall we represent the data from our poll?" Students and teacher negotiate a form, perhaps deciding on bar graphs.

## Closure

How will the student know when the learning experience is over? The end point can be defined in terms of time, quantity of material completed, or a certain kind of product being produced. Who determines these limits: teacher, student, or both together?

For certain experiences, closure is inherently determined by the student (examples are a painting or creative writing—except where the teacher says, "Write a four-page story"). For others it is clearly teacher determined ("Do the first three lines of problems"). But if closure is not inherently or explicitly delegated to the student, then failure to state it may lead us to conclude "none" on structuring of closure. The key questions are, "Which ways do we have for structuring closure to learning experiences?" and, "Are they used appropriately?"

Teachers who hand out folders containing pages of new worksheets and expect students to begin working are evidencing "none" for structuring of procedures and closure—and they often experience the consequences of that lack of structuring.

## Matching

One reason teachers treat students differently with regard to structure is learning effectiveness (see Colarusso and Green, 1972). Jimmy may be capable of designing his own procedures for collecting data from his science experiment, whereas Fred needs the teacher to structure procedures to maximize the benefit he gets from the experience. A certain group of students may be quite capable of picking their own reading material, whereas another is not (content).

But another reason might have to do with long-range goals. Some teachers have as a goal helping students become more independent, self-motivated learners. This means moving gradually from high to progressively lower structure. Such a teacher takes students where they are and provides the degree of structure necessary for learning to proceed efficiently. If this happens to be high structure, so be it. Over time, the teacher introduces negotiation of certain attributes, say, procedures and closure, with some students. Over the course of the year, more and more students become involved in more and more decision making about their learning as they show they are ready.

We feel that understanding structuring (and accountability) is the key to understanding the erratic record of open classrooms in the 1960s and 1970s. Those that worked were in control of structuring and matched it to the students in the class. Those that didn't offered too little structure to students who were unprepared to deal with it. The physical look and arrangement of the room, open versus traditional, is usually no clue to the level of structure and the degree of appropriateness for different students. Whole populations of students may be matched to a level of structure, or structure may be differentiated across different individuals and groups within the same class. Few American visitors to British infant schools in the early 1960s perceived the high degree of structure and accountability built into students' working routines, despite the open, child-centered, and apparently effortless flow of constructive activity (Berlak and others, 1975).

A robust line of research developed by David Hunt and his associates since 1966 has established the better learning that results when students experience a degree of imposed structure matched to their level of development. Numerous instruments are available for determining whether a student is suited to a high- or low-structure treatment (Hunt, 1971; Hunt and Sullivan, 1974; Rich and Bush, 1978). The possibilities we have sketched for who does the structuring—teacher, negotiated, or student—correspond to Hunt's ratings of high, moderate, and low degrees of imposed structure.

# Grouping and Interpersonal Complexity

## Definitions

Students may work alone, with a single peer, with a group of peers, with the total class, in a dyad with the teacher, with other adults (the principal, a visitor, a parent), or in a small group with the teacher. Any one or more of these possible combinations may characterize learning experiences over the course of a day or week. Each individual learning experience may have its own grouping. First, one can simply count the number of groupings evidenced to index a teacher's range.

## Significance

Characterizing the groupings in our teaching allows us to ask about what kinds of interpersonal complexity are consistent with the objectives of the curriculum. It also allows us to see how much congruence there is between intentions and reality. Notice we have replaced the word *grouping* with *interpersonal complexity*. This is because there is more to say about a group than how many people are in it.

It is also important to know what kind of interaction they are having with one another. Six students and a teacher may be answering recitation questions in a small group; these students have no interaction with each other and only simple interactions with the teacher as they give direct factual answers. Thus the interpersonal complexity is low. In that same group, however, the teacher may invite students to respond to or extend, interpret, or refute other students' answers. Students may begin speaking directly to one another without the teacher as intermediary between every student utterance. The teacher may still moderate the discussion and call on people, but the interpersonal complexity is now moderately complex and no longer simple. If the students are freely interacting with each other and create their own conversational rules and agendas as they go, the interpersonal complexity is high.

In a curriculum stressing social objectives—say, cooperation, listening to each other, or mutual respect—we would expect to see learning experiences with groups of students, dyads, and other combinations that brought students together without exclusive teacher direction. Whatever the themes of the curriculum, the types of interpersonal complexity displayed enable us to describe an important and real part of the learning environment and ask questions about the effect of those patterns on students' learning. Taken from the perspective of curriculum as planning, interpersonal complexity is a design feature of learning experiences that a teacher can tailor to the nature of the objectives and the needs of the learners.

## Matching

In studying our teaching, we can determine whether we discriminate among students in the kind of interpersonal complexity designed or allowed for in learning experiences (Colarusso and Green, 1972). Mehmet works well in large groups but tends to act out or be silly in small-group instruction. He does have a few peers with whom he seems able to work effectively. He allows these students to help him and can work cooperatively with them when he has to deal with them only one at a time. So we engineer teacher-Mehmet and peer-Mehmet learning situations as often as possible (while also working on his difficulties with being in groups) to maximize his productive learning time in the class. We have matched the interpersonal complexity in his learning experiences to observed characteristics of Mehmet.

We observe that this class attends poorly in a large group. So while making attention an objective for them, we make sure they have as many individual and small-group work situations as possible. That is a decision to match the needs of this particular class.

Ms. James notices her English class does not handle the high level of interpersonal complexity she encourages; they seem alternately to flounder or to attack each other when discussing the readings. She reduces the interpersonal complexity to moderate and increases her role as mediator. They prove quite capable of handling high-level literary analysis but require less interpersonal complexity than last year's class.

Where teachers show different patterns of grouping and interpersonal complexity for different children, we can note matching on this attribute.

How about the possibility of a mismatch? What would it look like so that we could defend such a judgment? Probably the learning experience wouldn't be going well. A mismatch means that something is wrong, and when something is wrong, we expect to see symptoms—usually disruptive behavior or inattention. Students are experiencing difficulty under these conditions, and we must be able to attribute this difficulty to inappropriate grouping or interpersonal complexity rather than to other causes (students' emotional baggage, inappropriate work, poor transition). How might an observer help to distinguish such causes?

Repeated observations over a long period of time might enable an observer to see groupings that were consistently successful for a certain student and others that were consistently unsuccessful. If the students were frequently placed in these failure settings, the observer could attribute mismatch to the grouping or interpersonal complexity. This would put the observer in the position of knowing, through repeated observation, something the teacher did not. Although such a situation is conceivable, a single observation is rarely enough to produce it. More likely the observer would be in a position to problem-solve with the teacher, exploring what the cause of the problem might be.

# Information Complexity

## Definition

"Students who are low in conceptual level (CL) are less capable of processing information in a complex way and less capable of dealing with information in a responsible fashion; students higher in CL are more capable of processing information in a complex way" (Hunt, 1971). It sounds simplistic, but it is not. The conceptual level of students, however, is not the same as their intelligence or ability. Often two youngsters who are both quite bright are different in conceptual level. What does it mean to process information in a complex way? We will define three levels of information complexity: *high, moderate,* and *low*.

At level 1, *low complexity,* information is linear and direct. One thing leads to another. Qualities of the learning tend to include remembering, sequence, performance, concepts, and skills. Learners are not asked to consider alternatives or make distinctions between points of view or such things as people's feelings or orientations. They have difficulty developing concepts on their own but can learn them receptively without difficulty.

At level 2, *moderate complexity*, the notion of alternatives appears. Students are asked to make distinctions and differentiate sources, points of view, courses of action, and possible explanations. They can assimilate the idea that there is more than one possible explanation for a phenomenon. Comparison and contrast enter the picture. Students can develop their own concepts from data.

At level 3, *high complexity*, students can consider several alternatives. Their ability to differentiate and distinguish increases and develops into the ability to see the relationships between different points of view or different explanations.

## Significance

Clearly there is a developmental quality to these three levels. (Five-year-olds are usually not ready to describe the relationships of different points of view.) Thus, this attribute reminds us to look at students and check if we are challenging them appropriately with the complexity of their tasks. It further challenges us to ask if they are ready to move toward the next level. And finally it challenges us to differentiate among students within a class and adjust their work appropriately.

Hunt's developmental model (1971) considers what we have called separately structuring, grouping/interpersonal complexity, and information complexity all at once. These are three facets of conceptual level, and they correlate with one another. That is, a student who is low in conceptual level (as measured by Hunt's paragraph completion test) will function best with a high degree of imposed structure, simple dynamics in groupings, and low information complexity. Conversely, a student high in conceptual level learns best with low

structure, more complex grouping interactions, and more complex information processing. The research supporting the effectiveness of this matching has been quite striking and quite consistent. It has proved applicable for adults as well as children and has been used successfully as a way to form classroom and instructional groupings (Gower and Resnick, 1979; Rich and Bush, 1978).

## Sensory Channels

### Definitions

This attribute of learning experiences is about the *perceptual modalities* and *motor expressions* students are called on to use as they engage new information or ideas and then make a product or express what they know. Sensory input channels may include one or more of the following: *visual, auditory,* or *tactile/kinesthetic.* Motor expressions that students exercise in the context of the learning experience may be *large motor muscles, small motor,* their *voice,* or nothing at all. Finally, the design of the learning experience may call for student output in the form of talk, writing, or performance of an observable skill.

### Significance and Matching

Matching students' optimum input and output channels is often cited as one way to individualize learning experiences for different students. Dunn and Dunn (1978) make a strong case for it. To the degree to which this is taking place, we would expect to see similar or identical objectives being worked on by students through input and output channels adjusted for their characteristics.

A count can be made of how many channels are used for input of information to students in learning experiences: visual, auditory, and tactile/kinesthetic. Regarding how students act in learning experiences (student output), the number of channels from among the following can be counted: talk, writing, or performance of some kind (such as drawing, building, manipulating, acting out motorically). Regarding motor use, one can record how many of the following muscle groups are used by students: large motor, small motor, voice, or passive (no motor).

One might use data about these three attributes of learning experiences to evaluate how active the learning was and how that level of physical activity fit goals for the learning program or for the needs of the students. But more likely the greatest significance of these data will be raising our awareness of the range we can create and the potential for matching that the range will offer.

Simply seeing a variety of perceptual channels operating differentially across students does not prove matching. To support a yes judgment on matching, there must be evidence that a particular mode is being used with a particular student or group of students and that there is not just random variety. Such evidence might be provided by a teacher remark or a systematic assignment system for directing certain students to a learning experience with a dominant perceptual mode different from other learning experiences being offered around the same objective to other students.

# Scale

## Definitions

Sometimes the scale of objects, print, or models used in learning experiences has been *enlarged* or *reduced.* The scale of materials used can be either of these two, or it can be *normal,* that is, as normally found. This attribute begins by a simple count of how many of these three possibilities are present.

## Significance

Like all the other attributes, scale is an attribute of a learning experience that affects the interaction of the learner with the environment, and that environment is under the control of the curriculum designer and the teacher. It can be controlled to effect. Examining this attribute of teaching brings it to consciousness and provokes questions about whether all the opportunities for scale manipulation in learning experiences have been taken. For example, by miniaturizing into models, we can bring concepts from the abstract to the iconic level to good effect for students who don't function well abstractly. Whole outdoor physical environments (a stream, a town, a valley) can be captured in paint on giant sheets of cardboard (3 feet by 4 feet) and unfolded around the periphery of a classroom to simulate the environment of the stream. By enlarging worksheets or other standard school tasks onto giant plastic-covered boards or using giant felt or plastic numbers, a teacher can provide variety to the conduct of otherwise standard learning experiences.

## Matching

When we see the scale of an object adjusted for use with a particular student or students, we can conclude "yes" on matching for scale. This can be particularly important for primary children for whom size of print and number of items on a page can be confusing.

# Summary

Table 18.1 summarizes the thirteen attributes of learning experiences discussed in this chapter. It can be used to profile a given learning experience

**Table 18.1.  Thirteen Attributes of Learning Experiences**

| | | | |
|---|---|---|---|
| 1. Source of information: | conventional | constructed | |
| 2. Resources used: | text | observation | |
| | teacher | audiovisual | |
| | peers | online services | |
| | parents | electronic devices | |
| | interviews | reference books | |
| | | imagination | |
| | | experience | |
| 3. Personal relevance: | contrived | simulated | real |
| 4. Competition: | competitive | individualized | cooperative |
| 5. Supervision: | supervised | facilitated | |
| | independent | matched | |
| 6. Expressing the self: | no | yes | matched |
| 7. Degree of abstraction: | concrete | representational | abstract |
| 8. Cognitive level: | recall | | |
| | comprehension | | |
| | analysis | | |
| | application | | |
| | synthesis | | |
| | evaluation | | |

| 9. Structuring: | none | teacher | student | negotiated |
|---|---|---|---|---|
| content | | | | |
| behavior | | | | |
| procedures | | | | |
| products | | | | |
| closure | | | | |

| | | | |
|---|---|---|---|
| 10. Grouping and | low | moderate | |
| interpersonal complexity: | high | matching | |
| 11. Information | low | moderate | |
| complexity: | high | matching | |
| 12. Sensory channels: | | | |
| Student input | visual | tactile/kinesthetic | |
| | auditory | matched | |
| Student motor use | large motor | small motor | |
| | voice | passive | |
| Student output | talk | writing | |
| | performance | matched | |
| 13. Scale | normal | miniaturized | |
| | enlarged | matched | |

**Research for Better Teaching, Inc.** • One Acton Place, Acton, MA 01720 • (978)263-9449 • www.RBTeach.com

from the student's point of view. It can also be used to profile a day or a unit of instruction to see how much variety and opportunity for matching your students are experiencing.

To check your knowledge about Learning Experiences see the quiz on our Web site at **www. RBTeach.com/rbteach/quiz/LExperiences.html.**

*Source Materials on Learning Experiences*

Anter, J., and Jenkins, J. "Differential Diagnosis—Prescription Teaching: A Critical Appraisal." *Review of Educational Research,* 1979, *49,* 517–555.

Aronson, E. *The Jigsaw Classroom.* Thousand Oaks, Calif.: Sage, 1978.

Bates, J. "Extrinsic Reward and Intrinsic Motivation: A Review with Implications for the Classroom." *Review of Educational Research,* 1979 *49,* 557–576.

Berlak, A., Berlak, H., Bagenstos, N., and Mikel, E. "Teaching and Learning in English Primary Schools." *School Review,* Feb. 1975, pp. 215–243.

Bloom, B. *Taxonomy of Educational Objectives, Handbook I.* New York: David McKay, 1956.

Bruner, J. *Toward a Theory of Instruction.* Cambridge, Mass.: Harvard University Press, 1966.

Bussis, A. M., Chittenden, E. A., and Amarel, M. *Beyond Surface Curriculum: An Interview Study of Teachers' Understandings.* Boulder, Colo.: Westview Press, 1976.

Colarusso, C., and Green, P. *Diagnostic Educational Grouping: Strategies for Teaching.* Bucks County (Pennsylvania) Public Schools, Doylestown, Mar. 1972.

Dale, E. "Cone of Learning." Unpublished paper, University of Ohio.

Davis, O. L. (ed.). *Perspectives on Curriculum Development.* Washington, D.C.: Association for Supervision and Curriculum Development, 1976.

Deutsch, M. "An Experimental Study of the Effects of Cooperation and Competition upon Group Process." *Human Relations,* 1949, *2,* 199–231.

Dunn, R., and Dunn, K. *Teaching Students Through Their Individualized Learning Styles: A Practical Approach.* Reston, Va.: Reston Publishing Co., 1978.

Gehlbach, R. D. "Individual Differences: Implications for Instructional Theory, Research and Innovation." *Educational Researcher,* 1979, *8,* 8–14.

Gower, R. R., and Resnick, H. *Theory and Research: Evaluation Results.* Washington, D.C.: U.S. Office of Education, Aug. 1979.

Gregorc, A. F., and Ward, H. B. "A New Definition for Individual." *MASSP Bulletin,* Feb. 1977, pp. 20–26.

Hunt, D. E. *Matching Models in Education.* Ontario, Canada: Ontario Institute for Studies in Education, 1971.

Hunt, D. E., and Sullivan, E. V. *Between Psychology and Education.* Hinsdale, Ill.: Dryden Press, 1974.

Johnson, D. W., and Johnson, R. T. *Learning Together and Alone.* (2nd ed.). Upper Saddle River, N.J.: Prentice Hall, 1987. Reprinted by permission.

Johnson, D. W., Johnson, R. T., and Holubec, E. J. *Advanced Cooperative Learning.* Edina, Minn.: Interaction Book Company, 1988.

Johnson, D. W., Skon, L., and Johnson, R. "Effects of Cooperative, Competitive, and Individualistic Conditions on Children's Problem-Solving Performance." *American Educational Research Journal,* 1980, *17,* 83–94.

Joyce, B. R. *A Guide to the Teacher-Innovator: A Program to Prepare Teachers.* Washington, D.C.: American Association of Colleges for Teacher Education, 1969.

Joyce, B. R. *Selecting Learning Experiences.* Washington, D.C.: Association for Supervision and Curriculum Development, 1978.

Rich, H. L., and Bush, A. J. "The Effect of Congruent Teacher-Student Characteristics on Instructional Outcomes." *American Educational Research Journal,* 1978, *15,* 451–458.

Rosenholtz, S. J., and Wilson, B. "The Effect of Classroom Structure on Shared Perceptions of Ability." *American Educational Research Journal,* 1980, *17,* 75–82.

Sharam, S. "Cooperation Learning in Small Groups." *Review of Educational Research,* 1980, *50,* 241–272.

Slavin, R. E. "Cooperative Learning." *Review of Educational Research,* 1980, *50,* 315–342.

Toepfer, C. F., Jr. *Brain Growth Periodization Research.* Washington, D.C.: Association for Supervision and Curriculum Development, 1981.

Tyler, R. *Basic Principles of Curriculum and Instruction.* Chicago: University of Chicago Press, 1949.

Winne, P. H. "Experiments in Relating Teachers' Use of Higher Cognitive Questions to Students' Achievement." *Review of Educational Research,* 1979a, *49*(1), 13–49.

Winne, P. H. "Aptitude-Treatment Interactions in an Experiment on Teacher Effectiveness." *American Educational Research Journal,* 1979b, *1,* 389–410.

# Assessment

Grant Wiggins once said that assessment was the Trojan horse of school reform. What he meant, we believe, is that if we did assessment properly and lined up all the soldiers it would take to do it well, we would open the gates to the rest of the army of improvement efforts waiting outside the city. Another way of looking at it is that certain changes have unusually large ripple effects into other practices, and good assessment is one of them. The view of what good classroom assessment is has undergone radical changes since the late twentieth century. We have shifted from the notion of using tests primarily as mechanisms to sort and grade students to using assessment in the following ways:

- to inform instruction
- to gather data about what students know prior to beginning instruction (preassessment)
- to continually gather data about how well students are understanding during instruction (formative assessment)
- to adjust instruction and reteach when necessary in an effort to ensure that all students can be successful in the end (summative assessment)

We have shifted from designing and administering tests after completing instruction to designing assessment tasks before we develop the instructional plan. We have shifted from having students "guess what will be on the test" to making criteria for success and assessment of learning public, precise, and understood by students prior to instruction. While in the past tests had been something done to students, we now see the need to make students partners in the assessment process by developing criteria with students, student self-assessment, student error analysis, student use of feedback, and student goal setting. We have shifted from an "every teacher for himself" orientation to conviction about the importance of common interim schoolwide assessments developed and used by all teachers who teach the same content. The primary purpose of classroom assessment is to increase student achievement rather than to simply measure it for reporting purposes.

Assessment that is designed to increase student achievement is crafted to accomplish three goals:

- Motivate students to want to do better
- Give students useful information they can use to do better
- Inform teachers' reteaching plans so students *can* do better

There are other reasons for doing assessment besides helping students learn more. And some of them are valid. Table 19.1 summarizes twelve purposes of assessment. In this chapter we focus on numbers 3 through 7: assessment as a vehicle for increasing student achievement. This means focusing on classroom assessment as done by teachers on a daily and weekly basis. Thus we begin the chapter with the question: What is it that a teacher needs to know about classroom assessment?

The foundation for productive classroom assessment is teachers of the same content agreeing on the most important learning standards for the course or semester (Reeves, 2004). This is the starting point of a chain of events that leads to good assessment. Without it, students don't receive cohesive schooling because what they learn will depend on their teachers' idiosyncratic choices. The logical next step among these same colleagues is to develop common interim assessments that can be used to measure student progress and make instructional adjustments.

Many of our colleagues who have had experience with this in the field, among them Rick DuFour at Adlai Stevenson High School in Illinois and Paul Bambrick-Santoyo and Jamey Verrilli at North Star Academy in Newark, New Jersey, report that common assessments across teachers who teach the same content, given quarterly and school-wide, are a powerful lever for elevating student achievement if teachers examine the students' responses closely and do error analysis to plan reteaching. How these meetings can be structured to maximum effect has been described thoroughly by Marshall (2006).

With long-term (course, semester, or yearly) learning goals established and quarterly assessments designed, we have laid the foundation to support ongoing and productive daily and weekly classroom assessment.

## Twelve Components of Good Classroom Assessment

Prior to planning assessment, of course, the teacher articulates lesson and unit objectives that are worth learning, shares with students what the objectives are and why they are worth learning, and clarifies them daily for students in a form comparable with statements such as "You (students) will demonstrate that you are able to . . . by . . ." This gives students something to aim at and the teachers a footing for evaluating the learning experiences. These actions set the stage for assessment planning and implementation.

**Table 19.1. Purposes of Assessment**

| | |
|---|---|
| 1. **To make summative statements:** | about how well students have done overall in meeting course or unit objectives |
| 2. **To certify students:** | as competent in a field of knowledge<br>as competent in a field of practice<br>as eligible for promotion |
| 3. **To signal clearly:** | what knowledge is important<br>what the criteria and standards are for quality work |
| 4. **To make instructional decisions:** | about where to start students with instruction<br>about which skills are mastered<br>about which skills or subskills to reteach to which students |
| 5. **To give feedback to students:** | about students' strengths, weaknesses, and interests |
| 6. **To give feedback to teachers:** | about the effectiveness of instruction<br>about the effectiveness of curriculum |
| 7. **To report progress to parents and communities:** | about any or all of the above |
| 8. **To elevate the curriculum so as to provide meaningful, higher-level thinking tasks for all students:** | |
| 9. **To sort, rank, or compare students:** | for honors and awards<br>for admissions into programs with limited enrollment |
| 10. **To norm students or groups of students:** | for comparative achievement in relation to national groups<br>for comparative achievement in relation to other populations |
| 11. **For placement:** | in courses, grades, or levels |
| 12. **To predict:** | success in a course<br>success in school<br>success in a job performance |

**Research for Better Teaching, Inc.** • One Acton Place, Acton, MA 01720 • (978)263-9449 • www.RBTeach.com

To accomplish the three goals mentioned previously (to motivate students to want to do better, to provide them useful information and support so they can, and to inform teachers' reteaching plans), classroom assessment must be composed of multiple components carried out in a sequence by students and teachers. Twelve components of good classroom assessment are enumerated in Exhibit 19.1.

To begin with, all successful assessment requires a clear understanding by both teachers and students of the learning expectations behind it, the criteria for success, and the expected level or standard of performance. Components 1 and 2 address these concerns. Classroom assessment itself starts at step 3, and each of the remaining steps brings students more closely into the game.

1. Determining the Assessment Task
The teacher generates or selects the type of product or performance students will be expected to produce (a lab report, a summarizing paragraph, a graphic organizer, a persuasive speech, a physical model, a volleyball serve) and describes or demonstrates the standards of performance that should be embedded in the product or performance.

**Exhibit 19.1. Twelve Components of Classroom Assessment**

1. Determining the assessment task
2. Communicating standards of performance
3. Assessing prior knowledge
4. Frequent data collection and record keeping by the teacher
5. Frequent high-quality feedback to students
6. Student self-assessment
7. Student record keeping about progress
8. Frequent error analysis by the teacher
9. Error analysis by the students
10. Planning and implementing reteaching
11. Goal setting and action planning by students
12. Reporting systems on student progress including three-way conferences

**Research for Better Teaching, Inc.** • One Acton Place, Acton, MA 01720 • (978) 263-9449 • www.RBTeach.com

2. Communicating Standards of Performance
The standards of performance and criteria for success in an assessment task are shared explicitly with students and described precisely prior to their work on the assessment task. Ideally there should be model products (exemplars) that exemplify the standards and criteria for success available for student examination.

3. Assessing Prior Knowledge
With this preparation, the next stage is some type of preassessment: finding out where students are in relation to the target objectives prior to beginning instruction. Students build new understandings—about anything from mathematics to video games—by making sense of new experiences in light of what they already know (Shepard, 2005). Hence we need to think of preassessment as a routine practice; it affords us the opportunity to assess readiness levels and surface misconceptions, and to determine what we need to address in order to clarify misconceptions, to scaffold instruction for those who don't have some of the prerequisite knowledge and skills, and differentiate learning experiences where necessary.

4. Frequent Data Collection and Record Keeping by the Teacher
Assessment is an ongoing process used to inform instruction. Hence there must be regular informal assessment events (observations of performance, short written or oral tasks) that yield data about how students are doing in relation to the target performance.

5. Frequent High-Quality Feedback to Students
Assessment must be frequent (Yeh, 2006), with students receiving daily feedback when possible on their work in relation to standards of performance. The feedback should be descriptive, nonjudgmental, and helpful for improving their performance. The frequency and immediacy of feedback allows students to refocus and redirect their efforts efficiently, just as instantaneous feedback from a computer game allows instant self-correction and improvement of performance. The descriptive and

nonjudgmental nature of the feedback provides information students can use to improve their work and prevents negative messages to students about their ability. Engineering such feedback is no small feat but is hugely important to successful instruction. There is a detailed discussion of feedback later in this chapter.

6. Student Self-Assessment

Students must be taught how to regularly use criteria for self-assessment and peer feedback. Applying the criteria forces the students to get to know what the criteria mean and doing self-assessment starts generating student ownership of their progress.

7. Student Record Keeping About Progress

Students regularly record or chart their learning progress. This makes students accountable, allows them to see progress visually, and becomes motivational in a class culture where everybody is doing the same.

8. Frequent Error Analysis by the Teacher

Error analysis, or figuring out what confusions, misconceptions, and gaps might lie behind student errors, is the prerequisite to productive reteaching. Error analysis is a potent activity for teams but must also be a part of every teacher's nightly planning.

9. Error Analysis by the Students

When tests, quizzes, and products are returned to students they are required to use the results and the feedback to do error analysis. This makes them think about what they know and don't know, and enables them to do the goal setting that is so important for student ownership and motivation.

10. Planning and Implementing Reteaching

The teacher uses the data on student performance to plan reteaching loops for students who didn't get it the first time. Reteaching must be done with verbal messages and with affect that make it a sign of good scholarship when students nominate themselves for the reteaching rather than a confirmation that they are "remedial" (read as inferior) students. We describe reteaching loops in Chapter Twelve, "Expectations."

11. Goal Setting and Action Planning by Students

Students use feedback and error analysis to set SMART goals for learning and specify an action plan. SMART goals are specific, measurable, attainable, realistic, and time-based, all characteristics that increase the chances that students will meet the goals. We discuss goal setting in Chapter Ten, "Principles of Learning."

12. Reporting Systems on Student Progress Including Three-Way Conferences

Teachers have a variety of vehicles for communicating to students and parents on student learning progress. Students report on their goals—and progress toward achieving those goals—at three-way conferences with teachers and parents. When parents are included in the goal-setting and reporting-out process, the stakes and the rewards get even higher.

So what does a teacher need to make all of these components happen?

- A commitment to use assessment to inform teaching on a daily basis. This means teachers need to become expert at data analysis and, most particularly, item-level error analysis so as to design precise and timely reteaching for students who didn't "get it" the first time around. We will expand on this shortly.

- A commitment to use assessment to inform students on what they need to do to improve their own learning [feedback systems that generate daily, useful information]
- A commitment to create mechanisms for student self-evaluation and goal setting so assessment practices can promote positive emotional engagement ("so students can experience winning streaks" [Stiggins, 2005]).

Figure 19.1 represents the ideal role of assessment in a twenty-four-hour cycle of teaching and learning in any class. The cycle starts on the left with "Assessment and Teaching." The intent is to show that these two activities are not separate: a thorough teacher is always assessing (and also recording) how students are doing with new learning, and doing so on the fly, while teaching.

In summary, what teachers need to know most is how to use assessment to inform teaching

**Figure 19.1. The Twenty-Four-Hour Cycle of Teaching and Learning**

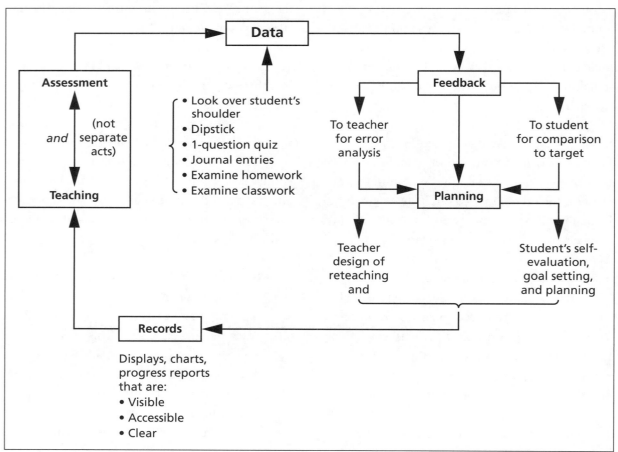

**Research for Better Teaching, Inc.** • One Acton Place, Acton, MA 01720 • (978)263-9449 • www.RBTeach.com

and learning on a daily basis and to use assessment as a motivation for students.

## Component 1: Determining the Assessment Task

Authenticity is a key idea in the assessment movement because authentic tasks amalgamate complex performances in the same way real-life problems do. Marzano, Pickering, and McTighe (1993) say that authentic assessment "conveys the idea that assessments should engage students in applying knowledge and skills in the same way they are used in the 'real world' outside of school." Wiggins (1993) adds "Assessment is authentic when we directly examine student performances on worthy intellectual tasks . . . engaging and worthy problems or questions of importance, in which students must use knowledge to fashion performances effectively and creatively. The tasks are either replicas of or analogous to the kinds of problems faced by adult citizens and consumers or professionals in the field" (p. 229). Or as Ann Johnson says, the task "replicates or parallels the experiences facing a consumer, citizen, worker, or professional in the field" (workshop handout, 1992).

Thus, a worthwhile assessment task has a student applying skills and knowledge in realistic, complex situations, integrated as closely as possible with something the student would have to do in the world outside school. What will be assessed will not be just subskills like the ability to decode words with short *a*, the ability to balance chemical equations given valences and quantities, or knowledge of facts or even comprehension of "the causes of the Civil War," at least as an isolated measurement. Rather, what will be assessed will be the ability to perform complex tasks that require higher-order thinking skills and the integration of knowledge: tasks that

are authentic because they are direct models of or simulations of tasks that people have to perform in the real world. In performing these complex tasks, of course, each of us must draw on our knowledge of subskills and facts, but they are put to use in service of a larger task that is realistic.

Jamentz (1993) offers the following criteria as a checklist for analyzing assessment tasks created for children:

- Does the task spark students' interest and motivation?
- Does the task require students to construct meaning?
- Does the task encourage demonstration of important habits of mind?
- Does the task encourage multiple modes of expression?
- Is the task free from arbitrary constraints?
- Does the task measure progress over time?
- Does the task require collaboration with others?
- Is the task a representative challenge, emphasizing depth rather than breadth of response?
- Does the task explore and identify hidden strengths?
- Does the task genuinely assess learning and effort rather than native talent?
- Do the standards for the task cover a wide range of knowledge, skills, and habits of mind considered important to the subject area or, if interdisciplinary, those that transcend a single discipline?
- Are the standards for good performance clear to students before they engage in the task?
- Are the standards for the task appropriately weighted?

- Are the standards for the task in harmony with shared school, district, state, or national goals?
- Does the task match the scoring framework?
- Is the task multidimensional, allowing for a single performance to be strong in some areas and weak in others?
- Is the assessment structured to provide prompt and useful feedback to the teacher and student?
- Does the task provide built-in opportunities for students to practice, rehearse, and retake it? [p. 29]

We think the first three characteristics on the list are particularly important. The anchor of the process for developing authentic assessments is getting clear on what we really want students to know or be able to do. Notice that the analytical criteria set out in "Exemplars" (see Exhibit 19.6) in the next section pertain to high-level thinking, problem solving, and communication skills. This does not mean that lower-level skills like mastering calculation skills, times tables, and the like are disregarded, but the value (and thus the assessment) is clearly keyed to reasoning strategies the writers believe are important to using math in life. These choices of higher-level, problem-solving skills thus guide the kinds of tasks that will be created.

Authentic assessment tasks are a far more valid measure of educational effectiveness than traditional paper and pencil assessment if we view education as the preparation of young minds for successful living. And they are more motivating to students.

Teachers who design authentic assessments find it a creative process that benefits from a high level of interaction with peers and often with students, too. Once they have discussed what they want students to know or be able to do, teachers then cast around for or create tasks that conform to as many of the criteria as possible.

Having piloted the assessment tasks, a group of teachers developing rubrics typically sit down with a large collection of student products. They quickly sort the student work into four piles representing poor, fair, good, and excellent levels of performance by examining the products with little or no discussion or analysis and grouping ones that seem at about the same level of performance. Placing a sample in a category is done by the sense of how the product strikes the teacher.

Then comes the most important part of the process, which carries the most inherent staff development meat for teachers. Going over student work samples in detail, the teachers describe in writing the characteristics of each category and thus produce the first draft of their rubric.

As the standards-based movement matures and we work through the next phase of what No Child Left Behind means for education, it will be important to remember that we want to leave no child behind in developing higher level thinking and problem-solving abilities as well. Thus generating authentic assessments of complex student performances will remain an important capacity for teachers to master.

## Component 2: Communicating the Standards of Performance

To give students a concrete image of what the words in the objective mean and what meeting standards looks like, students need to see, hear, and understand the standards (or criteria) by which their work will be assessed. Performance standards and criteria for success should be public, precise, prior, printed, and presented in models of exemplary work.

"Public" means there are no secrets: students (and parents) know exactly what will be the basis for evaluating the work. "Precise" means naming the qualities or characteristics that need to be present in their work—and explaining or describing them in sufficient detail such that students understand what each means and can determine whether or not and where each characteristic is present in a given piece of work. "Prior" means sharing this information with students when the assessment task is described at the beginning of the class, course, or unit of study and before they begin to work toward achievement of an objective. This enables students to focus on what is important during the learning experiences and to participate in assessing whether they are building the foundations for success in the end. "Printed" means written down for students to refer to as they participate in learning experiences and invest effort in an assessment task.

What is written might be a simple *bulleted list* of what must be addressed in a lab report or characteristics of an effective oral presentation. For more complex assessment tasks, tasks that assess multiple objectives, or tasks that will be practiced several to many times over, criteria might be communicated in a performance task list or a rubric. A *performance task list* (Exhibit 19.2) spells out the component parts of the task and assigns either a "yes" or "not yet" rating scale or a certain number of overall points that each component is worth, indicating the relative importance of each component to the final piece of work. A *rubric* (Table 19.2) specifies in matrix form the qualities or components on which a piece of work will be assessed and the specific indicators of proficiency (novice, practitioner, expert or below standards, meets standards, exceeds standards) that might be demonstrated in each component of the work. As is true of most everything else in teaching, these options

represent a repertoire of ways for representing criteria, from simple to more complex, and the option we choose for individual tasks is a matter of matching the complexity of the format to the nature and complexity of the task. A more detailed discussion of how to design rubrics appears later in this chapter.

"Presented in models of work" means that students see concrete models (pieces of work) that exemplify the standard of performance and criteria for success they are expected to achieve. These models (commonly referred to as *exemplars*) should be accompanied by a concrete explanation of how and why the exemplar meets the standards: "You should be able to do one that has these qualities!" The qualities are named specifically and pointed out in the exemplar. Or, once standards and criteria have been identified, students examine sample pieces of work and participate in identifying where and if those qualities appear. If exemplars are unavailable, criteria must either be presented and explained to students with a check for understanding or the students must help to generate criteria for proficient work with the particular assignment.

This same thinking applies to communicating images of good work for units of study, major projects, and year-long goals. At the macrolevel, students and parents might be given sample products that represent benchmarks of progress for a whole year in, say, reading and writing. Three samples that the Mather Elementary School in Boston uses to communicate standards for good work by the end of particular grade levels are shown in Exhibit 19.3.

When standards and criteria are public, precise, prior, printed, and presented in models of good work, we are offering students a comprehensive package to support them in focusing their effort effectively.

**Exhibit 19.2. Formats for Communicating Criteria for Success: Bulleted List and Performance Task List**

**BULLETED LIST: Summarizing a Historical Conflict**

Your summary should include *three paragraphs,* each of which:

- *Begins with a claim:* names one event that was a contributing cause to the conflict and names the parties involved and time frame of the event
- *Is supported by evidence:* 2-3 sentences explaining how/why that event was a contributing factor
- *Concludes with an impact statement* that is clearly connected to the conflict: As a result . . .

**PERFORMANCE TASK LIST: Delivering a Speech**

*Speaker* _____ *Date* _____

*Topic* _____ *Run time* _____

| *PREPARATION / STRUCTURE* | *Possible Points* | *Self* | *Teacher* |
|---|---|---|---|
| • engaging, inspirational topic | _____ | _____ | _____ |
| • gained attention and interest | _____ | _____ | _____ |
| • clear introduction of central idea | _____ | _____ | _____ |
| • indication of subject's value | _____ | _____ | _____ |
| • logical outline/order | _____ | _____ | _____ |
| • vivid, distinct main points | _____ | _____ | _____ |
| • sufficient support material | _____ | _____ | _____ |
| • well-structured conclusion | _____ | _____ | _____ |
| *DELIVERY AND STYLE* | | | |
| • voice quality: clarity and audibility | _____ | _____ | _____ |
| • rate of speech | _____ | _____ | _____ |
| • use of eye contact | _____ | _____ | _____ |
| • use of gestures | _____ | _____ | _____ |
| • relaxation, confidence | _____ | _____ | _____ |
| • sincerity, investment | _____ | _____ | _____ |
| • use of visual aids | _____ | _____ | _____ |
| *OVERALL* | | | |
| • held audience interest | _____ | _____ | _____ |

*Source:* Adapted and reprinted with permission from Gerry Speca, April 2007.

**Table 19.2. General Science Lab Rubric**

| | 4 | 3 | 2 | 1 |
|---|---|---|---|---|
| **FORMAT** | | | | |
| Title page | Contains title, name, date, course, period, teacher. | Has title and name. Missing one other. | Has title and name. Missing two others. | Missing title, name, or more than two others. |
| Sequence | Logically sequenced: Question, hypothesis, test, material, procedures, data, analysis/conclusion. All are present. | Only one category missing or out of sequence. | Two categories missing or out of sequence. | More than two categories missing or out of sequence. |
| **REPRODUCIBILITY** | | | | |
| Hypothesis | Clear explanation of purpose; provides context. | Gives correct purpose with some framework. | Declares purpose that is correct. | Purpose is incorrect. |
| Design | Clear step-by-step description of experimental procedures; labeled diagrams/drawings of devices used in experiment. | Step-by-step description missing only one key detail; diagrams/drawings included not labeled. | Step-by-step description missing not more than two key details; devices used are mentioned but not shown. | Description lacks more than two key details; not mention of devices used to carry out experiment. |
| **ACCURACY** | | | | |
| Units | Units are used correctly and consistently throughout the report. | Units generally used correctly in most of report. | Units used only in parts of report. | Units rarely used or generally incorrect. |
| Data Manipulation | Calculations are clearly laid out. Math correct. Figures display data correctly; all variables labeled. | Few calculation errors. Figures correct; variables unlabeled. | Calculations contain errors. Figures correct; no labels or legend. | Math not shown. Figures display data incorrectly. |
| **CONCLUSION** | | | | |
| Framework | Restates hypothesis, supports or refutes it and explains role of test in making decision. | Restates hypothesis and supports or refutes it. | Supports or refutes hypothesis without restating it. | Does not address hypothesis. |
| Evidence | Uses data powerfully as evidence. | Uses data to support statements. | Refers to data in the body of the report as support. | Does not use data to support arguments. |
| Logic | Conclusion logically follows from data. | Conclusion is logical but not thoroughly defended. | Conclusion is logical but poorly defended. | Conclusion is incorrect. |
| Context | Discusses scientific implications of experiment. Makes proposals for further investigations. | Cites a use for the work. Makes proposals for further investigations. | Describes work as useful but supplies no supporting evidence. | Provides no statement about relevance. |

*Source:* Access Excellence at The National Health Museum, 2007.

**Exhibit 19.3. Sample Exemplars for Communicating Standards**

*Writing* - The material below is what an average kindergartener should be able to write by the end of the year.

*Reading and listening* - The passage below, from *In a Dark Dark Wood* by June Meiser and Joy Cowley, is the level that a student at the completion of kindergarten should be able to listen to with good comprehension. Other books that kindergarteners should be able to understand include: *Caps for Sale, Farmer in the Dell, Blueberries for Sal, If You Made a Million, Stone Soup, The Hungry Crocodile,* and *Why Mosquitoes Buzz in People's Ears.*

In a dark dark wood, there was a dark dark path. And up that dark dark path, there was a dark dark house. And in that dark dark house, there was a dark dark stair. And up that dark dark stair, there was a dark dark room. And in that dark dark room, there was a dark dark cupboard. And in that dark dark cupboard, there was a dark dark box. And in that dark dark box there was a ghost!

A.

*Writing* - The piece below is the level expected of an average student at the completion of the second grade.

My Pet by Cathal Doherty
I have pet parrot. His name is Tweety. I like to chase him around. It is grey and white. It talks funny and it tickles you. We play together. It is fun to have a pet.

*Reading* - The passage below, taken from *City Mouse and Country Mouse* by Aesop is the level that a student at the completion of second grade should be able to read with accuracy, fluency, and comprehension. Other books that second graders should be able to read include: *Amelia Bedelia, Angel Child, Dragon Child, Blueberries for Sal, If You Made a Million, Stone Soup, The Hungry Crocodile,* and *Why Mosquitoes Buzz in People's Ears.*

The rugs were beautiful bright colors. In each room were beautiful chairs and tables and lights. Best of all was the kitchen. Country Mouse ran up and down everywhere. Everything in the kitchen was shining and bright. There, right in front of his eyes, was a mountain of food.

B.

*(Continued)*

**Exhibit 19.3.  Sample Exemplars for Communicating Standards** *(Continued)*

**Writing** · The piece below is the level expected of an average student at the completion of the fifth grade:

The Wolverine

I wake up screaming. Pain in my head so intense, I can't put a name to it, can't fight it, can't run away from it. I don't even know where I am. I'm in some kind of cave? Images flash through my brain. Memories, a jungle, a girl then a fight that I thought I won. I was wrong. Still fighting with my brain the pain unbearable like a million white hot needles digging into my skull. I'm beyond reason, beyond hope when that happens I turn animal.

The animal in me fights back pushing back at the needles. The strain takes its toll. I feel the darkness closing in. I thought I was dead only I'm not. I hear voices shouting then the lights come on! What I see in the mirror can't be real, but my senses tell me it is. I feel hard-packed dirt at my feet and sweat sliding down my back. I hear the buzzing of insects and crackling of fire. I see a beast out of hell, eyes blazing with arms like tree trunks. I still think I'm dreaming then reality sinks in. Boom! Aagh! I'm a wolverine.

**Reading** - The passage below, taken from *Island of the Blue Dolphins* by Scott O'Dell, is the level that a student at the completion of fifth grade should be able to read with accuracy, fluency, and comprehension. Other books that fifth graders should be able to read include: *Bridge to Terabithia, Roll of Thunder, Hear My Cry, Sarah, Plain and Tall, Stone Fox, Vampire Bat Girls' Club, Witch of Banneker School, Shiloh,* and *The Land I Lost.*

A short distance beyond the dune, near the cliff, I saw the pack of wild dogs. There were many of them and they were moving around in a circle.

In the middle of the circle was Ramo. He was lying on his back, and had a deep wound in his throat. He lay very still.

When I picked him up I knew that he was dead. There were other wounds on his body from the teeth of the wild dogs. He had been dead a long time and from his footsteps on the earth I could see that he had never reached the cliff.

Two dogs lay on the ground not far from him, and in the side of one of them was his broken spear.

I carried Ramo back to the village, reaching it when the sun was far down. The dogs followed me all the way, but when I had laid his down in the hut, and came out with a club in my hand, they trotted off to a low hill. A big gray dog with long curling hair and yellow eyes was their leader an he went last.

It was growing dark, but I followed them up the hill. Slowly they retreated in front of me, not making a sound. I followed them across two hills an a small valley to a third hill whose face was a ledge of rock. At one end of the ledge was a cave. One by one the dogs went into it.

C.

*Source:* Reprinted with permission. Excerpted from *Curriculum Exemplars for Writing and Reading.* Mather Elementary School, Boston, Massachusetts, 1994.

## The Relation of Rubrics to Exemplars and Criteria

*Rubrics* or *scoring rubrics* is the name given to the most detailed and comprehensive tool used to communicate criteria for success. Note that it is the criteria that are the central feature. Rubrics are communication devices for criteria. They break out different levels of quality to which the criteria have been met by student performances. They replace grades with specific information about a student performance. Usually in matrix form, a rubric identifies categories that define and describe the important components of the work to be produced. In a well-designed rubric, each component is accompanied by a progression of quality indicators (usually four) that contain precise descriptions of what criteria need to be met to demonstrate incremental levels of proficiency or competence (novice to expert) within that component. Exhibit 19.4 shows a rubric for scoring an essay.

The qualities to be assessed—that is, the components of a good essay—are organization, sentence structure, usage, mechanics, and format. Each is written down the left-hand side of the matrix. Each quality (component) has three paragraphs spelling out three different levels of performance. In between are two blank spots for scoring a student's work if it seems to fall between

**Exhibit 19.4. Rubric for Scoring an Essay**

| | 1 | 2 | 3 | 4 | 5 | |
|---|---|---|---|---|---|---|
| Organization | Little or nothing is written. The essay is disorganized, incoherent, and poorly developed. The essay does not stay on the topic. | | The essay is not complete. It lacks an introduction, well-developed body, or conclusion. The coherence and sequence are attempted, but not adequate. | | The essay is well-organized. It contains an introductory, supporting, and concluding paragraph. The essay is coherent, ordered logically, and fully developed. | X6 |
| Sent. Str. | The student writes frequent run-ons or fragments. | | The student makes occasional errors in sentence structure. Little variety in sentence length or structure exists. | | The sentences are complete and varied in length and structure. | X5 |
| Usage | The student makes frequent errors in word choice and agreement. | | The student makes occasional errors in word choice or agreement. | | The usage is correct. Word choice is appropriate. | X4 |
| Mechanics | The student makes frequent errors in spelling, punctuation, and capitalization. | | The student makes an occasional error in mechanics. | | The spelling, capitalization, and punctuation are correct. | X4 |
| Format | The format is sloppy. There are no margins or indentations. Handwriting is inconsistent. | | The handwriting, margins, and indentation have occasional inconsistencies—no title or inappropriate title. | | The format is correct. The title is appropriate. The handwriting, margins, and indentations are consistent. | X1 |

*Note:* The numbers in the right column indicate the weighting scheme.

*Source:* Reprinted with permission. Archbald, D., and Newmann, F. M. *Beyond Standardized Tests: Assessing Authentic Academic Achievement in Secondary School.* Reston, Va.: National Association of Secondary School Principals, 1988, p. 11. Copyright © 1988, National Association of Secondary School Principals. For more information on NASSP products and services to promote excellence in middle level and high school leadership, visit www.principals.org.

two descriptions. This arrangement yields a five-point scale for each quality. Notice also that some components are weighted more than others: organization is six times as important as format.

After examining this matrix students and parents know what the teacher is looking for and what the standards for good work are. And they will know even better if a sample of a well-done essay is provided with notes pointing out how and where each quality is manifested. There are many print and Web site resources available today for collecting sample rubrics to assess a wide range of products, performances, content, and skill areas. As is true of all available resources we have to be judicious and informed consumers, selecting the best or fine-tuning those that don't quite measure up. In other words, we need to look for exemplars of good rubrics. So what would we look for in selecting a rubric or what would we strive for in designing our own? Here are some guidelines we have found to be useful.

The best instructional rubrics:

- Address all relevant content and performance objectives
- Address different skills as separate criteria and assess them independently of one another
- Include gradations of quality (novice to expert) within each criterion
- Describe each gradation in specific detail, thus making obvious what differentiates one level from another
- Fit on one piece of paper
- Are easy to understand and use by both teacher and student
- Are accompanied by examples of student work that exemplify the levels described in the rubric
- Are always a work in progress

Rubrics can be used as formative or summative assessment tools. When used as formative tools rubrics enable students to self-assess and receive feedback on which level of proficiency is demonstrated in their work within each criterion in the moment; the feedback and the quality indicators can be used by students to determine where to invest their effort in improving the work and achieving higher levels of quality or proficiency. A rubric used in this way becomes a feedback mechanism that provides guidance about how to incrementally improve performance. Used as summative tools, rubrics clearly define the target for students and provide them with specific feedback on why they achieved a particular score or grade on a piece of work. If they should do that type of work again the feedback on the rubric can serve as a resource for goal-setting on the next piece of work.

Exhibit 19.5 is an example (developed by Penny Knox at Oak Creek Elementary School in Irvine, California) of a cross-curricular sixth-grade exhibition and the rubric that accompanies the project. In this case the teacher and students use the rubric for both formative and summative assessment purposes. The project gets scored four times on each criterion. Three times are labeled "Practice Date" (formative assessment) and the final (summative) assessment is simply called "Exhibition." This reflects a design in which students produce the final product (write the letter) three times and get detailed feedback each time on the quality of their work. The teacher can use the data to determine where reteaching needs to occur for some or all of the students. And the students can use the feedback to focus their effort on improving specific skills or in developing more background knowledge prior to the final exhibition. In this school, the children take the product home for one of the practice trials and work with their parents to apply the scoring rubric to the child's product. This is a particularly effective way to inform and involve parents in the education of their children.

## Exemplars

The complement to a good rubric is a set of samples of actual student work that exemplify the different cells of the rubric, accompanied by explanations of why each sample exemplifies the level of quality claimed for it. Exhibit 19.6 is a rubric found on Exemplars.com, a Web site that publishes collections of benchmark mathematical tasks, designed by teachers K–8, with actual student work produced for each task. (A benchmark task is one that calls for students to display a variety of competencies thought to be important. Such tasks aren't given every day but are saved for assessing student progress at certain key junctures.) The rubric is used to score student products as Novice, Apprentice, Practitioner, and Expert. An accompanying narrative explains how and why the samples exemplify one of the four levels of the rubric.

Behind all the mathematical tasks in the *Exemplars* collection are analytical criteria for good performance: problem solving, reasoning and proof, communication, connections and representation. These criteria serve as guidelines for creating good tasks as well as for scoring student work on the tasks.

The Appendix to this chapter shows a typical package that comes with an Exemplars task, including four samples of student work with explanations of their ratings. The samples show the kind of thoughtful analysis it takes to apply a rubric properly. Though the samples are for mathematics content, similar collections can be assembled for any discipline and any skill or concept within the discipline. Making those collections of exemplars is, in fact, exactly what we are advocating that teams of teachers do.

## Establishing Scoring Reliability

The last step in constructing good rubrics is establishing reliability across teachers in scoring student work samples. Reliability means that the rubrics are sufficiently clear and the teachers are sufficiently in agreement about the meaning of the levels of performance that different teachers would score a given work sample in the same way. This high level of reliability is established when teachers practice scoring students' work samples together, compare results, reconcile differences through discussion, and continue to practice until they are "reliable" in their scoring or until they have fine-tuned the language in the rubric to ensure common interpretation of criteria.

One writer notes that

> The conversation about standards inevitably stumbles over the degree to which standards should be explicitly stated. Is it enough to say student work should demonstrate "attention to detail"? Or should we describe the type and amount of detail we expect? There is little doubt that the latter provides students and teachers better guidance for planning teaching and learning, but capturing and agreeing on the former can be a significant step [Jamentz, 1994, p. 38].

If teachers take the time to work through to consensus on what the items in a rubric really mean and come up with exemplars of each level of performance, they can be clear with students about intended learnings. Even better, they can produce more precisely designed learning experiences

**Exhibit 19.5.  Rubric for a Cross-Curricular Sixth-Grade Exhibition**

**GOAL**

Student will communicate accumulated knowledge through creative and analytical writing.

**EXHIBITION**

Using class notes, individual research, literature, and information from audiovisual presentations, students will write a letter to their parents describing a trip to an assigned culture by including information on the following aspects of this culture:

- Art, architecture, literature
- Government
- Inventions and technology
- Social, economic, and political systems
- The daily lives of the common people
- Religion and ethical beliefs
- Importance of geography in the development of this culture
- Why this culture fell or declined

**EXPECTATION**

**Guidelines:**

- Correct grammar, spelling, capitalization, and punctuation must be used.
- Letter will be written in class.
- Final copy of the letter will be typed on school computer word processing program.
- Student will use appropriate note-taking skills and be able to organize ideas in proper outline format.
- Student is able to research notes to communicate knowledge creatively, establishing tone, point of view, and setting.

**Model:** Student letter is attached.

*Source:* Penny Knox, Oak Creek Elementary School, Irvine, California.

**Exhibit 19.5.** *(Continued)*

| | | | | | | | | | | | | | | | | |
|---|---|---|---|---|---|---|---|---|---|---|---|---|---|---|---|---|
| **Key:** | 1 Not Yet | | | | | | | | Student _____ | | | | | | | |
| | 2 Sometimes | | | | | | | | Teacher _____ | | | | | | | |
| | 3 Most of the time | | | | | | | | | | | | | | | |
| | 4 Always | | | | | | | | | | | | | | | |

**Observational category:** _____

| Skill | Practice Date | | | | Practice Date | | | | Practice Date | | | | Exhibition | | | |
|---|---|---|---|---|---|---|---|---|---|---|---|---|---|---|---|---|
| Student uses basic mechanics of writing, grammar, spelling, punctuation, and capitalization. | 1 | 2 | 3 | 4 | 1 | 2 | 3 | 4 | 1 | 2 | 3 | 4 | 1 | 2 | 3 | 4 |
| | | Comments: | | | | Comments: | | | | Comments: | | | | Comments: | | |
| Student is able to take notes from various sources (textbook, literature, encyclopedia) and effectively use them as a reference. | 1 | 2 | 3 | 4 | 1 | 2 | 3 | 4 | 1 | 2 | 3 | 4 | 1 | 2 | 3 | 4 |
| | | Comments: | | | | Comments: | | | | Comments: | | | | Comments: | | |
| Student is able to use research notes to communicate knowledge creatively, establishing tone, point of view, and setting. | 1 | 2 | 3 | 4 | 1 | 2 | 3 | 4 | 1 | 2 | 3 | 4 | 1 | 2 | 3 | 4 |
| | | Comments: | | | | Comments: | | | | Comments: | | | | Comments: | | |
| Student is able to outline and follow basic format of an expository essay. | 1 | 2 | 3 | 4 | 1 | 2 | 3 | 4 | 1 | 2 | 3 | 4 | 1 | 2 | 3 | 4 |
| | | Comments: | | | | Comments: | | | | Comments: | | | | Comments: | | |
| Student is able to use wordprocessing program. | 1 | 2 | 3 | 4 | 1 | 2 | 3 | 4 | 1 | 2 | 3 | 4 | 1 | 2 | 3 | 4 |
| | | Comments: | | | | Comments: | | | | Comments: | | | | Comments: | | |

Exhibit 19.6. The Rubric in *Exemplars*

| Levels | Problem Solving | Reasoning and Proof | Communication | Connections | Representation |
|---|---|---|---|---|---|
| **Novice** | No strategy is chosen, or a strategy is chosen that will not lead to a solution.<br><br>Little or no evidence of engagement in the task is present. | Arguments are made with no mathematical basis.<br><br>No correct reasoning or justification for reasoning is present. | No awareness of audience or purpose is communicated.<br><br>Little or no communication of an approach is evident. Everyday, familiar language is used to communicate ideas. | No connections are made. | No attempt is made to construct mathematical representations. |
| **Apprentice** | A partially correct strategy is chosen or a correct strategy for only solving part of the task is chosen.<br><br>Evidence of drawing on some relevant previous knowledge is present, showing some relevant engagement in the task. | Arguments are made with some mathematical basis.<br><br>Some correct reasoning or justification for reasoning is present with trial and error or unsystematic trying of several cases. | Some awareness of audience or purpose is communicated, and may take place in the form of paraphrasing of the task.<br><br>Some communication of an approach is evident through verbal/written accounts and explanations, use of diagrams or objects, writing, and using mathematical symbols.<br><br>Some formal math language is used, and examples are provided to communicate ideas. | Some attempt to relate the task to other subjects or to own interests and experiences is made. | An attempt is made to construct mathematical representations to record and communicate problem solving. |

| Levels | Problem Solving | Reasoning and Proof | Communication | Connections | Representation |
|---|---|---|---|---|---|
| **Practitioner**<br>*Note:* The practitioner must achieve a correct answer. | A correct strategy is chosen based on the mathematical situation in the task.<br><br>Planning or monitoring of strategy is evident.<br><br>Evidence of solidifying prior knowledge and applying it to the problem-solving situation is present. | Arguments are constructed with adequate mathematical basis.<br><br>A systematic approach and/or justification of correct reasoning is present. This may lead to:<br>1. Clarification of the task<br>2. Exploration of mathematical phenomenon<br>3. Noting patterns, structures, and regularities | A sense of audience or purpose is communicated.<br><br>Communication of an approach is evident through a methodical, organized, coherent, sequenced, and labeled response.<br><br>Formal math language is used throughout the solution to share and clarify ideas. | Mathematical connections or observations are recognized. | Appropriate and accurate mathematical representations are constructed and refined to solve problems or portray solutions. |
| **Expert**<br>*Note:* The practitioner must achieve a correct answer. | An efficient strategy is chosen and progress toward a solution is evaluated.<br><br>Adjustments in strategy, if necessary, are made along the way, and/or alternative strategies are considered.<br><br>Evidence of analyzing the situation in mathematical terms, and extending prior knowledge is present. | Deductive arguments are used to justify decisions and may result in more formal proofs.<br><br>Evidence is used to justify and support decisions made and conclusions reached. This may lead to:<br>1. Testing and accepting or rejecting of a hypothesis or conjecture.<br>2. Explanation of phenomenon.<br>3. Generalizing and extending the solution to other cases. | A sense of audience and purpose is communicated.<br><br>Communication at the practitioner level is achieved, and communication of arguments is supported by mathematical properties used.<br><br>Precise math language and symbolic notation are used to consolidate math thinking and to communicate ideas. | Mathematical connections or observations are used to extend the solution. | Abstract or symbolic mathematical representations are constructed to analyze relationships, extend thinking, and clarify or interpret phenomenon. |

*Source:* Reprinted with permission. www.Exemplars.com.

whose activities are more likely to enable students to learn what they want. To summarize, the sequence for developing a rubric goes like this:

1. Establish criteria for success.
2. Identify and spell out levels of performance.
3. Construct authentic tasks.
4. Select and display exemplars.
5. Establish reliability across teachers in scoring student work.

Well-designed rubrics and clear criteria in advance are essential for communicating the three messages of expectations: "This is important; you can do it; I won't give up on you." Without clear criteria for comparing student work, there is no way to make feedback full and informative enough for low-performing students. And without adults who take the time to give this full feedback, along with help to use it, students too easily can conclude they are incapable. It is not fair to students who do not have a clear image of what quality looks like to ask them to guess. They certainly won't figure it out from being told repetitively that they are not making the grade.

Collaborative planning time for groups of teachers is required for the process we have described. In fact, what we are really trying to do is "develop a professional culture in which teacher analysis of student work is expected and valued" (California Assessment Collaborative, in Jamentz, 1993). Principals and department chairs play a key role in communicating that message through what they say, model, and facilitate through scheduling, use of meeting time, and the resources they make available to teachers for this work of building rubrics. The administrator as a "school culture builder" (Saphier and King, 1985) plays a crucial role in the development of authentic assessments and in building the capacity of teachers to use the assessment process to improve instruction.

## Involving Students in Establishing Standards

Students can play a big part in developing criteria for the products they are about to create and, in the process, become clear about the goals and be motivated to meet them. Involving students in the process of identifying important standards of performance can eliminate the student complaint that got Chris Gustafson (1994) started on her assessment project. A student said to her after class one day, "I don't understand why I got this grade." Chris decided to get her students involved in defining standards at the beginning of a unit on immigration:

> I handed out a list of topics and asked the students to select one. The next day students who had chosen the same project formed groups that would write a grading standard by which their projects would be evaluated. I explained that a project completed as described on the project sheet [which she had provided] would receive a C. Each group was to decide what they would need to add to my criteria in order to receive a B or an A. As an example, we set a grading standard together for a writing project. That gave me a chance to discourage responses that were too ambitious: everyone's journal did not have to be typed, but more than a half page of writing on each sheet would be required, and so on.
>
> After writing the journal grading standard as a class, each group decided what [their particular] projects would have to include to receive a B or an A. I took all their suggestions and typed one grading standard for each project. The next day, I handed each person his or her group's grading standard sheet. Now, before students even began the project, they knew how it would be evaluated.

This time, when I took the projects home, each one had a grading standard attached to it. And what a difference that made: because my students didn't have to guess what to do to get a high grade, they were more successful; our high standards resulted in better projects; and although I still made comments, evaluation was easier. Parents could also see exactly how the evaluations had been done. The process was open to all, and the students had had a part in creating it [Gustafson, 1994].

## Component 3: Assessing Current Knowledge Before Instruction

Prior to introducing a new skill, topic, or concept, some type of preassessment can yield data about where students are in relation to where we want them to be. A ninth grade life science teacher uses an Anticipation Guide containing true/false statements about photosynthesis (including some commonly held misconceptions) to determine what students believe to be true based on prior experience. A third grade teacher asks students to write "the number that represents three thousand and forty two" and to label what each digit stands for, and uses several more examples like this to gather data about student understanding of place value. An art teacher asks students to draw a picture that includes some objects in the foreground, on the horizon, and off in the distance to assess students' level of understanding and skill with perspective drawing. What is common to all three of these is that they happen prior to instruction and are used as data sources to inform how the topic will be introduced and pursued and to determine the need to differentiate some aspects of instruction or form flexible skill groups along the way. Assessing prior knowledge gives us essential information about what background knowledge to teach, to

whom, and how long to spend on it so that our students can learn the intended curriculum.

## Component 4: Frequent Data Collection and Teacher Record Keeping

Once instruction is underway there must be ongoing data collection to keep students on track and support them in investing their effort effectively. It is not enough to say, "I am always assessing my students," unless you have some daily data record that shows you actually did so. The data can come from looking over students' shoulders as they work: walking around with a class list while students are learning to use certain commands in a software program, or walking around while students are solving one long division problem, checking off names of students who demonstrate mastery while making notes about types of errors that caused you to intervene and offer guidance. Data might come from listening to students read aloud one on one, from asking a well-planned combination of recall and comprehension questions of many students during whole class instruction to get information about which students not only recognize halves and quarters, but which know they always have to be comparing the same whole for fractional equivalents to be valid.

Certain kinds of data collection and error detection can happen very quickly using whiteboards and posing a series of examples with the same multiple-choice set of answers to ascertain understanding. (You've just reviewed the spelling and uses of "their," "they're," and "there" and want to determine whether or not students got it. You project a sentence on the wall ["I want to be_____ in the morning."] and ask students to write the correct spelling on their whiteboards and show their response on the count of three. After a series of ten or so examples you have noted where there is still uncertainty and confusion and will use the data to decide what to review and with whom.) Other sources of data about student mastery might come from analysis of products students have produced in a class, or from written student responses to a one-question quiz ("Based on the discussion so far, what do you think were the most important causes of the Civil War?").

The main point about collecting assessment data is that it is ongoing and we must use the information to inform our teaching: to determine who "has it," who doesn't, where students are in relation to the objective, and what reteaching needs to occur with whom.

## Record Keeping

Records can take the form of checklists or profiles; logs, journals, or anecdotal records; or portfolios. What is important is that the form of the record be appropriate for the assessment methodology and a good fit for the content or skill being assessed.

**Checklists and Profiles**  Teachers have traditionally used checklists in the elementary grades to track student skill acquisition, such as mastering multiplication tables, mechanical writing skills, or developmental levels of literacy. The checklist in Exhibit 19.7 represents a record-keeping device in which a check signals the student's developmental point on a particular behavior.

Checklists represent the idea that important academic behaviors develop over time and can be assessed along a continuum from emerging to fully developed. Although most developmental checklists are found in the areas of reading and writing, many districts have created them for other areas, including mathematics and science competencies.

Checklists are useful components in assessment because they allow teachers, students, and parents to summarize in compact form a student's level of skill acquisition and to see on the same form the next target skill. Anyone who shares these checklists with students must be careful not to overwhelm them. Certain children may interpret a sea of empty check boxes as a huge and unattainable roster of things to be learned and throw up their hands in despair.

**Logs, Journals, and Anecdotal Records**  Observation of student performance is often best recorded in anecdotal records of some sort that are easy to create, access, and interpret. These records may capture observations of anything from student social behavior to comments on their class participation or skill at interpreting books read. Hill and Ruptic (1994) describe systems that use triple-ring binders, folders, file cards, computers, sticky notes, and mailing labels.

The more repetitive the comments become, the more a teacher may be inclined to move to a checklist. It is more efficient to write a behavior once and check off when a student can do it. The more individual or idiosyncratic the comments, however, the more useful an anecdotal record is. Exhibit 19.8 shows two sheets that allow individual, original entries. The record forms in Exhibit 19.9 are designed as check-offs for skills displayed but still allow space for anecdotal comments.

Behind the choice of which record form to use must be clear teacher thinking about what is being assessed. The design of the recording instrument should meet the criteria of ease of use, clarity, accessibility, and appropriateness.

On another note, "data walls" have become popular as a form of teacher record keeping that makes student results visible and public. In New York City, Kinnari Patel displays the current levels and recent changes in students' reading levels for

**Exhibit 19.7. Assessment Checklist**

| READING | First Noticed | Developing | Independent |
|---|---|---|---|
| (Motivational) | | | |
| • Expresses a desire to own or borrow books | | | |
| • Recommends books or stories to other people | | | |
| • Keeps a book close by to be read in spare moments | | | |
| • Chooses books at an independent reading level | | | |
| • Develops preferences for different genres and for specific authors and illustrators | | | |
| (Listening) | | | |
| • Listens for increasingly longer times to stories read aloud | | | |
| • Listens to stories without interrupting and takes turns in responding | | | |
| (Conventions of Print) | | | |
| • Understands more complex punctuation during story reading (e.g., quotation marks, period after abbreviation, and so on) | | | |
| • Continues to build on knowledge of sight words | | | |
| (Linguistics) | | | |
| • Uses all cuing systems in a balanced and integrated way when working out unknown words in a story (e.g., context, picture, and letter/sounds cues) | | | |
| • Self-corrects when reading | | | |
| • Uses a variety of strategies when in difficulty (e.g., reads onto the end of the sentence, starts sentence again (the rerun strategy), substitutes a word that makes sense for an unknown word and reads on, and so on) | | | |
| • Rereads for additional information, clarification, or pleasure | | | |
| • Reads familiar material aloud expressively to enhance meaning | | | |

*Source: The Cambridge Handbook of Documentation and Assessment: Child Portfolios and Teacher Records in the Primary Grades.* Edited by Lynne Hall, Lynn Stuart, and Brenda Engel. University of North Dakota, Grand Forks, February 1995. Used by permission.

**Exhibit 19.8. Two Examples of Anecdotal Records**

ANECDOTAL RECORDS for *Susan*

| | | | |
|---|---|---|---|
| 12/17 Had to go home w/mom; crying right at 8:45 – called her to take her home – "big fight" Mom/Dad re work | 12/18 Home again at 8:45 Back at 9:30 to "help do things for others" after calming down | 1/4 Crying again during "Attendance" job... difficult goodbye w/Mo. Stress connected w/ Dad's lay-off and holidays | 1/7 Tearless, normal start Even able to take redirects at writing (off-talk) calmly |
| 1/11 Very helpful getting Tory caught up after long illness. Good "teacher" shows heart then does own work side-by-side ready to assist "student" | 1/21 Having trouble finishing SACAJAWEA she can read it, but it is a real challenge and seems not to hold her interest. Rdg level maturity level issue? | 2/1 "I'm not sure I want to do these tubs again" Offered options: Latin cubes ★ Estimating ! recording w/ >< = ★ chose this | 2/2 Working on chapter book of her own autobiography – 4 chapters so far |
| 2/12 Good compromising in problem solving activity w/ Theo, Trent and Alanna | 3/1 Author's circle for her autobiography; planning to use comments/questions for revision | | |
| | | | |
| | | | |

**ANECDOTAL RECORDS for** *Cindy's Conference Group (teacher)*

| Alice | Brad | David | Dylan |
|---|---|---|---|
| 1/19 Beginning to read more difficult (Nate the Great) chapter books competently w/ minimal help... __hard work__, but can do it! | 1/11 Talked about getting off the video game words and stretching yourself — me exasperated about his being stuck in the mire of copying w/ Harry. Took it well — contrite; agreed w/ me, made commitment to do more | 1/15 Needing to go to the bathroom a lot. He also noticed this — said he would speak to his parents | 1/15 Serious about taking responsibility for his own learning. Stayed in at recess to finish. Only took 5 minutes. Well done |

| Elizabeth | Harry | Jeri | Kathleen |
|---|---|---|---|
| 1/12 Off the wall all AM! Popping up and down, interrupting, off-task, noises and other sounds, repeated redirections necessary. "respectful behavior" discussed | 1/17 Writing story about "Baseball Diamond Mystery" w/ Andy — Prominent swastikas ?? all over it and drawing of what looks like Hitler... nothing said yet, but watching this. | 1/8 w/ Kleenex reading Annie Sullivan — "This is sad." "Do any more people die?" Talked about whether to continue — it's okay to cry/feel sad w/ books | 1/11 Finished "Kathleen Wore Her..." book. Nudged to correct the few misspelled words — 1st time. |

| Lawrence | Mandy | Michael | Nancy |
|---|---|---|---|
|  | 1/12 Really pleased first day to bring lunch packed at home rather than buying school lunch. "I made it myself!" | 1/17 __Making a book__ about fishing trip w/ lift-up flaps showing fish + names of them |  |

| Paul | Randy | Ricky | Susan |
|---|---|---|---|
| His went to Lawrence's on the bus, but Mom still came by at the end of the day... to check on him? | 1/19 On time __every day__ this week... maybe we've licked the tardiness problem? |  | 1/11 Very helpful getting Tory caught up after long illness. Good "teacher", shows how to, then does own work side-by-side ready to assist "student". |

| Thomas | Tory | Vince | Zoey |
|---|---|---|---|
|  |  |  | 1/13 Shocked and wanted to share with me what she was reading about M.L. King jr.. |

**Exhibit 19.9. Two Examples of Check-Off Record Forms**

# Reading Conference Record

Student_____

| | Date: 12/8 | Date: 12/17 | Date: | Date: | Date: | Date: |
|---|---|---|---|---|---|---|
| | Title: Two Little Dogs (G) | Title: Sleeping out (F) | Title: | Title: | Title: | Title: |
| Level Appropriate | Instructional Frustration ✓ | Instructional Independent ✓ | | | | |
| Strategies: Whole idea | | | | | | |
| Picture clues | ✓ | | | | | |
| Pattern | | | | | | |
| Sight Words | ✓ | ✓ | | | | |
| First letter | | | | | | |
| Decodes | ✓ | ✓ | | | | |
| Context clues | ✓ | ✓ | | | | |
| Skip return | | | | | | |
| Rereads | ✓ | ✓ | | | | |
| | | | | | | |
| Reads Fluently | | ✓ | | | | |
| With Inflection | | ✓ | | | | |
| Literal Comprehension | ✓ | + | | | | |
| Interpretive Comprehension | ✓ | + | | | | |
| Strategy Taught | contractions context | contractions speech marks | | | | |
| Comments | door's = door is that's gate's won't = will not don't = do not isn't = is not I noticed you used context to self-correct over (after) the (they) | It's = it is what's = what is she's = she is Ways to show speech: Word bubbles speech marks (quotation marks) | | | | |

CODES: + consistently
✓ sometimes

READING CONFERENCE RECORD

Name _____

| Date and Title | Miscues & Comments<br>book » said | Skills/Strategies<br>Taught | Fluency | Comprehension | |
|---|---|---|---|---|---|
| | | | | Factual | Inferred |
| 10/19<br>The Witch's Christmas | with → witch<br>wreath → w<br>very → every | wr = r<br>Look at pictures | ✓ | + | ✓ |
| 10/21<br>The Enormous Egg | me → my s/c<br>when → than<br>→ what makes sense? | | — | ✓ | ✓ |
| 10/26<br>scary Stories | many miscues<br>Read to Demo Dan!<br>Picked book from library · proud | syllables<br>-oi | — | ✓ | ✓ |
| 11/2 The Return of the 3rd Grade Ghostbusters | enough<br>check → jack<br>discovered how he could<br>"read" periods → expression | gh = ph<br>context | + | + | ✓ |

CODES: + = Very Good<br>✓ = Average<br>— = Needs Improvement

© 1993 Jan Peacoe. Bainbridge Island, WA

all the students in grades K–3 on a board in the teachers' lounge (Figure 19.2). Across the top of the display, the big letters represent the reading level of the student's current book. Students' names are on sticky notes and are placed in the column under their reading level. Thus, there is a big, visual display of the spread in each class and a way to compare the spread and levels between classes at the same grade level.

Whenever a student moves up a level, the teacher moves that student's sticky note and writes the previous level's letter and the date of move-up on the back of the note. Thus, at any time, an observer can turn over any student's sticky note and see how many levels he or she has moved through this year and on what date each move took place. This is a clear way of identifying which students are making progress and which are not.

When a teacher moves a student's sticky note, it leaves a gap in the column it came from. The gaps at the end of each day show the principal, Ms. Patel, where movement has occurred. She then moves up sticky notes to fill in any gaps in any column so that the next day if any gaps appear, she is informed visually that a child in a given class has moved up a level in reading. This form of record keeping enables different teachers of the same content and grade level to compare notes on how students are doing. It also provokes questions early on about why certain students are moving slowly or stuck.

## Component 5: Frequent High-Quality Feedback to Students

"Academic feedback is more strongly and consistently related to achievement than any other teaching behavior. This relationship is consistent regardless of grade, socioeconomic status, race, or school setting" (Bellon, Bellon, and Blank, 1997, p. 277).

**Figure 19.2. Data Wall**

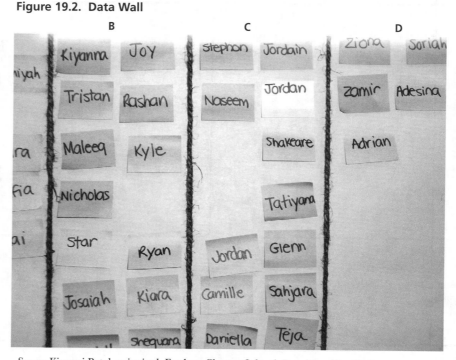

*Source:* Kinnari Patel, principal, Explore Charter School, Brooklyn, New York.

"The most powerful single modification that enhances achievement," writes Hattie (in Ainsworth and Viegut, 2006, p. 89), "is feedback. The simplest prescription for improving education must be 'dollops of feedback.'"

These assertions are backed by a considerable body of research including a number of studies reporting the good-size effect feedback systems can have on student performance. The ranges reported are between .5 and 1.8 (Black and Wiliam, 1998, 2004; Meisels and others, 2003; Rodriguez, 2004). An effect-size of 1 standard deviation translates into approximately 35 percentile points on a standardized test and 100 points on the SAT.

The research cited above is based on a technical definition of feedback that is narrower than the way in which people tend to use the word *feedback* in everyday talk. We adhere to that definition when we use the term in this text. We also discuss other ways of responding to student work that can have a place and a purpose.

## Feedback Defined

So what exactly is this more technical definition of feedback? "Feedback is information about how we did in light of some goal" (Wiggins, 2004). Feedback is descriptive of performance in relation to a standard or to criteria for success that have been clearly communicated.

You have seen examples of feedback with computer games, tennis lessons (or other forms of one-to-one athletic coaching), flight simulators, music lessons, and choral rehearsals. The choral director says, "I am hearing the altos a split second before the tenors are coming in and before I give the signal." The piano teacher says, "Your middle finger is hitting the F rather than the F# when you play that chord."

Pure feedback is nonevaluative information delivered directly to a student about how his or her performance or some aspect of it compares to a model of good work. "You have shown every step of your solution; your calculations are accurate. But your units aren't labeled." Feedback is value neutral; it has no praise or blame attached. It objectively compares a sample of student work to a specified criterion or an exemplar, pointing out specific ways or places where the student work meets or doesn't meet the standards. Wiggins (2004) defines feedback in an educative sense as *facts* (events or behavior that happened related to a goal), *impact* (a description of the effects of the facts or results), and *commentary* (facts and impact explained in the context of the goal). Here is an example of what that might sound like: "During your speech you consistently made eye contact with your audience, paused for one to two seconds each time you presented a new point, gave an example for each of your first three points, then went through the last three points without pauses or examples. You ended without a conclusion or closing thought. The audience wasn't prepared for the ending, which explains why they sat completely silent—and seemed nonresponsive at first when you finished."

Feedback that increases student learning significantly is:

- direct
- specific
- timely
- in the appropriate amount
- able to be understood (developmentally appropriate)
- credible
- frequent and ongoing
- nonjudgmental

- not advice or guidance
- used by students to self-adjust, modify, or augment their work

### Feedback Squared: Concurrent, Frequent, and Ongoing

Most of the attributes listed above describe qualities or characteristics of individual bits of feedback that would make it a good feedback event. But the challenge is to create a feedback system that is concurrent with (occurs during, not after) performance (Wiggins, 2004), combines sources to maximize the number of good feedback events students get in a period of time, and enables students to self-adjust and improve. We like the term *data stream,* coined by Jeff Howard of the Efficacy Institute, to characterize this systemic attribute of good feedback.

Good feedback systems produce a stream of data to students about how they're doing—a flow of pieces of information that is hourly and daily as opposed to weekly and monthly (which is the rate of feedback produced by systems that rely on tests). The total amount of feedback students get can consist of many individual moments or episodes when they receive information about their work, as with this teacher comment about a piece of writing: "Your point is clearly stated here, but I don't see the evidence that led you to it."

Feedback can come from teachers, other students, electronic devices, answer books, self-comparison of one's work with exemplars, and other sources. It can be written, verbal, visual, or on audiotape. But if we're not giving it frequently, we're not maximizing its power.

How does one create such a stream? Here are a few possibilities:

- Answers are available to students for use in checking their own work immediately after completion. In some cases, students check answers after each item they complete. Answers may be found in answer books, on the board or projected on screen, in databases, or in other quickly available sources.
- Students compare responses with each other for similarities and differences and then reconcile the differences.
- Students check their own or each other's completed work against lists of criteria, against exemplars, or self-scoring with rubrics.

Here are a few examples of multisource systems in action:

Mrs. Dunlap is working with a group of five fourth-grade students at a table on equivalent fractions. They are using manipulatives to create equivalent models of 2/3, 4/6, and 6/9 of the same size whole. Meanwhile, the rest of her class is working on paper-and-pencil exercises for the same topic. Seventeen students are at their desks or tables; there are two different assignments for students who are at different points in the curriculum. We will refer to them as the red and blue groups for purposes of clarity. Blue students are working on pictures of equivalent fractions. As blue students finish their problems, they sign in on the whiteboard. The next student who finishes signs in and the two get together to compare their answers and reconcile any differences by talking through the problem. If a student finds a mistake, he or she circles it and writes the correction above it on the paper. When the pair agrees on all answers, they put their papers in Mrs. Dunlap's in-box and return to their desks, where they resume other work. If they can't come to agreement they code the item for teacher help.

The red students are working on problems that require calculation and use of common denominators. They check their answers in an answer book on a front table when they have completed their examples. They mark them all and return to their desks to fix the ones they got wrong. When they find their mistakes, they write a note, usually one sentence, indicating what their mistake was (for example, "I forgot to convert the 3/6 into ninths"). If they can't figure out the mistake, they put up a red flag at their desks. One of the two designated "math mavens" for the day comes over to help. Alternately, students can get help from Mrs. Dunlap in the after-lunch period.

Students get equal credit for correcting a mistake as for getting it the first time around. Once a week Mrs. Dunlap gives out "Great Misteak" Awards (spelled that way on purpose) to students who have made mistakes, found them, and can explain what they discovered. A "Great Misteak" is a mistake from which everyone can learn.

For all of the students, data about the correctness of their answers comes quickly. The feedback is timely, specific, and used to modify their work. It might not be nonjudgmental feedback, however, if the students working in pairs are sarcastic to one another. Mrs. Dunlap explained the attributes of good feedback to her students earlier in the year, and they have role-played giving a fellow student feedback on work without judgmental words.

In language arts, her students are completing a unit on writing letters. For this week, they are writing a final draft of a letter to someone in their family who lives far away, telling them the family news for the month. Each student checks his or her completed letter against a visual template of proper form (see Exhibit 19.10). The template has boxes that students check off when they have verified that the element is done correctly in their own letter.

Students' letters are also read for content by peers. The three criteria for response (clear, inter-

**Exhibit 19.10.  The Five Parts of a Letter Checklist**

NAME:                                      DATE:

**The Five Parts of a Letter Checklist**

1.  Heading:
    - ❑  Right justified
    - ❑  Name
    - ❑  Street address
    - ❑  City, State Zip (include comma)
    - ❑  Month date, year (include comma)
2.  Greeting:
    - ❑  Left justified_
    - ❑  Comma after name
3.  Body:
    - ❑  Paragraphs indented
    - ❑  Capital letters
    - ❑  Correct punctuation
4.  Closing:
    - ❑  Comma after name
5.  Signature:
    - ❑  First letter of each name capital
    - ❑  All other letters lowercase

esting, paragraphs) are on a chart on the wall. The "paragraphs" item means that each paragraph is about a different topic, event, or aspect of a topic or event. In groups of three, the children read each other's letters, scoring each criterion either "yes" or "not yet." To score any item "not yet," students have to explain why and where something occurred. Following this activity, students revise their letters, attach the feedback from their peers, and place them in Mrs. Dunlap's language arts in-box.

Another example comes from Mr. Ramirez's Spanish II class. He is giving feedback one group at a time to the four groups that have done travel folder projects. As he rotates around to each group, the students in the other three groups are working individually on translations of English-to-Spanish passages from their textbook. As they complete their translations, they go to one of the three online computers in the room and sign on to Babblefish.com. They scan in the English text of their passage and print out the translation the site gives them. They compare the translation from the site, phrase for phrase, with their own translation and mark discrepancies. They decide whether theirs is correct, make changes if needed in green pen, and place it in the in-box on Mr. Ramirez's desk.

Babblefish.com is a Web site that does real-time translations between English and many other languages, including Spanish. In Mr. Ramirez's class, this site is the feedback mechanism. But because translation is an art that requires choices (several synonyms in Spanish could be used to translate the word *trip* depending on the purpose of the trip), Babblefish isn't perfect. That very imperfection is just what Mr. Ramirez likes about it. It always uses perfect grammar; thus, it catches any errors his students make, for example, in verb tense or adjective agreement. But the word choice Babblefish makes may not be on target for what his student intended. Thus, when they disagree with Babblefish, the students can evaluate whether they want to go with their original word choice or that of the site. Mr. Ramirez gets the best of both worlds: an immediate feedback mechanism on grammar that also makes his students think, evaluate, and make decisions.

The payoff for creating conditions of high-quality feedback in academic settings promises to be great: feedback is positively related to student engagement rate. Students who are given accurate information about the correctness and quality of their work spend more time working on academic assignments.

## Beyond Feedback: Guidance and Evaluation

Frequently when we define feedback and its powerful impact on student achievement teachers ask, "Is that all we are supposed to say to students to help them improve their performance? What if they don't know what to do with the feedback to improve their performance? Can't I ever congratulate them for what they have accomplished?" And the answer is that there are a number of other kinds of responses to student performance that can be meaningful—just as is the case in all aspects of teaching; there is never only one way to do anything. It is just that feedback is the essential component in any of our responses if students are to get the information they need to make adjustments and modifications until they have succeeded in meeting the standards set for quality work. So what are some other meaningful ways of responding that might accompany the feedback?

Wiggins (2004) talks about feedback, guidance, and evaluation. While feedback is information about what happened, guidance gives future direction, and evaluation judges the overall performance in light of a standard. "Feedback tells me whether I am on course. Guidance tells me the most likely ways to achieve my goal. Evaluation tells me whether I am or have been sufficiently on course to be deemed competent or successful." Figure 19.3, designed by our colleague Ann Stern, further delineates a repertoire of response options. When feedback should be accompanied by any one of the other response options is a matter of matching: taking into account the work the student has produced, the extent to which you determine that the student might need more than feedback in order to take the next steps and invest her effort effectively, and the amount of encouragement, praise, or recognition you deem necessary to motivate a student to continue to invest her effort. The

**Figure 19.3. Feedback and Beyond: Response Categories**

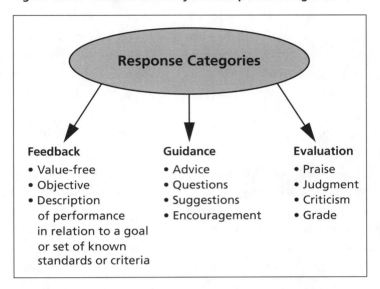

**Response Categories**

**Feedback**
- Value-free
- Objective
- Description of performance in relation to a goal or set of known standards or criteria

**Guidance**
- Advice
- Questions
- Suggestions
- Encouragement

**Evaluation**
- Praise
- Judgment
- Criticism
- Grade

bottom line is that "guidance and evaluation make little difference unless there is prior clarity (for the student) about goals, means and feedback" (Wiggins, 2004).

When teachers respond to student writing they have an opportunity to apply the attributes of feedback described above. But responding to students' writing calls for us to do much more than give pure "feedback" as defined previously. Response to writing should often (1) give students credible information about what they've done that is effective and why and (2) give them useful input about how to make it better. That is more than feedback.

Teachers skilled at responding to student writing have a hierarchy of purposes in mind, and different ones of these purposes may show up at a given time. Responding to students' mechanical and spelling errors for editing purposes, for example, may be reserved for a later draft and not occur at all in responding to an early draft. What thoughtful teachers do in responding to student writing is give help, specific suggestions, or some kind of guidance that students can use to improve their next draft.

Here are some different purposes skilled writing teachers have in mind in responding to students' writing.

1. To show what resonated for the teacher-reader as an audience
2. To highlight specifically the things students are doing that are appropriate, skillful, or effective in their impact on a reader and explain why
3. To lead the student to the next most appropriate stretch or improvement in their writing with suggestions or guidance, using the technical language of writers to do so ["show, don't tell" "strong verbs . . ."]. This kind of response is not solely objective, that is, only comparing student products to exemplars. It also seeks to help the student improve by giving direct leads or asking focused questions that guide the student to improvement.

Examine the three different sets of comments on the same paper from professional development materials published by The Writers' Express (www.WEX.org) shown in Exhibit 19.11. Compare the first two examples to the third one.

The first teacher catches every error. This could be appropriate for a piece of writing that was rich and complete, needing only technical repairs. But for this particular early draft the effect on the student might well be discouraging. Instead of asking for a thesis statement, the teacher supplies it for the student. There is the assumption that the student knows "frag" means sentence fragment and can use that cue as sufficient to self-remedy that. There is little shown that the student can build on, nothing to motivate the student to improve the writing, only an implied injunction to fix myriad technical errors.

The second teacher tries to be encouraging in her comment, but winds up being wishy-washy and vague, offering no specific suggestions except the vague "keep going." What reason would the student have for keeping going? "Watch those fragments" may not be enough to help the student see where she's written one or know how to fix it. Because the comments don't respectfully engage with the student's work, they don't encourage him to continue writing. And because they don't make clear what they want him to do next, they can't improve his skills.

The third teacher has crafted responses more likely to support good writing habits and also lead to improvement. She does self-reports of the impact of specific words: "Yum. My mouth is watering." and underlines the words that produced that effect, thus identifying the specifics. She shows she is attending to the content by responding to an arguing point of the student ("I also feel like sleeping helps me to focus."). The teacher then challenges the student to improve her piece by focusing on a specific skill ("Show, don't tell") and gives her

guidance for doing so: "Pretend you are in school after not getting enough sleep. Write 3 sentences to convince me . . ." The exercise is constructed to highlight the right size bite for the student, which the teacher decides is writing the sentences to show, not tell—just that. So the exercise represents a diagnostically determined focus for this student in this piece of writing to improve the next most important skill as determined by the teacher. And what we hope is that the technical errors highlighted by the first teacher response are noted by this third teacher and that they will be targets for skill development in later feedback and remediation.

Responses to writing that show the teacher is thinking diagnostically, providing guidance for improvement, and matching response to students' particular needs is applicable in any academic discipline where writing is called for: social studies analysis, science lab reports, music, art, and physical education. Guidance is also appropriate in response to student performance in any discipline even when writing is not called for!

"When you swung your arms while going stage-left [teacher starts with data], it strongly conveyed the character's cockiness [communicates effect of the behavior]. Try it again at a slower pace so we can see what the effect is." [teacher gives suggestion]—Drama

"The sudden bright color here [data] draws the eye to the sun [effect] much as Van Gogh would do. Try muting the color down here so the competition for attention isn't too distracting to the viewer." [suggestion]—Art class

"You adjusted the scale to highlight the similarities and differences in the treatments [data]. That made your data collection and graphic display very clear and accessible [effect on reader]. One can look at both your matrix and your bar graphs and see your points [more on effect and why]. But I cannot tell so clearly from your "conclusion" what

**Exhibit 19.11.**

# The Impact of Teacher Comments

### Approach 1: Catch Every Mistake

#### "Why School Should Start Later" (excerpt)

*two words* · *colloquial*

We need to stop feeling pressured everyday to be in school so early I mean sure we get

*you*

out early but what is the point of going if your are not ready to learn all the time?  We

*Frag.*

need to feel comfortable and willing to work. Focused and we need to take on

*our* · *or*

challenges.  We do not need to dream about how nice are bed would be right now of the

yummy breakfast that we missed because we were too late.   A few times I have dreamed

about being asleep and walking up to a huge ham, cheese, and tomato omlet with a giant

*colloquial* · *to school*

café colada to wash it down.  If we are feeling this way, then who really wants to go?  I

know that school can be pretty boring to students anyway, but maybe we just don't want

*too*

to go because we are to tired.  It is the perfect theory.

*No questions in persuasive writing.*

*You haven't stated your thesis/theory:*

*"School should start later because students are too tired to concentrate when they wake up early."*

*(Continued)*

you think the meaning of the data is for action in power plants." [feedback]—Science class.

Exhibit 19.12 shows an example of a different kind of response in which the teacher focuses on asking good questions to push the writer, Christian, to expand both his plot and his character development. Note the progress of the student's writing between the first two drafts. Only on the third draft (not shown here) will the teacher focus on technical and grammatical elements.

**Exhibit 19.11.** *(Continued)*

## The Impact of Teacher Comments

### Approach 2: Encourage and Nudge

### "Why School Should Start Later" (excerpt)

We need to stop feeling pressured everyday to be in school so early, I mean sure we get

out early but what is the point of going if your are not ready to learn all the time? We

need to feel comfortable and willing to work. Focused and we need to take on *Good attitude*

challenges. We do not need to dream about how nice are bed would be right now of the *Watch those fragment*

yummy breakfast that we missed because we were too late. A few times I have dreamed

about being asleep and walking up to a huge ham, cheese, and tomato omlet with a giant *Funny.*

café colada to wash it down. If we are feeling this way, then who really wants to go? I

know that school can be pretty boring to students anyway, but maybe we just don't want

to go because we are to tired. It is the perfect theory!

*You said it! Good start. I look forward to more. Keep going!*

# The Impact of Teacher Comments

**Approach 3:** Respond as a Reader; Instruct as a Teacher

## "Why School Should Start Later" (excerpt)

We need to stop feeling pressured everyday to be in school so early, I mean sure we get

out early but what is the point of going if your are not ready to learn all the time?  We

need to feel comfortable and willing to work.  Focused and we need to take on sleeping *I also feel like sleeping helps me to focus.*

challenges.  We do not need to dream about how nice are bed would be right now of the

yummy breakfast that we missed because we were too late.   A few times I have dreamed

about being asleep and walking up to a huge ham, cheese, and tomato omlet with a giant

*Yum. My mouth is watering.* café colada to wash it down.  If we are feeling this way, then who really wants to go?  I

know that school can be pretty boring to students anyway, but maybe we just don't want

to go because we are to tired.  It is the perfect theory!

*Beatriz,*
*you're starting to convince me that a later start time*
*would make us all more focused on school. I'm especially excited*
*for the possibility of an Omlette and coolata! ☺ Carli*

*SHowing Drill: Pretend you are in school after not getting enough sleep.*
*Write 3 sentences to convince me that you're not focused.*
*SHOW how you look and feel.*

**Exhibit 19.12.**

Mark is outside, walking around, he has to go to work, but he is thinking about going to the chess invitational.  He is not worried about winning or losing.  Mark can't cross the street because there are so many cars passing by.  Mark starts yelling "Come on, Already!" waiting for the walk signal to show up, he pushed the walk signal 5 times.  Mark starts to punch the pole just to hurt his right hand.  Some people came by and started to make fun of him.  They giggled silently and laughed hard when they got far away from him.  It was even worse when he continuously punched the open box at the bottom.  Still no walk signal.

*Why would Mark punch the pole to hurt himself on purpose?*

Christian — this is a good start for putting your character, Mark, in a situation. Mark is an interesting guy. He has a job and is a chess player, but I can also see by the way he "punches" the walk button that he is impatient, angry, and worried about what people think. Why is Mark so impatient. What might happen to him on the street that might CHANGE him or make him less angry. Think about CLIMAX. Let's talk!

Nice work.

Kate

Mark is outside his house, walking back and forth on his street, he has to go to

work behind a hardware store's counter, but he is thinking about going to the

*the chess invitational is a great idea - it makes Mark an interesting character!*

chess invitational. He is not worried about winning or losing because he is not

supposed to be at the invitational. He called in sick and had someone else

*wow, chess is important to Mark! Does he really not care if he wins or loses?*

substitute for him in his false absence. Mark cannot cross the street because

there are so many cars passing by. Mark starts to yell, "Come on already, not

wanting to wait patiently for the walk signal to show up. The walk signal does not

show up on the screen so Mark presses the button five more times, it still doesn't

*Your strong verbs show me how angry Mark is. Why is he angry? Did something happen?*

show so he starts to kick the pole, releasing his anger. His face turns completely

red as he continues to wait. Some people come by and start to make fun of Mark

and his troubles. They whisper to each other as soon as they get far enough

from him, they laugh hard because Mark is a man with problems, big problems.

*what problems?*

He finally gets across the street when thee is a green light, Mark walks slowly to

the other side of the street. Suddenly, a Black Lincoln Continental with the

*good description!*

windows all black and a black man wearing a black suit, not saying a word,

stares Mark down as he waits for him to pass. Once he gets there, he sprints

away fast to get away from him. There are no cars or people in sight, which

*why does this man scare Mark?*

scared Mark, and the light is red. The Driver drives away, before he did, he

pulled out a pack of Virginia Slims Cigarettes and began smoking. The driver

*(Continued)*

**Exhibit 19.12.** *(Continued)*

was really angry, he drove when there was a red light, there was nobody to catch

him drive on the red light.  Mark still sprints.

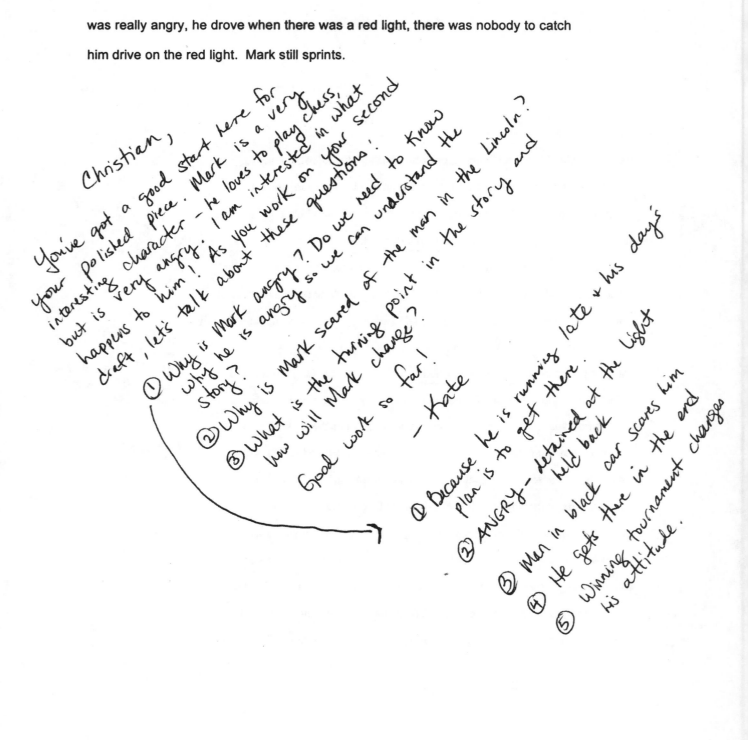

Christian,

You've got a good start here for your polished piece. Mark is a very interesting character – he loves to play chess, but is very angry. I am interested in what happens to him! As you work on your second draft, let's talk about these questions:

① Why is Mark angry? Do we need to know why he is angry so we can understand the story?

② Why is Mark scared of the man in the Lincoln?

③ What is the turning point in the story and how will Mark change?

Good work so far!

– Kate

① Because he is running late + his days plan is to get there.

② ANGRY – detained at the light held back

③ Man in black car scares him

④ He gets there in the end

⑤ Winning tournament changes his attitude.

Note that there is an underlying belief in these transactions between teacher and student. The belief is that learning to write is a process of steady growth and it has many different elements. Doing a piece of writing in this teacher's class is not an event that ends when an assignment is turned in. The message to the student is consistently invitational and encouraging. It is also respectful because it attends to helping the student develop characters and stories in which that student is interested. The intention of the response is to help the student develop some skills related to learning to write, not necessarily to produce a "correct" or finished product.

### Feedback as the Intersection of Objectives, Assessment, and Standards

Practicing good feedback is a critical element of successful teaching. It is part and parcel of a complex array of interactive and interdependent practices that successful teachers do. Another of our colleagues, Caroline Tripp, shows in Figure 19.4 that the development of effective feedback systems is the product of and dependent on strength in three areas: objectives, assessment, and standards of performance and expectations.

First, clear objectives must be communicated to the students in advance. No one can give (or use) specific and detailed feedback without a clear image of what students are supposed to be aiming for. Second, teachers have to have identified or developed appropriate assessment tasks or devices for observing and measuring student performance. Third, they have to have determined the specific standards of performance (or criteria for success) that will indicate proficiency and ensure that students know and understand the criteria so they will be able to use the feedback they are given to improve their performance. Finally is the issue of expectations: teachers have to believe in the stu-

dent's capacity to succeed in order to expend the energy it takes to create good feedback systems or implement them assiduously with all students.

We need to make feedback a regular and ongoing event for students because it will keep them focused on what's important and support them in investing their effort in incremental improvement and achievement. The effort we invest in providing specific, detailed, timely, and personal feedback to students signals to them that we think the work is important, that they can do it, and that we are there to support them in investing their effort effectively.

For feedback to have maximum effect, students have to be expected to use it to improve their work and in many cases taught how to do so. This is where student self-assessment and goal setting become part of the package.

## Component 6: Student Self-Assessment

The act of assessment should be an act of learning. "There are enormous instructional payoffs," says Popham (2006, p. 14), "in making students active, assessment-informed partners in the learning process." This requires that students be continually self-assessing and reorienting their efforts as a result of examining their own work, feedback from peers, and feedback from teachers and it has implications for both skills and dispositions we need to cultivate in students.

Earlier in this chapter we described some of the skills and conditions involved in being "assessment-informed": students must have a clear understanding of performance standards and criteria for good work and know how to apply those standards to work samples (their own or those created by others); they need to know how to analyze the nature and cause of their errors, search for clues on how

**Figure 19.4. Feedback on Product, Progress, and Process**

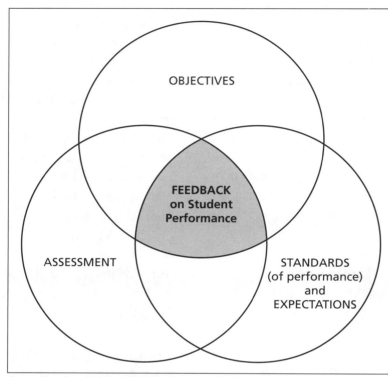

*Source:* Reprinted with permission from Caroline Tripp, 2000.

to correct their errors, decide how to reorient their efforts, and chart a course of action (set goals). They need to receive specific and ongoing feedback and use the feedback to set goals. We need to teach students how to do error analysis and also the techniques of goal setting. (See Chapter Ten, "Principles of Learning," for more on goal setting.)

There are also dispositions we need to cultivate if students are to be "active, assessment-informed" partners. Students need to understand and accept that when they first start to learn something, they're probably not very good at it. Stiggins (2005) says, ". . . while they're learning, it's got to be OK *not* to be good at it at first. We don't want the word 'failure' coming into play." We want students to see that errors are opportunities for learn-

ing, not confirmations of stupidity; that learning is a process—a steady accumulation of knowledge and skill over time—not an event; that achievement occurs along a continuum of incremental progress; that the continuum is not a scale of worthiness or smartness but rather it indicates where they are in the moment in relation to a goal they are working to achieve; that assessment tells them where they are in the journey and what they need to do next, not how good they are as students. We want students to develop an understanding that they aren't supposed to understand everything the first time around; that it is perseverance, quality, and care that lead to achievement; that they have plenty of ability to achieve the goals we set for them but consistent effort and effective strategies are necessary ingredients that add to the recipe for success; that good students solicit help and get lots of feedback on their work and use the feedback to improve their performance. Well beyond assessment these represent beliefs that we consider to be life-liberating because they reorient some counterproductive negative assumptions like mistakes are a sign of weakness, good students can do it by themselves, the faster you learn something the smarter you are, and only a few who are smart can achieve at high levels. (See Chapter Fourteen, "Classroom Climate.")

## Component 7: Student Record Keeping About Progress

Beyond teaching students how to do error analysis and goal setting, another way to build student confidence and ownership of learning is through record keeping and making their performance and progress visible, accessible, and clear to them. Rick Stiggins (2005) makes the point that properly done, this builds "positive emotional engagement" of students with academic work. "It feels good to succeed," says Stiggins. "When the human brain experiences success, it feels good and we're wired to want more. The trick is to take advantage of students' intrinsic love of self-improvement and give them a scaffold they can ascend, step by step." As part of a list of strategies for making assessment "a vehicle to deepen learning and to reveal to students their developing proficiencies . . ." Stiggins and Chappuis (2005, p. 15) recommend several practices that illustrate the way in which teaching students the skills or processes of self-assessment simultaneously reinforces some of the abovementioned dispositions:

- A teacher arranges items on a test according to specific learning targets and prepares a "test analysis" chart for students, with three boxes: "my strengths," "quick review," and "further study." After handing back the corrected test, students identify learning targets they have mastered and write them in the "my strengths" box. Next, students categorize their wrong answers as either "simple mistakes" or "further study." Then students list the simple mistakes in the "quick review" box. Last, students write the rest of the learning targets represented by wrong answers in the "further study" box.
- Students review a collection of their work over time and reflect on their growth. "I have become a better reader this quarter. I used to . . . but now I . . ."
- Students use a collection of their self-assessments to summarize their learning and set goals for future learning: "Here is what I have learned . . . Here is what I need to work on . . ." [Stiggins and Chappuis, 2005].

Linda Hunt, teacher at Bonny Eagle High School in Standish, Maine, has made visible records of student progress, error analysis, reteaching, and goal setting all an integral part of her everyday work with students. She tracks class progress on a test-retest cycle. While individual student scores are not identifiable in the public chart, the number of students scoring at each level is. Linda uses the charts to identify and plan with students what concepts are tripping them up and involves the students in planning where and how reteaching needs to take place. Reteaching (often using peers) and test retakes are normative practices in her class; retakes occur only after reteaching and the highest grade a student gets on a retake replaces any lower grade on the same material. When it comes to self-assessment, the important thing is that she starts with posting the data and having students participate in analyzing trouble spots and identifying focus areas for reteaching.

Linda displays the results of tests and retests on a leaf and branch chart. The top-scoring students do not elect to retake the test. Their scores, if added to a second chart, would put almost all the scores in the top three ranks. All but one of the bottom range scores from the first test have been dramatically improved. Another chart shows an item analysis of the questions on the first test and enumerates how many students missed that item. The class has used this chart to identify concepts they want retaught and to set individual goals.

A third chart records possible actions students are going to take individually. In their personal notebooks they pick a strategy to pursue and make a commitment to it. So in Ms. Hunt's self-assessment mechanisms we see the juncture of two arenas from Chapter Twelve ("Retakes and Redos" and "Grading Practices" with the public display of student data on tests), both for the positive purpose of student motivation. In this class, effective effort is rewarded, and the assessment practices are used to do so.

At this point we return to our beginning premise in Figure 19.1: that teaching, assessment, and learning are intricately intertwined; that "a good assessment makes a good teaching activity, and a good teaching activity makes a good assessment" (Shavelson et al., 1992); and that high quality assessment for learning is an ongoing cycle that involves teachers and students working as partners in the processes of ongoing data collection, feedback, and error analysis.

## Component 8: Frequent Error Analysis by the Teacher

Our most powerful reteaching begins when we analyze the errors of those students who did not show mastery and design reteaching based on under-standing the student thinking that led to the error. There are five key questions to ask when doing error analysis. They are worded here for a team of teachers who are analyzing errors together though they could just as easily be used by an individual teacher.

1. What might the students have been thinking to make this error?
2. How can we find out which of our hypotheses is right?
3. What different reteaching strategies could we use to fix this?
4. How will we plan and manage tasks and time in the period to get fifteen minutes for reteaching a few times a week?
5. How can the team help?

What follows is an excerpt from a "think aloud" error analysis session between a pair of colleagues looking at the test item in Exhibit 19.13 and the data on how ninety-nine students responded to this item. Thirty-nine students had the correct answer (B) and sixty didn't. (The numerical tally was generated by Kim Marshall, at the time principal of the Mather Elementary School in Boston.)

TEACHER A: Twenty-seven students incorrectly chose answer C. What might they have been thinking to pick that one?

TEACHER B: Perhaps they did not know that they need to zero a linear object on a ruler when measuring its length. That is quite common in elementary children. And rulers don't help, since many of them place the first hash marks for measuring one-quarter inch inward from the physical edge of the ruler.

TEACHER B: So maybe the problem is the children don't know they have to put the beginning of

**Exhibit 19.13. Fourth-Grade Mathematics Question**

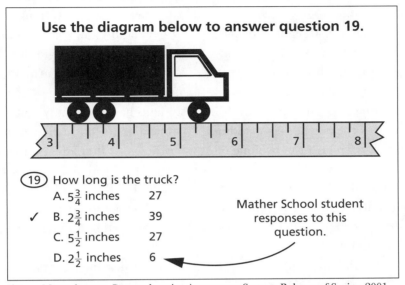

Use the diagram below to answer question 19.

19) How long is the truck?

    A. $5\frac{3}{4}$ inches    27

✓  B. $2\frac{3}{4}$ inches    39

    C. $5\frac{1}{2}$ inches    27

    D. $2\frac{1}{2}$ inches    6

Mather School student responses to this question.

*Source:* Massachusetts Comprehensive Assessment System: Release of Spring 2001 test items.

the object at the exact zero point on the ruler and that zero point might not be the physical left end point of the ruler.

TEACHER A: Or maybe they were just careless and didn't look carefully enough to notice that the truck in the picture was placed at 3 inches instead of 0.

TEACHER B: Or maybe some children are making a mixture of both these two errors.

TEACHER A: So for reteaching we will need to think about what fix-it strategies we could use for tomorrow . . .

TEACHER B: And they should be quite different depending on which error the student was making.

TEACHER A: Let's work out what to do for the children who don't know or don't remember to zero the object on the ruler. We could make up some pretend rulers on oak tag where the

first hash mark was at different distances in from the edge. We could cue the kids that they had to zero the object (say we will have different-size blocks for them to measure) and tell them that it won't be easy to do because these are "trick" rulers.

TEACHER B: We could say you have to measure each object with a different one of the trick rulers and have the kids pass the rulers and the objects around the circle

TEACHER A: Maybe put kids in groups of five . . .

The scenario continues while these teachers analyze the thinking of children who answered C and D. (D is the "best" error. Can you tell why?) And the conversation moves to how to gather data about who made which types of error and how to manage the reteaching.

This think-aloud could also be a teacher looking at her own data and thinking by herself. But imagine the power if teachers had regular collaborative opportunities with dialogue like this to examine data and plan how to reteach a concept!

Prior to reteaching, the teacher (or the team of teachers) will do a little data gathering with the students to see which of their hypotheses about the cause of the error is true. That can be done in minutes by simply asking a few children to think out loud about how they did the problem. This is also a golden opportunity for the teacher to share with students how she or he went about error analysis in preparation for teaching students, and how students can do the same with their own work.

## Component 9: Error Analysis by Students

Teaching students how to do error analysis is a fundamental skill in effective self-assessment and is one of the most significant ways in which we can make assessment an act of learning.

Examine the record in Exhibit 19.14 created by Deborah Levitsky for her eighth-grade team. Weekly quizzes are returned to students the day after the quiz and students fill in their score. Then students have to identify which problems they got wrong and do a form of error analysis in the third box down, as they attempt to analyze the types of errors or confusion their incorrect responses represent. Exhibit 19.15 contains a record filled in well by a student after a quiz on adding fractions followed by an example of a record filled in poorly.

The negative example in Exhibit 19.15 is negative because the student hasn't figured out what is different about the ones he got wrong from the ones he got right. In the positive example, the student has looked closely at the problems she got wrong to see what is throwing her off. A fourth box could be added asking the student what he or she

**Exhibit 19.14.  Test Record**

| Name: | Date _____ | Date _____ | Date _____ | Date _____ |
|---|---|---|---|---|
| What was your score, as a fraction? (e.g., 8/10) | | | | |
| Which problems did you get wrong? (Give the number for each.) | | | | |
| What caught your eye? OR What did you notice? OR What concept did you have problems with? | | | | |
| Plan for improvement | | | | |

*Source:* Deborah Levitsky, New Leaders for New Schools.

**Exhibit 19.15. Student Self-Assessment**

| Name: Positive | Date _____ | Name: Negative | Date _____ |
|---|---|---|---|
| What was your score, as a fraction? (e.g., 8/10) | 7/10 | What was your score, as a fraction? (e.g., 8/10) | 7/10 |
| Which problems did you get wrong? (Give the number for each) | #4, 6, 9 | Which problems did you get wrong? (Give the number for each) | #4, 6, 9 |
| What caught your eye? OR What did you notice? OR What concept did you have problems with? | Getting the common denominator when the numbers are big | What caught your eye? OR What did you notice? OR What concept did you have problems with? | Adding fractions |
| Plan for improvement | Come for extra help in G Block | Plan for improvement | Work harder |

*Source:* Deborah Levitsky, New Leaders for New Schools.

is going to do to learn the item, fill the gap, or prevent the error in the future.

As the negative example in Exhibit 19.13 suggests, students need to be taught how to analyze errors effectively and may need side-by-side coaching by their teacher to really internalize the skill. In fact, whole class lessons in error analysis are a necessity and are very productive when introducing this kind of self-assessment mechanism. A class activity can be students doing error analysis in pairs or in small groups. They help each other identify what went wrong when something went wrong. Teachers can make instructor answer books available in class for students to use after they do exercises or tasks. After checking their responses against the answer books, students have to explain their errors; when they do so, they can get full credit for the item.

Making error analysis the focus of a whole class lesson tacitly sanctions errors as normal and error analysis as a critical vehicle for identifying where we need to focus future effort to improve performance. Thus, student self-assessment and error analysis are a direct manifestation of the belief that effective effort is the key to success.

## Component 10: Planning and Reteaching

Our exploration of assessment thus far underscores how dramatically the job description of teachers has changed. It used to be that teachers would teach and then assess which students learned what was taught. In addition, they would grade students to differentiate who learned the most. Then the class would move on to the next topic.

Now the purpose of assessment is different, and teachers are required to stick with all the students until they reach proficiency, at least in literacy and mathematics, and to accelerate the learning of students who enter behind in academic attainment. This is both a moral and a legal imperative whose requirements stem from law (No Child Left Behind), moral conscience, our democracy's promise of equal opportunity, and economic necessity to compete successfully in the "flat world" (Friedman,

2005). Therefore, the prime purpose of assessment is to inform instruction in order to bring all students to proficiency.

Thus skills and concepts that students didn't get the first time around must be retaught. Thoughtful error analysis sets the stage for meaningful and productive reteaching with those students.

In an era when teachers are feeling pressure to cover curriculum, keep up with pacing guides, and prepare for standardized high-stakes tests, reteaching creates an additional challenge: how to afford the time to reteach and how to manage reteaching with one group while those who "got it" are productively engaged in meaningful work. Here are two examples from secondary teachers:

> In her eleventh grade American history class after a twenty-minute discussion of a current Supreme Court case, Ms. G takes aside five students who showed confusion in yesterday's quiz: they don't understand how some analysts think the Court is tacitly legislating morality. At yesterday afternoon's team meeting with the other history teachers, she got the idea of making an analogy to a family situation where parental rules get interpreted by other caregivers. While she is trying this out, the rest of the class is in groups preparing briefs they would use in arguing before the Court on the case she and they have spent the first twenty minutes explicating. They are going to hand in a flowchart of how their arguments flow logically and indicate what evidence and precedents they would cite.

An earth science teacher describes another scenario:

> In my earth science class we have been watching sections of Al Gore's movie, *An Inconve-*

> *nient Truth,* as part of our study of global warming. I am also using it as a way to show how powerful visual displays can make data more real for audiences. I gathered from yesterday's class discussion that a few students don't really understand why two particular graphs are different ways of representing the same data on temperature change. This is a problem, because these two graphic forms will come up many times over the coming year. Everybody needs to be fluent with them. I have gotten an idea from my science teammates about how to use an animation feature of PowerPoint to show side by side how the two templates could be tracking the same data. While I try this with the three students who are confused, the rest of the class will use a data table from Gore's book to construct a graphic display they think would be persuasive. They can choose from among four forms used in the film or another one if they can justify it. Pairs will make class presentations in the final fifteen minutes of class.

Although we believe that nothing will be as effective as reteaching another way by the students' own teacher (who knows the students, the content of the work, and what was done before), settings outside regular class hours can and should be created for students to fill in missing ideas or skills from recent classes: settings like extra help blocks, tutoring centers, Saturday school, and homework help centers.

The commitment to reteaching and to making it an integral part of classroom life is a poignant reminder of where professional knowledge and beliefs intersect: as a professional community we have to believe that all students are capable of reaching proficiency and that it is our most important work to continue to figure out how to make that possible for all students. Only then will we be tenaciously motivated to invest our creative and collective effort to develop the management and instructional skills requisite for in-class reteaching and to tackle the institutional obstacles (schedules, isolation of teachers, and so on) that stand in the way of making it feasible. Note that in both previous examples, the teacher got the idea for a reteaching strategy from colleagues. Helping each other plan reteaching strategies and useful short activities for the rest of the class is high-leverage use of common planning time among teachers. It is the penultimate indicator of a high-functioning professional learning community.

## Component 11: Goal Setting and Action Planning by Students

It's one thing to set a goal and another to set a goal in such a way that you will work hard on it and attain it. Both the motivational and the technical planning aspects of goal setting are explained at length in Chapter Ten, "Principles of Learning."

## Component 12: Reporting Systems Including Three-Way Conferences

The final component of good classroom assessment is three-way conferences with students, teachers, and parents that are *led by the students*. As readers of this chapter will see, the steps prior to this one lay the groundwork for student-led conferences because they develop a great deal of student involvement through participation in generating criteria, student self-assessment, error analysis, and goal setting. As Rick Stiggins says in his excellent *Student Involved Assessment for Learning* (2005), "We cannot simply plug in student-led parent conferences in a traditional teacher-centered assessment

environment, where students have little idea what the expectations are or how they are doing with respect to those targets. . . . We must set students up to succeed at conferences or such conferences are not worth conducting" (p. 350).

Stiggins goes on describe what it takes to make these conferences productive. The early steps include tasks described previously in this chapter: ensuring that learning expectations are public and clear to everyone and aligned with assessments and helping students self-assess and build collections of quality work (portfolios) that represent their progress.

He recommends sending portfolios or parts of portfolios home periodically, before three-way conferences, to keep parents informed of student progress and invite parent-student conversations. As conference time approaches, have a conference with each student to review their assembled portfolio of products and help them become articulate about how these products compare with the criteria for this kind of work as well as their analysis of what they need to work on next. Role play a good and a bad student-led conference with the entire class. Develop criteria for a good one. Make students responsible for inviting participants and for following up on the invitation so that all are informed. Gregory, Cameron, and Davies (2001) give a sample of a useful letter to send home explaining the purpose of these student-led conferences to parents (pp. 32 and 34). They also give additional useful guidelines for conducting the conference (p. 45).

"When the event happens, make sure students welcome all participants, handle introductions, review the objectives of the meeting, coordinate meeting events, . . . and summarize results" (Stiggins, 1995, p. 353). Thus preparing students to lead the conference is not time lost to instruction, but an episode of instruction itself.

Stiggins also recommends soliciting a follow-up written review of the experience from the parents—perhaps a questionnaire—to help them suggest future learning targets for their child. And he also recommends a debriefing with the students about the experience by writing about it or large-group discussions. Stiggins's chapter on this topic is well worth reading (Chapter Thirteen, pp. 340–356). It includes tips on how to make these student-led conferences practical in high schools and middle schools by only doing one quarter of the class each quarter of the school year; having "substitute" adults available for students without a parent or guardian to show up; and other creative ideas for managing the logistics and timing of such conferences. Readers can probably see that conferences such as these can be powerful motivators for students to focus on their learning goals.

Another important topic is the form of written reports that go home to parents. Numerical and letter grades do not give much information. They represent nonspecific indicators of their children's performance against some unknown set of criteria. Worse, they represent a ranking of their children in a normal distribution curve; that kind of a grade reports only how well the student has done in relation to others with no reference to actual learning at all.

Reports to parents should be as varied as the examples presented in this book, including portfolios, checklists, rubrics, and anecdotal comments. This kind of information-rich report can build the support and involvement of parents in their children's education unavailable in any other way.

It is now part of the conventional wisdom that children do better when their parents are positive partners with the school in their children's education. They cannot do this without information about what their children are supposed to be learn-

ing and about what quality work should look like. Similarly, feedback and reporting generated through authentic assessment give parents specific information and cues about how to help and with what to help their children. No system of letter grades can build this kind of home-school partnership that is now known to be so important for successful schooling.

One of the forces commonly cited as standing in the way of eliminating number and letter grades is that colleges demand grades for their admission process. High schools can't abandon class rank and letter grades, it is argued, because the colleges demand them. Is this really true? Alfie Kohn (1995) reported:

> I wrote letters to the Dean of Admission at Harvard and Brown and said, "What would you do if you got an application from a student who went to a school where there were no grades given at all (much less those unbelievably pernicious additive things like Honor Societies and class ranking), where there was only a sheaf of qualitative assessments of the kid? Would you consider such an applicant?" And both Harvard and Brown wrote back and said, "We not only would, we do." In fact, the guy from Brown added that such a student would probably be at a relative advantage because we would have a lot more information about that student than they would with a 3.6 (what the hell does that mean?). Now at state schools it becomes more problematic, to be sure. At least let's pull the plug on this pseudoargument that says, "We have to continue to destroy kids' interest in learning because the colleges demand it." It's more complicated when you look up close.

Another force to preserve letter and number grades is that they are easily manipulated into summative figures that can be used to compare the effectiveness of schools and districts by magazines, newspapers, and political interests.

There is not at the moment a great call from parents for anecdotal reports or for the use of rubrics. Many parents are satisfied by the simplicity of the letter grading system because they are used to it and because it appears to answer their bottom-line question: "How is my child doing?" Letter grades allow short answers like, "Doing well" (my kid is getting an A); "Fair" (my kid is getting Bs); "Poor" (my kid is getting Cs or Ds). Those kinds of data also invite quick and easy responses by parents: rewards or praise for doing well and punishments, restrictions, or injunctions to buckle down for not doing well. But this kind of reporting also excludes them from involvement in their child's education in any substantive way. Only through examination of real samples of their child's work in comparison to models of what he or she is supposed to be producing (with specific criteria for what is expected) can they see exactly how to help.

Side by side with this call for authentic reporting is the reality of parents' time in a society with many single-parent and two-job families: parents want to be able to digest information about their children's progress quickly. This factor will call for reporting systems that do not overwhelm parents with mounds of rubrics and samples, so teachers should select key products at important benchmarks to share with parents and illustrate the criteria for quality work concisely and compactly. This effort will be rewarded by more support from parents in helping students master what is important.

In describing what reports look like that meet these standards of being informative but time efficient for teachers and for parents, Wiggins (1996) writes:

> Over time what matters is whether Johnny can make discernible progress toward authentic

standards, irrespective of the grades teachers are most comfortable giving. But a single score, like a single grade, is inadequate feedback. A more helpful report would disaggregate performance into its many separate elements: Susan is thorough and accurate at laboratory work, though weak on tests; she is very conscientious and accurate in her homework problems. Jamie's labwork is spotty but indicative of understanding; he does extremely well on tests; and his homework, when done, is excellent—but it isn't always turned in on time, and careless mistakes are made in it.

He then goes on to present models of such reports that could disaggregate performances. In the process, he distinguishes three kinds of data they would provide for each performance element: achievement levels, work quality, and progress:

> Achievement levels refers to exit-level standards of performance. Work quality refers to the caliber of the products produced, at any level (thus allowing us to make the apt kind of distinction made in diving, figure skating, and music competition: degree of difficulty vs. quality points). Progress is measured backwards from exit standards. Progress would thus be charted along multiyear continuums so that a 3rd grader would know how she was doing against 5th grade and (sometimes) 12th grade standards, just as we find in such performance areas as diving, chess, and band.

He then provides an excellent example from Victoria, Australia (Exhibit 19.16). Note that the heavier the shading, the more frequently the student performs at that level. This format allows parents and students to see at a glance the upper limits of what a student can produce and the range of performance level he or she usually does produce.

**Exhibit 19.16. Language Arts Report**

Student: John Doe

Level of Performance: Writing: semester (2/93–6/93)

| A | B | C | D | E | F | G | H | I |

shading is proportional to frequency of scores

Level of Performance: Writing: year (9/92–6/93)

| A | B | C | D | E | F | G | H | I |

shading is proportional to frequency of scores

Progress in Writing: 4/5 (Good, relative to class)

Quality of Work Products: 3/5 (Satisfactory; slightly below average)

Consistency of Work Product Quality: 2/5 (Well below average of class)

Class Data: Writing

Class Range: Writing 5/93

| A | B | C | D | E | F | G | H | I |

Class Performance: Writing 5/93

1. Criteria scores (average of scores on all five leading criteria):
   3.6 (out of 5)

2. Most difficult criterion: "revision leading to polished work":
   2.6 (out of 5)

Please refer to exemplar book for samples of student papers for each level of performance and quality of work, summary of the six genres of writing and five criteria used in scoring, and description of performance

**Work This Quarter**

4 stories, poems
6 analytic papers
1 formal research paper
reflection journal

**Writing Profile**

Genres of writing
strength: persuasive
weakness: analytic
most progress: description

Critieria scores
strength: vitality of ideas (3.6)
weakness: mechanics (2.3)
greatest gain:
   focus (2.4 ➤ 3.2)

Each criterion is judged using a 5-point scale:
5 = top score

Score in parentheses = student's average score

## ENGLISH PROFILES IN WRITING

*Writing Band A*

Uses implements to make marks on paper.

Copies "words" from signs in immediate environment.

Explains the meaning of marks.

Writing shows understanding of difference between print and picture.

*Writing Band B*

Holds pencil/pen using satisfactory grip.

Writes own name.

Writing shows use of vocabulary of print.

Use of letters and other conventional symbols.

*Writing Band F*

Narratives contain introduction, complication, and resolution in logical order.

Complex sentences—principal and subordinate clauses: use of both active and passive voice.

Corrects most spelling, punctuation, grammatical errors in editing other's written work.

A range of vocabulary and grammatical structures.

Understanding of the difference between narrative and other forms of writing.

Consults available sources to improve or enhance writing.

*Writing Band H*

Vocabulary shows awareness of ambiguities and shades of meaning.

Meaning is expressed precisely.

Edits and revises own work to enhance effect of vocabulary, text organization, and layout.

Organization and layout or written text is accurate and appropriate for purpose, situation, and audience.

Figurative language, such as metaphor, is used to convey meaning.

Edits and revises others' writing, improving presentation and structure without losing meaning or message.

*Wiring Band I*

Writes with ease in both short passages and extended writing on most familiar topics.

Extension beyond the conventions of standard English writing in a skillful and effective way.

Uses analogies, symbolism, and irony.

Structures a convincing argument in writing.

*Source:* Reprinted with permission. Wiggins, G. "Honesty and Fairness: Toward Better Grading and Reporting." In T. Guskey (ed.), *1996 A.S.C.D. Workbook.* Alexandria, Va.: Association for Supervision and Curriculum Development, 1996, pp. 173–174. The Association for Supervision and Curriculum Development is a worldwide community of educators advocating sound policies and sharing best practices to achieve the success of each learner. To learn more, visit ASCD at www.ascd.org.

Immediately below these shaded bands of levels are compact statements of the student's progress relative to the class and overall quality of care and thoroughness in the work. To the right is a summary of the types and number of assignments that were given and a profile of strengths and weaknesses (disaggregating the elements of performance). All of this information is laid out on one page and is visually clear.

As a backup to the report form itself is a page that explains the meaning of the nine bands (levels) of student performance. And there is also a background booklet for parents developed by the district that shows by example what the nine levels mean. It contains performance samples of work at each level, rubrics, and sample teacher comments on the work samples. Thus, Wiggins develops a set of criteria for good reporting systems well worth attending to.

Good reporting systems:

- Disaggregate performance into its elements (not, for example, calling "language arts" one global entity).
- Report separately students' achievement level, work quality, and progress (the sample in Exhibit 19.16 also reports consistency).
- Are based on clear descriptions of what each level of performance means, including booklets for parents that spell out quality performance with examples at different levels.

Creating such reporting systems takes considerable effort and time, especially for such steps as creating the background booklet with good examples of performance at each level plus teacher comments highlighting the way in which each paper or sample illustrates the level. Good reporting systems to parents, however, can create their own market. Until people have experienced something new and useful, they don't know they want it. The better it

is, the more they come to feel they can't do without it. Some critics may see this position as naive, believing more cynically that the majority of people will always cling to the easier way: the traditional grading system. It is our belief, however, that parents are likely to want the extra data to help their children perform well and achieve at higher standards. These data will be available only when assessment and reporting systems spring from authentic roots.

Now that we have finished the exposition of the twelve events in good classroom assessment, there are a few areas of general teacher knowledge left to discuss: validity and reliability and methods of gathering data on student learning.

## Validity and Reliability

Now we come to the topics of validity (Is the assessment assessing what we really want to measure?) and reliability (Would the assessment give the same result or score if we administered it again to the same subjects?). For complex performance assessments, validity is a particularly important issue as teachers design assessment tasks. Any assessment task requires a range of student behaviors: perhaps reading or listening to directions or gathering information from sources that require more or less initiative and perseverance, then acting cognitively on the information, then representing the output of that cognition in writing, speaking, or other expressive forms. The more complex the assignment is, the more it resembles a chain where any weak link can cause a break. Complexity is an asset when assessments are used as opportunities for teaching and learning. But a "mastery/not yet" benchmark assessment—that is, an assessment used to signify attainment of some important level of learning for students—must be sure not to contain confounding variables of student performance that are off to the side of what we want to measure. For example, assignments containing a great deal of essay writing to assess science knowledge are good as learning experiences yet may obscure the data on what the student really knows about, say, using microscopes.

The following questions need to be answered satisfactorily if assessments are to be technically sound. The questions include checks (where applicable) on criteria, sample size, objectivity, reliability, and validity:

- Are pre- and posttest measures taken? (Student behavior should be assessed before instruction begins to see if students already know the material or part of the material.)
- Is assessment repeated at some future date after the end of instruction to measure the permanence of the learning?
- Is the sample of items big enough (enough questions on each area) so that chance error doesn't mask what students really know or can do?
- Is the assessment administered objectively, without bias, distractions, or confusion to individuals?
- Are assessments scored or judged accurately?
- Is the assessment reliable?
- Is the assessment device appropriate to students with diverse learning styles, and does it thus represent multiple intelligences? Are assessments culturally responsive?

## Methods of Data Gathering on Student Learning

Fleming and Chambers discovered in 1983 that short-answer paper-and-pencil tests at the fact level dominated assessment in American schools at all levels, K–12. And Goodlad's (1984) data revealed that recitation structures—cycles of teacher questions and student answers, a form of ongoing oral assessment—accounted for over 80 percent of all lessons observed. We can't cite a study more recent than those—so let us all hope those studies truly represent a picture of the past and that when they are replicated one day in the classrooms of our twenty-first century American schools the landscape will be qualitatively different. It is not that there is anything inherently wrong with assessing students' knowledge of facts, or in doing so orally; it is surely one kind of data we want to gather from time to time. Rather it is the pervasiveness of those limited practices—and the relatively superficial nature of the data they yield—that is troubling. Like every other area of teaching examined in this book, there is no one right or best way to gather data about student learning; there exists a repertoire of methods for doing so and that is what we will explore here.

It is the responsibility of every teacher to develop a wide repertoire of ways to assess student learning because it enables us to assess various types of learners and learning styles. But more than that, it enables us to match assessment format to the cognitive level of objectives being assessed, and to align assessment practices with the demands of twenty-first century curricula. These demands include knowing how to use knowledge and skills, thinking globally and critically, applying knowledge to novel situations, analyzing information, communicating, collaborating, solving problems, making decisions, using technology as a tool for learning, functioning as a productive contributor within an organizational setting, and using all of these skills to understand and address global issues (Saltpeter, 2003). Obviously more than paper-and-pencil short-answer tests, essays, and written reports are needed (though these will remain part of our map).

We are going to describe a number of assessment devices and the kind of learning for which they are appropriate. Each device has a place including short-answer tests, essays, and written reports. But teachers must now have the capacity to design and use a much wider range of assessment devices because they will be aiming squarely for the kinds of learning the devices measure. Figure 19.5 identifies the repertoire of assessment devices and shows their relationships.

## Written Tests

### Short Answer

There is a place for short-answer tests (fill in the blank, true-false, multiple choice) in educational practice, but it is much smaller than the place it once held. Though they are not "authentic," short-answer quizzes, where students respond with right answers (like facts on timed tests, a series of recall questions involving content knowledge, and so on), enable us to gather data about whether students have basic foundation knowledge or mastery of certain skills. Short-answer quizzes can be appropriate whenever students need feedback on their factual knowledge to identify what to study. Short-answer quizzes can also be oral, a much neglected medium. Short-answer oral quizzes can allow students' assessment to be individualized, and they can also be given by students to one another. Then benchmark certification quizzes can be given by the teacher when students declare themselves ready for certification (such as ready for the multiplication fact mastery test on tables).

When the characteristics of good assessment are applied to short-answer quizzes, students know what the criteria for success are (for example, the pack of math flash cards in sixty seconds, knowledge of all the states and capitals without error).

Perhaps they keep track of their own progress and use the data on each set of results to plan what and how to study next to reach the criteria.

### Essays

An essay test is a highly verbal task, performed orally or in writing, that asks students to do higher-level thinking using information acquired over a period of time. The thinking task may ask students to take and defend a point of view, providing specific evidence, or to show relationships of cause and effect between events or conditions and actions or outcomes.

Essays should continue to play a significant role in assessment, but paper-and-pencil essays are only one format. There are new questions in the literature these days about the reliability of handwritten essays in an era when many students are accustomed to using the computer as their primary writing tool. There is speculation and a growing body of research that being required to handwrite essay responses creates a handicapping condition that interferes with student expression. Increased use of keyboard technology may alleviate this problem, but oral presentations also could be used much more frequently, and student performance could be assessed on the same criteria of organization, evidence to support claims, sentence structure, and so forth. Curry and Samara (1994) present a product guide for oral reports:

*Introduction*—speaker introduced; topic described; impetus for project explained; expected outcomes discussed

*Beginning*—topic described in general terms; major points outlined; audience involved

*Middle*—major points supported with details; intermittent summarizations; transition statements link major points; audience involved with content

**Figure 19.5. Assessment Devices for Gathering Data on Student Learning**

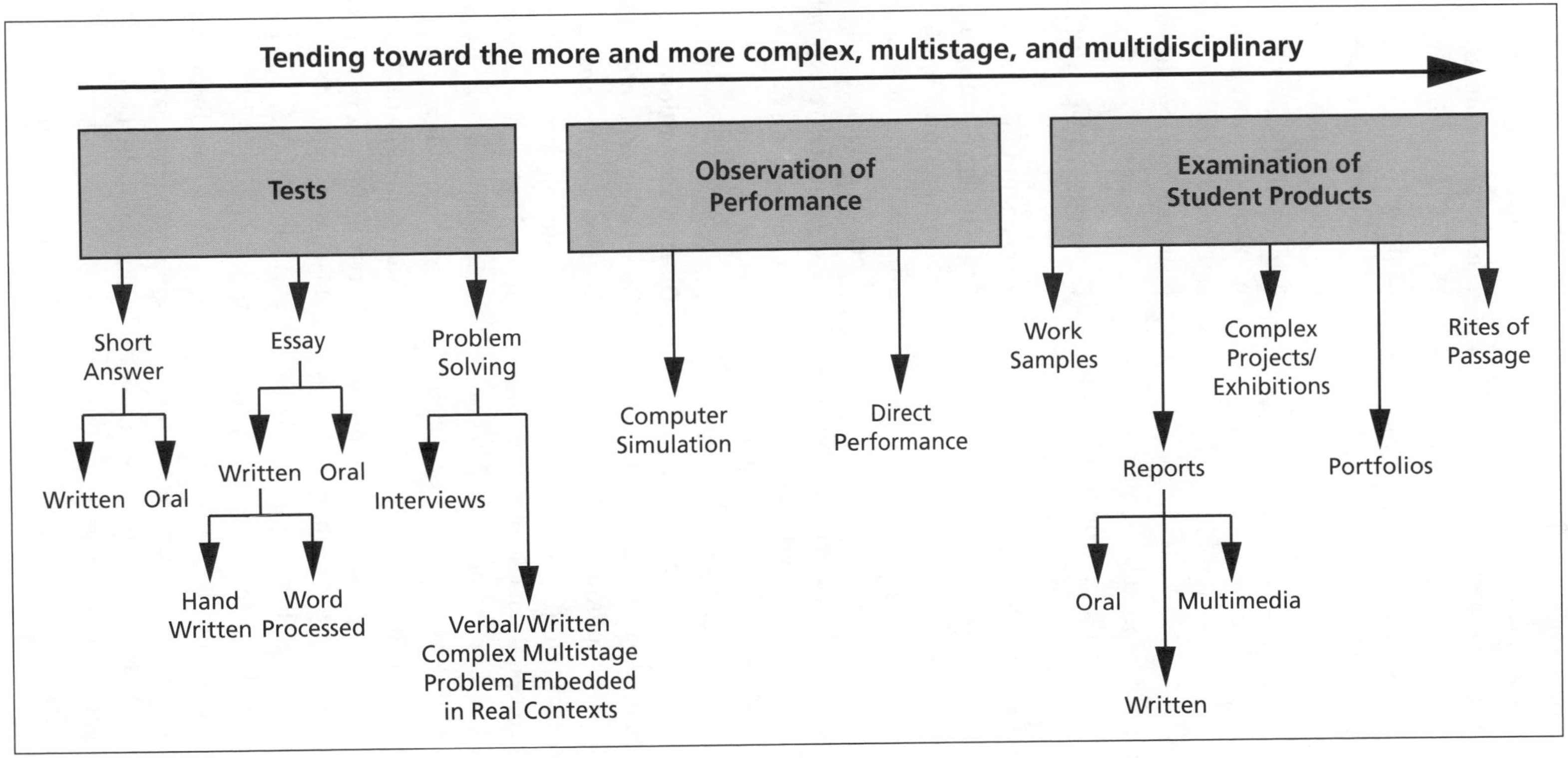

Tending toward the more and more complex, multistage, and multidisciplinary

*Summary*—major points reviewed; call to action/ask for acceptance of concepts/beliefs/positions

*Body language*—sustained eye contact with each member of the audience; formal posture; natural gestures/expressions, clear/well-paced voice

*Use of visual aids*—to support major points; intermittent use; limited

This guide could be used by teachers or students, or both, as criteria for giving feedback to students on their performances. It would also be a formative guide for students in preparing their oral reports.

### Problem-Solving Tasks

Complex problems embedded in real-life situations can be found in many current development efforts at national, state, and district levels. Exhibit 19.17 is an example drawn from the National Assessment of Educational Progress Pilot Study of Higher-Order Thinking Skills Assessment Techniques in Science and Mathematics (NAEP, 1987).

Tasks like these tend to be engaging to students because of their personal relevance. But they also go beyond traditional word problems. This one demands that students invent some sort of protocol for converting performances in the three events to individual scores of some kind. No such protocol or guideline is given in the problem; the student has to create it. A student might decide to assign points for first-place finishes, second-place finishes, and so on and then add up the totals for each competitor (being careful to have most points for first place and not assigning 1 to first—unless the lowest point total would be the winner, another piece of sophisticated thinking). At another

level, a student might create a weighting scheme for actual results in the events, regardless of what place someone finished in the event. In either case, explaining the solution is as important as the actual answer.

This sort of item assesses a range of student capacities. In this case, they need the ability to read and interpret a table of data, analyze the scores and interpret them into rank order for each event, and invent a scoring rule for comparing overall performance and to explain that rule.

## Observation of Performance

Assessment of performances gathers data on students in the act of doing something—solving a problem, conducting a science experiment, doing a drawing—and thus avoids the possible mediating effects of language skills called for in traditional tests. The data are as much about how the student was performing the operation as about the final results.

### Direct Observation

Direct observation of student performance allows teachers to observe exactly what they want to assess without injecting confounding variables into the process as written tests usually do. Suppose you want to know if students understand what variables in science really are; in addition you want to know if they can apply that knowledge to designing and carrying out an experiment that controls the variables and uses consistency and preciseness to reach a conclusion. Then you might design a task like the following.

Shavelson, Baxter, and Pine (1992) cite a task where students have to figure out which of three brands of paper towels will hold the most water. To do that task, students take samples from each of the three rolls of paper towel, making sure the samples

**Exhibit 19.17. Problem-Solving Assessment Task**

### Triathlon: Interpreting Data

Students are required by this paper-and-pencil task to examine data about five children competing in three athletic events and decide which of the five children would be the all-around winner. Students must devise their own approach for computing and interpreting the data and explain why they have selected a particular "winner." Students must be careful in their interpretation, because the lower scores are better in the 50-yard dash, while the converse is true in the frisbee and weight lift.

### Student Assessment Sheet

Joe, Sarah, Jose, Zabi, and Kim decided to hold their own Olympics after watching the Olympics on TV. They needed to decide what events to have at their Olympics. Joe and Jose wanted a weight lift and frisbee toss event. Sarah, Zabi, and Kim thought running a race would be fun. The children decided to have all three events. They also decided to make each event of the same importance. They held their Olympics one day after school. The children's parents were the judges and kept the children's scores on each of the events.

The children's scores for each of the events are listed below:

| Child's Name | Frisbee Toss | Weight Lift | 50-Yard Dash |
|---|---|---|---|
| Joe | 40 yards | 205 pounds | 9.5 seconds |
| Jose | 30 yards | 170 pounds | 8.0 seconds |
| Kim | 45 yards | 130 pounds | 9.0 seconds |
| Sarah | 28 yards | 120 pounds | 7.6 seconds |
| Zabi | 48 yards | 140 pounds | 8.3 seconds |

**Record Findings:** (A) Who will be the all-around winner?

(B) Explain how you decided who would be the all-around winner. Be sure to show all your work.

**Account for Findings:**

_____

_____

_____

*Source:* Reprinted with permission. Archbald, D., and Newmann, F. M. *Beyond Standardized Tests: Assessing Authentic Academic Achievement in Secondary School.* Reston, Va.: National Association of Secondary School Principals, 1988, pp. 15–16. Copyright © 1988, National Association of Secondary School Principals. For more information on NASSP products and services to promote excellence in middle level and high school leadership, visit www.principals.org.

are the same size; saturate each with water, making sure they are completely saturated; then measure how much water each saturated towel holds, either by weighing or squeezing out the towel and measuring the volume of water squeezed out (a slightly less reliable method since the towels may be unequal in how much water they retain). If there is only one scale to do the weighing, the student has to be sure excess water from the previous weighing is removed before weighing the second towel.

For such tasks it is relatively simple to develop a protocol (that is, a form with places for an observer to record checks or scores) that records how well the student did on various dimensions of the task (equal-size samples, completeness in saturation, care in measuring and weighing, recording of results). (See Exhibit 19.18.) "Moreover," say Shavelson and Baxter, "the scoring scheme should capture the procedure used and could thereby characterize performance in terms of both processes and outcomes."

Doing large-scale standardized assessments of large numbers of students on activities such as the paper towel task is expensive and time-consuming compared to paper-and-pencil tests. Rooms have to be set up with stations for each task, and a trained observer has to score individual students as they rotate through the stations. Despite the cost, Shavelson and Baxter's own research has made it clear that such performance assessments yield valid and reliable measurement results. They also point out, however, that "performance tasks vary on a number of factors, especially knowledge-domain specificity and requirements for students to monitor their own performance as they proceed on a task. Some are inherently more difficult than others. More importantly, some students perform well on one task and others perform well on another task. Consequently, a number of assessment tasks are needed to gener-

alize, with any degree of confidence, from students' performance to the science domain of interest" (p. 358).

This sort of assessment provides such a direct and realistic measure of the thinking skills students should be learning that it remains valuable for states to sample populations of their students on an annual basis. This sampling will give a reliable statistical report card on how well particular districts are doing in developing the skills and work habits that are valued, even if expense prohibits assessing all children by direct observation in the near future.

Individual teachers can use direct observation of performance much more in assessing their own students, and not only in science. For example, in math, how many times does a teacher have to observe a student doing a complicated long division problem successfully to know the child can do long division? Maybe twice. And he or she can record mastery on a checklist. Suppose you have a student who thinks aloud as she does a word problem. How many such problems do you have to witness the student solving to know that she follows orderly steps: identifies the real problem, searches to separate relevant from irrelevant data, and identifies the operation that is called for by the problem? Probably not very many.

### Computer Simulation

To simplify and make more economical the observation of student performance, many performances can be converted into computer simulations, which avoid the confounding variables of written tests and get straight to what we want to assess. (This remains true as long as students know how to operate the computer adequately.)

Shavelson, Baxter, and Pine (1992) have constructed a task where students connect batteries, bulbs, and wires in a circuit to determine the contents of a set of mystery boxes:

**Exhibit 19.18.  Paper Towels Score Form**

**Paper Towels Score Form**

*Student* _____ *Observer* _____ *Score* ____

1. Method for getting towel wet

| A. Container | B. Drops | C. Tray (surface) | D. No Method |
|---|---|---|---|
| Put towel in/pour water in/ | | Towel on tray/pour water on | |
| 1 pitcher or 3 beakers/glasses | | Pour water on tray/put towel in | |

2. Saturation

| A. Yes | B. No | C. Controlled (same amount of water—all towels) |
|---|---|---|

3. Determine Result

   A. Weigh towel

   B. Squeeze towel/measure water (weight or volume)

   C. Measure water in/out

   D. Count # drops until saturated

   E. Irrelevant measurement (i.e., time to soak up water, see how far drops spread out, feel thickness)

   F. Other

4. Care in saturation and/or measuring Yes No A little sloppy (+/−)

5. Correct result                        Most                                    Least

| Grade | Method | Saturate | Determine Result | Care in Measuring | Correct Answers |
|---|---|---|---|---|---|
| A | Yes | Yes | Yes | Yes | Both |
| B | Yes | Yes | Yes | No | One or Both |
| C | Yes | Controlled | Yes | Yes/No | One or Both |
| D | Yes | No or Inconsistent | | Yes/No | One or Both |
| F | Inconsistent or | No and Irrelevant | | Yes/No | One or Both |

*Source:* Reprinted with permission. Shavelson, R. J., Baster, G. P., and Pine, J. "Performance Assessment in Science." *Applied Measurement in Education,* 1991, *4,* 353.

For the electric circuits investigation, students used a Macintosh computer with a mouse to connect circuits with the mystery boxes to determine their contents [see Figure 19.6].

The intensity of the luminosity of the bulb in a real external circuit was accurately simulated. Students connected a multitude of circuits if they so desired. Alternatively, they could leave one completed circuit on the screen for comparative purposes. Instructions on how to record answers, erase wires, save their work, or look at a previous page of their work on the screen were given in a teacher-directed tutorial format prior to the test. The computer recorded every move the student made [p. 355].

Similar computer simulations have been developed in physics, chemistry, and mathematics and should prove exciting and flexible ways to augment assessment of student performance. An

**Figure 19.6. Computer Simulation for Assessment**

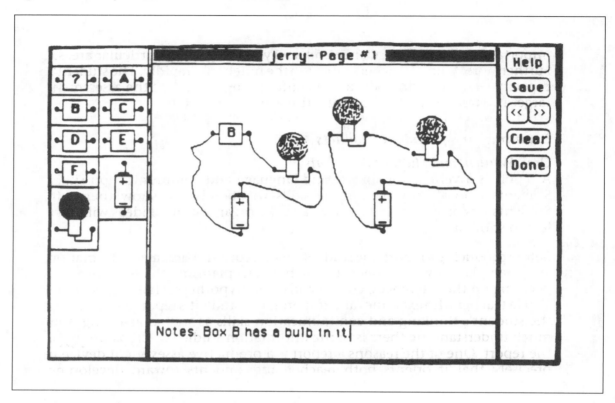

added benefit is that students can schedule taking tests on computers at any time agreeable to them and their teachers.

## Examination of Student Products

### Notebooks

An alternative way to get direct data on student performance is through notebooks in which students record their actions and their thinking. Students are asked to use the notebooks while they conduct hands-on investigations. Shavelson (Shavelson, Baxter, and Pine, 1992, p. 352) praises this methodology because it is inexpensive and "provides an opportunity for students to express themselves in writing, an important skill in doing science and a

way of integrating curricular areas." Furthermore, trained teachers can score the notebooks rapidly. The student's capacity to write clearly becomes a confounding variable if the assessment target is purely related to scientific thinking.

### Reports: Oral, Written, and Multimedia

A report is a vehicle for showcasing language and communication skills. Students who already have these skills will be able to show them off. Students less proficient in language and the organization of ideas will have less to showcase.

Before producing a report, the student must record and organize information and then plan how to present it, which means planning the sequence and deciding on the inferences, conclusions, and hypotheses that will be in it. Studies of writers writing show that the drafting and revision process itself produces some of the steps above. Report writing, like other forms of creative writing, is not the orderly process one might think. "I write what I know to find out what I think," said Henry Glassie in *Passing the Time in Ballymenone*, an anthropological study of Irish village life. Thus, a teacher who examines and responds to a student's report is examining the student's thinking and communication skills as well as assessing how much understanding there is of the information studied in preparation for the report. One of the reasons a report is a productive assessment device is precisely that it orients both teacher and students toward developing communication skills. A teacher is implicitly stating an objective to improve research, organization, and communication skills when assigning a report.

A report is supposed to be a way for students to show they have internalized a body of knowledge and can do something intellectual with it beyond reciting facts. Thus, reports typically ask students to go beyond information and do any one or several of the following operations: make inferences, give conclusions supported by appropriately selected evidence, make reasoned and supportable predictions or hypotheses, give opinions, surface assumptions, and sometimes make original connections. (These thinking operations can be called for and successfully produced by primary grade children given appropriate experiences and guidance.) Thus, the nature of the report assigned makes the report as assessment a potential vehicle for teaching organization and thinking skills. Getting ready to produce the report should therefore be an "episode of learning" (Wolf, LeMahieu, and Eresh, 1992).

Report writing is not something students are born knowing how to do or learn to do by being assigned the task. Teachers are obligated to teach students how to produce reports, and that means breaking down the task into component parts. The link between assessment and the teaching of report writing is the model of good performance provided at the beginning and the explicit analysis of those good products with the students: "What about this good report we are looking at makes it a good report?"

Similarly, if the report is oral or multimedia, videotapes of former students delivering good reports or a preserved exemplar of an excellent multimedia report need to be presented to students and analyzed for their good points. Analysis means showing exactly where examples of criterion behaviors occur—for example: "Now see how this sentence summarizes the main points of the previous four paragraphs? That's what I'm looking for in your reports when I say 'summary sentences' on your criteria sheet. Can anyone find a sentence like that in the second section of the paper?" Here is an example for a multimedia report: "Notice how she uses the music to set a mood at the beginning before saying any words but then brings music back with the jazz piece when the mood she wants is different. Be looking for music that fits with your message in a similar way."

The teacher-student dialogue might go like this:

TEACHER: What did you notice about this student's use of visual material?

STUDENT: I noticed that for every main idea there was a different visual—either a chart or a picture—to go with it.

TEACHER: Right, and that's something I'll be looking for in your reports too. But the visuals have to be a good fit with the point you're making. How were these a good fit?

STUDENT:  Well, when she had a chart with the words, it wasn't really a good fit. It was just having the words printed neatly and using different colors. But when she had the picture of the riot, that was a good fit to show how violent the reaction to the draft really was!

## Exhibitions

An exhibition is a complex project that displays the student's capacity to perform a set of higher-level thinking skills that the school thinks are important. The sixth-grade project developed by Penny Knox (Exhibit 19.5) in which students write a letter describing a culture is an exhibition. It takes the students all year to gather the knowledge and skills required to do it well. All students are expected to do it, and the criteria for success are clearly spelled out in a rubric. In addition, they have several trial runs at the final product before they produce the version that "counts."

In the vision of high school articulated by Ted Sizer's Coalition of Essential Schools, an exhibition is both a gateway to graduation and a target for the student's four years of high school. Each student must present an exhibition, and it must meet minimum standards if that student is to graduate.

An exhibition also serves as a powerful stimulus to faculty dialogue about what these skills for graduation should be. The list almost always includes higher-level thinking and communication skills as with the item, "Can state assumptions and argue a point of view with clear evidence." Graduation targets like these push across departmental boundaries and cause teachers to plan within their disciplines for how they can teach for them. They also increase interdepartmental communication and open the door for integration of curriculum. Thus, "graduation by exhibition" becomes a genuine force for bringing a school together and shaping practices around certain core outcomes it wants for students (Saphier and D'Auria, 1993).

When an exhibition is required for graduation, its magnitude and complexity vary from school to school. Sid Smith and his faculty moved English High School in Boston a significant step forward when they instituted an exhibition requiring all students to write a two-page position paper on a controversial issue of their choice: "It formed the basis of English High School's commitment to decide what its students must know and be able to do to earn their high school diploma. It was the start of the school's effort to require all its students to publicly demonstrate their skills and knowledge" (Smith, 1993, p. 17). That an exhibition requirement applies to all students for graduation and that it is assessed by competency rather than by grades and numbers makes it a lever for raising standards for all. It also makes schools gauge both the strength of their belief that all students can achieve to a high level and their determination to get them there.

If a position paper is a start on the process of developing graduation by exhibition, the multiple exhibitions collected in a portfolio that are required for graduation from Walden III High School in Racine, Wisconsin, represent maturity. Archbald and Newman, drawing on the student handbook written by Tom Feeney, a teacher at the school, summarize the exhibition requirements in Exhibit 19.19.

Requiring a wide-ranging portfolio of this magnitude takes years of faculty collaboration on developing the topics, standards, scoring rubrics, and procedures for students to navigate their way to successful completion. A school that has thought out graduation requirements this far and expressed them in terms of performance knows what it stands for. It is also clear that to prepare students to succeed on these assessments requires substantial integration and coherence between

**Exhibit 19.19. Exhibition Requirements at Walden III High School**

*EXHIBITION REQUIREMENTS AT WALDEN III HIGH SCHOOL, RACINE, WISCONSIN*

**The Portfolio.** The portfolio, developed during the first semester of the senior year, is intended to be "a reflection and analysis of the graduating senior's own life and times." Its requirements are:

1. *A written autobiography,* descriptive, introspective, and analytical. School records and other indicators of participation may be included.
2. *A reflection of work,* including an analysis of the significance of the work experiences for the graduating senior's life. A resume can be included.
3. *Two letters of recommendation* (at minimum) from any sources chosen by the student.
4. *A reading record* including a bibliography, annotated if desired, and two mini book reports. Reading test scores may be included.
5. *An essay on ethics* exhibiting contemplation of the subject and describing the student's own ethical code.
6. *An artistic product or written report* on art and an *essay on artistic standards* for judging quality in a chosen area of art.
7. *A written report analyzing mass media*: who or what controls mass media, toward what ends, and with what effects. Evidence of experience with mass media may be included.
8. *A written summary and evaluation of the student's coursework in science/technology; a written description of a scientific experiment* illustrating the application of the scientific method; an *analytical essay* (with examples) on social consequences of science and technology; and an *essay* on the nature and use of computers in modern society.

**The Project.** Every graduating senior must write a library-research-based paper that analyzes an event, set of events, or theme in American history. A national comparative approach can be used in the analysis. The student must be prepared to field questions about the paper in the overview of American history during the presentations, which are given in the second semester of the senior year.

**The Presentations.** Each of the above eight components of the portfolio, plus the project, must be presented orally and in writing to the ROPE committee.

Six additional oral presentations are also required. However, there are no written reports or new products required by the committee. Supporting documents or other forms of evidence may be used. Assessment of proficiency is based on the demonstration of knowledge and skills during the presentations in each of the following areas:

9. *Mathematics knowledge and skills* should be demonstrated by a combination of course evaluations, test results, and worksheets presented before the committee; and by the ability to competently field mathematics questions asked during the demonstration.
10. Knowledge of American government should be demonstrated by discussion of the purpose of government; the individual's relationship to the state; the ideals, functions, and problems of American political institutions; and selected contemporary issues and political events. Supporting materials can be used.
11. The personal proficiency demonstration requires the student to think about and organize a presentation about the requirements of adult living in our society in terms of personal fulfillment, social skills, and practical competencies; and to discuss his or her own strengths and weaknesses in everyday living skills (health, home economics, mechanics, etc.) and interpersonal relations.
12. Knowledge of geography should be demonstrated in a presentation that covers the basic principles and questions of the discipline; identification of basic landforms, places and names; and the scientific and social significance of geographical information.
13. Evidence of the graduating senior's successful completion of a physical challenge must be presented to the ROPE committee.
14. A demonstration of competency in English (written and spoken) is provided in virtually all the portfolio and project requirements. These, and any additional evidence the graduating senior may wish to present to the committee, fulfill the requirements of the presentation in the English competency area.

*Source:* Reprinted with permission. Archbald, D., and Newmann, F. M. *Beyond Standardized Tests: Assessing Authentic Academic Achievement in Secondary School.* Reston, Va.: National Association of Secondary School Principals, 1988, pp. 24–25.

departments. Such is the promise of the authentic assessment movement.

## Portfolios

A portfolio is a "purposeful collection of student work that tells the story of a student's efforts, progress or achievement in a given area" (Stiggins and Conklin, 1992). Portfolios provide the database for teachers to continue exploring and refining successful performance directly with students. They also provide a tangible bank of products over time that reveal (ideally) how far students have come. Thus, they become a credible record of progress that can provoke "wow!" responses from parents and students alike in a way grades or compliments never could.

"The feature that defines a portfolio and differentiates it from a folder or collection of work is the selection mechanism. Based on the purpose or purposes, pieces are included to demonstrate progress toward a stated aim. A portfolio is a subset of all work done; something must be rejected for it to be constructed" (Mitchell, 1992, p. 107). What makes portfolios an important tool in the framework developed in this chapter is that students do a self-assessment and choose what goes into the portfolio.

A crucial role for the teacher is to pose questions that the students use to select items for inclusion. Ruth Mitchell (1992) supplies one set of questions that might be used in having students reflect on a selection:

1. Why did you select this particular piece of writing? (Why does this piece stand out from the rest of your work?)
2. What do you see as the special strengths of this work?
3. What was especially important to you when you were writing this piece?
4. What have you learned about writing from your work on this piece?
5. If you could go on working on this piece, what would you do?
6. What kind of writing would you like to do in the future?
7. Now that you have looked at your collection of writing and answered these questions, can you identify a particular technique or interest that you would like to try out or investigate in future pieces of writing? If so, what is it? [p. 110].

These questions show how portfolios set the stage for goal setting as well as self-evaluation. The last question is actually asking the student to set a goal.

Portfolios also enable a powerful form of parent involvement. They can be sent home periodically with students and parents asked to read them thoroughly. Then they are asked to write back (or communicate in some other way) what they noticed, enjoyed, or were concerned about in their child's work. Kathryn Howard uses the form in Exhibit 19.20 to invite parents to participate in portfolios in her eighth-grade writing course.

The concept of involving students in self-evaluation and goal setting makes portfolios desirable vehicles for student development in any subject area, including math and science. Knight (1992) and others show how having students save their best tests, best labs, and other best pieces that show forms of their mathematical and scientific knowledge can provoke the kind of self-examination and goal setting that goes with being an effective student.

Developing a climate of self-examination and reflection does not come without its costs. One author writes:

**Exhibit 19.20.  Parent Portfolio Review and Reflection**

*Student* _____

*Reader*   _____

*Date*     _____

Please read everything in your child's writing folder, including drafts and commentary. Each piece is set up in back-to-front order, from rough draft to final copy. Further, each piece is accompanied by both student and teacher comments on the piece and writing process. Finally, the folders also include written questionnaires where students write about their strengths and weaknesses as writers.

When you have read the folders, please talk to your children about their writing. In addition, please take a few minutes to respond to these questions:

- Which piece of writing in the folder tells you most about your child's writing?
- What does it tell you?
- What do you see as the strengths in your child's writing?
- What do you see as needing to be addressed in your child's growth and development as a writer?
- What suggestions do you have that might aid the class's growth as writers?
- Other comments or suggestions?

Thank you so much for investing this time in your child's writing.

*Source:* Reprinted with the permission of the Free Press, a division of Simon & Schuster, from Kathryn Howard in *Testing for Learning: How New Approaches to Evaluation Can Improve American Schools,* by Ruth Mitchell. Copyright © 1992 by Ruth Mitchell, p. 112.

Portfolios are messy. They demand intimate and often frighteningly subjective talk with students. Portfolios are work. Teachers who ask students to read their own progress in the "footprints" of their works have to coax and bicker with individuals who are used to being assessed [by others]. Halfway through the semester, at least a half dozen recalcitrants will lose every paper or sketch they have ever owned. More important, teachers have to struggle to read and make sense of whole works and patterns of growth. Hence, hard questions arise: "Why bother? What comes out of portfolio assessment?" The immediate answer lies in integrity and the validity of the information we gain about how and what students learn [Wolf, 1992].

Judith Warren Little once commented in an audiotaped interview (Sparks, 1993) that the most powerful form of staff development might be to put a group of teachers in one room with samples of student work. Her point was that in comparing and debating the merits of actual student performances, teachers refine their concepts of standards; in addition, teachers inevitably get hooked into discussions of which learning experiences to use to develop specific student capacities.

It has been our experience that in these situations, teachers go on to invent learning experiences together. Through the examination of student work, teachers are drawn into authentic and productive conversations about teaching that comprise true collegiality. Portfolios of student work provide the raw material in organized form for this kind of collegial sharing, refining, and curriculum development. Thus it is reasonable to assume that use of student portfolios can encourage more collaborative work among teachers. It would certainly be a useful practice in schools that are seeking to develop a collaborative culture.

# Reflecting on Assessment

Many prominent thinkers in the assessment movement (Wolf, 1992; Zessoules and Gardner, 1991) use the phrase "assessment as a moment for learning" to convey the point that assessment should be integral to planning lessons, not end points. Others have made the point that assessment is an occasion for learning. This is because when students are given a challenging problem they are able to see relationships and connections that were not obvious to them before. The learning that takes place is a function of the interaction between the student(s) and the task or the students and each other. It does not take place because the teacher is actively mediating the students' thinking (Baron, 1989, p. 315).

Those are the beliefs behind "assessment as a moment for learning," and they are reflected in the following statements:

> Less noticed is that tests routinely fail to inform learning. The efficient collection of data about a sample of student performance for an outside audience has come to dominate over the first audiences and obligations for assessment: to make students and teachers acute critics of the quality of work and able discussants of what should count as excellence. . . . Students infrequently have the opportunity to make use of what they learn from earlier performances to inform a second try. In essence, rarely are school assessments the occasion for making

public the standards and strategies for doing good work. Yet all we know regarding the generation of worthwhile work tells us that it requires incubation, revision, collaboration, and the public display of and debate about failure, risk, and excellence.

The implication for the redesign of current testing is that a major portion of school-based assessment should be conceived as an episode in which students learn how to write or experiment, or do research, using the power of assessment to push them along the "zigzag path" that Magdeline Lampert cites in her presentations to her students at the University of Michigan. In more specific terms, assessment ought to:

- Be live: that is, conducted in the face and threat and promise of serious and ongoing work of consequence for the student.
- Take the form of a series of iterative episodes of work followed by time for personal reflection and the gathering of responses from peers, mentors, and judges.
- Allow an individual ways and time for making use of the resulting chorus of opinion so as to make it possible to decide what in the criticism is apt, and what misses the mark.
- Permit that individual to plow the fruits of critique and reflection back into his or her final response [or next try] [Wolf, 1992].

These recommendations imply that teachers must create the time and place in class for students to critique one another's work—and not just writing. They apply as well to dinosaur fact sheets produced by ninth graders, geometry proofs of tenth graders, and science experiments of fifth graders. This collaboration and critique is characteristic of a "portfolio culture, that is, a setting where there is frequent and public discussion about what makes for good work and a clear sense that good work takes a long time to emerge." It thus becomes incumbent on teachers to create frequent opportunities for these public discussions about good work.

In these discussions, "students have access to the criteria that will be used to score their work and those criteria are explained, even debated" (Wolfe, 1992). The point is that they learn about the place of qualities like the ability to pose an interesting problem. Modern assessment puts the teacher, not the testing company, in charge because assessment is built systematically into instruction. Because what is assessed is students' evolving and improving process, not just one-time performances, the data collected are about process and strategy as well as product. Student self-assessment is at the core.

In a tenth-grade geometry class, for example, each student is assigned different proofs for homework. Twice a week at the beginning of class, students show their proofs to a partner, who reads the proof and critiques it according to the criteria of logical order, completeness, and readability. (Readability includes neatness and also whether abbreviations and references can be understood.) The teacher periodically models how to do these critiques with proofs at the board; students change partners each day when they critique each other.

In another classroom, the teacher uses self-evaluation to collect data about eighth graders' ability to play different roles in discussion groups (for example, summarizing, stating issues, breaking tension). She has told the students she is collecting the self-evaluations to see whether they have increased their ability to play multiple roles and so that she can identify students who need more help. Each role has been explained and modeled by the teacher, and students have practiced them in structured exercises. Now students are asked to participate supportively in a new group discussion. In their self-evaluation, they are to record what role or

roles they see themselves as having played and the roles played by every other member of their group. They have succeeded when they can claim three or more different roles and the majority of their group supports their claims. One instance of role-appropriate behavior is enough to claim that role. The teacher meets with students who play fewer than three roles and has them pick an additional one to try in the next discussion. Students who claim more roles than their group testifies to are asked to write examples of the unsupported roles, which the teacher may accept as evidence. In her grade book she keeps a checklist of students who meet the criteria. For comparative purposes she has her own observational records of which roles individuals played before instruction.

Self-evaluation can also yield added dividends of more student involvement, more awareness of criteria, and better discrimination of quality. Waters, MacMullen, and Glade (1992) have students periodically isolate their best work from the collections in their writing folders. As they explain, "The making of this collection provides students with an on-going opportunity to review and analyze their best work, choose what best represents him or her, establish a sense of progress, [and] establish a base line from which to move ahead." It also creates the groundwork for individual teacher-student conferences around the collection. Such conferences are unmatched opportunities for involving students in goal setting and helping them generate ownership for their own learning.

## Parting Thoughts

### Teaching Teams and Assessments

It is rare in teacher training for candidates to study the design of assessment instruments, and yet we are arguing here that the kind of thinking that goes into the design and creation of assessment instruments (whatever their form—written tests, performances, exhibitions, essays, or something else) is the foundation of good instruction. Put another way, the detailed conceptualization, design of assessment criteria, and assessment tasks enable teachers to "plan backward" (Sizer, 1992, p. 102). The design of effective learning experiences flows from thinking that starts with the students' point of view and flows from clarity about what teachers want the students to know and be able to do at the end of the experience. Thus, the clearest articulation of the objective appears in the assessment task and its criteria for success. In fact, the objective is not fully conceptualized until its assessment is defined.

From this perspective, then, expanding the ability to design different kinds of high-quality assessment tasks is essential to the professional teacher. If teaching is not a profession but rather a trade that any competent person can do with a year of basic training, then we can let others make the decisions and do the design work on assessments. But if we are a profession, we must develop the capacity to design and continually refine our own assessments based on changing students and changing curricula.

## Standards

On observing the proliferation of the use of standardized tests in 1920, Walter Lippmann, the noted journalist, wrote: "We will breed generations of students and educators who don't believe that those who begin weak can ever become strong." He was right.

Standardized tests are designed to produce normal distributions, not to represent standards that all students could reach. Normal distributions, by definition, must always have a lower half, and

within the lower half there must always be a bottom stanine. Lippmann accurately foresaw that the design of standardized testing inevitably led to sorting, and that sorting would produce losers (bottom-scoring students), who would form permanent low opinions of their own intellectual capacity. The structure of the assessment system and the view of unevenly distributed intellectual gifts behind it was inherently incompatible with success for all and, in fact, damned many to a permanent intellectual underclass.

Authentic assessment might have given Lippmann heart, for here he would have seen a form of testing where everyone can be winners. The location and the look of the finish line—standards clearly laid out for all to see—and periodic feedback and self-evaluation can allow all students to self-correct and chart a course to success.

The authentic assessment movement has gone into seclusion as the press for high standardized test scores from the No Child Left Behind law has washed over the nation. We have much work to do before No Child Left Behind becomes the force for equity some of its authors hoped for. When this equity goal is back on center screen, so will be the commitment to developing thinking skills in all our students and the connection to authentic assessment.

Authentic assessment provides the map for children to identify the learning targets and track their progress toward the standard. They will take advantage of such a map, however, only if they believe errors are opportunities for learning as opposed to confirmation of their inadequacy (Dweck, 1991). Authentic assessment is philosophically aligned with mastery learning because it encourages sustained effort to reach criterion levels of performance. Coupled with teachers who send high and positive expectations to students, one would now have designed an environment where the structures of the school are consistent with a belief in all students' capacity to learn to a high level. If we really want to prepare all students for the demands of this century, nothing less than this marriage will do.

## What's Next?

The gap between the practices advocated in this chapter and the practices found in most schools is about the size of the Grand Canyon, and to close it takes extensive teacher planning time, usually in grade or department groups. Our advice is to start slowly as individuals with natural partners (say, the teachers in a high school who teach biology) and to work simultaneously with administrators to devote allocated meeting time to instructional topics—for example, comparing student work samples for quality. Here are some other useful steps that can be begun immediately:

1. Make a special effort to present students with clear criteria for success and models of good performance for each important topic and assignment. Take the time to help the students understand exactly what about the models of good performance makes them good.

2. Get students involved regularly in self-evaluation and peer feedback using the criteria for good performance.

3. Review which methods of assessment and record-keeping devices you are using. Stretch for diversifying and expanding the repertoire. Do you use one-minute interviews or oral presentations as a way of finding out if students have mastered objectives? Do you use direct observation and checklists as a way to record student progress where appropriate?

4. Explore the possibilities of exhibitions across grades or for graduation as ways of bringing it all together for students.

5. Develop and refine portfolios as comprehensive collections of authentic student performance including self-evaluation.

The liberator for authentic assessment will arrive when teachers and administrators devote planning time to compare samples of student work and develop clear exemplars that define what they believe to be the most important student learnings.

To check your knowledge about Assessment see the quiz on our Web site at **www.RBTeach.com/ rbteach/quiz/assessment.html.**

*Sources for Assessment*

Ainsworth, L., and Viegut, D. *Common Formative Assessments.* Thousand Oaks, Calif.: Corwin Press, 2006.

Baron, J. "Performance Testing in Connecticut." *Educational Leadership,* 1989, *46*(7), 23–25.

Bellon, J. J., Bellon, E. C., and Blank, M. A. *Teaching from a Research Knowledge Base: A Development and Renewal Process.* Upper Saddle River, N.J.: Pearson Education, 1997.

Black, P., and Wiliam, D. "Assessment and Classroom Learning." *Education Assessment: Principles, Policy, and Practice,* 1998, *5*(1), 7–74.

Black, P., and Wiliam, D. "The Formative Purpose: Assessment Must First Promote Learning." In M. Willson (ed.), *NSSE 2004 Yearbook: Toward Coherence Between Classroom Assessment and Accountability.* Schaumberg, Ill.: National Study of School Evaluation, 2004.

Bloom, B., Madaus, G., and Hastings, J. *Evaluation to Improve Learning.* New York: McGraw-Hill, 1981.

Curry, J., and Samara, J. Workshop handouts at the NSDC Annual Conference, 1994.

Davies, A. *Making Classroom Assessment Work.* Merville, B.C.: Classroom Connections International, 2000.

DuFour, R. Eaker, R., Karhanek, G., and DuFour R.. *Whatever It Takes.* Bloomington, Ind.: Solution Tree: 2002.

Dweck, C. "Self-Theories and Goals: Their Role in Motivation, Personality, and Development." In R. Dienstbier (ed.), *Nebraska Symposium on Motivation.* Lincoln: University of Nebraska Press, 1991.

Fleming, M., and Chambers, B. "Teacher-Made Tests: Windows on the Classroom." *New Directions for Testing and Measurement (Testing in the Schools),* 1983, *19,* 29–38.

Friedman, T. *The World Is Flat. A Brief History of the 21st Century.* New York: Farrar, Straus, & Giroux, 2005.

Goodlad, J. *A Place Called School.* Princeton, N.J.: McGraw-Hill, 1984.

Gore, A. *An Inconvenient Truth.* New York: Rodale, 2006.

Gregory, K., Cameron, C., and Davies, A. *Setting and Using Criteria.* Merville, B.C.: Classroom Connections International, 1997.

Gregory, K., Cameron, C., and Davies, A. *Self-Assessment and Goal Setting.* Merville, B.C.: Classroom Connections International, 2000.

Gregory, K., Cameron, C., and Davies, A. *Conferencing and Reporting.* Merville, B.C.: Classroom Connections International, 2001.

Gustafson, C. "A Lesson from Stacey." *Educational Leadership, 1994, 52*(2), 22–23. © 1994 by ASCD. All rights reserved.

Hill, P., and Ruptic, B. *Practical Aspects of Authentic Assessment.* Norwood, Mass.: Christopher-Gordon Publishers, 1994.

Jamentz, K. *Charting the Course Toward Instructionally Sound Assessment.* San Francisco: California Assessment Collaborative, 1994.

Kohn, A. "From DeGrading to DeGrading: Basic Questions about Assessment and Learning." Audiotape. 95-3213. Alexandria, Va.: ASCD, 1995.

Knight, P. "How I Use Portfolios in Mathematics?" *Educational Leadership,* 1992, *49*(8), 71–72.

"Making Sure That Assessment Improves Performance." *Educational Leadership,* 1994, *51*(6), 55–57.

Marshall, K. *Interim Assessments: Keys to Successful Implementation.* New York: New Leaders for New Schools, 2006.

Marzano, R. J., Pickering, D., and McTighe, J. *Assessing Student Outcomes.* Alexandria, Va.: Association for Supervision and Curriculum Development, 1993.

McTighe, J., and O'Connor, K. "Assessment to Promote Learning: Seven Practices for Effective Learning." *Educational Leadership,* 2005, *63*(3), 10–17.

Meisels, S. J., Atkins-Burnett, S., Xue, Y., Nicholson, J., Bickel, D. D., and Son, S. "Creating a System of Accountability: The Impact of Instructional Assessment on Elementary Children's Achievement Test Scores." *Education Policy Analysis Archives,* 2003, *11*(9). Available Sept. 13, 2007, from http://epaa.asu.edu/epaa/v11n9.

Mitchell, R. *Testing for Learning.* New York: Free Press, 1992.

Perrone, V. *Expanding Student Assessment.* Alexandria, Va.: ASCD, 1991.

Popham, J. "A Tale of Two Test Types." *Principal,* 2006, *85*(4), 12–16.

Reeves, D. B. *Accountability in Action: A Blueprint for Learning Organizations.* (2nd ed.). Englewood, Colo.: Advanced Learning Press, 2004.

Riggins, C. "Embracing Assessment, Erasing Failure." *Principal,* 2006, *85*(4), 8.

Rodriguez, M. "The Role of Classroom Assessment in Student Performance on TIMMS." *Applied Measurements in Education,* 2004, *17*(1), 1–24.

Saltpeter, J. "21st Century Skills: Will Our Students Be Prepared?" *TechLearning,* October, 2003.

Saphier, J. *Bonfires and Magic Bullets.* Carlisle, Mass.: Research for Better Teaching, 1994.

Saphier, J., and D'Auria, J. *How to Bring Vision to School Improvement.* Carlisle, Mass.: Research for Better Teaching, 1993.

Saphier, J., and King, M. "Good Seeds Grow in Strong Cultures." *Educational Leadership,* 1985, *42*(6), 67–74.

Shavelson, R., Baxter, G., and Pine, J. "Performance Assessments: Political Rhetoric and Measurement and Reality." *Educational Researcher,* 1992, *21*(4), 22–27.

Shepard, L. "Linking Formative Assessment to Scaffolding." *Educational Leadership,* 2005, *63*(3), 66–70.

Sizer, T. R. *Horace's School.* Boston: Houghton Mifflin, 1992.

Sparks, D. "Dennis Sparks Interviews Judith Warren Little on Professional Development in School Reform." Audiotape. Oxford, Ohio: NSDC, 1993.

Stiggins, R. *Student-Involved Assessment for Learning.* Upper Saddle River, N.J.: Pearson, 2005.

Stiggins, R., and Chappuis, J. "Using Student Involved Classroom Assessment to Close the Achievement Gap." *Theory into Practice,* 2005, *44*(1), 11–18. © 2005. Reproduced by permission of Ohio State University. http://www.osu.edu.

Stiggins, R., and Conklin, N. *In Teachers' Hands: Investigating the Practices of Classroom Assessment.* Albany, N.Y.: State University of New York Press, 1992.

Waters, F., MacMullen, M., and Glade, J. *Intelligent Learning.* Unionville, N.Y.: KAV Books, 1992.

Wiggins, G. *Assessing Student Performance.* San Francisco: Jossey-Bass, 1993.

Wiggins, G. "Assessment as Feedback." *New Horizons for Learning,* March 2004, *10*(2). Available June 21, 2007, at www.newhorizons.org/strategies/assess/wiggins.htm.

Wiggins, G. "Honesty and Fairness: Toward Better Grading and Reporting." In T. Guskey (ed.), *1996 ASCD Yearbook.* Alexandria, Va.: ASCD, 1996.

Wolf, D., LeMahieu, P., and Eresh, J. "Good Measure: Assessment as a Tool for Educational Reform." *Educational Leadership,* 1992, *49*(8), 8–13.

Yeh, S. "High-Stakes Testing: Can Rapid Assessment Reduce the Pressure?" *Teachers College Record,* 2006, *108*(4), 621–661.

Zessoules, R., and Gardner, H. "Authentic Assessment: Beyond the Buzzword and into the Classroom." In V. Perrone (ed.), *Expanding Student Assessment* (pp. 47–71). Alexandria, Va.: ASCD, 1991.

# Appendix to Assessment

## The Missing Key Dilemma
### Grade Level 3–5

**Task**

Woe is me!!!!! My calculator does not have a 3 key that works!!!! How can I use this broken calculator to do this problem? Explain your reasoning carefully and clearly.

$$\begin{array}{r} 23 \\ \times\, 45 \\ \hline \end{array}$$

**Context**

We had been studying multiplication and doing some mental math and talking about different strategies. I wanted to know if my students knew the theory behind multiplication, not just how accurate they were with the algorithm.

**What This Task Accomplishes**

This task will tell me what students really know about what multiplication does, how it works, and how flexible their thinking is.

**What the Student Will Do**

Most students solved the problem using the algorithm first. Then they began to try different strategies. Some students had to test out their theories to be sure they worked. Other students were confident that their strategy would work.

**Time Required for Task**

This task takes about 15 or 20 minutes.

**Interdisciplinary Links**

This task is purely mathematical; there are no interdisciplinary links.

**Teaching Tips**

You might want to include this task as part of a test on multiplication. It reinforces the fact that algorithms need to be understood, not just memorized.

**Concepts to Be Assessed
and Skills to Be Developed**

Problem solving

Reasoning

Communication

Connections

Number theory

Computation

---

*Source:* Reprinted with permission from Exemplars. To view more like these visit www.exemplars.com.

### Suggested Materials

None

### Possible Solutions

There are so many ways to approach this problem. Some possible solutions are:

$22 \times 45 + 45$      $24 \times 45 - 45$

$11.5 \times 90$      $22.5 \times 46$

(use two numbers whose sum is 23) $\times 45$

45 added 23 times or 23 added 45 times

### Rubrics and Benchmarks

#### Novice

Inappropriate concepts are applied. The student thinks that the strategy for addition (move one number up on the number line and the other number down on the number line) will also work with multiplication. Her mathematical reasoning is faulty.

#### Apprentice

The solution is not complete. The student found an estimate, not the exact answer. The student's solution is partially useful, leading some way to the solution, but not a full solution.

#### Practitioner

This student has a broad understanding of the problem. S/he uses a strategy that leads to a solution of the problem and uses effective reasoning in a clear explanation.

#### Expert

This student has multiple solutions showing a deep understanding of the problem. S/he has the ability to identify the appropriate mathematical concepts.

### *AUTHOR*

Clare Forseth developed this task, which was done by students at the Marion Cross School in Norwich, Vermont. Clare is a member of the Vermont Mathematics Portfolio Committee. She has consulted and worked with many school districts. She is a member of the Mathematics Advisory Committee of the New Standards Project as well as its mathematics portfolio working group.

**NOVICE**

$$
\begin{array}{r}
23 \\
\times\ 45 \\
\hline
\end{array}
$$

Move one dubel diget down three on the number line* so you wont have to use three, and you'll get the same ansore as 3×45

* and one up thre on the number line.

**APPRENTICE**

$$23 \approx 20$$
$$X \quad 45 \qquad \times 45$$
$$\overline{115} \qquad \overline{100}$$
$$+920 \qquad +800$$
$$\overline{1035} \qquad \overline{900}$$

Estimate 23 to 20. Then multiply 20×45 on your caculator, You can still use your caculator.

**PRACTITIONER**

$$\begin{array}{r} 23 \\ \times\ 45 \end{array}$$

$$\begin{array}{r} \overset{2}{2}4 \\ \times 45 \\ \hline 120 \\ 960 \\ \hline 1080 \\ 45 \\ \hline 1035 \end{array}$$

$$23 \rightarrow \overset{2}{2}4$$
$$45 \rightarrow 45$$

$$\begin{array}{r} 120 \\ 960 \\ \hline 1080 \\ 45 \\ \hline 1035 \end{array}$$

If your Calculator doesnot have a three button and you want to multiply 23×45 you obviously can't do 23. So you make 23 to 24 and you multiply 24 ×45. I got 1080 but I knew that since the you added 45 to the problem you would have to subtract the divisor (45) from the problem to get the answer. My Answer is

$$1,035$$

<u>Rule</u>

For any problem like this (that you can't use a number for example 3) you just raise the number higher (23→24) and when you get your answer subtract the divisor. This to you makes it possible to something to any problem. I just raised 43→ to 44 and got 2244 but I had to subtract 51 and not 4192 ———————— over

$$\begin{array}{r} \overset{2}{4}4 \\ 51 \\ \hline 44 \\ 2200 \\ \hline 2244 \\ 51 \\ \hline 7100 \end{array}$$

$$\begin{array}{r} 43 \\ 51 \\ \hline 43 \\ 2150 \\ \hline 2193 \end{array}$$

**EXPERT**

$$\begin{array}{r} 23 \\ \times\ 45 \\ \hline 1,035 \end{array}$$

Look at #4

$$\begin{array}{r} 22 \\ \times 45 \\ \hline 110 \\ \cancel{880} \\ \hline 990 \\ +\ 45 \\ \hline 1035 \end{array}$$

① First you do 22×45 because it is very close to 23×45. Your answere will be 990. But you still have 1 more 45 to add on. So you do 990+45. That equals 1,035. You got the;s answere without using the three button.

② You could do 45+45 23 times and get your answere without using the three button.

③ You could do the same thir as #1 except do 24×45. Then you'd have to subtract 45 instead of adding it

④ You could do 46×40 and divide by 2

☆ ☆ ☆ ☆ ☆ ☆

---

*Source:* © Exemplars. These tasks are from Exemplars. To view more like these, visit www.exemplars.com.

# Wrapping Mom's Lamp

## Grade Level 6–8

### Task

Sarah's mom needs to wrap a lamp she bought for Sarah's birthday. The lamp is 26 inches tall, including the shade, and 8 inches across the circular base. What are the dimensions of the smallest sheet of wrapping paper she will need to wrap the lamp? (Hint: the lamp is fragile, so you might want to put it in a box before wrapping.)

### Context

This problem can be given to students with a knowledge of perimeter and area, but this is not necessary to find a solution. It is open ended in that some students will make allowance for the size of the lamp shade and whether or not to use a box with the same dimensions as the lamp.

### What This Task Accomplishes

This task will show whether the student has a basic understanding of area and perimeter and can apply it in a practical situation. On a higher level, it will show reasoning, which goes beyond computation with the dimensions that are given.

### What the Student Will Do

The student will need to decide what size box to use and consider that the top and bottom must be covered. They may allow for some overlap for neatness or may take the directions literally to find the smallest piece of wrapping paper that will cover the box. They may consider the width of the shade.

### Time Required for Task

45 minutes to allow time to actually wrap a package before or after recording the solution.

### Interdisciplinary Links

Links can be made to the many practical situations that involve surface area and perimeter of a three-dimensional figure.

### Teaching Tips

This task could be done hands-on with wrapping paper and a box followed by a written explanation with pictures or diagrams of how the students arrived at their solution, or the actual wrapping could be done *after* the solution and explanation have been written to test the accuracy of the solution and make corrections as needed.

### Concepts to Be Assessed and Skills to Be Developed

Problem-solving skills
Reasoning and decision making
Spatial visualization
Multiplication in context
Understanding the term "dimensions"
Understanding of area and perimeter
Communication

### Suggested Materials

You could make available rectangular boxes and wrapping paper.

### Possible Solutions

The basic solution is to add 8 inches to the height to allow 4 inches to cover the top from the front and 4 from the back and likewise for the bottom. The length of the paper would thus be 34 inches. The width would be found by multiplying 4 times 8, which is the width of each side of the box. Thus the dimensions are 34 inches X 32 inches. Other solutions would be to allow for some overlap in the width or to use a larger box in order to pack the lamp securely. Finally, some students might consider that the shade would probably be wider than the base and could even be packed in a separate box.

### Rubrics and Benchmarks

#### Novice

The solution shows experience with computing area, but a lack of understanding of when to use it. S/he does not take into consideration that the top and bottom have different dimensions from the sides.

#### Apprentice

The solution is not clearly explained in written communication or by the picture. While the 42 inches is probably the result of adding 8 inches to cover the top and bottom to the height of 26 inches, the student does not explain this reasoning for this or the 32-inch width.

#### Practitioner

The practitioner shows a broad understanding of the task. The communication is clear and the second picture adds to the understanding of the solution.

#### Expert

The expert shows the student has a clear understanding of the task and has taken into consideration the size of the shade. The written communication explains each step clearly, and an alternative solution is given. The student uses mathematical language and pictures. The explanation and pictures are easy to read and understand. A real-world application is included.

### AUTHOR

Deena Serafin is an eighth grade teacher at Snellville Middle School in Snellville, Georgia.

**NOVICE**

11-26-93

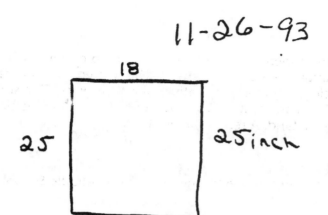

A= LW
Area=Lenghth·Wedth
A = 6(LW)
   Because there is 6 sides

A = 6(25 · 18)
A = 2,700 inches of Paper

you caun use this elon this Season with all of the Hoelday plesent that need to Bewhaped

(But alf al had to wRape it, it would take me 3 rolls) I Can't wRape

**APPRENTICE**

the answer to this question would
be a box 26 inches tall and 8 inches
wid on all sides and top and bottom
becouse the lamp is 26 inches
tall and 8 inches wide in a
circuler base

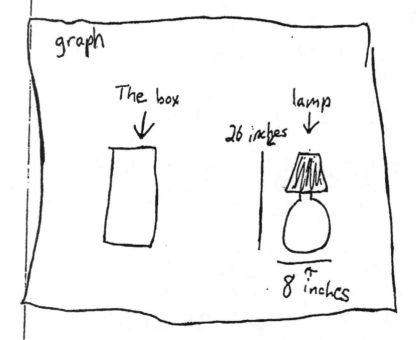

The sheet of wrapping paper would
be 32 inches long and 42 inches wide

**PRACTITIONER**

November 28, 1993

Non-Routine Problem

problem: Sarah's mom needs to wrap a lamp she bought for Sarah's birthday. The lamp is 26 inches tall, including the shade, and 8 inches across the circular base. What are the demensions of the smallest sheet of wrapping paper she will need to wrap the lamp? (Hint: The lamp is fragile, so you might want to put it in a box before wrapping.)

Solution: I got 32 × 34 inches for my final answer. I got this by first imagining the size of a box that the lamp would fit in. (26 × 8). I drew a picture of a box.....

8 inches

26 inches

To find the width of the box, I took 8 inches and multiplied it by 4 to get 32 inches, (because there are ~~3~~ 4 sides).

To find the height of the box I had 26 inches and added 8. Because for the top and bottom of the box you would need to add 4 for the bottom and 4 to the top.

these will fold over to cover the top and bottom.

So my final answer is 34 by 32 inches. This is an example of a real life situation, If you really did want to know the dimensions of the wrapping paper.

**EXPERT**

Answer: Area 1088 in²
↓ 34 x 32

Algebra

dimensions of box
8 × 8 × 26

■ = box

■ = paper

■ = paper direction

formulas
* 34 in long × 32 in wide
  68 in long × 16 in wide

(Possibilities are
very numerous.
Starred is most
likely to be found.)

26

← 8 →

(We are
assuming
that if the
base will fit,
so will the
shade.)

# Diagram

A: covers top + bottom of box (34)
B: covers height of box (32)

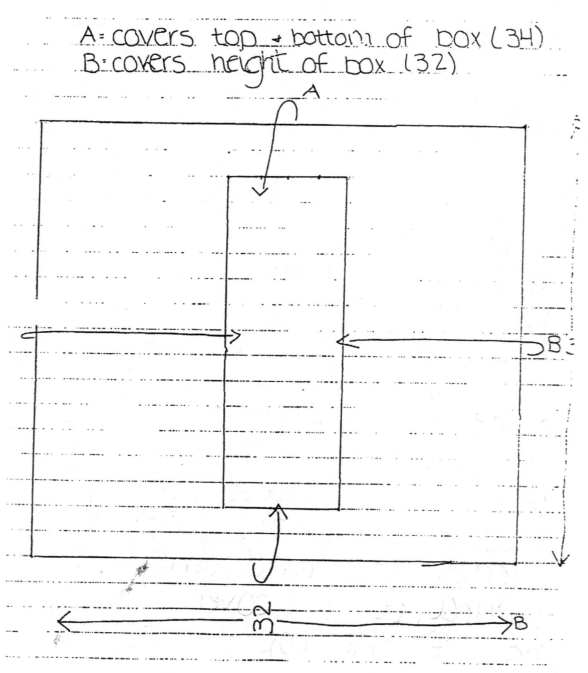

Explanation

(A) 26 inches is height of box. You must have this number in this part of the equation so the box heighth will be covered. This is only added once because it will make the whole paper this heighth. Then you add 1/2 of the boxes width, which is eight, so you add four. You do this to cover the top of the box; do the same (1/2 of width) once more to cover the bottom. You only add half, because again, it makes the whole paper 34 inches tall, and when wrapped around, it will cover the other half of the top + bottom of the box.

B. To get 32, you notice that the length of the box is eight. You must simply multiply this by four. You do this because the box has 4 sides that are this length, _and not yet covered_. This will cover the remaining uncovered part of the box

## Association

On birthdays this is a problem we all face. I never go into this much detail about this much wrapping. I think I don't need to explain a real life association because this is one

# Overarching Objectives

Many of you reading this book came into teaching because you had something particular you wanted to give to students. You had a passion for it, and you built everything you did around it. You had an overarching objective.

Maybe what you wanted was that your students would leave loving books and believing that books have something of value for them. Or maybe you wanted your students to be critical thinkers who could size up situations with care and be deliberate in their decisions. Or maybe you wanted your students to know what it is like to walk in someone else's shoes: developing empathy for other humans. No matter what else you were teaching, that was always in the back of your mind and somehow visible in your choices.

Not all teachers have overarching objectives, but those who do stand out from the crowd. Overarching objectives are those big picture outcomes for students that, if a teacher actually has them, shape core practices and account for much of what we see in their classrooms. They come from teachers who have asked themselves: "What do I most want for my students? When they leave me at the end of the year, what is the most important thing I want them to carry away from the experience?" These overarching objectives may not show up in unit or lesson plans, but they permeate everything the teacher does. They show up in interactive behavior and decisions about learning experiences. Overarching objectives are stated in sentences like the following:

When my students leave me at the end of the year,

- They will know how to work effectively in groups.
- They will have the motivation and the skills to be lifelong learners.
- They will be slow to judge and adept at critical thinking.
- They will know how to confront without hostility and resolve conflicts without rancor.
- They will understand the balance of life on the planet and be willing to do their part to preserve it.
- They will understand and appreciate the differences between people in the world—differences of color, culture, language, thinking style—and respond with tolerance and inclusion rather than with prejudice and exclusion.

This list is meant to exemplify the concept of overarching objectives, not be an all-inclusive or a recommended list. Although one may value all the statements, it is rare that an individual will really be seen in practice to stand for more than one of them. If you stand for an objective, it permeates your practice and influences everything you do. It is always in the back of your mind and serves as a backboard against which you make all your decisions.

A person can have only a very few overarching objectives at this level of commitment—usually one and maybe two or three at most. Otherwise one becomes simply too diffuse in one's efforts and makes little progress on any front.

Individual teachers who have overarching objectives may give lasting gifts to their students. It

would be possible also for teams of teachers or houses within a larger school to have an overarching objective in common and achieve even more by virtue of their consistency and congruence with one another. And beyond that, it would be possible for a whole school to share an overarching objective and create an environment so supportive and total in its commitment as to be an incredible engine for change. In such places, the objective becomes a beacon for structuring arenas throughout the school that go well beyond individual classroom practices—arenas like the cafeteria, school reward systems, faculty meeting time, extracurricular activities, student government. We have written elsewhere in detail (Saphier and D'Auria, 1993) about the process of creating such a school. It is not easy or quick, but it can be done. In this chapter, however, we focus on the classroom dimension of overarching objectives.

How does a teacher go about pursuing such a large objective in his or her own classroom? How does it influence interactive teaching, his or her choices of strategies from the other areas of performance? How does it influence the way a teacher treats curriculum if the overarching objective is unique to that teacher and is not part of the curriculum as written?

## Interactive Teaching

The overarching objective becomes the set for instruction, the charter, the guidelines for which items to pluck from the repertoires of each area of performance. And the overarching objective highlights certain areas of performance themselves. This section shows how the light from an overarching objective illuminates choices from the repertoires in certain areas of performance. Because we will run only one overarching objective through this exercise, we will highlight only one set of choices. It is our hope that readers, singly or in groups, will repeat the exercise for different overarching objectives that represent their personal commitments.

Suppose a teacher has an overarching objective that students leave at the end of the year with an appreciation of human differences so that they not only tolerate differences but embrace them. This teacher will be particularly active with the Classroom Climate area of performance. Developing Strand 1, community among the students with acceptance and inclusion, will be particularly important to this person. This teacher will also want to recognize differences in learning style among students and have the students themselves understand how learning styles influence behavior and students' reaction to different kinds of tasks (Strand 3). Thus, this teacher might explicitly teach the students about learning style, their own and others, and be explicit about calling for the students to value and honor the differences between themselves and their peers.

Models of teaching that bring students together in groups and teach them how to work well with those different from themselves will be prized by this teacher. Thus, Group Investigation, the Johnson Brothers (1988) version of cooperative learning with social skills training, and Slavin's (1990) S/T/A/D will be valued. Certain strategies from Clarity that bring students together with peers will be used often because this teacher will see them as an opportunity to bring students from different backgrounds into joint work situations where they need and can help one another. This teacher would tend to choose strategies like Round the Clock Learning Buddies and numerous other activators and summarizers.

Classroom routines might be structured with content that emphasizes the human differences theme. For example, a daily news routine may highlight events from around the world where racial or ethnic differences have been respected or disrespected. Students could be expected to bring in clippings or articles for posting on a bulletin board and later discussion in the class. Routines might be created for students to get help from one another where peers with different strengths—art, organization, video editing, writing—were available to peers to help with projects and assignments.

The Personal Relationship Building area of performance would be important to this teacher. The teacher's desire to value differences would require as a foundation that each student felt acknowledged and valued personally by the teacher. This teacher would rank high on the application of fairness, respect, and active listening with all students, especially those who might be different—physically or mentally disabled, learning disabled, or racial minorities.

In addition to choices like those within areas of performance previously, an overarching objective will influence choices of curriculum units and materials and how the teacher deals with the materials.

## Curricular Choices and Materials

A teacher who has respect for human differences as an agenda might be expected to highlight issues of race in social studies or in literature and deal with them in a way that forced students to think. For example, characters or episodes in *Huckleberry Finn* could be placed on a grid as they came up during the novel and discussed in terms of racist or antiracist behavior (Figure 20.1). One of the revelations in this exercise is that there is no such thing as "passive antiracist" behavior. Being passive in the presence of racism and disapproving without speaking or acting supports and perpetuates the racism.

**Figure 20.1.  Forms of Racist and Antiracist Behavior**

| | Racist Behavior | Antiracist Behavior |
|---|---|---|
| **Active** | | |
| **Passive** | | |

*Source:* Reprinted with permission by Beverly Daniel Tatum and Andrea Ayvaziam. Mount Holyoke College, South Hadley, Massachusetts.

These discussions would not replace others but would be woven throughout the unit on *Huckleberry Finn* by a teacher who had an overarching objective pertaining to human differences. Both the racist and antiracist actors and actions in this book could be addressed within a context of understanding and dismantling racism.

The stories and novels a teacher chooses for students is an obvious place to locate an overarching objective. Whether it be courage, perseverance, respect for difference, or any other character trait, excellent bibliographies can be found to aid selection of books.

Overarching objectives that pertain to attitudes and habits of mind tend to show up in specific skill lessons and units. For example, if the overarching objective is love of learning and the skills to pursue one's own questions, the teacher is likely to teach interviewing skills explicitly to children because interviewing is a major way to find out what one wants to know. This same teacher is likely to make it a high priority that students learn how to use library resources, online services, and Internet browsers. These skills are in direct support of the overarching objective and might not have entered the curriculum at all but for the big picture objective. The larger point here is that a teacher's overarching objective may easily have direct implications for the skills that the teacher chooses to emphasize or teach at all.

## The Hidden Curriculum

Overarching objectives may be understood and classified through a set of lenses set forth by Gower and Scott (1977). They describe five realities present in any classroom (or, for that matter, any other human interaction) at all times: *social, personal, moral, political,* and *information processing realities.* These five dimensions could be used to classify overarching objectives teachers may have for individuals. Objectives may be primarily social in nature (for example, students learn to resolve conflicts nonviolently) or moral (respect for human differences). These objectives can be aimed at personal development (students become risk takers) or political outcomes (students become active environmentalists). Finally these objectives may aim to develop certain thinking skills or ways of processing information that students use whatever the content they're studying (for example, they will be able to restrain the rush to judge and will exercise critical thinking skills).

Another way to use these five lenses from Gower and Scott is to analyze the classroom realities that teachers create on each of the dimensions from an inductive point of view. Even without a deliberate overarching objective in any of these five categories, a certain reality for students in each of the five dimensions is created in every classroom by every teacher. Each has attributes, and each can be described. Switching gears now from the prescriptive and intentional (overarching objectives) to the descriptive and perhaps unintentional, let us examine these five realities, which form a hidden but describable curriculum in every classroom in every school.

## Social Reality

What is the social reality in a class at any given moment? Social reality has to do with the way *people interact.* We can inquire into *group dynamics, norms, roles, expectations,* and *interpersonal transactions* from any one of a number of points of view. But the point remains that at every moment, there is a social reality present, whether or not we attend to it. It has been constructed or allowed to develop and can be described. And its form may or may not be a deliberate creation of the teaching. A group of students working together cooperatively on a group project constitutes a very different social reality with respect to norms, roles, and interpersonal transactions from the same group working with a teacher as director.

## Personal Reality

Every one of us has a personal reality at any moment that consists of how we are feeling and reacting. Our *hopes, fears, dreams,* and *goals,* which we carry with us at all times, are touched to a greater or lesser degree by the events of the moment. Each student in a classroom, at every moment, has a personal interior state of feeling. That state is complex, changeable, and real. Each individual's feelings at the moment are the personal reality for him or her. When we seek to understand or provide for personal reality in the classroom, we are examining the changeable, interior, personal world of individuals and their feelings of well-being.

## Moral Reality

We enter the moral dimension in a classroom when we ask about the *concepts of right and wrong,* of *duty, justice,* and *obligation,* that exist—that are embedded in curriculum materials, teacher behavior, class norms and procedures, and students' judgments and choices. Such concepts exist, they function, and they are describable and analyzable in any class, whether or not the teacher is aware of and deliberate about them. Sometimes in more recent curriculum packages, moral considerations are taken up head-on in learning experiences (Shaftel and Shaftel, 1967; Lickona, 1972, 1991).

## Political Reality

The political dimension of reality has to do with *power, influence,* and *control.* When we examine this dimension we ask questions like: Who has power? How is influence exerted? On whom, by whom? How are decisions made? Who influences the course of events and their form? How does one person (the teacher or a student) get another to behave in a certain way? Who decides what will be done next? What are the students learning in this class about their role in relation to power?

## Information Processing Reality

The information processing reality in schools has to do with *academics.* How is information dealt with? How is it presented, acquired, received, manipulated, and used? The answers are quite different when one contrasts a discovery orientation with an advance organizer orientation, or a Socratic discussion with a laboratory experience, or programmed instruction with self-directed research.

The nature of each of these five realities can be described for a given class period. In addition, one could comment over time on how much variance there was within each of the five dimensions. By variance, we mean the range of ways to be on one dimension, the number of different realities observable over time when the classroom is examined through a particular dimension's lens. The social reality of a class may remain constant, such as always one large teacher-directed group; or it may have two social realities: a large teacher-directed group and a large democratic discussion group with emphasis on interpersonal transactions. (This distinction is not one that would be picked up by the attribute interpersonal complexity of learning experiences.) One may see a variety of social realities over a class day or week or year. The social reality within a small group changes if the teacher ceases being a direct skill lesson leader and becomes an equal participant and facilitator in a discussion of, say, states' rights.

Moral reality may be invariant: community norms and expectations that students do their work (the good, duty, obligation) are maintained and enforced by the teacher without discussion. Or a different moral reality may be observed at different times, as when children consider ethical issues as a learning activity or when groups are permitted to problem-solve with the teacher acting as a mediator.

## Emphasis Within Dimensions

The hidden curriculum can be seen as those social, personal, moral, and political learnings that accrue to students as a result of the environment in which

they function, in both the classroom and the broader school at large. These learnings may be built in unconsciously, or they may be deliberate and orchestrated by the teacher. Either way, they are happening and in all five dimensions.

When they are deliberate, we find teachers who can talk explicitly about their ideas of social curriculum, personal or psychological curriculum, and, less often, moral curriculum and political curriculum. These people may be so clear as to have an overarching objective related to that dimension and curriculum to go with it. This curriculum may evince itself in explicit learning experiences or, more subtly, in intentional aspects of the learning environment the teacher constructs or allows to exist (for reasons he or she attributes to social goals or moral goals). Emphasis in any dimension usually manifests in awareness, deliberateness, and objectives for that dimension. As we observe teaching and interview teachers about their teaching, we have found that we can identify dimensions that are being emphasized in the design of the learning environment or in personal interactions with certain students.

We commented before that there is some describable reality on each dimension at all times, regardless of the teacher's awareness or deliberateness about what it is. When a dimension is emphasized, even if it has only one form, it means that the dimensional reality figures prominently in learning experiences and one would expect the teacher to be able to say why. For example, some teachers may provide a high frequency of negotiation and choices by students because they have a philosophical commitment to developing student ownership and influence (a commitment from the political dimension). If we observe students in frequent debate, stating and defending positions on issues with the teacher as facilitator and clarifier, we would expect the teacher to have something to say about getting students to be independent thinkers, or critical thinkers, or effective speakers, or some such goal.

## Matching Dimensions to Needs of Classes or Individuals

Although they stop short of forming overarching objectives, many teachers pursue personalized objectives for particular students that are outside the formal boundaries of their academic agendas. These goals could be from any of the five dimensions and could show up in individual choices or interactions. They are, in fact, usually highly personalized moves and reflect a high level of matching.

For many teachers these moves are quick and spontaneous. Although it often takes probing to get people to even remember they did them, the moves may come from deep and consistent wells. Experienced and well-developed teachers may have a large number of such individual objectives from the five dimensions for different students.

If a teacher has a social goal for a child, that teacher wants the student to develop or increase some particular interpersonal capacity or insight. "Well, I stopped and asked Jane how she saw the issue because I wanted her group to hear her thinking. She's too shy to offer it on her own and needs an opening. I want to help raise her status in her group." This teacher has a social goal for the student.

If a teacher has a personal goal for a student, that teacher wants the student to develop some personal capacity or inner strength. "Jimmy, I'd like you to see if there is any pattern to the ones you got wrong. If there is, how about setting a goal and checking it out with me before lunch?" This teacher has a personal objective for Jimmy to learn how to self-analyze and set goals.

If a teacher has a moral goal for a student, that teacher wants the student to learn something about justice, right, duty, or obligation. Charmaine has several students sent to her today for help during the ninety-minute period. The teacher has arranged in advance with Charmaine by negotiation that she, who is skilled at analyzing and setting up word problems, will be willing to help others in this difficult problem set. This arrangement is not an attempt to boost Charmaine's self-esteem. Her self-esteem is already at the point of arrogance. The teacher is systematically trying to help Charmaine develop a sense of responsibility for the success of others. This is a moral objective.

When a teacher has a political goal for a child, that teacher wants that student to learn something about power or influence. Mrs. James has had Peter read a chapter on mediation during the class study of the labor movement. She has asked him to conduct a mock mediation in front of the class in which he explicitly models the mediation skills in the chapter. Later when Peter gets into one of his frequent high-pitched arguments with a classmate that he usually wins by bullying, Mrs. James intervenes and says, "Peter, let's mediate. Coach me through the steps." She does this frequently over the first term in an attempt to teach Peter an alternative way to exert his influence in a dispute.

Notice that in these examples, some of the teachers' actions were spontaneous, as in the case of Jane and the goal to increase her status in the group. Others were deliberate and planned, such as the last example with Peter. What all the examples share in common, however, is individualized thinking about objectives for the child's growth. These objectives are in realms that include academic and thinking skills, but also go beyond into other dimensions.

In the teaching ranks of our schools there are thousands of unheralded virtuosos of the five dimensions profiled in this chapter. These people make subtle and deliberate on-the-fly moves with individual students. These moves are keyed to social, personal, moral, and political objectives that rarely show up in lesson plans but are alive as perceptual filters the teachers use to catch teachable moments with particular students. These teachers are complex thinkers who can and who do address multiple objectives simultaneously.

Understanding this aspect of sophisticated teaching may give observers a new lens for inquiring into those quick little comments and moves that teachers make almost in passing with individual students. This lens can serve as a foundation for interesting questions in conferences as observers help teachers debrief and interpret the complex reality of interactive classroom teaching.

For teachers, this chapter may provide a frame for thinking about their students, one by one, and for sorting through the multiple ways their teaching can match the needs of individuals.

To check your knowledge about Overarching Objectives see the quiz on our Web site at **www. RBTeach.com/rbteach/quiz/OObjective.html.**

*Source Materials on Overarching Objectives*

Gower, R. R., and Scott, M. B. *Five Essential Dimensions of Curriculum Design.* Dubuque, Iowa: Kendall Hunt, 1977.

Johnson, R. T., and Johnson, D. W. "Cooperative Learning: Two Heads *Learn* Better Than One." *In Context,* 1988, *18,* 34.

Lickona, T. *A Strategy for Teaching Values.* Pleasantville, N.Y.: Guidance Associates, 1972.

Lickona, T. *Educating for Character.* New York: Bantam Books, 1991.

Saphier, J., and D'Auria, J. *The Core Value Process: Bringing Vision to School Improvement.* Carlisle, Mass.: Research for Better Teaching, 1993.

Shaftel, G., and Shaftel, F. *Role Playing for Social Values.* Upper Saddle River, N.J.: Prentice Hall, 1967.

Slavin, R. *Cooperative Learning: Theory, Research, and Practice.* Upper Saddle River, N.J.: Prentice Hall, 1990.

Stanford, G. *Developing Effective Classroom Groups.* New York: Hart Publishing Co., 1977.

Tatum, B. D., and Ayvazian, A. *Forms of Racist and Anti-racist Behavior.* South Hadley, Mass.: Mount Holyoke College, 1994.

# Name Index

# Subject Index

## THE SKILLFUL LEADER II: *Confronting Conditions That Undermine Learning*  2008
### by Alexander D. Platt, Caroline E. Tripp, Robert G. Fraser, James R. Warnock & Rachel E. Curtis

A practical, strategy-filled handbook to help district, school, and classroom leaders who are trying to pull adults together to accomplish large-scale improvements in student learning. Case profiles, models, legal notes, and tips all focus on recognizing cultures and practices that become obstacles to change and taking them on as a professional community or as a supervisor and evaluator.

## THE SKILLFUL LEADER: *Confronting Mediocre Teaching*  2000
### by Alexander D. Platt, Caroline E.Tripp, Wayne R. Ogden & Robert G. Fraser

Based on *The Skillful Teacher* framework, this book is targeted to evaluators and supervisors who want a field-tested tool kit of strategies to improve, rather than remove, underperforming teachers. The text includes valuable legal notes and a model contract, case studies, assessment tools, and personal accounts of leaders in action.

## THE DATA COACH'S GUIDE *to Improving Learning for All Students*  2008
### by Nancy Love, Katherine E. Stiles, Susan Mundry, & Kathryn DiRanna

This resource helps data-team facilitators move schools away from unproductive data practices and toward examining data for systematic and continuous improvement in instruction and learning. The book includes a CD-ROM with slides and reproducibles.

## JOHN ADAMS' PROMISE: *How to Have Good Schools for All Our Children,*
### *Not Just for Some*  2005
### by Jon Saphier

Curriculum reform, structural reform, funding reform, organization reform – all these 20th century efforts have failed to make a significant dent in the achievement gap and the performance of disadvantaged students, especially in cities and poor rural areas. What are the most important targets for school improvement?

## TALK SENSE: *Communicating to Lead and Learn*  2007
### by Barry Jentz

Barry Jentz shows how leaders can build the requisite trust and credibility for improving organizational performance. Typically, leaders *Talk Tough* to improve performance. When that doesn't work, they *Talk Nice* (or vice-versa). By learning to *Talk Sense*, leaders can succeed in their efforts to improve performance.

## ACTIVATORS: *Activity Structures to Engage Students' Thinking Before Instruction*  1993
### by Jon Saphier & Mary Ann Haley

This book is a collection of classroom-tested, practical activity structures for getting students' minds active and engaged prior to introducing new content or skills. Each structure is designed to elicit what students already know about a topic, to surface misconceptions, and to create cognitive hooks when new material is presented.

## SUMMARIZERS: *Activity Structures to Support Integration and Retention of New*
### *Learning*  1993
### by Jon Saphier & Mary Ann Haley

This book is a collection of classroom-tested, practical activity structures for getting students cognitively active during and after periods of instruction. Each structure provides a framework for guiding students to summarize for themselves what is important, what they have learned, and/or how it fits with what they already know.

## HOW TO BRING VISION TO SCHOOL IMPROVEMENT *Through Core*
### *Outcomes, Commitments, and Beliefs*  1993
### by Jon Saphier & John D'Auria

This practical guide provides a proven step-by-step sequence for generating consensus among parents and staff about some of the valued core outcomes they want for all children. Then it shows how to achieve them through concrete areas in school and family life.

## HOW TO MAKE SUPERVISION AND EVALUATION REALLY WORK:
### *Supervision and Evaluation in the Context of Strengthening School Culture*  1993
### by Jon Saphier

This book offers school leaders a carefully integrated approach for transforming often divisive supervision and evaluation systems into a positive force for strengthening school culture. Specific guidelines lead to meaningful, multifaceted teacher evaluation systems.

### RESEARCH FOR BETTER TEACHING
One Acton Place     Acton, MA 01720
978.263.9449 *voice*     978.263.9959 *fax*     www.RBTeach.com